THE MIRAGES

OF

MARRIAGE

D0169428

Le pays du mariage a cela de particulier que les estrangers ont envie de l'habiter, & les habitans naturels voudroient en etre exiles.

The land of marriage has this peculiarity, that strangers are desirous of inhabiting it, whilst its natural inhabitants would willingly be banished from thence.

—MONTAIGNE

THE MIRAGES

OF

MARRIAGE

———

BY

William J. Lederer

&

Don D. Jackson, M.D.

W · W · NORTON & COMPANY
New York · London

ISBN 0-393-30632-1

W. W. Norton & Company, Inc., 500 Fifth Avenue, New York, N.Y. 10010
W. W. Norton & Company Ltd., 37 Great Russell Street, London WC1B 3NU

PRINTED IN THE UNITED STATES OF AMERICA

1 2 3 4 5 6 7 8 9 0

Publisher's Note

The conception of this book is, like most conceptions, difficult to time with precision. However, it began in William J. Lederer's mind and at Harvard University after he had been exposed to the lectures of Percy Bridgman and Norbert Wiener. He was struck by Professor Bridgman's application of mathematics to social problems and by Professor Wiener's discussions of cybernetics and in particular the systems concept.

It occurred to Mr. Lederer that marriage is a system in which the partners act and react to each other and the total relationship in definable ways and that marriage cannot be dealt with by dealing with the partners as separate individuals. At about the time Mr. Lederer had begun to formulate his ideas for a book on the subject, he met Dr. Don D. Jackson. Dr. Jackson was one of the most meteoric of the younger psychiatrists. His speciality was human communications and in particular family relationships. His work as director of the Mental Research Institute in Palo Alto had gained him world renown in professional circles. When Mr. Lederer told Dr. Jackson of his thoughts on a new approach to the problems of marriage, he discovered that Dr. Jackson had begun to work along the same lines. They agreed to write the book together.

Contents

7

Acknowledgments

Shortly before Dr. Don Jackson—my dear friend, my book-collaborator, and my philosophy-collaborator—died, we spent a happy week together at Harvard University. It was a hectic time; we both had many things to do. But it was a joyful week. Long into the nights we discussed: the pathology of the U.S. foreign-relations process (I was then writing *Our Own Worst Enemy*); the various processes by which human beings communicate with each other (Don was then preparing the Salmon Lectures); the people to whom credit should be given here for their help in the creation of this book.

Don wanted to acknowledge everyone, including the many people who had permitted us to test our concepts on them. The trouble was that Don's proposed list—in his scrawly, red-ink handwriting—contained literally hundreds of names.

At the bottom Don had put "PS—Bill, I guess we haven't space to give credit to our hundreds of experimentees and all those whose counsel we sought, but those who helped us in research and in idea—their names *must* go in."

Finally, we compromised. Following is the result.

We are obliged to Professor Percy Bridgman at Harvard, who taught me the application of mathematics to social problems, and to Professor Norbert Wiener of MIT, who simultaneously influenced us with his systems concept and cybernetics (1950–51).

We are indebted to Dr. Karl Menninger, who encouraged us during the trying times when we were testing our ideas.

We are obliged to the staff of the Mental Research Institute in Palo Alto, California, for countless acts of assistance. Special notice is deserved by Dee Barlow, who was Dr. Jackson's editorial and research assistant. She went through the manuscript line by line, contributed many useful suggestions, and often helped the two authors avoid the danger of a male bias.

We are obliged to hundreds of married couples who permitted us to observe in depth their behavior and communication, and who candidly discussed their fears, discords, and hopes. We also are obliged to the hundreds of couples who permitted us to interview them before and after marriage.

We are indebted to Angie Jackson for acting out and taping examples of marital dialogues, and we owe much gratitude to Corinne Lederer for her constructive thoughts and for her care in reading the manuscript for our mistakes.

We received much help from the members of the Harvard University community. We were helped also by several score clergymen of all faiths, teachers, and doctors who tried this book out on their parishioners, friends, and patients.

We give special thanks to Katharine Schwager, who typed the entire manuscript and made many good suggestions, and to Esther Jacobson, the copy reader who with patience and extraordinary skill polished and organized our many-times-rewritten manuscript into an orderly and logical book.

W. J. LEDERER

Foreword

In October 1966 the authors of this book visited The Menninger Foundation and delighted the faculty and Fellows of The Menninger School of Psychiatry and the Clinical Psychology and social work trainees with their infectious enthusiasm, their dedication, and their talent. They discussed with me, at that time, the book about marriage counseling which they were writing and out of that conversation I developed a personal interest in and expectation of the book.

From time to time I heard that it was progressing. Early in December 1967 Dr. David Levy, Dr. Stanley Cobb, and I were honored by the New York Psychiatric Society. We were happy to hear that Don Jackson was coming to deliver the main address of the evening. When we arrived for the banquet at the Academy of Medicine, however, we learned with regret from Dr. Francis Braceland, the president, that Dr. Jackson had been taken ill and would not be able to be present.

A few days later, in Chicago, I received a letter from Don saying in part: "After the holidays you will be receiving a manuscript of the marriage book which Bill Lederer and I have labored on since 1964. We would consider it a great honor if you could do a brief Foreword to this book. Naturally it would only be if the volume seems to you to have something to say and in a different manner than the hundreds of trashy marriage books that are available. Your interest in pioneering new areas and urging new looks at psychiatric and emotional problems has made us think of you first."

The manuscript arrived in January and while I was reading it, there came the sad and shocking news of Don's death. He was only forty-eight, cut off midcourse in a brilliant career of research and education. We miss him for his great personal charm, his earnestness, his devotion to people, and his place in psychiatry.

This book represents a monument to him, which he and his able co-author built with their minds and hearts and hands. It shows forth their concern for couples and their wish to go beyond vague advice to prescribe definite procedures and techniques which have been tried and found helpful in improving marriages.

For a great many years I have been interested in bibliotherapy: therapeutic help received from the reading of books. Quite a number of people have written me attributing a crucial turning point in their lives to the experience of reading something in our field I or someone else had written. This will be the effect of Bill Lederer and Don Jackson's book for many, I trust; the spirit of the authors will be experienced through these pages. Thus, Don will live on, and Bill, too, and their many friends will find their book a joy and a consolation.

Chicago   KARL MENNINGER, M.D.
March 1968

INTRODUCTION –
WHAT THIS BOOK
IS ABOUT

Year after year, in the United States, marriage has been discussed
in public print and private session with undiminished confusion
and increasing pessimism. Calamity always attracts attention, and
in the United States the state of marriage is a calamity. One third
of all marriages end in divorce within ten years,[1] and no one
knows how many of the remaining two thirds are calamitous.
Recent surveys indicate that in an affluent community like San
Mateo, California, seven out of ten marriages fail.

The Mirages of Marriage makes use of a recently codified theory
called the systems concept. During the last ten years the systems concept has revolutionized both the physical and the
social sciences. The pioneer work in "system orientation" was
done by the brilliant philosopher and mathematician Norbert
Wiener, of the Massachusetts Institute of Technology, and Lud-
wig Von Bertalanffy, of Alberta University. This new concept has
already radically altered technology. In the social sciences it is

[1] Interim Report, Judicial Committee, Legislature, State of California,
1966.

modifying the traditional orientation toward the individual, or the "intrapsychic" point of view, as well as the chemical, hormonal, and brain-oriented biases which have dominated psychology and psychiatry for the past hundred years.

The systems concept helps explain much of the previously mysterious behavior which results whenever two or more human beings relate to one another. We now know that the family is a unit in which all individuals have an important influence—whether they like it or not and whether they know it or not. The family is an interacting communications network in which every member from the day-old baby to the seventy-year-old grandmother influences the nature of the entire system and in turn is influenced by it. For example, if someone in the family feels ill, another member may function more effectively than he usually does. The system tends, by nature, to keep itself in balance. An unusual action by one member invariably results in a compensating reaction by another member. If mother hates to take Sunday drives but hides this feeling from her husband, the message is nevertheless somehow broadcast throughout the family communications network, and it may be Johnny, the four-year-old, who becomes "carsick" and ruins the Sunday drive.

There is an understandable resistance to new ideas and techniques (such as the systems concept) which clash with traditional thinking and behavior. Throughout the history of medicine, for example, innovation has been bitterly opposed by the majority of physicians. Freud was ridiculed and harassed. Pasteur was ostracized by his fellow physicians and accused of being a quack because he believed in little bugs no one could see.

The reluctance to accept advances exists in the twentieth century even though it is the age of rapid progress and change. We therefore anticipate that some marriage counselors (including psychiatrists) will be upset by *The Mirages of Marriage*. We hope so. Many of them deserve to be upset.

We, the authors, are *for* marriage—workable, harmonious marriage. If this end is to be achieved, current mirages about marriage must be eliminated. The customs and biases which now dominate attitudes toward marriage grew out of conditions appropriate to the past, *not* the present. This influence of the past is most easily apparent in the legal aspects of marriage. Our current laws concerning marriage, divorce, alimony, and custody were taken en masse from English common law, some of which is more than five hundred years old. In most of our fifty states, these laws have been altered very little, and nowhere have they been adapted to meet the demands of twentieth-century America.

We believe that the current concept of marriage is anchored socially, legally, and psychologically in anachronisms and therefore is widely unworkable. Marriage today, by and large, is a disappointment. It is a relationship too frequently not relished but endured.

On their wedding day, a young man and a young woman, standing before the priest, minister, or justice of the peace, usually have a high opinion of one another. They overflow with joyous thoughts. Each has a firm intention of pleasing and nourishing the cherished person who is about to become a partner for life.

Some years later (the highest incidence of divorce, excluding teenagers, is after ten or so years), these same two people may be living in a chronic situation of hate, fear, and confusion. Each spouse in such a marriage may blame the other and defensively emphasize how hard he* tried to be loving, tried to make the marriage a success, and tried to keep the other from sabotaging the effort.

What causes such frightful changes? What brings about such startling emotional and behavioral metamorphoses?

The most easily apparent causes are the failure to pick a suitable mate, and the failure—once a mate has been chosen—to work out relationship rules that will be durable and equitable.

There are about 400,000 divorces annually in the United States. Some counties in this nation have divorce rates as high as 70 per cent. But these figures do not reveal the entire marital tragedy. More often than spouses care to admit, marriage results in years of dislike and mutual destruction—rather than love and mutual growth. In interviews with hundreds of average marital pairs we learned that approximately 80 per cent of the couples had seriously considered divorce at one time or another, and many of

---

* To avoid the awkward repetition of "he or she," the terms "he," "him," and "his" have been employed throughout the book to refer to either spouse —husband or wife.

them still think about it frequently. Often, only the existence of children, the restrictions of poverty, the edicts of religion, or a lack of courage blocks the decision to get divorced.

Clearly, then, the marriage process in America is ailing. It is to the need for an understanding of the ailment and of what can be done about it that *The Mirages of Marriage* is addressed. This book has four main goals: to diagnose the maladies of modern marriage; to show readers how to diagnose their own problems, or how to seek outside diagnostic help when they cannot identify their own marital ailments; to suggest methods of bringing sick marriages back to health; and—if the marriage is in the grave— to show how to recognize that it is a corpse so that it can be buried with grace and maturity, and to do so within the framework of current laws and religious beliefs.

We repeat, we are *for* marriage. But we are *against* destructive relationships and ill health perpetuated in order to meet the requirements of antiquated social expectations. We shall try to explode the prevalent myths and erroneous assumptions regarding marriage in our present-day culture—the myths and assumptions which doom a marriage even before it starts. We are *for* couples learning about the marriage process and autonomously creating their own workable union. We are also *for* skilled, mature, and well-trained marriage counselors. But we are *against* the very many insufficiently trained therapists and the well-intentioned but ill-informed do-gooders who foist themselves upon the couple seeking solutions for a troubled marriage. One of the most destructive forces operating in our culture today is the out-of-date marriage counselor who works unilaterally, with only one of the spouses. In so doing he neglects the basic irritant of the marital mess—the interactional pattern in which the spouses attack and counterattack each other. Some psychiatrists refer to these patterns as "games." Games of this sort have nothing to do with recreation or amusement. They are often forms of combat and competition—the behavior modes of spouses trying to gain power over each other. The result, inevitably, is mutual debilitation.

In this book we shall demonstrate the necessity for "equality" in marriage. This kind of equality is not based on the absurd belief that spouses need to have the same IQ or the same interests, or to work equally hard. It is based on the more subtle notion that close, enduring human relationships depend on an interplay of behavior which signals to each spouse that whatever he receives has been forthcoming in response to something given. In other words, a *quid pro quo* (something for something) agreement is in effect: to live in reasonable harmony the spouses negotiate with respect to their behavior and responsibilities. Perhaps this kind of relationship appears selfish and unromantic, yet in our view it is the single most required and most overlooked aspect of any marriage. It seems all too clear that most Americans believe that "love" and "romance" plus plenty of gadgets will keep a couple happy. Americans tend to enter marriage with a grinning, false-face concept of what married life will be like. From this delusion has come our mass marital failure.

As we shall show, the question of who has the right to do what to whom—and when—is the pervasive, nagging issue which must be worked out by every couple, for it arises daily. A set of relationship rules must be agreed upon. In the formulation of these rules each individual must feel that he has a right, equal to the other's right, to determine what goes on. A person who feels that he is being controlled, denied the rights of reasonable self-determination, will fight—overtly or covertly—to regain control. History (of both marriages and nations) repeatedly has shown that systems based on an unequal division of power eventually fall. To survive a system requires mutual responsibility, reward, security, and dignity.

If the backgrounds, the values, and the needs of the husband and wife are so different and rigid that a *quid pro quo* negotiation is impossible, disaster usually results. Some forms of it may be illness, constant arguing, desertion, slow marital death caused by silence, divorce, or even murder.

We are *against* most of the books, magazine articles, and newspaper columns which concern marriage and which usually promise solutions. Almost all of these are trash. They are of no more value to individuals seeking answers than an Ouija board would be. It tells the individual what to do, but neglects the central issue in every marriage—the relationship.

We have briefly mentioned the *apparent* reasons for so much marital discord—the failure to choose a suitable mate and the failure to adjust to the one that is chosen. But these are more symptoms than causes. The underlying cause is that American thinking patterns and traditional American values concerning marriage are rusty, broken-down, obsolete.

If workable marriages are to exist in this latter part of the twentieth century, the artificially determined roles of male and female (developed during the Middle Ages) must be discarded and replaced. The rigid, male-dictated marital structure of the eleventh and twelfth centuries cannot function in today's environment. Neither can the extreme feminist dream of female domination. Modern marriage requires equality, just as world history indicates a trend toward equality among people regardless of sex, race, or creed.

To approach equality, each spouse should perform the roles for which he is best suited *regardless of custom or tradition*. The culture determines what are the appropriate marital roles, but in an egalitarian culture like the United States, a great deal of flexibility is possible. One of the most satisfying marriages we know is between the successful owner of a hardware store and an extremely pretty, gentle woman of the top social order, a graduate of an eastern boarding school and Vassar College, active in the Red Cross and Girl Scouts. They have three children. This happy couple has assigned an unusual distribution of roles. In the late afternoon, the husband cooks dinner while the wife works in the vegetable garden or does repair jobs about the house. The husband dislikes gardening, and is tired of tools by the end of the day. But he is a fine chef and gets pleasure from preparing dinner. The wife is a mediocre cook, but a skilled gardener and handy woman.

If modern marriage is to be successful, not only the assignment of roles, but other traditional attitudes and practices as well must be revised. For example, husbands and wives are frequently led into destructive interactions by the need for denying, or avoiding many kinds of human behavior which society and tradition label as bad—such as losing one's temper and showing it. In reality, some of these "bad" reactions can turn out to be the strengths of a marriage. We shall describe how to make constructive use of the so-called bad behavior. Also, we shall catalog and show how to identify the really destructive elements in a marriage, and suggest ways in which married people often can eliminate them. Finally, we shall indicate at what point the partners of a destructive marriage should see a professional counselor, and how to find the right one.

Our major efforts will be to present an up-to-date concept of marriage, and to demonstrate structure and processes of personal interrelationships. In the future, perhaps grammar-school students will take courses in relationships just as they now do in math and English. The adults of today do not have such a background. They know only what they have observed from their own parents' marriages, and have little or no training in how to develop functional methods of relating to others. Therefore, people have to work hard to get rid of the old destructive ideas and learn from scratch what marital growth and interaction is all about. This book offers *one* such beginning.

We do not claim that bad marriages can easily be transformed into wondrous, ecstatic, heavenly love matches. We do not claim that marriages can (or should) be devoid of friction or problems. All we claim is that in many cases, discordant marriages can be made into workable, reasonably satisfying relationships.

We have pointed out that as practiced today, marriage is in some ways an archaic and unworkable institution, but the alternatives to marriage are not too attractive either. The fact is that relationships generally based upon marriage are to be found in most of the civilized world, and in a good bit of the uncivilized world. Monogamy is not essential for the existence of the family, but the alternatives (polyandry and polygamy) have, in general, been unworkable except in very small groups, such as the Tivs in the Nigerian area of Africa.

Marriage, then, is a contractual arrangement entered into (even if it doesn't make sense) by most of the people in the civilized world. Granting that there is no such thing as perfection in marriage, what can be done to make it more workable and provide the greatest satisfaction possible for all concerned?

Those contemplating divorce should try to see marriage as a process, a system. They should recognize the destructiveness of the widespread biases and myths regarding the differences between men and women and the inevitability of the battle of the sexes. Once such biases and myths are believed, all the transactions of a marriage (or a divorce) become more difficult because they are based on unreality.

Spouses considering divorce *must* realize that people have unconscious reasons for selecting each other; and it is not rare, except in cultures where marriages are arranged by a third party, for an individual who has known another just a few days to have unconsciously selected him as the desired mate. When someone with marital problems says, "My wife is a bitch, and she's this, and that . . . " he can go on for hours without remembering that *this is the woman he chose.*

In every marital situation we have ever seen, each partner has contributed to both the assets and the liabilities. Blaming the other spouse accomplishes nothing. Yet we know of coffee klatches in Palo Alto, in Honolulu, in Cambridge, where women gather in the morning to bitch about their husbands; their husbands gather for a drink before they come home, and do the same thing about their wives. This sort of collective complaining is getting to be an extremely common and destructive phenomenon. The participants in these conversations are completely oblivious to the fact that they agreed to the marital contract with their eyes wide open.

Although people speak of having to work at marriage, probably just as much work—energy, strength, and time—is required to support a bad marriage as to support a good one. There is simply a difference in the ways in which the energy is used, not in the total amount of energy spent.

Assume for a moment that for a thousand dollars one can buy either a 1935 Chevrolet with a hundred thousand miles on it or a brand-new Cadillac. Why would anybody buy the Chevrolet when he could buy the Cadillac? The same question can be asked about marriage. If as much energy must be expended in a miserable marriage as in a happy, satisfying, successful marriage, why does anybody have a miserable marriage?

We believe that husband and wife in a discordant marriage can do the greater part of the healing and growing for themselves. There is no doctor or counselor who can—for any amount of money—give "instant" love or marital harmony. The partners involved must do the work. Advisers can only make them more conscious of interactional behavior and suggest ways of bringing about changes.

Part I

THE MIRAGES OF MARRIAGE

1

THE ORIGINS OF MARRIAGE AND THE FAMILY—AND THEIR DISINTEGRATION IN THE MODERN WORLD

At the beginning of man's existence, over a million years ago, it seems that members of the human race procreated in the same random manner as almost all other animals do. A female and a male met by chance, and if both had a strong sexual drive, they copulated. After a short period of intimacy, the male wandered off to continue his usual activities—hunting and fighting. Several months later, the female perhaps noticed that she was pregnant. It is probable that for many millennia pregnancy was not associated with the sex act. Furthermore, in those ancient days (as in some of the more impoverished rural nations today), the condition of pregnancy probably did not diminish the daily activities of the female until the point of actual delivery. When labor pains

began, the female assumed as comfortable a position as possible
—wherever she happened to be—and gave birth to the infant.
Perhaps within a day or two she was foraging for food as usual,
with the additional burden of nursing and caring for the child.
The father was totally uninvolved and didn't know his own child.

After almost an aeon, human beings (most likely the females
of the species) learned that certain fruits and grains and vegetables could be cultivated and stored for the winter months. Small
gardens were started, and shelters were built nearby. Probably
the females tended the gardens and built the shelters. Gradually
these females must have gathered together in groups, clustering
their temporary homes near one another, and the first community
developed. The male still was the hunter and the warrior, probably roaming wherever game was most plentiful during the
spring and summer months, and during his wanderings copulat-
ing with any female he might happen to fancy. But the female,
under the necessity of rearing children, accumulated the food to
last through the winter, developed skill at turning animal hides
into protective clothing, maintained fires, and created shelters. It
is probable, therefore, at least in the northern countries, that
itinerant males migrated toward the communities of females
sometime in the late autumn.

With warm weather, the males wandered off again, stopping at
the abodes of females in a random fashion. Finally, in some
groups, the association between sex and childbirth became
known. But still the human species continued the random sexual
pattern. It is likely that the first human social group consisted of
women who learned to help each other during labor and take
turns at minding the children.

Under this social system there was no concern about paternity.
Eventually, probably because of the invention of tools and the
further development of agriculture, men began to spend more
time around the camp and a simple social group evolved in which
they played a fixed part. A primitive law, or taboo, slowly formed,
which forbade mating in directly ascending and descending lines
of consanguinity—in other words, the incest taboo developed.
We find this taboo among peoples and races all over the world; it
is probably the first socio-marital regulation imposed by man
upon himself. The origins of the incest taboo have been discussed

at length by anthropologists, but none have found undebatable answers. It is possible that after generations of loose social organization, man acquired some general understanding of heredity, but this is not an easy assumption since most diseases of proven genetic causation occur only about once in a population of ten thousand unless both parents carry the offending gene. It is not difficult, however, to see how an incest taboo would simplify and strengthen the social structure by allowing relatives to band together into a "clan," whose members could trust each other and support each other in fights or other mutual endeavors. The ban against incest allowed males to avoid battles over their own sisters and mothers and to have a common link with other males (brothers-in-law). Since evidence indicates that polygamy and polyandry were common among primitive people, the early family units would have been different from those we know today and would have consisted of several women with a relatively close tie to one another and a looser tie to one or more men. Even today, in some African tribes, there is no word for "mother," but the child uses the word "auntie" for a number of women. An older man, perhaps his actual grandfather, is the male whom the child respects, and "father" as such does not exist. These ties reflect the fact that the younger men are mobile, while older men and the women stay at camp.

There is evidence that man existed for many thousands of years without clothing; the need for warmth was another factor which slowly led to the development of settled communities. In order to keep warm, he had traditionally been forced to migrate with the seasons. Some groups, such as the Australian bushmen, eventually located an agreeable climate and a large land mass suitable for foraging, and they were able to establish permanent settlements. Evidence derived from studies of the bushmen indicates that a particular kind of social organization was probably necessary for the migration and survival of the human race in early times. The men had to forage for game and yet find a camp when the hunt was over or women could not become impregnated and perpetuate the race. The long period of gestation in the human animal made possible the absence of men for considerable periods of time without a resulting decline in the birth rate.

Since the life-span of primitive man was probably less than

thirty years (man's life-span was approximately thirty-seven years in Roman days), it was advantageous to mate indiscriminately. A man could thus be the father of many children by a number of women, instead of waiting as much as twelve to eighteen months for one woman to become fecund again. (Probably less than half of the children survived infancy.) If twenty men went on a hunting and foraging expedition and only five returned, there were at least four women for each survivor to impregnate in the service of the tribe. Objects relating to fertility rites have been found by anthropologists among almost all primitive and nomadic people studied; thus, it seems likely that man took great interest in the survival of the race at an early date in his history.

Today we may see indiscriminate mating as immoral and crude, but it was necessary for the preservation of the species under primitive conditions of life. The larger the gene pool from which an offspring emerged, the more likely he was to possess adaptive potentialities. When, by chance, "bad" genes (that is, those transmitting characteristics not favorable to survival in a particular environment) were inherited from mother or father, the offspring usually did not survive for long, so there was a tendency for these characteristics not to be perpetuated.

Another factor must have entered the picture at some point many thousands of years ago. Changing atmospheric and soil conditions made possible the advent of tall grasses; shelter and food became more available within a given geographical area, and with the domestication of animals and especially with the acquisition of control over fire, a "camp" could be maintained for relatively long periods of time.

Consider now in a speculative fashion the kind of organization which such circumstances might require. Women tied down by childbirth and child rearing would be likely to remain close to the camp. Men would hunt but return to the camp, either at nightfall (for protection and warmth) or after longer periods of hunting. Individuals would begin to have for their neighbors, though to a lesser extent, the kind of feeling that a mother has for her child. People would be regarded as belonging in one of two categories—those whom one knew and those whom one didn't know. The latter probably were killed whenever possible, but gradually larger groups collected where the land would support them. And as their numbers increased, people found it necessary to develop tolerance for one another.

About this time, speech probably developed. The utterance of vocal noises appears to have evolved as one method available to primitive man for finding his camp and identifying his own kind. Thus, the rudiments of human speech probably derived from crude calls which identified the location of the camp and gradually came to indicate danger or success in hunting by varying inflections of tonality. Differences in vocalization also distinguished one tribe from another, and probably promoted a developing sense of clan membership.

As long as society remained primitive, the relationship between married male and female was a practical one: *the family unit was a unit for physical survival.* Almost everyone in it had to work long and hard. A male and a female who became partners and had children normally had greater chances for survival and more advantages than they would have had if they had stayed alone. The first young children were a survival liability, but as they grew up the original "couple" became a group—with all of its members participating in the survival activities. "Love" was not important. In primitive vocabularies there was no word for "love."

It was not until the Middle Ages that the word "love" (in the sense in which it is used today) became current. Communities developed under the protection of the nobles in their great castles. The lady of a castle assumed the same prestigious position as her husband, the lord. Other people did the work, but the lady of the castle had leisure time to learn to read and practice the arts. Usually she was more educated than her husband, and if she had duties, they were light and principally administrative. Having so much spare time, she often became egocentric, and she began to adorn herself.

She also became bored.

When the Crusades began in the eleventh century, many of the nobles went off to war, leaving their wives at home. The men who did not go on the Crusades tried to amuse the ladies; they wooed them usually with extramarital sex in mind. During this period there arose the phenomenon of the troubadour, usually a noble, who went from castle to castle to entertain. These troubadours sang songs and ballads about "romance" to entertain the lady of the castle.

There is much literature that suggests that sex outside of marriage became the fashion with these ladies. Probably these married women were the aggressors and initiators in these sex activities. The women were bored. They were intellectually and artistically superior to their husbands, and probably resented the inferior, nonproductive position into which they had been forced by a male-dominated society. *Extramarital passion was defined by them as "love."*

These ladies of the Middle Ages, in their excessive leisure, gathered into groups called Courts of Love, which defined the current rules and traditions of "love." The example which follows is a code of love agreed upon by a court of women under the leadership of the Countess of Champagne, in May, 1174.

CODE OF LOVE OF THE 12TH CENTURY

1. Marriage is no good excuse against loving.
2. Whoever cannot conceal a thing, cannot love.
3. No one can bind himself to two loves at once.
4. Love must always grow greater or grow less.
5. There is no savour in what a lover takes by force.
6. The male does not love until he has attained a complete manhood.
7. A widowhood of two years is prescribed to one lover for the other's death.
8. No one, without abundant reason, ought to be deprived of his own love.
9. No one can love unless urged thereto by the hope of being loved.
10. Love is always exiled from its dwelling by avarice.
11. It is not decent to love one whom one would be ashamed to marry.
12. The true lover does not desire embraces from any but the co-lover.
13. Love that is known publicly rarely lasts.
14. An easy conquest renders love despised, a difficult one makes it desired.
15. Every lover turns pale in the sight of the co-lover.

16. The lover's heart trembles, at the unexpected sight of the co-lover.
17. A new love makes one quit the old.
18. Probity alone makes a man worthy of love.
19. If love lessens, ít dies speedily and rarely regains health.
20. The man prone to love is always prone to fear.
21. Real jealousy always increases the worth of love.
22. Suspicion and the jealousy it kindles increase love's worth.
23. Whom thought of love plagues, eats less and sleeps less.
24. Whatever a lover does ends with thinking of the co-lover.
25. The true lover thinks naught good but what he believes pleases the co-lover.
26. Love can deny love nothing.
27. The lover cannot be satiated by the delights of the co-lover.
28. The least presumption compels the lover to suspect evil of the co-lover.
29. He is not wont to love, whom too much abundance of plea-sure annoys.
30. The true lover is haunted by the co-lover's image unceasingly.
31. Nothing prevents one woman from being loved by two men, or one man by two women.

We pronounce and decree by the tenour of these presents, that love cannot extend its powers over two married persons; for lovers must grant everything, mutually and gratuitously the one to the other without being constrained thereunto by any motive of neces-sity; while husband and wife are bound by duty to agree the one with the other and deny each other nothing. Let this judgement, which we have passed with extreme caution and with the advice of a great number of other ladies, be held by you as the truth, unquestionable and unalterable.

In the year 1174, the third day from the Calends of May.[1]

Here we have the genesis of "romantic" love. Like most human beliefs, attitudes, and ways of behaving, it grew out of the *social conditions* and requirements of an era, and represented an adjust-ment to these conditions. In turn, it influenced the conditions themselves, and triggered a series of changes which exert influ-ence on attitudes and behavior even today.

The phenomenon of "romance" grew even stronger when there

---

[1] John Langdon-Davies, *A Short History of Women*, New York, Literary Guild of America, 1927, pp. 266–267.

were powerful female monarchs on the throne—for example, Queen Elizabeth and later Queen Victoria in Great Britain. The romantic environment was utilized *during the courting of the female by the male,* but after marriage the male became dominant, even tyrannical. Romantic love had nothing to do with married love—which was something else—and still is.

This romance-before-marriage tradition was brought to the American Colonies from England. But in America its practice was not restricted to the elite. The romantic courtship became a common custom, largely because of the scarcity of women in the pioneer days. This early shortage had an enormous influence on American male-female relationships, an influence that still lingers. In pioneer days males competed for the few females, using romantic-love behavior as a persuader. Also, the widespread belief (whether true or not) that the male was stronger, more vigorous, more courageous, and more aggressive than the female placed emphasis, both directly and indirectly, on romantic love. The few females for whom the pioneers competed appeared "small and helpless." They had to be "protected" by the males. This view reinforced romantic attitudes *before marriage.*

During the periods of World War I and World War II, a revolution occurred in the relationship between men and women. Women learned that they could do almost anything men could do—as well as, and in many instances better. It was realized that women live longer, are healthier, have a higher threshold of pain than men, and can successfully compete with men scholastically.

This realization offered to women a new spectrum of satisfactions and opportunities, based in large measure on an improved self-image, which had long been denied them. For them it indicated the end of the primarily male-dominated and male-structured society. The modern woman in the first half of the twentieth century desired equality in every way, beginning with sex and the vote.

At about the same time, contraceptive devices were perfected. Now woman could be man's equal not only in society, in business, and in scholarship, but also in sexual convenience; the sex act could be enjoyed by both without the woman's having to fear an unwanted pregnancy.

In past centuries in Western society, it has been considered important for a bride to be a virgin, whereas this condition seldom was required of the male, or even considered desirable. Today, though people may pay lip service to the idea of the virgin bride, in practice it is not generally considered important. Evidence from Kinsey and other authorities indicates that during the past thirty years women have practiced premarital sexual relations at an increasing rate.

Probably promiscuity has always been common in certain lower socio-economic groups, but in the upper middle class it was considered relatively rare until twenty years ago; at least it was not as obvious. The desire for extramarital intercourse has been increased by the advent of mass-communication media, particularly television and advertising. These have tended to make sex—both in and out of marriage—appear to be the most important thing in the lives of most Americans. The effect of the growing sex emphasis is shown, for example, in the fact that in the year 1962 in California 57,000 babies were born to "child-mothers" twelve to eighteen years old.

Thousands of high-school students are being married annually. In California, one third of these are in the ninth and tenth grades. A great many of these couples marry not because they wish to, but because the girl is pregnant. The frequency of premarital intercourse among these California high-school students has considerable significance because it indicates a corresponding trend among adults—a trend less clearly reflected in statistics concerning adult women, despite their greater opportunities for sexual activity, because they have easy access to contraceptives and sexual information usually unavailable to their teen-age counterparts.

Two forces remain to be considered in this survey of the history of marriage. The first is religion: When the Holy Roman Empire was at its peak, the Church exerted control over all facets of human life in Western Europe by means of canonical law. The most stringent canonical laws concerned marriage. For many ages marriage laws and customs had been civil, but then the Church moved in and took control. The first step was to make marriage a Holy Sacrament, for in the New Testament there is no proviso for this.

The hold of the Church for many centuries was so complete throughout Western Europe that almost everyone believed and accepted anything (religious or nonreligious) which came from Rome. One breach occurred in the sixteenth century with the discoveries of Copernicus. His declaration that the planets, including the earth, revolve about the sun, that the earth is *not* the center of the universe, *as the Church maintained,* was heard throughout Europe. More and more, men of learning doubted some of the edicts which came from Rome. Also, with the emergence of the Protestant Churches, Roman Catholic control over many aspects of life was reduced. It became possible for the elite to divorce without having the Pope's permission.

The growing disbelief in the Church's infallibility also resulted in time in the rejection of the Church's definition of male and female characteristics, including the evil nature of woman and the natural superiority of man.

Another force which influences marriage is economics. Until the nineteenth century, the European family was a unit of economic survival. Most people lived on the land or maintained family industries. The larger the family, the more hands there were to work at home. This arrangement may have been hard on the wife, but no one seemed to care about that in the male-dominated society.

In 1769 the first great economic-technological explosion began. With the development of the modern steam engine by James Watt, an economic metamorphosis was initiated which led to corresponding changes in family life and marriage. The steam engine made factories possible, and the factories took the husband out of the home, keeping him away all day and often into the night. The full burden of maintaining the home and family life fell upon the woman. Hitherto, she had at least been able to depend on her husband to discipline the older children and to make major household decisions. In his absence, she was forced to assume almost all of the responsibility for the family.

The construction of factories also affected marriage in another way. It caused families to move from their rural homes, where they could always live off the land in times of depression, into cities and slums which provided no place to forage for food or to grow it. Workers and their families were crowded in the slum

areas. Homes were small (often consisting of one room) and un-
heated; children had no place either to work or to play, and they
were exposed to more contagious illnesses. At the age of eight
they too went to work in the factories. Children longed for
the day when they could leave their parents' shabby quarters,
and the family was splintered in a fashion unheard of in rural
communities.

The effects of slum living on family life were calamitous. The
mother suffered the humiliation and despair of seeing her children grow hungry, ill, or quarrelsome. She was prevented from
performing her usual nurturing role without a continuous, ex-
hausting struggle. The slums and factories also brought humiliation to the father. Pay was so low and depressions were so frequent that he could not provide for his children or his wife.
Unable to fulfill their traditional roles adequately, parents coped
with hardship and disillusionment in the various ways which are
common to human beings under stress. Some became lethargic
and pretended not to care; some deserted the family rather than
face utter failure; some stayed and continued the struggle, often
at the price of illness, bitterness, and chronic fear. Women began
to work and seek more education so that they could help ensure
adequate care for themselves and their children when their husbands could not. Men began to seek new ways to maintain their
dominance and self-respect in the home. At that time, English
law, from which our own family law derives, gave the wife
and mother no legal protection—let alone community property.
Women in such a legally helpless condition learned to distrust
men and began to seek ways to look out for themselves.
According to some authorities many of these women moved to
the United States as contract wives and subsequently influenced the development of American family structure along more
egalitarian lines.

During this era, which lasted approximately a hundred years,
we find the disintegration of the traditional home. For centuries
in Western Europe the traditional home was congruent with a
particular form of marriage. With the fracturing of the customary
roles in the home, the institution of marriage—inevitably—also
came into serious question.

In Western culture the male had always been dominant over

the female. The "real man" was the individual who could use
heavy tools, could hunt, and was a good physical fighter. Physical
strength, having been the basis of survival, also placed men in
the positions of power: they made the rules and decisions. But
after the Industrial Revolution a man's value began to be measured in terms of his technical skill and intellectual productiveness,
as shown by the amount of money he made. And as the twentieth
century moved on, the female was able to develop the same skills
and intellectual powers, and make money almost as well as the
man. In the United States today, the women control and spend
more money than do the men.* In other words, as men's roles
became less dependent upon physical strength and more related
to skill and intellect, they also became more accessible to women.
Birth control made it increasingly possible for both men and
women to seek new avenues of expression. To women, with their
increased education in nondomestic areas, the new male role
seemed attractive. By contrast, the traditional female roles often
were regarded as unchallenging and servile—perhaps less because of their inherent nature than because of their association
with the concept of women as inferior beings capable of filling
only these roles and no others.

Drastic changes in family life were inevitable. One such major
change has completely altered marital expectations and behavior:
marriage has become more than a purely functional process.
People today seldom enter marriage *because it will help them
survive physically,* or because it is generally more advantageous
for a male and female to join in a collaborative partnership than
to live alone.

The relationship problems evinced in complex industrialized
societies have led some people to wish for the "good old days"
when social and sexual roles were rigidly defined by the society
and just as rigidly enforced. Also, one often hears: "If the youngsters had more *real* problems to worry about, they'd stay out of
trouble."

Both of these nostalgic sentiments are based on some truth. In
more primitive societies—those social groupings in which sheer
physical survival is the consciously understood central focus of

* Women own more than half of all stocks traded on the New York Stock
Exchange.

communal living—active collaboration with others and submergence of the individual interests to group interests become a necessity. Quarreling and separation such as occur in divorce or desertion are threats to individual survival and are controlled by the group in its own interest. In these societies, the socialization process is such that individual needs are adjusted to group needs. Indeed this adjustment is the goal of socialization and education in all societies; but in modern civilizations the variety of conflicting divergent groups makes it impossible for an individual to gear his needs and aims to those of all groups. The groups which capture his allegiance, or the allegiance of his parents, generally determine his social behavior.

In modern industrial society, couples facing a crisis affecting survival often stick together, only to separate when the emergency has passed.

The battle for survival in modern societies is usually a battle for emotional survival and the tools of war are correspondingly psychological, aimed at maiming the enemy's self-esteem or causing him shame rather than at killing him.

In such psychological warfare (for example, the battle of the sexes between spouses), it is difficult to decide who is the winner and who is the loser. There may be other parties in the picture operating unwittingly in subtle ways (the mother-in-law gets most of the blame), so that it is difficult to name the players without a program.

The institution of marriage has failed to adapt itself sufficiently to current requirements. The constant battle of the sexes and the family turmoil raging today are evidence of the haphazard efforts of individuals to reconcile their traditional role images with current realities. With little help from any social quarter, men and women are fighting lonely battles to find their place in the sun. Plagued by guilt and uncertainty, they struggle to discover their "identity" yet are unable to *accept* themselves if they do catch a glimpse of their genuine needs, desires, and goals. For what they glimpse is not what they have been conditioned to believe is "good" or "right" according to age-old systems of beliefs, developed on the basis of requirements which died at the time of the Industrial Revolution.

The man who, through education and training, has learned to

find his greatest fulfillment in reading or art or hairstyling or general scholarship rather than in athletic or business competition, must find ways to reconcile his preference with many age-old images regarding "masculinity." The college-educated woman who finds happiness and self-respect in professional achievement has the task of reconciling her learned needs and preferences with the "feminine" image which continues to define womanliness in terms of domestic and mothering abilities.

Today both sexes can perform *most* social functions equally well, and the rigid social resistance to role diffusion is becoming a genuine frustration to those who seek self-expression in roles outside the boundaries of their defined sex roles.

Members of the younger generation today often shock and frighten their parents and grandparents by their apparent determination to break through traditional role designations. But it is a major task of this and future generations to find solutions to the sex-role problems which their parents have left unresolved. The extreme manifestations of what parents see as sex-role confusion—such as boys dressing more like girls, girls dressing more like boys, and the increase in homosexuality—frighten parents because they cannot imagine a future different from the past they have known.

The Industrial Revolution has indeed been accompanied by a trend toward the development of great similarity in the social roles of males and females. This does not mean that the biological differences between men and women have been destroyed or that homosexuality will be the eventual outcome. We tend to forget that *there is a difference between social roles and the players who fulfill those roles*. For example work done by Robert Hess (and others) illustrates a considerable consistency in the manner in which second-grade children describe fathers, presidents, and Uncle Sam. Yet the *ideal* father they picture may be very different from the actual man at home who is their biological father. A mother may be playing what is thought of as the father's role when she disciplines children, but there is no implication that she is being more masculine because of this. Studies of families where the father was overseas for at least two years during World War II indicate that where the mother had a clear and essentially loving picture of her husband, the children immediately related to the father upon his return as if he had never left. Yet while he was gone, it was the mother who was fulfilling both parental roles.

However, it is possible for our basic conception of a role to change. Many of the important roles in our society are dependent upon intelligence, the ability to operate machines, the ability to work for or with other people, or the power to utilize certain specialized knowledge, like the mathematics of physics; these are capacities which both men and women possess. Therefore, role distinctions are being made less on a sexual than on a functional basis. It would be difficult for the average American to accept the situation in Russia, where two thirds of all physicians are women, and yet a few years of living in such a society would have to at least partially destroy our cultural bias that male physicians are superior.

Some of the young people today who are vehemently against marriage are actually struggling to find new attitudes to match new social realities. Accomplishment of this aim will necessarily involve vast changes in the marriage process and in family structure.

In summary, marriage used to be an institution for the *physical* survival and well-being of two people and their offspring. This function gave rise to a particular rule-governed structure suitable to the situation. Today, except in time of war or accident, the struggle for survival in industrialized societies does not require purely physical strength. Instead, we have primarily the struggle for *psychological* and *emotional* survival. The family unit is the natural unit for human survival regardless of what the hazard is. But so far, the changes in the structure, form, and processes of marriage have been too few and too unsystematic to cope with the new psychological and emotional problems. Marriage still is an anachronism from the days of the jungle, or at least from the days of small farms and home industries.

Divorce, marital strife, desertion, and emotional and physical illness are a few symptoms of this cultural lag in the institution of marriage, and they seem to be on the increase. We cannot return to the "simple" life of an agricultural or primitive community in

this atomic, industrial age; we must modify our outmoded attitudes, beliefs, and institutions to accommodate current social
realities.

Marriage is still a necessary institution. But it must be adjusted
to new social and economic conditions. Above all, the new roles
and relationships of men and women must be recognized. It is
not surprising that an anachronistic social institution cannot function; nevertheless, it is tragic that so many marriages fail and so
little is being done about it.

2

THE MYTHS OF
MARRIAGE

Both individual experience and statistical surveys make it clear that almost everyone suffers severe disappointment within a few months after marriage. A study conducted by the Mental Research Institute with couples married for an average of one year indicated that they felt marriage was different from what they had expected.

One young woman said, "Marriage is not what I had assumed it would be. One premarital assumption after another has crashed down on my head. I am going to make my marriage work, but it's going to take a lot of hard work and readjusting. Marriage is like taking an airplane to Florida for a relaxing vacation in January, and when you get off the plane you find you're in the Swiss Alps. There is cold and snow instead of swimming and sunshine. Well, after you buy winter clothes and learn how to ski and learn how to talk a new foreign language, I guess you can have just as good a vacation in the Swiss Alps as you can in Florida. But I can tell you, doctor, it's one hell of a surprise when you get off that marital airplane and find that everything is far different from what one had assumed."

This realistic and candid young woman is now happy in her marriage. But for her to reach this point required two years of patient working and changing, and of expensive visits by herself and her husband to a competent marriage counselor for a once-a-month "checkup." She learned that the institution of modern marriage is based on many false assumptions and untrue beliefs.

Whenever a decision or a system is based on false assumptions it is almost certain to be a failure. And marriage is no exception. We believe that if men and women were acquainted with the realities of marriage before they entered it, and if they accepted these realities, the divorce rate in the United States would diminish markedly.

To understand the realities of the marital relationship it is essential first to recognize the unrealities. What follows is a discussion of seven of the major myths of marriage.

3

FALSE ASSUMPTION 1

That People Marry Because They Love Each Other

The first myth is the belief that people get married because they are "in love." It is extremely difficult to define love satisfactorily. Dictionaries disagree. Psychiatrists and psychologists who specialize in marital problems usually are unable to define love. When they are asked the question by a client, they usually evade the issue by asking, "What do *you* think love is?"

The definition of perfect love which is most cherished in the Western world is the one given by St. Paul in the thirteenth chapter of First Corinthians. True, it is a Christian definition; but it is so universal that its almost exact equivalent is used by Muslims, Hindus, Buddhists, and Jews.

Love* suffereth long, *and* is kind; love envieth not; love vaunteth not itself, is not puffed up,
Doth not behave itself unseemly, seeketh not her own, is not easily provoked, thinketh no evil;

---

* Some versions use the word "charity" instead of "love." But they mean the same thing. Both refer to the act of cherishing dearly and giving unstintingly without wishing anything in return.

Rejoiceth not in iniquity, but rejoiceth in the truth;
Beareth all things, believeth all things, hopeth all things, en-
dureth all things.
Love never faileth.

The authors have never met a person who is consistently loving
according to St. Paul's definition. We have known many decent
people, people who have integrity and who are kind most of the
time; but they are not consistently loving in this biblical sense. It
is our opinion that it would be too difficult for spouses to practice
this kind of relationship described by St. Paul—unless both were
saints.

A more practical definition of love has been given by the great
American psychiatrist Harry Stack Sullivan: *"When the satisfaction or the security of another person becomes as significant to
one as is one's own satisfaction or security, then the state of love
exists."*[1]

The state of love described by Sullivan is possible in marriage
—but few spouses are prepared for it, or capable of experiencing
it, right after the wedding. Its coming, if it comes at all, is the
result of luck or of years of hard work and patience—as we hope
to demonstrate later. Observation of hundreds of married couples
shows that very few experience love.

It is a false assumption that people marry for love. *They like
to think of themselves as being in love;* but by and large the
emotion they interpret as love is in reality some other emotion—
often a strong sex drive, fear, or a hunger for approval.

If they are not in love, then why are they impelled to marry?
There are several reasons.

During courtship, individuals lose most of their judgment.
People who believe themselves to be in love describe their emotion as ecstasy. "Ecstasy"—from the Greek *ekstasis,* which means
"derange"—is defined as the "state of being beside oneself; state
of being beyond all reason and self-control." When an emotional
courtship starts, the man and woman appear to relinquish whatever sense of balance and reality they ordinarily possess.

Courtship—the time of ecstatic paralysis—has been cleverly

[1] Harry Stack Sullivan, *Conceptions of Modern Psychiatry,* New York,
W. W. Norton & Company, 1953, pp. 42–43.

designed by Nature to lure members of the species into repro-
ducing themselves. Courtship is a powerful manifestation of
sexual excitement. In Western culture, it has well-defined rituals;
these are simple steps leading up to the ultimate goal—legal
breeding. The man and the woman are in a trance. By the magic
of Nature, they have become wonderfully attractive to each other.

It is marvelous to observe how ruthless and cunning Nature is
in her effort to perpetuate the species. Individuals are in such a
dizzy state that they become reckless. The problems of marriage
are not noticed or considered. The frightful divorce statistics
mean nothing; it seems obvious that bad marriages, like death,
are for others only. Frequently, the partners-to-be know that they
are marrying the wrong persons, but they are in such a passion
(some call it romance), and are being driven so hard by the
applause of society, that they cannot help themselves. For example, they may realize that the man is unable, as yet, to earn a
living; or that the woman is incompetent to manage a home; or
that each has radically different tastes and values from the other.
These and many other obstacles to a workable marriage usually
have no significance to a couple in the courtship stage. The courting individuals are obsessed by one desire only—to mate. And
society ordains that a ceremony must sanctify the mating. Although in a majority of marriages the magic and marvelous attractiveness of courtship diminishes (and often vanishes entirely)
within a brief time after the honeymoon, it is obvious that the
instinct to reproduce—the sex drive (which mistakenly is called
love)—lures a great many individuals into marriage.

People often marry because society expects it of them. In our
society a spinster is frequently regarded as an unattractive failure; and a middle-aged bachelor is suspected of being a homosexual, or of having a mother complex. Society encourages marriage in many ways and for many reasons. For example, marriage
is—to put it crudely—good for business. It gives employment to
ministers, justices of the peace, caterers, florists, dressmakers,
printers, jewelers, furniture manufacturers, architects, landlords,
obstetricians, and so on almost endlessly. Whenever there is a
wedding a hundred cash registers tinkle. Therefore members of
the profit-making multitude smile and applaud, frequently in
honest approval. This approval adds to the myth that the very act

of marriage is a good thing; it brings prestige in society's eyes to the young couple.

For the clergy and for officials, marriage is a source of power and control, a means of perpetuating loyalty to the Church through the children. Certain historical necessities—which in point of fact may no longer exist—are also reflected in the attitudes of society. For example, in earlier days, when mortality rates were high, a "big family" meant more people in the community and thus a greater chance for survival; and marriage was prerequisite for the existence of the big family. Though circumstances have changed now, the approbation of marriage has not. In short, almost all segments of society disapprove of the single state but approve of marriage. This universal attitude tends to cause people who think they are in love to be impetuous, hurried, and careless in getting married. Marriage, they have been taught, is a "good thing."

The pressures and the maneuverings of parents often push their children into premature and careless marriages. Parents maneuver, manipulate, and meddle. Fathers and mothers claim that they meddle for their children's benefit. The truth is that parents often feel failure or disgrace if their children aren't married at the conventional age. And parents are seldom fully honest to their children about their own relationships. Therefore, most youngsters believe that their parents are or were in love, and that they must be emulated in this respect.

Romantic literature, tradition, and social hysteria have given marriage false values which the excited male and female often accept as true. They enter wedlock expecting a high level of constant joy from that moment on. Although they take an oath to love and cherish each other throughout all adversity, in fact they do not expect any serious adversity. They have been persuaded that love (which they cannot even define) automatically will make it possible to solve all problems.

Loneliness often drives people into marriage. Many individuals simply cannot bear to be alone. They get bored and restless, and they think that having somebody of the opposite sex in the house will stop them from being miserable. Thus they marry because of desperation, not love.

Many people are fearful concerning their economic future. Men may believe that the responsibility involved in supporting a wife and children will automatically motivate them to produce more than they would if they remained single. Women often feel they will find financial security through marriage, regardless of the current ability of their fiancés to provide for their needs.

Some individuals marry because of an unconscious desire to improve themselves. Almost all human beings have a mental image—called the ego ideal—of what they would like to be. In reality an individual seldom develops into this ideal person. But when he meets someone of the opposite sex who has the qualities which he desires, then up pops another false assumption. The individual unconsciously concludes that if he marries, he will, without effort, acquire the missing desirable characteristics or talents. For this reason a drunk sometimes is attracted to an abstainer; an inherent liar may be drawn to a simple, naïve person; a man with poor physical coordination often marries a slender, athletic woman; a person who cannot carry a tune often marries one who can sing well; and so forth. After the marriage the spouses learn that intimacy does not bring about the desired self-improvement. Each blames the other and the discord begins.

Many marriages are motivated by neuroses. Certain individuals pick as mates those who make it possible for them to exercise their neuroses. These people do not wish to be happy in the normal sense. If they enjoy suffering, they unconsciously choose partners with whom they can fight, or who will abuse or degrade them. Some of these marriages endure for a considerable time because the partners get pleasure from discord, but this type of perversion can hardly be called an expression of love.

Some people miss their father or mother and cannot live without a parental symbol. Therefore they find—and marry—a person of the opposite sex who will play the parental role.

In summary, then, it may be said that people generally enter matrimony thinking they are in love and believing that marriage will bring them "instant happiness," which will solve all problems. Actually, in most instances they are swept into marriage on a tidal wave of romance, not love. Romance is usually ephemeral; it is selfish. Romantic "lovers" are distraught and miserable when separated, and this misery is caused by selfishness of the most egocentric type. The "lover" is sorry for himself and is grieving over his loss of pleasure and intimacy. This state of mind is closely related to another selfish emotion—jealousy. Romance is exciting —but it is no relation to love, no kin to that generous concern for someone else which Harry Stack Sullivan defines as love.

Most people believe they are marrying for love. This is a false assumption and a dangerous myth.

4

FALSE ASSUMPTION 2

That Most Married People
Love Each Other

Both our own research and a review of publications by many social scientists have led us to the conclusion that spouses who have been married for more than three or four years rarely state spontaneously to an interviewer that they are in love with one another. They are more apt to speak in utilitarian terms or to make unilateral statements like "John is a good provider" or "Jane is a good mother to our children." Yet in many marriages, especially discordant ones, each partner tenaciously and stubbornly believes that he is a loving individual—more loving than his spouse.

Each partner strongly feels that he is trying, with courage and self-sacrifice, to make the marriage work; and that if there is friction, the other partner is causing it. Each may cite specific episodes which demonstrate that he is loving, patient, and good (and that the other is selfish, unkind, and unreasonable).

In many cases, spouses who believe their behavior to be generous and loving, are unwittingly lying to themselves. A large percentage of what they believe to be loving acts are in truth profoundly destructive acts, the expression of an unconscious hypocrisy. The spouses usually are not aware they are murdering their marriages and mangling their partners under the guise of love.

The pattern, in brief, is this: Spouse A believes (consciously) that he is behaving in a loving, benevolent manner to spouse B. In reality (unconsciously) A is behaving in a harmful manner. If B labels the behavior as harmful rather than benevolent, A is hurt and replies, "I was only trying to be helpful."

The accusations, misunderstandings, and fights now begin. Here are three examples.

1. Michael Young (who was a bachelor until he was thirty-two) is a marvelous cook and an efficient housekeeper. His wife, Martha, knows almost nothing about domestic science. She has lived abroad most of her life. Her family had servants for all chores. Michael is unhappy over Martha's low-grade performance in cooking and home maintenance.

"I will show you how to do it," says Michael. "I will teach you."

On weekends Michael puts on a brilliant performance, cleaning the house with efficiency and speed, and concocting gourmet meals effortlessly. He repeats the act whenever there are guests present ("because that's when Martha needs help most") and frequently reminds her that he is helping her.

Actually he is showing her up, nagging her, making her feel even more helpless and incompetent. He is making her afraid to try to learn, and is convincing her that no matter what heroic efforts she makes, she will be a failure. He is unconsciously persuading her that she will never be able to equal his own performance and satisfy him. But he says—and believes—he is helping her and being loving.

2. Joan Dalrymple is a great cook. She majored in domestic science at a women's school and later studied cooking in Paris and Vienna. Preparing things to eat—the fancier the better—is the passion of her life. She bakes her own bread, makes her own mayonnaise, grows her own herbs, livens up vegetables and meats with rich egg and cream sauces. Her desserts are famous. People are eager to be invited to the Dalrymple home.

Joan is proud of her skill. She has elaborate dinner parties regularly, which she regards as her way of exhibiting her love for Howard and of helping him in his business. She forgets how much she enjoys receiving the praise of her guests, and their requests for recipes.

Howard is getting fatter by the month. His blood cholesterol is up; his physician wants him to lose weight. But Howard's health requirements do not take precedence over Joan's determination to nourish her own ego by impressing others with her skill as a cook and as a thoughtful loving wife, nor over her wish to advertise how much she is helping Howard professionally.

Howard tries to follow his doctor's advice, but finds it hard to refuse eating in front of guests; or to appear difficult after listening to Joan enthusiastically describe how she drove twenty miles to a farm to obtain absolutely fresh cream.

Howard may, with tired despair, eat the food and hope to reduce in other ways. Paradoxically, Howard believes *he* is being loving when he does so, because he doesn't wish to hurt Joan's feelings—especially in front of guests. In this way he is compounding Joan's deceit and destructive behavior. He is not only permitting Joan's "loving" actions and attitudes to destroy him; he is assisting her.

3. Joe, who has been married about three years, works hard in his advertising office. He comes home at night extremely fatigued. At his moment of arrival his wife greets him effusively and insists on "relaxing him and taking care of him." During the summer she always meets him at the garden gate, kisses him affectionately, puts her arm around him, and leads him to the chaise longue in the shade beneath the apple tree. There, waiting for him, are a glass of freshly made lemonade and two aspirins.

"But, Marie, I don't want to. . . ."

"Now, darling, you're exhausted and nervous, and I know what's good for you. That's my sole function in life—to take care of you. . . ."

Observed objectively, this dialogue sounds like part of a comic opera, but variations of it occur daily in thousands of homes.

Joe may be flattered, but he is also irritated. What he would like to do is have a martini, a hot tub, and about a half hour of quiet. But Marie insists, and Joe usually gives in. Yet each evening, driving home from work and thinking about the reception he'll receive from Marie, he feels extremely angry. Sometimes he even wishes his wife would die: "If she were dead, I could get into the house without being molested." This thought recurs so often that Joe finally feels he is losing his mind, and goes to a psychiatrist.

The psychiatrist interviews both Joe and Marie.

Here is part of his private report: "Marie is a 'sweet' person who has firm ideas about what a wife should do for her husband. When her determined benevolence violates her husband's concepts, Joe resists and tells her to stop managing him. Marie responds by bursting into tears, clinging to Joe, and pathetically sobbing that he is rejecting her and does not love her."

And indeed after several years of Marie's "benevolence" Joe does reject her and dislike her. Marie has "loved" him into a nasty divorce.

Joe's friends are shocked. How can he leave such a loving wife? Joe shakes his head with the unmistakable air of a man misunderstood. "Yes," he is able to reply, after several months of seeing the psychiatrist, "Marie worked hard to make a good marriage. She worked so hard she forgot about *me* as an individual."

There are many other examples of behavior which appears to be loving but is really selfish. Consider, for instance, the spouse who "loves" the other so much that whenever they are separated he frets, phones, telegraphs, writes his partner to distraction. Or examine the behavior of the individual who believes he wishes to make the other proud of him—but really desires to exhibit his fine intelligence and talents. In a group with the spouse, he will dominate all conversation, answer all questions addressed to the spouse, and even steal all the punch lines, all with the air of being supportive and helpful, of trying to make "both of us" look intelligent.

The husband who picks out a new car and gives it to his wife as a surprise birthday present is proud of his generosity and his loving behavior. He looks ahead for the flash of joy which will light her face when she finds the car with her initials on it waiting in the garage. But this desire for an enthusiastic response, a look of joyful surprise, is selfish—he is nourishing his own ego. Were his wife's happiness and pride as significant to him as his own, he would have told her to pick out the automobile which *she* wanted, giving her the pleasure of choosing the make, model, color, accessories, and so forth. Or he would have suggested that they both go out and look at cars together. We do not mean to imply, however, that the occasional, spontaneous acts of giving which occur in marriage are harmful.

The generalized recommendation to "be loving" offered by counselors is too vague to be helpful and often simply makes the worried spouse feel guilty about being human and occasionally unloving. And when giving is spontaneous rather than forced, it brings joy to both the giver and the receiver. And when a so-called marriage counselor recommends a "loving" act which one spouse performs independently (without discussion and mutual agreement), he is leading the spouse into debilitating behavior. The "loving" spouse is here unilaterally deciding the nature of the marriage relationship. This kind of behavior unequivocally leads to trouble.

Yet just such behavior—which we call loving self-deception— is recommended by many writers on marriage in newspapers, magazines, and books, and by many marriage counselors, some of whom have an M.D. or a Ph.D. after their name. The advice goes something like this: "If you want to make your wife happy, send her roses once a week." But the wife may resent the spending of seven dollars a week on flowers. She may prefer to spend the money at a beauty parlor or on new clothes. Consider the following (paraphrased) remarks of a nationally syndicated marriage counselor to a woman who seeks advice on how to behave toward her husband, whom she has just caught making love to another woman:

> Dear Madam:
> It is obvious that you have not been providing your spouse with sufficient stimulation [sic!] at home. How long has it been since you've had your hair restyled? Do you wear a dirty wrapper to the breakfast table—your hair still in curlers?
>
> I suggest you say nothing about the situation to your husband. Simply make it a practice to arise a half hour before he does in the morning and start his day off right by being a charming, attractive wife.

It is not obvious why the expert chose *appearance* as the focal point for his cure, but he is treating the situation as if it were solely the wife's fault. There are many reasons why his advice is unfortunate—if not actually harmful—including such obvious possibilities as the following:

1. The husband's fondness for his paramour may indicate not sexual dissatisfaction, but a desire for intellectual companionship; he may already feel his wife is too vain and resent her lack of interest in intellectual activities. The columnist's advice, in this case, will only increase their problems.

2. If the wife is suddenly "loving" and charming and the husband is feeling guilty for having behaved badly, what will he think of his wife's inappropriate behavior? He may easily imagine that she is simply biding her time before letting the ax fall—by secretly making legal arrangements for separation or divorce. In the meantime, with no honest communication between them, his suspicions and guilt and her suspicions and anger will only drive them further apart.

3. Most important, how does this advice aid the couple to examine their total relationship—which is, after all, the key to the reasons for any form of infidelity?

Thus behavior which *appears to be loving* may in reality be a form of one-upmanship, selfishness, and lack of consideration. Deception of oneself and others is destructive, and accelerates the disintegration of a marriage.

All human beings perform unilateral and selfish acts. To do so is not always bad; it sometimes can be wholesome if the individual knows what is happening. But under no circumstances can these acts be regarded as loving, and the first requirement for a workable marriage is to live and relate on a basis of reality, not of myths, obsolete and meaningless traditions, and self-deceit.

5

FALSE ASSUMPTION 3

*That Love Is Necessary
for a Satisfactory Marriage*

Even though people are reluctant to admit it, most husbands and wives are disappointed in their marriages. There is overwhelming evidence to confirm this.

At least one person out of every three who gets married will be divorced within about ten years. Many of these will indulge in legal polygamy—that is, they will marry and divorce several times. All told, the divorce rate in the United States is 41 per cent.

Marriage is so turbulent an institution that articles on how to patch up disintegrating marriages can be found in almost every issue of our family magazines and daily newspapers, with titles such as "How to Keep Your Husband Happy," "How to Make Your Wife Feel Loved." Surveys show that this sort of article frequently attracts more readers than anything else in the publication. It appears because of public demand, a demand which must originate from millions of unhappy, confused, and dissatisfied couples. Evidently the dreamed-of marriage often does not materialize. There are unexpected shortcomings, bickerings, misunderstandings. Most spouses to varying degrees are frustrated, confused, belligerent, and disappointed.

Almost every expression of our culture, including advertisements, has something to say about how to improve female-male relationships. Motion pictures, plays, television, radio, feature the friction between wife and husband more than any other subject.

The offices of marriage counselors, psychologists, and psychiatrists are crowded with clients who are concerned over problems which mainly involve marriage, and who pay from twenty-five dollars to fifty dollars an hour for assistance. But these troubled people usually cannot identify their problems; even worse, they usually do not sincerely seek solutions. What each one wants is confirmation that he is correct and good, and that his spouse is the one at fault!

One reason for this marital disenchantment is the prevalence of the mistaken belief that "love" is necessary for a satisfying and workable marriage. Usually when the word "love" is used, reference is actually being made to romance—that hypnotic, ecstatic condition enjoyed during courtship. Romance and love are different. Romance is based usually on minimum knowledge of the other person (restricted frequently to the fact that being around him is a wonderful, beatific, stimulating experience). Romance is built on a foundation of quicksilver nonlogic. It consists of attributing to the other person—blindly, hopefully, but without much basis in fact—the qualities one *wishes* him to have, though they may not even be desirable, in actuality. Most people who select mates on the basis of imputed qualities later find themselves disappointed, if the qualities are not present in fact, or discover that they are unable to tolerate the implication of the longed-for qualities in actual life. For example, the man who is attracted by his fiancée's cuteness and sexiness may spend tormented hours after they are married worrying about the effect of these very characteristics on other men. It is a dream relationship, an unrealistic relationship with a dream person imagined in terms of one's own needs.

Romance is essentially selfish, though it is expressed in terms of glittering sentiment and generous promises, which usually cannot be fulfilled. ("I'll be the happiest man in the world for the rest of my life." "I'll make you the best wife any man ever had.")

Romance—*which most spouses mistake for love*—is not necessary for a good marriage. The sparkle some couples manage to preserve in a satisfying marriage—based on genuine pleasure in one another's company, affection and sexual attraction for the spouse as he really is—can be called love.

If romance is different than love, then what *is* love? We do best to return to the definition of Harry Stack Sullivan: "When the satisfaction or the security of another person becomes as significant to one as is one's own satisfaction or security, then the state of love exists." In this sense, love consists of a devotion and respect for the spouse that is equal to one's own self-love.

We have already shown that people usually marry on a wave of romance having nothing to do with love. When the average American (not long from the altar) lives with the spouse in the intimacy of morning bad breath from too much smoking, of annoying habits previously not known, when he is hampered by the limitations of a small income (compared with the lavishness of the honeymoon), or encounters the unexpected irritability of premenstrual tension or of business frustration and fatigue, a change in attitude begins to occur. The previously romantic person begins to have doubts about the wonderful attributes with which his spouse has been so blindly credited.

These doubts are particularly disturbing at the start. Not very long ago, after all, the spouse believed that "love" (romance) was heavenly, all-consuming, immutable, and that beautiful relationships and behavior were *voluntary* and *spontaneous*. Now, if doubts and criticism are permitted to intrude upon this perfect dream, the foundations begin to shake in a giddy manner. To the husband or wife the doubts seem to be evidence that one of them is inadequate or not to be trusted. The doubts imply that the relationship is suffering from an unsuspected malignancy.

To live with another person in a state of love (as defined by Sullivan) is a different experience from whirling around in a tornado of romance. A loving union is perhaps best seen in elderly couples who have been married for a long time. Their children have grown, the pressure of business has been relieved, and the specter of death is not far away. By now, they have achieved a set of realistic values. These elderly spouses respect each other's idiosyncracies. They need and treasure companionship. Differences between them have been either accepted or worked out; they are no longer destructive elements. In such instances each has as much interest in the well-being and security of the other as he has in himself. Here is true symbiosis: a union where each admittedly feeds off the other. Those who give together really live together!

But it is possible to have a productive and workable marriage without love (although love is desirable) as well as without romance. One can have a functioning marriage which includes doubts and criticisms of the spouse and occasional inclinations toward divorce. The husband or wife may even think about how much fun it might be to flirt with an attractive neighbor. Such thoughts can occur without being disastrous to the marriage. *In many workable marriages both spouses get a good deal of mileage out of fantasy.*

How, then, can we describe this functional union which can bring reasonable satisfaction and well-being to both partners? It has four major elements: tolerance, respect, honesty, and the desire to stay together for mutual advantage. One can prefer the spouse's company to all others', and even be lonely in his absence, without experiencing either the wild passion inherent in romance, or the totally unselfish, unswerving devotion that is basic in true love.

In a workable marriage both parties may be better off together than they would have been on their own. They may not be ecstatically happy because of their union, and they may not be "in love," but they are not lonely and they have areas of shared contentment. They feel reasonably satisfied with their levels of personal and interpersonal functioning. They can count their blessings and, like a sage, philosophically realize that nothing is perfect.

We must return once again to the meaning of the word "love," for no other word in English carries more misleading connotations. The following is an actual example of how distorted the thinking of an individual may become when he believes he is in love.

A young woman and her fiancé visiting a marriage counselor had completed an interpersonal test which told much about their behavior and how they viewed each other. The counselor, after studying the data, asked why the woman wished to marry this man, who was an admitted alcoholic. She said she had sought the counselor's help because she did have some doubts. Her previous husband, from whom she had recently been divorced, was weak and passive. Now she was looking for a man strong enough to take care of her.

The marriage counselor explained that he could not understand why she had picked an alcoholic—obviously a weak man who could not possibly look after her. She would have to look after *him*.

Her fiancé sat passively by and did not enter the conversation.

The counselor asked again, "Why do you want to marry this man who appears to be just the opposite of the spouse you say you need?"

The young woman shrugged her shoulders, smiled happily, and said, with dogmatic conviction, "Because I love him."

Her fiancé smiled and nodded in support of her unsupportable statement.

It is obvious that this woman did not know what she meant by "I love him." She did not even know how she felt about him. Because of her complex neurotic needs she had a desire for this man—and it could probably be shown that this was a unilateral and totally selfish desire. Her choice of someone to "love" had nothing to do with her prospects for having a workable or satisfying marriage. The word "love" was a cover-up for an emotional mix-up which she did not understand.

Often "I love you" is an unconscious excuse for some form of emotional destructiveness. Sometimes it is a camouflage for a status struggle, which may continue even after a couple has separated. A spouse who has been deserted (especially for another) may covertly or unconsciously wish to be identified and applauded as the good and loyal partner. The jilted spouse assumes a saintly, pious behavior—especially in public—and makes certain everyone knows he still "loves" the other and will lovingly and patiently wait forever until the other comes to his senses. This can be accomplished with operatic flamboyance while the individual simultaneously has a well-hidden affair with someone else's husband or wife; and the apparent inconsistency later can be rationalized away: "After John's [or Mary's] departure there was such a hole in my life I *had* to do something to stay on an even keel. If I had had a breakdown it would have hurt the children. But my behavior didn't alter the fact that I loved him."

This type of "love" is especially likely to manifest itself when one spouse believes he received ill-treatment from the other for some years prior to the final desertion. The "injured" spouse (for so he regards himself no matter what he did to hurt and destroy the other) will loudly maintain with grief: "But I still love him." It takes little clinical experience or psychological brilliance to recognize that usually this person really is exhibiting hurt pride and rage at being the one who was left, rather than the one who did the leaving.

"Love" may also be used as an excuse for domination and control. The expression "I love you" has such an immutable place in our traditions that it can serve as an excuse for anything, even for selfishness and evil. Who can protest against something done "because I love you," especially if the assertion is made with histrionic skill and in a tone of sincerity? The victim—the one on the receiving end—may intuitively realize that he is being misused. Yet he often finds it impossible to remonstrate.

Sullivan's definition of love is important. It describes not a unilateral process, but a two-way street, a bilateral process in which two individuals function in relation to each other as equals. Their shared behavior interlocks to form a compages* that represents *mutual* respect and devotion. One spouse alone cannot achieve this relationship. Both must participate to the same degree. The necessity for both spouses to "give" equally is one of the reasons that a marriage built upon mutual love is so rare.

People naturally wish to have a happy marriage to a loving spouse. But such a union is hard to come by without knowledge of the anatomy of marriage, plus much patience, work—and luck. Many people fail to face the fact that if their parents' marriage was unhappy or their childhood was neurotic, they do not possess the prerequisite experience for choosing the correct mate. Where have they observed a good model for marriage? How can they possibly know what a loving marriage is like—and what elements must be *put into* it?

Most Americans enter marriage expecting to have love without having asked themselves the question, Am I lovable? Following close behind is another question: If I am not lovable, is it not likely that I have married an unloving person?

* "A whole formed by the compaction or juncture of parts, a framework or system of conjoined parts, a complex structure."—*O.E.D.*

There is another misuse of the word "love." Some people believe that they can love generously even if doing so requires behaving like a martyr. They believe their rewards will come not on earth but in heaven, or at least in some mystical, unusual way. Therefore they seem able to love unilaterally and want nothing for themselves. They suffer happily and enjoy making sacrifices while pouring their love out on another. The more undeserving the other is, the more of this love there is to be poured.

This situation is deceptive. Martyrdom is actually one of the most blatant types of self-centeredness. No one can be more difficult to deal with than the one-way benevolent person who frantically, zealously, and flamboyantly tries to help someone else, and apparently seeks nothing for himself.

Nathan Epstein, William Westley, Murray Bowen, John Workentin, Don Jackson, and others who have conducted research on couples who are content with their marriages and have reared apparently healthy, successful children, agree that *companionability* and *respect* are the key words in the lexicon these couples use to describe their marriages. A husband interviewed in one study stated: "In love? Well, I guess so—haven't really thought about it. I suppose I would, though, if Martha and I were having troubles. The Chinese have a saying, 'One hand washes the other.' That sort of describes us, but I don't know if that's what you mean by love."

The happy, workable, productive marriage does not require love as defined in this book, or even the practice of the Golden Rule. To maintain continuously a union based on love is not feasible for most people. Nor is it possible to live in a permanent state of romance. Normal people should not be frustrated or disappointed if they are not in a *constant* state of love. If they experience the joy of love (or imagine they do) for ten per cent of the time they are married, attempt to treat each other with as much courtesy as they do distinguished strangers, and attempt to make the marriage a workable affair—one where there are some practical advantages and satisfactions for each—the chances are that the marriage will endure longer and with more strength than the so-called love matches.

6

FALSE ASSUMPTION 4

*That There Are Inherent Behavioral and
Attitudinal Differences Between Female and
Male, and That These Differences Cause
Most Marital Troubles*

———————————————

Ever since history was first well recorded (mostly by the male)
men and women in civilized nations have based their behavior
on an unprovable belief. Their relations to each other have been
founded on the assumption that women and men are vastly different emotionally, intellectually, and spiritually. They have considered each other almost as different species of *Homo sapiens*.

The myth breaks down into many specific false assumptions
(some of which are embraced by men only, some by women
only). Here are some examples:

1. Women are more emotional than men.
2. Men are better at abstract thinking than are women.
3. Women are more intuitive than men.
4. **Men are more skillful with their hands (and in using tools)**
than women.
5. Women are more hypochondriacal than men, but men are
little boys at heart, especially when they're ill.

6. It is almost always the man who indulges in infidelity and breaks up the marriage.

7. Homosexuality is practiced more by men than by women.

8. The female usually snares the male.

9. Women are slier and more cunning than men.

10. Men are bolder, more physically vigorous, more courageous than women.

11. Women are more loving than men.

Believers in these myths often try to support their view by asking questions like the following: Why have there been no famous women chess players? Why so few great female mathematicians, composers, violinists, artists? Why is the male such a beast of infidelity while the woman is usually loyal and chaste? Why do more men have ulcers than women? Why do more men remain emotionally immature all their lives? Why do men start all the wars? It is supposed to be self-evident that these observations are explained by the inherent differences between the sexes.

Rousseau, the great French philosopher, wrote, "Woman is especially constituted to please men. . . . to please them, to be useful to them, to make themselves loved and honored by them, to educate them when young, to care for them when grown, to counsel them, to console them and to make life agreeable and sweet to them—these are the duties of women at all times, and what should be taught them from infancy."

A woman author in nineteenth-century England, who signed herself "Lady of Distinction," wrote, "The most perfect and implicit faith in the superiority of a husband's judgement, and the most absolute obedience to his desires, is not only the conduct that will ensure the greatest success, but will give the most entire satisfaction. . . ."

Blackstone, the jurist, wrote in his famous *Commentaries*, ". . . the very being or legal existence of woman is incorporated and consolidated into that of the husband; under whose wing, protection and *cover*, she performs everything. . . ."

Milton, the great English poet, wrote, "It is no small glory to him [man], that a creature so like him should be made subject to him."

Aristotle wrote, "The male is by nature superior, and the female inferior; and the one rules and the other is ruled. . . . The male is

by nature fitter for command than the female. . . . We must look
to the female as being a sort of natural deficiency."

Even the Christian church downgraded and stereotyped the
female. "What is woman but an enemy to friendship, and unavoidable punishment, a necessary evil, a natural temptation—a
wicked work of nature covered with shining varnish," wrote
St. John Chrysostom. A canonical decree prohibited women from
approaching the altar or ministering to the priest. "A woman is
incapable of true spiritual jurisdiction," said a Pope.

All of these statements were made during the last 2,400 years,
well into the era in which the male has been dominant in most
civilized countries. During this period he has had roles in society
which make him *appear* stronger, wiser, superior.

There are several explanations for the present acceptance of
the natural superiority of men.

First is the fact that in the past the members of the two sexes
have found themselves in different social roles. These roles have
given the impression that the type of work done by the individual,
and his social position, indicate his character and talents. For a
long time, man was by necessity the hunter; therefore, he was
believed to be more courageous and bold. Woman was immobi-
lized by pregnancy, child rearing, and home duties. Because she
was for biological reasons assigned to a domiciliary role, it was
assumed that she had a passive nature, and she was treated
accordingly. This kind of reasoning is called the *self-fulfilling
prophecy*. The individual believes a certain thing—then unconsciously arranges life so that what he believes becomes a fact.

Because laws and customs usually gave power, property, and
authority to the male, the female found that her only obvious
avenue of survival was patience, cunning, sex allurement. So she
began to exhibit these characteristics even though inherently she
possessed them to no greater degree than did the male.

Woman had almost no opportunities to exhibit her abilities in
physical activity, intellectual creativity, and invention—abilities
usually regarded as being uniquely male. Therefore woman has
been considered lacking in these areas.

There is evidence that in prehistoric days (which lasted much
longer than the historically recorded period) society was matri-
archal—managed by the female. Agriculture, spinning, weaving,

pottery—all activities except war and hunting—were carried on by the female. In those days women were the inventive ones, the abstract thinkers who from necessity created tools for turning plant fiber into yarn and yarn into cloth, discovered such complicated processes as baking and fabricating clay into pottery, and developed the crude instruments for sewing, erecting movable shelters, and so forth. The basic inventions which allowed man to change from a half-animal caveman into a civilized being were made by females because technology was their area of concern. Both men and women long have scoffed at the idea of a female being a political leader. Yet when a woman takes on such a role she often does well. Witness Queen Elizabeth, Cleopatra, Queen Victoria, and Queen Liliuokalani.

It is mainly the pressure of society that determines what roles, attitudes, kinds of behavior, the members of each sex will embrace. These roles, attitudes, and kinds of behavior have almost nothing to do with the sex of the individual—but many males refuse to accept this fact.

The way a person's role in society influences his status can easily be illustrated. In Hawaii, for example, an Army enlisted man generally is treated as a socially inferior person (except by the merchants who want his money). If a young lady goes out with an enlisted man, friends may raise eyebrows. It is assumed that the enlisted man usually drinks a lot and is not well educated, and that his only reason for dating a local girl is to sleep with her. The status of the Navy enlisted man in Norfolk, Virginia, is even worse.

But observe Private John Smith closely. See how attractive he is? Even though he is the lowest of the enlisted men, Private Smith—like many other servicemen—is a college graduate, from a fine, loving family. He is a person of integrity, gentleness, ambition; and he has a clear, brilliant mind. Yet regardless of his talents and fine character, when people see Private Smith, in his enlisted-man's uniform, walking down Kalakaua Avenue, they assume that he has the undesirable behavioral tendencies traditionally associated with enlisted men. *And they treat him accordingly.*

However, if Private Smith is suddenly promoted and becomes Lieutenant John Smith, he *ipso facto* becomes socially acceptable even to the elite. His role in society has changed. People now assume he is more decent, has better manners, a better mind, than the John Smith who wore a different uniform (and hence played a different role) only a few days before. At neither time do the observers have any information about John Smith. They estimate his worth from the role he is in, according to traditional, anachronistic values. Also, John Smith's opportunities to exhibit his talents when he was an enlisted man were limited (although not insurmountably) by the social role in which he found himself. Even the wife he chooses will be influenced by whether or not he wears a silver bar.

The same method of assuming that the nature of a role reflects the inherent characteristics of the one playing it has been employed in judgments about the qualities of the male and the female. People have assumed man and woman to be vastly different simply because historically they have carried out different duties in society. It is not usually realized that when the roles of male and female are reversed, each acquires many of the mannerisms and personality traits usually associated with the other. In certain areas in Greece during the Nazi invasion there were no able-bodied men left. The Greek women fought the Germans ferociously and vigorously with rifles, swords, hatchets. The old Greek men stayed home to care for the children and assumed the women's role. In the same way, the effect of a reversal of roles is strikingly exemplified by young Israeli women who fought bravely in war, swore, cut their hair very short, and dug ditches alongside the men with whom they served. History supplies many instances of this kind.

Another factor which has promoted the belief in rigid male-female differences is the influence of publications by scientists—most of them men—who unwittingly biased their own experiments to conform to their preconceptions about female inferiority. Their bias created a distortion similar to that which results when Negro children are tested for intelligence by Southern examiners; the children evidence lower I.Q.'s than a similar group tested by Northern examiners. We have learned only recently that experiments are influenced by the natural bias of the experimenter and by the environment in which the experiment takes place. The experimenter, without knowing it, affects the behavior of the person he is examining. *Often this influence is so great that the response of the subject is almost entirely created by the already-held beliefs of the experimenter.* It is well established now, for example, that the hallucinations of subjects taking the drug LSD vary with the personality and beliefs of the *experimenter* and with the environment in which the session is held.

Likewise, when a person has hallucinations as a result of sensory deprivation (in experiments where the subject, with eyes and ears covered, is placed in a quiet, dark room—devoid of any kind of external stimulus), the hallucinations vary according to what the subject has been told he may expect.

It is obvious, of course, that there are physical differences between men and women. There are also psychological differences; but it is difficult to estimate them, let alone measure them accurately. The slight hormonal differences between them relate mainly to sexual functioning. But what happens when the sex hormones are altered? Does this change cause the individuals to be radically incompetent in their present social roles, or make it impossible for them to maintain their status in society, or change their sex patterns? It does not. It has been well demonstrated that both male and female castrates (those having testicles or ovaries removed for medical reasons) can function adequately in their normal social roles if they have internalized the roles before being castrated. They can even achieve sexual satisfaction and orgasms. Perhaps most convincing of all is the work done by Hampton, Money, and Money, in the studies they originated at Johns Hopkins University, concerning hermaphroditic children. Hermaphrodites are physically closer to one sex than the other. But, it has been found, the hermaphrodite child makes a better adjustment to the sex with which its parents have identified it than to the sex to which it is biologically closer. For example, such a child may have functioning ovaries and only rudimentary testicles. In such a case, by hormonal and surgical treatment a physician can most easily bring about a biologically—that is physically—female child; but if the parents have been treating it like a boy and wishing it to be a boy, there will be trouble: the child may turn out to be a homosexual. *The psychological trend established by the parents in such cases is more influential than the anatomical situation.*

In an example like that of the hermaphroditic children, we are dealing with the extreme end of the continuum; such drastic changes in the bio-psychological nature of human beings can be made only after years of hormone treatments, surgery, and by psychological consultations.

The anthropologist Margaret Mead shows in her books *Male and Female* and *Sex and Temperament in Three Primitive Societies* that masculine and feminine behavior is conditioned by the attitude of society. In *Sex and Temperament in Three Primitive Societies* she discusses her observations of three tribes:

> These three situations [in the three tribes] suggest, then, a very definite conclusion. If those temperamental attitudes which we have traditionally regarded as feminine—such as passivity, responsiveness, and a willingness to cherish children—can so easily be set up as the masculine pattern in one tribe, and in another [the second tribe] be outlawed for the majority of men, we no longer have any basis for regarding such aspects of behavior as sex-linked. And this conclusion becomes even stronger when we consider the actual reversal in Tchambuli [the third tribe] of the position of dominance of the two sexes, in spite of the existence of formal patrilineal institutions [in which children carry the name of the father].

Today, in our Western culture, we have our own tribal laws about sex roles. In early life both parents, wittingly and unwittingly, transmit the cultural values to the child by indicating that "boys don't cry," "girls don't fight," and so on. Mothers tell their daughters, "The trouble with men is . . ." Fathers implore sons, "For God's sake, don't let 'em sucker you. . . ."

Later on, when dating is culturally appropriate, mothers pass their attitudes toward the opposite sex on to their daughters, and fathers pass their attitudes on to their sons. Mothers seldom discuss dating with their sons, and fathers seldom discuss it with their daughters. In this manner, the parents help perpetuate the myth of the separation of the sexes.

In summary, it is debilitatingly erroneous to believe that there are vast differences between the male and the female and that these differences cause most of the troubles in marriage. There are no vast, innate differences. The behavior patterns, attitudes, and temperaments of the male and the female are not inherently rigid. Despite the habits and cumulative forces of society, the man and woman can determine for themselves what role each will have in marriage. When they are unable to do this, then the marriage either will fail, or will be merely a numb, routine affair. Trouble is caused not by vast differences (which don't exist), *but by the inability to choose and activate the desirable or necessary role.*

7

FALSE ASSUMPTION 5

*That the Advent of Children Automatically
Improves a Potentially Difficult or an
Unfulfilled Marriage*

This is a book about marriage, not about families; yet it would be an injustice to any description of the marital system to assume that the child plays no role in the making or breaking of the marriage.[1] To have children is one of the explicit reasons for marrying; indeed, in some religious groups, sexual intercourse between spouses is supposed to occur only for the purpose of procreation. It is easily observed that some spouses are totally child-oriented: they live for their children. In return, the children keep the marriage alive by providing the parents a *raison d'être* for the marriage, and help fill the emotional and physical distance between the spouses, so that the expression of tension and friction

[1] For those readers who want information about family functioning, especially in relation to severe emotional problems, the following books are recommended: Virginia Satir, *Conjoint Family Therapy*, Palo Alto, California, Science and Behavior Books, 1965; Don D. Jackson, *Myths of Madness*, New York, Macmillan, 1964; G. Zuk and B. Nagy, editors, *The Psychotherapy of Disturbed Families*, Palo Alto, California, Science and Behavior Books, 1966; Nathan Ackerman, *Treating the Troubled Family*, New York, Basic Books, 1966.

between them is kept at a minimum. When the children leave home, these marriages typically are in serious difficulties—unless the parents are fortunate enough to have developed outside interests sufficient to maintain the protective distance between them.

Certain basic questions, propositions, and observations concerning the effects of children on marriage merit special discussion. Let us consider, first, whether childless marriages are less successful than marriages which beget offspring. This is a real *yes-and-no* proposition despite the public's general belief that marriages which result in children are more successful. For example, spouses who marry relatively late in life tend not to have children and yet appear to have a higher average of functional marriages than couples marrying earlier. But it is the fact that they do not marry until later than their peers that has most to do with how the marriages turn out; the fact that they do not have children is accessory. Several studies also indicate that professional women who marry later than their peers and choose not to have children have a better marital record than their undergraduate college classmates. Successful professional women who marry later than their collegiate peers tend to hold satisfying, well-paying jobs, so they do not rush into marriage for financial reasons and feel they must have children, in part, to hold their husbands. In the lower classes, a father may desert his family when he staggers under the realization of how many mouths there are to feed. Here the presence of children is clearly a liability.

Thus, one cannot generalize with certitude about the proposition that children help or hinder a marriage. Instead, the question becomes meaningful only when specific types of marital interaction within varying ethnic and socio-economic groups are studied. It is obvious, for example, that conventional, middle-class Midwesterners in agricultural areas are quite likely to marry, to stay married once they have said "I do," and to have children—because their values teach them to do so. Again, one cannot say that they have more successful marriages than other groups because they usually have children; having children is just part of their larger cultural context and value system.

Another observation often made is that it is desirable for married couples to wait a year or two before starting a family. This statement, for a number of reasons, deserves a nearly unequivocal *yes*. Now that we have "the pill," family planning should be as frankly discussed as the budget, and it should be as forthrightly carried out as the inevitable purchase of a television set.

Young people who marry because the girl is pregnant are very often doomed to find themselves parties to a divorce or an annulment. Marriages in which the wife becomes pregnant on the honeymoon seem to be much less risky than those beginning with a shotgun wedding. However, though there is no convincing set of statistics to indicate that these couples divorce more frequently than couples who postpone pregnancy, marriage experts agree that early pregnancy destroys (or at least maims) the important "getting-to-know-you" period of the first year or so of marriage.

Often serious problems result from the purely fiscal or physical aspects of early pregnancy. For example, the husband may have to quit school and get a job because there is an unexpected mouth to feed. Correspondingly, if pregnancy forces the wife to leave a job from which she derives a great deal of satisfaction, she may have a good many negative feelings about her new role as a mother. Pregnancy may throw the couple's beginning sexual adjustment out of whack because the girl is resentful of what he "did" to her, and the young husband may feel trapped because of what she "allowed to happen."

But what about couples that have been married for a number of years? Can a correlation be found between their chances for marital success and the number of offspring?

In Puerto Rico, India, and other countries where devices preventing pregnancy have been in use for five or more years, statistics are becoming available. These indicate that most couples do *not* wish large families, and that there is a higher percentage of happy, productive marriages among couples who have no children. Recent research suggests that the same situation exists in the United States, and that the parents of five or more children who so proudly point to their huge brood may be putting on an act.

In countries where the new contraceptives (pills and intrauterine contraceptive devices) are utilized, evidence is accumulating that not even those who traditionally have large families

—such as Catholics, Negroes, and the poor—necessarily want a great many children. In the United States the difference in family size between poor people and the well-to-do used to be sizable. Now it is diminishing rapidly.

Our picture of the large, happy family (the poor and shoeless) was based on myth. Instead, it appears that desertion rate among fathers *diminishes* when family size is controlled—when the very size of the family doesn't panic the father into leaving.

These facts do not mean that the presence of children reduces the chance for success of any particular marriage. However, it is clear that the begetting of children is not a magic which will improve an already shaky marriage; instead, it will help to destroy it even further.

One aspect of the myth that children will automatically improve a marriage stems from the parent's unconscious (sometimes even conscious) belief that he can experience through his child the things he was denied or failed at as a child. Or, perhaps, from the belief that he can develop in the youngster those desirable qualities lacking in the other spouse. For example, a man who is secretly ashamed of his wife's dowdiness may work extra hard to earn money to buy attractive outfits for his infant daughter. His wife may share his enthusiasm for their "cute little girl" and take pride in the neighbor's comments about the daughter's outfits, but she also understands (often unconsciously) her husband's opinion that she is dowdy—even though he may not tell her so directly.

Childless couples can sometimes reconcile their marital differences and disappointments by ignoring the discords, pretending they do not exist. They can seek compensating gratifications elsewhere, perhaps in their work—it is simple for both of them to have jobs. However, when there is a child, this shift of emphasis is impossible, and the child becomes living evidence of the dissatisfaction in the marital relationship.

Children by their presence may aggravate an already unhappy marriage by virtue of the role which they play in the relationship between spouses that may be labeled the battle of the sexes. The power struggle between the sexes often focuses upon the question of who—husband or wife—does the more important work. Should the husband have certain prerogatives because he earns the money? Should the wife, who stays at home doing routine work and does not meet new people daily as her husband does, have some compensating rewards? Should she be taken out often, or have several nights off to attend motion pictures, or to play bridge with the girls? By finding some chore which the father may logically be expected to do for the child, the wife may be indicating to the husband that he is neglecting an important part of *his* function and that even if he earns the money and is important in his office, he is no better than she is. Conversely, the man who wishes to put his wife one down, can always find some instance of child neglect, particularly if the child becomes noisy or ill.

It is obvious that sacrificing or compromising one's personal desires in order to meet the needs and wishes of another can create a sense of deprivation and become abrasive in any relationship. Children require a great deal of care and attention which often conflicts with their parents' own needs and desires. Yet in our culture fathers and mothers cannot often admit their sense of personal deprivation. Therefore, since they cannot feel guilty about having children, they end up blaming each other.

If when a child is conceived the parents hope the infant will mend a fractured marriage, the disappointment may be excruciatingly painful. The child's presence in a discordant union, therefore, may instigate new troubles and the marital relationship may deteriorate even more.

For example, a young woman feels that her amorously adventurous husband will be "steadied" by becoming a father. Within a year she gives birth to a baby girl. The husband is pleased and proud of the little girl. He pours the majority of his affection on her, thus rejecting the wife in a blatant manner. The mother begins disliking the child almost to the point of hate.

At first the wife thinks it cute when the little girl (at eighteen months of age) refuses to obey her and waits for Daddy to come home and arbitrate matters between her and her mother. It is not so funny when the little girl becomes an accomplished enough actress to stage tearful scenes. If her mother appears adamant, the daughter, now four years old, dramatically tells other adults how bad Mommy is and declares that she and Daddy are going to live somewhere else. The father is usually flattered by this behavior and rarely interferes. Occasionally he becomes embarrassed and even frightened by the situation, and in a rage, punishes the child. The mother then attempts to protect her daughter and again the parents are caught up in mutually destructive behavior.

In another situation, common in white upper-middle-class marriages, the wife uses the children to undermine the husband's authority and power. She manages this by unwittingly encouraging or assisting the children to break the rules established by the father when he is trying hard to be "in charge."

For example, as the father backs out of the garage on his way to work, he notices the children's toys in the driveway. He gets out, throws bicycles, skates, toys, and baseball bats out of the way, then dashes to the kitchen and shouts, "Goddamn it, Martha, you tell the kids to put their stuff in the playshed and the next time anyone leaves anything out he'll spend the day in his room."

That night he is late for dinner. When he drives into the garage, he hears the crunch of wheels rolling over a skate board and a bicycle. He storms into the house. His family has begun eating. Martha is looking fresh, clean, and relaxed.

He screams, "Martha, who in the goddamn hell left the toys in the garage? This morning . . ."

Martha replies, "Oh dear, that's probably my fault. I chased the twins in to get their baths and didn't think about the bicycle and toys. Dear, is that such a terrible crime?" The husband turns on his heel and leaves, loudly slamming the back door. Another devastating battle has begun with the usual first act, "The Defeat of Dad."

All these examples illustrate flaws in the basic myth that when two people are about to be married and there are potential problems (caused, for example, by little money, different racial backgrounds, or different cultural levels), these major problems will be solved by the couple's sheer joy in having a child. True, they may find pleasure in the youngster, *but the presence of the child probably will not eliminate existing difficulties.* The adults must find solutions on their own. And unfortunately, the child may well aggravate the problems.

The truth of this observation becomes apparent when one considers that the family is a system and that every person in a system is equally important in maintaining it. Just when Martha

has forgiven John for one of his occasional temperamental outbursts, John junior puts on an act which Martha associates with
his father, and she is angry at her husband all over again. When
John senior comes home that night seeking solace, his wife attacks
him for being temperamental; he feels, "But I haven't done anything," and has a temper tantrum. John junior, watching this
outburst, has his own temperamental behavior reinforced. The
three individuals are caught up in a system which will repeat
itself, and Martha's blaming John's heredity for his being temperamental—or John's blaming Martha's physiology for producing "bad times" each month—will only obscure the nature of the
system in which they are caught.

8

FALSE ASSUMPTION 6

That Loneliness Will Be Cured by Marriage

Once upon a time there was a well-received television drama (it later became a motion picture) called *Marty*. At the conclusion of the performance, the viewer experienced a feeling of satisfaction and general good feeling, the same sense of well-being and joy that a person has when he has read a fairy tale, such as *Snow White and the Seven Dwarfs* or *Little Red Riding Hood*.

The story of *Marty* concerns a lonely, shy boy, Marty, who finds, or is found by, a lonely, shy girl. They supply each other's needs, decide to marry, presumably live happily ever after. It could be wonderful if such events could take place frequently in the lives of lonely people. But the action in *Marty* represents—for most people—fantasies, not reality. Lonely people who marry each other to correct their situation usually discover that the most intense and excruciating loneliness is the loneliness that is shared with another.

There are several types of loneliness.

First is the loneliness of individuals who have a limited behavioral repertoire. The "behavioral repertoire" is the accumulation of behavioral acts that have been learned since birth and are at the individual's command. People afflicted with this type of loneliness find themselves to be strangers in a more than normal number of situations involving relationships. They yearn to be on a cheerful, or perhaps competitive, or perhaps collaborative, action-interaction basis with other people. But they have difficulty because their behavioral repertoire is limited and therefore in many cases they do not understand other people and other people do not understand them. So they are strangers—and lonely.

When such lonely people marry each other, each has expectations of his spouse, and neither realizes that the other is paralyzed by a limited behavioral repertoire. Neither of these individuals has much to give to the other, unless the behavioral repertoire is enlarged and developed. If lonely spouses recognize this problem, they may have a chance for a workable marriage; if they are cognizant of their limitations, perhaps they can form a team and slowly and painfully increase the range of their behavior. Usually, however, each expects satisfying behavior from the other—the kind of action which is beyond the capability of his spouse. As a result, both of them end up more lonely than ever before. And to this loneliness, a bitterness frequently is added. For each of them is vulnerable, and when he does not receive the behavior he expects from the spouse, he believes he has been given a rebuff. Usually it is not a rebuff at all, but merely a reflection of social inadequacy. What happens next? The "rebuffed" spouse draws back and then the other feels that now he is being rebuffed and rejected; and thus the distance between the two quickly increases.

An extreme example of the result of limited behavioral range in marriage occurred with a couple known to the authors. The situation described here actually existed. A shy young woman married a shy young man. His mother and sister had reared him much as one would raise a hothouse plant. Several years after the marriage, the girl formed a close friendship with the young lady who lived next door. From her she learned that sexual intercourse was supposed to take place in a normal marriage. She and her husband had been so ill informed that they had merely embraced. Neither of them had been brave enough to bring up the question of how babies were made.

When the young wife learned the facts about sex, she felt humiliated and cheated. Vituperatively, she scolded her surprised husband, and as a result they experienced so much turmoil that it became necessary for them to seek the help of a psychiatrist.

One of the mysteries of this situation is why the young woman did not recognize that she was just as uninformed as was her husband, and why he did not point this out to her.

A second type of loneliness (more prevalent among males than females) frequently characterizes the individual who lost his mother at a very early age. This type of person has been denied love as a child and unconsciously seeks "triumphs" over others as a love substitute. He cannot get along with anyone over whom he cannot triumph in some way, or except in some rare instances in which he collaborates with someone else to triumph against society.

Within this category we find many "successes" in the arts, in industry, and in business. These are the perfectionists, the people who are obsessed with becoming champions or innovators, or the top person in a field. Such people have limited emotional repertoires. Usually they can be loving and kind and considerate only to those who are useful to them; and they define usefulness only in terms of their drive for perfection or success. In the marriage of such a person nothing which the spouse does is ever good enough. He is constantly critical of the spouse's performance level. People of this sort trust no one to do anything well. They suspect that almost everyone will impede their gallop toward success. They require almost everything to revolve around themselves; and as this seldom happens in married life, these individuals drift from one marriage to another, always looking for the impossible and becoming more and more suspicious and more and more lonely.

The third type of loneliness is perhaps the most painful of all. It is usually experienced by individuals who have had an intelligent, dominant mother and a passive father who behaved as if he were her inferior. These people are obsessed with the desire to be popular and well thought of. They have bright personalities and well-developed social skills. Frequently they are glib talkers and good dancers, and dress attractively. Often they are excellent salesmen, advertising personnel, and social leaders, and they tend to be gossips. By gossiping (transmitting malicious information about somebody else) they bribe others to approve of them. A high percentage of these people give the appearance of being flirtatious and "sexy," but really are sexually unskilled, and often frigid, even though they act passionate and may have had more than the normal number of affairs. This type of individual finds it difficult to be intimate and collaborative with anyone unless their mutual behavior results in his being the center of attraction. This can happen only if he marries a passive person, probably his inferior. But the fact is that in marriage—and in relations with people in general—unless one can participate in behavioral inter-actions which are characterized by equality, one is lonely despite the appearance one may give of being very gregarious and a great mixer.

Loneliness cannot be cured by marriage. Loneliness is better tolerated by those who live alone; they have no expectations, and thus no disappointments. Lonely people who live together have about the same chance of realizing their expectations as the host who insists that everybody have a good time at his party.

9

FALSE ASSUMPTION 7

*That If You Tell Your Spouse to Go to Hell
You Have a Poor Marriage*

Most of us in this country are taught diplomacy, decorum, and the art of self-restraint. Many husbands and wives believe that politeness, consideration, and benevolence are important in a marriage, and not wishing to be rejected, they may attempt to practice these arts unremittingly.

If spouses are thoughtful of each other on all occasions, the likelihood is that they have a sick marriage. It is obvious that individuals have competing tendencies—different interests, different ways of using time, different biological rhythms, and so on —and they cannot always have the same desires, needs, wishes, or whatever at the same time. The problem then is: What should they do when conflicts arise?

There are several possible answers, but the most important one is that the individual should do *what he feels he has to do* at this particular moment, and should believe enough in the durability of the marriage to withstand even a period of hate from the other spouse. When such conflicts do not ever arise, it must be concluded either that the spouses are peculiarly lucky in having chosen partners with exactly the same values, tastes, needs, and so on, or that somebody is sacrificing quietly and will unwittingly pay the other spouse back.

This may sound like explosive propaganda. But the alternative is a relationship in which one spouse thinks so little of his partner that he cannot permit an independent act that happens to displease him for the time being. How can spouses trust each other if they never have any disagreements? How does each know what the other really thinks and feels if he is accommodating and thoughtful all the time? For all anyone can tell, one spouse may secretly hate the other's guts.

Tom Henderson was a successful insurance executive with a mad passion for golf. He had been planning for some time to attend a golf clinic being given in Concord, Massachusetts, by his favorite professional. Not only was he delighted to have the opportunity to work with his favorite pro, but knowing this geographical area he realized that coming here would be very pleasant for his wife and two children; they could rent an attractive older home, swim in a nearby lake, and engage in many of the pleasant activities of the city. Mary, his wife, was a bit reluctant, particularly because she was not well acquainted with the East and wasn't sure what she was getting into. However, Tom's enthusiasm overcame her reluctance, and the kids were always eager for a vacation.

But over the next few months a subtle campaign of propaganda was beamed toward Tom Henderson. It came from all directions. For example, Mrs. Smythe, Mary's mother, had taken an apartment in Honolulu, near the beach. She wrote to her daughter that she wished the whole family would visit her, and described what a wonderful time the children would have. Thereafter, the advantages for the children formed the core of Mary's propaganda campaign. Magazines with pictures of brown-skinned, lithe surfers lay exposed on the coffee table and occasionally at the writing desk. Also, knowing Tom's interest in golf, Mary one morning read him an article about a recent golfing match at the Waialae Country Club. She mentioned with a shy smile that her friend Nancy, who lived in Honolulu, had told her that golfers consider a round at the course of the Oahu Country Club one of the great golfing experiences of all time.

While Mary spoke, Tom was hastily reading his mail and finishing his last mouthful of coffee. Not until he had nearly reached his office did it occur to him to wonder, "How come Mary's interested in golf all of a sudden?"

"Oh, well." He turned to the tasks of the day. His errant thought lay untended and died.

When Jane, their oldest daughter, celebrated her birthday in May, Mary presented her with a ukelele and a book of twelve easy lessons.

Now the propaganda had reached the stage where it became obvious even to Tom. One night he confronted his wife. "Darling," he said, "I thought we had agreed we were going to Concord this summer for our vacation. Now I get the impression that you're pushing for Honolulu."

Mary regarded him with her wide, startlingly blue eyes much as she would a man from Mars suddenly appearing in her bedroom. "Why, Tom, whatever, do you mean? I know how much you're counting on going to the golf clinic in Concord, and the children and I won't really mind."

Tom absently nodded and went into the bathroom to brush his teeth. He felt like a bit of a stinker for having raised the question, but something was still tugging at his mind and he was not satisfied. When he got to bed he went right to sleep, with no thought of being amorous. Mary didn't rest well that night, for the hand that grasps for power is always a bit shaky.

As the days went by, Tom was reminded by both children of what a wonderful place Hawaii is. He suspected that Mary was putting them up to this, but where was the evidence? Jane seemed to have a new-found interest in hula lessons, and Tom junior spoke with wonder of the intricacies of surfing. Then one day Mary brought Tom a somewhat pleading letter from her mother describing her wish to see them and stating that a lovely apartment would become available close by during August—the very month that they were planning to spend in Concord. Now Tom was no longer in doubt. He recognized the nature of the enemy, but almost as quickly as he turned to fight he found his resistance fading. What father likes to deny his children? What husband wishes to keep his wife separated from her aged mother (whom she may never see alive again), and from school chums whom she hasn't seen in many years? Who can deny the beauty of

Hawaii and the excellence of its golfing spots? And so Tom suc-
cumbed and erected in place of the defeat in the Battle of
Concord an icon at which he daily worshiped: the image of Tom
Henderson, Family Man.

Mary's mother was waiting for them at the airport in Honolulu.
Although the Henderson family had been surfeited with food and
drink, everyone accepted grandma's gracious hospitality as she
took them to lunch at the Outrigger Club. Leaning against the
back of his chair and looking out at the sparkling Pacific, Tom
sipped his favorite beer, hoping that some appetite would come
so that he would not have the embarrassment of being the only
one not eating. He half listened to the cheery conversation as
grandma told the children about the wonders they would soon
behold. Mary interrupted, running in and out of the conversation
like a track star with what Tom considered wife-type questions:
"Where can you get this?" "Where's the best place to buy that?"

Since first getting on the plane Tom had been aware of a slow
ball of dread forming in his stomach, and now it felt distended.
He had been helped on the flight by two vodka martinis and half
a bottle of Chablis, but the liquor hadn't dissolved the lump in his
gut. It had only anesthetized the surrounding area. Tom sat there,
and to his horror he began to feel hate—not for the children, not
for his mother-in-law, but for Mary. Suddenly, for the first time
in the months of propaganda and the weeks of knowing that he
had been hoodwinked, he experienced a surge of resoluteness. He
sat straighter, and gulped his beer instead of swishing it around
like mouthwash.

Tom had a plan, but he said nothing about it. He allowed his
mother-in-law to pay for the lunch, and made arrangements for
transporting their huge pile of baggage to the apartment. He
worked hard helping the family get settled and even went with
Mary to the supermarket to lay in a stock of food. He had time
for these things because his plane did not leave until midnight.

Mrs. Smythe had them over to supper. Tom went through the
routine of replying to meaningless questions about his work and
how his golf game was faring, and played an All About Hawaii
word game with the kids. Finally the Hendersons left grandma's.
When they reached their own apartment, Tom called his family

into the small living room and told them, as dispassionately and kindly as he could, that he was leaving on that midnight plane for San Francisco and had been lucky enough to secure a connecting flight to New York. When his wife, with her white, stricken face, started to open her mouth, Tom held up his hand and said, in a tone stronger than he usually employed, "Let me finish." Talking to the children, so that Mary could listen without feeling so attacked, he explained that he was not leaving the family, but was doing something that he felt he had to do. He recognized that his decision was expensive, would upset the rest of the family, and would ruin him forever in his mother-in-law's eyes. He would like to rejoin them in two weeks, and would be very sad if they were so immutably angry about his decision that he was no longer welcome; however, this was a chance he would have to take. He had counted on this golf vacation for a long time and—he reminded them without an air of martyrdom—it had been many years since they had taken the vacation *he* wanted. He stated that at times it was necessary to do something drastic to break a pattern that was forming, and this one threatened to encrust not just the marriage, but the interrelationships of the entire family.

Then he told them that he was not willing to discuss the matter, since his decision was irrevocable. Here he was wise, for there is nothing more useless than beating and bloodying a *fait accompli* with hopeless argumentation. His wife's response was to run crying from the room. Tom had expected this, and it did not curb his resolution. He kissed the children and, sad but erect, walked down the long stairs.

All this occurred ten years ago. The Hendersons are still married, and enjoy a mutual respect that was formerly missing. During her husband's absence Mary recognized that she was something of a spoiled child. She recalled that her own father had rarely gotten his way, and did not fight for it. As a result, Mrs. Smythe had grown more and more into a skillful manipulator and dictator, often using the excuse that something was "best for Mary" to get her own way. The parallel was very obvious to Mary, and she respected Tom for breaking the mold. They eventually agreed that for them the only workable system would be

to take turns in making decisions, since this would eliminate the
need for covert maneuvering and propagandizing through the
children.

The Honolulu episode also proved useful in another way. During the two weeks Tom was in Concord, Mary performed su-
perbly. To her own surprise she found that her anger at him gave
her the strength to enjoy the children in a manner she had not
experienced before.

The Henderson story came close to having a very different
ending. But great changes are built upon risk taking.

Part II

THE ANATOMY OF MARRIAGE

10

THE SYSTEMS CONCEPT

The principle of the systems concept has been understood for a long time. A Babylonian astronomer said, "Heaven is more than the stars alone. It is the stars *and* their movements." According to the systems concept, the whole is *more* than the sum of its parts. The whole consists of all the parts *plus* the way the parts operate in relation to one another.

A simple example is oxygen. Each molecule of the oxygen we breath (O_2) is composed of two atoms which maintain their relationship as a pair. If this arrangement is changed, even though the atoms are still close together, a different kind of oxygen is formed. Called nascent oxygen, it has properties different from those of ordinary oxygen: it is unstable and combines more easily with other substances. In this case nothing physical has been added or removed. *The component parts remain the same.* But the relationship between the two atoms has been altered.

According to the systems concept, a change occurs when related parts are rearranged—be they atoms or the behavior of closely associated human beings, such as two people who are married.

Everything in the universe interacts. A sunspot (which is an area of turbulent gas on the surface of the sun) can affect crops on the earth almost a hundred million miles away. Statistics indicate that the irritability of human beings increases during sunspot intervals, as do the rates for suicide, accidents, and acts of delinquency.

The poet John Donne said, "No man is an island." We now know that nothing in the universe is an island. There are no self-contained actions. Every action has some influence on everything else, although the influence may be so minor that it is unnoticeable and unmeasurable. Frequently an event may be incomprehensible when observed alone, but takes on significance when associated with a related occurrence. For example, in Canada an official in the wildlife study bureau observed that the rabbit population in one area had diminished considerably. Scientists tried to discover what illness had attacked the rabbits, but found none. A few years later the rabbit population increased; then later, again, it diminished. The scientists could find no illness, the reason for these cycles in the rabbit population remained a mystery. At approximately the same time, other officials in the wildlife bureau noticed population fluctuations among foxes. They too sought—and did not find—epidemics among the foxes which might explain these cycles.

By chance, the reports about the varying rabbit population and the varying fox population got to the desk of the same scientist, and having both reports he soon solved the mystery. When the rabbit population increased, so did the fox population. When there were a great many rabbits, the foxes had plenty of food, so they multiplied. But when the large numbers of foxes ate the large numbers of rabbits, the rabbit population declined. Now there was not enough food to support a large fox population, and the number of foxes declined. When the fox population declined, the rabbits could multiply; then there again was plenty of food for the foxes, and it was their turn to increase in number.

The systems concept postulates that there is a constant action-reaction between associated things. The closer the association, the more obvious is the action-reaction. If an influence upsets the balance between the associated entities, then a compensating factor is provided *by the system,* to regain balance. This is known as "feedback." A person who goes blind soon acquires extraordinary facility in hearing. A blind person uses sounds almost like radar, and he can teach his fingers to be sensitive enough to read braille.

The kind of interaction referred to by the systems concept is also illustrated by the body's mechanism for maintaining the right amount of fluid and the proper body temperature. In the normal course of events, a certain amount of perspiration comes to the large skin surface of the body. Here it evaporates and thus cools the body, for evaporation is a cooling process. The warmer the body, the more it perspires, in the effort to maintain a temperature of 98.6 degrees. As the perspiration leaves the body and evaporates from the skin, fluid is lost, which must be replaced. But perspiration also contains salt, and the salt too must be replaced, not only because the body needs a certain salt content, but because water cannot be retained unless salt is present. In turn, the salt cannot be retained unless small amounts of potassium are present. Under these circumstances, the individual normally craves foods which contain both the sodium and the potassium required, thereby providing the necessary feedback for homeostatic balance.

In this example, the salt balance, the potassium balance, the fluid-content balance, the body temperature, the perspiring process, the desire for salt, thirst, all are directly related to each other. They are part of the system.

Let us go a step further. People in a warm climate where there is a high humidity tend to be sleepy and lazy. Once again the systems concept is demonstrated. On a humid day the evaporation process is slowed because the air already has a high moisture content. Therefore, the cooling effect of evaporation is limited. Without even thinking about it, the individual becomes lazy and sleepy. When he moves slowly or sleeps he is physically inactive, generates less body heat, and requires less cooling to keep the body temperature constant.

The systems concept applies to marriage as unequivocally as it applies to the oxygen atoms, or to the relationship of salt, potassium, perspiration, body temperature, and body water. To grasp this, one must realize that in its totality *marriage is not just a rigid relationship between two rigid individuals.* Marriage is a fluid relationship between two spouses and their two individual systems of behavior. The totality of marriage is determined by how the spouses operate (behave) in relation to each other. Put John Smith alone on an isolated island and he will have a specific behavioral pattern. Place John in an office with a harsh boss and John will have another—a different—behavioral pattern. Put John into the intimate relationship of marriage and he will have still another, one largely depending on the behavioral pattern of his wife. No matter how strong a personality John has, his behavior will be influenced by his wife's behavior (and vice versa). In physics it is accepted that for every action there is an equal reaction. The same law holds in psychology—in human relationships.

It is obvious that human behavior seldom is constant for long. An individual may be cheerful one morning, irritable the next. He may be generous and benevolent one afternoon, stingy and mean the next. A person may feel amorous one evening and frigid the following night. The systems concept makes it clear that a change in the behavior of one spouse is usually a reaction to changes in his partner's behavior, and in turn causes additional change in the partner's behavior. This action-reaction system operates in a *circular* fashion (sometimes vicious, sometimes positive). However, changes in a system can also be introduced by factors *outside* the system, such as one spouse's loss of a parent by death. In such cases, the unilateral change in one partner must be dealt with and incorporated into the family system. The other spouse will respond (perhaps unconsciously) in a manner designed to keep both himself and the system in balance, in homeostasis. Suppose, for example, that the husband is a drunk, so that the wife has to earn money, drag him home from bars, nurse him, and suffer humiliation and sometimes physical damage. The wife one day, because of a chance encounter with an old friend who has just divorced her own alcoholic husband, decides she has had enough and insists that the husband see a doctor. Several months later the husband is cured. In many such cases the wife then has a nervous breakdown at worst, or at least a prolonged depression. Her role in the marriage has changed—her status has changed—and it will take her some time to adjust. There is a constant motion in personalities and hence in the marital system, a changing of emotional levels and intensities. Compare the totality of marriage of a male and a female to the physical compages of the human body—the combination of arms, legs, internal organs, eyes, ears, tongue, nose, and so forth. When the individual goes blind, his hearing functions at a higher level. Likewise, when one spouse becomes "discordant" (angry, less sensitive, thoughtless, or the like), there must be a compensating mood or action (usually in the other spouse) or both the individuals and the system will get out of balance.

The phenomenon of the marriage system appears even more complicated when one realizes that when a person joins the company of *any* other person, a new system is generated. When husband and wife go out together and meet other people, their behavior patterns are different from what they are when the two are alone. The presence of others feeds new stimuli into the joint wife-husband system and it becomes *a new system* as long as the other persons are present. Husbands and wives often wonder why they behave differently in public than when they are home alone, or why they behave differently when they are together with their children than when each is alone with the children. This apparent inconsistency often causes trouble. Each spouse notices the changes in the other but not in himself. An objective observer would see that they both change. These alterations are unavoidable because all additions or departures from a group in some way change the system of the group as a whole.

This changing of systems and behavioral patterns is demonstrated by an experiment with chicks. When chicks are alone, they cheep at different time intervals. One chick may cheep every two seconds; another (in another location) may cheep every seven seconds. The interval is constant for each individual chick. But when the chicks are placed in a group, all have the same time interval (or oscillation) between cheeps. They do not cheep in unison, but the time lapse between sounds—once individually determined—now becomes standard for all members of the flock. The phenomenon can be observed also in the croaking of frogs and even in the light flashes of fireflies.

The systems concept applies to everything from the atoms of inanimate objects to the relationships among people, elephants, or penguins. Once a person is conscious of this, he may ask, "If I behave in such and such a manner, what will it do to the system? How will it alter the tone or the behavioral pattern of my marriage?"

In a marriage, each partner tries to maintain behavioral systems which provide himself with maximum satisfaction. Sometimes the satisfaction assumes neurotic dimensions, such as finding pleasure in illness because it can be used as a weapon against the spouse. When both partners are in a state of satisfaction, there is present an emotional and psychic balance, a homeostasis. That is what they strive for. But human behavior changes frequently and radically, and every action and mood of one spouse begets a reaction from the other. Therefore, to remain in balance, the marriage system always is in a state of flux. The forces in it move this way and then that way, go up and down to various levels, increase and decrease in intensity. The systems concept makes this situation clear and can be used to describe the process mathematically.

When people marry, the first important action which takes place is the attempt of each spouse to determine the nature of the relationship; that is, each wants the system to be satisfying to himself, and would prefer to achieve this end without changing his already established behavioral pattern. Each wants the other partner to make the accommodations. Usually a spouse approves of his own ways of behaving, his own mannerisms, habits, and performances, and finds fault with those of the other. For this reason almost all marriages—at least at first—have friction. And to reduce this friction is difficult, because of "behavioral blindness." The individuals contribute not only their *conscious* behavioral tendencies, tastes, and so on to the joint system, but also the greater part of their total personality—the part about which they know nothing, which is motivated *unconsciously*. Nevertheless, each spouse attempts to shape the relationship, to influence how the joint system will operate, and determine the limits of acceptable behavior. Once a system is established, it tends to remain in homeostasis.

Here is an example of the operation of balance, or homeostasis, in a marital system. Assume that through their interaction up to this time, a newly married man and woman, on their honeymoon, have established an unspoken "rule" that each is to fill the other's needs without being asked. Mary prepares John's favorite meals, compliments him, straightens his clothes; and John buys small gifts for Mary, compliments her cooking, makes all travel arrangements, and so forth. In this interaction neither has to ask the other to fulfill his role according to their mutual expectations.

Now suppose that on the fifth day of the honeymoon, Mary (having already received a number of small gifts from John without asking for them) sees a ring which she would like to own and asks John if he will buy it for her. At this point, one unspoken rule of their relationship has been broken. *Mary has asked for a gift.* The system is temporarily *out of balance.* Now any number of things can happen, depending on John's reaction to Mary's rule breaking.

John may comply cheerfully with Mary's request; in this case the system is in balance again, but a new rule has been established: Mary has the "right" to make requests of John.

But the action may go in another direction. John may agree to purchase the ring, but make it clear by his grumbling that he is not happy about the new turn of events. In this case, balance is reestablished on the basis of a rule which implies that Mary may ask for things, but must pay the price for this privilege by tolerating John's grumbling.

Reactions belonging to a third category are provoked if John refuses to purchase the ring. Now the establishment of homeostasis becomes dependent upon *Mary's* reaction to John's reaction to her original action. Mary may choose passively to let John define the nature of the relationship, or she may choose to fight.

If Mary accepts John's refusal cheerfully ("You're right, dear, I shouldn't have asked"), the original system is reestablished and the rule of not asking remains in force. If Mary accepts his refusal but is quietly unhappy about it, balance is reestablished, but Mary is learning a new kind of behavior necessary to keep the system operating: she is learning to withdraw in order to avoid rocking the boat. John is learning that the price of his refusal is to be temporarily isolated by Mary's silence. In this case, as in the case of John's grumbling, no real agreement on the ring issue has been reached, but they have temporarily agreed to accept the disagreement without pressing it. The system is in balance again, but the balance is exceedingly precarious.

Another possible reaction of Mary's may lead to what is called a runaway. Suppose Mary refuses to accept John's refusal to buy the ring. She may express anger, stubborn insistence, hurt, at his refusal, casting the responsibility back on John to accept her new definition of the relationship or accept her angry behavior, each of which implies a new rule. She may say something like, "Why can't I have the ring? I made your favorite dinner last night and didn't even ask to go out. You can certainly do this one small thing for me." John may reconsider and agree to buy the ring, thereby reestablishing the balance with a new rule: Mary can ask for what she wants and she will get it. But John may become angered by her anger and lack of appreciation for what he's done for her under the old system (without being asked). He may accuse her of being "a typical woman," "unreasonable," "selfish." If the argument continues to escalate in this fashion, the situation is called a runaway; the balance can be reestablished only when some agreement is reached on a new rule or rules for the relationship. Balance in a system lasts only until a new challenge to the system is presented. If no agreement is reached and the escalation continues until it is completely out of hand, the runaway eventually ends in divorce, desertion, murder, or suicide—in the complete breakup of the system or relationship.

MORE ON THE SYSTEMS CONCEPT

Social scientists often borrow concepts from the physical sciences because the latter are believed to be so much more precise. In this book, we are stressing the systems concept because it is the most useful way of viewing marital interaction that has yet been developed. Our theoretical language is still faulty and imprecise, but this defect will eventually be overcome by social-science research. Not even the physical scientists have solved all of their thorny theoretical problems. The physicist can tell us what energy a collection of atoms will give off, or indicate the total amount of the Brownian movement of a group of particles. He cannot specify which particular electron will collide with which other electron, nor which particle in a cloud-chamber study will move in what direction. What the physicist does is to give us in mathematical formulas the description of a group interaction or a prediction concerning its outcome; the random behavior of the individuals forming the group, however, is not separately describable or predictable.

We are in a similar situation in describing marital interaction. We cannot say, "Mr. Jones will light a cigarette at 8:00 P.M. Sunday evening and Mrs. Jones will give him hell because he is smoking on the Sabbath." We *can* say that the Joneses have an interacting rule-governed system, one particular *quid pro quo* of which is *his* right to violate certain of their shared principles in return for allowing *her* to feel superior to him and to express that feeling in criticism. We can, then, describe rules which indicate the probable outcome of the interactions of a married pair, but not the particular acts the couple perform or the specific events or contingencies which may occur in the marriage.

The way in which this rule-governed system develops can be clarified by reference to Darwin's notion of natural selection. He stated that species of animals or plants which were originally close enough to one another to interbreed freely became for various reasons more and more differentiated in the course of time until the possibility of free interbreeding was lost, and the breeding continuity broke up into several separate communities. Some of these new species had a good adaptive balance with their environment and they flourished and multiplied, giving rise in turn to other new species. Others were not well adjusted to the environment and sooner or later dwindled and became extinct. Darwin thus gave us one of the first hints of how random developments may lead to an apparently well-defined pattern. The process he described corresponds to the "behavioral exploration" of a couple. At first the man and woman randomly exchange a wide variety of behavior; eventually, they work out mutually acceptable ways of labeling and of interrelating their behavior, so that each individual feels he is an equal. In a workable marriage, as in Darwin's natural selection, the maladaptive patterns die out. If both develop a satisfactory relationship, by the time the marriage is some years old they probably will have forgotten this period of probing, vacillation, and behavioral juggling, and they probably will not recall the action-reaction complexities. They may say, "We were always well adjusted to one another."

"Cybernetics" is the name coined by Norbert Wiener for the

science that specifically considers the application of control principles to the biological organism. The name came from a Greek
word meaning "steersman" or "governor." Wiener felt that randomly distributed objects or particles in a state of rhythmic
oscillation can affect one another through interactions, these interactions between them generally consisting of a feedback of information that tends to stabilize the system. In an "error-activated
system" overdeviation is corrected by what is known as negative
feedback. A good example is the thermostat on a furnace. As soon
as the heat drops below, let us say, 68 degrees, an electrical impulse activates the furnace, which goes on and brings the temperature of the room back to 68.

Married couples may act upon each other in just such a fashion
and thus keep the deviations of behavior within their marriage to
a comfortable range.

Positive feedback is a deviation-amplifying mechanism that can
lead to a breakdown or a so-called runaway in the system. If the
wires on a furnace thermostat become crossed so that when the
furnace reached 68 a positive impulse was sent by the thermostat,
the heat would keep climbing until the house (or at least the
furnace) burned up. An actual example of this kind of feedback
in a marriage was discussed earlier in this chapter.

It has sometimes been pointed out that married couples begin
to look like each other over the years. This may be an extreme
example of interaction, but it is perfectly clear in interviewing
married couples that they are not the same when interviewed
singly as they are when interviewed jointly. The friendly, humorous, joke-cracking husband may become very dour when near his
wife—not merely because he dislikes her, but because his dourness is part of their system's oscillation. By being dour he may
keep her at the peak of her performance, since nothing she does
ever pleases him. Yet she keeps trying because although he is
dour he continues to live with her, which indicates to her that she
must not be as bad as his expression suggests. She also gains some
sense of equal status by her attempts, as her husband's dourness
makes her social skills seems superior by contrast.

There is one further aspect of cybernetics that should be mentioned in relation to marriage. Wiener and, later, Duncan Luce
and others have demonstrated two types of games for which they

developed cybernetic models. One is called the zero-sum game and the other, the non-zero-sum game.

In the zero-sum game if someone wins, someone else loses an equivalent amount and thus the sums cancel each other out. In the non-zero-sum game both people may win or both may lose. It is difficult to find actual examples of the zero-sum games in marriage, although some individuals insist on acting as if they were common. Usually in a marriage either both people win or both lose. The marriage in which one takes and the other gives is either a sick marriage or a very recent one.

Probably every reader has seen in a Western or police film the situation where two robbers are apprehended by the sheriff or the police but there is not enough evidence to guarantee their conviction. They are placed in separate rooms, and each is told that the other has already confessed and that if he will confess also he will be allowed to turn state's evidence and shorten his sentence. Both men know that if they remain silent they may defeat the attempts to place blame on them. But what if A has already confessed? Then won't B look like the uncooperative one? So B is tempted to confess even though A has, in fact, remained mute. This typical situation has been called "the prisoner's dilemma." Its application in marriage will probably be recognized by most married readers. If the husband is late for dinner and thinks his wife is going to jump on him, he may beat her to the punch by exclaiming as he comes in, "Why in hell don't you sweep the walkway someday?" His wife may not have been upset by his being late, but she certainly is upset now by his criticism, and when she retorts angrily, "Because that's your job," the husband is convinced that she was in a bad mood anyway. These individuals do not have a stable system and hence are doubtful about their ability to form a coalition. Therefore, like the prisoners, they believe that the best defense is a good offense. And so on and on this nasty game is played.

11

COMMUNICATION IN MARRIAGE

All Behavior Is Communicative

Communication in marriage is a constant exchange of information —of messages—between the two spouses by speech, letter writing, talking on the telephone, the exhibition of bodily or facial expressions, and other methods as well. The information may be straightforward and factual, conveyed by words ("I want coffee"; "It is raining"; "Here is five dollars"), or it may indicate, by tone of voice and by gesture, the nature of the relationship between the parties involved. Receiving a message is not a matter of understanding spoken words alone: the rattling of pots in the kitchen or the slamming of a door may telegraph the mood of a spouse.

During the time a husband and wife are asleep in different beds, they are neither in conflict nor sharing anything. When they awaken, the interactions begin, because now the two people are able to hear and observe each other.

People in our culture believe that the most important communications are spoken or written. This view is erroneous. Scientists have estimated that fifty to a hundred bits of information are exchanged *each second* between individuals communicating actively. Everything which a person does in relation to another is some kind of message. *There is no* NOT *communicating. Even silence is communication.*

If a wife asks her husband, "What are you thinking?" he may answer by looking at her tenderly and smiling. The message here is, "I am thinking of you, darling." The tender look and the smile are more eloquent than speech.

Suppose his response is silence and a blank look. The wife repeats, "Did you hear me? I asked you what you're thinking about." And her husband says, "Yes, I heard you," and lapses back into his silence and his blank stare. What does this mean? He is telling her at least that there is something he will not share with her; at worst, he is saying, "Will you shut up and stop bothering me! Whatever I say now might incriminate me."

If a husband comes home late for dinner, his wife may not comment. Yet her silence can be a worse scolding than an angry verbal reminder that his tardiness caused the steaks to burn or the soufflé to fall would have been. He may recognize in her silence the message, "Why in hell didn't you telephone to say you would be late; and when will you learn to have some consideration for me?"

The raising of eyebrows, a frown, the bringing of flowers, the cooking of a favorite dessert, a handshake, a surly grumble, an unexpected holding of the hand, a kiss, all these are examples of nonverbal behavior that sends a message to the other person.

In relating to another person it is *impossible* NOT to communicate. If one turns away or is silent, one conveys a message. The way one behaves, moves, hold oneself, all these transmit messages. Some people cross and uncross their legs when they are angry. Some bite their lips. Some rub their fingers together.

Thus communication occurs at several different levels, often simultaneously. Every message has at least three aspects—the report aspect, the command aspect, and the context aspect.

The *report* aspect consists of what is said or written, the actual meaning of the words, the content of the message—what is literally asked for, reported, and so on.

The *command* aspect helps define the nature and meaning of the message, indicating how it is supposed to be heard, how the sender is attempting to influence the nature of his relationship with the receiver. The sender's intentions may be suggested by the tone of his voice, by its loudness or softness, by the speed with which he speaks, or by nonverbal behavior—gestures and the like. When "Go to hell" is said with a snarl and a menacing glance, the report and command aspects reinforce each other. A very different message is conveyed by "Go to hell" said with a smile. Here the report and the command aspects may be easily separated.

The *context* aspect is determined by the cultural implications of the situation of the communicants. For instance, if a lifeguard yells "I'll save you" to a drowning boy, the boy can safely assume that the lifeguard means to pull him out of the pool. If a little old lady working in an apostolic mission says "I'll save you," the listener can assume that she means to help him to become a good Christian. In a famous old Western, the Virginian says to the bad guy, "When you call me that, *smile!*" This is a complex message in which the context is all-important. The scene occurs in the old West, where violence was expected and returned without awaiting due process of the law.

Frequently there is a conflict of messages. The sender of the message may include words which purposely confuse the ostensible message, for example: "I'd love to have your mother visit, but I just don't know if I can find time in my schedule." The spoken words may say one thing, but behavior, gestures, responses, may say something else. An unfaithful wife may tell her husband she has spent the evening with a sorority sister when, in reality, she has been in a motel with a man. If the husband questions the wife, she may fabricate details of the meeting with the sorority sister—when they met, where they had dinner, and so on. The husband intellectually may accept the account; but it is also possible, and perhaps probable, that he will receive a score of other messages from his wife: her excited behavior, her extraordinary concern over him, her unusually well-groomed appearance, her interest in subjects to which she previously paid no attention, these all convey messages. At first he may not understand them; he may not even be conscious of their presence. But they are sent, and he does receive them.

A young man in a bar may see an attractive young lady. He approaches her and says, "It's a nice day, isn't it?" or "Whew, this place sure is noisy," or "Do you happen to have a match?" Taken literally, his words have a certain meaning. But the quite different message he is trying to send is, "Hello, I'd like to meet you."

The girl probably will receive the message as intended. She may reply to the young man by looking at her watch and saying, "Yes, it is a nice day," and then adding, "My boy friend is always late." This may mean, "If you want to invite me for a drink while I wait for my boy friend that's okay with me," or it may mean, "I don't want to get picked up." The expression on her face, the tone of her voice, or other nonverbal methods of communication will clarify her meaning. But the girl may be naïve and take the message literally. In that case she replies, "Yes, I do have some matches." *There are many instances when the message received is not the message sent.*

This faulty communication is one of the major causes of breakdown in otherwise workable marriages. A wife may have had a hard day and be utterly fatigued when she and her husband go to bed. When the husband, feeling amorous, begins to caress his wife, she may turn away and yawn. She is trying to say, "I'm terribly tired. Do you mind if we go to sleep?" But the husband may receive a different message, one of personal rejection.

Thus one of the greatest difficulties in communication between individuals is recognizing what the other person *really* means. There is no infallible way of determining this. Even the polygraph, or lie detector, can be fooled by some individuals, and therefore evidence obtained by use of the polygraph is not admissible in courts of law. As is widely known, Freud demonstrated that people are motivated by unconscious factors. We would express this idea somewhat differently: an individual reacts to a communicated message according to his own perception of the nature of that message, and the appropriateness of his reaction is directly related to the clarity and explicitness of the message. Since most messages are not very explicit, most responses appear to be "unconsciously motivated" because neither the action nor the reaction is clearly understood by both parties. Often the message is misunderstood because the sender and the receiver, like the amorous husband and his tired wife, interpret it in terms of quite different contexts.

Freud's theory about unconscious motivation has nevertheless

created a large number of self-appointed motivation hunters who
feel that they can spot their quarry in the other person's unconscious and bag it by announcing, "You don't mean what you say.
What you really mean is . . ." Or "You say that, but I don't believe
you mean it—unconsciously you mean just the opposite."

Once we accept the idea that we can't *really* guess with any
accuracy what someone else means, it becomes obvious that what
we must count on is *behavior*. Centuries ago, men learned to shake
hands because they could not read each other's intentions but
could "scientifically" determine if the sword hand was empty, by
testing it with a handshake. Behavior consists of more than a
single act or even a series of acts on a single day. Our actions
vary, and it is the long-term haul that gives evidence of our real
intentions.

In the Pacific there are a large number of tropical fish called
tangs. These beautiful multicolored creatures are noted for a spot
of intense color near the dorsolateral fin. In certain of the tangs,
this spot conceals a poison spur, and in others, a sharp spur which
is used for defensive protection. Finally, there are the tangs with
the brightest, most luminescent and striking dorsolateral spots of
all, and *these tangs have no stinger whatsoever*. Yet, even so, other
fish give them a wide berth.

The message received by the fish is that they should beware of
a tang's bright-colored spot. The fact that some tangs don't really
have a defensive spur cannot be known by the other fish until
they actually test the expectation by encountering the tangs in
combat. Since they avoid such explicit encounters, they never
learn which tangs have the stinger. The story has a moral for
married couples: Don't condemn it until you've tried it!

Analysis of slow-motion films of couples in various situations
reveals that the two individuals continually "speak" to each other
by nonverbal methods (gestures, actions, facial expressions, and
the like). When people have been married for a period of time—
even a few weeks or months—they develop a mutually understood labeling system. Certain gestures are assumed to indicate
specific moods or emotions. This process of classification is natural, but it has a serious flaw. It ignores *equifinality*, which means
that a particular end result may arise from one of several different
beginnings; thus, if a wife rubs her nose whenever she is getting

angry at her husband, he will soon recognize the connection. But suppose she also rubs her nose when it itches? His immediate defensive behavior (when he believes she is angry) may set off in the wife a spark of annoyance that then convinces him that indeed she was angry. Old patterns, unlike soldiers, don't die or fade away. They remain, unless clarified by the wisdom and experience of the spouses.

This misunderstood nose rubbing illustrates once again the fact that the message sent is not always the message received—the lack of clarity of communication which is one of the major problems in marriage. It is inevitable that spouses will miscommunicate occasionally, perhaps even 20 per cent of the time. But when miscommunication begins to overpower clear communication, the marriage is in trouble, and probably will get worse. Poor communication tends to breed more of the same.

What happens between troubled spouses is that they do not communicate effectively. The spouses do not exchange clear, useful information. Instead, they attack each other with hypocritical messages which may mean one thing literally, but in effect mean something else. These come in a repetitive pattern—which triggers double-meaning, destructive responses from the other spouse. "Everything would have worked out fine if you hadn't upset me."

"The hell you say—you just don't give a damn about my feelings."

This is a familiar kind of exchange, which may be yelled, signaled by angry glances, or telegraphed by hurt silence.

Yet as has been suggested earlier in this chapter, the breakdown of communication between spouses usually does not arise from deception. The greatest single cause of breakdown is the exchange of information which is culturally clear to one spouse and culturally foreign to the other. Spouses usually have different backgrounds; therefore, they have learned to label things differently. For example, their definitions of what is meant by "good" behavior or "good" taste may be divergent. To the shy, puritanical husband, his gregarious wife may seem immoral when she kisses men she knows upon meeting them at parties. And the wife, whose family always ate breakfast (consisting of cereal and coffee) in the kitchen, may believe that her husband is an unrea-

sonable snob when he insists on having a well-cooked breakfast
served on white linen in the dining room.

At times the standpoint of one spouse—the context in which he
is thinking or acting, which determines the labels he utilizes—
may be very different from that of the other, and therefore the
message sent will not be the message that is received. For example, the husband in a happy mood who tells jokes to his depressed wife may feel that he is attempting to cheer her up; but
she may conclude that she is being ridiculed.

When there has been for some time a burning issue in a
marriage, such as whether the husband is really faithful, or
whether the wife is smarter than the husband, or whether they
married each other because she was possibly pregnant rather than
because they were in love, every exchange of information can be
interpreted in terms of the central unsettled question.

For example, if a husband had affairs before he married, his
wife may still worry about the possibility of promiscuity, although
he is currently monogamous. The husband may label his behavior
from the standpoint of the participant in a relationship based
upon fidelity and trust, but the wife may label his behavior with a
degree of suspicion. Consequently, their discussions about a business trip may be troubled by misunderstandings. The wife may
say she wants to accompany her husband in order to look after
him—when she really means that she wants to check up on him.
The husband with no thought of being unfaithful, is not aware of
his wife's message. He knows that he does not require looking after
on a two-day trip. His company furnishes a room at a good hotel,
transportation, meals, and so on, and his schedule of appointments will keep him busy from nine in the morning until midnight.
He may thank his wife for offering to look after him, and tell her
how pleasant it would be to have her—but he will go on to say
that it is impossible for her to come. The company would not pay
her way and they cannot afford the expense; also, since it would
not be appropriate for her to sit in on his continual round of
business meetings, they'd hardly even see each other except on
the plane. Therefore, she can't come.

It can be seen that a great many mislabeled communications
will pass between husband and wife on this issue, and that each
destructive communication will lead to still others. Time after

time, each spouse will be sure that *his* message is true and good, and that the other spouse's message is false and bad.

Communicating is a skill which can be learned. There are simple techniques for guaranteeing that the message sent is the message received. These will be discussed later.

12

TRUST IN MARRIAGE

One of the necessary ingredients of a workable marriage is trust. "Trust" is defined as "confidence in or reliance on some quality or attribute of a person or thing, or the truth of a statement." It is also defined as "the quality of being trustworthy; fidelity; loyalty; trustiness."

More immediately applicable to the marital situation are the definitions of the verb, "to trust": "to have faith or confidence that something desired is or will be the case," and "to invest with a charge; to confide or entrust something to the care or disposal of the other."

The trouble with these definitions is that they imply that trust can be unilateral, as when the infant trusts his mother because he is tiny and she is large and he has no other choice. Trust in marriage is different. It is formed on the basis of exchanges of behavior (and hence, information) which go on all the time between the spouses. When the spouses, by their behavior, are communicating clearly to each other, there is no "noise" on the line between them; then there is trust, because they read each other clearly. Each spouse can understand and accept the significance, the intent, the values, and the meanings of the other's behavioral repertoire; and if there is any doubt, he feels free to clarify the matter immediately.

Trust is not something that one or the other spouse has as a personal quality or character trait; it is present between the two if it is warranted by their exchange of behavior. Naturally, during stress, unclear communication, or confusion, the trust existing between a couple may temporarily diminish, but the experience may fortify trust over the long run if they successfully handle the situation. Thus, trust is developed over a period of time as a result of experience. If spouse A's behavior generally is consistent and clear, spouse B will feel trust because he has learned to depend on this behavior. When two people trust one another each can relax, for he knows what kind of behavior to expect from the other; mutual confidence develops.

Trust has to be distinguished from labeling. If one labels one's spouse as ungenerous and unkind, one may be said to "trust" him always to behave selfishly and unkindly. This attitude, which might be called negative trust, is a huge barrier to efforts by one or both spouses to change or improve their behavior. Unlike the positive trust we have been discussing, it is not based on clearly communicative exchanges of behavior.

"Love, honor, and obey . . . 'til death do us part" is an unrealistic part of the Christian marriage vow because it suggests that trust is static. In the mystique of the marriage ceremony, spouses assume that by saying "I do" they have signed a rigid and unalterable pact, and therefore they *expect* trust from each other. Trust is not created by expectations. It develops as a result of mutual shared experiences which are clarified between the spouses. The Christian marital vow is based on the fallacy that nothing will change. Trust in marriage does *not* mean, "I am certain that you, my darling spouse, will always be exactly the same as I estimated you to be the day we were married." Trust is the result of a flexible, developmental bargain between spouses which endures because it is able to accommodate change.

The word "trust" originally came from the Scandinavian language and meant "to comfort," "to console," "to confide in." It seems to have first appeared about the ninth or tenth century in a Nordic society in which men and women lived, in a state of relative equality, in an environment requiring a desperate struggle for survival. To "trust" then meant to give comfort and cheer when needed. It had nothing to do with estimating another's behavior. This original definition of the word represents the first step toward Sullivan's definition of love.

The modern meaning of "trust" is quite different from its original significance. Today spouses who trust have learned to depend on each other's behavior because experience has taught them that their relationship is predictable. But they do not necessarily demonstrate comforting or succoring behavior, simply because behavior of this sort may be foreign to their personalities, experience, values, or mutual expectations.

If a wife commits adultery and is questioned about it by her husband, should she lie and attempt to deceive him further? Or should she admit the adultery, openly explain the circumstances and causes, and tell him whether it was a single chance occurrence or whether it reflects feelings which make the continuance of the marriage undesirable? If either spouse wishes the relationship to grow, it is essential that they both be truthful, even at the risk of painful scenes or possible violence. Decisions about continuing the relationship can only be made by both parties if both know the truth of the situation. A person remaining with his spouse for expediency's sake—for instance, a mother with five children who stays with her breadwinner because she has no hope of gainful employment, and who wants nothing from the marriage except financial support—may lie in order to continue the relationship as it is. But those who wish to improve their marriage and foster growth and trust through the relationship must overcome their fear of honesty, because every lie begets another lie. It is always necessary to cover the cover-up, and in a close relationship, the attempts at deception are likely to be unsuccessful, for the other spouse is only deceived *if* he or she *wishes* to be.

The practice of honesty and clear communication in marriage is likely to result in an extra dividend, for it encourages spouses to be generous, comforting, and consoling. If the spouses can be truthful and open about themselves—for example, if a husband can admit he is afraid that he is failing at his job instead of attacking his wife for spending too much money—mutual support and helpfulness are possible. Tolerance and generosity in relation to others' mistakes become easier when one learns that others can be generous in return. If a person can be honest enough to recognize and admit his own weaknesses—and finds he is forgiven by others for his lapses—it then becomes possible for him to be tolerant in relation to the weaknesses of others. We are able to give to people we trust because we have received from them and know that we will again; thus trust and generosity are both causes and results of a genuine give-and-take, or in our terms, *quid pro quo.*

Those couples who enjoy trust, who give trust to each other, probably are among the most fortunate people alive. Note that we say "couples," not "individuals." It is obvious that for trust to exist *both* spouses must be completely open and truthful with each other. This is difficult. People in our culture are taught to lie from childhood, whether their instruction is overt or implicit. Children learn that if they tell the truth (for example, comment on all that they observe, such as the behavior of adults) they will be rejected or punished. Dishonesty is so greatly expected in our society that courts require witnesses to testify "under oath." Much of the training that a trial lawyer receives is intended to give him skill in exposing dishonesty on the part of those testifying. Psychiatrists know that many patients lie to them—and pay a fee for the privilege. The Internal Revenue Service is organized in the expectation of falsified income-tax returns.

Because we are reared in dishonesty (largely the dishonesty of omission, as in politeness or diplomacy), complete truthfulness is most unusual. Even as noble an institution as the Catholic church encourages dishonest behavior. Edwin F. Healy, S.J., in his *Moral Guidance,* interprets the commandment "Thou shalt not bear false witness against thy neighbor" as follows:

> [on lying] . . . If one tells falsehoods to a child who is wholly unable to perceive one's meaning, there is no lie involved, for one is equivalently talking to oneself. . . .[1]

> [on mental reservation]   One is never justified in telling a lie. Still at times one is obliged in conscience to veil the truth, for there are secrets to be guarded and detractions to be avoided. Sometimes silence will not suffice to maintain the secret which one is trying to guard. In fact, it may happen that silence would betray the secret. Hence there must be some licit means of concealing the truth when necessary. This licit means is the broad mental reservation.

[1] Edwin F. Healy, *Moral Guidance,* Chicago, Loyola University Press, 1960, pp. 232–233.
[2] *Ibid.,* p. 235.

. . . If a suspicious husband asks his wife whether or not she has committed adultery, she may licitly answer, "no," even though she has actually sinned thus many times. Her answer really means: "No, I have committed no crime of adultery that I must reveal." The question is rightly aimed only at knowledge that is not secret, and so the wife may reply accordingly.[3]

. . . One way of putting the question is to ask if a false statement is always a lie. Some theologians answer in the negative. When a child tells a caller that mother is not at home, he makes a statement which is objectively false and speaks contrary to what he knows to be true, yet no one would accuse him of lying. Sometimes it is necessary to make a false statement in order to protect secret knowledge. Silence or the use of mental reservation is not sufficient; the only way to protect the secret is to make a statement contrary to what you know to be true.[4]

We do not agree with this advice. We believe that it is *wrong and destructive* to deceive—even for the sake of expediency.

Unfortunately, honesty is even more complex and difficult to achieve than verbal truthfulness. For example, if a husband verbally states to his wife that he "loves" her, yet by his daily behavior communicates only selfishness, lack of consideration, irritability, and the like, how is the wife to learn trust? He may sincerely believe that he loves his wife, and that he is speaking truly when he says so, but his *behavior* belies his words. If a wife tells her husband that she trusts him implicitly to care for her, yet spends hours each day voicing her concern about financial and other problems, can the husband be expected to *trust* his wife's statement that she *trusts* him?

Honesty is complicated by the fact that messages are communicated both verbally and nonverbally, by words and by other behavior. When a person's words are not supported by his nonverbal behavior, trust is not possible, even though the speaker believes that his words transmit his real feelings.

A couple recently seen in therapy provide a good example of the complexities involved in honesty. The husband repeatedly said that he did not trust his wife. His wife could not understand why, because she believed in honesty and tried never to lie. At

---

[3] *Ibid.*, p. 237.
[4] *Ibid.*, p. 238.

one of the sessions, the problem became clear. The husband had occasion to state that he could not like his wife very much because she criticized him constantly. The wife said she did not, and was thereupon instructed by the therapist to refrain from criticism for the remainder of the session (about fifteen minutes). After promising to do so, she turned with a large smile to her husband and suggested that they attend a group activity that weekend involving yoga-type bodily-sensory exercises and the discussion of personal problems. The therapist knew from past sessions that this kind of activity was much enjoyed by the wife but hated by the husband. Asked why she had proposed this activity when she knew her husband didn't like it, the wife angrily replied that she knew he disliked it, but thought that he would benefit from it and that he needed to learn to be more open with people. By presenting this seemingly pleasant invitation, the wife had indeed criticized her husband—immediately following her promise not to do so—by implying that he "should" like such activities and was lacking in some way if he did not. After some exploration, the husband was able to pin down verbally the reason for his lack of faith and trust in his wife: *she broke many verbal promises through discrepant behavior.* He recalled, for example, the time he was ill and she visited him in the hospital. At that time she had spoken of her great concern and love for him, but though he was hospitalized for four days, she only paid him one visit. The wife "honestly" had been unaware of the double messages she delivered repeatedly, by saying one thing and doing another.

Honesty involves, therefore, not simply saying what one believes, but also doing what one says. It requires consistency. Trust is possible when verbal and nonverbal behavior are consistent and are communicated clearly. Being predictable and consistent does *not* mean that one must never change. A person who remained the same for fifty years would bore the mildest spouse to tears. It *does* mean that the growth and change, the reversals in opinions, attitudes, and desires which are inevitable in living human beings, are clarified honestly for the spouse as they occur, so that the changed behavior can be understood, adjusted to, or commented on. Only then can change occur without fear—fear of the unknown.

Here we come to another requirement for the development of trust in marriage: both spouses must be realistic. They must accept the fact that everyone changes in the course of time and under varying circumstances. Change is inevitable, yet many spouses interpret change in their partners as a betrayal of their trust. If a spouse becomes a cripple or is told he has cancer, this change can be accepted because it is so obvious, and it is not usually interpreted as reflecting the affected partner's feelings for his spouse. Yet few marital partners are prepared to accept the subtler changes that come with time and altered life situations. Such changes, whether pleasant or not, should be expected and acknowledged just as an unpleasant physical disease would be. But the explicit acknowledgment of the true state of affairs is all too rare in most marriages. Instead, both spouses pretend, or one is "frank" while the other is "quiet." Trust in only one of two spouses is sheer idiocy. One should always be on guard against the person who says, "But I trust *you!*" Trust, like love, is only possible as a mutual relationship; it cannot be the sole property of one or the other spouse. The spouse who trusts an unloving (hence untrustworthy) partner is usually a prideful, scared person—not a trusting one.

In a marriage where the spouses trust each other, the significance of their vows might be something like this: "We have voluntarily agreed to form a marital partnership for our mutual benefit. We are human beings, and will grow and change with age and with circumstance. Neither of us is perfect. We are not afraid of being fallible and therefore we will be honest and open with each other, and reveal ourselves and our changes or failures; we will disclose the hidden things when they unexpectedly emerge from the unconscious or from the forgotten past. If what happens is joyful (as we have faith it will be most of the time), we will treasure this good fortune. But if events are painful or harmful, we will adjust and accept the change because it is a fact. Instead of exhibiting frustration and being punitive toward each other, we will be consoling and encouraging. We will discuss realistically whatever has happened and see how it relates to us mutually, and as equals, we will decide what action is required. We also will discuss, if necessary, how both of us may change or adjust for our mutual benefit. More important than ourselves as individuals is our marital compages."

The conception of trust presented here—which returns to the original Scandinavian meaning of the word—is still the most realistic and effective there is. It supplies the best definition we know for a workable marriage. Unfortunately, marriages based on this kind of trust are rare, but they give the rest of us something to hope for and try for.

Paradoxically, those spouses who have not experienced trust in their relationship may find it occurs under surprising circumstances. For example, an incident or an act involving one spouse may cause the other to recoil with horror or shame and say, "I can never trust him again." Yet, this may be the beginning, instead of the end, of a growing relationship. Up to now, each of the spouses may have assumed the other to be static, like a placid cow, and the disturbing piece of behavior may shock them both out of their emotional *rigor mortis.* Or unilateral change due to forces outside of the marriage (a job, relatives, friends, and so on) may shake a frozen, static relationship into motion, for the mutual benefit, growth, and learning of both spouses.

Trust requires the constant exercise of intelligence, truthfulness, and courage. Perhaps that is why it is so rare.

When the word is applied to relationships other than marriage, we are usually speaking about a specific aspect of the situation, as when a businessman says, "I trust him to pay his bills." In business, individuals are dealing with money and power—material matters—and they do not always care about the growth and feelings of those with whom they deal as long as they are honest or reliable in a business sense. But businessmen can afford to engage in a socially sanctioned struggle for prestige and power, while two spouses who live in constant competition will end up with a bankrupt marriage.

Trust is not granted as part of a dowry, and it is not built into the legal contract that binds the couple. It is something that is worked out and developed by mutual conscious effort, often by taking two steps forward and one back, but its rewards are great and more than worth the effort.

13

SEX IN MARRIAGE

What is the role of sex in marriage?

Like every other element in the marital relationship, sex involves behavior between individuals. The response of each partner varies with his mood, his physical state, and the oscillations of the relationship.

Given adequate physiological and anatomical equipment (which Nature rarely fails to provide) and a modicum of knowledge of sexual techniques, the spouses will enjoy sexual union *when both are in a collaborative mood.* The collaborative mood exists when each is adding something to the sexual act, not just submitting. When the spouses are not in a loving mood, they still may find in sex a release from tension and thus derive another type of pleasure from it, especially if they are in agreement about what they expect, but it is likely to be less fulfilling and often may be frustrating, because one partner has contrary needs which are left unmet.

This sex act—a comparably simple matter—has become the most written about, the most talked of, and the most muddled aspect of marriage. There are several reasons why the role of sex in marriage has become excessively emphasized and distorted.

A cultural fear of sex's losing its effective status in the social structure. This fear is as ancient at least as the Old Testament dictum that "a man . . . shall cleave unto his wife." The expectation is that if this pronouncement is violated the species will not fulfill its obligation to procreate in a familial or nurturing setting.

The fear of desertion and abandonment. In our culture, this fear is stronger in women than in men. Women are tied down by the processes of childbearing and childbirth and require assistance physically and emotionally. In response to this fear, and to provide a weapon for fighting it, the belief has developed in our culture that if one is "sexy" enough, one's mate will *not* desert. The result has been an exaggerated consciousness of sexual performance as a ritual to increase personal security in marriage or to induce marriage. Yet if one is "sexy" enough there is the danger of being *too* "sexy" and violating the ancient commandments.

The female's simulation of sexiness. The male requires an erection to enter into the sex act. If he is uninterested in sex, or afraid of it, he will not have an erection. However, a woman does not have any obvious physiological indications of spontaneous readiness. She can fake sexual spontaneity, and the male (at least for a time) may not be aware of the deceit. The female extends this stimulation of sexual interest into parasexual areas by means of hair dyes, falsies, girdles, cosmetics, perfumes, and high heels. These parasexual devices scream, "Look, I'm sexy. I'm desirable." This may or may not be true, but it is probable that women resent their need to advertise and would prefer to be accepted as they really are; men resent the necessity for sexual deception even though they foster it.

The economic forces in our culture sustain and stimulate these hypocritical actions. Any attempt to alter the pattern involves resisting the advertising and other merchandising techniques used by multibillion-dollar businesses to peddle false female sexuality. The women who attempt to retain a "natural" appearance, with undoctored hair, no makeup, and so forth, are few in number, and they may (because of cultural conditioning) be regarded by both men and women as deviates. Most of the people who might be inclined to rebel against this type of sexual mores are intimidated by cultural pressures and mass value judgments.

Furthermore, the emphasis upon female sexual paraphernalia is an inherited social custom which long has been associated with the elite. In past ages, makeup, breast accentuators, and the like were worn mainly by the ruling classes, and the tendency to show upward social mobility by imitating the elite still exists. Even today, the wealthier the spouses, the more they exaggerate the difference between the sexes. The wife wears elegant gowns, elaborate hairdos, scintillating jewelry, and expensive furs and perfumes. Her husband may favor dark conservative suits, homburgs, and thick-soled, handmade English shoes.

The erroneous belief that unsatisfactory sexual relations are the major cause of bad marriages. The speciousness here is clear. Unsatisfactory sexual relations are a symptom of marital discord, not the cause of it. It is difficult for the victims to see this because of the mass of propaganda about sex that attacks them day and night, on the street, in the home, in the office. We are such an absurd culture that even mouthwashes and Lysol are related to the sexual aspects of marriage.

John Jones, for example, is dissatisfied with his marriage. On his way to work he may look up and see a billboard with a picture of a nearly nude, beautiful woman, advertising a brand of stockings. John is stimulated sexually and says to himself, "Boy, I'd like to have an affair with something like that." He knows this is wishful thinking, and may even recognize that the beautiful model might be incompatible with him. Next he retreats from the daydream and his thoughts turn toward his wife. But the sexual fantasy he has had about the girl in the ad colors his reflections about his marriage relationship, and he thinks, "Golly, Mary's legs might look better in that kind of hosiery." What he means is, "If Mary were a better sexpot we'd both have a happier marriage." He is caught in a double error: the appearance of Mary's legs has nothing to do with the couple's sexual satisfaction, *and* he has forgotten his *own* function in achieving a successful union.

Such a process may be repeated frequently during the day, for John is never permitted to escape advertisements which suggest that sexuality is the key to happiness. Yet there is considerable evidence that an individual's *perception* of the sexual relationship is more related to marital satisfaction than the sexual act itself.

In a survey conducted at an Ohio university, interviews of several hundred couples showed that by and large those who reported their marriages as "satisfactory" gave the frequency of their intercourse as twice a week. Those who reported their marriages as "unsatisfactory" also reported a frequency of twice a week, yet among the unhappy couples the husbands said that twice a week was more than their wives wished but satisfactory from their point of view, and the wives said it was less than their husbands wished but just right for them personally. The "happy" husbands and wives said the frequency of twice a week was satisfying to both themselves *and* their spouses. In other words, the problem was in the couples' communication and not in the actual frequency of their sexual relations.

While sexual problems are often blamed for marital difficulties, one is seldom made aware of the other side of the coin: sexual relations may keep some marriages going, providing virtually the only kind of contact which the spouses have. Psychiatrists and other professionals who treat marital problems are aware that some individuals have been able to establish successful sexual relations with each other although they cannot get together in any other context. Many of these couples have the experience of waking at night to discover themselves involved in sex, with neither partner aware of who took the initiative.

The differences between male and female. The physical differences between male and female contribute to the novelty and adventure of sex. Heterosexuality is extrafascinating and carries with it the illusion of intrigue. At the same time, the differences make understanding one another more difficult. Also, the excessive emphasis on sex as the major factor in marriage results in a distorted viewpoint. The natural differences between male and female are made to appear crucial for the success of a marriage. Actually, a woman will not improve her marriage by achieving a voluptuous bust, legs like a model, and an aura of exotic perfume. If her marriage is an unhappy one, her husband may develop a preference for small-breasted women who dress plainly and do not wear perfume.

Having reviewed some reasons for mistaken attitudes toward sexual intercourse, let us now take a look at its actual role in marriage. What is special about sexual intercourse, a highly satisfying male-female symbiosis, is that it requires a higher degree of collaborative communication than any other kind of behavior exchanged between the spouses. Sex is consequently precious, but also perilous. It is the only relationship act which must have mutual spontaneity for mutual satisfaction. It can only be a conjoint union, and it represents a common goal which is clear and understood by both.

The reason people keep asking where sex fits into marriage is that they have been hoodwinked, bamboozled, pressured, conned, and persuaded that the sexual act is compulsory in their lives and *must be performed alike by everyone;* the "standards" are established by advertisers, publicity for sexpot motion-picture stars, literature, movies, plays, television, and so on. But these are standards of fantasy. Therefore people ask silly questions: How often should we have sex? What is the best position? How intense should it be? Should we scratch and bite each other? What time of day should it be done? The questions sound like inquiries about the type of gymnastic procedures to be followed for attaining muscles like Mr. America's or a rear end or bust like Miss America's. Perhaps even worse off are the myriads of couples who don't dare ask questions and just assume they *must* be abnormal because their own practice differs from some so-called standard.

The problem is obvious. In sex, trying to keep up with the Joneses is the road to disaster. To decide where sex fits into their particular marriage, a couple must look inward at the marriage, not outward at the deceptive advice and make-believe standards set by others. There are no standards, and most "advice" from friends or family is misleading, for few people can speak honestly about their own sex life. Rather than admit their own sex problems and misgivings, friends often let one assume that their sex experiences are indeed superior; otherwise, the implication is, they wouldn't be giving advice.

Can women and men live without sex and still stay healthy?

Yes, they can. People cast away on isolated islands have gone for years without sex and have not experienced any physiological or psychological breakdowns or deficiencies as a result. Priests, nuns, and many mystics, such as the great Mahatma Gandhi have eschewed sexual union and not damaged their health or decreased their longevity.

Sex, of course, is necessary for propagation; nature has provided this instinctual drive so that the species will survive. The drive is effective because of the variety of intense pleasures derived from its fulfillment. But no harm will occur to the normal individual to whom sex is denied.

Almost all adult human beings somehow have the feeling that experiencing sex frequently is a requirement for good physical and mental health, even if intellectually they know better. Both men and women who have enjoyed sex at regular intervals become frustrated, sometimes desperate, when it is withheld for (what seems to them) a long time. The sex aggressions of men at war in foreign lands and of sailors who have been at sea for months are well known. Such behavior stems more from a feeling of deprivation than from pure physical necessity. A person who voluntarily renounces or limits sexual intercourse—as priests, nuns, and others do for varied reasons—suffers no ill health or mental anguish as long as the renunciation corresponds to his emotional needs. If, however, a person desires sexual union and has deep, unmet needs for this form of human intimacy, yet is unable for some reason to meet the need, the resulting sense of deprivation and frustration may create emotional problems.

Sometimes unusual sex actions are stimulated by nonsexual deficiencies. For example, male children with a dread of being abandoned by their mother often will masturbate excessively. Men who have repressed homosexual tendencies (frequently the result of having a passive—or dead—father and a dominant mother) often are inclined to act oversexed in order to "prove their manhood."

The *beliefs* (most of them specious) which most individuals have on "what kind" of sex is desirable, and "how much," have several sources:

1. So-called "scientific" information obtained from books, articles, and lectures.
2. Customs, traditions, and advice conveyed by relatives and friends.
3. Customs, traditions, and examples transmitted by literature, radio, television, movies, and advertising.

Tradition molds many beliefs and habits having to do with sex in marriage. For example, consider the barbaric custom of the honeymoon—particularly in past centuries, when the girl's chastity was treasured and important. In those days the bride and groom, who hardly knew each other, departed to a strange geographical area and into sexual intimacy. Usually the bride possessed only hearsay information on sexual matters and the husband's sexual experience had not necessarily prepared him to understand the needs of a virginal bride. They hurried away from the courtship milieu of jollity, gregariousness, and traditional optimism into a new sexual environment of their own, and were expected to emerge a week or ten days later with all the tenderness, love, and devotion needed to create a successful, happy marriage—whether or not the sexual experience had been traumatic for one or both of them.

A modern version of the same ritual occurs today, with an additional cultural expectation introduced: the newlyweds are expected to achieve *mutual* sexual satisfaction during the honeymoon. The young couple usually is launched with a lavish wedding and a tremendous amount of effort and expense on the part of both their families. The newlyweds are under pressure to "have fun" on their honeymoon and to return looking radiant and serene. Frequently the opposite happens. We estimate that most honeymoons are periods of frustrating sexual disappointment. The honeymoon may be an exciting novelty, but usually it results in confusion even when there has been premarital sexual experience. The situation of the bride who cried all through her honeymoon is a common one. Sex, like anything else, has to be learned; and even if the two have had relations before marriage, the marriage state places them in a new psychological milieu to which they must adjust. Now they are "legitimate," and they believe that their sexual experience will therefore be better. Now they are legally tied; they cannot walk away from each other. They feel the sex act *must* be a success every time; otherwise, the marriage is disintegrating.

This situation is aggravated by the pronouncements of most sex consultants, books, and articles on marriage. They usually indicate that sex is the keystone of marital success. We disagree. Sex is significant; and good sex is satisfying and emotionally nourishing. Sex is highly desirable, but it is not the only vital force in marriage, either during the honeymoon or later.

The situation is muddied further by the conflicting views of "experts" who give "scientific" information on sex. It is important that all "expert" opinions on sex be taken with a grain of skepticism.

Most "scientific" information on sex comes from two sources:

psychiatrists and other physicians writing about data obtained from the experiences of their patients, and social scientists generalizing from data obtained in surveys conducted by means of some type of questionnaire.

In point of fact, conclusions based upon the medical data obtained from patients are not necessarily applicable to most people. Patients go to doctors for the treatment of one or more problems. If they have come for psychiatric therapy, they expect to spend many hours discussing sex and exploring the negative aspects of themselves, their spouses, their friends, and so on. Few (if any) will pay twenty-five or thirty dollars an hour and then spend the time discussing pleasant and satisfactory experiences. The gynecologist or the family physician who writes a sex book is scientific only in regard to anatomy. The nonanatomical aspects of the text are based upon his own personal sex experiences plus whatever his ailing patients have told him.

Some of the most popular tracts on sex and marriage are written by gynecologists whose practices consist to a great extent of women who *spontaneously and voluntarily* talk freely to the physician in their efforts to describe their personal discords. The fact that a person talks and answers questions in a doctor's office (instead of in a public bar or a living room) does not prove that the individual is accurate or objective, and certainly does not indicate that his conclusions are generally applicable. Almost all patients' views on sex are subjective and weighted, especially since those who feel the need to discuss their sex lives usually have special problems.

The same difficulty causes the flaws in the Kinsey reports (and in most other studies whose data comes from question-and-answer procedures). Although Kinsey made an important study, one that required courage to initiate, we cannot overlook one important fact: he depended primarily on *volunteers* to answer his questions. Can we be sure that the people who volunteer to answer sex questions are representative? Some of the Kinsey interviewees talked two or three hours about their experiences—evidently revealing intimacies was fun for some.

Also, there were considerable differences in experience and ability among Kinsey's interviewers. Only recently, the work of the Department of Psychiatry at Harvard has demonstrated that the nature of an interviewing context (including the interviewer's attitude) has a tremendous influence on the interviewee's response. An interviewer who strongly believes that, say, many wives have intercourse with other men when their husbands are on trips, will come up with much more evidence to support this view than will an interviewer who holds the opposite opinion at the start of the investigation.

Nevertheless, the Kinsey material provides the most complete and reliable data we have on the sexual practices of middle- and upper-class Americans. It reveals that increasingly in our culture, sexual intercourse is not confined to married people; and it is certainly not limited to sexual congress between men and women.

The bulk of the Kinsey material and of other surveys (which primarily relate to college students) concerns homosexuality, masturbation, premarital intercourse, perversion, post-divorce sexual activities, the activities of spinsters and bachelors, and adultery. To our knowledge, *no one has studied a sample of normogenic (average) married couples in significant numbers* and scientifically determined what married people think and do in relation to sex. Little is known about socio-economic class differences, let alone ethnic idiosyncrasies.

Where does sex fit into marriage? It is almost impossible to estimate (except with respect to a specific married couple, after many hours of interviews) because so few studies have been made on the subject, and those which do exist are limited in scope and objectivity.

The answer to this question also depends upon time and circumstances, for sexual needs are fundamentally psychological. Middle-income spouses who have been married for a year and have no children, but want some, may have different sexual needs from the husband and wife without jobs, so poor they can't pay the rent, who therefore are afraid to have children. A couple married for thirty years, with four children in college, may have different sexual needs from a couple married for five years, with only one child. Such differences are not merely due to age. Boredom plays a more significant role in decreasing the frequency of intercourse than do withering sex glands. Also, a couple whose sex experience is beautiful and satisfying may engage in sex less frequently than an unhappy pair frantically experimenting for a solution to their discord.

There is no accurate sex information which gives exact answers for everyone, since there are so many variables. Yet in the United States, the sex ethic has become all important. As we have already stressed, the fallacious concept that sex determines our lives is spread far and wide by those promoting the tremendous sales of products supposed to enhance sexual attractiveness. Also, "authorities" on sex lecture, write, and give sexual advice *for a fee*. Naturally, they exaggerate the importance of sex in marriage. Offering complicated sex techniques is a profitable profession, and the more difficult the techniques, the longer the expensive counseling will last. The most popular sex manual has been through countless revisions and has outsold all other books except the Bible!

The myth that perfect and heavenly sex must be experienced by an individual before he can consider himself normal has become the foundation for a national mania. Sex success is the theme of social instruction and of almost all advertising, even for products not in any way associated with the sex act.

Spouses who are disappointed in sex are profoundly concerned about their difficulty. This is a reasonable reaction, if the disappointment is well founded. Men often wonder about their manhood or suspect that their wives are frigid or malicious. Wives wonder about their frigidity and suspect that perhaps their husbands are having affairs or that they are effeminate or at least inconsiderate or ignorant of satisfying sexual techniques.

Spouses will try anything to bring about a happier union, *one closer to the sex-success image* which is our national demigod. Many a man and wife have spent a small fortune to go to a posh luxury lodge where they hoped they would miraculously achieve a sexual congress they couldn't bring about in their own bedroom. If the weather is nice and the view is good, something may come of the weekend, but it is not apt to result in unusual sexual satisfaction. People frequently buy new houses, hire interior decorators—with the hope that a fresh environment will improve sexual relations.

If the various manifestations of sex were accepted as natural, and if people could abandon the view that there is a single absolute standard to be reached by all who are normal, the unhappiness of many couples would decrease—*and their performance would automatically improve.*

Our concern in this chapter has been with the problem: Is great, *great*, GREAT sex necessary for a satisfactory marriage, for a workable marriage? If sex is not up to culturally created expectations, is the marriage a failure?

It need not be a failure. It can be a good marriage even if the partners don't find heaven in bed.

Next, is a less-than-heavenly sex performance "normal"?

No one knows the answer, neither clergymen nor doctors. No one knows what normogenic sex performances are in marriage. Scientists have studied pathological marriages, but not normal ones. Small-sample research (such as that by Epstein and Westley at McGill University) supports our contention that sex is not essential; it has been found that some apparently well-adjusted spouses have "given up" sex after a few years of marriage.

In summary, the important thing to remember is that there is no absolute standard against which the success of married sex can be measured as one would clock a hundred-yard dash. Occasionally, there are medical abnormalities (such as disfigured or diseased genitals, impotence, a pathological fear of sex), but assuming that these are not present, there is only one important question: Is sex a source of pleasure—in the spouses' own judgment?

What is a satisfying sex experience for two people may well be undesirable for two others, and vice versa. For example, it is estimated by most physicians that more than half of all women married an average of ten years and having three children have never experienced an orgasm. In a sampling made of such cases most of the women were not aware that they had not had a full sex act. They derived varying degrees of pleasure from the physical intimacy with their husbands. Equally interesting is the fact that the husbands frequently did not know that their wives voluntarily made the same noises and motions which they *had heard or read* were performed by passionate women; the husbands had accepted these as spontaneous and derived satisfaction from them as evidence of the wives' pleasure.

Spouses should not permit their satisfactions to be influenced by authority figures (such as actors and actresses), advertising, art, literature, and social customs and traditions. Personal sex values concern the two people involved. For example, we know a couple in their seventies. Every evening they bathe and dress elegantly for dinner. They treat each other with the dignity and courtesy of a blossoming courtship. At night when they go to bed they hold each other throughout the night, even though they have not exercised their genitalia for years. The elderly gentleman has described their experience as "having a ten-hour orgasm every night." For these two, it is a complete and wonderful sex act, and a very satisfying and nourishing one. Who is to differ with them?

Is sex important in married life? Yes, it is. It is *one* of the cements which hold the bricks of married life together. But the when, the how, the how often, and the quality can only be determined by the people involved.

14

THE
MARITAL SPECTRUM

The Different Types of Marriage

Spouses who can identify their marriage as belonging to a certain type find it easier to hold discussions concerning marital problems. Once they have agreed on the general category of their marriage, the perspective in which they see particular marital processes and ways of behaving seems to become clearer. We shall therefore attempt to describe the "spectrum of marriage"—a broad classification of marriages from the "best" down to the "worst." This spectrum is not a scientific classification, but merely a way of thinking about marriage which we hope will be helpful.

Throughout this book, there are frequent references to the functional, or workable marriage. The concept of the functional marriage is especially important in this chapter. Such a marriage is not necessarily "happy," and cannot be described in terms of its specific goals. A functional marital system is one which is functioning, or operating, without debilitating blockage or impasses, despite the variety of both positive and negative elements it contains.

One cannot accurately categorize a particular marriage as "happy" or "violent." The outside appearance of a marriage is often social camouflage; the packaging often fails to indicate the contents of the box. Homicides have occurred among spouses who were never known to quarrel. Many discordant marriages appear happy, and sometimes, on the other hand, spouses who quarrel in public have achieved a functional union, occasionally even a joyous one. The analysis-in-depth of a marriage must go far beyond the apparent mood or appearance of the partners. Marriage is a process and a relationship between two people. Therefore, to analyze the marriage it is necessary to examine the process and the relationship interactions.

Three avenues must be explored in order to define marital categories:

First, *functionality*. How functional is the relationship? How well can the spouses work together in complementary fashion? How wide a range of behavior can they achieve, or have they brought into the marriage? How appropriately does their behavior fulfill the needs and expectations of both parties? How suitable is their behavior for achieving the various common goals of the relationship, with impasses and blockages kept to a minimum?

Second, *temporal compatibility*. How are the two spouses oriented temporally? That is, in terms of time, what are their views, their desires, their ambitions? Are the short-term and long-range goals of each compatible with those of the other?

And third, *vector relations*. In what direction and at what speed is the marriage changing? Are the spouses developing a collaborative relationship, or are they headed toward irreversible discord because they agree less and less on the direction and rate of change of the relationship?

In seeking answers to these questions, the reader must understand that the human being is a goal-oriented animal, and that the attempt to achieve goals involves a complicated and sometimes incompatible or antithetical use of time and energy. *Homo sapiens* is often a perverse creature who may desire one thing, and yet, paradoxically, behave in a manner which makes the realization of his desire impossible.

As yet no scientist has come up with a *wholly* reliable classifi-

catory description of marriage. In the social sciences there are
bound to be some hazy areas. But this is no reason for not presenting the principles of a system. Therefore, in the following
pages we sketch—in broad strokes—a spectrum of marriage. We
feel it is important to do this. Most people require a landmark, a
frame of reference, with which to orient themselves with respect
to any philosophical or behavioral system which involves them
deeply and objectively.

CLASSIFICATION OF MARRIAGES

The following classification is based on the concept that at any
one moment in time a marriage can be regarded as belonging
more or less in one of the listed categories. The categories are
arranged in order of desirability and functionality. The one at the
top is the "best," and the one at the bottom is the "worst." Each
category has two subcategories.

    I. The Stable-Satisfactory Marriage
        1. The Heavenly Twins
        2. The Collaborative Geniuses
    II. The Unstable-Satisfactory Marriage
        1. The Spare-Time Battlers
        2. The Pawnbrokers
    III. The Unstable-Unsatisfactory Marriage
        1. The Weary Wranglers
        2. The Psychosomatic Avoiders
    IV. The Stable-Unsatisfactory Marriage
        1. The Gruesome Twosome
        2. The Paranoid Predators

It is easy to place a marriage in one of these categories. But as
one does so, it is important to remember that they represent segments of a *continuum*. Marriage is a continuous process, involving constant growth and metamorphosis. As the partners change,
or their relationship changes, or the status of one partner changes,
or the external pressures or environment changes, the marital
state may move from one category into another. One of the purposes of this book is to assist the reader to recognize the trends of
his own marriage, to halt those which are destructive, and to
stimulate and nourish those which promise functionality and
satisfaction.

A particular marriage may wobble from one category to another and then back again. No category is absolute. The "best" category, the Stable-Satisfactory, marks the upper limit of the continuum and represents a marital state probably never achieved in its pure form. This perfect, harmonious relationship, this absolute compatibility, is extremely rare because no two spouses are ever completely alike, nor do they have total congruity of backgrounds, nor absolute similarity of tastes and interests. Minor tensions based on conflicting interests, requiring some degree of change and compromise, occur at some time in all marriages. Differing periods of a marriage require different modes of adjustment.

Likewise, marriages classified as belonging to the "worst" category, the Stable-Unsatisfactory, hardly ever reach complete implosion. A totally destructive relationship is impossible. The husband and wife in a miserable marriage are certain to enjoy at least a few pleasant moments and small mutual triumphs, even if their pleasure consists of hurting each other.

The position of marriages along the continuum is determined by their relative success, with most falling in a cluster somewhere in the middle two categories. The extreme marital types which approach the two ends probably constitute only from 5 to 10 per cent of all marriages.

15

THE STABLE-
SATISFACTORY
MARRIAGE

This relationship is almost hypothetical. Such a harmonious and
collaborative union has seldom been directly observed by the
authors, and then only between elderly men and women who
have been married for thirty or more years—or who have remarried late in life some years after being widowed—and who either
have had no children, or have grown-up children living in homes
of their own. We have never observed a generally constant collaborative union between spouses during the period when they
are raising children. This raises some interesting speculation—but
to resolve them into valid conclusions would demand extensive
research and a separate book.

Having observed the Stable-Satisfactory relationship among
some older people who are living alone without children, we
shall attempt to show, by extension and deductive reasoning,
what it would be like within the framework of a young marriage.

The Stable-Satisfactory marriage represents the ultimate in
collaboration. When it occurs, it is made possible by the hand-in-
glove fit of the two spouses. Their backgrounds must be similar

enough so that each partner clearly reads the other's signals, and in turn, responds with unambiguous messages. This effective communication makes possible the establishment of trust. With trust, comes the acceptance of each other's differences. *They are regarded as indications of varying tastes or values, not as symbols of a hostile relationship.* Mary knows her way will be cheerfully accepted a good part of the time by her husband, John. Therefore, it is not difficult for her to do the same for him. The spouses' ready acceptance of each other's differences makes it possible for them to be "creative"—to develop and project their own identities. The recognition of basic equality gives partners the self-assurance and courage to exercise their individuality with respect to outsiders and to the world in general.

The collaboration of the Stable-Satisfactory couple, based on mutual trust, allows them time, energy, interest, and confidence to engage in activities and avocations outside of the marital milieu. They become free to enjoy not only each other, but everyone and everything else which may interest them mutually or individually. They can work together when discipline or decisions regarding a child are involved; and they are able, as individuals, to enjoy and share the children without jealousy. They can form coalitions and make joint decisions—whether the issue involves work, play, friends, relatives, or organizations—and on occasion they may act as autonomous individuals. In contrast, the spouse who *isn't sure* of the other's love or trust or devotion may be unable to let the other out of his sight. Sometimes, the marital novice will mistake the watchful wariness of an untrusting and suspicious partner for love and devotion. The partner's C.I.A.-type sleuthing or oleaginous protectiveness and feigned interest usually disguise serious problems in the relationship.

In a collaborative relationship the man and woman may not always agree, but when they do not, they accept the disagreement comfortably and seek a *team solution* permitting recognition of both parties. If an impasse is reached, they resort to flipping coins or taking turns, in the recognition that neither is right nor wrong but a decision must be made. Their noncompetitive relationship makes possible close interaction with almost all people and situations.

As the years of marriage pass, the trust continues to reinforce itself and strengthen the spouses. Anyone who knows an older couple in this marital category is familiar with the serenity and certitude which these rare couples radiate.

Within the Stable-Satisfactory group there are two subcategories—the Heavenly Twins and the Collaborative Geniuses.

The Heavenly Twins are spouses who appear to have been "born for each other." We recall an elderly man and woman who seemed to be totally collaborative, who loved and were loved. They told us that they had been this way since they were first married forty-three years ago.

Both were second-generation Armenians whose fathers had been doctors and whose mothers had been nurses. Both came from large, happy families, which had lived on the same block in the same city. Both families had been in the same income group. Every member of both families had married someone of Armenian extraction. Husband and wife had the same tastes, the same values, the same background. Following the familial pattern, the husband in this couple was a doctor, and the wife was a nurse, and had worked in her husband's office for four years, until she became pregnant. They had been engaged for two years before they were married.

Such couples are extremely rare. In this era of geographical, economic, social, and vocational mobility, of family disintegration, the probability of finding such a match is exceedingly slim.

This type of couple is most frequent in those geographical areas where the divorce rate is lowest. These are also the areas where spouses are apt to come from similar backgrounds. The divorce rate is lowest in Midwestern farm communities, where spouses are likely to share the same values concerning almost everything from food to religion. In some agricultural communities, such as the Amish and the Mormon, where religion is a dominant influence and hard work is the accepted ethic, divorce is almost unknown. However, we do not assume that a low divorce rate means that *all* the intact marriages are happy or even working well.

The Collaborative Geniuses are spouses who did not have extremely similar backgrounds, yet still developed a Stable-Satisfactory union early in the marriage. We *assume* that this breed of marriage must occasionally exist, but we have not observed such a couple, perhaps because these people do not seek marital therapy, or because they tend to be engrossed in creative team endeavors which keep them somewhat outside the areas of conventional living.

But even the Collaborative Geniuses probably begin marriage with a greater-than-average similarity in basic tastes, values, and background, and an unusual degree of flexibility. One major key to "love" (the life spirit of a highly collaborative marriage) is the ability to agree on important ways of behaving with respect to one another. To "know someone well" means to be free to meet new situations or novel contingencies knowing that one will function with one's partner together, as a team. This is possible because the couple has largely reduced the red tape of ritual and formality, and the strain of trying to make predictions about each other's behavior. Shared *experience* with one's spouse may result in a highly functional relationship after years of effort and compromise. But the Stable-Satisfactory relationship, the extraordinarily collaborative one, usually results not only from experiences occurring solely *within* the limits of married life, but also from similarities in background, parental and family experiences, interests, ethnic lines, subcultures, and so forth—in other words, important basic shared experiences occurring *before the marriage* begins. It also seems probable that those who develop the Collaborative-Genius relationship have experienced and observed some basic rules of cooperation in their parental homes, acquiring the fundamental ability to give and take without great rigidity or fear. Learning the basic rules of cooperation from their own parents, they have a beginning from which they can develop the art further and become *collaborators* rather than just *cooperators*.

People who are about to get married dream of being Heavenly Twins or Collaborative Geniuses, but the cards are stacked against them. In today's world of big cities, fast transport, and instant communication, almost everyone has more to do with strangers than with "the boy next door." Therefore, in almost all marriages the partners begin with foundations of dissimilar experiences, backgrounds, values, and tastes. These differences eliminate the possibility of easy communications and shared assumptions. Consequently, almost all marriages require that the spouses work hard to keep the union functional, expending much time, energy, and vitality in trying to stay together. Change and compromise by both partners are required from day to day. The result is tension and conflict, and a determined commitment is needed to keep the relationship going. The majority cannot enjoy the easy collaboration, the swift, merry communication, the trusting individualism, with which the Heavenly Twins and the Collaborative Geniuses are blessed. They burn up most of their energies in the everyday battle for marital survival.

Average spouses, dissimilar people who stay married by diligent effort and application, may feel that they have a relatively functional and satisfactory marriage—and they may. But they rarely achieve the gracious stability of the Heavenly Twins or the Collaborative Geniuses. Quarrels and "games" in the initial period make wounds which are often reopened later on, frequently by children who suffered through the early years of the marriage. What had appeared to be a stable relationship may again become unstable—until by work and compromise, the couple bring it back to another period of equilibrium. If the "happiness" factor of this type of oscillatory marriage were graphed over the years, it probably would resemble a sine curve. Marriages of this sort are grouped in the second category; they are Unstable-Satisfactory marriages.

16

THE UNSTABLE-
SATISFACTORY
MARRIAGE

Probably most marriages which last more than five or ten years are in this category. In many marriages of this sort, though the spouses believe they have a comfortable relationship, their disappointment with each other on occasion is obvious. In times of stress, hostility and buried resentment emerge. There are periodic outbursts of subtle or open aggression. The spouses attack each other emotionally and inflict fresh wounds. Some of the wounds heal; and even though scabbing and scarring occur the marriage remains basically sound. These people are the Spare-Time Battlers.

The Spare-Time Battlers have a wide field of conflict. They may get into a limited status struggle (the symmetrical relationship, to be discussed in a later chapter), which frequently has overtones of the battle of the sexes. If John loses money playing poker, Mary may insist on spending an equal amount for new clothes. If Mary goes to a music festival for several nights in a row and neglects to fix John's dinner, John may go off on a weekend fishing

trip just when Mary's relatives are visiting and she needs help to
entertain them.

The Spare-Time Battlers may show hostile competitiveness with
each other at the bridge table or in budgeting, or may try to out-
shine each other during conversations with friends. However,
there is an underlying network of agreement about what each is
willing to do, reciprocally, for the other. Therefore, the unpleasant skirmishes usually are seen within the context of the total
marriage. In the spouses' eyes, the importance of the marriage
outweighs the periodic hostilities or disappointments. The assets
are remembered even during the battles over liabilities.

Examples of Unstable-Satisfactory marriages are as numerous
as our friends and relatives; we can find them wherever we have
the wits to look. These are the ordinary marriages, which really
differ greatly from one another, though they all seem alike because the spouses live in similar ticky-tacky boxlike houses and
drive similar overfed children to school in similar cars.

But the marriages seldom seem "ordinary" to their participants,
who feel themselves in hell some days, in heaven other days, and
just plain "married" most days. The intricacies of such marriages
are not well known by behavioral scientists because on the whole
the Spare-Time Battlers don't seek professional help. They expect
marriage to have its ups and downs, and meanwhile, their attention is focused upon children, money, security, and status.

One such couple we know well. John and Johnnie have three
children and fourteen years of marriage behind them. They claim
they have never considered divorce, yet they admit to numerous
quarrels and plenty of dissatisfaction. John has told us he's never
been unfaithful. Typically, for our culture, we forgot to ask
Johnnie.

John is a busy surgeon. His patients adore him and his colleagues like and respect him. Johnnie is proud of him, too, and
likes to spend his earnings, but she does wish that he could be
home a little more often and that he would not insist on having
his mother over so frequently. John thinks his wife wastes time
and ("like all women") tends to be hypochrondriac. He does not
attribute any of her chronic fatigue to the hectic pace of their
life, and they don't discuss such questions because they "just end
up fighting."

It is not difficult to spot how Johnnie gets back at her husband covertly. When he is at home he attempts the paterfamilias role, and Johnnie cuts him down by sabotaging his efforts to discipline and instruct the children. He appears unaware of this technique and blows up at the kids instead of his wife. They are used to these outbursts, and simply wait them out. Yet John and Johnnie love their children and spend much of their time together discussing the children's problems and futures. How they will manage together when the children have left home is questionable, and cannot be predicted at present.

There are many pleasures and rewards in the marriage. For example, their sex life seems quite satisfactory to both and they like to go out socially, even though when they do they typically stay away from each other throughout the evening, perhaps seeking someone with whom they can discuss subjects outside of the spouse's repertoire. While such behavior may be desirable, it also seems to be a social protest against admitting dependency. In some social gatherings, being "happily married" is often interpreted as indicating weakness or overdomestication. At cocktail parties, in particular, men and women tend to separate into two distinct groups. In seating her guests at dinner, a hostess must alternate men and women in order to break up this cultural division of the sexes.

One thing is obvious. John and Johnnie do not spend much time together, and except in the bedroom they are seldom alone with each other. They would consider no other life, and have little tolerance for friends who have marital problems requiring professional help, or who become divorced. In their own way they feel that they are the backbone of our nation, and to them this is a position of solemn responsibility. They think more in terms of procreation than of creativity, and their values are relatively fixed. Marriage is difficult—but what else is there? Their moments of joy are only occasional, but they are generally content with their lives. When changed circumstances cause a couple of this sort to become less satisfied—as when the children leave home or one spouse meets someone who opens up new vistas and dreams—the marriage may stumble down one level to the Unstable-Unsatisfactory category.

One other type of marriage, this one *nearly* stable, is classified as Unstable-Satisfactory. Here the partners, whom we call the Pawnbrokers, know they are not in love. One or both of the Pawnbrokers recognize that they have compromised or limited their efforts to seek an "ideal" partner; yet they wish to remain married anyway, usually because the other spouse, despite his perceived limitations, provides something very much desired (money, social status, security, companionship, sex, assistance to a coveted goal, an unusual professional situation, and so forth). One or both spouses believe the limited satisfaction gained by staying married is preferable to the uncertain rewards which may or may not be found by looking further for another mate or by returning to the single state.

Since, as we have indicated, people cannot *not* communicate, the message "I am not really in love with you" gets across, and the marriages of the Pawnbrokers are consequently unstable. Continual unspoken adjustments must be made to compensate for the lack of romantic emotional attachment. Mary may actually dislike her husband, or she may be fond of him but find sexual intercourse with him distasteful. However, Mary may seek sexual activity more often than she naturally desires it—to fulfill her part of the bargain, to "show" her husband that she *is* fond of him in many ways, to compensate for her lack of genuine pleasure, or perhaps to get the sex act over with quickly and routinely.

In one way or another Mary's message will reach the husband, but he may accept the situation for his own reasons. Perhaps he too is ambivalent about sex, and Mary's aggressive, regular advances disguise his own ambivalence. Perhaps he directs the major portion of his interest into his profession, and does not wish a deeper emotional involvement with a woman. Thus spouses of this type have themselves in hock to each other. They are willing to pay the required interest, and refuse to take themselves out of marital pawn because the payment they receive from the pawnbroker seems to them to be a fair exchange for what they give. It is for this reason that we call them the Pawnbrokers.

Many novels, motion pictures, and plays present characters in this category. Frequently, the plot has concerned a rather extreme example of the expedient marriage—the marriage of a beautiful young girl to an older wealthy man. She knows the old buzzard has been attracted by her beauty and youth, and she lets him enjoy these (usually *until* they marry). He tries to please her by spoiling her with attention, with expensive gifts and entertainment.

In some of these stories, the drama is provided by a runaway situation. The girl cheats on her elderly husband and then is killed by him; or she is rejected by her lover and returns to her husband with abject apologies, or, in the fairy-story movie, she decides she loves her spouse after all, returns eagerly—and they live happily ever after. However, in actuality most Big Daddy–Baby Doll marriages are eventually doomed. There are only so many gifts possible before the girl begins to feel saturated and looks for pleasure elsewhere, and the husband can certainly become bored with being told that he is a "great big man." Baby Doll grows older and Big Daddy looks at new young chicks; or conversely, Baby Doll finds an even bigger Daddy and kisses off number one.

Among some professional people (for example, physicians and politicians), the deliberately expedient marriage still occurs. But the general rise in affluence, the increasing equality of women (sexual, financial, and social), and the growing acceptance of spinsterhood and bachelorhood have combined to diminish the number of blatantly expedient marriages. Correspondingly, fewer and fewer movies, television shows, and the like depict Big Daddy–Baby Doll situations. Today the motives for expedient union are usually subtle and complicated, and this complexity is reflected in many of the "new look" movies and dramas.

During the nineteenth century there were more women than men in Pawnbroker status. The numbers have equalized now that women can earn their own living and have outlets other than marriage to an ambitious man for their own personal ambition. Also, with the greater sexual freedom of women today, the sharp distinction between "loose" women and "nice" women has broken down. Men today are able to establish meaningful relationships with intelligent, sensitive women without necessarily having to fear being rushed into premature marriage. The mature man searching for love, beauty, and companionship is therefore free to be more selective. He does not have to settle for a purely sexual relationship with a woman interested primarily in what she can get out of it financially or socially.

Thus, most Pawnbroker marriages which occur today are not

even remotely similar to the old Big Daddy-Baby Doll type so common at the turn of the century. At that time, though women were soon to be legally equal, they remained socially unequal. But gradually they began to have glimpses of their right to expect more out of life for themselves than a house full of children and dishes, and a secondary position based upon the reflected glory of the husband's successes. The wife in this position was often left out of her husband's life emotionally, and had to exercise considerable inventiveness to find substitutes for self-respect based on personal achievement and companionship with equals. This situation also placed severe limitations on the husband's satisfaction. With a wife at home who was usually tired of housework and talking to three-year-olds, frustrated by the narrow confines of a small house and limited circle of housewife-friends, the man seeking camaraderie and stimulation frequently had to look for it outside his home. Often he was attracted to country clubs, men's bars, or "illicit" relations with single women whose sparkle had not yet been dimmed by a relatively dull social routine.

Through the years, this situation has indeed improved, though haphazardly and irregularly. Today, men and women continue to experiment with finding a "middle ground" making possible varied experiences and social and professional opportunities for both. Despite the growing divorce rate, cooperative, or collaborative, marriages appear to be increasing.

Unfortunately, the lessons of cooperation and collaboration are frequently learned through pain, marital failures, and hard knocks. Many Pawnbroker marriages today occur between spouses who have been married before, and seek a second relationship permitting greater freedom-with-camaraderie than the first marriage (based on romance and "falling in love") allowed. Many Pawnbroker marriages occur between professional people who are getting older and have lost their early visions of the perfect love. Such marriages appear to be expedient in the more conventional sense, but are often very satisfactory for the people involved. Still an unstable element remains because the vision of eternal romance is so ingrained in our culture that even those people who feel they are beyond it are never sure that they or their spouse may not lock eyes across the room with someone else someday.

17

THE UNSTABLE-
UNSATISFACTORY
MARRIAGE

The Weary Wranglers and the Psychosomatic Avoiders—and their situations are as unattractive as these names suggest—form a considerable proportion of the American married population. The spouses in this Unstable-Unsatisfactory category make up the majority of couples seen by counselors, psychologists, or psychiatrists.

The Weary Wranglers reach their condition after years of preliminary bouts. It takes them some time to discover how to hurt each other frequently and with finesse. By the time the spouses have become competent Weary Wranglers—if the marriage has not been terminated by uxorcide, suicide, desertion, or divorce—each usually finds satisfaction in seeing the other make mistakes or experience failures, for these count as defeats in the continuing war.

The Weary Wranglers may recognize that they have a miserable marriage, but usually they are unwilling or unable to do anything about it. Often they need or desire the combat which their marriage provides. Frequently the Weary Wranglers are angry people who are not prone to introspection or self-accusation. Directing hostility outward is one of the ways in which an individual relieves the discomfort of anxiety and frustration. The Weary Wranglers find a degree of comfort in being hostile to each other, for the situation enables each to shift the responsibility for his unhappiness to the other. In fact, it is sometimes for this advantage that people are drawn to each other in the first place. Another major attraction of this mutual hostility is that it prevents personal change by keeping the participant's attention focused away from himself. But the Weary Wranglers do not know that hostility and anger are not self-limiting. Once the trend has started, it accelerates geometrically; often the anger runs away with the contenders and damages both equally.

One reason the Weary Wranglers have such a shaky future is that the spouses do not know how to stop their argumentative games and begin to form coalitions. In any discussion or activity each is more interested in winning than in dealing effectively with the matter at hand. Indeed, carried along by the need to win every game, they may not even be able to stick to a single topic. A third party listening may experience an eerie sense of unreality as the topic changes with every sentence. By contrast, couples able to form coalitions and to collaborate can explore a situation as a team, each in turn contributing and building upon what his spouse has contributed.

The Weary Wranglers tend to blame each other explicitly (verbally) for the failures and disappointments in their relationship. Often, they involve the children in their conflict. Sometimes the wife picks one child for special favor and the husband picks another; but sometimes they bid for the same offspring, and he may end up feeling he is God's special gift to the world. On the other hand, a child's life may be extremely miserable because his parents are competing to find fault with him (the "fault," allegedly, being "inherited" from the other spouse). In either case the child is apt to suffer from severe psychopathology. Often the children of such a marriage who are not forced into the role of scapegoat or of parents' favorite seem to survive the marital mess, because the parents' battling is relatively overt and the children are aware of the parents' discontent. Children can adjust to what is obvious, even though they look ahead to the day when they will be old enough to leave home.

Not all spouses in the Unstable-Unsatisfactory category are continuously battling and agitating openly. Many couples in this group begin as Weary Wranglers, but after a few years they grow tired of arguing and become Psychosomatic Avoiders. Some spouses who are unable to express anger openly at all *never* try to fight it out and are Psychosomatic Avoiders from the beginning of the relationship. The primary characteristic of such couples is that they wage their battles covertly, expressing their anger and disappointment primarily through subtle sarcasm, double-edged humor, tangentialization, or nonverbal means. A few of the more common nonverbal methods of expressing their frustration are illness, alcoholism, and frigidity. Both parties unconsciously recognize that the disturbed spouse is expressing discontent with the marriage, but our health-oriented culture allows them to focus on doctors, pills, and heating pads. The *sine qua non* of this group is the pill-filled bathroom where a careful reading of labels on containers shows frequent changes of medication. Partially empty jars, bottles, and boxes are mute testimony to the fact that the doctor has no prescription for a bad marriage.

Many of these spouses eventually find their way into the offices of psychiatrists. Normally just one spouse of the couple seeks therapy for his psychosomatic symptoms, drinking problems, or frigidity—while the other spouse looks on sympathetically and believes himself to be perfectly healthy by comparison.

Some spouses among the Psychosomatic Avoiders work out an unconventional *modus vivendi*. For example, the wife permits her husband to have a mistress, while in order to achieve a temporary, uneasy peace he allows his wife to spend large amounts of money on clothes, entertainment, and psychoanalysis. Of course, their apparent acceptance of such a destructive agreement does not mean they are happy about it. Not only does the wife pay heavily with her illness, but the husband normally would prefer to have a loving, healthy wife rather than a mistress. Psychosomatic Avoiders, unfortunately, find it easier to bear their pain alone than to argue openly.

Many Unstable-Unsatisfactory couples attack each other over the years—either overtly or covertly—with a determined destructiveness increasing in geometric progression, so that the fifth year may be sixteen times as bad as the first. One common cause for this kind of escalating marital antagonism is the husband's increasing financial success. More rarely the financial, social, or professional success of both spouses precipitates the conflict. The problem is so widespread that many large industrial companies insist on interviewing the wives of prospective executives. The Young Presidents' Organization (a national association of men who have become presidents of million-dollar-gross companies by age forty) makes its contribution to marital harmony by planning most of its regional and national meetings for the executive *and* his wife. In the United States various estimates have been made of the loss of productivity caused by marital problems. The figure is especially high when it includes the huge sums spent to train executives whose effectiveness is subsequently reduced or destroyed by discord at home. Some educated guesses have put it as high as *one and a half billion dollars per year.*

The pattern of this kind of difficulty is often so familiar to the experienced clinician that he can fill in the middle part of the story after hearing the first few minutes of the beginning from a distraught couple.

Typically, the young man and woman meet in college and marry shortly after graduation or when he has returned from military service. Often, he goes to graduate school while she supports him, and during this period they are equally busy and fairly broke, with little time to dwell on their spats and quarrels. Then comes his first offer—excitement, the vision of a joyous future of color television and wall-to-wall expenses and country clubs, and eventually Europe!

Maybe Sally doesn't like the thought of living in Kalamazoo, but after a few days of quarreling and tears she keeps her prim little mouth shut and tries to share Walter's delight in being selected by such an up-and-coming outfit. Then her little secret is added to the dice they're rolling. She is pregnant! Probably it does make sense for Walter to go ahead to Kalamazoo while Sally goes to Houston to have her child and let her mother help in those trying days. Then Walter, of course, plans to fly down to Houston to bring Sally and the baby to Kalamazoo to start the nest, and Sally's mother will come along to help out until Sally is strong again. Walt is unhappy about the arrangement and feels

Sally is not being supportive enough. He is also hurt by her inability to share equally in his excitement over the job, but since she did give in to the move he now feels he has no choice but to let her go to her mother's. He has always liked Sally's mother, but the situation changes soon after they arrive in Kalamazoo. Mrs. Hanson seems too eager to keep him from the baby (as if all men were clumsy oafs knowing nothing about children). Sally seems petulant and demanding and her mother responds, while Walt worries about whether indeed this too shall pass. After a few months, Sally's mother departs. The quarrels Walt and Sally had in the privacy of their bedroom during Mother's visit have left them angry and drained. Sally becomes tight-lipped and resolves not to argue with Walt any more, since she feels she never wins anyway. Walt becomes equally guarded, since he feels Sally never gives in, and he begins to spend more time at work.

Things at the plant are going swimmingly. Walt and his immedate superior get along together like an up-and-coming kid and his wise older brother. Of course, late some afternoon Mr. Eccler may suggest, "Say, Walt, why don't we grab a drink and a quick meal and come back here and go over the Choosey Chews account? I think it'll open your eyes to some of the problems and their solutions." So a happy and guilty Walt calls home, filled with the knowledge that Sally is alone now that his mother-in-law has left, and informs his hurt, trying-to-understand wife that the boss insists he go over the Choosey account instead of coming home.

"But I had planned . . ."

"Really, it's an opportunity I can't miss."

Sally says, "All right, Walt. If you must, I suppose that nothing I say will matter," and turns off the oven. She sits before the television munching cheese and crackers (they have a great martyr quality about them, in contrast to the filet Hubby is presumed to be eating), and wonders from time to time what she has done wrong. And so the unfortunate pattern is set: each spouse, responding to cultural pressures, sees himself as reasonable and the other as unreasonable, and believes that the other is becoming angry because he knows he is in the wrong. Wishing confirmation, they discuss the situation with friends. Each finds comfort and support in his particular clique, unaware that this "understanding" increases the space between himself and his spouse.

Once a pattern of "victim versus victimizer" becomes established, even a sincere attempt on the part of one spouse to "make up" is likely to be misinterpreted as just another trick. For example, Walt may have been working every night for a month to complete a difficult assignment. He is rewarded with a raise, and gaily sweeps Sally off on an expensive holiday to compensate for his past neglect. Sally is thereby caught in a conflict which she dares not discuss, in order not to ruin the holiday. She may be suspicious, wondering if Walt is indulging in such a trip because he feels guilty. If so, of what is he guilty? Was he really working every night last month? If Sally becomes convinced that Walt is just being loving, she is now unable to express her frustration and resentment over his earlier neglect, for she finds it impossible to criticize him when he is taking her on an expensive holiday. Perhaps some aspect of their unsent messages steals out and delivers itself, resulting in further misunderstanding and hurt feelings. Walt may now be angry because Sally's response to his conciliatory gesture is not altogether enthusiastic. Halfway through the holiday, Sally becomes ill with a headache and stomach cramps, and has to be taken home. Both are disappointed, Walt is quietly angry, and Sally feels misunderstood and guilty. By this time, they have started down the path of the Psychosomatic Avoiders, having become weary of wrangling.

As their situation worsens, they have only the child in common, and the specter of that day in the future when the child will leave home begins to hang over their heads. Despair, unfortunately, does not always breed solutions—instead it may beget further despair.

The end of this particular story is of little importance. It may adopt several conventional forms; the spouses may resort to booze, blondes, illness, separate beds, "he doesn't understand me," or "I'm on my way to my first million and she couldn't care less." The crucial thing is that time and the pyramiding misunderstandings have created a gap very difficult to bridge. Each spouse is equally convinced of the righteousness of his position. Angry defensiveness replaces the biblical injunction "Come now, and let us reason together."

Frequently the inability of spouses in the Unstable-Unsatisfactory category to improve their situation is a reflection of the gamesmanship which they employ. For example, the wife may attempt suicide for fear that her husband will leave her. The attempt fails, but the husband feels guilty and assures the wife that he will stay with her, "only please don't kill yourself." She promises him never to do such a thing again. The wife has won the game for the moment and the couple push their rowboat back onto the stormy sea and continue the journey. But the husband knows that now it's his turn to win a game, and he starts looking for one. Couples of this sort are surprisingly easy to find in our society.

The Unstable-Unsatisfactory couples often stick together because each partner hopes to collect unpaid emotional bills from the past. There is a vague but persistent dream of what the other spouse could be like if he really tried. "Someday he'll realize how I've been wronged and he'll be more loving and appreciative; then we can be happy. Before we married [this theme continues] he gave every evidence that he would love me and do so and so..." These individuals usually end up severely disappointed, frustrated, and angrier than they ever were prior to marriage. As they get older they realize that time is running out and they still have not received what they feel the other spouse owes them.

One other important characteristic of many Unstable-Unsatisfactory marriages should be mentioned. These couples often give the impression of togetherness when in fact they live in quite separate emotional, and perhaps also physical, worlds. In most couples, this deception takes one of two forms. These appear to be quite opposite, but serve the same function—disguising the separateness of husband and wife.

The first form is typified by the man and wife who individually maintain active, absorbing lives, each having professional and social roles so demanding that he literally sees little of the other, and yet preserve the façade of an integrated marriage through such accouterments as a large house, several children, and a dog. As long as they do not see too much of one another, they appear to get along quite well. But inevitably there are occasions when the distance between them cannot be maintained because the wishes or needs of the two at that moment are on a collision course.

Two young married physicians with small children, for example, appear to have a surprisingly intact marriage. A considerable

amount of their success in maintaining the marriage is due to the
presence of a matronly, tenderhearted housekeeper who lives in
and is virtually one of the family. She fulfills most of the household and mothering functions, so that the wife-physician is free
to pursue her career. However, just before an important medical
meeting which both spouses wish to attend, the housekeeper is
forced to go to the hospital for a kidney operation. The husband
immediately assumes that his wife will find another babysitter or,
failing this, will stay home from the meeting and take care of the
children. The wife, on the other hand, feels her professional responsibilities make it just as important for her to attend the meeting as it is for her husband, and before they have even attempted
to find a satisfactory babysitter, they break out into violent
quarreling which changes the entire cast of their relationship.

This kind of clash of interests is inevitable from time to time in
such a marriage, but the spouses may get enough enjoyment from
the relative "independence" their marital arrangement gives them
to tolerate each other when they are together. We do not mean to
suggest that *all* or even *most* couples in which both partners are
active are less close than they appear. Some couples can be busy
and often separate physically, yet be close emotionally and in
genuine agreement. But for many active couples this is not the
case. Furthermore, if in the course of time one spouse's career or
local social importance becomes relatively greater than the other
spouse's, the marriage will have a smaller chance of survival.
Often the frightening thing about the occasions when one spouse's
career is on the upswing while the other's is on the downswing, is
the sudden recognition of how little marital glue they really have
to hold them together in a crisis. There may be an outbreak of
despair about their ability to overcome the current situation and
carry on.

The other common manifestation of this characteristic of deceptive togetherness among Unstable-Unsatisfactory couples is
more difficult to spot. Certain couples consist of individuals who
have developed common interests or strong causes to which they
can devote enormous amounts of time and energy. Because the
spouses in such a marriage are seen together a great deal, and to
some extent believe in the value of what they are jointly doing,
the casual observer may think them a wonderfully companionable

couple. A more intimate examination of their marital situation often reveals that they are virtually never alone with each other, and that when they are, the momentary absence of the joint cause leaves them each feeling quite separate. This is frequently the case when the children of "professional parents," who devote their lives to the children, go away for the summer, and the husband and wife find themselves feeling quite "lost" and are unable to enjoy activities as a couple. Couples who rely on causes for their togetherness have no time for intimate talk or occasional chit-chat and may even enter into a kind of competition by occupying their free time with *preparation* for the cause, by doing research for reports to be presented later on, for example, or by attending lectures related to their *cause célèbre*. Again, so long as they remain relatively equal in the eyes of their peers, the marriage may appear quite sound.

It is probable that in most of these couples, one spouse is more intimately involved in the cause than the other, while the second spouse is able to conceal the fact that his involvement is slighter, or even to convince himself that he is as interested as the other. But as the years go by, it usually becomes apparent that he is only secondarily concerned. Both find it more and more difficult to hide their emotional distance. This sort of relationship is sometimes portrayed in fictional presentations of missionaries; the missionary couple in James Michener's book *Hawaii* is one example. In many such instances, it turns out that one of the spouses, either the husband or the wife, is more able to endure the hardships of missionary life, or has the greater "faith," and the second spouse becomes increasingly ill, martyred, or complaining. Or the martyred one (often the wife) becomes ill and dies and the other spouse is free to carry on the great work, while sanctifying his "good wife" for her martyrdom.

In a nonmissionary couple—perhaps active in politics, or "professional parents" devoted exclusively to their children—one spouse may suddenly walk out on the other after years of an apparently close working relationship and mutual agreement on "their" goals. This may occur because the more dominant spouse has found someone who is a greater "believer" in his goals than the current partner, and feels the need for refueling. Or the opposite may occur; the apparently more subservient spouse, who in order to keep the relationship going has been pushed into a way of life that he does not wish, is finally fed up and leaves the whole situation behind—to everyone's astonishment!

A beautiful example of the latter situation—one which is very common in our culture—occurs in Elia Kazan's novel *The Arrangement*. The central figure of the story has become increasingly dissatisfied with his marriage and at forty-three engages in a serious affair with a younger woman. He cannot understand his own behavior and feels guilty because he cannot admit that his wife's apparent benevolence is driving him into a rage and leaving his most basic needs unfulfilled. His wife arranges a plan, a "way of life," at this point for the two of them, in the belief that it will "cure" her husband's "illness." The husband tries, and for eleven months they share this new style of life, closely resembling that of two sorority sisters. Their arrangement is appropriately called the "fortress": it is designed to protect the couple from material and carnal desires and dangerous independence—chinks in their imaginary togetherness. The wife's emphasis on the "pure" life and spiritual values is intended to eliminate her husband's carnal feelings for *other* women, but as is to be expected, the husband sabotages her dominance by becoming impotent.

During the fortress period, they become the envy of all their friends who do not see the covert aspects of the relationship. Such sharing! Such devotion! What the friends do not realize, as the reader does, is that the togetherness, the shared style of life, represents only the wife's dream, *not* the husband's. After eleven months, the husband has a serious auto accident which forces him to recognize a suicidal impulse. That's the beginning of the end of the relationship, for the husband leaves the wife after his recovery.

Although a husband and wife may *appear* to be sharing, if their goals in life or their ways of behaving are based on the wishes of one spouse rather than both, they are not actually sharing. Togetherness without genuine *agreement* is like a sand castle built too close to the water's edge. When the tide of change comes in, the castle crumbles, and when it goes out, one resident of the castle often goes with it—to swim toward new shores which he sees with his own eyes.

Today, almost everyone has known at least one couple which

broke up after years of apparent togetherness. Usually, the long-suffering spouse who leaves the "fortress" is labeled the "bad guy," and in one sense, he is. By going along with another's dream —out of passivity or sheer exhaustion or denial of his own real desires—such a person has lulled his spouse into a false sense of control and security. When one spouse passively refuses to set limits to the other's demands, by refusing to fight it out and choosing withdrawal as the better means of survival, and when the dominant spouse refuses to heed the many clues and messages that the other is only going along because he can't win, and that he is not really in agreement, the husband and wife lead each other on and on into the woods of imaginary togetherness. Then when night falls, and the suffering, passive spouse "can't take it another minute" he walks out, leaving the dominant spouse behind. They would have done better never to enter the woods at all, or to fight things out earlier, while there was still some daylight and a chance to try to make necessary changes. It is not uncommon in a sharply dominant-submissive marriage for the dominant spouse to become increasingly hysterical or dictatorial, to the point of losing all self-control, as he slowly discovers that the submissive spouse neither loves nor respects him and that the passivity is simply based on loathing. Kazan also depicts this "arrangement" in his description of the hero's mother and father. The submissive, downtrodden mother holds her tongue and survives. The domineering father dies in hysterical self-defeat.

Many Unstable-Unsatisfactory couples do not break up, although the increase of divorce in this category is alarming. Couples in this category vary widely, ranging from those who exchange quite a bit of information by "fighting it out" day after day, to those who exchange practically no explicit information and ignore much of the information that is exchanged (leaving one spouse's needs unfulfilled much of the time because he won't or can't fight the dominant spouse effectively). But many of these spouses stick together physically despite the lack of emotional closeness, and the amount of consequent psychosomatic illness, infidelity, disturbance in children, and general misery is great.

A small number of Unstable-Unsatisfactory couples do manage eventually to make a workable union. Fortunately, aided by acts of God, or wise counsel, or understanding bosses or relatives, they realize that they do not have black-and-white differences, and that compromises are possible. Sometimes a painful crisis or blowup threatening a runaway shocks each spouse into renouncing his righteous, misunderstood position, and then the partners begin to communicate.

What, nevertheless, remains important is *when* (i.e., how early in the marriage) something useful in the way of change is attempted. Years are not of equal length in marriage, and sick patterns, once fixed, are increasingly difficult to extirpate. If positive change occurs early enough, these couples may work up the ladder to an Unstable-Satisfactory marriage. If it comes late, their chances for developing a satisfying give-and-take relationship are seriously diminished.

18

THE STABLE-
UNSATISFACTORY
MARRIAGE

Though marriages in this category are stable, they are the "worst" of the lot. In a quiet, socially respectable manner the people in this group suffer more pain, hate more profoundly, and cause more discomfort to others than do the members of the other three groups. *Yet the spouses appear to be unaware of their behavior.* There is a deadly virulent glue of hate that is only visible to the keen eye of the behavioral scientist or the brilliant novelist.

One of the most obvious types is the Gruesome Twosome. This consists of individuals who are growing old together in an unsatisfactory marriage which is quite stable because neither is able nor willing to acknowledge his dissatisfaction. Indeed, very often both will claim they have a wonderful marriage. They do not recognize their inability to live either with or without each other.

Such couples consult marital counselors or other therapists usually because of problems with their children. The spouses themselves would not seek help because they are not conscious of the nature of their marital relationship; but they force themselves, or are forced by their physician, to seek help for the children.

One of the common ways in which such spouses attempt to minimize their pain is by becoming cultists of some sort. The wife in a Gruesome Twosome we know attends church twice every day. She seeks the counsel of the minister on everyday matters "so that my wonderful family can live in a way that is a glory to God." In the meanwhile, she has bullied her husband to the point of tragic passivity. She identifies her bullying as "looking after poor Tom." The husband has developed into a helpless person—unable to fry an egg, to initiate even the simplest activities, to manage his finances—and often says "My wife is the dearest person in the world, the most wonderful wife a man could be blessed with."

Both assert as loudly as possible, at every opportunity, how much they love each other and how happy they are. But observe an incident from their life together:

Their only daughter was being married on July 4, in Buenos Aires. This event was of intense interest to the parents. On the afternoon of July 4, the husband, who was fond of baseball, went to a neighbor's house to watch a game on television. During his absence, the daughter telephoned from South America to tell her father and mother about her marriage and to have her husband say hello.

When the father returned, the mother said, "Tom, if you hadn't cared more about baseball than about the welfare of your daughter, you would have been here when Betsy and her husband telephoned from Buenos Aires."

A look of shock came over the husband. Neither of them had known the daughter would telephone, and he was extremely disappointed to have missed her; now he was startled by his wife's cruel and untrue accusation.

After a few moments he put his arms around his wife, wiped his tears off on her shoulder and said, "What would I do without you, darling? You take care of everything for me. Thank God, you were here for the call."

"You must be tired," said the wife. "I'll fix you some tea and then I'll tell you what Betsy and her husband said *to me* in their long-distance call from South America."

Holding each other's hands, they walked into the kitchen.

This Gruesome Twosome constantly repeats the game just described, regardless of the issue. But they tell everyone how happy they are. She is disappointed in her husband's failures both as a man and as a businessman. He is disappointed in his wife's performance as a supportive person. Yet they never admit this situation to the world, to each other, or even, consciously, to themselves. As is to be expected, their three children all have miserable marriages.

Another man and woman we met became human vegetables in the course of maintaining their union. Before marriage, the woman was aggressive and competent, and she had done very well in high school. She was unhappy at home, however, and married a muscular young marine private who was a high-school dropout and a fearful underachiever. She hoped to help him "realize his potential." After five years of marriage, the wife weighed close to three hundred pounds and was so afraid to meet people that she locked herself in the house, with the heat up to 90 degrees and all the shades down. She spent her time watching television and knitting endlessly. Her husband remained in the Marine Corps, with a menial base job; he was always the last man in his specialty to progress in rank; but he eventually advanced enough to remain in service because he was dependable and gave no reason to be expelled.

The couple had no sexual life or outside interests. They had no children. Although their behavior *appeared* to be saccharine and supportive most of the time, it was punctuated on the wife's part by occasional outbursts of anger followed by guilt and remorse. The dull, passive husband was awkward and inadequate when in his wife's company; he would go to bed when he came home from work, sleep until supper, watch two television shows, and then return to bed. *Once,* in a semidrunken state, the wife revealed to one of us that she was afraid that if she lost weight, went to work, and met other people, she would leave her husband. Except for this one moment of truth, the couple always assured everyone that they were happy. The wife's hermitlike, fearful behavior produced such uncertainty and lack of self-confidence in the husband that he felt helpless without her, and made it difficult or impossible for him fully to utilize his minimal drive and obtain advancement. In turn his inability to achieve and progress in his employment made his wife feel a need to protect him and appear more inferior by contrast, and so each pulled the other downward. The wife succeeded, at great personal expense, in appearing more helpless than he did; he, at least, was able to hold a job.

Environmental factors played a part here too, for the wife's lack of formal education limited her ability to achieve in accordance with her own expectations. Also, the husband had a job which provided security and permanent employment, even though he was not doing particularly well. Had one of these or of a number of other factors changed, the balance of this relationship would have had to undergo change also if the marriage was to stay intact. At the time of our contact with this couple, the husband and wife were twenty-five years old. If they could achieve such a condition in six years of marriage, the chances of any dramatic improvement occurring in the future—barring death —are very slim.

The members of a Gruesome Twosome live in accordance with the old proverb "People who live in glass houses shouldn't throw stones." Neither spouse dares to comment on the other's behavior or on the nature of their marriage except to forgive and offer unrequested succor. Each is afraid of what the other may do or say in response to a critical or openly attacking remark. The children are taught not to mention unpleasant matters or even notice the nature of their parents' relationship. For by doing so they might bring distasteful or uncontrollable material to their parents' attention, and then the children would feel the repercussions. These couples form a rigid coalition on one point only— that they will not admit the condition of their marriage or of their true feelings—but that point they defend against all intruders. The children often grow up to be cautious and reserved, and unable to judge the quality of any relationship. They justify their denials and lies by insisting that "it is better to tell a small falsehood than hurt someone's feelings." When a child gets into difficulties (the couple whose daughter was married in Buenos Aires also had one son who drank excessively and another who was expelled from college for spending the night in a girl's room), the parents form their usual coalition of denial and insist that nothing can be wrong with their baby. The school system is at fault, the police department is incompetent, or perhaps there is something wrong with the child's health. A child of theirs who manifests emotional problems must, they are sure, have suffered a brain injury during childhood.

In the second subcategory of Stable-Unsatisfactory marriages are husbands and wives who exist by avoiding each other, without its being evident that they do so. Thus, in a different way from the Gruesome Twosome, they are able to dissemble a miserable relationship. The husband may be zealously involved in his business and the wife in civic activities, the church, and so forth, but their activity possesses a quality which marks them as different from the busy Unstable-Unsatisfactory couples. We call these men and women the Paranoid Predators, for they both take a stand against a world perceived as hostile and form a team to fight it. The man may practice ruthless business methods because he is obsessed by the notion that "in our society today everyone hates a poor man. To survive you have to have dough and screw the other guy before he screws you." The wife supports this attitude. The wife may work ten hours a day for militant anti-Communist organizations "because it is our duty as good Americans to stop the Communists from destroying freedom and Christianity." The husband agrees with her and carries this attitude also into his own activities.

The intense activity of the Paranoid Predators is motivated by their need to avoid each other by focusing on something outside themselves, which can unite them in a common goal or attitude, and thereby keep the marriage intact. They accomplish this by seeing little of each other and by being mutually disdainful and suspicious of others. Together they may criticize other individuals or groups, support extremist organizations, and so on. In doing so they deny the misery and emptiness of their own relationship.

Paranoid Predators employ extremely destructive behavior. Their two-against-the-world approach to life enables them to maintain the marriage, but only at tremendous cost to themselves, their children, and society as a whole.

In one such case, the husband was an alcoholic merchant seaman who was promiscuous in every port. After some years, a severe case of syphilis brought his Southern Baptist conscience to the fore, and he left the sea, returned to his wife and two children, and became a part-time minister and carpenter.

The family lived in mortal terror of offending the Lord, and spent their days working together to ferret out possible enemies of Christianity. They succeeded in organizing their small community to avoid one sixteen-year-old out-of-wedlock mother, who later committed suicide! The husband and wife had renounced sex as sinful since they had already procreated (and the husband wasn't sure whether syphilis had rendered him sterile). Finally, the odd behavior of their oldest boy brought the parents to the school's attention. The parents refused to cooperate and moved to a different community. We do not know what befell them, but hazard a guess that the son went to a mental hospital and the marriage survived.

This material has been included so that spouses may identify their own marital type in general terms, so that they may have some frame of reference in which to locate themselves—simply to aid them in their own discussions. There is no undeviating classificatory description of marriage, and the categories are given in broad strokes only.

In reviewing the various categories into which marriages can be divided, it is important to remember that no one knows for sure what a normal marriage is. Surveys do reveal those qualities that seem to be related to workable marriages, but there have been no in-depth studies—let alone longitudinal studies—of marriages which are actually happy and collaborative, or the opposite.

Therefore, a person who becomes envious when a friend or neighbor describes how ecstatic his marriage is, or feels depressed after reading about the joys of certain wedded Hollywood stars, is probably trying to apply to his own marriage some sort of standard or gauge which does not really exist. Most of us have some kind of fairy-story image of the ideal marriage because our parents weren't frank with us about their own marital problems and because our culture is so loaded with movies, television programs, magazine articles, and books about marital bliss.

We have attempted to offer a kind of classification of marriage, based not on ideals of "happiness" or "perfection" (which everyone defines differently), but on the exchanges of behavior between spouses which result in a more or less workable relationship. A marriage is regarded as "workable" when it is sustained without great personal loss of mental or physical health by either spouse.

The categories we have presented in semianecdotal form could also be distinguished in terms of the *clarity of communication* between spouses. Communication is clear when the amount of explicit information exchanged is great compared to the amount of noise (or meaningless communication, as when a code is heard that cannot be deciphered).

Defined in terms of communication, the Stable-Unsatisfactory marriage is one in which virtually no relationship information is exchanged between the spouses. Their lives together are usually quiet, separate, and distant, and the manifold problems in the marriage are represented nonverbally by the emotionally sick children, who are usually regarded by their parents as having organic disorders rather than severe emotional problems.

The Unstable-Unsatisfactory marriage does include some exchange of information between the spouses, but it is limited, frequently inappropriate or out of context, and new information introduced into the system (often by the children) causes upheaval. The spouses have difficulty exchanging information without precipitating serious battling or psychosomatic flareups, but they may nevertheless actually be able to exchange information during times of upheaval. The children often suffer from being scapegoated or from getting caught in the middle and becoming wise old diplomats before their time. This quality often separates them from their peers, leaving them feeling lonely, "different," and vaguely inadequate.

The partners in an Unstable-Satisfactory marriage can exchange some information and can occasionally collaborate. New information, new problems or challenges, initially may cause dissension, but this will usually quiet down, be denied, or be handled by edict. Thereafter, it seems to be forgotten; but it is filed away in the unconscious and the reason that many of these marriages slowly become Unstable-Unsatisfactory is often that what was supposed to be forgiven and forgotten has accumulated underground, until one spouse suddenly finds that he is "out of love" and can't live the rest of his life that way. He abruptly walks out, to the amazement of the other, who wails that "there was so much good in our marriage!" The mental health of the children of such couples can be relatively good despite a considerable amount of disagreement between the parents because the conflict is overt often enough for the children to see what is really going on. Frequently the best communication between the Unstable-Satisfactory married spouses occurs after an upheaval, when they are in the process of making up and are willing to listen to each other.

The Stable-Satisfactory spouses are able to exchange information easily, often in part because of similarities in their backgrounds. They know each other so well that long dissertations or lengthy harangues are unnecessary; a smile, a nod of the head, or a disapproving glance is sufficient. Such husbands and wives are able to collaborate, but they are also able clearly to distinguish the circumstances in which it is important to them to be autonomous. The children of such marriages are fortunate and look forward to getting married themselves. Because the parents are able to collaborate, they do not fear intervention by the children (i.e., they do not fear that their coalition will be split apart) and thus the children can be taken seriously and their opinions can be given whatever consideration is suitable. The most important single element observable in such marriages is the operation of trust.

19

BASIC MODES OF
RELATIONSHIP

Symmetrical, Complementary, and Parallel

A *symmetrical* marital relationship is one in which the spouses continually need to state to each other behaviorally, "I am as good as you are." We refer to such couples as status strugglers.

A *complementary* marital relationship is one in which (at the extreme) one spouse is in charge and the other obeys. Fully complementary marriages are virtually unknown in our culture. Instead, typically one spouse is in charge of certain *areas* of the relationship, while the other spouse has other areas of control.

In a *parallel* marital relationship the spouses alternate between symmetrical and complementary relationships, in response to changing situations. There may be episodes of conflict concerning particular areas, but since the spouses feel equal to each other, they can be both supportive *and* competitive without fear, knowing that neither will win *all* issues at the expense of the other. The parallel relationship is therefore the most desirable one for our egalitarian culture. The ability to be honest and open in regard to both agreement and disagreement makes for trust, since each spouse knows where he stands in relation to the other.

The word "symmetrical" was first used in the sense defined here
by the anthropologist Gregory Bateson, who went to New Guinea
in the 1930's and lived with primitive tribes there. At the start he
could not understand the reasons behind their many formal ceremonies, rituals, and myths. (Anthropologists who had been there
earlier had found sexual significance in their patterns of behavior.
They saw phallic symbolism in every carving, headdress, and
ceremony.) But Bateson patiently and objectively observed the
culture until he recognized that the varied—and apparently un-
related—patterns of behavior had profound similarities which
joined them into a single category of human action. He called
these *symmetrical.*

One tribe might suddenly collect all its spears and rush up to
the camp of the next tribe. But instead of having a battle, the
warriors would simply shake their spears and shout curses at
their neighbors. After they had returned to their camp, the members of the other tribe might retaliate in exactly the same way, or
they might hold a ceremony in which they communicated with
their gods, as if to show that they were on better terms with the
deities than their neighbors were.

According to Bateson, the primary message in this behavior
pattern appears to be, "I am as good as you are." The difficulty is
that if A says, "You can't scare me, I've got a gun," and B retorts,
"Well, you can't scare me either, I've got two guns," there is
danger that this behavior will escalate until the only solution is
for A and B to demonstrate their equality by shooting each
other.

An analogy to the symmetrical relationship between individuals
is the armament race among competitive nations. A less powerful
nation, for example, France, says, "I am the equal of Russia,
China, and the United States. Therefore, I should have a nuclear-
bomb stockpile." France accordingly goes to enormous expense
(which she cannot afford) to manufacture nuclear weapons. In
the meantime, both Russia and the United States put men into
space (an achievement with potential military applications). In
response, France struggles and makes economic sacrifices to do
the same. But she also attempts to take leadership in other areas
of international life. France is almost obsessed with the idea that
she must prove her equality, and works hard to maintain a sym-

metrical relationship. Her efforts, in turn, stimulate other nations to show that they are equal or superior to France.

Historically, the upshot has typically been that a nation having a difficult time proving its equality one day uses its weapons in war—expecting to establish its equality or superiority through a military victory. The danger, then, in symmetrical behavior is that attempts to prove equality often end in open hostilities.

When the term "symmetrical" is applied to relationships between individuals, it means that both of them are indicating simultaneously their wish to determine the nature of the relationship. Each by his behavior indicates that he is determined to have *at least equal* control.

We have said "indicates" because the signs, the messages, which they transmit to each other are not necessarily verbal. Messages can be sent by gestures, facial expressions, and other nonverbal methods. Sometimes the intention of attempting symmetry is transmitted without the sender's being conscious of his action or the receiver's being aware that he has received the message.

Symmetrical behavior is a competitive pattern. It is the opposite of collaborative behavior. It may also be described as a status struggle, for each individual is constantly trying to prove to himself and to his partner that he is the other's equal—or superior.

In infancy and early childhood the human being experiences helplessness and dependency, partly associated with not being able to assuage his own hunger and partly associated with his inability to control his space situation. In his struggle against helplessness, the infant soons learns that by crying he can cause his mother to bring the bottle. In young children, this fight against helplessness can be seen in games (such as dragon slaying or Cops and Robbers) in which they pretend to have control over their environment. However, as the child begins to grow up and experience relationships with his peers, he finds that unless he *shares* control of many situations with others, he will be left alone. To a psychiatrist, the presence of the "only child" syndrome does not necessarily indicate that a person is an only child, but it does show that he has not *learned to take his turn and to share*. Obviously, in marriage—a continuous series of interactions—it is important that the spouses have some *alternating control* over the situations which arise, whether in disciplining the children or in selecting the evening's entertainment. Part of the noncompetitive quality which exists in cultures having well-defined roles for male and female is due to the fact that since these roles are established and accepted, the area in which competition can occur is relatively small. In our culture, as we have pointed out elsewhere, affluence, mobility, emphasis on education, and democratization have led to a general loosening of role definition, leaving much more room in which symmetrical behavior can occur.

The process of the status struggle, or symmetrical behavior, usually starts when one person states or indicates an opinion, or specifies the way something should be done, or unilaterally initiates an action which involves both parties. The other person receives the message and—either consciously or unconsciously—concludes, "My spouse doesn't believe I am as competent or as good or as skilled as he is. I don't like that. I am equal." This conclusion frequently has a postscript: "I am equal—and probably superior."

In marriage, the status struggle ("I am just as good as you are") is easily identified by the back-and-forth arguments and interruptions of the spouses. This struggle to establish an apparent equality indicates fear of inferiority, or to be more precise, it indicates a fear that the other person does not consider one his equal.

At a time when such a situation is present between Mary and her husband, John, it may be said that Mary (in this instance) is trying to persuade or to maneuver or to battle John into concluding, "Yes, Mary is my equal. In fact, Mary may even be ahead of me in some ways."

If Mary's behavior causes John to sense what she is attempting to do, what is the next step in their status-struggle relationship? John now wonders, "Gracious, can it be possible that Mary believes I am inferior to her? I had better do something to make certain she knows I am *her* equal."

At the same time, John may not be consciously aware of his symmetrical behavior with respect to Mary, any more than he understands why he is terribly angry at the stranger behind him at a football game with whom he starts trading escalating insults until one or the other backs off or a third party intervenes.

In the status-struggle relationship, the subject of the argument makes no difference. The spouses may be disputing about what stock to purchase, how to win a war, how to bring up children, or the most efficient method of cleaning a bathtub.

Listen to a status-struggle dialogue between John and his wife, Mary, in a restaurant in New York:

JOHN: Darling, you're so fond of good meat, you really should try the rib-eye steak.

MARY: Thank you, darling, but I'd much prefer the filet mignon. It's a little more expensive than rib-eye, but I do think it has a better taste.

JOHN (*sensing that Mary has not accepted his superior knowledge of meat*): But people order filet mignon because of snob appeal; only connoisseurs really know about the rib-eye cut. You'll be missing an opportunity if you don't order it. Many restaurants don't even carry it.

MARY: I really appreciate your advice, John, but I do feel like having a filet mignon tonight.

JOHN: I'm not giving you advice. I'm just telling you facts.

MARY: You are giving me advice, and I don't need it. If it's all right with you, I'd like filet mignon—or do I have to order fish?

JOHN: Order what you damn-well please!

(*The rest of the meal is spent in angry silence. Each feels the other is an unreasonable bastard and refuses to make the first conciliatory gesture.*)

In all marriages with which we have had any experience, there are some symmetrical exchanges between the partners—particularly in those areas which have not been covered by the couples' rules. When new situations arise, the spouses must engage in bargaining behavior in order to work out who has the right to do what in relation to whom.

Also, as we have pointed out, marriage is a game where both parties win or both lose. When spouses are caught up in a continuous status struggle, each insists he has an equal right to dictate the nature of the marital behavior; each finds it necessary continually to dictate that he is the equal of the other spouse, thus perpetually renewing the struggle. Most of these spouses are destined for a lifetime of fighting, or perhaps more likely, they will end up in the divorce court. However, not all of these marriages end up in the divorce court, not only because divorce may cost too much money, but because *even agreeing to a divorce* may not be possible for individuals truly bonded to a status struggle. For example, neither may wish to play "bad guy" or "home wrecker" in front of the children, so they stick together in order not to let the other have the advantage. Little thought is given to what such an arrangement actually does to the children.

Such spouses are easy for marital therapists to recognize. The key is that regardless of the situation, the spouses respond by engaging in a struggle much the same as the one that occurred earlier for some other reason. In other words, status-struggle spouses do not quarrel over specific issues so much as they quarrel over *who has the right to say what* concerning the issue; one spouse may feel that the other is indicating superiority, and the response is to fight him on these grounds rather than on the merits of the particular case. Or a couple may argue about something which cannot be objectively resolved. Imagine a couple coming to blows about their respective attainment of "masculinity" and "femininity"! How can these qualities be measured, unless one estimates biceps size and how many thousands are spent on cold creams and dresses?

How does such a relationship arise in the first place? One apparent answer is that in our culture the marital circumstances set up a condition that neither spouse expected. For one thing, as pointed out by Jay Haley,[1] once the legal ceremony of marriage has taken place, the question may arise at any point as to whether the spouses are now together because they *must* be, or whether the relationship is still one that they really desire and would continue voluntarily. The social pressure on people to regard marriage as sacred and eternal (at least until death intervenes) functions almost as a third party in the relationship. This third party may be felt vaguely as "society" or "they," or it may take the quite specific form of relatives or in-laws on one or the other side of the family. There are also financial pressures to stay married, and the necessity of maintaining the marriage may seem to one or both spouses a compulsory fact of life. They persuade

---

[1] Jay Haley, "Marriage Therapy," *Archives of General Psychiatry*, Vol. VIII (1963), pp. 213–234. The author is a Research Associate at the Mental Research Institute, Palo Alto, California.

themselves that they would have to stay together even if they hated each other. Naturally, in such a relationship each spouse has reason to doubt the trustworthiness of the other's feelings toward himself. The husband thinks, "Maybe she doesn't really love me. She is just afraid of the disgrace of getting divorced." Or perhaps, "She really despises me. She's just looking for a meal ticket for herself and the kids. She thinks she's too old to get a job."

Similarly, the wife may feel that the husband's signs of affection for her are phony, that he is going through the motions because he is afraid of being "taken for a ride" in the divorce court. Thus, couples who apparently got together voluntarily in the first place, suddenly find themselves faced with the consideration that their union is now inalterable. If they have children, an extra pressure to stay married exists, providing another source of doubt regarding the real feelings prevailing in the marriage. Thus, for a variety of reasons the marriage becomes compulsory; it drags on, whereas the spouses might separate if they only had no children, or a low-cost opportunity, or less guilt, or less social pressure.

If Mary and John feel a compulsory note in their relationship, Mary may try in many ways to show John that he is inferior and that she is just being responsible and stoic in staying. John, having been made to feel inferior, now needs to indicate that he is Mary's equal.

Status-struggle relationships often include intimidating or threatening behavior which is used to keep the other spouse tied to the marriage, even though such behavior increases the likelihood that the marriage will break up. For example, suppose John has taken Mary on a business trip. John may be busy, and since he sees Mary's role as that of enhancing his business interests *independently* and *actively,* he pays little attention to her. Perhaps Mary is uncertain and less gregarious in this situation than at home among her own acquaintances. Feeling inadequate and neglected, Mary may force John to notice her by, let us say, being late for appointments, sitting silently in a corner at the businessmen's cocktail party, and so on. John may say that Mary's behavior is upsetting him and that she should take the next train home. Mary begins packing as she listens to John angrily say that it was a mistake to take her on the trip, and that perhaps it was a mistake to get married. Mary agrees. She says she is glad to leave and adds, "But I'm not going straight home. I'll be gone for a week."

"Where are you going?"

"You may think I'm a lousy mixer here, but it's all your fault. I assure you that, on my own, plenty of people will find me interesting," and she snaps her suitcase shut.

We do not know what Mary intends to do for the week, but John understands her to mean that she'll have a wild old time, perhaps picking up a strange man or looking up an old boyfriend.

Mary is using one of marriage's most successful threats and intimidative techniques. Unfortunately, two can play the game, and then the status struggle begins again on this issue—who can be the more socially desirable in the absence of the other.

Spouses who get caught up in symmetrical struggles often are individuals who come from emotionally lopsided homes where one parent was overtly dominant and the other tried to maintain some sense of equality by undermining and undercutting the efforts of the dominant spouse, while appearing to be passive and martyred. The child of such a union has no model for developing a collaborative relationship. As he grows to adulthood, he chooses a partner he consciously feels is different from the parent of the opposite sex, but who in fact is similar to the parent in many important ways. Once the honeymoon is over and he begins to see the old familiar tactics being used, he fears getting caught up in the same patterns, and the struggles begin. Usually neither he *nor* his spouse ever learned how to behave cooperatively, as people tend to choose spouses with many patterns similar to their own. One can only do what one knows *how* to do! The marital state comes as something of a shock to them—especially if the marriage follows a romantic period of courtship during which each was exceedingly receptive to the wishes of the other and the symmetrical struggles had not yet occurred.

Once a status struggle begins, it often spreads and becomes more and more pervasive, often vicious. Each spouse continues trying to prove that he is just as good (or powerful, or skillful, or intelligent) as the other. The spiral goes up and up. In rare instances, the spouses may consciously recognize the pattern and agree that they are equal and can afford to desist. Usually, the battle continues indefinitely. It sometimes ends *overtly* when one of the parties says (in effect), "Okay, you are superior to me. You take charge. I'll follow." This withdrawal from the battle leads to serious problems, because few people of either sex can be satisfied in a completely submissive role and the one who yields will find ways to undercut subtly the control of the dominant spouse. The battle simply *goes underground,* where it is more difficult to deal with.

A more functional (and more genuine) solution is for the spouses to divide the areas of responsibility between them. The relationship may then change to a *complementary,* interdependent, one. In this kind of relationship each spouse's behavior (at least in some important areas of living) complements or mutually enhances the behavior of the other spouse—as when one spouse wishes to receive and the other, at that moment, is willing to give. When the behavior of a man and woman is complementary, one individual defines the relationship and the other accepts the definition. Its keynote might be: "Okay, you take charge now."

Thus, if a husband says, "Let's go to a movie," and his wife replies "Fine!" their exchange can be labeled as interdependent. Sometimes, the wife may add, "However, after the movie I'd like to have a beer at Joe's place," and the husband may then say, "That's okay with me." Now the wife is in the complementary position which was occupied by her husband just a moment before.

If we sample Bob's and Sue's behavior in a wide range of situations and at different periods, we may find that sometimes one spouse and sometimes the other takes the initiative and is in the complementary dominant position. We also will usually find that there are periods of symmetrical behavior, when Bob and Sue are working out (or even battling out) the nature of their relationship at that moment. This combination of interdependent behavior (with the spouses alternating in the complementary position) and occasional status struggles is called the *parallel* relationship. Such a marital system, which might also be called the give-and-take marriage, is the most durable, workable form. The spouses allow each other equal opportunities to determine the nature of the relationship. Naturally, they are competitive some of the time, but they are also able to exchange interdependent behavior—and this is mutually enhancing.

To carry the example further, if we continue to sample the behavior of Sue and Bob we will notice almost invariably that Sue is in charge in some areas and Bob in others. Some gray areas may remain to which neither has an absolute claim, and in these, temporary symmetrical behavior will be necessary before one or the other is able to take over. The reader may wonder why it is necessary for someone to take charge in every aspect of life. We do not mean that one partner must be bossy and the other passive; however, if work is to be accomplished and the relationship remain functional, acceptable behavior patterns must be insti-tuted and in some way be agreed upon. Even if two individuals were identical, carbon copies of each other, someone still would have to "take charge." For example, the first time they tried to go through a doorway together, someone would have to decide who was to go first.

All couples quickly try to work out rules about who is to take charge of which area and under what circumstances. The rules of some couples may be durable, workable, and ubiquitous; but other spouses may never agree on the rules, or may make agreements fraught with pathological consequences. For example, suppose a husband and wife have very different backgrounds, the man being the son of a German physician and the wife the daughter of an American farmer. As soon as they are married, the more immediately forceful husband devises the rule that he is to be in charge of all decisions. His position is given support by prevailing cultural pressures and as the bride is also subject to cultural role definitions, she accepts this rule for their relationship, expecting her dear husband's natural kindness and love to make the situation pleasurable. The husband does allow her to run the household as she wishes, discipline and supervise the children, spend whatever funds she deems necessary to care for the family. If she wants money for "permissible" purchases, she need only go to her husband and ask for it, but her husband makes the decision as to what is "permissible." When they are out together, the wife acts devoted and gentle. Other men may secretly admire them as the "perfect couple," and women may

despise the husband and resent the wife for appearing to welcome the prescribed cultural role which they dislike.

Such an arrangement is culturally prescribed in most societies,
but even so the more submissive spouse usually finds ways to
bring the relationship into more equal balance—normally by
sabotaging the rules and efforts of the dominant spouse. What
happens, for instance, when the physician and his farm-bred wife
go to bed together? The husband can insist that his wife have
intercourse with him, but he cannot insist that she enjoy it.
Despite arrogant domination and threats, there is no way he can
force her to get pleasure from intercourse, and when she does not,
he feels defeated and castrated. There may be other kinds of
enjoyment that are important to him too, like the opera, sports,
television, art, or movies. In none of these areas can he effectively
insist that she share with him the satisfaction and joy of real
companionship. The more he tries to dominate her subjective
feelings (for example, sexual pleasure), the more persistent she
becomes, thus appearing increasingly passive but in reality, defeating her husband's domination in the most effective way
possible.

What is the outcome likely to be in this situation? In many
parts of the world (in South America or in southern Europe, for
example) the husband may find a mistress who can be a companion and give him a feeling of being a superior lover, while he
and his wife share certain limited activities (thus, they may eat
meals together), find pleasure in recreation away from each other,
achieve separate bedrooms and a *détente* in the sexual area. But
if this arrangement cannot be afforded economically or, as in the
United States, if it is fraught with censure and legal difficulties,
the husband probably will begin to interfere in decisions that
formerly were left to his wife—partly to get even, but partly too
because the power he cannot now demonstrate in sexual intercourse has to be exerted in another area in which he also partici-
pates. He may then take over the function of scolding the children
whereas he formerly left their management to his wife. The children may react by becoming upset, his wife may look at him as if
he were a brute, and consequently he may feel guilty and become
angry at her. Now their formerly stable situation has become
chaotic. There are many possible destructive outcomes (including

physical violence) unless they can reach an agreement regarding who is in charge of what.

The point then, is that the nature of their rules will determine the chance a husband and wife have for maintaining a marriage in our present complicated society. In earlier days, when most spouses were attempting to survive under adverse conditions, marital stability was easier to maintain. The husband worked long hours, usually outside the home, to earn his family's keep, and the wife worked long hours inside the home to care for the family needs. Under these conditions, marital rules could be relatively simple and the areas of autonomy for each spouse were relatively fixed and obvious. Nowadays, with leisure increasing, the situation is no longer this simple, and couples who succeed in building a workable marriage have to have rules which are flexible and cover a wide number of possibilities.

When the spouses cannot develop these rules, cannot stop a status struggle, the marriage gets into trouble. Each is trying to have the other consider him an equal, but as we pointed out earlier, each often behaves (in the eyes of the spouse) as if he wished to be considered superior, so the partner who has been "challenged" returns a similar challenge. This situation is common because most people have little *practice or experience* in cooperative, equal-status relationships. History has been a tale not of equality, but of dominance and competition. The results of such power struggles are repeatedly tragic and markedly impair human growth and progress.

Paradoxically, husbands and wives caught in the struggles of the symmetrical relationship often cannot leave each other, no matter how savage their behavior. Often, the reason is that the one who would like to initiate the departure or divorce feels that doing so would be an admission that he is inferior (wrong) and that the other is right after all. Or if one does decide to leave, the "deserted" partner may try to prevent the departure in order to avoid the suggestion that he, having been abandoned, is inferior, and the spouse who left is superior. So, many couples cling to each other because of hate—which can be as binding as love. As an attractive, intelligent young woman with excellent chances of remarriage said, "I'd leave the S.O.B. in a moment, except that I'll be damned before I give him the satisfaction of being the injured party in court." Or as a woman who had had an unhappy second marriage said, "If I get divorced for the second time everyone will think that my first smashup was all my fault—even though I divorced him—or else why should my second husband want to leave me?"

For a marriage to last as a reasonable and workable relationship, the pattern of continuous status struggle *must* be broken. This can be done, and techniques which help in terminating these struggles are described in Part IV.

20

TIME AND GOALS
IN MARRIAGE

The human being is a goal-oriented animal. Goals are imposed
upon individuals by their culture from birth to death; and when
two individuals are joined together in matrimony, the complex
combination of two sets of goals forms a joint system. This new
joint system develops its own shared goals, which often clash with
the individual goals of the spouses. The results are limitless and
unpredictable. The new joint system may become a conflict-
ridden compages capable of goading the most selfless person into
battle; or it may turn out to be capable of humanizing the most
hopeless egotist.

It is generally recognized that most married couples have
mutually agreed upon purposes and goals—for example, raising
healthy children, living frugally in order to save money to retire
in Florida, or establishing a reputation as solid citizens in the
community. But it is often overlooked that goal achievement involves a highly complicated and sometimes incompatible or antithetical use of time and energy. Most people are constantly
plagued by conflicts consuming the use of time and the use of
energy. A major problem of life is how much—if any—time and
energy should be devoted, for example, to making money, learning, making love, seeking other sorts of pleasure, caring for chil-

dren, serving one's country, worshiping one's God, and so on. It is improbable that any two people will be so much alike that their ideas on the use of time and energy will always be compatible.

Also, even if their ideas on this matter—whether in general or at any given moment—are identical, they may lack the abilities and the behavioral repertoires necessary for using the available time and energy as they desire. For example, a couple may agree that they wish to concentrate on the pursuit of a high income. Yet the wife may not have the ability to entertain her husband's business associates graciously or to help him meet the right people. The husband may not have the skill or astuteness to rise to the top of his company. Therefore, even though they agree regarding the use of their time and energy, they may blame each other more and more viciously as time passes and it becomes clear that they cannot achieve the high income which is their long-range goal.

Matters become more complicated still when the couple's long-term goals are vague, or—worse—both vague and incompatible. For example, consider a wife who has, without realizing it, a burning desire for the "perfect love," something which is as unreal as the land of Oz. This desire is an obsessive, unconscious force which dictates much of her behavior without her being aware of it.

Her husband saw her initially as a pleasing, devoted person; his goal was to succeed rapidly in the business world, and he pictured her as the perfect hostess and helpmate. She was also facile with a typewriter, and since love to her meant willingness to please the spouse in order to be given love in return, she was always only too glad to be helpful. It is easy to see that a marriage in these circumstances is doomed to failure. The person who is seeking the perfect love and attempting to achieve it by being sweet, thoughtful, and giving, usually ends up feeling used. The person who is looking for a helpmate in his quest for success is not giving love, but is expecting his spouse to accept status and achievement as reward enough for her efforts.

When a husband and wife of this type have limited functionality, so that they have difficulty adapting to changing situations, they cannot vary or change their goals significantly and are

largely unable to communicate in such a way that the disparity
between their goals becomes clear to them. They cling to each
other, each hoping to get blood out of a turnip eventually; as the
years pass, each feels increasingly cheated by the other, but
cannot give up the notion that someday his goal will be realized.

Short-term goals (involving a very limited time expectation)
also play a part in this kind of Gruesome-Twosome relationship.
For example, the wife looking for the perfect love (her long-term
goal) may give her husband the feeling that he has been using
her, so as compensation he offers her a night on the town (short-
term fulfillment). The problem here is that, compared to the
perfect love she desires, such an offer seems irritatingly trivial—
a crumb instead of a loaf. When she shows no enthusiasm for the
invitation, he feels angry and hurt and withdraws it. On the other
hand, if she attempts to please him by making an extra-special
fancy dinner (short-term fulfillment), he may show little appreciation because he cannot connect a pleasant meal with his drive
to succeed (his long-term goal). Perhaps he would have preferred her to save her energies for a time when they were enter-
taining his boss. Now it is her turn to feel hurt and angry.

However talented, bright, capable, or sophisticated the spouses
may be, their differences in *time orientation* may preclude a
smoothly functioning relationship. How often one hears the comment, "But why can't he behave that way with me?" Here the
difficulty usually has to do with time. The husband may feel like
letting go and living it up at a party since this is something he
does only occasionally. In this way he interacts with a large
group of people over a brief time period. The "fun-loving" aspect
of his personality does not include intimate tête-à-têtes, which his
wife would prefer. To her husband, the time spent together in
"intimacy" is more suitably devoted to worrying about bills,
making plans, and the like.

21

RECIPROCAL BEHAVIOR

The Quid Pro Quo,
or the Marital Bargaining Table

Marriage is an interlocking, self-contained system. The behavior and the attitudes of one partner *always* stimulate some sort of reaction from the other. A slight half-smile, a lifted eyebrow, a quick wrinkling of the forehead, will beget *some* response, though not necessarily a verbal one. Even silence can be a forceful message. Neither spouse may be aware of the action and reaction, for these usually originate at the unconscious level. Much of the interaction between the two consists of what might be considered behavioral reflexes, manifested without conscious knowledge.

In the course of time, as partners experience recurring patterns of behavior in their relationship, certain predictable successions of events are established. The wife's left eyelid may quiver almost imperceptibly when the husband has badgered her too much about how boring her parents are. After this sequence has been repeated a few times, they both "know" that if husband continues nagging, the wife will lose her temper and may walk out. At this point, the husband may say, "Let me make you some coffee," to indicate that he is sorry and will change the subject, yet neither party is consciously aware of the nature of their exchange. In this situation they are an error-activated system; they are behaving exactly like the thermostat on a furnace—when it becomes too cold, on goes the heat; when it becomes too warm, it shuts off. The spouses govern each other's behavior to maintain the expected or usual emotional temperature for their relationship.

After several years, this type of behavior pattern between two people appears to the skilled observer as constant and predictable —exactly as if it had been consciously planned and both parties were aware of it. This reciprocal behavior is to be found wherever two people have a close relationship. They may be business partners, a father and son, two homosexuals living together, two women working as nurses on the same ward, and so forth. Marriage has been studied more than other relationships and we are apt to forget it has much in common with all relationships.

We call this system of behavioral responses the *quid pro quo*. *Quid pro quo* literally means "something for something." In the marriage process, it means that if you do so-and-so, then I automatically will respond with such-and-such. It might be called "tit for tat," or "point and counterpoint," or "reciprocal behavior," but some of these names imply nasty or opprobrious responses, whereas by *quid pro quo* we imply shared, or exchanged, behavior—much of it unconscious.

Regularly occurring patterns of interaction evidencing unspoken *quid pro quo*'s are obvious if one observes families carefully. In one instance, a family having a discussion in a psychiatrist's office was photographed by a motion picture camera. During the short discussion, father, mother, and daughter crossed their legs one after the other fourteen times. Invariably, first the mother crossed her right leg over her left, then daughter did the same thing, and finally father, who was sitting in a chair opposite them, followed through with the same motion. This behavior on the mother's part always followed a pronouncement by the father about what sort of action the family should take; in other words, it occurred whenever the father "took charge." It might thus be said that whereas he was the titular leader, the mother was demonstrating by her nonverbal behavior that she had an equal right to lead a family movement—and was capable of doing so. None of the three was aware of the leg movement. Even when they knew they were "on camera" the members of this family, like most others, could not hide their nonverbal messages.

Manifestations of the *quid pro quo* are endless. For example, a husband insists that the spare bedroom be converted into a study for his use even though the renovation is expensive. Several days later, his wife engages a cleaning woman. Previously both had considered a maid too expensive. When the husband gets the bill for the maid at the end of the month, he goes into his now-comfortable study, writes a check for the maid (even though he previously felt he could not afford one), lights a good cigar, and congratulates his wife on how clean the house is. Something-for-something behavior has occurred—a *quid pro quo*—without spoken acknowledgment by either spouse. Yet this exchange of behavior is more than a single event. It also serves as a model for future exchanges between these spouses. It is part of the marriage continuum.

Soon after a marriage, both partners become conditioned to the *quid pro quo* pattern. They may not realize it, yet each informs the other of his response pattern by little clues—hints and innuendos which suggest what must be done to keep the partnership in balance. For example, when the husband wanted the bedroom made into a study, the wife may have responded with, "Yes, dear, with a study you'll be able to get more work done." The implication then was that he'd make more money and she'd spend more of it—perhaps by getting the maid.

The *quid pro quo* process is an unconscious effort of both partners to assure themselves that they are equals, that they are peers. It is a technique enabling each to preserve his dignity and self-esteem. Their equality may not be apparent to the world at large; it may be based upon values meaningless to anyone else, yet serve to maintain the relationship because the people involved perceive their behavioral balance as fair and mutually satisfying.

After the marriage (or any other human relationship) has been operating for awhile, the *quid pro quo* pattern becomes an unwritten (usually not consciously recognized) set of ground rules. The wife unconsciously knows that if she behaves in manner A, her husband will respond in manner B; and the husband unconsciously knows that if he behaves in manner K, his wife will respond with attitude L. This recognition can reach the conscious level, but it seldom does. One of the techniques for diminishing a destructive *quid pro quo* is to bring it from the unconscious to the conscious level. Later we shall demonstrate how to do this. Some *quid pro quo*'s are destructive and some are nourishing—just as some laws are hindrances and some are helpful to societal health, progress, and growth.

Once the *quid pro quo* pattern has been established and *accepted* (no matter how bizarre the exchanges are), each partner can live from day to day with some sense of security because he knows what to expect from the other partner. Each has tacitly agreed to a behavior complex which he believes protects his own dignity, self-respect, and self-esteem in relation to the other party. Whether the actions are cruel or loving is irrelevant; both partners accept them, once the pattern is established. Later we shall suggest techniques for establishing a functional *quid pro quo*.

Under certain circumstances, the *quid pro quo* becomes destructive.

First, there may be a situation in which, from courtship, the spouses think they have an agreed-upon set of rules. After marriage, one or both spouses may suddenly reveal that they "didn't mean it" and not accept the *quid pro quo*'s that the other spouse has felt were workable. For example, during courting days a young man spends much time with his fiancée. Immediately after marriage he ignores her in favor of his job. When she complains, he tells her he is only looking out for her welfare by working so hard, and is hurt that she is so "selfish."

Second, one or both partners may be incapable of understanding the signals and therefore may ignore them. This may occur when there is enormous intellectual disparity between spouses, or a wide difference in background—resulting in different tastes, behavior patterns, social habits, moral values, and so on—which causes much of both the spoken and the nonverbal communication to be as incomprehensible as a foreign language.

Third, one partner may break the rules after the *quid pro quo* has been consciously or unconsciously accepted by both. This is what occurs in the play *Who's Afraid of Virginia Woolf*. Martha, the wife, breaks the rules by publicly discussing their imaginary son. Her husband, George, then proceeds to violate his share of their agreement and publicly humiliates her. Their "sharing" of an imaginary son gave them something in common. Now they will have to develop a new game; or if one or both will not, the marriage will be devoid of any but destructive qualities.

Finally, if the nature of the *quid pro quo*'s is such that it ~~i~~ously limits the behavior, creativity, or growth of one or both ~~u~~ses, then there is a premature freezing, or jelling, of the mar~~riag~~e which probably will result in one or the other spouse's ~~bre~~aking away; or both will grow old together stuck in an emotional morass, which usually is characterized by a rigid, unchanging, negative relationship.

All of these examples demonstrate that acceptable *quid pro quo*'s can only be determined over a significant time span. *Quid pro quo*'s made within narrow temporal limits quickly become dysfunctional because they do not allow for the ever-present factor of change. Inflexible, nonutilitarian rules for the *quid pro quo* are bound to become destructive because people and marriages change in the course of time. Spouses may (and should) shift their *quid pro quo*'s as the marriage grows older, even if doing so is temporarily upsetting, instead of allowing fear of change to dominate the relationship and keep them trapped in their fixed patterns.

When the *quid pro quo* ground rules are violated by either party, trouble begins. Such violations may occur when an unexpected outside influence pressures the marriage, or when there is a change in the behavior or expectations of one of the partners. The predictable behavior pattern is no longer predictable. Confusion and discord unbalance the partnership.

If one of the spouses violates the ground rules, the other one, without knowing why, feels that he has been betrayed. He now (often unconsciously) attempts to create a new *quid pro quo* which will protect his interest. For example, if a husband comes home from a business trip and finds that his wife, without consulting him, has invited her mother to live with them for two months, and that the mother is occupying his new study, he feels betrayed. The study is *his,* and no one in the family was supposed even to enter it. A *quid pro quo* ground rule has been broken by the wife. The way the husband responds here will depend on the nature of their relationship. He may react by insisting that the newly hired maid be fired. He may be surly and rude to his wife's mother (although he agreed a long time ago to be always courteous to her even though he doesn't like her). He may start complaining about how bad business is and insist on unreasonable cuts in the household budget. He may start nagging his wife, saying that his boss is angry because he hasn't properly completed some work which he brought home. Thus he implies that he is failing at his job because his mother-in-law is in his study, and that his wife is to blame.

Diplomats recognize that the *quid pro quo* process also applies to relations between nations, as seen in the institutionalized behavioral limitation (a conscious *quid pro quo*) called protocol. Protocol may seem old-fashioned, ridiculous, or even humorous to someone outside of the diplomatic world, but it is very useful, enabling nations to observe a lawful,* predictable system of behavior. Thus, as is well known in diplomatic circles, a violation of protocol conveys a significant message.

If the spouses' verbal and nonverbal behavior did not occur redundantly, forming a pattern, each individual would have to learn about the other individual (or some aspect of him) all over again every time they met. Someone who is "highly unpredictable" may be interesting for brief periods of time, but usually is not the sort of person one would choose for a spouse. Unpredictable individuals are rare in our society. People noted for their erratic behavior (such as a few famous movie actors) actually are predictably unpredictable, and therefore the label is a misnomer. Nevertheless, their notorious multiple marriages testify to the fact that such people are hard to live with.

The occurrence of the *quid pro quo* action-reaction pattern is inevitable. In these exchanges the man and woman negotiate their total conjoint behavior, and at the same time each becomes acquainted with the other's total personality. This is why a long and intimate courtship is desirable. The short or "good time" courtship, confined to wooing activities in which each attempts to appear as attractive as possible to the other, exhibits only a small percentage of the behavioral range of each. It is a common experience for someone to be shocked after marriage by the discovery that he has married a "stranger."

Behavioral scientists have often observed this phenomenon in the case of individuals who indulge in extramarital sexual relations. The relationship with the mistress or lover resembles court-

---

* "Lawful" as used in this book means "regularly occurring"; in the same way, a scientific "law" describes a regularly occurring phenomenon. The term "redundant" in systems theory is another synonym.

ship. Each limits himself to a narrow behavioral and social repertoire aimed at pleasing the other. Often this pleasing repertoire consists precisely of kinds of behavior which are missed at home—those which the legal spouse seems to lack. In addition, there is the excitement of "mistress and lover against the world." There are secret trips, sojourns at hotels under false names, and so on. The lover and mistress are certain that the affair is the high point of their lives. On the basis of this conclusion, they often divorce their spouses and marry each other. Then they *really* get to know each other, becoming acquainted with the entire range of conscious behavior and of *quid pro quo* exchanges. At this point, the former wife or husband may appear very, very desirable.

One of the functions of a long premarital engagement is to determine whether the interlocking patterns of behavior which will become regularized between the two individuals are acceptable to both. For example, individuals from two widely disparate cultures rarely marry, because they are not able to read each other's signals and cannot properly label the kinds of behavior they are exchanging. They cannot develop *quid pro quo*'s. An Eskimo woman may be offended by a Frenchman's attempt to kiss her, and the Frenchman may be equally puzzled and displeased when the Eskimo woman insists on rubbing noses. It is not likely that two with such differences in social background will end up as spouses; the fact that just this does happen on occasion is due to another phenomenon, which confuses the courtship (premarital engagement) situation. The two people will usually excuse each other's strange or unacceptable behavior because of the "romance" and excitement born of novelty. If the girl wants to rub noses, the boy may see her desire as cute and inventive; but he probably will become irritated by it once they have decided to get married.

Quickie marriages, especially between young people, have the highest divorce rate.* The two are attracted to each other by "romance"; and not until after the wedding ceremony do they learn that they just "don't understand" each other. The cultural and behavioral patterns of husband and wife are often so different

* In California, 40 per cent of all divorces occur among those aged twenty or less. In addition, there are numerous annulments.

that each is unable to receive and understand (either consciously or unconsciously) the messages which the other sends. The two are unable to establish a workable *quid pro quo*. When they become conscious of failure, and frantically try to do "something" to ameliorate the problem, it often gets worse. A high percentage of annulments, desertions, and divorces occur in marriages in which the bride was pregnant. The man marries to fulfill his part of the bargain ("After all, you got me into this") and having done so, takes off for other parts.

As has been suggested, the operation of the *quid pro quo* is largely unconscious. Indeed, it might be compared to breathing. The process of breathing is described by behavioral scientists as "institutionalized." It works so perfectly that the individual doesn't even think about it. If someone is told, "Do you realize you are breathing exactly fourteen times per minute and have been doing so for the last half hour?" his first reaction is to hold his breath. If he then tries to count his own rate of breathing, the regularity disappears. Usually the rate of breathing increases once it has been brought to consciousness.

In the same way marital rules and interactions often exist in an evenly working fashion without either spouse's being aware of their presence. Indeed, should the spouses accidentally (not by mutual effort) become aware of their own rules, problems are introduced, just as breathing loses its regularity when brought to the individual's notice. If John realizes that he does *X* in return for Mary's doing *Y*, he may then for the first time attempt to see if they balance. If he concludes that he is receiving less than he is giving, he usually will try to alter the relationship unilaterally by deciding what a fair exchange is and trying to force acceptance of his view. Now if his spouse feels that she is being shortchanged, she will attempt to bring the behavioral exchange back to what, *in her estimation,* is fair. Each spouse acts unilaterally, and each concludes that the other considers himself to be superior and is trying to win the upper hand. At this point, the behavior of both becomes destructive.

Since a couple spending a whole day together probably will complete many thousands of exchanges during that period, it becomes obvious how quickly the destructive actions can increase and how the balanced, workable *quid pro quo*'s can soon be replaced by discord. Therefore, spouses must learn how to diminish the destructive *quid pro quo*'s and become aware of, and emphasize, those that are functional.

A case which illustrates inadequate *quid pro quo* formulation follows.

John feels he may have to leave his wife, Mary, because there is a basic antagonism between her demands on him for attention and his passionate involvement in his chosen profession. Mary is often upset if John works late. If he is completely tied up in his job for several days in a row, she becomes irritable and behaves in a manner guaranteed to disturb him. If he takes her on a short business trip (as she usually wishes him to do) she becomes jealous when he devotes his energy and attention to his business associates; she is likely to make a scene, for example, just before he goes off to a conference or a business meeting. As a result, John has decided he will not take Mary on any more trips, and she therefore feels more left out than ever.

On one occasion, Mary makes a particularly urgent appeal for John to arrange to be with the family over the weekend and to take care of a number of chores about the house. He does as she requests, yet on Sunday evening she attacks him, accusing him of ignoring her over the weekend. John is startled because he believes he has devoted the weekend to Mary's wishes. The next day, John sees a psychiatrist. During the session with the doctor John recognizes that even though he was at home for two days, doing what he had been asked to do, he hardly thought about Mary during the entire weekend, and gave her no personal attention. On the other hand (he remembers) he frequently thinks of Mary while he is at work, and particularly when he is away on a trip.

John further recognizes that he obtains enormous satisfaction (both personal and monetary) from his job and enjoys being busy. When he is with Mary and the family he does not feel useful, and becomes restless. Mary runs the house in her own way, and John, who is used to being in charge at work, becomes irritable and withdrawn. He has been interpreting her refusal to let him "run things" at home as an indication of her disapproval, and as negative behavior on her part.

John has failed to recognize that his wife's moods and behavior largely depend on his acknowledging her as a capable homemaker and desirable wife, and that this acknowledgment must take the form not of doing something *for* her, but of an unequivocal personal demonstration that he loves and admires her as a person, and that she is as important to him as his work. This situation is complicated by the fact that Mary, like John, often thinks of their being together as an opportunity for doing projects around the house or with the children or with each other; by this attitude she unwittingly collaborates in John's particular game. John's reaction is that as long as he is going to have to work, he might as well work at his job (which he enjoys) instead of at household repairs and so forth.

Such a couple exhibits automatic, repetitious behavior which may be compared to that of an electronic computer which has been incorrectly programmed for a particular kind of data processing. The errors in the program cannot be rectified by the computer, they can be corrected *only from outside the computer, by a human being feeding in new instructions.* The computer itself does not observe its own mistakes; neither do most married couples see their own pattern; they are caught up within the system and are not able to look at themselves from a vantage point outside.

It is our view, however, that some couples can look at their marital system from a new viewpoint, such as the *quid pro quo* theory provides, for example, and as a result come to understand their interaction in a way that they had not previously. Of course, in difficult situations, the aid of a third party is required.

22

AUTONOMY VERSUS SYMBIOSIS

"I'd Rather Do It Alone" Versus "Togetherness"

The discussion of the autonomy-symbiosis dichotomy requires some precise, scientific words. The major terms used in this chapter, with their definitions, are as follows:

Autonomy (as used in this book). The exercise by the individual of independence with respect to some matters which relate to the marriage, or which the other spouse *considers* to be integral parts of their marriage.

Symbiosis. An association of two organisms (in this case, wife and husband) living attached to each other and contributing to each other's support. They cannot function autonomously; and if they are separated will function inefficiently, if at all. Recently the word "togetherness" has often been used to imply symbiosis.

Dichogamous. Characterized (as a hermaphroditic plant or animal may be) by the production of male and female organs which become mature at different times, so that self-fertilization is impossible. A marital union so described is one in which the two spouses are so out of phase that collaboration, even cooperation, becomes difficult or impossible.

Dichotomy. The division of a whole into two independent parts, as when a limb forms two separate branches.

Compages. A whole formed by the compaction or juncture of parts, a framework or system of conjoined parts, a complex structure.

Marriage is a complex unity made up of at least three different but interdependent systems: the system of the male (his total being); the system of the female (her total being); and the marital system, deriving from the interaction of the male and female systems joined together (the compages, or relationship). The marital system springs into being spontaneously when the systems of male and female join. It is a good example of the whole being *more* than the sum of its parts, of one plus one equaling three.

Too many marriage books and "helpful" newspaper and magazine columns treat the step across the threshold to marriage as a glorious advance into complete and monolithic union. But the union is not complete, for after individuals are married they continue to strive to remain individuals, even while they attempt to make their marriage grow.

The picture is dismal only if the husband and wife fail to face up to the fact that both of them will struggle with the concepts of "me" and "we" all their lives. If they can recognize this, accept it, and negotiate practical *quid pro quo*'s, a workable marriage is possible.

The relationships can be expressed diagrammatically (Figure 1). Perfect collaboration, as shown in *C*, is rare indeed and generally is sustained only during a limited period of a marriage, characterized by special circumstances.

For example, such perfect union may be essential for physical survival, as when two people in a leaking boat join unreservedly in bailing out water as fast as they both are able because otherwise the boat will sink and they will drown. It may also occur when man and wife share the passion of an intense collaborative effort, like the Curies in their experiments to isolate radium. Or it may result when a couple is completely child-oriented, as parents might be who were mutually absorbed in an effort to care for their seriously ill child.

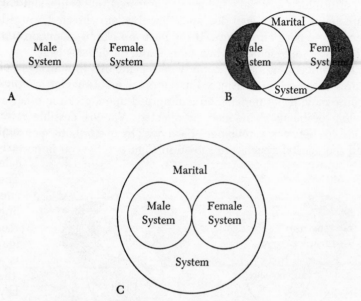

Figure 1. Relationships Between Systems.
  A. Before a relationship has developed. The two systems
     function independently.
  B. After a relationship has developed. The more collaborative
     the couple, the smaller will be the portions (shaded) of
     their individual systems which function independently of
     the marital relationship system.
  C. A near-perfect collaborative relationship.

When situations like these exist, the symbiotic marital system
is dominant over the two individual systems. Otherwise, the
triadic marital system (consisting of the two individual systems
and the marital compages) is in a state of constant flux. The
percentage of symbiosis as opposed to autonomy varies with
changes in the spouses' moods, attitudes, and communication
effectiveness that are generated by the problems and circumstances confronting husband and wife.

Sometimes one of the individuals in a marriage may be egocentric and behave like someone who is not married. For example,
if a wife has a passion for singing or music, during the time she

is performing (especially before an audience), she is in a state of autonomy. All her energies and thoughts are directed toward herself and her performance. If the husband climbs mountains all alone, he is autonomous when he is scaling a difficult peak.

The functioning of autonomy versus symbiosis in marriage requires clarification because the autonomous behavior of one spouse may, if not understood and agreed upon, give the other a feeling of being abandoned or rejected. Various possible relationships between autonomous behavior (by one or both spouses) and the marital system are shown in Figure 2. Several important

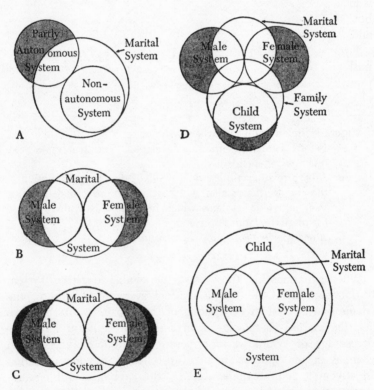

Figure 2. Possible Relationships Between Autonomous Behavior and the Marital System.

    A. Part (shaded) of one spouse's system is operating autonomously, independently of the marital system, and the nonautonomous spouse is left at home feeling abandoned.

questions may be asked: At what point will the amount of genuine autonomy be excessive? That is, when will it transform a workable marriage into one in which the spouses either separate from each other or live separately under one roof; when does autonomy turn a workable marriage into a dichogamous situation or a dichotomy? When is behavior truly autonomous, and when is it "relationship" behavior which emits the message, "I don't like you and therefore wish to be independent of you"?

The notion of marriage based on romantic love dwells on complete symbiosis (or togetherness). In actuality, unless the individuals are perfectly congruent, the development of some autonomy is inevitable and obviously desirable under most circumstances— but some forms are more acceptable to any particular husband and wife than others.

For example, Mary does not feel abandoned or rejected if her husband, John, attends night school to study law and improve his prestige and earning capacity. But if he spends the same amount of time playing pool (or in any other activity which she can't, or

---

B. Part (unshaded) of each spouse's system is operating in symbiosis with the other; the remainder (shaded) is operating autonomously, independently of the marital system.

C. An increment (blackened area) is added to each spouse's autonomy by a well-functioning marital system. Functioning well, however, depends on each being *equally* autonomous. A feeling of abandonment would occur if one began to be *more* autonomous than the other; this could escalate into competition as to who could be more autonomous, and end in separation or divorce.

D. The "egalitarian" family, in which both parents and child(ren) function autonomously to some degree, but parts of their systems operate in symbiosis. "Togetherness" provides room for independent growth for all.

E. The extreme example in which the child's system engulfs both parents' systems and the marital system, so that the child's system dominates any autonomy the parents have in relation to each other. In this case, the parents compete for the child, and if one gains unequal favor with the child, the other feels abandoned or rejected by both spouse and child. If there are several children, each parent may "choose" one, so that the family may split into multiple coalitions.

doesn't want to, participate in, or which yields benefits she cannot share), she may feel abandoned or rejected. Likewise, if Mary takes singing lessons five nights a week, leaving John home alone, John may feel that their togetherness has been destroyed by Mary's autonomy, and he may feel rejected or abandoned, especially if he does not enjoy music. But if Mary is out studying typing and stenography (to help John), he will not feel rejected or abandoned.

Let us examine the case a bit further.

Before John and Mary were married, especially if their courtship was highly romantic, they seldom found enough time to be together. School, work, or other commitments—even the need to sleep—seemed like terrible distractions to keep the lovers apart. The urge for as much togetherness as possible is normal under these circumstances. Usually there is an absence of autonomous behavior during the courtship period.

But after the wedding . . .

If John has been an enthusiastic golfer, Mary naturally expects him to continue playing after they are married, even if she doesn't play. But how often? Shall he play when she is pregnant and ill? Or when their finances are strained? Suppose that John meets a friend with whom he has had a long history of competition in golf and they play an extra nine holes to settle a bet. When he returns from golfing at 4 P.M., two hours later than usual, will Mary assume that he has deliberately avoided or punished her because they had an argument at breakfast?

Or observe Mary on the day after the golfing incident. She discovers that one of her favorite authors is lecturing at 4 P.M., and goes to hear him. As a result, dinner is a half hour late and consists of quickly warmed up beans and frankfurters. Is Mary being understandably autonomous? Or is she punishing John because of the golf episode?

It is not easy for a person to indicate that he wishes to be alone (or to do something independently) without making his spouse feel unwanted. Some people tend to feel rejected if they are left out of anything; even when they do not particularly want to be involved, they still want to be invited.

Here is another example of the trouble caused by the inability to discriminate between a genuine desire for autonomy and a negative relationship message. Frank has learned that he will have a more productive day if he does *not* eat breakfast at home; going to a quiet restaurant is better for him. Here he can order the food he likes (at home he has no choice); but more important, instead of participating in hurried and noisy household activity, he can spend a restful hour reading the newspaper and making plans for his busy day at the office. Then his eight hours at the office are usually characterized by serenity, high concentration, and efficiency. Thus, by an hour's autonomous action at breakfast, Frank directly benefits himself; but indirectly his wife also benefits, for his high performance level in the office will result in his more rapid promotion, increased earning power, and a pleasant mood during the evening.

Further, Irene enjoys sleeping in the morning. It appears, therefore, that Frank's having breakfast in the restaurant is good for everyone. However, unless communications between Irene and Frank are excellent, Irene (despite the facts) may interpret Frank's morning behavior as meaning, "I don't like you early in the morning," or "Your performance as a mother and a cook stinks, and I simply don't want to be upset; therefore, I'll eat elsewhere."

In defining the problem of autonomy versus symbiosis, one cannot simply assume that autonomy is synonymous with physical separation and that symbiosis occurs whenever the spouses are together. We are concerned rather with the fact that the autonomous behavior of one spouse may cause the other to feel abandoned or rejected in some manner. This may occur even when husband and wife are next to each other physically.

The reader is invited to consider for a moment whether the autonomy-symbiosis problem exists in his own home. For example, after the guests have departed from a dinner party, perhaps one spouse says to the other, "You spent the whole evening playing up to Mr. Big [or Miss Cutie]. You never looked at me once. You deliberately tried to humiliate me."

It is possible that the speaker is correct: the intended message may have been something like, "I didn't want this party. We can't afford it. You forced me into it. Therefore I got even with you by publicly rejecting you," or "You've been turning me down sexually lately. I'll show you I'm attractive to someone else."

On the other hand, the "playing up" to Mr. Big or Miss Cutie may have been an honest effort to make the guest of honor feel important, to include a new person in the group, to be especially nice to the husband's boss or co-worker or the wife's best friend, or something of that sort.

The problem of independent action versus togetherness may become extraordinarily significant to a couple when one spouse is involved in a complicated activity requiring unusual amounts of time and energy. Many highly productive people (male or female) isolate themselves from their families in order to accomplish what they feel they must do—sometimes not just to acquire time or quiet for concentration, but because they believe that there is not sufficient vitality to nourish both a family relationship and a creative activity. Most highly creative individuals must be autonomous while engaged in their work, and exhaust themselves in the creative process.

People of this sort may be unable or unwilling to change or compromise their behavioral patterns and tastes, with the result that genuine relationships with them are impossible. The most individualistic people in any society are generally those least amenable to personal change or to the compromise of cherished goals or ideals. Such individuals, often called loners, may be highly creative people or leaders, or they may be "outsiders," destructive rebels or hermits. Unwillingness to compromise does not guarantee creative ability, but it is often characteristic of creative people. Many such people refuse to sacrifice the time, energy, or dilution of their central aims necessary to maintain prolonged personal relationships. Even if such an individual has a following, so that he seems to be intimately involved with many others, the involvement is illusory. His followers do not ask him to change in any fundamental way. Quite the opposite, the followers generally support whatever position the leader is maintaining, and if a few dissenters do challenge his position, they must either acquiesce or be banished from the group. In rarer instances, the leader is overthrown but departs from his followers still upholding his original position. This is equally true whether the loner is a leader of a rebel gang or the leader of a great nation, like Mao in China. For the most part, loners in positions of leadership have few intimate friends, and the relationships they do have are with the devotees, or followers, who impose few or no demands of their own on the "master," not requiring him to undergo change.

Such individuals, perhaps aware of their place in history, or desiring a place in history, have highly developed inner resources which make it possible for them to substitute for intimate give-and-take relationships with people, relationships of another sort. For example, the artist may relate to his canvas or clay, the scholar to his books, the scientist to his mathematical investigations. The picture of the creative genius or scientist or artist with the devoted spouse in the background supporting his creativity is lovely to contemplate, but especially since the advent of mass education, such relationships are not at all common. Some of the most individualistic creators known to recent history either never married or were separated or divorced. Few individuals are satisfied to be passive in relation to others, particularly as increased education has prepared more and more people to plan and to make judgments with some degree of confidence that their judgments are at least as good as the next person's. Unfortunately, tension and conflict are bound to occur *when two individuals seeking self-expression* commit themselves to maintaining a relationship to each other over a period of time. The needs or interests of one or the other have to take first place, and the left-out spouse is seldom satisfied to come in second. If the "noncreative" spouse does stay with the relationship he may become passive and thus incur the disdain of the more creative or more recognized spouse.

In certain instances, a spouse will forgive "excessive" autonomy in the busy partner when the activity is utilitarian or when it provides rewards (prestige, money, respect) which can be shared. Mahatma Gandhi was famous for his devotion to India, but he was not a normal husband. Early in his marriage he renounced sexual intercourse because he said he needed his total energies—psychic, emotional, and physical—for working on national problems (he also used this sacrifice as a magnificent political ploy). This deprivation may have caused his wife dissatisfaction, but she remained a willing member of his family, presumably because her role offered sufficient compensation for what she might have lost. Also, who could have withstood the shame of abandoning the great Mahatma? After all, the word "family" derives from the Latin *familias,* meaning "servants of a household."

By and large, however, the biographies of creature geniuses are filled with accounts of marital discord. Part of this is caused by the individual's egocentricities and his passion for his work, but still another cause of marital discord in such cases is the reaction of the husband or wife to autonomous activity, the spouse's feeling of being abandoned, even though abandonment may not have been intended. *Usually, when spouses do not behave according to traditional roles, abandonment or rejection is suspected.*

In this era of increased leisure, there are more opportunities than ever before for individual hobbies and for other kinds of autonomous behavior; and accordingly, there is more marital suspicion and discord resulting from the autonomy-symbiosis conflict. Because of the difference existing even today between the male and the female roles in our society, only rarely do spouses have identical outside interests.

The situation is further complicated by man's paradoxical desire to be both autonomous and gregarious. Most civilized individuals like to be alone for periods of time; they enjoy having some independent activities. But shortly after withdrawing into independent behavior, they wish to be back with other people. The pendulum keeps swinging back and forth: the effort and strain of interacting with others stimulates their desire for independence; then the loneliness of autonomy drives them back to the social groups. And so on.

In a workable marriage, the autonomy-symbiosis phenomenon does not become a debilitating problem, even though difficulties do arise. The frictions created in any personal relationship by dissimilarities or conflicting needs, different interests, idiosyncracies, and so forth, are often handled by understanding, acceptance, sacrifice, and compromise. When reference is made to an individual's "commitment" to marriage, what is being described is the degree to which that person is willing to compromise self-interest, personal ideals of perfection, indulgence in tastes, and so forth, so that a particular relationship can continue. The alternative to making a commitment is not having a relationship—that is, remaining alone. Most people dread being alone, and are therefore willing to make considerable sacrifices for the relationship commitment.

In a functional marriage, the spouses have agreed upon the rules of the relationship—that they will discuss hurt feelings or misunderstandings, that they will circulate at parties, and so on. They have discussed who will do what, and when. Here again we can see the importance of mutual agreement (after negotiation) concerning most aspects of a marriage. Unilateral autonomy is almost always dangerous to a marriage because it implies rejection, abandonment, or inequality. The spouses must be in accord about most of the behavior of each, and compromises must be made. The firm hands of *quid pro quo* are always at the steering wheel of the workable marriage. When there is no agreement about where it is going, the marriage is almost certain to run into a ditch.

23

THE MAJOR ELEMENTS
OF A SATISFACTORY
MARRIAGE

The studies of ordinary workable marriages in middle-class society indicate that many different patterns of marital relations appear to function successfully. There is no *one* way for two people to relate in order to have a satisfactory marriage, but the following elements appear to be common to the various patterns.

First, the spouses in a workable marriage respect each other. Each spouse finds some important quality or ability to respect in the other—being a good parent, making a lot of money, writing beautiful music, or whatever. The greater the number of areas of respect, the more satisfactory is the marriage.

Second, the spouses are tolerant of each other. They see themselves as fallible, vulnerable human beings and can therefore accept each other's shortcomings.

Third, the key ingredient in a successful marriage is the effort of the spouses to make the most of its assets and minimize its liabilities. We have tried to show that if the spouses have enough cultural values in common (and usually they would not have married if they did not *think* they did) workability depends on *learning to communicate* in order to negotiate *quid pro quo's.* This allows them to agree on common goals and progress toward these goals. Further, workability requires the recognition that a marital relationship is not static. Relationship is a process involving constant change; and constant change requires the spouses to *keep working on their relationship until the day they die.*

Somehow, a myth has arisen in this country which teaches that the first few years of marriage form the period during which all problems "get ironed out." The implication seems to be that thereafter the spouses sit passively while the marital wagon rolls along through life. This conception of the relationship is nonsense, as we have tried to show. Divorce figures indicate how fallacious this myth really is. Interviews with hundreds of couples clearly show that those who resign themselves to a static relationship are inviting divorce, desertion, or disaster. Disaster comes in many forms in marriage, from psychosomatic and mental illness all the way to the grim life of the Gruesome Twosome.

Perhaps in the rapidly changing world of the twentieth century the traditional family and marriage structure may become anachronistic. But at present the family unit and monogamous marriage still are the keystones of our culture, and we believe they are worth a lot of effort.

Part III

DESTRUCTIVE ELEMENTS IN MARRIAGE

24

THE MYTH OF
NORMALITY

Society has created artificial standards defining the good marriage, the bad marriage, the normal marriage. Many spouses are
upset because they are afraid their relationship doesn't "measure
up." This fear is unnecessary; it diminishes the value of their real
assets and limits the spouses' functionality.

Psychiatrists, psychologists, and others laboring in the arena of
mental-health research or service, constantly make judgments
about the relative degree of sickness of an individual. The public,
too, accepts the concept of normality and assumes that personalities and relationships can be classified as normal or abnormal.
Yet, surprisingly enough, there is no standard of normality which
can be used as a yardstick.

For some years, the Mental Research Institute in Palo Alto,
California, has been studying average families, obtained at
random either from the phone book or through the school system.
While no absolute standards have been determined, a few generalizations relevant to the consideration of normality and ab-
normality can be drawn from these studies. There appear to be
many different styles of family living, and many different child-
rearing practices, so that it is meaningless to say, for example,
that spanking is or is not good, or that the child should or should

not be treated in some particular fashion. There are families with
whom one would prefer to spend Christmas Day, and others who
would be better company on News Year's Eve, but one cannot
conclude that some of these are therefore superior, or more normal, than others. There are parents who appear to live together
in extreme harmony but have nervous children, and parents who
get along miserably but have children who seem to function quite
well. The underlying currents in the family are often subtle and
not discernible by talking to the family members individually.

Much child-rearing advice is based on the individual's recon-
struction of his own childhood. This is an unreliable approach—
not only because the years disguise what actually occurred, but
because family living is a game where not all of the rules are
known to the players. Much of the research on marriage and the
family has depended heavily or entirely on retrospective data
(the individual is asked, for example, to describe various aspects
of his childhood). Yet mothers have been known to have almost
totally unreliable memories concerning such relatively simple
matters as the ages at which their children walked, were toilet
trained, spoke, and so forth—even when the events occurred as
recently as five years earlier, and even though the mothers were
certain of the validity of their answers.

So, once more we caution spouses not to feel that their marriage
is a failure because it does not measure up to the "normal." There
is no such thing.

Nevertheless, even when artificial standards of judgment are
abandoned, it is of course evident that some marriages are less
successful than the participants would like them to be. In the
chapters that follow, various common difficulties are discussed.
Some of these, if allowed to persist, may eventually have a deeply
corrosive effect on the marital relationship. However, once the
spouses become aware of these destructive elements, they may
take steps to eliminate them; specific suggestions about how to do
so are included in our discussion.

25

THE FALLEN DOMINO

Some marriages are so fraught with nagging, destructive behavior, and the imputation of motives, that they seem to smoke from discord. The spouses appear to be on the point either of obtaining a divorce or of murdering each other. Yet, even in such cases it frequently happens that the relationship is reasonably sound. What has happened may resemble the collapse of a line of dominoes when the first one is hit—except that in this case the behavior is reversible. If the head domino is straightened up, the others may jump back into an upright position on their own. The problem, then, is to get that first domino straightened up.

In other words, in many instances of marital difficulty one powerful irritant has poisoned the relationship, and because both parties are perhaps stubborn or defensively rigid, this one destructive element contaminates the entire spectrum of marital behavior.

An example is the case of Cynthia and Joseph Special.

Cynthia and Joe had been happily married for four years. They didn't have much money and they had no children. Cynthia worked as a librarian and Joe worked for a paper-manufacturing company. Very slowly during the first four years they furnished their own home, paying cash for everything.

At the end of the four years, two things happened. A child was born—followed in a year by another—and Joe became assistant manager of the paper plant. Now Cynthia had of course left her

interesting job at the library and was home all day with two
infants. Joe, as assistant manager, no longer was able to leave the
office at five o'clock. He had to stay behind to check up on that
day's production, or to see about personnel, and attend the
executive meeting at six o'clock.

When Joe came home at about seven thirty, he was fatigued.
Cynthia was also fatigued. With two young children, the small
house was always untidy, and Cynthia didn't have time to prepare the kind of meals Joe was fond of. They no longer spent a
pleasant hour drinking a couple of cocktails, discussing the interesting things which happened during the day, followed by a
simple but elegant meal, eaten in leisurely fashion, and then a
play or a motion picture. Joe had his drink at the executive meeting, and when he arrived home he was eager to eat quickly and
go to bed. Slowly, Cynthia began to believe that they no longer
were companions or equals, that Joe had more interest in his
business than in his family. Joe felt that Cynthia was being selfish
when she wanted to go out after the children were asleep. He
became irritable when she asked him to skip having drinks with
the executives and, instead, go back to the old system of spending
an hour before dinner with her in the evening.

The situation is one with which most people are quite familiar.
Slowly, Cynthia began to take less interest in preparing even
reasonably fancy meals for dinner. Joe gulped his food and no
longer commented on her efforts. And when Joe was amorous in
bed, Cynthia said she was too tired from looking after the children, feeling vaguely angry that Joe seemed to be interested only
when *he* was in the mood, and was unresponsive to *her* needs
when she showed the initiative.

Joe started eating out with other executives two or three times
a week. Slowly, their needs became divergent in one area of their
relationship after another, and Cynthia and Joe were about ready
for a divorce.

Cynthia and Joe decided to consult a professional counselor
before they saw a lawyer. He recognized the falling-domino pattern almost immediately. He perceived that one basic, relatively
small irritant was poisoning the whole marriage system, and he
was able to suggest a solution. Here is what they did.

At the executive meetings at six o'clock, Joe abstained from having his cocktail and instead had what Franklin Delano Roosevelt called a horse's neck, ginger ale with a piece of lemon in it. Joe found he could now enjoy a drink a little bit later with his wife.

Instead of eating immediately upon returning home from the office, Joe took a hot shower and rested for almost an hour. The children were already asleep, and Cynthia too was able to shower and nap. When they got up, both put on fresh clothes and had a cocktail and dinner. What difference did it make if they ate at eight thirty every evening instead of seven thirty? The delay enabled them to refresh themselves and enjoy the evening.

When Joe had his two-week vacation, Cynthia visited her mother for two or three days while Joe stayed at home and took care of the children. The experience gave him some perspective on what a time-consuming job and intellectually unstimulating day Cynthia usually had.

At one of the office executive meetings, Joe pointed out that the problem of working late and getting home tired was probably common to all executives. He suggested that the wives be permitted to spend a day at the office, one at a time, to gain some understanding of their husbands' work and responsibilities. The president thought this was a good idea. Soon Cynthia spent a day watching Joe.

One night a week Cynthia hired a responsible baby-sitter and she and Joe went out to a restaurant. They gussied up, and had a gay evening just like old times.

Cynthia and Joe had a discussion as to whether his particular job with its extraordinarily long hours was worth keeping. Should he quit and find another one? Cynthia volunteered that since Joe had been promoted quite recently, it seemed normal for him to have long hours in the new position, but presumably when he became more familiar with the routine he would be able to maintain a more normal schedule again. Cynthia recognized that this was the difficult period in Joe's career, and she was happy to share the extra hard work. Joe responded sincerely that he knew caring for two small children was the most trying part of the family-raising cycle for Cynthia, and wondered what he could do to make life easier and more pleasant for her. In their discussion neither of them came up with any suggestions for making

Cynthia's labors less arduous and long, but in the mysterious manner of positive reinforcement, Joe's interest and appreciation made her work more acceptable.

How to Handle the Falling-Domino Pattern

To determine if a falling-domino situation exists in their own marriage, spouses should sit down together and each answer the following question (after tossing a coin to see who will go first):

"What is the one thing which annoys me the most about you?"

If the major complaints involve physical circumstances or clearly defined ways of behaving, the spouses may be able to correct them without outside help. Here are some examples of such complaints.

"I can't stand to make love when you've been drinking too much. It destroys your attractiveness."

"You always eat with your mouth open at the table, and it makes me sick to my stomach."

"Your bad breath drives me crazy."

"The house always looks like a pigsty."

"You're a slob. No matter how much I clean up the house, you always drop your clothes and ashes all over."

"Half the time you're late for dinner and you never telephone to let me know. Half our meals get burned."

"You've put on twenty pounds and I'm repulsed by fat people."

All of these complaints and annoyances are reasonably correctable. Yet if they are not corrected, they will cause problems in other areas. If a person registers a valid complaint of a correctable nature and the spouse—from stubbornness or lethargy—refuses to alter his behavior, it is likely that the complainer will in turn refuse to make changes requested by the other. The message here seems to be, "If you won't change for me, then I won't change for you." Most people actually fear giving in to another repeatedly because they sense that this will become a one-sided pattern and they will have to give in on everything henceforth. In many cases, this fear is justified. Only when the fear is proven to be ungrounded in fact, when the other party evidences an equal willingness to compromise and to change, can the fear be relinquished and relaxed flexibility take its place.

Once reasonable complaints are remedied, quite frequently other negative factors disappear. Just the act of getting together and discussing how to improve the marriage has a general therapeutic effect on many areas of behavior. The spouses are *trying* to have a functional relationship and that's half the victory. It's one big step toward realistic trust in a responsible partnership.

26

HOW TO DRIVE YOUR
SPOUSE CRAZY

In the discussion of the symmetrical relationship and the status struggle we mentioned that certain statements or actions may unconsciously be directed at the spouse in a derogatory, attacking manner by a person who is attempting to establish that he is the peer or the superior of the other, in order to build his self-esteem, his self-respect, his dignity. This behavior is often of the you-hurt-me-so-I'll-hurt-you variety; in many instances it becomes a form of mental plundering, pillaging, and weakening.

The cause of this sort of conduct is likely to be vague, hidden, or camouflaged. It may be something which the other partner is believed—whether correctly or not—to have done or to have omitted doing. Perhaps one of the spouses suffers from his own sense of inferiority and in compensation attempts to elevate himself by stepping on his partner. Often an individual may attack his spouse on any insignificant issue when his real criticism is related to something entirely different. For instance, a husband may nag his wife for being a mediocre cook (even though he really doesn't mind her cooking) because he is jealous of her social success. He is shy and awkward socially, but may unconsciously sense that if he attacks her on this issue, he automatically will expose his own feeling of inadequacy and his envy. In order to avoid painful self-disclosure, he chooses to pick on one of his wife's sensitive areas—her cooking. He is probably not even aware that he is doing it, and certainly does not understand *why*.

Attacks of this kind are not restricted to husbands and wives. They may involve employer and employee, brother and sister, two congressmen who happen to sit next to each other. But they are most obvious and (probably most damaging) in the case of marital partners simply because marriage lasts so long and is so intimate. Spouses cannot keep up a front with each other, no matter how much they wish to do so, or how hard they try to deceive themselves.

The symptoms of this type of human aggressiveness—though not necessarily the causes—have been reasonably well identified by psychiatrists and psychologists. In most cases in which marriages break up, several varieties of this destructive kind of behavior have been at work. It is probable that these patterns of behavior are present in almost all marriages, but they need not be damaging. In the same way, the germs of tuberculosis and pneumonia are present in the bodies of most human beings, but these pathogenic germs are kept under control and do not become pernicious unless the body becomes weakened by fatigue, other illnesses, or the malfunction of an organ. Correspondingly, in a healthy marriage the natural defense system of the individual can handle the derogatory attacks, sometimes by tolerance, sometimes by *quid pro quo* techniques, sometimes by rendering the attacks harmless through personal change or a good old-fashioned fight.

Many a spouse, after spending expensive months with a psychiatrist or marriage counselor, has at least become aware of the extreme, constant attacks that he unconsciously makes on the other. It is one of the great rewards of psychiatry to witness the client's explosive surprise upon recognizing that he has unconsciously been beating his partner into an emotional pulp. Usually the response is, "But I love my wife (or husband); how could I have done such a terrible thing for so many years?"

If this illumination comes before the partner has erected permanent defenses against the tormentor, there usually follows a satisfying revitalization of the marriage. Because the marriage process is an interlocking system, any one action which has been fed into it has effects in a dozen different ways. When a person.

recognizes and understands the attack he has been making on the other, he is likely, almost in a moment of revelation, to understand a variety of past experiences which were discordant and confusing.

In the hope that some readers will experience illuminations of this sort, we present in the following sections on "How to Drive Your Spouse Crazy" examples and analyses of the most common methods by which one partner attacks and cripples the other, without even knowing what he is doing.

Yet the reader should recognize that it is incorrect to say that one spouse has "ruined" or "castrated" or "undermined" the other. A law of physics states that every action has an equal and opposing reaction; correspondingly, while there is no victim without a victimizer, it is equally true that the victimizer requires a *willing subject*. For instance, there can be no aggressive or dominating husband unless there is an accepting or passive wife. However, in each of the following examples we are concerned only with techniques employed by one of the spouses; it is up to the reader to remember that this approach is used for the sake of simplicity, so that the reader perhaps will be able to recognize the complexities of actual life.

27

TECHNIQUE 1

The Incomplete Transaction

This destructive technique is especially effective against the spouse who is naturally aggressive and imaginative and seldom has the time to do everything he wants to do. The more the person is a success in his profession or business, and wants the same degree of control in his home, the more effectively this destructive technique can be used against him. It consists of subtly undercutting the efforts of the aggressive spouse in a frustrating manner which can't be readily identified. Here is an example.

John Z. Alderson has a deep feeling of resentment toward his wife, Eloise. Whenever they are together he is ill at ease, frustrated, and in a smoldering sort of way, angry at her. John thinks about this often, with a sense of shame and guilt, for he cannot understand his feeling of frustration and annoyance at his wife.

"Why should I feel this way?" his thoughts run. "Poor Eloise works so hard. She is a sweet, thoughtful person and certainly a good mother. I really have little excuse for being so angry at her so much of the time, especially since the things which annoy me are so trivial."

The reader is now invited into the Alderson home.

It is seven thirty in the morning. John has just finished shaving

and in a few minutes will go down to have breakfast with
Eloise. He reaches into his dresser drawer for a clean shirt, but
the drawer is empty.

"Eloise!"

"Yes, dear."

"How come I'm out of shirts again?"

"But, dear," Eloise says, "by having the laundryman come just
every other week, we're saving considerable money on the
laundry."

Eloise's remark doesn't seem quite logical to John. He
scratches his head and begins thinking that perhaps his own
logic is faulty, although he doesn't know what the error is. He
grunts to himself, looks in the mirror, shrugs his shoulders, and
rummages around in the laundry basket for an already used shirt.
He puts it on, and selected a bow tie instead of a four-in-hand,
because the bow tie hides the wrinkles in the soiled collar a
little better.

When John has finished dressing he goes into the kitchen.
Eloise is humming happily to herself as she spoons coffee out of
a two-pound can.

"Eloise, for God's sake, I've asked you not to buy two-pound
cans of coffee. The damn stuff gets stale on us and loses its
flavor. You know how much a good cup of coffee means to me."

Eloise looks at him somewhat maternally. She shakes her
head and smiles patiently. "But, darling, I couldn't resist; I save
twenty cents a can when I buy it on sale."

"Eloise, I don't give a damn if you save five dollars a can.
Stale coffee is stale coffee. Please don't buy two-pound cans
anymore."

"Yes, darling."

Twenty minutes later, as John is leaving for the office, he
notices some cobwebs in the corner behind the sofa. Now he
starts looking. His eyes go around the room, and he observes (as
he has several times recently) that there is dirt behind all the
furniture.

"Eloise!"

"Yes, darling."

"When are we going to get the cleaning service?"

"But we've talked about it before; remember, the day after your birthday we outlined the whole plan. . . ."

"Oh? Eloise, I think you work hard enough as it is, and if we both want a clean house, which I certainly do, why can't we employ the cleaning service?"

"Oh, darling, you know how spooky I feel about having strangers in the house. Those cleaning men are always underfoot. They shove the furniture around, and I can't do a thing while they're here except stand around and bite my fingernails. Really, darling, I'd much rather do the cleaning myself."

"I know, Eloise, but you're terribly busy as it is now, with the children, and the PTA, and your reorganization at the Red Cross, and that business you're doing for senile elderly people. I understand how important all these things are. But after all, there are only so many hours in the day, and you can't be so active and keep the house clean too."

Eloise looks at John. Her eyes grow watery. She bites her lips and says, "That's all right, darling, I'll do the very best I can. Anything I can do to help you by being a good wife, is what I want to do." With this Eloise turns and walks into the bedroom to make the bed hastily before leaving for a meeting of the local Red Cross chapter.

John leaves the house and heads for his automobile. All the way to the office he finds his stomach growling. A throbbing ache is beginning at the back of his neck and spreading up into the occipital region. He feels rather bitter toward the world at large—but he knows only vaguely that it is related to his wife.

However oversimplified the above incident may seem, it does exemplify a particular behavior pattern commonplace in many marriages.

In this case, Eloise is a master tactician, even though she doesn't realize it. By assuming the "one-down" position, by ~~being~~ considerate, thoughtful, and above all patient, she is slowly driving John nuts. He is angry and frustrated for no apparent reason, and so can only conclude (unbelievingly) that something must be wrong with him alone.

What has characterized their conversation is *the absence of a completed transaction.* No decisions have been made.

Eloise's manner suggests to John that she will do *anything he desires*, but the logic of his past experiences with her indicates that *she will not*. He is completely frustrated and angry and doesn't know how to deal with the situation. His own conclusions about it swing from one extreme to the other; sometimes he believes his wife is a liar, and at other times he feels there is something terribly wrong with him.

Both of his conclusions are correct. But husband and wife alike are unaware of what they are doing.

How to Handle the Incomplete Transaction

There is a place in the best of marriages for occasional bluntness or even rudeness. Occasionally, even an out-and-out fight may be in order; as long as it falls short of homicide, it will probably leave both spouses refreshed. At times we all let relationships become complacent and limited by incomplete transactions. Our garage man, for example, may take us for granted, and for a while we accept his "Sure, sure, Mr. Smith, I'll take care of it," but often he does not take care of it, and makes endless reasonable excuses instead. Finally, one day we blow up and say, "God damn it, Barney, get that carburetor fixed or I'll take my business elsewhere." As a result of this explosion he has more respect for us, we have more respect for ourselves, and the limits of the relationship have been clarified.

Similarly, in marriage there is no miraculous method for carving out a relationship without occasional struggles. One cannot make an omelet without breaking eggs, and one cannot make a marital relationship without breaking some of the other spouse's expectations and built-in preconceptions, and forestalling his very human tendency to try for a foot when a few inches have just been offered.

In the case of Eloise and John, the issues John raises are never dealt with directly by Eloise; when a conversation ends John never knows whether or not he has scored a point, whether or not his wife has understood him.

It is important to remember that Eloise doesn't recognize what she is doing. As far as she is concerned, she is attempting to mollify an unreasonable man and to delay his demands by placating him. Her manner suggests to John that she will do anything he desires, but somehow or other, she usually manages to change the subject under discussion, and she never fulfills her implied promise to do what he wants. By behaving inconsiderately while *appearing* to be considerate, thoughtful, and patient, she is slowly driving John to distraction: he never knows definitely what he can realistically expect from her.

This pattern of behavior is a tried and true one, used in diplomacy when one nation is trying to stall another on some urgent matter. Attempting to drag out an incomplete transaction, the nation will counter the other's proposal with something like, "But do you really think that such a thing is moral?" or "Please define precisely what you mean by 'peace.'"

The incomplete transaction is a serious form of faulty communication. The reader will recall from a previous chapter that every message has at least three aspects: the report aspect, the command aspect, and the context aspect. For two people to communicate effectively, the listener must understand all three aspects of a message correctly. If they conflict or are incongruous, understanding is impossible. The person receiving an incongruous message must ask for clarification if he is to understand and react appropriately.

In the example of Eloise and John, there is an incongruity in Eloise's messages. The report aspect says one thing, and the command and context aspects say something else. What John has failed to do is to clarify the command aspects of her messages. When she says, "I'll do the very best I can," the report she is giving appears to be one of willingness. When she did not act accordingly, it becomes clear that though the report aspect conveys one message, the command aspect conveys another: "I don't think it's good for you," or "I don't think it's necessary," or something of that sort. Each time John accepts the report aspect of her message without clarifying the command aspect, the problem increases.

John is just as culpable as Eloise. He says he needs more clean shirts, and Eloise states benevolently that she is saving money. The issue of money is irrelevant and tangential. John has sufficient income, and laundry bills are no problem. Yet he fails to respond to this issue because Eloise's benevolent tone sidetracks him. Possibly the circumstances of his own rearing have made him susceptible to apparent benevolence, and his experience with Eloise had reinforced this response.

Spouses who wish to eliminate the destructive pattern of incomplete transactions, should practice the following exercise.

If both spouses are collaborating in the effort to change this pattern, each must make a special effort to listen to the other's statements; and when a statement is not absolutely clear, the confused spouse must query it, indicating, for example, that the meaning or the context is obscure, or that the tone of voice seems to imply something that doesn't fit with the words.

If a spouse feels that this method is too dangerous or confusing, or that he is not up to practicing together, he can practice by himself, analyzing in writing the kinds of things the other spouse does with words and meanings that are confounding and confusing.

If a spouse finds himself the recipient of a tangential answer, like Eloise's response to John about his shirts, he must firmly insist on the substantive outcome. For example, if Eloise states with her persuasive and benevolent pleading, "But, honey, even if you have plenty of money it's silly to throw it away on laundry!" John must reply with something like, "Perhaps I'm misunderstanding you. What I hear you saying is that you refuse to send my shirts to the laundry and would rather have me wear a dirty shirt to the office than spend another quarter. Is that what you mean?"

Eloise probably will say that this is not what she means; she is just trying to be a good wife and help John save money. If John accepts this answer, the result once again is an incomplete transaction, and the destructive effects of her apparent benevolence spread out a little further. Here John must reply with something like, "I know, Eloise, and I appreciate your point of view, but I definitely need more shirts, and I want the laundry to come to the house every week to pick them up. From my point of view, you'll be a good wife if you arrange to have my shirts clean. Now will you or won't you do this for me?"

If this method is followed, the incomplete transaction pattern will gradually be eliminated. The vice president of a large company reported in an article that after simple techniques of this sort for clarity of communication were introduced throughout the organization, the board of the company estimated that within several months efficiency rose 40 per cent.

Unfortunately, our American notions of romance, chivalry, and ladylike and gentlemanly behavior make it difficult for young couples to believe that fighting is permissible—and may even be necessary. If husbands and wives are to clarify what each other's limits are—determining how much can be asked for in any one time period without evidence of immediate return, and who (correctly or not) believes he is doing more of the giving—and if they are to find answers for the many other relationship questions that arise, there is no alternative to frank talk or action, even at the risk of temporarily damaging the relationship.

To put it simply, the motto of young spouses (or any two people) trying to work out a relationship should be, "If you can't tell someone to go to hell, you can't love him very much." It takes courage to shake the status quo, but if the relationship isn't worth a risk to improve it, it is bound to be forever limited and burdened by its own stagnation.

28

TECHNIQUE 2

"Thank You for Nothing, Darling"

Here is another spouse-killing technique employed frequently in our affluent society.

Marge Edgeworth looks across the settee at her husband, who is engrossed in the evening paper. Between them sits a tinkling martini pitcher, and Marge is sipping her second drink. This is her method of gaining courage, and she needs it, for earlier in the afternoon she decided to put an end to a situation which has been bothering her.

She clenches her fists, sits up straight.

"George, put down that paper," she says in a loud half-command, half-whine.

"Eh, what?"

"Put down that damned paper," shouts Marge.

"Oh, oh . . . sure."

George lets the newspaper fall to his lap, removes his glasses, and says, "Well, what's up?"

"George," Marge says, trying to speak calmly, "why don't we ever talk together anymore?"

George looks at her quizzically and drops his shoulders, a sign of constraint. "I didn't know we weren't talking to each other, dear."

"Oh, come now, you know what I mean. You used to tell me about things, your work and all. That was when you always used to say you loved me."

George looks at his wife as if he were about to curse. He scratches his ear and with effort forces a smile. "Well, dear, what would you like to talk about?"

This routine of George's deserves the label of "the perfect squelch."

Marge twirls her martini glass because she finds herself unable to think of anything to say. She wants to get some conversation from her husband, not to make a speech herself. She doesn't know, has never yet learned, that one *cannot* compel a "spontaneous" response.

"Well, I don't know," she says after a long pause. "Did anything interesting happen today?"

"No, no, dear, not a thing. Just the usual routine."

George starts to pick up the paper. He hesitates, looking over the top of his spectacles.

"Oh, by the way, Marge, we'll be going to the Waterhouses tomorrow night and I think it would be a good idea if you got a new dress. You've been much too conservative about spending money on yourself, and I think you've got a new dress coming."

"Oh, thank you, dear," says Marge with a grateful smile. "I'll take a look and see what I can find."

While she is speaking, George has returned to his paper. Marge reaches for the pitcher to start her third martini.

If a psychiatrist were to step into their living room at that moment and say, "Look here, George, old fellow, you're being destructive," this husband would be startled. George regards himself as a generous man. He considers his wife's life easy and pleasant. And he is absolutely sure that his business success is responsible for the pleasant life that Marge is leading. How can she complain when he is working so hard and doing so much for her? "Why," he thinks to himself, "it's almost a shame how hard executives work to maintain their families. The coronary rate of executives is the highest in the nation." The fact that this has nothing to do with what Marge is talking about is completely ignored.

Somehow Marge is unable to bring her complaint into the

open. If she does buy a dress for the Waterhouse party, especially
if it's an expensive one, she has further contributed to her own
problem. How can you complain about a man who allows you to
buy whatever you want?

Characteristic of this type of marital combat is the way in
which George suggests—almost requires—Marge to buy things
for herself. Or he may encourage her to visit her sister twice a
week or to take a class at the local college in order to entertain
herself, thereby reducing her demands on him for companionship.
*More and more Marge will learn to wait for these suggestions
before she takes action.* Particularly when one receives a reward—
such as a new dress—for following another's dictates, loss of
initiative is the usual result. For example, animals are trained
to obey commands instantly by being given food each time they
obey. After a few weeks or months of this reinforcement by
rewards, they rely heavily on their masters' commands to determine their behavior. A "well-trained" animal has *learned to* not
take initiative. Marge, also, under a "reward" system such as that
used by George, begins to lose her initiative, and this loss in turn
places more responsibility on George to arrange her life for her.

A vicious cycle develops, for she gets from George only the
bare victuals of life, not the emotional nourishment she desires
and needs. But rather than get nothing at all from him she plays
the game "Thanks, darling." At the same time she does not help
George solve *their* problem, because by accepting, she gives him
the illusion that he is doing what she wants and thus has satisfied
her. George also has *learned* his role. If Marge refuses the gifts
and insists on more companionship instead, George will have to
learn a new role because he will then know that the gifts are not
those Marge desires most and that therefore, although they may
be effective in silencing her complaints for the moment, she will
soon be dissatisfied again.

Many women, too, take George's role in this game.

How to Handle the "Thank-You-for-Nothing" Pattern

What can be done to break up a "thank-you-for-nothing" behavior pattern? As in any of the marital misery games, it is essen-

tial to change the old routine. First of all, Marge must begin to take more initiative in determining her own behavior. One way is for her to respond each time George proposes that she buy something by saying, in effect, "A new dress? No, thank you, but I'll take the money because I'm going to spend the weekend in New York with Mary so we can see some Broadway shows." This technique accomplishes two things. It allows Marge to refuse and yet not to be denied, and it causes George to realize that he does not make his offer because he is completely benevolent, that he is not simply trying to please his wife. Marge, in order to change their relationship, should plan or buy something at least equal in value to whatever George has offered—but chosen by herself. If when Marge asks George to talk to her he suggests that she might go to a movie with her sister, Marge is to say, for example, "No thank you, dear, but I think I'll ask some of my friends to come over for a game of bridge."

Concurrently, a technique should be employed that is planned to reduce the repetitious aspect of this pattern, the routine meals and the nightly hiding-behind-the-newspaper act. Marge should take the initiative and responsibility for deliberately planning activities for the two of them—going to the theater, dinner parties, movies, or whatever. Marge should anticipate that they may not enjoy themselves, that there may not even be good conversation. The point is not that they have a good time, for like spontaneity, enjoyment cannot be compelled. Rather, the purpose is to initiate changes which will help break up the old patterns.

If George requires even more confrontation to make a change, Marge should aggressively arrange, and press, their going out two or three times a week, within the limit of their finances, until George rebels and thus becomes conscious of the repetitiousness of their past behavior. They can then negotiate a "happy medium" that will be acceptable and reasonable for both. As in most bargaining it is often wise to set one's initial "price" a little higher than one requires, expecting to come down in the course of the negotiations.

29

TECHNIQUE 3

The Mind-Reading Act

Sue Bernard is sweet, bright, and cute. At 105 pounds, five feet one inch tall, she seems incapable of driving Sam, her 220 pound ex-tackle husband, into frantic confusion. Yet she can, and she is very, very good at it.

Every day, Sam Bernard returns home on the five-thirty commuter train. All the way up from the station, he thinks of getting home, of a Scotch and soda, some soft music, and his sweet Sue, who can be fragile, cuddly, a small but strong bulwark against the nasty competitive world of stocks and bonds.

It is now 6:05 P.M. at the Bernard residence. Sue has seen Sam come up the walk. She opens the front door just as Sam reaches for it with his key. The welcoming is thus a bit unnerving, especially as she gasps, "Oh, darling, you look so tired!"

Thus doubly taken aback, Sam feels a bit vulnerable. He responds without protest to her mothering invitation to sit in his favorite chair while she gets him a drink.

Her wide brown eyes peer steadily over the rim of her gin and tonic (Sam also has one, since she didn't ask—and he didn't say—that he preferred a Scotch and soda).

"Darling, you're angry about something. Yes," continues Sue

before Sam has a chance to reply, "you are. You forget how well I know you. Why don't you tell me what it's about?"

"Sue, I don't know what you're getting at. I am a little *tired.* I am not angry." His voice starts to get strident.

"All right, if you won't say. I don't see why you can't share anything with me any more. I just wanted to help."

"Damn it, I don't need help. I'd like to listen to Miles Davis and relax a bit before dinner. Is that asking too much?"

"Well, I like that! I told you you were angry. Now you're taking it out on me. You're mean and nasty and I'm getting sick and tired of it," says Sue petulantly, flouncing off to the kitchen.

Sam can hear the clanging of pots and the mild banging of dishes, a sure sign that sweet Sue is sour. Sitting and sipping the bitter gin and tonic, Sam feels his stomach ache as if a big tackle had put an elbow into his gut. He is puzzled and despairing.

Sam has unwittingly encouraged Sue's destructive "mind reading" by not dealing with it specifically. He has permitted Sue to control and anger him almost any time she wishes.

Husbands play the mind-reading game too. This vicious process could have worked the other way around. For example Sue might have been looking ahead to Sam's return, and he might have entered the front door saying, "Oh, I see you've had a bad day?"

"No, as a matter of fact . . ."

"The house always looks a mess when you've been feeling bad. Are you beginning to be premenstrual?" And then it would have started.

Sometimes both spouses practice this arcane art. While it makes for interesting listening for a marital therapist, it is hell for both participants, who join the world's most misunderstood people.

How to Break Up the Mind-Reading Act

What can be done to help the mind reader refrain from practicing this destructive technique?

The spouse who wishes to correct this behavior in his mate can do so *if* he skillfully and consistently follows the proper method, even for a short period. He must *always agree* with the mind reader. In fact, it is desirable to *over agree,* as in the following dialogue.

SUE: Oh darling, I know you're just beat. You must sit down here.

SAM: Thanks, darling. You're right. I've *never* been so tired. Could you get me a drink while I lie down?

SUE: Certainly, sweetheart. You've had a bad day, I can see that.

SAM: You don't know the half of it. Everything went wrong. To begin with, I may have to fire my secretary. Did I tell you some of the things that girl did?

SUE: Oh, excuse me, darling, I must see to supper. I'm sure you'll feel better after a hot meal.

SAM: Well, I don't know if I'll be able to eat anything, but I can try.

SUE (*Retreating in confusion*): Oh, that's fine, hon. I'll call you.

This technique depends on the principle of the *reductio ad absurdum*, in which by carrying something to its logical conclusion one shows it to be ridiculous. What the mind reader says is usually irrefutable, so argument does no good. But he doesn't expect agreement, and when he gets it he becomes confused, for he depends on omnipotence and surprise in order to retain the advantage. Now he is suddenly afraid to continue; he doesn't know where his remarks may lead.

This is not an easy technique to use, but some practice before a mirror will help.

30

TECHNIQUE 4

The Handy Heart and the Convenient Cancer

HIGH BLOOD
PRESSURE
- ABUSE

The Jewish mother is not the only one among our kind who uses the threat of imminent demise to achieve mastery over someone else. In the caricatures she is shown bending her children to her will by clutching at her chest and crying out in martyred tones, "Go ahead, do what you want to, don't mind me!" the implication being that she won't be around much longer anyway. One classic is the story of the young Jewish boy who called his mother to inform her that he was about to elope with a Catholic girl. His mother listened patiently and congratulated her son upon his choice. He was surprised and a little suspicious. Then the mother went on to say that they should come back to live in her apartment after the honeymoon. The son said, "But Mom, you only have one bedroom."

And Mom replied, "So who's gonna need two bedrooms? After I've jumped off the bridge, the two of you will be living here by yourselves."

Spouses have been known to attempt mastery over each other by the utilization of subtle symptoms. Unfortunately for the one who uses illness as a weapon, he eventually begins to fool himself and does indeed feel "poorly" even when there is no physical reason for it. One of the classics, of course, is the headache which prevents the acceptance of an unwanted invitation or means that the husband must take his unexpected visitor out to dinner because his wife is lying down in the bedroom with a "migraine." The husband who is unable to do anything around the house because of his "weak heart" or "murmur" or "sick stomach" is not uncommon in our society. Then there is the pale, tired husband or wife who "suffers" quietly and by doing so maintains control over the other spouse. The implication is that early death can be expected from mysterious ailments which the doctors can't quite diagnose. The more cheerful and energetic the "healthy" spouse becomes, the "sicker" the sufferer gets.

Unfortunately, this game can be played by both partners at the same time, and then it is just that much more difficult to correct. In one situation we knew, the husband was going to college while the energetic wife worked and kept house. The husband complained more and more frequently of vague pains and exhaustion, even though he studied only sporadically, made rather poor grades, and spent hours watching television. As time went on, the wife began to feel more and more used, particularly as the husband refused to help her around the house, claiming "exhaustion," and would study only at night, when she had returned from work and wanted help and companionship. Before long, the wife too, began to come home from work "exhausted," with stomach cramps and aches and pains which prevented her preparing dinner or cleaning house. By the end of the school year, the husband was failing his studies and the couple ate out four or five times a week; both felt exhausted, and television had become their sole source of "companionship." Each was so determined to master the other, that the problem was never solved. The day the husband finished school, his wife left him. Within weeks, the wife was busier than ever in her profession and feeling fine, and the husband began to swim and play tennis regularly. In this unfortunate case, the solution used to prevent "chronic illness and death by exhaustion" in two healthy people was divorce.

How to Counteract the Handy-Heart Technique

The following method is helpful in reducing the impact of this destructive technique in a marriage.

The "healthy" spouse insists that the "sick" spouse visit a competent physician, and accompanies him on the visit. If he is already under a physician's care, arrangements must be made for a consultation with a specialist not known socially by either husband or wife. This is necessary because the family physician too can be fooled, as a result of his wish to be helpful and of his own doubts. *He may unwittingly be helping the "victim" to preserve the "illness."*

If a clean bill of health is forthcoming, the complaining spouse must be forced to live in a way befitting a healthy person. If some chronic physical condition is present, clear rules on diet, the amount of exercise permitted, and so forth, should be obtained from the physician, so that the "sick" spouse cannot exaggerate the degree of his illness. It is not unkind to push a spouse into good health. It is far less kind to nourish and encourage illness by falling for such a destructive technique.

One of our colleagues was upset by his wife's constant use of vague aches and pains to avoid any activity which did not interest her, and decided to do something about it. First he took time off from work to have his wife thoroughly checked at the Mayo Clinic. The physicians reported her as "healthy in all respects." When they returned home, he made careful arrangements for his wife's financial care, and moved out of the house, telling his wife that he would not return because her imaginary illnesses were too much for him.

After several weeks the spouse recognized that he meant what he said. She began to play golf and engage in other activities possible for a healthy female. Nearly a year, and one girl friend, later the husband invited her to go on a trip to Europe with him. When they returned after six weeks, they moved to a different house together. Now, some ten years later, they have apparently passed the critical years and the marriage has prospered. While it is unusual for a spouse to be so direct, action of the sort taken by this husband is the basis for many cures.

31

TECHNIQUE 5

The Pseudobenevolent Dictatorship

Some people are just so good it hurts—really hurts. The technique which we call pseudobenevolence is one that can drive a spouse crazy in no time, and it is common in our society.

The pseudobenevolent dictator may be the husband or the wife, or both; his identifying characteristic is that he *imagines* that he is an abundant giver and can anticipate or *know* the needs of his spouse. The problem is that the victimizer fails to recognize and show approval of the expressed needs or real desires of his partner. This behavior has something in common with the mind-reading act described earlier, in that both rest on unclear communication and the assumption that one person "knows" what the other is really feeling, wishing, or thinking.

In one young couple we knew (whose marriage lasted less than five years), the husband brought frequent little gifts to his wife. One day he would burst in with a chocolate malt (his wife was on a diet) and say boyishly, "I thought you needed a treat!" A few weeks later, he would bring home two tickets to a night baseball game because his wife had been wanting a night out (his wife hated sports and for months had been nagging to be taken dancing; her husband hated dancing). This went on and on. If the wife needed new clothes, the husband might surprise her by picking out a dress on sale which he "knew" was just right for her, even though she preferred to do her own clothes shopping. After every such gift, the husband would look expectant, proud, and pleased because he was being such a considerate person.

The wife played right into the game. Not about to be labeled the "bad guy" in this twosome, she would praise the husband for his thoughtfulness, and accept the gift. She seldom had the courage to object.

The pseudobenevolent dictator sometimes senses that the happiness of his spouse is only feigned, so he may end up feeling just as depressed as the recipient. Since neither realizes what is happening, the giver may regard the receiver as ungrateful, while the receiver thinks the giver is super-selfish.

The person who believes he is benevolent usually does not recognize the discrepancy in his behavior. He overlooks the fact that "benevolence" based on *one's own fantasy* of what the other person wants, or *one's own need* to give, turns out to be dictatorship. It cuts the other person out, and any hints or clues the other delivers that he feels left out are ignored, or simply not heard, or seen as lack of appreciation. If the victim tries to press his point, the conversation may go something like this:

"What do you mean I never do anything for you? I took you to the movies two nights ago."

"But, darling, you forget I didn't want to see that movie. I was tired that night and told you I'd rather go to bed early."

"You did not. You just said you were tired, and I thought the movie would relax you."

"But *you* were the one who wanted to see that movie! I hate John Wayne movies!"

"Boy, see if I ever do anything for you again. Other wives never get taken out, and when I try to do better, you nag me for it. That's the last time."

The imputation of desire as illustrated here, is not the same as responding to the spouse's *real needs*, expressed or unexpressed. In some cases, a spouse may certainly give spontaneously without being asked, because as a result of past experience he knows that his partner desires a particular gift, or loves to cuddle at bedtime, or likes a certain meal especially well. If a person is genuinely sensitive to another's needs, and gives to fulfill these rather than his own, he should rightfully be called—not a pseudobenevolent dictator—but in romantic terms, a lover!

How to Overthrow a Pseudobenevolent Dictator

When next the pseudobenevolent dictator offers an unwelcome gift or proposes some undesirable recreation, his spouse must refuse politely and follow up by saying, for example, "But since you are in a giving mood, I would appreciate it if we could go to a show," or "Thanks so much for the sweater, darling. I notice, however, that it's your favorite color—olive green—and I've been telling you that I plan to buy a pink one. I hope you won't be disappointed when I exchange it tomorrow."

The recipient of phony benevolence is as guilty as the giver— if he accepts what is offered. The recipient *must* object, thanking the giver but firmly stating that he prefers to determine the nature of the gift or favor. If the pseudobenevolent spouse is *really* trying to please or cooperate, he will accept the change, for if he doesn't he demonstrates that he was indeed being a dictator. If he does not accept the suggestions, the spouse may have to be insistent.

32

TECHNIQUE 6

"I Could Be the Best Husband (Wife) in the World, If Only My Spouse Would Be Different"

There are many spouses who operate according to a tit-for-tat system. If Mary performs and behaves in a manner which John desires, then John will behave in a manner which Mary desires. But if Mary displeases John (and sometimes he requires the impossible), then John will, with effort and planning, behave so as to make Mary as miserable as he can. Unlike the *quid pro quo* process, in which the relationship agreements originate largely out of awareness, the tit-for-tat system implies a revengeful kind of conscious motivation which seeks equality in a punitive way that cannot possibly succeed. (Unfortunately, even nations seem not to have learned this elementary distinction.)

The following statements are characteristic expressions of the tit-for-tat relationship.

"If you treated me as if you really loved me, I could stand anything, accomplish anything."

"You are negative about everything I do. Whether I swing a big deal or take the children camping, you suggest that it could have been done better. When we do things together, you always try to take charge, making it clear that my method is no good. If you encouraged me, the sky would be the limit in our relationship."

"If you'd only make a good home, I'd be here all the time, and I'd be loving."

"If only you wouldn't drink so much, I wouldn't be so nervous and bitchy."

"If you didn't interrupt me whenever I started talking, I'm sure I could cure myself of the habit of using filthy language about the house."

"If you didn't shout at me or embarrass me in front of strangers, and if you'd hold my hand and look after me at parties, I'm sure I'd never flirt again in my life."

"If you'd only read a few important books and some good newspapers, maybe we could find something to talk about."

"If you'd stop going to those damned bridge parties every afternoon and stay home more . . ."

"If you didn't watch television day and night and would talk to me just a little . . ."

"If you'd stop apologizing to guests about the miserable house, the poor meals . . ."

"If you'd only go to cooking school and learn how to prepare a meal . . ."

"If you'd only be a little neater and stop dropping your ashes all over the house . . ."

"If you'd only stop pampering the children . . ."

In each of these statements, one spouse indicates that he feels his own behavior depends on that of his partner.

Here we have the old chicken-and-egg problem. Even if it would help for the husband to be neater and for the wife to play less bridge, *who will make the first move?* And if someone *does* take the initiative, will his spouse regard this as an admission that he is the villain? More important, are these complaints valid, or do they really represent oversimplified attacks based on more general relationship problems? There are ways to avoid *some* of these traps, and we shall describe suitable methods. But in any event, if *you* find yourself simply blaming your spouse for all your problems, you had better seek a new constructive approach. For whatever else you do, you would have a hard time picking a *worse* technique to help a bad situation.

How to Handle the "If-Only-You . . ." Situation

One of the most common complaints that a marriage counselor hears begins with the words, "If only John [or Mary] would . . ." Here one spouse presents the need for a unilateral change on the part of the other. The person who has been labeled as inadequate usually responds by presenting alibis, or by attacking his spouse on some other grounds in an attempt to change the subject. In doing so, he is making a mistake. Instead, he should recognize that if he *did* make the particular change requested, the other spouse would probably discover that it didn't alter their relationship as much as he had expected.

Therefore, the attacked spouse (the one considered to be in the wrong) should insist that the natural consequences of making the suggested change be considered. He should point out that a change on his part will also require a change on the part of the other spouse, and should attempt to project what these changes would be like. The question then would be, are these projected changes desirable or undesirable? Are the husband and wife even prepared to handle them?

For example, a man who is well informed and is respected for his obvious intelligence may feel that his wife should be better read and better able to hold her own in a discussion. It is true that if his wife became more intellectually competent, they might share more together, but is he willing to pay the price? If she sharpened her powers, perhaps the man would find his own self-esteem and sense of importance, derived from being the "smart" one in the family, suffering greatly. Is he really prepared for her competition? Can he relinquish his position in the spotlight at social functions? Is he ready to *help* his wife contribute to conversations by listening intelligently to her, or does he expect her to attempt to shine despite his continuing efforts to appear smarter than she is?

In other words, we are urging the spouse who is told to change to evaluate this request in terms of how it will affect the other partner, and to insist that change involves a joint effort and is not up to him alone. Equally, the critical spouse is urged to evaluate his request in terms of what corresponding changes will be necessary on his part and to *refrain from asking for changes to which he cannot adapt.*

This concept may, at first, be hard to grasp because it is completely antithetical to our usual way of thinking about marriage. We assume that if we wish our spouse to change in a particular way, he will—if he is loving—immediately attempt to oblige. But actually, in a marriage most of the important behavior patterns (we are not speaking of such minor annoying habits as dropping ashes or leaving hair in the wash basin) are products of the relationship and not just manifestations of traits peculiar to one spouse.

Consider, for example, a gentleman we know who has become increasingly vociferous in his comments about his wife's slovenly housekeeping. He neglects to mention to his friends, during his numerous complaints, that his wife accompanies him in many activities (far more than the usual). For example, they often go sailing together, they hunt, and they fly a private plane in which she is the navigator. Since there is not enough money for a maid, the housework just remains undone.

The question here is why the condition of the house is so important to the husband. Is he simply a person of compulsive neatness, or is he protesting that his wife's role is becoming too close to his own and that he is uncomfortable about this closeness and would like to push her back to a more "feminine" role? If she simply takes the blame for the untidy house, they will never face the question of the shared-role conflict, which may be the important issue in their marriage. As long as he is free to complain about a slovenly house he has the feeling that he is asserting his control over her, while at the same time nothing can actually happen, so there is no danger of an upsetting change.

The spouse who is being criticized in this case might appropriately wonder why her husband doesn't pitch in more and help clean up the house since it seems important to him and since it also seems important to him to have her share in his many activities. Does she sense that he requires this kind of complaint in order to keep their marriage workable? To test this hypothesis she might propose that during the next several weeks she give up all her other activities and concentrate on pleasing her husband, by keeping the house immaculate. If the husband's complaint is functional—that is, if it is related to the marital system and does not simply reflect his liking for cleanliness—some other source for complaint will emerge to take the place of the no-longer-dirty house. When it becomes evident that the complaining is related to a larger relationship pattern, the couple is in a position to discuss the larger problems with some chance of making *basic changes* to improve the relationship, and can learn to avoid repetitious arguments over topical and insignificant issues.

It is important now to take a closer look at the behavior of the spouse who asks for changes in the other by complaining. Such an individual contributes to the other's unwanted behavior by *permitting it and complaining afterward.* The tendency to nag and complain instead of refusing to tolerate unwanted behavior is widespread in marriages in our culture. A husband may accuse his wife of being inconsiderate because she repeatedly interrupts him. But how often will he prevent this behavior *at the time it occurs* by saying, "You interrupted me, Jane. Please let me finish what I was saying"? If this didn't work, he might simply get up and leave the room, saying, "You apparently aren't interested in what I'm trying to tell you now. When you do want to hear it, let me know." A few such episodes would get the point across quickly and without unnecessary anger. This type of behavior may seem harsh and rude, but it does work. The practice of nagging and complaining does not, because it never *deals explicitly with the unwanted behavior at the time it occurs.* However, people prefer complaining just because it is futile: if they actually enforced a change in the other's behavior, they would have to change their own behavior as well. If Bill is firmer than he used to be about Jane's interruptions, he must also give up the privilege of interrupting *her,* or else risk having her walk out on him in her turn.

Mary may harbor burning resentment toward John because he makes jokes or sarcastic remarks about her intelligence or physical appearance in front of acquaintances. Yet if this behavior on John's part continues over a long period of time, it is a sure bet that she has done nothing to stop it. Perhaps she smiles or laughs with embarrassment in response to these remarks, or perhaps she counterattacks with nasty remarks of her own about John's messy living habits, his bald spot, and so on. Later, when they are alone once more, Mary may just sulk, or she may explode and tell John his behavior makes her furious, so that their nastiness escalates into a fight, or mutual withdrawal, or whatever. If Mary really wants to put a stop to John's unkind actions, she must be willing to change her own behavior. The next time they are with friends and John is insulting, Mary might say, *in front of the friends,* "John, your remarks are humiliating and inappropriate. I suspect they make our friends as uncomfortable as they do me. If you have something to tell me, wait until we get home and can discuss it in privacy." If John persists in his behavior, Mary can rightfully say, "I asked you once to stop your unpleasant remarks, John. I won't argue with you here and embarrass our friends, but neither will I tolerate this kind of talk. I'm taking a cab home and I'll see you there later." One or two such confrontations evidencing Mary's determination and willingness to change *her own* behavior in relation to his undesirable behavior will force John to make a corresponding change.

Again, the reader may shudder at such tough, harsh recommendations, but marriage is so important, and so difficult to make workable, that there is no place for half-truths and half-hearted actions.

One of the most useful ways for spouses to correct unwanted behavior patterns and improve a marriage is always to act on the assumption that their actions are bilateral, not unilateral. There is no action involving them both to which they haven't both contributed. Therefore, any change must be made by both.

33

TECHNIQUE 7

The Disaster Seeker

There are more disaster seekers in our society than most people realize. In the symmetrical, or status-struggle, type of relationship, disaster seeking is frequently employed, for it is a clever technique for proving one's equality or superiority. For example, Mary Bicker throws a dinner party and works hard to make it a success. She may lack the cultural polish and the experience of her husband, John, in this sort of thing, but she *tries her best.* Her husband, the disaster seeker, begins looking around for something that has gone wrong. Everybody may be having a pretty good time, but John discovers that the meat should have been browned a little more, or perhaps the cheese sauce needs another herb, or he makes sarcastic remarks because there are no guest towels in the bathroom or they are not set out where the guests can find them, and so forth. *Consciously,* John thinks that he's doing a good thing. He feels that he's improving the quality of the party and that Mary, who comes from a lower-middle-class family, will never learn how to throw a party properly if he doesn't show her. Moreover, he suspects that left to herself, she would be satisfied with a mediocre performance and would continue to entertain in that way.

As a result of John's constant heckling, Mary becomes tense and makes some real mistakes. The tense and frenetic feeling that

John is stimulating with his disaster seeking soon spreads to the guests.

Having created a disaster, John is satisfied. Suddenly he becomes benevolent and tender; he takes charge of the party, corrects everything, and ends up a big hero, while his wife looks like a fool. John would have been very disappointed if he had *not* found something wrong with Mary's party techniques.

Another variety of disaster seeker is known as the killjoy.

Al has just been invited to New York City to deliver a lecture, and he decides to take Carol along. Al's lecture turns out to be a tremendous success, and he receives much applause. In his exuberance, he suggests that they go out to a well-known restaurant and celebrate with a wonderful meal. Carol counters, "But Al, can we really afford it? I'd feel guilty spending fifty dollars on a fancy dinner when I know that little Madeline is crying her eyes out for a pair of skates and the dentist's bill hasn't been paid yet."

Al persuades her that they have both earned this celebration and so they go to the expensive French restaurant. Al is chatting away about how the pioneering ideas he has developed were accepted by the entire profession at his lecture, when Carol breaks in with "Why in hell can't they write these menus in English?"

Al calls the waiter and gets him to translate the menu. When he is through, Carol asks him petulantly, "Are you sure the oysters are fresh?"

She continues along this line, and by the conclusion of the meal Al is convinced that he made a terrible mistake in coming to this restaurant. He feels guilty for having spent so much money, and is no longer holding forth about his very successful lecture and his plans for the future. He retreats into his shell and stops talking. When he begins to appear definitely glum, Carol reaches over, pats his hand, and tells him how proud she is of him. Now Carol becomes genuinely merry. She has not only searched for disaster; she has found it.

How to Handle the Disaster Seeker

There are two approaches to this problem. The first is meant for the situation in which one spouse labels the other a disaster seeker, but the other spouse does not agree. The second is useful when both spouses are in agreement that one or both of them have this trait.

If one spouse is attempting unilaterally to change the other, who refuses to admit to being a disaster seeker, he must be willing to take a chance on being a troublemaker.

Basically, the disaster seeker is afraid of being abandoned. He is unconsciously afraid that the other spouse will grow apart from him, becoming too independent or successful. By employing the gloom-and-danger ploy, the disaster seeker attempts to keep the other spouse in line. Thus the spouse who would cure the situation must convince the other that this technique won't work and is harmful to the relationship, and he must do the convincing by means of *action*, not by complaining or nagging.

The approach is simple. The healer chooses an area in which there has been past evidence of disaster seeking. He makes it clear that the spouse is welcome to attend this convention, fly on this trip, or whatever, but that the plans will be carried out regardless of what the disaster seeker does or says.

A variation open to the healer is to invite the disaster seeker on a short vacation that he knows from their past experience should be pleasant. However, he must stipulate: "If you so much as make *one* negative comment about the trip, I will end it." If this stipulation is to be effective, it must be carried out the first time the disaster seeker utters an unpleasant remark, even if the result is that they return home a half hour after departure. This action must then be carried out so that the message is, "I am not going to desert you, but I am going ahead with these plans that are important to me."

The first few times, the disaster seeker may pout and be sullen upon the other spouse's return, but this reaction is to be expected. If it does not deter the spouse from his course of action, it will disappear.

If both spouses agree that there is a need for remedying a disaster-seeking attitude, and will work together, it can be accomplished easily. Two techniques are employed.

First, the disaster seeker accepts punishment each time he commits the sin of announcing disaster. In this way he is made aware of the frequency with which he makes remarks of this sort.

Ordinarily, it is easy to overlook gloomy predictions because if they are incorrect (as they usually are) they are soon forgotten; only if a disaster occurs is the prediction recounted over and over. As Disraeli pointed out, it is easier to be critical than to be correct. The punishment can be of any sort as long as it is genuinely annoying—for example, having to set the alarm and do twenty push-ups at three in the morning, or (for the husband) doing the dishes for a week.

Second, the disaster seeker is required by the other spouse to predict everything (in detail) that will go wrong with the projected activity. The other spouse notes these remarks down and has the forecaster initial them. After the event, the couple reviews the list together, checking the accuracy of the predictions. Usually, the disaster seeker cannot bring about the fulfillment of all his gloomy prophesies.

What has to be recognized about the disaster seeker in order to cure him is that, much like the average neurotic described by Freud, "he makes worse the very thing he seeks to cure." The disaster seeker may have a temporary feeling of independent security when he is able to exert control over his spouse's actions by the use of dire predictions, but he also loses, since he gives up the privilege and pleasure of being able to be dependent, to count on someone else whom he has placed in a position of authority or confidence. He cannot downgrade his spouse without reducing his own chances of finding succor in the marriage.

34

TECHNIQUE 8

The Cross Complainer

———————————

Harry Swenson is a patient man—or so it seems. His blood pressure indicates he is more *restrained* than patient. Living with Shirley is one cause of his difficulty, for Shirley is a master of conversational finesse and timing, particularly in the art of "cross complaining."

For example, when Harry brings up what he believes is a reasonable complaint, such as, "Dear, can't we ever have lamb any more?" Shirley quickly replies with something like this: "Harry, you can't keep nagging me about the money I spend and then tell me to buy lamb at today's prices. You are terribly inconsistent." (Shirley knows perfectly well that Harry actually only brings up the question of spending money when she buys expensive clothes impetuously and without having budgeted for them.) If Harry begins to complain about Shirley's arranging a bridge party on Sunday afternoon, she says something like, "What's the matter, Harry? Don't you want the girls to see how sloppy you are on weekends?"

So Harry retracts and the subject is changed.

How to Handle a Cross Complainer

Harry should insist that Shirley observe one of the marital imperatives: *Don't argue with me on my own time.*

By this we mean that when one spouse is making a complaint, he should not allow the other to answer with a cross complaint. The two complaints simply cancel each other out, and nothing has been settled. If Shirley also has a complaint, let her bring it up on her own time, not while Harry is asking for a change.

This is a simple but important marital imperative. *Never break this rule,* for each infraction invites another infraction! Remind each other, hold up a hand and say "Beep-Beep"! *Do anything,* but don't exchange complaints at the same time!

Harry should be firm about his right to complain even if Shirley appears not to recognize that she is cross complaining. Consciously or unconsciously, the cross complainer is aware of the nature of his tactics. If he refuses to admit what he is doing, more stringent methods of confrontation must be employed. A simple yet effective device is the following. When one spouse has identified the other as a cross complainer but the other will not cease the practice, the first spouse should announce: "I think you are capable of recognizing my right to complain *on my own time!* The next time you cut into one of my complaints, I'm simply going to leave the room. If you follow me, I'll simply leave the house." This apparently rude behavior is very effective because the cross complainer *needs an audience* to reassure himself that the other's complaint has been stifled by his cross complaint. When there is nobody in the room, the transaction is incomplete; the cross complainer is frustrated, and therefore in a better position to see the destructive nature of his tactics.

35

THE WRECKING
OF THE MARRIAGE

The disintegration of a marriage occurs so gradually, so incre-
mentally, so naturally, that most spouses do not recognize the
calamity for several months or years, and then only after it has
reached very difficult proportions. Actually, however, most marriages begin to fall apart during the honeymoon.

The moment the spouses say "I do," the relationship becomes
compulsory instead of voluntary. Almost everything within the
newly formed joint system is viewed within a perspective different from that of the happy courting days. The change is profound.
During the wooing, both people constantly attempt to be as
attractive as possible; each tries to exhibit only those parts of
himself which will please and capture the other. For example,
during courtship, a man who is bored by opera may get tickets
for an opening night, put on uncomfortable clothes, and spend
more money than he can afford for the grand occasion, if that's
what his woman wants.

Women behave in a similar manner. For example, a city woman
who dislikes walking even three blocks to the subway and who
enjoys staying up half the night and sleeping the next morning,
may when "in love" get up before sunrise and go fishing with her
young man—even though the sight of a flopping fish may disgust

her and the pitching boat may make her seasick. Romantic love and the desire to "capture" the other stimulates this type of behavior.

During the courting period, the male (in our culture) usually assumes the initiative. He woos the female. The female generally encourages this by playing the traditionally feminine role—that of joyfully accepting the male's aggression.

But after the marriage the average husband has to get about his chore of making a living. His romantic aggressiveness diminishes. Certain of his behavioral and material contributions to the woman's well-being are discontinued. Instead, the husband now believes his wife has an added responsibility—that of "taking care" of him; he tacitly assumes that she will henceforth be a mother to him as well as a mistress and a wife.

In the romantic passion of the courting period, the female had assumed (or at least had hoped) that the male's ardent wooing would continue forever. But it does not, and so the wife usually begins to ask for the courtship courtesies the male once gave her voluntarily. She indicates that for him not to give them is a breach of contract. He resents this, regarding her demands as showing a lack of consideration and therefore themselves constituting a breach of the courtship contract. He gradually finds excuses for decreasing his wooing activities even further, sometimes substituting indifference or stubbornness. The wife retaliates by withdrawing some of the tendernesses and loving niceties she had provided during their premarital days.

As the novelty of the relationship begins to wear off, the effort to change one's idiosyncracies in order to be accommodating becomes more difficult. The husband says he is too fatigued to go to the opera; and the wife feels ill when it's time to get up early to go fishing. In the course of day-to-day living, the spouses cease being actors trying hard to please an audience of one; and the habits and tastes acquired during a lifetime begin to show and to clash. The situation is further complicated by the development of new needs, new patterns of behavior, and resistance to change, provoked through the new relationship itself. Once married, people often are surprised by themselves and will say, "But I *wasn't* like this before we married, so it must be *you* who make me like this." Perhaps the wife can't stand the husband's habit of sleeping in his underclothes and of bathing only in the morning. He may feel insulted when she comes to dinner with rollers in her hair. The husband may get annoyed when his wife leaves the kitchen a mess at night, and she loses her temper when he refuses to cut the lawn.

Their differences seem numberless. The wife rolls the toothpaste tube up from the bottom; the husband squeezes it in the middle. He hates hairs in the sink; she neglects to wash out the basin after she has combed her hair. She learns that he tells the same stories over and over, which becomes a bore; he finds that she laughs at other men's jokes more than she does at his. And so the clashes occur repeatedly through the variety of behavior patterns which occur daily.

Starting with the honeymoon, sex also is usually a disappointment, if not a complete failure, or even a tragedy, as we saw in Chapter 13; so in this respect too, marriage contrasts sharply with the courtship period.

Slowly, the battles begin. If the wife has a headache just when her husband feels especially eager for sex, he may well conclude, "She's using sex as a weapon to get her own way. That's just like a woman!" If the husband loses his temper over the wife's behavior, she may think, "He's too damned domineering. What does he think I am, his slave?" Whatever the areas of difference, they are almost certain to be enlarged by the advice and comments of friends and relatives who enjoy vicarious participation in the battle of the sexes.

Interviews with normogenic (average) families make it clear that the disintegrating process in a marriage is usually triggered not by consciously malevolent behavior, but by what the spouses neglect to say and do. *The first steps toward destruction result mostly from omissions,* failures to bring the spouse's untested expectations into conformity with reality. It is important, then, that spouses recognize the conduct and transactions whose absence may be sabotaging their marriage.

Let us consider the two destructive omissions which occur most frequently.

Destructive Omission 1

The failure of spouses to identify, determine, and mutually assign areas of competence and responsibility, of who is in charge of what.

Married people are involved in an almost endless number of activities. In some, the determination of which partner is more competent and responsible can usually be made without question. For example, infant rearing is generally regarded as a female function, while chopping wood is assumed to be the responsibility of the male. In other activities such as, say, finances, both spouses may participate. One may do the bookkeeping, while the other pays the bills.

But there are many areas in which the competence and responsibility of each are difficult to determine. They range from relatively unimportant matters such as sweeping the leaves off the walk, or chaperoning a children's party, to activities of major importance, such as making out the family budget. In certain pursuits each partner believes himself to have superior competence. Certain others—often bothersome and disagreeable—are regarded by each as the responsibility of the other.

These issues must be *decided* and *agreed upon* by the spouses. Frequently the decision involves negotiations, discussions, and compromises. Suggestions on how to accomplish the negotiations are given in Part IV. Of course, cultural cues, social pressures and mores, influence the spouses in their mutual decision making; and husband and wife often are dominated by social pressures even when they sense that the socially directed methods won't work. They often forget that social patterns and mores change; indeed, in this era entire cultures may change within a decade. It is far more common today than it was a few years ago for the husband to cook (his special gourmet dish) when the pair entertains. In some homes the father may not be the sole wage earner; both mother and father go to work, and both share the housework.

Often the myth (deriving from tradition and social habit) that the male *must* be in charge of certain things and the woman in charge of others frightens the couple from independently determining areas of competence and responsibility. This myth has such a hold on people that they usually cannot shake it off. The situation breeds trouble.

When the spouses' temperaments, abilities, and training make an established cultural prescription unnatural, husband and wife may find that they can neither change the rule (as established by society) nor follow it. They may then resort to subterfuge. Perhaps a husband goes to the PTA meeting only if his wife has a headache—and she usually develops a headache on PTA night. In this case there has been no agreement on who should stay home with the children and who should go to the meeting. Therefore, the husband may one day feel that he is being "done in," even though he enjoys the meetings. Or, as happens more often than is realized, the wife may resent having to feel sick to get her husband to do something which she senses that he wants to do anyway. A rule-making session would eliminate discord here.

It is imperative that the spouses deliberately and mutually develop rules to guide their behavior. Omission of this procedure can destroy a marriage. Husband and wife should operate in ways which mutually assist each other—*regardless of custom or tradition*. Decisions must be made, for example, about who washes the dishes and when, who takes the children out on weekends, who mows the lawn, who goes to PTA meetings, who takes care of minor repairs, and so forth. If spouses fail to make such arrangements, then every time a question of who does what comes up, it must be renegotiated, even if it has arisen many times before. The result is squandered energy—and destructive power struggles. What might have been a mutually helpful interaction turns into an argument in which each says, in effect, "I must have my way, you stupid, stubborn idiot!" Examples are common. Suppose a husband and wife have not decided on early-morning rush-period rules concerning who gets up first, who uses the bathroom first, and at what time, who fixes breakfast, who feeds the children, who sees that they get to school. If there are no rules, there will be bedlam every morning—and in most homes there is. A mother with several small children may believe it is her husband's duty to help in the morning. However, *he* may feel that he should have a quiet, leisurely breakfast, reading the paper in peace, to prepare him for a day of decision making at the office.

Arrangements for situations like this should therefore be worked out and agreed upon.

Molding the marriage into a rule-governed system may seem unromantic and boorish. But people are misled by the myth that if there is "love," all problems will work themselves out automatically. It just doesn't happen that way.

A workable relationship (which is the first step toward a loving, enduring union) requires order, not chaos. If the rules and the resulting order do not come naturally—and they seldom do—they must be established through conscious effort. One cannot just go on hoping that they will grow spontaneously and satisfactorily. This principle applies to all relationships, whether between spouses, between business partners, or between nations. Part of the satisfaction and security of a workable marriage originates in the development of agreed-upon predictable behavior in basic family activities—the everyday chores, responsibilities, emotional exchanges, and exercises of taste. Accomplishing this is one of the great triumphs of a successful marriage. It is the cornerstone of survival in this age of rapid change, loosening cultural role assignments, and increased education tending toward the equalization of all people.

It is this predictable behavior that breeds trust, which is the greatest cohesive strength of a lasting, mutually nourishing marriage, as the discussion of trust in Chapter 12 makes clear. The reader must recall, however, that *negative trust* will develop if one repeatedly does not live up to his bargains and promises. An individual can be predictable by *never* being trustworthy. The kind of predictability that breeds *positive trust* is based on the fulfillment of one's responsibilities, promises, and agreements.

In the establishment of order, not only who does what, but also how it is to be done must be determined. The spouses can only perform tasks within the limits of their behavioral repertoires and acquired skills. These limits must be discussed. In any particular area, either the performance level must be accepted by both, or steps, mutually agreed upon, must be taken to improve the skill. For example, if a wife cannot cook well enough to please her husband, perhaps the husband will do some of the wife's chores while she attends cooking school. If both decide that the husband needs more education to increase his earning power, perhaps the wife will take a part-time job while he goes to school.

The clear assignment of authority and responsibility by the spouses does not result in a rigid relationship. Quite the contrary, it creates a flexibility which is impossible in a chaotic marriage. When behavior and performances are predictable, exceptions to the rules are possible—without suspicion or haggling.

Deciding who does what also conserves energy and time, thus leaving room for humor, good cheer, experimentation, and emotional virility. In contrast, if there is a failure to make and abide by rules, then the "business" of marriage saps the energy from the spouses and little is left for enjoyment and loving.

Destructive Omission 2

The failure of spouses to evaluate their differences as being only differences—not marks of inferiority.

A Frenchman considers himself superior to an Italian, and an Englishman feels superior to both of them. The Italian, in turn, looks down on both the French and the British. Most people evaluate cultural differences as better or worse, inferior or superior, good or bad, instead of simply accepting them as differences.

In many marriages, one spouse considers certain aspects of his rearing or traditions or tastes as superior to those of the other spouse. Naturally, the other spouse resents this attitude. The resulting tension is like a pebble in the shoe. At first it is only uncomfortable, but after some miles it breaks the skin and may cause a painful lesion.

This tendency to make the mistake of evaluating differences as inferiorities is most easily illustrated by the misunderstanding between nations and races. For example, before World War II, the Chinese thought American motion pictures which showed men and women kissing were in bad taste, and indeed, obscene. Partially for this reason, the Chinese considered Americans to be inferior barbarians. Yet in Chungking a respectable Chinese woman might, only a few yards from a highway, lift her skirts, squat over a "honey pot," and defecate. This custom originated because in this part of the world human feces were prized as fertilizer and were collected. Also, Western-style plumbing was considered expensive and unnecessary. To the Chinese, their custom appeared practical and wise. Yet almost all Americans who saw Chinese publicly crouching over the smelly "honey pots" turned away in disgust. They ridiculed the Chinese as an inferior and backward people not sufficiently civilized to use modern plumbing.

This kind of misunderstanding is not self-limiting. Once started, it grows and grows. In marriage (with its day-after-day intimacy) the negative value judgments made by one spouse about the habits and traditions of the other constitute a slur on his background, a disparagement of his family, a slander on his breeding, and even an insult to his intelligence. The expression of such judgments is a cruel and effective way of repeating in endless ways, "You are inferior! You are inferior!"

Often the barbs are disguised as wit. For example, listen:

"Damn it, no one but poor white trash eats parsnips. If you had any taste . . ."

"Hell no. It's simply that no one in your family ever knew how to prepare parsnips properly."

Whether deliberately or not, one spouse is telling the other that he is inferior. If this message is taken seriously (and it usually is), it raises the crucial question, "If I'm no damned good, why did you marry me in the first place?"

And then the battle and the deterioration begin.

36

DIVORCE, DESERTION, AND DESPAIR

Marriage may be difficult, but divorce is difficult too. Married people often feel trapped, for divorce is frightening, painful, expensive, and subject to social disapproval, and it is one of the few important institutions in our culture for which there is no formal ritual. Birth, marriage, death, all have formal cultural rituals associated with them—divorce does not. Furthermore, there is evidence that even when divorce is feasible, it is not always the ideal solution for marital difficulties. Among white people, those who have been divorced have the highest suicide rate, and there are often emotional problems in children whose parents have experienced divorce or desertion. Most divorced people can't stand loneliness—they try promiscuity and booze, and become more despairing; then they try remarriage, and here the divorce rate is still high, though some do better in the second marriage than they did in the first. When a person moves on into second, third, fourth, and fifth marriages, the chance that he will succeed becomes increasingly small. We end up saying that marriage is hard to live with and hard to live without.

On February 1, 1966, the state of California began a massive attempt to gather information on the background of divorces, in order to provide data for professionals trying to develop ways to

lower the incredible divorce rate. Each of the major counties in
California had over a thousand divorces in 1965, and San
Mateo County reached seventy divorces for every one hundred
marriages.

In California all lawsuits for divorce, annulment, and separate
maintenance now are to be accompanied by a comprehensive
questionnaire completed by both the husband and the wife. The
state hopes to find out what factors are particularly important in
divorce. Religious differences, ages of the spouses, race, finances,
and so on, will be examined.

The resulting statistics may also have other uses. In January,
1966, in San Francisco, a young widow and her son sued the city
for $500,000 in damages because her husband of one month had
been killed in a traffic accident on the city's streetcar system.
However, the city called in an expert from the University of
California. He examined the case, considering such factors as the
different religions of husband and wife, the fact that the girl
was pregnant before marriage, and the fact that both she and her
husband were teenagers and that both had been raised in Marin
County, where the divorce rate is exceedingly high, and concluded that the marriage would probably have been doomed even
if the man had lived. The jury, deciding that the expert knew at
least something about the matter, awarded the widow $145,000
instead of $500,000.

There soon may be a constitutional proposal in California for
the creation of a State Department of Family Relations. This
amendment, generally known as the Sitton-Winterfeld Initiative,
is backed by a number of people throughout the state who feel
that the present divorce procedures are terribly unfair and create
more dissension among divorced people than is necessary. In
particular, opponents of the existing divorce laws object strenu-
ously to the adversary system, in which one of the separating
mates, usually the husband, must be found guilty of some degree
of cruelty—"extreme," "mental," or whatever—before a divorce
can be granted. (Desertion and adultery are also grounds for
divorce in California, but are rarely used.) The resulting court-
room confrontations produce perjured testimony and lasting bitterness that forever precludes reconciliation and leaves the
children caught between two parents, who remain bitter and
antagonistic even though divorced and living apart.

The backers (largely male) of this bill are also concerned about the monetary considerations involved. In particular, they feel that citizens are at the mercy of avaricious lawyers who provide quick divorces for couples with limited financial resources, but manage to introduce long, complicated procedures, with correspondingly large fees, when their clients are wealthy. They feel that the child-support payments in general are fair, but that provisions for the settlement of the estate and for alimony are way out of line.

The proposed State Department of Family Relations would have a governing board of six elected directors, and regional boards in family-relation centers which could establish educational programs in family-relations matters. The department would have exclusive jurisdiction, subject to an appellate-court review, over divorce, annulment, and separate-maintenance proceedings. Parties could be represented by agents who were not attorneys. Divorces would be granted without regard to "guilt," and they would be effective immediately; the current one-year interlocutory decree would be abolished. Alimony and support payments would be based on the ability to pay and on need.

The sponsors of the measure say the plan would work as follows:

> The plan operates on a local basis in the county with a board of three county directors. These will be psychologists, sociologists, marriage counselors so they will have related educational backgrounds with experience in human relations.
>
> A staff of referees-investigators, accountants, social workers and other specialists will handle individual cases. The emphasis at this level is on premarital and post-marital education and direct aid in altering problems.
>
> Individuals in need of help may come to family arbitration center for informal discussion of their problems. If reconciliation methods fail and it is found advisable to terminate the marriage, divorce, annulment or separate maintenance will be granted by the three members of the Family Arbitration Board in an equitable and just manner. The rulings would have the same force and effect as a court of law.

The sponsors of the bill feel that obtaining divorces will not be "easier" under their proposed setup, and no increase in the divorce rate is anticipated. They claim instead that a complete and thorough investigation will be required, and divorces will be granted only when it is determined that the marriage should not continue. Counseling *prior* to the initiation of divorce proceedings should, by all accounts, act as a deterrent to the irresponsible or impetuous divorce begun in an escalating breakdown of communication. The sponsors feel that the program will be geared to prevent family breakups, and that there will be savings in welfare costs, juvenile-crime costs, legal fees, and other related costs. Operating revenue will be obtained from fees charged by the department.

It is likely that the proposed bill will stimulate great opposition. It is also apparent that many of the bill's proponents are males who have been burned by the financial inequities of the present legal system. Nevertheless, it is a healthy and important sign that people are looking critically at the divorce situation. Under a brilliant and facile attorney, Robert Furlong, the judicial committee of the state assembly in California recently held hearings on divorce procedures and accumulated a great deal of evidence about current methods, trends, and inequities.

There is little doubt that the present system in most states strongly favors the woman as far as financial matters are concerned. Consequently, a man may enter marriage already on the defensive, since no one gets married without at least thinking about the possibility of divorce. The legal situation thus encourages the battle of the sexes. The popular idea that making divorce financially punitive for the man will reduce its frequency is an ill-conceived notion, to say the least, and belongs in the same destructive social category as capital punishment.*

Psychiatrists, psychologists, and marriage counselors have recognized for some time that often the process of marital separation is relatively smooth, with due consideration shown by the spouses for the children and for each other, until attorneys enter the picture and the man and woman are forced to squabble over

---

* Divorce laws among the fifty states vary widely, and we have used those of California simply as an example. The authors are not implying approval or disapproval of any particular state's family laws. However, in our opinion, these laws should be similar in all states. All men may have been created equal, but when divorce occurs, they find themselves in vastly *un*equal—and perhaps inequitable—situations, depending upon the states in which they happen to live.

money. One of our acquaintances who was arranging to get a divorce attempted to be extremely fair to his wife and children, and was thoroughly rebuked by his attorney for being too generous. He had only recovered from this lecture when his wife's attorney called to ask how he could be such a cold-hearted skinflint. In this case, the behavior of both attorneys was so untoward that the spouses finally came together to discuss their problems in person, and worked out their own settlement. Then they looked hard and long for a single attorney to represent them both.

In war, we encourage the bravery which leads men to get themselves killed, for example, by superb performance in the face of enemy fire, and then we go to fantastic lengths to save the lives of those who are wounded. This behavior is not paradoxical; we are saying, "We want you to be brave, and you may thereby die; but if you are brave and live, we will see that you receive all the rewards we can offer."

Marriage too, is encouraged by the culture, but there have been few compensations for the wounded; they are just told that they shouldn't have been hurt in the first place and it's their own fault if they were. Even the "cooling-off" period provided by the interlocutory decree is of little use; by the time it is obtained, the preceding legal maneuverings have so stirred up the roaring fires that it is often too late for cooling off.

The Australian system seems far more realistic. In Australia, divorce is not permitted until a marriage has been in existence at least three years (annulments may be granted sooner under certain unusual circumstances). Thus people are not able to rush in and out of marriage. Before a divorce is granted, conciliation is attempted and every resource which might help save the marriage is utilized. But if a divorce is obtained, it becomes effective immediately. Our system reminds one of capital punishment; we cling to it despite years of testimony that punishment does not serve as a deterrent.

When a divorce is necessary, the separation should be amicable. This is particularly important if there are children, since they become cross monitors; that is, all unawares, they transmit messages from one parent to the other—often hateful messages.

The traditional practice among psychiatrists and marriage therapists has been neither to recommend divorce nor to stand in the way of a couple wishing a divorce. This canniness is desirable. There are so many complicated factors in any marital breakup that it is difficult to see the situation as a coherent whole. Often it is only after a person has been divorced that he can look at the marriage and decide realistically whether he is better or worse off than he was before it was dissolved. If a third person enters the picture, he is apt to be blamed for causing the divorce, even if, in fact, the couple had wished it but lacked the guts to go through with it until they were on the brink and called in the third party to act as a go-between.

In our opinion, there is one fact that stands out in most family breakdowns. The best reason for divorce is *that the man and wife cannot function together without serious damage to one or both,* physically or emotionally.

Part IV

HOW TO TRY
TO MAKE THE
MARRIAGE WORK

37

YOUR MARRIAGE MAY
NOT BE AS BAD
AS YOU THINK

Marriage is a process involving two complex and ever-changing sets of behavior; therefore, continuous and perfect harmony in marriage is impossible. It is possible, however, to achieve a useful, livable, and workable relationship. Most marriages are characterized by discord; reversing the trend toward destructiveness and taking steps toward learning to work as a team requires patience and courage. *Most of all, it requires the desire to change.*

When the two systems (male and female) are abrading each other, it is difficult for the parties to sit down and straighten things out in the same mechanical way that one would clean out a flue or change a tire. There are too many subtle variables. Some are in the realm of the unconscious. Even a trained and dedicated psychiatrist might need considerable time to analyze the conditions and prescribe effective therapy, and still further time to guide the couple's efforts at changing.

The do-it-yourself material which follows will not *guarantee* a perfect marriage, or even a workable marriage. However, if the suggestions are studied and seriously applied they may stimulate a pattern and pace of thinking which may:

1. prevent constant repetition of old, destructive patterns;

2. stop small problems from becoming big problems;

3. point toward broad relationship goals;

4. force spouses or prospective spouses to explore certain areas which they have avoided or which social customs have formerly forbidden them to explore;

5. assist couples in recognizing that a large number of so-called experts are giving (and charging for) tests and counsel that are not effective; and that the nature of much of this counsel leads people into easy—but spurious—conclusions which often are destructive to the marriage.

You may find that your marriage is much better than you think!

38

HOW TO ARREST SYMMETRICAL BEHAVIOR IN A MARITAL RELATIONSHIP

If a husband and wife—Miriam and Ken Thompson, let us say —agree that they are predominantly a status-struggle type of couple and are frequently engaged in stressful competition, they can learn to enjoy great cooperation and to function less competitively by practicing the series of exercises which follows. These techniques will not completely eliminate status struggles, for such struggles are necessary from time to time when issues arise for which rules have not yet been agreed upon. But the practices we suggest can help limit the struggles to appropriate areas, and make the marriage correspondingly more workable. Let us stress that the spouses must go slowly. They *must not* attempt to change their marriage overnight. After all, psychoanalysis not infrequently takes six to eight years. These exercises should therefore be taken slowly, step by step, over a period of weeks.

First, Miriam and Ken are to sit down together and compile a list of the various duties performed and roles filled when they are home together over a weekend. Such activities as cooking, cleaning, entertainment, and helping the kids with schoolwork will be listed. Miriam and Ken probably will discover that status struggles occur when both attack the same problem at just about the same time, as when Ken is helping Johnnie, their son, with his homework and Miriam cannot refrain from putting her two cents' worth in.

For the sake of experience and practice they should plan for the next several weekends to divide functions and tasks rigorously, agreeing in advance about which spouse is to take charge of each particular duty. For example, it may be Ken's job to drive the kids to their swimming lesson every Saturday and to mow the lawn, while Miriam goes to the laundromat and arranges for a baby-sitter for Saturday evening. (The matter of choosing the type of entertainment will be discussed later because this is one function that cannot be assigned to a particular spouse as part of a role.) Miriam and Ken may find during several weeks' trial that they have to do some shifting of tasks. Perhaps Miriam is better at helping the kids with their English homework, and Ken with their mathematics. If Miriam accepts the task of attending the PTA meeting on Wednesday evening, perhaps it will be desirable for Ken to take charge of providing for dinner on that night. Since he does not cook, this may mean taking the family out to dinner, or having a simple barbecue.

The procedure described here sounds very simple and mechanized, but in carrying it out, most couples will find to their surprise that although they have been assuming that each has his assigned tasks, actually—except for the most obvious ones—tasks have not been clearly assigned, and that status struggles occur when husband and wife attempt to take over a task at the same time, or when one interferes with the other's performance.

The couple will soon discover that even after weekend functions and tasks have been divided, many areas of dissatisfaction remain. This is most often the case in matters involving idiosyncratic taste or choice such as the selection of a movie. *Status struggles occur in the choice of anything upon which one places cultural value.* It is always possible to argue that it's better to go see a Shakespearean play than a gangster film.

In situations of this sort, many unnecessary status struggles can be eliminated if the spouses agree to alternate in choosing the evening's activity, with each in turn accepting without adverse comment the selection of the other.

After the status strugglers have weathered a weekend in which the labor was broken up into tasks for each, they are ready for the next step, the assignment of *areas of competence* rather than specific duties. This change introduced a relative freedom into the system, because areas are not as confining and controlling as specific duties. The trick here is to realize that a good cook is no greater than a good accountant, that the successful gardener isn't superior to the careful housekeeper. In order to work out areas of competence, the spouses must have made enough progress to be able to agree on a number of important areas which must be taken care of if the family work is to get done, to recognize that the question of someone being better than someone else is not relevant.

Here is a method for assigning areas of competence. The spouses sit down together, and one tells the other what he did best—what situation he handled most competently—over the weekend. If the other agrees, this may be considered one of his areas of competence. For example, the wife may say to the husband, "The way you kept the children from quarreling was marvelous. I think it would be a great thing if you could take over the discipline of the kids over the weekend because by the end of the week I'm somewhat weak and frustrated with them and probably not very effective." If he assents, she is free to take over another matter; the husband may now suggest that she keep the family financial records, since she handled them neatly and systematically over the weekend and he finds bookkeeping a boring chore.

After trying a weekend during which areas rather than tasks are assigned, the spouses review the allotment of areas; some shifting, or at least a few slight changes will probably be necessary and these should be discussed at this time. The next step will then be to decide how to share responsibility in those areas in which some overlapping is inevitable. One such area is shopping, since an individual out for other reasons may stop to "pick up" something, thus doing part of this job. Child rearing is another area in which both parents are usually involved.

Many status struggles involve the question of who is doing a better job of disciplining the children. The fact is that the mother is with the children a great deal more than the father is, therefore her values will predominate despite her husband's best efforts unless he has intimidated her completely, and the husband's frustration is evident when he tries to impose his values upon the children during the infrequent periods when he is with them. In the effort to eliminate status struggles over the children a good first step is to assign the father complete charge of their discipline when he is present on weekends. His wife will often be dissatisfied with his approach, but only by stepping out of the picture does she make it possible for him to experience the burden of total responsibility for child discipline. The chances for settling into a compromise are much improved once one recognizes that it is all very well to wish the children were behaving in a certain way, but it is quite another matter to put forth the effort to get them to do so.

Spouses who attempt exercises of the sort just described will recognize, in all likelihood, that in their efforts to bargain and to divide responsibilities, they end up competing over who can fulfill his share of the bargain *better*. But though it is still competition, *competing to cooperate* is one step forward, for it leads toward more positive interactional patterns and gives one less of a sense of struggling with the other spouse over fruitless and never-ending "issues." Issues are usually smoke screens hiding a more basic disagreement over who "cares the most" or who is being "more thoughtful." The many status struggles occurring over particular issues may, indeed, be reflections of the basic status struggle implied in this central question.

For most people, the main difficulty in being thoughtful is that they experience a hurt vulnerability when their thoughtfulness is not returned, or when they fear that it will not be returned. The result is the defensiveness described elsewhere in the book as reverse vulnerability. To avoid this fear of being thoughtful, and hence this reverse vulnerability, spouses should divide tasks and

areas of responsibility in such a manner that neither can claim that
he is being more thoughtful than the other or is being denied
thoughtfulness by the other. If the reader will think back on
recent arguments with his own spouse about who has done the
most or who has worked the hardest or had the hardest day, he
will recognize that the discussion rarely concerns actual man
hours spent in labor; it usually involves some ill-defined question
of who "cares" the most or who "gives" the most. Such scrapping
represents the desire of each for recognition that he has contributed at least his share, the desire for a display of thoughtfulness and appreciation on the other's part, but usually it leads only
to further argument, recrimination, and status struggling. Therefore, it is desirable for each spouse to avoid merely thinking
competitively about how to "beat out" the other spouse, and try
instead to put himself in the other's position and imagine how he
feels, asking, "If I do so and so, how will Jane (or John) be made
to feel?" This approach introduces a forward look into relationship behavior and drives home the knowledge that cooperation
is not just a moment-to-moment thing, but also affects the future.

Some additional exercises to break down destructive status
struggles over who is "more thoughtful" and who is "less appreciative" of the other's thoughtfulness can be found in the discussion of reverse vulnerability in Chapter 44.

39

AGGRESSIONS
AND QUARRELS

Aggressions and quarrels are, in some degree, present in almost all marriages. They have many causes, but are most likely to arise out of a symmetrical struggle. Since they are particularly apt to occur when a couple is working to form a *quid pro quo*, as described in subsequent chapters, a brief word on "battles" is appropriate at this point. Some aggressions and quarrels may be regarded as helpful to a marriage; others are destructive.

Aggression is the act of intimidating the other spouse into taking a direction or agreeing to a decision that has been made unilaterally. Aggression can be helpful when, for example, one spouse knows a situation or topic better than the other and takes charge simply because of his obviously superior knowledge. It can also be useful if both spouses have been paralyzed by doubts or debate and one of them finally emerges from the paralysis and settles the matter by edict. For example, when Sue invites the Smiths to dinner without asking John's permission, he may understand that they have been stalling too long in trying to decide whom to entertain.

A quarrel is a disagreement over fact, or a struggle over who has the right to do what to whom. It is generally a self-limiting situation because escalation frightens the spouses into finding some way to break off the argument. The "deadly" quarrels, which are not self-limiting, will be considered shortly.

Like aggressions, quarrels are sometimes helpful. For many couples, battling may be the only means of sharing private feelings and thoughts. During a quarrel spouses may lose or reduce their reserve and give each other information which they would otherwise keep hidden. Correspondingly, some couples deliberately get drunk together in order to "come clean." Even if moderate physical violence occurs—violence not requiring repair work by a dentist or physician—the quarreling may still be useful, serving to define the extremes of the spouses' relationship and to place their total behavior in some kind of perspective. Thus a wife who feels neglected and unloved may be reassured when her husband cares enough about her to strike her in anger because she has been too flirtatious at a party.

Destructive quarrels and aggressions, on the other hand, are those which have no point: they solve no mutual problems and contribute nothing to the joint system. At their worst, these become deadly quarrels. In a symmetrical struggle one spouse may destroy another's mail, be late for dinner, or burn the potatoes, simply to be mean. A spouse may commit acts of aggression in public so that the other is too embarrassed to retaliate, or may start secret conspiracies with relatives, friends, or even the most available of all pawns, the children.

Naturally, the meanness in destructive quarrels and aggressions begets meanness, even when the other appears to be a "good sport" about it. A woman who had been married for twenty-five years asked her psychotherapist in considerable wonderment why her husband was still so loving and good to her when she had been mean and nasty for a quarter of a century. The therapist asked if she could think of a better way to make her look like an ass.

If one believes that meanness is an innate character trait, there appears to be no recourse for nasty couples except to split up or continue their nastiness. But according to the systems concept, nastiness begets nastiness: it is part of the system, not an expression of the individual's personality. This point of view has been corroborated in psychiatrists' offices. For example, a therapist may instruct an aggressive or quarrelsome husband and wife to treat each other with reserve and suspicion but *without any nasty acts* until he meets with them again in a week or two. During this time if either feels the *other* has shown meanness, he is to phone the therapist and report the incident (thus each spouse reinforces the instructions given for the other). Under these conditions the spouses may discover that they do not feel mean or nasty. It may occur to them that hitherto each one believed the other would be mean and therefore tried to move first in self-defense. The built-in vulnerability and defensiveness in this system thus keep it self-perpetuating. The restraint demanded by the therapist (with his method of checking up on it) often breaks the negative chain.

40

THE NEED
TO BARGAIN

It is implicitly held by most married couples and explicitly stated by numerous authorities that bargaining is bad in marriage. Pastoral counselors, in particular, seem to err in the direction of urging people to "make sacrifices," "give," "do it for his sake." Women's magazines in numerous articles have urged their hundreds of thousands of readers to "be more attractive," "stop being selfish," "be more loving," "take up fishing, you may learn to like it," and so on. We feel that in attempting to follow such instructions people only make themselves feel guilty and frustrated for not being able to do the impossible. Should they succeed by some supreme effort, they also succeed in making the spouse feel pressured to rise to the occasion—and inadequate if he is unable to do so. For instance, if the wife decides she is not pretty enough to please her husband, having just read the newest copy of *Vogue* magazine, she may suddenly go shopping and buy an elegant new dress for the next neighborhood barbecue. Her husband is likely to feel unhappy about such a unilateral action—not only because the dress cost too much, but also because he had planned to wear his usual old sport shirt and khaki trousers. By the same token, if the wife decides to take up fishing to please him, he may well feel she is interfering in the one activity which he enjoys with other men, and which he looks forward to each year as a break in his routine.

We state vigorously and unequivocally that bargaining is an essential part of the workable marriage. In fact, the marriage relationship requires constant and continuing bargaining between the spouses, because attempts at adjustment are inevitable and occur daily or perhaps even hourly. The cultural preconceptions of the roles of husband and wife are so different from the actualities of the working relationship that must be maintained that bargaining is essential if each spouse is to get the other to cooperate.

Before we explore the methods of conscious negotiation, a word of caution about bargaining behavior is appropriate. A rather frequent method of bargaining which is nevertheless the least efficacious involves the use of some kind of outside standard. For example, the wife may say, "We're the only family in the whole block that doesn't have a new car." Or the husband may say, "I'm the only man in the office whose wife doesn't get up and fix his breakfast."

The trouble with using outside standards as a starting point is that they can be manipulated. The individual can quote the standard or statistic that most fits his own case. Also, since each of us believes he is idiosyncratic and individualistic enough not to be guided by other people's standards, the spouse at whom the standard is directed will resist it. The couple therefore drifts from the issue over which negotiations began, and ends up squabbling over something irrelevant.

The best kind of bargaining behavior is that which is not immediately "time bound." That is, the couple recognizes that if one spouse does something for the other, the benefited spouse need not *immediately* turn around and pay off his debt. It is assumed that there will be an opportunity for paying back in the future. This kind of arrangement is ideal, but unfortunately, as with most things, it sometimes also carries the seed of its own destruction within it. It is quite possible that A may keep encouraging B to believe that he will do something in the future, but never get around to it. This sort of unkept promise is the material for marital disharmony and bitterness. It is more apt to occur when spouses do not trust each other; or when one spouse has an extremely selective memory—recalling every detail of what he has contributed, but forgetting or undervaluing what the other has done, or what he himself has neglected to do.

We knew one miserable woman who after supporting her husband through law school also financed a boat trip to Hawaii because he was worn out from taking the bar examinations. The wife thought her day would come when he was earning a good living and she would have the house and life of her dreams. Unfortunately, he met another woman on the boat, and ended up divorcing his wife.

Since marriage is a series of adjustments, some of which may best be achieved through debate, it is imperative that spouses do three things:

First, they must examine their relationship to see if their bargaining has been overt or has been conducted obscurely underground. When spouses are trying to straighten out a discordant marriage, the bargaining must be brought above ground and be accomplished deliberately, consciously, and with stated goals. Underground bargaining too often is not bargaining at all, but manipulation for control.

Second, each spouse must examine his own attitudes to determine if he is placing his promises of repayment too far in the future. For one thing, it is possible that these repayments may never be made, but more important is the fact that such an arrangement interferes with the realistic day-to-day acceptance of "you scratch my back and I'll scratch yours." Of course, the setting of mutual goals for the future—owning a home, for example, or returning to college after the children are married—is quite another matter. What we are discussing here is negotiation concerning things, attitudes, or behavior over which there is a difference of opinion. Each spouse wants his own way, and since this is impossible, they are negotiating a compatible compromise.

Third, they must estimate whether they as a couple are able to bargain. Their differing opinions may be so great and their capacity for behavior control so small, that they are incapable of negotiating a compatible compromise. An extreme example might be a marriage in which the husband has a series of behavior patterns which irritate the wife. He may chew at the table with his mouth open, and dislike having his wife's intellectual friends about the house (because he never even graduated from grammar school), wishing instead to watch television every evening; and when his wife's friends come, the husband may dislike wearing a necktie and coat, and sit about in his shirt sleeves, sulking. He may prefer eating in the kitchen with bottles of ketchup and mustard on the table, rushing through a supper of fried steak, mashed potatoes, and ice cream, while his wife insists on eating off linen in the dining room—with candles, wine, and good conversation. In such a case the cultural difference is so great that successful bargaining is improbable.

One general indication of whether bargaining can be successful for the spouses is their ability to get through the exercises for the *quid pro quo* described in Chapters 42 and 43. If the spouses are able to accomplish this kind of cooperation, they may have enough cooperative spirit to bargain with each other without using meat cleavers and without causing hurt feelings and tears that make bargaining impossible. If, because they cannot get through the exercises and because they have great differences of opinion, the spouses are convinced that they are unable to bargain, they must either find an objective third person to act as an arbiter (for example, a therapist), split up, or allow one spouse to assume the complementary relationship, in which he runs the show and the other is apparently totally passive. The latter is a difficult situation to maintain but some couples deliberately do so.

If the spouses feel that they don't really know much about bargaining, or do not understand how it functions as a behavior experience, the following kind of practice (which may seem trivial or even ridiculous) is in order before attempting the *quid pro quo* exercises.

The two spouses meet under the *quid pro quo* rules set forth in Chapter 42. After a flip of the coin each chooses an opposite position on an obvious topic such as, Which is better, a Lincoln or a Cadillac? Where would you rather go, to Honolulu or to San Juan, Puerto Rico? Which kind of pie is preferable, apple or coconut custard? Even the process of deciding which topic to argue about will give them a chance to learn about bargaining. They then begin this totally unimportant debate, with the idea of learning about each other's debating tricks, verbal skills, use of emotional ploys, and so on. Usually three or four minutes of such activity are enough to destroy boredom and to show how each behaves in this kind of situation.

In the second exercise one spouse (again chosen by a flip of a coin) is to convince the other that he should have such-and-such, or be allowed to do such-and-such; the other spouse is required to be totally silent, just listening. Even a man and woman married for many years may be surprised to discover how little each has noted about the way the other behaves when he is attempting to get his own way. So often we close our minds at the first few words or first sentence of a bargaining session and consequently know very little about the other spouse's behavior.

The third exercise, to be carried out on a subsequent evening, requires complete honesty from one of the spouses. A flip of the coin determines which spouse is to have the privilege of talking the other spouse into agreeing to something that he really wants to do or have. This "something" should be actually feasible for the couple. The spouse who is to listen flips the coin again, *without letting the other see it.* If the toss is heads, he is to end up agreeing with the other regardless of how good or bad the bargaining has been. If tails, he is to end up disagreeing. About this he must be completely honest with himself and obey the dictates of the coin even if he would prefer to ignore the toss and decide on the basis of his spouse's argument.

The first spouse then will never know whether his eloquence and debating ability would have won the day if the decision had not been determined by a flip of the coin. Here we are teaching the spouses something important, namely, that since bargaining in marriage is a constantly occurring affair, it is not simply a matter of someone winning or losing. When one spouse yields to the other's blandishments, he does so primarily so that he will be yielded to in turn.

To put it differently, even though on any particular day bargaining may appear to be a matter of winning or losing, over the long run it is all a matter of negotiation.

41

HOW TO ESTABLISH
COMMUNICATION

There are two major ways in which communication between individuals breaks down. The absence of clear and workable communication almost always involves both parties.

The first type of breakdown is in a sense physical. The spouses speak to each other, but neither "hears" what the other says. Sometimes this failure is the result of a lifetime of "nonlistening" —a practice unfortunately common in the United States. The nonlistening habit can also develop between spouses after they have been fighting for several months or years. Both spouses are on the defensive, and as soon as one begins to speak, the other starts preparing to defend himself against an attack; his mind is concentrating on what the reply will be, not on what is being said.

The physical breakdown of communication is present in almost every marriage in which there is trouble. We know of one New England housewife who, on a cold January evening, got a screwdriver and removed the front door from its hinges. The cold air and the snow began blowing into the house, and her surprised husband came out bellowing, "What the hell have you done?"

"I asked you three times to shut the door when you come in," said the wife.

"You never said any such thing."

"When you left the house at eight o'clock this morning," said the wife, "you left the door open. I ran out and knocked on the car window and said to you, 'Please shut the door when you leave the house; you're freezing the place out.'"

The husband said angrily, "I don't remember your saying any such thing."

"Do you remember my coming out to the car and shouting at you?"

"Yes, but I thought you were still bitching because I didn't eat any of the pancakes you made for breakfast."

The wife said, "You rolled the window down while I was talking and looked me right in the eye."

"Well, I don't remember you saying anything about closing the door."

"But," said the wife, shouting, "I told you the same thing when you came home for lunch, and I told you the same thing when you left to go back to the office, and every time you were looking right at me."

"I don't remember hearing you tell me about shutting the door."

Probably this husband did *not* hear his wife tell him to shut the door, even though the sound reached his ears. Variations of this episode occur several times a day in most unhappy families. Fortunately, this kind of breakdown is easily repaired. If both spouses agree to improve their communication, there is a small exercise which will help.

A completed communication consists of the statement made by the first speaker, the acknowledgment by the recipient of the message, showing that he has heard it, and then the acknowledgment by the original speaker that he has heard the acknowledgment. If for about two weeks a husband and wife will conscientiously make certain that every message is a completed one, even though it sounds forced and silly at the beginning, the chances are that their physical communication will improve greatly. But this exercise, with its exaggerated emphasis, must be performed with every communication, no matter how small.

For example:

MARY: My, how blue the sky is. (*This is the original statement.*)

JOHN (*acknowledging that he has heard*): Yes, it certainly is a beautiful blue.

MARY (*acknowledging* JOHN's *acknowledgment*): I'm glad you like it too.

Spouses will make many short statements like Mary's in the course of a day—"Gracious, this must be the coldest day of the year;" "Phew, but I'm exhausted;" "Something smells good in the kitchen;" "I had a hell of a day at the office."

The usual response to statements of this sort is a grunt, a nod of the head, or perhaps nothing at all. If one of the spouses tends to be a chatterbox, the other may easily get into the habit of not listening to anything, thereby only reinforcing the chattering behavior, which doesn't require a response.

When an attempt is made to complete all messages (so that each consists of statement, acknowledgment, and second acknowledgment), the amount of "nothing" talk is soon reduced. Spouses learn not to speak unless they desire to have a completed communication. Some examples of the completed communication follow.

MARY (*original statement*): Please shut the door when you come in or go out. It's damn cold outside.

JOHN (*acknowledgment*): I'll try to remember, and if I forget, will you remind me again?

MARY (*acknowledgment of the acknowledgment*): Thank you, John. Yes, I'll remind you if you forget.

Another example:

JOHN (*original message*): Something smells good in the kitchen.

MARY (*acknowledgment*): Yes, I have an apple pie in the oven.

JOHN (*acknowledgment of the acknowledgment*): Oh, good, I hope we're having it for dinner.

Even if the messages are negative, they must be completed:

MARY (*original message*): John, will you bring me ten pounds of potatoes on the way home from the office?

JOHN (*acknowledgment*): I'd rather not. I work late today,

and if I stop at the supermarket there's a hell of a long line at half past six.

MARY (*acknowledgment of the acknowledgment*): Oh, all right, I guess we can hold off till I go to the store the day after tomorrow myself.

It is unnatural for most couples to complete every communication in this way, and at the beginning of the exercise the routine will frequently be forgotten. Spouses must help each other to remember. If Mary makes a statement and John grunts an answer, Mary must say, in a courteous manner, "John are you going to acknowledge?" If John has acknowledged and Mary simply nods her head, John must remind her: "Mary, are you going to acknowledge my acknowledgment?"

For spouses intending to improve their marriage, the development of a functional communications pattern is the first step to be taken. Furthermore, the exercise just described can be a great deal of fun. It can be a good game; and when it is done quietly in public, the participants frequently gain a great feeling of shared understanding, because as they look around they see that other husbands and wives are usually paying no attention to what each says to the other. Besides, this little exercise can be of enormous benefit to all of one's human relationships. It gradually transforms the habitual "mumbo-jumbo" conversation into an I-am-thinking dialogue, which is an exciting experience.

The practice of mumbo-jumbo conversation is the basis of bad manners. In homes where there are several children, bedlam is common because when a child wants something he simply shouts until he gets it. The habit of shouting develops because the parents do not listen either to each other or to the children. Following the model set by the parents, the children may run in and out of others' conversations in track shoes.

One method of installing the principles of good communication in children can be practiced at mealtime. The parents can insist that when a family member wants something passed to him, something like the following dialogue must occur.

CHARLES: Joannie?

JOAN (*turning her head*): What? (*This is her way of saying, "I'm listening."*)

It is important that this little routine be practiced if there are several people present. If a name is not specified, no one knows who is being addressed. If the person who is named does not turn and acknowledge the communication, the original speaker, in this case Charles, doesn't know if he has been heard. We now continue the dialogue.

CHARLES   (*original message*): Will you pass the butter, please?
(JOAN *passes the butter to* CHARLES; *this is her acknowledgment of the original message.*)
CHARLES   (*acknowledging the acknowledgment*): Thank you, Joannie.

The second type of major breakdown in personal communications occurs when the message sent is not the message received, as was pointed out in an earlier chapter.

How do husbands and wives manage to misunderstand each other so completely and so successfully? The major reason is that people *are* separate one from the other, and can transmit the state of their feelings, desires, intentions, and expectations only by verbal or nonverbal communication.

It will be recalled that the significance of a message is determined not only by its literal meaning (the report aspect), but also by the accompanying gestures, facial expressions, and the like (the command aspect), and by the nature of the total situation in which the message is sent (the context aspect). Communication between intimates is especially difficult in some respects because the sender may not realize that the understanding of his message may be affected by his nonverbal behavior or by a misinterpretation of the context. The most practical method for clarification of a message is for the receiver to ask the sender to elucidate, if there is any doubt about its meaning. For example, if John comes home a little bit tired and angry and finds the house looking slovenly, he may say to Mary, "I had to call on the Hatfields, and my gracious, Louise Hatfield keeps a lovely home. It's a joy to be in it."

In this instance Mary may say, "John, you said that Louise Hatfield keeps a wonderful home. The message which I hear, what I think you're trying to tell me, is that our home looks like a pigpen. Is that right?" If John says yes, that's what his message was, then Mary can say, "I know the house looks a mess this afternoon, and I don't like it any more than you do, but the water pipes burst at four o'clock and I had to go after the plumber and I haven't had time to clean up." The ambiguity of the message is cleared up unless John feels that Mary's response is an old ploy; in that case they must continue struggling for a resolution.

A similar exchange may occur at a party when Mary says, "Isn't it wonderful the way Jim Power always holds his wife's hand and sticks with her throughout the party? It sure is nice to see people so much in love."

John can understand this message either as an expression of sincere admiration for the Powers or as a criticism of himself. He is not sure which interpretation is correct, so he says, "Are you implying that I'm neglecting you at the party, Mary? Does it bother you when I leave you and talk with the boys?"

Mary can answer "Yes" or "No," and again, the problem can be resolved because what they are talking about has been made clear.

Suppose John says instead, "Yes, the Powers are a lovely couple." He is choosing to take Mary's remark literally and thus while appearing to be in polite agreement, he is actually blocking off clear communication. When spouses repeatedly encounter obstructions of this sort, they begin to despair and lapse into permanently unclear communication.

As soon as families begin to squabble, the number of messages incorrectly received increases. People who are quarreling fall into the trap of saying one thing when they mean another, or of hearing one thing when something else has been said, because they are angry, hurt, or frightened. It has often been remarked that none are so blind as those who will not see. Unfortunately, we may say as well that none are so deaf as those who will not hear.

A communication problem occurs when a message has two or more possible meanings: The "meaning" is therefore dependent upon the interpretation of the listener, which may be different from the interpretation given by the speaker.

For example, one spouse may attempt to be witty at the expense of the other, either as a way of retaliating for previously incurred injuries, real or imagined, or to make himself look good in the company of others, without regard for the partner's feelings.

The spouse who is always making sarcastic jokes at the expense of his partner can usually be stopped if the victim says, "John, the message I get from that bit of humor of yours is as follows . . . ," and then spells out the message. The sender will usually try to laugh, and say, "Oh, you know I was only kidding."

"Well, maybe you were kidding, but that's the message I got."

"You shoudn't be so thin-skinned."

"Well, darling, would you please not pull that kind of joke on me in the future? I would consider it a great favor because it embarrasses the hell out of me. Or if you really are angry with me, let's talk about it and knock off the sarcasm. Otherwise, I won't be able to appreciate your humor because I'll always be watching out for digs at me."

The argument in this case arises over the nature of the command aspect of John's message. His spouse takes the message literally, while John insists he wanted it to be taken humorously.

A response of this sort may cause some small fights in which the sender of the "kidding" messages accuses the receiver of being thin-skinned and oversensitive or perhaps of having a persecution complex. It may result in an admission by the "teaser" that something is indeed "bugging" him or her. But the essential point is that this confrontation permits the couple to discuss their problems openly and explicitly, so they can be dealt with. The communication system has moved toward a higher degree of functionality.

One more thing. We do not claim that clear communication *always resolves* marital problems. The spouses may clearly agree that they disagree and are at an impasse. Even so, this recognition is preferable to spilling energy, fathering pain, and spreading gloom by obfuscation, incomplete transactions, hurtful "humor," and all the other destructive devices we have been attempting to analyze.

Here are some simple exercises for establishing clear communication. They should not be attempted until *both spouses* have read and understood the book, and agree that clear communication is an essential ingredient in a workable marriage.

If either becomes uncomfortable or feels that these exercises are "stupid," he should admit it and call off the session. He may want to try again later. In any case, the exercises may take more than one session.

In undertaking these exercises, the spouses recognize that clear communication is difficult and that even when working at it they are lucky to achieve noise-free communication 60 per cent of the time. Therefore, each assumes an attitude of mild skepticism about his understanding of the other and asks questions freely to establish what is actually meant.

Furthermore, they agree that mind reading, the imputation of motives, and digressions into past history, though they may be momentarily ego inflating, create noise and hamper communication. Each spouse watches out for the use of such ploys by the other. The spouse accused of using them should agree, for he cannot be sure that he didn't, and these exercises must take place in a spirit of mutual charity.

In the first exercise the spouses sit face to face in straight chairs with knees touching. Each puts his right hand over the spouse's left. They then look each other *directly* in the eyes and maintain this position for at least two minutes while they discuss trivia; if nothing occurs to either spontaneously, the husband is to introduce an unimportant topic. The spouses then ask themselves some questions: Is either (or both) able to admit discomfort in this position? Why should the discomfort occur when the subject is so unimportant? This discussion should occupy not more than one or two minutes.

Next, maintaining this position and looking directly into his wife's eyes, the husband tells his wife a deliberate lie. He can embellish it as much as he wishes, but he must attempt to sound convincing. Then the wife must do the same thing. As the spouses will quickly discover, it is difficult to tell a deliberate lie in this position. Isn't it possible—the spouses should ask themselves— that they avoid eye contact more than they realize and thus encourage distrust even when it is not warranted? Have they been saving physical contact for the sex act and thus not appreciating how important a form of communication it is?

In the next simple communication exercise the toss of a coin determines who goes first. The winner tells a story about something that happened that very day, and the spouse attempts to interrupt the story, using the following techniques. When the narrator-pauses to take a breath or find a word, the interrupter quickly makes a comment or asks a question. Whenever the storyteller uses a word that has more than one meaning, the interrupter shows that he assumes the inappropriate meaning is intended. And if the spouse uses a metaphor, the interrupter takes it literally (Speaker: "And it sure gave me a butterfly-in-the-stomach feeling." Interrupter: "How could you get butterflies in your stomach?").

After three minutes, the spouses switch roles. This time, the interrupter spouse looks for any opportunity to give a relationship comment (Speaker: "So then I decided I'd go to a show." Interrupter: "You're just the kind of person who'd go to a movie").

These exercises show how easy it is (and how frustrating for the speaker) to make someone's communication difficult. Yet spouses often spend a lot of time doing just that, even if unwittingly; none are so deaf as those who *do not wish to hear.*

When these exercises have been done, the spouses should transmit two completed messages—original communication, acknowledgment, and second acknowledgment. They are now ready to start—at their next session—the nonverbal communication exercises described in the following chapter.

42

ESTABLISHING A
QUID PRO QUO

In reorganizing a marriage so that it can operate with maximum workability, establishing a *quid pro quo* is essential. To achieve a *quid pro quo* it is necessary to understand two fundamentals:

First, the spouses must learn what their total communication facilities are. As we know, a marriage is an interlocking, self-contained system. The behavior and the attitudes of one partner always stimulate some sort of reaction from the other. Because these attitudes, and the resulting actions and reactions, usually originate at the unconscious level, both spouses may be unaware of them. In bringing the *quid pro quo* procedure to maximum functionality, each partner must learn to recognize his own behavior and attitudes and the reactions which they stimulate in the other. He must become fully conscious of the many aspects of communication with the other, and also of how the other one will respond to each communication, be it by a word, a lifted eyebrow, a silence, or a punch in the nose. One way to get started on this is for the spouses to read the communications chapter aloud to each other, alternating on paragraphs.

Second, it must be realized that with the exception of such rare couples as the Heavenly Twins, spouses have many differences in behavior—in attitudes, in tastes, in methods of performance, and in levels of performance. Therefore, if each behaves naturally and spontaneously, scores of conflicts between the spouses are inevitable. If the wife, for example, wishes to watch a variety show on the single television set at the same time that the husband wants to tune in the boxing matches, one of the spouses will have to yield. This is a simple example, but differences of this sort may be found with respect to food, to moods, to sex; they may permeate the entire range of behavior, tastes, and attitudes of a man and wife. Marriage may be a source of many advantages and many comforts, but it does *eliminate some of the spontaneous behavioral repertoire.* Perhaps that is why a spouse is often referred to as "the better half." This may well be a folk method of expressing the fact that in marriage one reduces by half the free and spontaneous ways of behaving which were available before marriage. If both spouses are rigid and insist that all of their desires be granted, the marriage cannot continue as a functional relationship. Day after day and night after night each of them will seek to exert power over the other, to gain his own way. Some of the maneuvers and ways of behaving which are instruments of this power struggle are unconscious; therefore, if the marriage is to be improved, they must be identified, as we indicated in the preceding paragraph.

In establishing a *quid pro quo* the spouses acknowledge that they have differences—at many levels, both conscious and unconscious—and that in order to maintain the marriage, in order to achieve the benefits of collaboration, each is willing to sacrifice a percentage of his natural and spontaneous behavior. The process of establishing a workable *quid pro quo* could well be called a "marital bargaining session" or "negotiations for the betterment of the marriage." Both spouses are saying "I can't have everything I want and you can't have everything you want, but let's arrange our behavior in such a manner that we each get the maximum; let's negotiate so that each has those things which are most important to him and at the same time tries to nourish the well-being of the other to the maximum extent." The establishment of a *quid pro quo* means the making of behavioral rules which are of the greatest mutual benefit. Only rules equitable to both work in marriage. It is a union in which both parties win or both lose.

Naturally, the more hate-filled the spouses, the more discordant the marriage, the more difficult it will be to start afresh
with a new *quid pro quo.*

Getting the marital process back in balance often can be a long
and arduous task. Even with professional help it may require a
year or more. In some cases, however, spouses working on their
own may be successful in only six to eight weeks, or perhaps a
few months, provided both have a keen desire to solve their
mutual problem. They may experience a certain zeal, a certain
zest for mutual victory, which might be lacking if they were
leaning on a professional counselor.

The danger in self-therapy is that the spouses may expect a
balanced marriage, a good functional *quid pro quo,* to appear
almost instantly. It will not. They should assume that at least six
or eight weekly sessions of an hour apiece will be necessary
before any degree of success is apparent. If after a reasonable
trial the spouses are convinced that they cannot bargain, their
alternatives, as has been mentioned, are to seek outside help, to
separate, or to permit one spouse to dominate entirely.

The sessions should be looked upon as an important ritual, a
ritual almost as important as the marriage ceremony itself, for in
many cases if these sessions are not successful, the marriage will
terminate. It is helpful if the spouses pick for the first session a
date coming roughly a week after they have completed this book,
and mark the appointment on the calendar. The circumstances of
the meeting should be as convenient as possible for both. For
example, it may be necessary to spend a night in a hotel to avoid
interruption by the children. Even if the meeting is conducted at
home, it should be approached as something very special. One
couple we knew took the attitude that they were now attempting
to make a beginning in their "real and lasting marriage," and
that their earlier wedding ceremony amounted to just a legal piece
of paper which didn't count in human terms. Though they had
been married for seven years and had three children (and many
problems), they prepared for their *quid pro quo* meetings as if for
a festivity, at which each wished to be at his very best. They
bathed, dressed up, and in every way tried to appear as attractive
as possible. At first they held their meetings at home after the
children had gone to sleep. Later, they learned that they made

more progress if they hired a baby-sitter, had dinner out, and conducted their discussion in a hotel room. The use of the hotel room is frequently advantageous because it is a neutral area without any personal associations; both spouses are certain there will be no distractions, and in many cases it brings back memories of courtship days. This couple also used a tape recorder so they could later listen to the sessions *separately*.

Married couples, in short, can do something for themselves, and if they exhibit patience and stick to certain ground rules they will not damage their marriage, but rather improve it. If *quid pro quo* formation is to be attempted, the procedures described below must be explicitly and conscientiously followed.

First, as has been stated, the spouses should pick a date and make a formal appointment with each other for the first meeting. They should choose a day when both can be relaxed and unhurried. If, for some reason a possibility develops that interruptions may occur, the meeting should be postponed to the following week. If there are several postponements, one or the other spouse should force agreement on a date, since one or both of them may be attempting to avoid this kind of confrontation.

The first session should be devoted to understanding the material, described at the end of the preceding chapter, on establishing communication. Readers who have previously performed these exercises will find some review sessions useful. This is a good way to start for several reasons. First, throughout the sessions to come, the highest degree of communication must be exercised. Second, learning to communicate fairly well can be done almost mechanically by following the instructions. If the exercises are performed with care, success is usually easy. We deliberately start these discussions with procedures which we are confident both spouses can accomplish. If they cannot, the reason is more apt to be unwillingness or sabotage than inability. If this is the case, the services of a therapist will probably be necessary.

Most people find the communication exercises to be fun, and are able to carry them on with considerable success, especially if they limit the use of the exercises to twice a week.

During the period required to complete these exercises, each spouse should observe the various methods of nonverbal communication employed by the other. Each should make notes specifying what behavior, attitudes, motions, grimaces, silences, and so forth are interpreted as messages and what these messages mean to the receiver. Here are some examples.

"When Mary sleeps in pajamas instead of her silk nightgown, I know she's annoyed. I wonder if she realizes this is how I know not to approach her sexually on certain nights."

"When John simply slides his eyes around at me without moving any part of his body, and says nothing, I know he disagrees with what I have said."

"When Mary fixes her hair in a bun on the top of her head early in the morning, I know she's happy."

"When John leaves the house without shining his shoes in the morning, I know he's in a bad mood."

"When John has little wrinkles by the side of his eyes and tugs on the end of his ear, I know he's about to play a practical joke."

"When Mary sits up very straight in the chair and stares straight at me when I'm telling her something important, I know she has something else on her mind and isn't even listening."

During the first week or two the spouses put down as many of these observations as possible, each listing at least six nonverbal communications, of which two or more give a happy, or positive, message. Spouses have an inclination to search out the nastier types of message, and competition as to who can obtain the most negative material should be avoided. At first, getting six nonverbal communications may appear difficult. But it is one of the most effective methods of increasing the number of objective communication channels.

When the verbal communication exercises (described earlier) have been completed, the spouses move on to the attempt to make each other aware of their nonverbal methods of communication. They flip a coin to see who goes first. Then, taking turns, they play a kind of charades. One spouse acts out a way of behaving which serves the other as a nonverbal communication and the other tries to guess what the acted-out behavior indicates. If the guessing is unsuccessful, the actor explains how he interprets this particular action, grimace, or whatever. Then the roles are reversed.

When this exercise has been completed, they move on to the next. One partner looks at his list of observations and calls out the message which he receives from one of his spouse's ways of behaving. For example, John says, "Mary, I'm telling you something very important, but you really don't want to hear it so you're pretending you're listening and you're really not."

The spouse responds, if he can, by acting out his nonverbal behavior for transmitting this message. In this instance, Mary sits up straight in the chair and stares at John. John then may say, good-naturedly, "Mary, that's pretty good. But usually you sit up a little bit straighter and you thrust your head forward just a little and you don't have that twinkle when you're staring at me. It's a sort of glazed look, as if you're starting right at the end of my nose." Then Mary tries acting her own behavior out again. If it turns out that Mary is not aware of what nonverbal method she uses to transmit some particular message, John describes it to her, and she then attempts to act it out.

Next, Mary may say, "John, it's Monday morning. You're in a bad mood, and the eggs which I fixed for your breakfast weren't quite right. Will you please act out your usual behavior in this situation?"

John pretends he's eating at a table. He frowns, looks at his wristwatch, and mutters, "There'll be a lot of traffic this morning. I'd better leave fifteen minutes early. I don't have time to eat everything." He stands up and walks to the end of the room, pretends he's opening a closet, looks down as if searching for the shoe-shining equipment, shakes his head, frowns, pretends he's tossing on his coat and hat, and mimics himself walking out the front door without saying anything.

Mary may clap her hands and say, "You did that very well, John, but you left out one thing. You usually mutter as you open up the closet, 'Nobody ever puts the goddamn shoe-shine gear back in the right place.'"

John now goes through the whole thing again, overemphasizing his scowling, perhaps caricaturing his swearing, and stamping out of the house.

This exercise can be an enormous amount of fun, and it is an easy and practical way for both spouses to become aware of their nonverbal methods of communication. The most difficult part of the exercise is the beginning—the observation and listing of the forms of nonverbal communication which are employed. At first they will be formed only after a good deal of looking, but once the spouses are caught by the spirit of this exercise, their recognition will become easier and easier.

A large movable mirror, in which each spouse can see himself as he reenacts his own nonverbal behavior, is desirable. Watching oneself in the mirror not only makes the exercise more enjoyable—for almost everyone is a ham actor—but also provides an opportunity for the other spouse to coach the one who is acting. Mary may say to John, "You're doing that very well, but, really, the corners of your mouth go down a little more when you're annoyed at me at breakfast." Here John will try to push the corners of his mouth down a little bit more and Mary will applaud him and say, "That's right." Now John is likely to respond with a burst of merriment, and he may caricature himself. Interplay of this sort helps individuals slowly to visualize their own nonverbal behavior and to begin to understand how this behavior sends powerful messages to the other spouse, and why sometimes the message received is not the one the sender believed he was transmitting.

When the spouses have completed the communication exercises they are ready for the actual *quid pro quo* practice sessions. The first of these should be started at the next meeting.

43

QUID PRO QUO
PRACTICE SESSION

Before proceeding, the spouses should review their performance in the communication sessions to make sure that neither has gotten into the habit of using the past adversely against his mate. Remarks like "I notice you started these sessions late just as you do everything else" can only lead to a series of infinite regressions back to Adam and Eve. We recommend that whenever one of the spouses is *unable* to avoid the adverse use of past history, the other should take the privilege of stopping the session at once.

First Session

This session is designed primarily to help each spouse listen to the other so that later on, when more substantive issues are discussed, the spouses have a better chance of *hearing* each other. It enables them to learn to control the tendency toward recriminations or alibis or the utilization of any sort of defensiveness. Accurate hearing means not only perceiving what is said, but also refraining from attributing to the speaker what he has not actually said at this particular time.

It is recommended that the first *quid pro quo* session be divided into three segments of fifteen minutes each. The spouse who speaks first is elected by flip of a coin, after which they alternate. During the first segment, each of the spouses has his turn to state as factually as possible what characteristics he would ideally like to see in the other, to make the marriage more workable. The spouse who does not have the floor remains completely silent, making every attempt to listen to what is being said.

The second segment begins when the spouse who last was silent summarizes what he has heard from the other and inquires if his summary is approximately correct. Then he adds supplementary comments, *but only about himself* (for example, "It seems to me that if I were in your position I would want me to be more prompt than I have a tendency to be"). Note that the spouse who is summarizing is *not* allowed to introduce defensive or attacking material. When he is through, then the other spouse does the same thing. At first, the habit of introducing such harmful material will be hard to break, but if both spouses are conscious of the problem, success will come.

The summary which opens the second segment should be easy to complete quickly. During the third segment (after again flipping a coin to see who starts) one spouse is required to spend exactly fifteen minutes (timed by the listening spouse) describing how he himself contributes destructively to the marriage and how he could change so as to improve the marital situation. If the individual cannot think of any ways in which he contributes destructively or is failing in the relationship, this fifteen-minute period must be spent in silence. It is surprisingly difficult to remain silent this long, but it is even more difficult to be so perfect in a marital relationship that one cannot think of a single fault in oneself. The fifteen minutes seldom pass silently.

If the spouses have reached this point in the practice sessions without destructiveness or mutual antagonism, they can feel they have made considerable progress and are urged not to hold any discussions of their marital problems until the next exercise—which is at least one week away. If either one brings up the topic of their marriage during this recess, the other is to remind him that the book says, "Thou shalt not."

Second Session

The second session consists essentially of one spouse's learning to take directions from the other. One of the most common and grievous problems in the ordinary marriage is that spouses cannot accept instruction from each other. In the course of any relationship, in the course of getting family work done, it is necessary for the spouses to divide areas of work responsibility and for each to be willing to cooperate by taking instruction from the other in the other's particular area. In actuality, however, *this is rarely done.* Usually, there is avoidance—"I'm doing it because I want to"—or a slight changing of the instructions so as to make them seem to have been issued by the spouse who is doing the work. The following exercise, then, is one in which one of the spouses learns to take instruction from the other.

On a morning shortly after the end of the rest period (approximately one week) the spouses again flip a coin. Then, in the course of the day, the winner plans in detail a weekend for the two of them; the children (if any) are *not* to accompany their parents. The other spouse is told about the plans that evening. He can make no suggestions, and during the weekend is expected to accept all of the arrangements made by his partner. The weekend is to consist of only two days and one night, for it is likely to be a difficult period for the couple. Couples frequently fail in their first try at the one-spouse-dominated weekend; the strain can be particularly great if the coin toss has resulted in a complete role reversal—as when the spouse who usually dominates becomes the follower, and the submissive spouse becomes the leader. Several attempts may be necessary before success is achieved. But when it is, the resulting relief and self-understanding will be recognized by both spouses.

One highly competitive couple achieved weekend success through humor. The husband, who had lost the toss of the coin, responded to his wife's detailed orders throughout the weekend with a cheery "Yes, boss!" Laughter followed, and suddenly both found the pattern easy to carry out.

The next exercise will be enlivened by recollection of the

weekend experience and should not take place before the following Wednesday or Thursday.

Third Session

In the third session, the spouses ask each other questions which must be answered by "Yes" or "No" and nothing more. If attempts are made to qualify or explain the answers, the value of the session is decreased. The spouse whose turn it is to lead asks two questions of the other, waiting for a reply to the first before proceeding to the second:

Do you believe that this marriage of ours can be improved?

Apparently we have to do a lot of work and perhaps give up some things in order to improve the marriage. Do you think our marriage is worth the enormous effort?

When these two questions have been asked by spouse A and answered by spouse B, then the roles are reversed. B asks and A answers the same two questions.

The next step is for spouse A, speaking out loud, to ask a series of questions of himself, answering each in turn by saying "Yes" or "No." Spouse B listens. The questions are as follows:

1. During the last few months, have I ever said, "If only you [the other spouse] would do so and so, our marriage would be much better?"

2. In the last few months have I often stated, "If you [the other spouse] had a different personality, I would be much better off and the marriage would be a much smoother one?"

3. Have I in the last few months used past history against you? Have I brought up your past errors and ways of behaving, things I didn't like about you in the past, in order to prove a point, or to intimidate you, or to get some degree of control over you?

[Remember, these are all to be answered by the spouse who is asking the questions.]

4. In the last few months have I generalized about some fault of the opposite sex? Have I done this either out loud or in my own thinking? [Here the speaker should try to recall whether he has

indulged in the common tendency to play the game of the battle of the sexes. It is easy to forget that our biases are reinforced constantly, and are thus enlarged, unless we become aware of this danger and learn to look around and think for ourselves.]

5. In the last few months have I felt vulnerable in relation to you? [Only by avoiding a sense of vulnerability can one be open, fully trusting, and nondefensive. The speaker should try to remember if he has withheld loving behavior for fear that it would be interpreted as approval of some of the disliked behavior of his spouse.]

6. In the last few months have I used the children against you at any time?

While spouse A has been asking and answering these questions, spouse B has been sitting silently. Now the procedure is reversed. Spouse B asks and answers the same questions, while spouse A listens.

After this has been done, the same questions are used once again, only in this instance, we start off with spouse A asking the questions of spouse B. For example, spouse A will ask, "During the last few months, have I ever said, "If only you would do so and so, our marriage would be much better'?" Spouse B answers with "Yes" or "No."

The procedure is then reversed; spouse B asks and spouse A does the answering.

Answering the questions is a sufficiently arduous task for one session. The reason for requiring a simple "Yes" or "No" is that it is important, at this time, for the spouses to avoid discussing the content of the questions. The urge to enlarge on the answers, and thus to become both defensive and aggressively destructive, is very great, and at this stage such behavior must be made impossible because one cannot truly evaluate marital interaction unilaterally: if A thinks that B is at fault, he is not considering how his own effect on B may have helped bring about that particular action.

During the next week the spouses are to think about the questions which they asked and answered, *but they are not to discuss them between themselves—or with anyone else.*

Fourth Session

At the next weekly meeting, the questions and answers of the previous session are discussed. Whenever an answer has been "Yes," the data supporting it is now presented. For example, if spouse A answered "Yes" when he asked the first question ("During the last few months, have I ever said, 'If only you would do so and so, our marriage would be much better'?"), he now gives as many examples of his making this remark as he can recall. For instance, Mary may say, "Yes, I said that if you, John, would be home the same time every evening, I wouldn't be so nervous about meals. I'd be more cheerful at dinner, and we'd have much happier evenings." Then she goes on to mention other statements of this sort which she has made. When she is through, spouse B— John, in this instance—lists further examples which he may remember but which spouse A forgot. Both spouses speak as dispassionately as possible, making statements of fact, without elaboration. The spouses do not discuss whether or not the remarks now recollected were justified. They do not discuss the effects of the statements. They simply list as many as possible. After A has gone through the list of questions and given examples, and B has supplied more examples, B takes his turn and goes through the same list, with A adding further illustrations. Even if the one spouse supplies examples which the other thinks are exaggerated or perhaps totally unfounded, there is to be no disagreement or arguing.

Once again, a mirror in the room is desirable, for the effect upon the spouses of watching themselves as they speak is enormous. The inclination to become angry or defensive during the dialogue is strong. If the spouses watch themselves in the mirror, they can see when they begin to look angry or grimace or make gestures of annoyance and are then able to control themselves. Even if the effort at control is not completely successful, just the fact that they have observed the development of anger in themselves, is a large step toward the establishment of a *quid pro quo*.

Most spouses can get through this dialogue in one session lasting about an hour and a half.

The participants will notice that the exercise has involved statements of facts *as seen by each spouse*. Nothing is argued about, defended, or fought over. This avoidance of argument is important to the process because neither spouse can eliminate the ideas or behavioral patterns of the other by arguing, defending, or fighting. Up until now the exercises have been intended only to get each spouse acquainted with the nature of the other's thinking. Attempts to play district attorney or instructor must be avoided at all cost. The spouses must approach this undertaking as equals, with neither feeling superior in any way to the other. They must remember that if things have gone wrong, both are equally to blame. There is no victim without a victimizer. There is no victimizer without a victim.

Fifth Session

The fifth session is by far the most difficult and can be attempted only if both spouses feel they have accomplished the following:

1. Decided that the marriage should be continued, and indicated a willingness to make a vigorous effort to develop a functional relationship.

2. Practiced the rudiments of effective verbal communication.

3. Become conscious of some of the nonverbal methods of communication utilized by each, bringing them into awareness and learning to identify what they mean.

4. Learned what each spouse believes he has done to create discord in the marriage.

5. Learned that one cannot evaluate marital interactions unilaterally.

6. Learned that the developing of a *quid pro quo* need not be a battle, *but can be satisfying*.

We now approach the bargaining table—which separates the adults from the children. Here one's capacity for maturity is put to a harsh test. Here it is possible to find out whether the spouses really wish to have a functional relationship, or whether they are only playing cruel games.

Both come to the bargaining table with paper and pencil. If

possible, a mirror should be placed where they can see themselves in it. At this meeting each spouse presents his wishes, desires, and needs.

Once more they flip a coin to see who will begin.

The first speaker then describes what he would like; he does not dictate how his spouse should behave, or criticize his past behavior. Some examples follow.

"I would like to learn to be more patient with the children."

"I would like to see myself have more time to practice the piano."

"I wish that we could get a station wagon."

"I wish that I had a feeling of greater importance in our marriage."

"I wish that we could have dinner at the same time every evening."

"I wish I were not so jealous of you whenever you go on a trip."

"I wish we had a greater income." (Here the speaker should specify any practical suggestions for implementing the desire, if possible.)

Since these are to be important items, from six to ten should generally be sufficient to convey the individual's principal wishes.

One of the major hazards here is that one or both of the spouses will tend to use the bargaining table to present what they do not want in the future instead of making simple, declarative statements of what they do want. This practice in reality is a way of condemning the other spouse and of bringing up the past.

At this stage, then, one spouse expresses his needs, wishes, and desires and the other simply listens, asking for clarification when necessary, but not arguing. As the items are mentioned, *both spouses write them down.*

When one spouse has finished, the other has his turn to present a list of wishes, desires, and needs.

After both spouses have spoken, they must spend about fifteen or twenty minutes studying the two lists. Then each (if possible) identifies the first desire or need of the other which he feels can be fulfilled. We are suggesting here that the spouses find at least one area for collaboration, if they can.

The extensive use of teaching machines in the last few years has confirmed the commonsense notion that success reinforces the learning process and accelerates the rate of learning. So too in "teaching" the *quid pro quo* we are suggesting that the spouses can learn more easily to trust each other enough to bargain if they are successful from the first. The simplest way to accomplish this is for one spouse to pick from the list of the other an item on which he can agree, or about which he at least has very little negative feeling. He will then find it easy to "aid" the other spouse in working out something in relation to his wish. The other, having had the pleasure of cooperation, will be in a mood to cooperate in return.

If the spouses (and we consider this highly unlikely) are unable to select even one area of agreement for a beginning collaborative effort, they require further discussion and training in *quid pro quo* formation.

For example, if they have been unsuccessful, they should quickly review the session in their own minds to see if they have employed any of the disaffilliative techniques most common in such discussions:

First, has either spouse made the assumption that he is right and the other is wrong? If so, and if he is unable to feel differently after independently reading the material on the *quid pro quo* to follow, he is in need of discussions with a third party before attempting further meetings with his spouse.

Second, has either spouse attacked the other with all-encompassing criticism which leaves the impression that there is no possibility of improvement? Such statements as "You never do anything right," or "You have always been like that," are fatal to this effort.

Third, has either spouse employed defensive withdrawal, a destructive though ineffectual way of behaving? In defensive withdrawal, one spouse breaks off contact and leaves the other feeling abandoned and righteous, like a modern-day Joan of Arc perishing in the flames of her own indignation. The wife who becomes silent and tearful as her husband's voice takes on a rasping, accusatory tone may feel she is trying to avoid making him even angrier, but she is, in fact, doing just the opposite. She is also indicating that she feels he is impossible, a message which does little to improve their communication.

As we have already indicated, these initial sessions will be difficult, especially since one spouse is required to sit silently while the other states how he would like to change the marriage. Hence, a failure the first go-around is not fatal to the process. The spouses must be sure they do not get carried away and continue the discussions over approximately an hour.

Sixth Session (a Full-Scale Discussion)

After each partner has at last been able to select an area of agreement with the other, and to develop a means of accomplishing the desire expressed, the spouses are ready for their first full-fledged *quid pro quo* discussion. At a time when they feel at ease and safe from interruption, they sit down together to exchange viewpoints about what each feels is necessary, to determine the extent to which these aims are compatible, and to decide what can be done to achieve them.

If through the preceding exercises they have developed clear communication and a spirit of cooperation, each should find it possible to yield on some points in return for concessions from his spouse on others, and to maintain the attitude that his purpose is not to gain more than the other, but to help make decisions which will be to the advantage of both.

The following is an example of a successful start in a *quid pro quo* discussion.

HUSBAND: I hate to sound like a tightwad, but I feel I must tell you that we have to cut down on our expenses at least until I get some of the new office equipment paid for.

WIFE: What particular items were you thinking of?

HUSBAND: I've been looking over the checkbook and I find that clothes make up a considerable item. I'm willing to forgo any new outfits. How about you?

WIFE: You know very well that I spend much more on clothes than you do. If you're telling me to cut down, why not come out and say so?

HUSBAND: Because something occurred to me and that was that you've spent more on clothes lately since you lost that weight. I was very much for your losing it, too.

WIFE: That's right, I did have to buy a number of things right after finishing the diet, but it was nice of you to remember it. How about reviewing this matter in a few months but agreeing not to buy anything in the meantime?

HUSBAND: Whew! I feel off the hook. I won't forget to bring it up when finances get better.

Note that although the husband begins tentatively, he manages to be at the same time specific and not attacking.

Complete examples of *quid pro quo* discussions, both unsuccessful and successful, are to be found in Chapters 45, 46, and 47.

44

SOME BEHAVIOR TO AVOID IN WORKING OUT THE *QUID PRO QUO*

A REVIEW OF THE DIFFICULTIES IN FORMING A *Quid Pro Quo*

The discussion of the difficulties which may occur in establishing a *quid pro quo* is not meant to imply that successful practice sessions will always remain mild and gentle in tone. Spouses can sometimes break through each other's defenses with passionate statements or pleas. By no means will emotion be eliminated from these sessions. It should however be contained.

One of the tactics most likely to produce anger in the discussions is reference to the past to illustrate what one does not want in the future, as in the following example.

HUSBAND: I think this would be a happier marriage if you would be more dependable.

WIFE: I don't know why you bring that up. You're one of the

most undependable people I know. You even managed to be late
to our wedding.

HUSBAND: I didn't say I was dependable. I was just asking if
you could try a little harder to do the few things that I ask.

Obviously, this conversation should stop at this point, for it's
going from bad to worse. This husband and wife should try
conversing again at another time, avoiding the errors which they
made in this attempt:

The husband has forgotten that a spouse should state very
specifically what he would like or desire, but should not dictate
how the other spouse should behave.

The wife has tried to undercut the husband by referring to the
past. She has forgotten that his interpretation of the past is different from hers. Neither can now say what really happened ten
years ago. It may even have been the wife who was late for the
wedding.

Instead of striking back with a criticism of his own, the spouse
to whom a request is directed should listen to the other's wishes,
ask (if necessary) why this particular thing is important to the
other, and see what he can do to help achieve it. Often the spouse
who has made the request will readily settle for a compromise
because it indicates an attempt at mutual cooperation. If the
spouse who receives the request is feeling defensive, he would be
wise to keep responses to a minimum.

There is in this conversation another hidden destructive element, which is easily overlooked. When the husband specifies how
his wife should behave and the wife retaliates by dredging up her
husband's alleged sin of being late for their wedding, the subtle
implication of each is that some else *would* have the desirable
trait, and *would not* have behaved so badly. In other words, an
unrealistic standard is being used, for neither spouse actually
knows that things would have been better with a different person.

One of the natural but destructive sins of spousehood is thinking that someone else would be easier to live with. One spouse
may notice the behavior of a friend and say to his mate, "Why
can't you be more like that?" The fact that the friend who seems
more desirable isn't living with the spouse doing the observing is
overlooked. He might not have this trait if he were a partner in a

different relationship (remember the systems concept!). In addition, the observed person may have many undesirable or annoying characteristics of which his friends are not aware. Directness makes a far better communication tool than do references to the past or to other persons.

In carrying on a discussion, spouses must beware of the tendency to fall into a vicious cycle of accusation, defense, and counteraccusation. How such a pattern can be broken is shown in the following episode, in which a man and wife were aided by a therapist, who acted deliberately and somewhat harshly (rather than indirectly). The wife had been destructively scolding her husband for not being more forceful in handling their thirteen-year-old son. As a result of the wife's nagging, the father was becoming defensive and the couple were splitting apart. They needed to join together as a coalition to handle the boy correctly. The therapist asked the father to change places with him, and induced the wife to pretend that he was her husband. Then, as mock husband and wife, they discussed an incident in which the boy had said "Shut up" to his parents and raced up the stairs to the second floor, locking himself in the bathroom before his father could reach him. The wife fell right into the spirit of the session and played her accustomed role as if the therapist were her husband. She berated him for not having punished the boy for his disrespect. She tried to generalize, recalling all sorts of other incidents and comparing what other fathers would have done. However, the therapist insisted that they stick to the particular episode. Acting as the husband, the therapist said. "Okay, you feel I'm a weak father. Then what do *you* suggest we do to punish George?" The wife was somewhat taken aback, but finally stated that she thought maybe taking his allowance away for two weeks would be helpful. The therapist-husband replied, "Look, that kid gets eight dollars a week by working Saturdays. He gets fifty cents a day for school lunches and you already told me that you don't think he spends it on lunch. His allowance is fifty cents a week. How in hell would it make any dent in his finances to stop his allowance?"

The wife was confused and surprised because she realized for the first time there were no easy answers. The problem had seemed hitherto simple because she transferred the blame to her husband, and he accepted it. She defensively tossed the ball back and asked the therapist-husband, "Okay, what would you suggest?"

"I suggest the next time he locks himself in the bathroom, I break the damn door down and paddle him."

"Break the door down?"

"Sure, you want me to take action! Okay, maybe it'll cost us twenty-five bucks to get the door fixed, but it's worth it if he's prevented from getting away with this kind of behavior."

"But isn't that a little drastic?" The wife was beginning to show alarm.

"No, goddamn it; we've got to put a stop to this rudeness of his. Now are you going to back me up or not? Just say so now in front of the doctor here (her husband acting the doctor's role) so I'll know whether I'm going to be made a fool of and have the rug pulled out from under me."

For a few moments the wife looked indecisive and uncomfortable, and then she stated weakly, "Okay, if it's necessary, I will back you."

At this point, the husband could not keep out of the picture any longer. He eagerly changed seats with the therapist and took over, spelling out with his wife the details of *when* she would agree that it was necessary to back him up and *how* she would back him up. Using what they had learned in this fairly brief exchange, the couple found during the next few weeks that they could apply the principles of specificity, direct action, and coalition formation to a number of situations which did not involve their son.

It is quite possible this couple could have worked out the same coalition pattern at home without the help of an expensive therapist *if* they could have broken, even for a few moments, their habitual pattern of accuse—defend—withdraw—accuse further —and so on, *ad nauseum.*

REVERSE VULNERABILITY

In a world that is becoming increasingly crowded, all of us have some need to protect ourselves from becoming too involved with too many people. We may, for example, plant a hedge between ourselves and our neighbors; or we may have the Joneses over only once a month, so that they will invite us back only once a month—and thus we avoid a relationship more intense and time-consuming than we wish to have with the Joneses.

People are often considerate and helpful to new acquaintances, thereby permitting themselves to be "vulnerable" (that is, open to behavior not yet predictable on the basis of experience with the other person). Frequently, somebody to whom one has been considerate will telephone a few weeks or months later to make further requests that the individual is unable or unwilling to carry out. The petitioner may then become disappointed and confused, calling the person (especially if he is prominent or influential) cold or snobbish, or saying he had no right to encourage him in the first place if he couldn't follow up. After a few such experiences, an individual is inclined to withhold most of his natural enthusiasm, courtesy, and kindness, thus insuring that he will not be vulnerable to this subsequent unpleasantness. He soon discovers that affiliative behavior is considered by others to be a commitment and that others may attempt to attach themselves to him socially, emotionally, or even commercially.

Most well-adjusted people learn to use various types of behavior that permit limited degrees of involvement. They attempt to walk a middle road, to keep the few aggressive people at a distance without becoming totally isolated themselves. By discriminating between personal and impersonal relationships, and between those people who are strangers or part of the "public" and those who are personally significant, they manage to retain a healthy degree of natural vulnerability.

In marriage, the excessive withholding of responses which are expected (and often needed) by the other spouse can be either a destructive act or a means of defense. We call this kind of behavior *reverse vulnerability*. In essence, it occurs when spouse A is afraid of making spouse B too loving or too dependent—thus putting a responsibility on spouse A for being equally loving and (in his view) excessively nurturing. Spouse A may fear that unless he withholds something, retains some latitude for independent actions and feeling, spouse B will expect the loving and nurturing behavior *at all times and under all circumstances.*

The spouse who functions according to the dictates of reverse vulnerability *cannot* (for whatever reason) *feel confident about his ability to discriminate between those times when he wishes to share loving behavior and those times when he wishes to enjoy what he regards as independence, separation, or withdrawal.* Consequently, his attitudes and behavior tend to be rigid. Spouse B is invariably confused by spouse A's double messages; and frequently the interpretation is, "He tells me he loves me, yet he is so cold to me. He must be either crazy, hostile, or a liar."

Another aspect of the problem is that the spouse who uses reverse vulnerability as a defense may think, "If I am loving, my spouse will conclude that I am accepting those things which I dislike and which in my opinion are causing discord in our marriage." In order to rationalize his withholding behavior, spouse A then keeps finding more and more fault with spouse B. But frequently the constant disapproval creates a vigorous competitiveness and rebelliousness in spouse B. Spouse A's response is to withdraw; he indulges, by keeping silent, in an even more cutting form of reverse vulnerability. *In this way spouse A allows behavior of which he disapproves or has grown tired to continue— out of fear that any change or comment will result in disaster.* The longer a pattern of this sort goes unchecked, the more difficult it is to change because its very history makes the idea of change all the more unacceptable.

Another variant of reverse vulnerability is exemplified by the individual who, virtually from the beginning of the marriage, *will not allow certain kinds of behavior to occur at all, for fear that a single occurrence will escalate irreversibly into a set pattern which he cannot change.* A common example is the husband who fears that unless he remains "in charge" at all times, his wife will "take advantage" of him. Such an individual becomes extremely rigid; *this practice of absolute avoidance is just as habit-forming as the consistent acceptance of disliked behavior would be.* Typical is the husband who never once does the dishes, even when his wife is ill, for fear that she will expect him to do them again. Or suppose a husband has had a great day at the office and comes home feeling like a gay Lothario and a big spender. He may be excited as he anticipates sharing his good mood with his wife. Too often, the wife will refuse to join in, or will in some way dampen his pleasure and spoil the prospect of an evening on the town, although she may sorely need and want the fun and companionship. Why? Because she fears he will think that he can wipe out all of his deficiencies as a husband and father just by playing the big shot *when he is in the mood.* Or she may be so angry about all those other evenings she wanted to go out and he insisted on watching television that she refuses to let him think this one grand gesture can make up for all the times he failed.

Thus, many a person indulges in reverse vulnerability by refusing to have fun with his spouse because he fears that doing so would be interpreted as blanket approval of the other's behavior. The flexible, vulnerable person, however, can have fun when fun is to be had and save the complaints for the times when particular issues warrant them!

A wealthy manufacturer we know married a very pretty girl. After the marriage, he developed a dislike for his mother-in-law because of her habit of becoming ill every time she wanted to control her husband. For example, at one time, the father-in-law bought a ranch—his life's dream. His wife, not wishing to live in the country, immediately became so ill that the doctor said she couldn't move out there. Without the personal supervision of the husband the ranch did not operate very well, and eventually it had to be sold because of heavy indebtedness. The moment the property was disposed of, the wife became healthy again. Our friend made up his mind that this would not happen to him. Therefore, even when his wife was genuinely ill and in pain, he paid little attention to her and gave her little comfort or help. He wanted to make it clear that he was not going to be controlled by her sickness as her father had been controlled by her mother. This reaction was a form of reverse vulnerability.

Reverse vulnerability is a destructive kind of behavior because it is not self-limiting. It may initially be caused by one specific stimulant, but it spreads throughout one's entire behavioral spectrum. It is a particularly insidious defense because in using it, one erects premature barriers to close relationships. It prevents the user from *testing the reality of his fears.* He lives in a defensive fantasy world behind fortress walls which long since may have become anachronistic.

The development of reverse vulnerability is sometimes indicated by the abrupt cessation of some kind of thoughtful or considerate behavior which was habitual in an individual. It is as if he feels that this pattern is becoming mandatory, that it will give rise to rigid expectations in the other spouse. So the practice—perhaps buying gifts or giving praise regularly—is suddenly stopped. This is most apt to occur early in a marriage.

There is a certain logic in this behavior. None of us wishes to perform always in a certain manner. The difficulty for a marriage lies in the fact that when spouse A suddenly stops behavior of this sort without explanation, spouse B is hurt and feels that A doesn't love him so much any more; then A is angry in return—having been "good" up to this point, A expects to receive "credit" for past kindnesses. Relationships unfortunately don't usually operate like savings-and-loan institutions, where one can build up a big account during prosperous times, withdraw portions of the investments during lean periods, and meanwhile collect interest!

HOW TO HANDLE REVERSE VULNERABILITY

Usually reverse vulnerability is recognized by one spouse, though both may be indulging in it. The spouse who identifies it should suggest a limited marital checkup session. (See Chapter 49 for full checkup.)

When the session has commenced, the spouses flip a coin to determine who speaks first. Then each asks the other four basic questions:

Has either of us developed certain behavior patterns sharply different from those which used to be habitual? For example, does the husband now come to breakfast in a foul mood, criticizing and swearing, when formerly he was cheerful and courteous? Or does the wife come to breakfast looking slovenly and serve only packaged cereal in the kitchen, when formerly she was well groomed and prepared a big breakfast which was beautifully served in the dining room? When were the changes in behavior first observed?

Have either of us been paralyzed into rigid and routine behavior which he is afraid to change because the change might be misunderstood? For example, does the family take a drive every Sunday even though it has become a chore and no one enjoys it? Does the husband come home to lunch every day even though he would prefer eating in the office lunchroom and the wife would prefer not to fix lunch?

Are there certain kinds of behavior which we would adopt if we felt completely free and were not afraid of being misunderstood?

Does either of us routinely refuse to engage in certain activities or types of behavior—even though he may not be well enough acquainted with them to dislike them—mainly because the other has suggested them? For example, perhaps the wife has never gone fishing in her life and continues to refuse to do so out of fear that if she goes fishing once, her husband will expect her to accompany him on every fishing trip. It is quite possible that after one fishing trip she will never go again, but it is also possible that she may find she enjoys this activity. Or perhaps the husband refuses to take his wife dancing (even though he enjoyed dancing before they were married), again out of fear that if he takes her dancing once she will expect to go often, and his refusal will lead to a blowup of serious proportions. He may be afraid that if he frequently stays out late he will be unable to function effectively at work the next day.

When the answers to the questions are positive—that is, when the spouses agree that they are caught in a reverse-vulnerability pattern—one partner may appear to be the aggressor, but actually *both are equal participants.* Frequently the spouse who is the apparent victim is equally culpable, for he may be passively aggressive, behaving in a manner which provokes the other's reverse vulnerability.

Once the reverse-vulnerability pattern has been identified, the spouses must ask each other three further questions:

First, can we tolerate the repeated small struggles caused by the fact that each of us wishes to do different things and has to "fight" for his preferences? Or are we perhaps avoiding such struggles by steering clear of joint activities or by always allowing the same spouse to determine where we are going? Clearly, these two ways of behaving are equally inflexible; both lead to problems, and are indicative of a reverse-vulnerability pattern.

Second, are our activities so rigidly patterned that we dread being together, or often look forward to being with others?

Third, does each feel that he is more appreciated and respected by others than by the spouse?

There is a particular kind of security, exemplified in the armed services, in which sameness of behavior (such as getting up each morning and putting on the same uniform) becomes an end in itself. Many marriages function in just this way—joylessly, routinely, soberly—until all of a sudden one or both partners can't take it any more. Marriage without novelty is like a salad without dressing—there is an enormous monotony in eating plain vegetables, even if one can live on them tastelessly for years. Some couples and individuals attempt to fight this kind of sameness by developing a variety of reverse vulnerability in which they interrupt patterns through fear of being forever stuck with them. By fighting monotony in this way, they get into traps as monotonous and isolating as the ones they are trying to avoid. However, if husband and wife work on the problem *openly* as a *team*, they may be able to avoid both monotony and defensive isolation and still live together.

If the spouses are convinced at this point that they have fallen into the reverse-vulnerability patterns described, the next question is how to reduce it. The suggestions that follow can almost be guaranteed to lead to temporary strife, but this is the kind of struggle which is well worth the pain it causes (usually considerably less than is anticipated).

The procedures may sound absurdly childlike and simple, but they are effective.

The spouses flip a coin, and the winner takes charge of their next joint activity, selecting a mutually acceptable time (a day, an afternoon, or an evening) and determining how it will be spent. As long as the activity is physically and financially feasible, the other spouse is bound to accept and go along. The activity may be just about anything. For example, they may go fishing, attend a concert, clean the attic together, go to the zoo with the children, visit a museum, plant tomatoes, and so on. The other spouse is *not expected* to have a good time or approve of the activity; but both, before the coin is flipped, must agree to play the game amenably. When this joint activity has been completed, the roles are reversed. The second spouse takes charge of the next joint activity.

Some readers may wonder what good it does to carry out such an artificial set of actions.

For one thing, many spouses have lived for years without *once* being able to agree (overtly or covertly) on anything. If they try giving in to each other, the chances are good that they may discover that doing so is not as frightening as they have imagined all along.

Second, many a married person who has occasionally gone along spontaneously with the wishes of the other spouse has only found himself in more hot water for his efforts, being accused of not really having a good time, or of "just doing it for my sake— you don't really mean it." Naturally, after such a negative response he is likely to wait a long time before trying to be conciliatory again. But when the spouses practice giving in *alternately*, no matter how artificial their behavior, each has the experience of *not fearing* to give in today, because he knows his turn will come tomorrow.

A pattern which is associated (even though it appears to be the opposite) also sometimes occurs. The spouses may—on weekends particularly—be "together" more than is wise. That is to say, they stay at home, spending their time in different parts of the house, engaged in separate activities, each feeling free neither to leave the other nor to participate collaboratively or even cooperatively with him. If the husband and wife pass much of each weekend spreading mutual gloom and being stuck in each other's orbits, a withholding or reverse vulnerability is likely to result. For this circumstance the following exercise is suggested.

On alternate weekends the spouse chosen by lot must arrange to engage in an outside activity for either Saturday or Sunday. He may visit friends, play golf, go to a movie, or sit miserable and alone in an empty park, but he must agree to leave the house and stay away until nightfall or a reasonable evening hour, without the other spouse.

The remaining form of reverse vulnerability—the withholding of approval—often can be reduced by the following exercise:

The spouses flip a coin to see who first is to be the "giver." For one week, the giver performs all the loving actions which the other desires. For example, a wife may wish her husband, when he is the giver, to demonstrate affection in public, to thank her for the many things she does all day long, to hold her chair, to take her to a movie, to ask her mother over for dinner, to stop using foul language, to help the children with homework, and so on. The husband, when his turn as recipient comes, may request that the sloppy house be made neat, that meals be cooked and served in a certain way, that the wife read certain magazine articles and discuss them with him, and the like.

During the week that the giver performs as requested—in a cheerful, skillful manner—the recipient *never* acknowledges what has been done, never gives thanks, and if possible, complains that things could have been done better. The following week the roles are reversed.

If this exercise is done with seriousness (no caricature) the results often are startling. The giver becomes aware that many of the things the other has asked for (and apparently believes he needs) are simple and are not degrading or difficult to provide. The recipient, because he is forced to withhold praise and is made to grumble, becomes conscious of this sort of behavior, and thereafter often finds it hard to withdraw and be negative.

At the end of two weeks, frequently there is a dissolution of the rigid patterns which have been paralyzing both of them and causing the destructive reverse vulnerability. Henceforth, the husband and wife are able to bring the subject up openly—without an inhibiting defensiveness—and corrective steps can be taken.

The second time this exercise is performed (we know one couple who do it every few months), it usually becomes an enjoyable game.

Some couples will have to seek professional help in breaking out of their reverse-vulnerability patterns. The need for help is indicated when the attempt to perform these exercises is unsuccessful because one or both cannot cooperate or remember to do what is required. "Not remembering" is usually a form of noncooperation—one repeatedly "remembers to forget!"

In sum, reverse vulnerability is a natural defense against the vulnerability all of us in our culture feel in an intimate relationship. However, it must be identified and then dealt with, as we suggest, by letting each spouse discover that vulnerability is as much a part of life as is breathing. It is extremely important to eliminate reverse vulnerability, for it produces relationships which leave one isolated, guarded, suspicious, and lonely. Only by being open to the unknown in others and testing the reality of our expectations by *experience,* can we make the real world more rewarding than our fantasies.

45

A *QUID PRO QUO* DISCUSSION WHICH FAILED

The difficulties inherent in the *quid pro quo* exercises should not be minimized. The following is an actual transcription of a dialogue between a husband and wife who were having problems. These two volunteered to attempt a *quid pro quo* discussion because they had been fighting for months, and were on the brink of divorce.

Although both had been carefully instructed in the use of the *quid pro quo* exercises, they unintentionally violated the rules. Their dialogue was a failure.

DIALOGUE

HUSBAND: Let us start off by defining what we want from life and marriage.

WIFE: I would like to be productive and healthy. I would particularly like to have a happy and fruitful relationship with you, Bud.

INTERPRETATION

The wife begins the discussion in broad, vague terms which need definition.

DIALOGUE

HUSBAND: I would like to be in harmony with everything, to be productive, efficient, joyful, spontaneous, and healthy. By productive I mean, for me, primarily to be creatively productive in my work as an architect. Is it clear to you when I say I want to be productive?

WIFE: Yes, I think you've made that very clear to me, and I believe I understand that. In terms of things I'd like to do in life when I say I'd like to be productive, I have a real desire to study art, to learn to paint, to learn to sew, to have a restful home and a healthy, happy, productive husband and, ultimately, children.

HUSBAND: It's my estimate that you are so competitive that you must always be on some new project and shine, even if it does not last long. You want to do a million things—what do you mean by being productive? Do you think you can do all that and still run a house?

WIFE: Well, I meant to take care of my other needs and interests in good time and in good order. There's a certain order for how these things would happen. When we married, I had the idea that the most important thing to be considered was the domestic area. I feel I could use a little help from you when you felt like doing it or giving it. But I'm not going to art school, start sewing, and painting, all at the same. If I can do these things and not end up slighting you, then that's nifty and I want to, but in proper order. But you criticize me so much and find fault with everything I do, that I don't feel you love me very much, or that I'm very important to you.

HUSBAND: Uh, just so my honesty is bright and shining, I have to disagree with you. Now, for me to be productive—and this is more important than anything else to me, even being married— did you hear me?

INTERPRETATION

The husband responds in kind, then begins to define the one concept which relates to his major concern for himself—productivity —without first relating his remarks to his wife's statement regarding her desires.

The wife follows his lead competitively by defining, both specifically and broadly, what productivity means *for her*. As her husband had not supported her earlier, she now fails to support him by giving attention to his need for productivity and exploring ways to help him achieve his stated goal, with the faith that her chance will come next. Instead, she helps turn the discussion toward competition as to whose needs are to be filled *first*, or who will grant the first *quid pro quo*.

The husband comments (*apparently* irrelevantly) on the wife's competitiveness, becoming more competitive himself. He challenges the wife in a way which can only make her defensive, implying that her definition of being a productive person is inferior and unrealistic. At the same time, he delivers the message that the domestic tasks should come first.

The wife does respond defensively, both by delivering a relationship message to the husband ("I could use a little help from you when you felt like doing it or giving it")—a covert complaint— and by confirming the husband's judgment about the primary importance of domesticity, though without seeming to be in genuine agreement, instead of persisting in making her own judgment about relative values. The wife's withdrawal clouds open communication, as does her counter-complaint regarding the husband's criticism of her.

The husband responds by ignoring the wife's statements, which could have led to the formulation of a *quid pro quo* (in this instance, suggestions about what he could do to make her feel more secure). Instead, the husband confirms the wife's doubts

WIFE: I know that, and I've always known it.

HUSBAND: . . . And if I'm productive, and can create functional
and beautiful buildings, I'm a pretty good guy to be around, I
believe, and if I'm not, then I'm an absolute bastard. Uh, let's not
analyze why, but I just want to have it clear. I wish you would
tell me what I have to do to make you feel important, whatever
that means.

WIFE: You sure know what it means when we are with other
people: you're *always* flattering other women and complimenting
them on their wonderful cooking, or something else—but all I
ever get is complaints.

HUSBAND: Baloney. But let's not get into that. I want to talk
about the problems between you and me. The initial one is that
I don't trust you. First, I don't know that when you say something, that is what you really mean—like you might say before
we were married, or even now, "I never want to see you again."
Are you making it up? And then I would say, "Screw you," and
walk out of the house. And then later you'd say, "I didn't really
mean that, I just have a hell of a bad temper." So it's my nature
that I don't have to solve a damn crossword puzzle to know what
you're talking about. As it comes out of your mouth, I believe it.
This spreads over a lot of our problems. I'll make a commitment
right now that from now on, I will accept everything you say
exactly as it hops out. I will not ever refer to anything in the past,
although one makes his conclusions and has faith by adding up
what's happened and projecting it into the future. Uh, I will
accept everything you say as absolutely being what you mean,
but up to now, I've been scared to trust you. What do you say
to that?

INTERPRETATION

about his commitment to the marriage by insisting that his productivity and work come before the marriage. The wife says she gets the message.

The husband warns the wife that he can be expected to be a bastard if he's not permitted (able?) to be productive in the marriage. He then shifts the topic, making a request which opens the door to discussion of a *quid pro quo*.

The wife fails to respond to the husband's request to discuss a *quid pro quo*, and instead uses his statement as a means of opening up on another sore subject of her own, thus inviting escalation. She has again become defensive because of the husband's implication that her feeling "important" is vague and silly.

The husband again avoids escalation; he makes a provocative statement and then runs, by changing the topic. Using this technique, the husband is able to provoke and challenge the wife, keeping her in an essentially defensive position and preventing her from really challenging or attacking him for his failures or shortcomings. One result of this kind of guerilla warfare is that the formulation of a *quid pro quo* becomes impossible; the sniping effectively eliminates any basis for teamwork or cooperation. The wife is kept so busy defending herself that she has no chance to initiate bargaining by asking her husband for a *quid*— the favor he would grant, the expectation he would fulfill, in exchange for something from her. Now the husband follows up by stating that he doesn't trust her. He then makes an apparent effort to suggest a *quid pro quo* by offering to take everything she says at face value, the implication being that she should reciprocate by actually being trustworthy from now on. But this obviously cannot become the basis of a *quid pro quo* since the wife hasn't agreed that she has ever been untrustworthy.

WIFE: I just think there's a fallacy in believing just what comes out of a person's mouth. People make predictions about others on the basis of knowledge of the other's character, not just on what she says. Now if I were to say, "I don't give a damn about how the house looks," you ought to know from your knowledge of me that, regardless of what I say, I keep house in a responsible way. When somebody is angry, he says things he doesn't mean. That's just human. I agree, ideally, that it would be nice if someone's words and actions were entirely consistent, but I'm not perfect and neither are you, and I don't know anyone who is.

HUSBAND: I understand you to say that I should never mind what you say and just in some sort of mystical way interpret you to be honest, trustworthy, loyal, no matter what you say. Now I ask you, can I really trust you?

WIFE: I think you can, and I think you have—in your stiff-necked way—miscontrued what I said. It is my responsibility to try to make my actions consistent with my speech, but I can't always when I'm mad, and I think you should consider this.

HUSBAND: Uh, please be loving here now, and don't be angry at this question—it's absolutely an intellectual one. Before we were married, you were engaged to Mike, yet you went away with me to Mexico without his learning about it, and wrote a letter to him saying that you loved and missed him. I saw the letter by accident. How do I know you won't do that to me?

INTERPRETATION

It seems evident also that the husband is simply offering to do what he has tried to do in the past—take her words at face value —so his suggestion is not an attempt at a genuine *quid pro quo* or compromise. It involves little change on his part and is something *he* wants to do, *not* something his wife wants him to do.

Instead of talking in terms of specific behavior which each could adopt to correct the problem of mutual lack of trust, the wife again reacts defensively, arguing about the basic premise. As in the previous exchanges, the wife's defensiveness simply escalates the arguments, which will continue until the husband drops the topic and runs to a fresh one, which then will put the wife on a new defensive, causing the argument to escalate until he drops the topic, *ad nauseum.*

Both spouses begin more and more to rake up the past, thereby breaking the cardinal rule of a *quid pro quo* discussion. The pattern repeats. The husband's statement, in spite of his plea that the question is a harmless "intellectual" one, is destined to provoke defensiveness, escalation, and so on.

DIALOGUE

WIFE: Well, how about the time you changed your weekend skiing plans with Joannie, saying your mother was ill, when you were really with me all weekend?

HUSBAND: I could get into an argument here over the message to Joannie, but I won't just now. Let's talk about . . .

The wife bites. Here we go again.

The husband runs, reconnoiters, launches an attack from another bush. This can, and almost did, go on forever.

As the comments accompanying this discussion make painfully clear, the old ways of interacting die hard. It takes more than a wish that things could be different to change patterns acquired over years of living together. It also requires determination, hard work, and willingness to change and to become vulnerable by temporarily or permanently giving up some destructive defenses which prevent change. It takes readiness to let some old hurts go by without expiation, in an effort to reduce future hurts.

The discussion transcribed here really took place—between two people who are extremely intelligent, well educated, capable, and eager to make their marriage more workable. They had discussed the nature of a *quid pro quo* exercise in advance of attempting it, and had decided together that they were going to consciously try very hard to develop a *quid pro quo*. They felt that they understood the process before they started. Yet their effort was unsuccessful. Let's take a look at some of the reasons this attempt at a *quid pro quo* discussion was doomed to failure from the beginning.

First, the couple could not agree upon who should be the first to state his concept of a workable *quid pro quo*. A flip of a coin could have better settled this problem, for contention begets contention; beginning with a conflict, they were torpedoed right from the start.

Second, there was a total absence of *teamwork*. Each spouse used the discussion as an opportunity to draw blood for old hurts, to register new complaints, to deliver messages he had not dared to state openly before. We saw a good example of two "closed systems," or "closed-off people," in conflict, each fighting for gains and defending himself against being changed by the other, competing for the position of being the last to give "something for something." Each wanted to receive first, before giving. To be successful, a *quid pro quo* discussion requires as participants "open systems," people open to change, working together to reach new, improved solutions which are more satisfying to both than what each started with. At no point in this couple's interchange was there any feeling of teamwork, of "Let's see what we two, working together, can do to guarantee the achievement of our mutual goals." They did begin with a broad, seemingly mutual goal, vaguely defined as a "happy" and "productive" relationship. But in order to reach such a goal, they would have had to make room for the fulfillment of the individual needs and goals of each party. Furthermore, neither one would let the private hurts of the past alone, so they ended up by fighting each other over whose were the more hideous hurts, and failed to capture the essence of teamwork and cooperation. The result was that each won the battle, but lost the war.

Third, in their discussion there was a striking absence of *behavioral specificity*. The couple began the dialogue in broad, vague terms and at almost no time did either one become specific about his expectations for future behavior. We heard, ". . . can I really trust you?" and "being made to feel important," rather than, "What can I *do*, how can I *behave* differently, in order to prove my trustworthiness or make you feel loved?" We heard, "I have a real desire to study art . . . to learn to sew," and "I would like . . . to be creatively productive in my work," without any follow-through on "What can you and I *do* to make these wishes a reality?"

Finally, the *quid pro quo* discussion requires a *present and future* orientation. This couple dwelled almost entirely on the past —past hurts, past battles, past failures. A workable *quid pro quo* demands arrival at *new* patterns of behavior, *new* techniques and methods of interaction, *new* agreements and solutions. The essential questions in the *quid pro quo* are, What can you and I do differently in the *future?* What can we do *now* to make these changes possible? Dwelling on past failures can only result in the continuance of old arguments and the resensitizing of old wounds. It does not produce changes in the old, faulty patterns of interaction.

This same couple tried again. They were disappointed at having failed to establish a *quid pro quo* relationship, and were determined and courageous enough to make another attempt after discussing the failure and defining more clearly the nature and requirements of this kind of discussion. The following chapter describes their second effort.

46

A SECOND

QUID PRO QUO

ATTEMPT WHICH

FAILED

After the failure of the *quid pro quo* session described in the previous chapter, the same couple tried again. The transcription of their second *quid pro quo* session follows. It, too, failed, although it is a distinct improvement over the first effort. A number of the errors previously discussed are in evidence once again. Especially dangerous is the tendency of one spouse to start lecturing the other. When this happens—with no third party present to stop it—the conversation may never recover from the initial direction it takes. As before, the advantages of the marriage are not referred to; instead, the general focus is on the faults of the other spouse. The question of trust recurs, especially when a spouse astonishingly makes a statement implying that he himself is trustworthy yet the other spouse must be assumed to be untrustworthy. There is a tendency for one spouse to become defensive because the other wishes for something and to respond as if the wish were a command which had to be obeyed. Above all, again note how frequently the discussion leaves present specific focuses for generalizations about the past.

HUSBAND: Now, we are going to try to reach agreement on some things we usually argue about. I'll begin. I assure you that, as long as you and I are married, you can depend on my fidelity. No matter how miserable our relationship might be, I will not sleep with anybody else. You can assume that as long as you and I are married, I will not knowingly flirt with anybody else and if I do and you bring it to my attention, I will apologize or stop it. Do you agree?

WIFE: Do I agree that you're going to do this?

HUSBAND: Yes.

WIFE: I accept that from you and I believe you will not do this.

HUSBAND: Now, I'm asking you if I can depend on you in this way.

WIFE: Well, I can agree that this is an area where we can reach agreement. (*Laughs.*) I think that the fidelity issue is one that we both feel the same way about, and I will not sleep with anyone else either, as long as we are married. And that flirting thing—I know that this is something you slipped in because I have a tendency to be extra cheerful and responsive in the company of others, which I have never thought was improper or an indication of infidelity. But I will agree to attempt to not flirt for the purpose of greater harmony in this marriage relationship. Is that good enough?

HUSBAND: Uh, there seems to be some doubt in your mind that, as a matter of principle, we both agree about flirting. But I expect that this is a behavioral area which we can define later and adhere to; so even though you showed some hesitancy, I will accept this.

WIFE: No, there was no hesitancy about the physical fidelity at all and this is very basic and completely agreed to. But there have been times in the past when you said I was flirting and I didn't feel I was. I wasn't aware of a flirtatious pattern, but we do agree in principle.

HUSBAND: So now we've agreed on one thing. Now let me take the lead here and try something else for the next step. I think that in most marriages and most friendships—in any action or reaction between humans before they get married or before they form a partnership—each one, right or wrong, understands that certain contracts have been made. Maybe they misunderstood, but in the minds of each individual there were certain things that he felt the other was promising to do after marriage. For you, I expect—and if I'm wrong, stop me—you felt that I had made a contract to make you feel important, to make you feel loved, to make you feel really wanted.

WIFE: By you.

HUSBAND: By me. Whether you got this impression correctly or not, whether I spoke it, whether I had intended it or not is irrelevant—this is the impression you had. And I judge that you feel at this stage that I have broken my contract on it.

WIFE: Yes.

HUSBAND: You agree that I have—I mean that you feel that I have?

WIFE: Yes.

HUSBAND: I agree that I have not been effective in this—unconsciously or because I wanted to—but I have not been completely effective in making you feel important, loved, and wanted by me. So I agree with you that you *feel*—right or wrong—I've let you down. Next, you believed, I think, that when we got married I would "look after you," that you would have financial security now during the marriage and afterward, that is, after I'm dead, and I will not argue here whether or not I promised this or implied this or said the opposite. The point is that I believe that you had it fixed in your head that it was part of the contract, and now at this stage of our marriage you are apprehensive and anxious over what is going to happen to you financially.

WIFE: I'd like to qualify that a bit. I think it would be more correct to say that I expected that we would share, and whatever the financial situation was it would be a shared one. If there were hard times, we'd share hard times, and if there were good times, we'd share good times, and I feel I did not expect to be taken care of quite in the way you've said it. I don't think I expected a free ride or a high standard of living but I expected—I guess I have to say it again—that we'd be sharing, we'd be equal in the thing, the standard of living and the finances that were available. I feel that you have not been fair on the financial——

HUSBAND (*interrupting*): I gather that you have not been happy because I spend money on business equipment, and hold this more important than I do your new clothes. . . .

WIFE: Well, whether it's business or not, specifically I believe at this point that there has been a unilateral handling of the financial arrangements in which I have had very little to say.

HUSBAND: All right. Now can you give other areas in which you feel I've failed you?

WIFE: Most of the things that come into my mind fall generally into either of these two categories you've already mentioned. In the area of loyalty, I feel this has been abused by you, in that I had expected that we would be devoted to each other and loyal to each other. But when you discuss our intimate problems with your friends and other outside people, I don't think you're being loyal. You let me down here. Actually, I guess the same goes for you. I believe that you thought that I would be helpful in your work. The house and the wife and the specifics of this I don't think were clear in your mind necessarily, but I think there was a general overall expectation of help and assistance from me whether it would be just psychological or more in terms of being an assistant or hostess or whatever the things might have been might not be clear, but I believe there was a general expectation on your part that when we married, somehow I would be an instrument to increase your productivity and be a real aid and assistance in your work and I believe that you are convinced now, at this point in time, that you feel that this has not materialized. This expectation on your part has not come to pass. Am I correct in my evaluation of this as an expectation?

HUSBAND: Yes, you are.

WIFE: Which has not come to pass and it was something that you expected to happen?

HUSBAND: That is correct. Okay, we each identified areas in which we thought the other one was let down. Now we step into a little bit of hazard here and we have to be damned careful to stay objective. You were let down by not having a feeling that

I loved you, desired you, and wanted you to feel important, and——

WIFE: Don't forget the one about loyalty.

HUSBAND: Yes, the one about loyalty. Now, I'm speaking here and you're going to do the same thing to me, so don't get your back up. Now about your disappointments. I believe that you are correct on number one, the one about your being loved and desired. The one on the finances I disagree on. Uh—the one on loyalty is debatable. I mean in *my* mind—it is not debatable with you. So we have one area of agreement that is complete here, one I disagree on, and one that's debatable; and a natural step later is to discuss what can be done about it.

WIFE: Now, I'm interested in how my behavior has led to your being disappointed. Let's take the area of your work. I knew that you felt that I would increase your productivity. But I'm having a problem figuring out how my behavior per se has been a factor in your trouble with productivity. Now I know that before we were married, I painted too rosy a picture of our getting married and living happily ever after, which was romantic idealism. I talked about being good for you and making you happy and all this other stuff, which I realize on looking back was ridiculous. Was that behavior which contributed to the loss of your expectation?

HUSBAND: Yes.

WIFE: Because I did believe that it was all going to be so much better than it has been. And I was thinking just of our being together and our being married; we'd been having this affair for over a year and I had always wanted to be married and get through this irregular relationship to a more stable, normal type of thing; and I just thought that would be the greatest thing in the world when it happened and that was unrealistic and silly, I suppose, but it was a genuine feeling.

HUSBAND: I am now taking the role of the psychologist, not as the husband or as the participant. "Patty, if you had this image in your mind that this was the way your marriage with Bud would be and if you feel that he is disappointed in the areas which you have defined earlier, then there must be some reason why he feels disappointed. Perhaps it is your behavior. Perhaps it is not. Perhaps some unseen factor entered which you had not expected, but you must admit that if there is a differential between what he expected and what, in his mind, happened—I emphasize in his mind—there must be a stimulus which made it."

WIFE: Yes.

HUSBAND: "If you will think about it a little, I think it will help." I am no longer the psychologist.

WIFE: I'm facing it. I'm thinking. Now I expect that I have—I don't know whether it's a behavior pattern or a personality pattern or what—not been totally or even sufficiently absorbed in what you are doing and I think you've felt this sometimes when you've asked me to help you and I might have had something else on my mind—I would not give total devotion to your work. I, uh—there's a terrible temptation to go back and say I never—I was never—I was not thinking in terms of being devoted to your work even before we married. I was thinking in terms of being devoted to *you* as a human being, so again I can't determine the behavior—the specific behavior on my part—that let you down in your expectation that your work would be improved. I did *not* make direct contributions in the sense of being a working partner. Now these things are behaviors—these things I did *not* do. Uh, will they qualify or is it a feeling perhaps—is it a lack of feeling about your work?

HUSBAND: The psychologist is again speaking.

WIFE: Oh, can't you speak for yourself?

HUSBAND: All right. I'll speak as me but then it will tend to create defensiveness. But I will. The key here is what you said earlier, that I expected the whole household to revolve around me and my work, instead of which you are messing around with paints, or sewing, or things *you* want to do.

WIFE: Well, uh, yes, uh, well, my behavior—how did this come about?

HUSBAND: Now don't get defensive here. Say anything you want. I will not get defensive no matter what you say—or at least I will try not to.

WIFE: Well, uh, I'm trying to think what I might have done that I didn't do, and I guess you'll have to help me here, cause I think I did try. But the one expectation above all that *I* wanted and was let down on was, in my opinion, so *easy* to perform because it was simply a matter of your being gentle and tender and loving. But I don't think this approach is very constructive anyway, Bud. I want to propose that we make a ground rule or come to an agreement for the future, that we not go back any more over the territory of the past, because this always leads to defensiveness. I did this because you did that and you did that because I did this and we each want the other guy to say, "Okay, I was wrong and you were right," and neither one of us is probably going to do this because we don't feel that either of us is right or wrong. At least, each of us personally is more interested in defending his position, I believe, and I don't know whether anything constructive can come out of it. So now we understand these great expectations and how they have not been realized, and I think it would be much better if we could go from here into—and using the same technique—what each of us could do to try to make the expectation come about, and then open up an area of discussion—a give-and-take just on this subject without any reference to what has been done or not been done in the past. Then, too, I do not think it was necessary to talk about those areas where we failed. Can we agree on this? We could move into the future or the area of today and say "What could I do, now that your expectations have been clearly outlined and I have acknowledged that I know these have not been met, and you have agreed that this is so?" Then I might say that I will do X, Y, and Z. Do you think that will help? And you could say I'd like you to do A, B, and C, or yes, X, Y, and Z would be great, or vice versa. Now, okay, it's yours.

HUSBAND: I'm not in a very great mood this evening. What I read you as having said is, "The things you outlined to me before we got married as your requirements, Bud, are impossible, but my requirements are very easy to fulfill. Neither has fulfilled the other so we will wipe the slate clean, old boy, and without trying to understand why these things didn't operate. Mine is possible and easy, Bud, and you can do it, but now we must negotiate as to how to downgrade *your* requirements; in short you'll have to change them. That's how I read you."

WIFE: Well, that's unfortunate because that's not what I said at all. I just tried to suggest a way to improve this discussion—because I don't think you really understand the *quid pro quo* thing at all—and you ignore my suggestion. But now that you brought it up, I think one of the problems as far as this relationship is concerned, at least in my opinion, is that I've got a lot more things that I would like to get out of this relationship but I've become terribly realistic and I know what is possible and what isn't possible and many of the dreams that I had . . . Well, anyway, perhaps that was my error in not going back and mentioning more of the ways you let me down. But the one that I need most to happen is the one that I think you are capable of and you have been able to do, but you haven't. Now you're going to get mad. I'm just telling you that I'm not even discussing the areas in which I already know you simply can never produce or can never do for me—there's no point in doing that. Of course, that may be going back to who was more realistic when we married. And when we took that test up at Columbia with I don't know who it was——

HUSBAND: The psychologist.

WIFE: He indicated that I was much more realistic about your nature than you were about mine. But anyway——

HUSBAND: He what?

WIFE: Well, about how important your work is. Now, let's try to be a little more constructive. Anyway, how would you like me to act so that you would feel more productive?

HUSBAND: I greatly admire your inventing such a ballsy question and the answer is that there is probably nothing that you can do, given your selfish nature. We should never have gotten married to begin with.

WIFE: You did not want to get married, then?

HUSBAND: No, I didn't. I wanted to just live with you without being married.

WIFE: Well, I don't see how we can be constructive at this point, because you had the choice to marry me, or to not do so.

HUSBAND: This is true.

WIFE: You made the choice to marry me. Now I don't think it's fair to go back and say, "I had so much more before that I simply can't have now," and the implication is that it's because of my nature to restrict you in some way.

HUSBAND: No, I did this thing voluntarily. This is true, but, on the other hand, I was in love with you, and in this condition you conned—and I use this word "conned"—you conned me into believing that——

(*At this point the wife switched off the tape recorder and wisely refused to continue.*)

Note that one reason this *quid pro quo* discussion failed from the start was that the husband took over at the beginning, as in the first attempt. If the spouses had flipped a coin and hence started out as equals, the wife would not have battled so belligerently to regain control.

Thus again the couple sustained their pride and wrecked the *quid pro quo* session.

47

A *QUID PRO QUO* ATTEMPT WHICH SUCCEEDED

We have given two examples of *quid pro quo* discussions which failed. Following is one which was quite successful. It is not completely typical in that it occurred between a man and a woman who were engaged, rather than between spouses who had been married for some years and who had set up rigid patterns. Both participants had had previous unsuccessful marriages. The man in the example is a Spanish professor from Vermont, and the woman is an anthropologist from Los Angeles. We are using this example because both parties were familiar with the *quid pro quo* process. They recognized that each of them had slightly different cultural and geographical backgrounds and different needs. Within the past year, after separating from their previous spouses, both had moved to Denver, and they were employed there. The man had four children by his previous marriage, and the children were living with their mother about a hundred miles from Denver.

Our two prospective spouses, John and Mary, had been going out together a great deal during most of the period that they had been in Denver. They lived in different apartments, but frequently enjoyed sexual relations. They believed they loved each other, and wanted to marry, but their professional ambitions and their memories of painful past marriages made them wary. Therefore, they decided to establish a *quid pro quo* for their present relationship—that is, for the relationship which would exist, say, for the next year, pending their divorces. They taped their session, and it is reproduced here with their permission. It should be noted that in these *quid pro quo* negotiations, little mention is made of marriage. But this is precisely the kind of discussion (even though the problems may be different) which should take place *before* marriage is contemplated.

JOHN: The question I would like to raise is, let us assume that this relationship is operating next fall. It is unlikely by that time that either of us would be free legally, although it is conceivable since there are still places like Reno. I would like to take six months off from teaching to finish the paper I'm writing on Guatemala, and this would necessitate living in Central America for at least three or fourth months. And I'm quite convinced from past experience that I could not do this on my own, since I couldn't hole up in a castle somewhere and write day and night by the light of a coal lamp. Now this situation poses problems for you because you also have your own life and career interests and there is also the legal status that interferes socially to some extent. Let me stop there and ask what your reaction is to this kind of general area.

MARY: The assumption is that we are trying to work out something where we do plan to try to work together?

JOHN: Ah, to work together is not absolutely necessary, but I think that would be great.

MARY: Plan to be together.

JOHN: Be together is what I was really talking about, yes.

MARY: Well, let me see, um, this doesn't necessarily have to conflict with my interests. Assuming that there is a school offering anthropology in Guatemala, it seems to me I could pursue my interests and still be of some help to you and you could be of some help to me too in my effort to finish my Ph.D.

JOHN: Assume that there is no school of anthropology. Do you feel strongly enough about the possibilities of the relationship that you would undertake other courses that would be furthering your career but not in as direct a way as finishing your Ph.D.?

MARY: The only difference, the only problem here, is this sort of switches the focus of what we are working on. That throws it back to the continued course of relationship. We don't have Tom's and Paula's advantage right now in that we are not married and we don't *have* to work these things out. So our relationship has a more tentative element to it. But assuming that the relationship is going to continue, as we expect it to, then I think it would be possible, yes, for me to go ahead and take other courses. I feel strongly about finishing the Ph.D. I'd like to do it now, but I also know that this is not necessarily the best or the only preparation for what I want to do. I have a lot of interests. And so there is that possibility that I could go to Guatemala anyway and take courses, and look forward to finishing the Ph.D. at a future date.

JOHN: What do you see as a reasonable *quo* for the *quid* of your putting off for a year the schooling, the finishing of the Ph.D.? This would be giving up something.

MARY: Yes, and a good *quo* would be simply that you and I somehow would find a way to guarantee that I am learning professionally in another way. If you and I could see to it that while you're writing and studying I could also be there, because I want to write too. So for me, helping you write would be part of the *quo*. So that I could help you write and learn from it at the same time, and we could do this together. And just somehow form associations and be with people where I could have some feeling of real progress in learning about society and group patterns. I would also have to have freedom to become involved in some anthropological research, so if I wanted to go out digging in the ruins—even for a few days at a time—you would need to be tolerant. And probably I think it might be important for me to have some personal associations which do not include you and vice versa, because I think I do need that now to establish myself, to get a sense of my own identity, and I think it might be important for me to take classes separately from you as well as together and have friends in my own field, who maybe might not

appeal to you too much. But I need a little latitude, a little freedom, especially since we probably would not be legally free to
marry at that time.

JOHN: How much of a guarantee would you feel you require at
this time to know that finishing the Ph.D. would not be put off
indefinitely, in which case you would be doing something for me
but not getting your requirements taken care of?

MARY: How long do I think I could put this off? Well, there is
a practical problem here, John; I'm getting older, you know, and
need to finish the Ph.D. soon or take a back seat professionally.
I think I could wait two years probably, without a severe blow
to my career. So you could take a two-year leave if you wanted
to; then we could go some place where I could finish up my
education. Or, if you couldn't leave, I could always leave by
myself, finish my degree (nearby, if possible), and then return
to wherever you were at that time. Or another possibility is that
within the next year or two my goals would change, my professional goals, so that perhaps I may never want to finish the
degree. So it's not that rigid. I'm not that rigid, but I'd have to
feel I was going somewhere professionally.

JOHN: Well, I think you have a third alternative. The second
one I think would be totally unacceptable to me. It means we
would be apart for a year or nine months—the school year. Ah,
the other real consideration is, what kind of situation could possibly arise where I would *have* to stay in Guatemala? I can't
imagine what that would be because either I would finish the
paper soon or return to my university job in Denver.

MARY: Well, I was thinking of another possibility. After you
finish your paper, maybe we could come back some place else,
say, like Los Angeles. There's lots going on there professionally
that would interest you and you could teach there and I could go
back to U.C.L.A. to finish the Ph.D. I'm not sure I'd want to
return to Denver.

JOHN: Yah, that's a possibility, but I wonder what sort of relationship, if we lived in Los Angeles, you would require with your
family in order to not feel torn. What would they expect of me
in relation to them, assuming that I didn't particularly want to
get involved with them, which I don't know because I've not met
them. I might enjoy them thoroughly. I might have some reaction

to your reaction to your family. You might find I'm making you nervous or something. But assuming that you enjoyed being near them, and since the area made sense both because of the school there and professional opportunities, what would you expect in the way of behavior on my part?

MARY: I'm going to sound overly optimistic here. First of all, I don't require a great deal of association with my family. I've lived in Los Angeles before in a separate apartment, and I did while I was married to Wayne, and at the most, I saw them once every two weeks. I'd drop over for a few hours once every couple of weeks. And I don't, you know, don't even call them regularly. They don't require a lot of physical proximity and don't visit me much when I'm in the area. But assuming that maybe everything wasn't ideal, that you didn't feel any real wish to be around them, I think I could very happily go see my folks by myself and you would not have to participate to any great extent, but I would expect of you that when you *were* with them once every few months, if we got together once a month or at Christmas time or something like that, that you would make an effort to enter into it and not make me feel uncomfortable or guilty for forcing you to do something against your wishes. I would expect some cheerful cooperation because I wouldn't require you to visit very much and when I did, I think I would expect a reasonable attitude on your part in terms of being gracious and warm to them and not setting up artificial barriers. But I wouldn't put excessive demands on you in terms of visiting them once a week. What do you think?

JOHN: I think that sounds quite reasonable. It's the sort of thing I'm used to carrying out because I certainly was not that close to Kim's family, nor was she to mine, and the way we worked it out was primarily by separate visiting with some arranged visits, which would be odious except it didn't come that often. Two other areas strike me as important. One is that there would be a period in which you would expect to behave as a wife even though you wouldn't have the legal protection of being a wife. The other area that strikes me is that it would be necessary, indeed essential, for my self-respect to do something with the kids. Both of these could be potentially sticky areas depending on how they're handled.

MARY: What was the first one?

JOHN: The nonlegal status.

MARY: Right. With regard to this, I think that when we leave Denver I will have to ask for a number of *quids* probably. One is that until there is a legal marriage, I will require a separate residence for my own feelings of freedom, social acceptability, this sort of thing. And also, I think I'll probably want some financial support, in the sense of feeling somehow that I am cared for, that it isn't just sort of now and then. So in terms of finances, it would probably take the form of something like paying for my apartment and that in dating situations, it wouldn't be dutch. I would give a *quid* also, and I'd want to hear what you would expect in return. I would not take all the benefits of being a wife in terms of your footing all the bills, this sort of thing. First of all, I think I need a sense of independence in the situation in order to feel comfortable with it, so I would certainly expect to pay for my own schooling and food and this sort of thing. But on the other hand, I woudn't want you to get the feeling of being a sugar daddy or being used. I think that this is a delicate area and we would need somehow to be able to give to each other without being taken advantage of.

JOHN: Well, my own feeling about that is that I would not make such a trip unless it were with the idea of matrimony in mind. But it seems to me the financial business just makes simple good sense, since you wouldn't be financially contemplating such a move if you didn't expect financial help. I'm the one who's pushing it. The least I could do is see to that. Ah, the area I think is a little stickier or foggier is this one about independence. For example, I don't think it would be tolerable to have separate dating somehow, since this kind of a relationship is set up for a very particular reason, not so that we can just date, but to see if marriage seems desirable for us. How much independence is the kind of independence you're talking about?

MARY: Yes, I agree with you about dating. If we go to Guatemala under this firm an agreement I won't go for separate dating either. In that case I'd have to have complete independence, financial independence. I'd go on my own and I'd date freely. So assuming we would be going under the circumstances being discussed, I agree as to the dating. When I talk about independence, I'm thinking of having a little life of my own in the sense of having some friendships separate from you, either male or female, in relation to my profession, but it would be strictly for professional and learning purposes. I can't become completely dependent on you for my life's blood. If you were the one who was teaching me everything, you were financially supporting me, only your friends were my friends, etcetera, I just don't think I could salvage any self-respect out of this sort of situation because I am relatively independent. And I am also thinking in terms of minimal financial independence so that I don't get the feeling that I'm using you too much, which would put a real strain on my feelings for you. I can't tolerate this sort of thing either because I'm not that calculating. Also, I would need a sense of security too for the future—knowing that I was doing part of this myself so I wasn't getting in such a symbiotic, dependent relationship that if anything did happen in our relationship and we decided to terminate, that I would be absolutely helpless and have to go out and really start from scratch, you know, not having taken care of myself at all. Is that plain?

JOHN: Yes, and I think the kind of independence you're talking about is quite acceptable because there are times when you know I'd be happy to sit at home with a book and not feel the need to entertain somebody else.

MARY: Well, at the same time my degree of independence would also free you because I know you have interests and are going to have friends and people who perhaps are fairly specific and outside of my general interests. So it gives you freedom too.

JOHN: Now what about the children problem? How does that grab you?

MARY: I know it's necessary. I think this would be hard for me, one of the harder areas. But I understand it certainly theoretically and emotionally because I would be the same way; I know how important they are to you, and it's important to the kids too. And I feel quite a bit of concern and affection for the children even though I don't know them very well. So this is something I'm recognizing I might not always be terribly understanding about in a particular situation, say, if you wanted to leave and come back to Denver for three weeks by yourself to be with them or something. It would be a little hard for me to take, and on this point more than on any other we've discussed so far I might be a little more sensitive, having to cope with it as it came up. But at least now I say yes, I do understand, and I also feel enough affection for the kids that I would not object at all; in fact, I'd rather like to become friends with them and have them come over and this sort of thing, except that our situation legally would be so precarious that it might not be comfortable for the kids.

JOHN: Initially, yes, that's true.

MARY: I don't think I could play mother to the kids, but I do think I could become friends if they wanted to.

JOHN: Yeah, they have a mother, but also their relationship with their mother is different. Are there any areas offhand that—oh yeah, there is one other that occurred to me. My standard of income will be down from what it has been because of alimony and child support. But it seems to me that what you've been used to has been little so it would still be increased over what you've been used to. But how do you feel about money and about seeing those checks every month being sent to Denver?

MARY: Let me say something more about the kids. In terms of a specific event, you know, like wanting to be with the kids for an evening, this sort of thing, I do think that I would be certainly as understanding as I could possibly be and would try to give you plenty of freedom to be with the kids. But I think as a *quo* I would have to expect, too, that the kids wouldn't always come first. They wouldn't *always* come before me. I don't know if I could be a sacrificial lamb in the sense of stepping back and letting the kids take over. I think I would require some consideration on your part in the sense that sometimes the kids would come first because their needs were particularly grave or something important would come up, but there might be other times when my needs would be great and I would expect somehow to feel that I were equal with the kids in your consideration.

JOHN: Yeah, I think the very fact that I don't feel sacrificial enough to them to remain married to Kim, which is what they would prefer, is already an indication that I don't feel that sacrificial and one of the encouraging signs to me of the possibility of handling them in a fair manner and being with them only at certain times and in certain specific contexts, such as, let's say, Tony's getting pregnant and suddenly being in a crisis and my flying over and getting into it.

MARY: This I could see. But I think it would be important to me not to somehow get labeled or feel as if I were getting labeled as a selfish bitch if I at some times said, "Look, I know the kids need you right now but I don't think it's that urgent and I need you now too." Not that we couldn't work it out and maybe the kids would win, you know, in this particular situation, or you would go to the kids, but it's just that I wouldn't get labeled somehow as being selfish because I didn't give them all the hundred per cent privilege of being the most important thing to you. But I do know they're terribly important and I don't see there is any possibility of replacing the kids. I don't think it's necessary 'cause they're different and my role with you is certainly different from the children's role. So I don't think I'd feel competitive, but that's not necessarily true on one particular issue. I think it would take an awful lot of understanding on both sides.

But about the finances, I would prefer ideally, I guess, not to see checks go to Denver, but I also again have enough understanding and care about the kids enough that I think it's necessary and they need it. Even if financially they didn't need it, I think emotionally they need it to know that you are investing in them. And you're right; your income even if it is cut in half, is still substantially above what I'm used to. I don't think I'm that materialistic. I enjoy things, but I'm not greedy, and it doesn't take a hell of a lot really to satisfy me; as long as I'm happy in other ways, the money does not concern me. And I'm also not a rigid person in the sense of needing a steady income every month, everything, you know, on time. I'm not panicky or compulsive about bookkeeping, and I also am not made terribly insecure by not knowing when the next check is coming. I'm used to handling crisis situations, and I'm very comfortable in them. More than that; I'm very happy in them. It's a challenge for me and I enjoy them. So in terms of your taking time off from teaching, and having a less regular income, I think this is something I could live with very easily and mostly because I do trust you and your competence and I think, whatever you do is, you know, you'll do fine. I just don't think that I'd ever have to fear about not having any beans for lunch with you. Does that make sense?

JOHN: Yes. In some ways I think the only area that is not workable right now in terms of a *quid pro quo*, probably because there are some months to go, is the idea of separate residences.

This would bug me; how much I can't really say at this time, partly because I don't think that it's socially that much of a stigma when people understand the reasons for the situation, but I can also expect that the woman feels somewhat differently about this than the man does in our culture. And I think that this is the one area of those that we've brought up that is still kind of a question mark, although, as I say, I may be more in agreement on it than I can tell right now. It may be less important when I learn to depend on you, because then I don't have to see you quite as much in order to get the reassurance you're still around and want to get married.

MARY: Well, I see the separate residences would be important to me and it would be very difficult for me to live openly with you and be happy and be casual and, you know, not get all tied up with ulcers over not being "legal." This would be the only thing, I think, that could take care of that for me. I just think our relationship would suffer because of my embarrassment about the thing if we didn't have the separate residences, but as a sort of compromise, we could certainly be not very far away and, you know, from my point of view, a lot of it would be strictly in name only. But I think I'd need that reassurance somehow even if I weren't there a good deal of the time; I'd need to be able to have a separate residence for myself.

JOHN: Well, I think we have covered a number of areas that have occurred to me in the past week or two and I also have to get back to the university because I've got a two o'clock class. So here's your chance for a last word.

MARY: No word—we'll stop while we're ahead.

48

THE USE OF A
THIRD PARTY IN A
MARITAL DIALOGUE

When spouses have difficulty in conducting a dialogue, the presence of an objective third party may be desirable. However, even with the best of intentions, this individual may sometimes find himself unable to be helpful. In the following example, Mary and Bill Parson have been having a violent marital problem. They believe it concerns money. For weeks they have been shouting at each other, accusing each other of being selfish and stupid. Now they have decided that discussion with a third party may help to ameliorate the problem.

They have known John True for several years. Both Mary and Bill respect him, and they agree that he is the one with whom they would like to air their troubles. Both hope that he will assist them to find a solution. The following dialogue takes place in John True's living room. It will be observed that although John True, the third party, gives Mary and Bill temporary relief by taking the heat out of the immediate problem—by means of edict and by dividing and conquering—he fails to help them resolve their fundamental difficulty. He permits the content of their dialogue to remain in the terms in which they present it to him, not recognizing that their fighting is a status struggle—and that the money issue is just the current manifestation of that struggle. (Later on, the Parsons visit a professional, Dr. Smith. The dialogue which takes place at that time provides a contrast in third party technique.)

BILL: Well, we started to argue this morning and things got out of hand kind of fast and I guess we got all shook up by it, and we thought, why not take advantage of somebody like you, and your experiences, and, you know, and I gathered that before your wife died you were very happily married. And maybe you could help us out a little bit here because I know if we start again, things are going to get a little bit rough.

THIRD PARTY: What have you been arguing about?

BILL: Well——

MARY: The point we started talking about we aren't even talking about any more.

THIRD PARTY: What you're doing here is starting to fight all over again. Will somebody please answer the question?

BILL: I think we're fighting over money.

THIRD PARTY: That's what you're squabbling about? Well, I know you're making thirty-five thousand and you only have one youngster. What's the matter?

BILL: Well, I've been working as a CPA in a crummy office and I'm just beginning to get some more expensive clients and I think I've got to put some money into the office.

MARY: Which I can understand! But he can't wait five minutes and he won't talk about anything else and he won't get off my back until he has it and we don't have the money at this time. Our little girl is——

BILL: Has got colitis, yes.

MARY: . . . has had a terrific case of the flu in the last couple of weeks and we've had medical bills that we don't normally have, and I've been putting off buying clothes for more than two years and my wardrobe is absolutely empty because of the sailboat that he insisted on getting about a year ago and because I put off all my shopping that I needed to do. Really——

BILL: I haven't bought anything lately, either.

THIRD PARTY: Let me interrupt you here. Just a moment here;

you came here and so let me horn in. Mary, do you think that Bill is competent to run his office?

MARY: Sure he is.

THIRD PARTY: Do you think he knows what equipment he needs?

MARY: I haven't any argument, Bill, about your new equipment. I'm just thinking about a few months. If you'll just put it off until—the season is changing and I don't have any clothes. I've got about three dresses and two pairs of slacks for the season. I can't go around naked. If he'll just put it off for two months, that's all I ask. I put off my shopping.

BILL: I think it's damned foolishness, in business, spending money begets money. We're not just talking about some clothes that wear out.

MARY: I'm just saying that when you decide you have to have something, you have to have it right this minute. You did the same thing about the sailboat.

BILL: Just a minute. The boat thing has nothing to do with it.

THIRD PARTY: I don't want to make it look like I'm on your husband's side, because I'm not, and you know I've always had my eye on you anyhow, but the thing you're squawking over is that *he'd* like to spend money right now and *you'd* like to spend money right now.

MARY: The boat does have something to do with it, because I put off buying some new clothes last year and I went without them all during the summer and I thought that next year——

THIRD PARTY: Mary, we're getting no place. I'd just like you two to sit down and write out how much money you have, and how much is spent each week, and where.

MARY: We have our budget worked out. There's no problem there. It's just that we don't have the money in the next couple of months, we really don't, for both.

THIRD PARTY: Mary says you have a budget. Write it out as it is now and let me look at it. I'll be back in a little while.

BILL: Okay.

(*A half hour has gone by now, and Mr. True rejoins Bill and Mary.*)

THIRD PARTY: Hey there, have you got that budget all made out?

BILL: Here it is. Our net income after taxes is about twenty-eight thousand, take or leave a few dollars. That's not going to buy her the kind of clothes she wants. Okay, with the payments and all that, she gets four hundred a month to run the house on. We've got the automobile payments listed here, you see, and the medical bills. We have this protective coverage, we have my life insurance, and so on and so on, and you can see right now that after I pay my quarterly installment, what we are talking about is roughly six hundred dollars that we'll have left over.

THIRD PARTY: All right, what will your equipment cost?

BILL: I haven't looked into it because I didn't want to go ahead without consulting Mary.

MARY: What do you think? What do you want?

BILL: I think it would take around two hundred dollars to get the office painted and two fifty to three hundred to get a new dictating machine.

THIRD PARTY: All right. And, Mary, how much will your clothes cost?

MARY: Well, if I go down to the—well, I don't have to get anything special,,just if I go down to the—just if I have something to get by in during the summer. So, if I had about four hundred dollars, that would take care of everything.

THIRD PARTY: Well, it seems to me that you could have two hundred and his office expenses will be about four hundred——

MARY: Well, they're not. They're going to be about five hundred, which leaves me a hundred lousy dollars.

BILL: Well, maybe four fifty, if I really pare it down.

THIRD PARTY: Why can't you?

BILL: But this is a capital investment. She can't seem to get that through her head.

MARY: But I do.

THIRD PARTY: Never mind. It's a small amount of money. Why can't she have two fifty for clothes and you have three fifty for the office?

BILL: Then we'll just have to be going through this again some time. It's the principle of the thing. I'm not spending any money on clothes. It's not fifty dollars for a fly rod for me.

MARY: You don't need clothes right now.

BILL: Yes, I can get along with this. This suit's only two years old. Huh?

THIRD PARTY: Now, look here, neighbors, you stopped in here, and my counsel is to stop your squawking. Two thirds of the money to go for the office and one third for Mary. That is my counsel. Please don't argue. Either take it or leave it. And if you'd like another cup of coffee, you may have it.

BILL: Okay.

MARY: What would that amount to? Hell, no! I'd get taken *again*, just like always.

Some weeks later, the Parsons visit a professional therapist, Dr. Smith. Note how he continually attempts to direct them toward *some* area of agreement.

THERAPIST: Good afternoon, won't you come in and sit down, please?

MARY: Good afternoon.

THERAPIST: What's brought you here?

BILL: Well, my wife and I have been squabbling. We went to see a neighbor and he tried to act as middleman. He recommended that we come and see you.

THERAPIST: Right. He called briefly and told me that you had talked to him about money, but he didn't think you were getting any place with it.

MARY: He was really nice and I felt sorry about him because it didn't do any good and we just went on home and fought harder.

BILL: Yeah.

THERAPIST: And you're still fighting?

MARY: Yes, sir.

THERAPIST: You don't seem like you're fighting this morning. Does it stop sometimes?

MARY (*laughing*): We hate to hit you with it all at once. We have to warm up a little.

BILL: We had a battle on the way over here and we're still kind of stewing about it. And I thought it might be good to let you take the lead here because you're a doctor—because every time one of us opens our mouth, we start to scream.

THERAPIST: Uh huh. Well, let's start where you guys left off. What were you arguing about?

MARY: Money, as usual.

THERAPIST: Money, in relation to what?

BILL: Here's how——

MARY: Why don't you let me?

BILL: All right.

MARY: My husband gets extremely angry with me sometimes because I spend money to call my parents long distance.

THERAPIST: Um-hum.

BILL (*bursting out*): Sixty dollars in the last month!

MARY: This is a perfect example. He never lets me finish. First of all——

THERAPIST: Did you know the bill was sixty dollars?

MARY: Yes, I know. But my husband earns thirty-five thousand a year.

BILL: Well, I don't spend that calling my family.

MARY: All right. I call long distance. And if he'll be quiet, I'll tell you what he does that makes me feel that this is all right. First of all, he makes about thirty-five thousand a year, and my husband is an avid golfer and a sports fan and he spends about a good—a *good*—two hundred a month at the country club, golfing and buying the fellows drinks and whatnot. That's his form of recreation. I don't have anything like that. I'm not a big spender.

BILL: Goddamn it, recreation, my eye. I hate to play golf, but my biggest client is a golfer.

MARY: Well, this is something that means a lot to me, and I have good reason for calling my family. They've been having difficulties for years, and it means a great deal to my family to have me call and talk to them.

BILL: I don't object if she'd call about once a week and keep it to five minutes. But sixty bucks and she calls in the morning and the afternoon and she talks for an hour.

THERAPIST: Your wife mentioned that you spend two hundred a month on golfing. It seems like a fantastic amount.

MARY: Plus the drinks.

THERAPIST: I understand—but it does bring up another thing. How do you people decide who is to spend how much in a month?

MARY: We never do decide. That's the point. We just end up fighting every time over something that has been done and it just keeps recurring and——

BILL: I'm working as a CPA and my office looks crummy. I want to fix it up and my wife spends all my money, so I can't. In order to make money, you've got to spend some—on business, I mean.

THERAPIST: You sound like your wife—that sort of complaining but self-justifying tone. I think that somebody who wants to call his parents is very fortunate. Lots of us won't have anything to do with our parents.

BILL: Doctor, you asked me a question—how you figure out how much money is spent in one spot—and I'm trying to answer it.

THERAPIST: But you know that I know that it takes money to make money.

BILL: Wait a minute. I don't get this.

MARY: He means, why do we have to apologize when we've got the money? For the most part, we do have the money and that's all that counts.

THERAPIST: You mean, you eat well, and this won't make any difference?

MARY: Yah, and yet he criticizes me for calling my mother.

THERAPIST: Do you agree with that?

BILL: No, I don't at all. In order to build up a business you've got to build and build, and I'm sticking all our money back into it. Sixty bucks comes to a lot of money, and I'll be honest with you, it's the goddamn principle of it, spending sixty bucks every time she's lonely—she just picks up the phone and calls her goddamn mother in Los Angeles. And it has nothing to do with whether you've got the money or not; it isn't necessary to call one's family that much.

THERAPIST: Why do you feel that your wife's family is better than your family?

BILL: I don't have any family. I'm an orphan.

THERAPIST: So then almost any family is a better family than the one you've got?

BILL: I despise her family. Just to watch her mother eat. Jesus Christ!

MARY: I like them. And about the only time I call my mother is when he's out playing golf. But he takes *all* the money, the extra money, and wants to invest it and then he criticizes me for taking money because he says he wants to invest it. To him, business is everything.

THERAPIST: What else does he do?

MARY: First, he's never at home. He doesn't ever have anything to do with the kids because he's too busy making money. They need a father a lot more than they need a new bicycle. And he doesn't like my family. He's rude to them under all circumstances.

THERAPIST: How often does he have to see them?

MARY: Not more than once every five or six months. That's why I call them. We don't see them very often.

THERAPIST: So, he's only interested in making money and he doesn't pay any attention to the kids. What else? This business of making money distracts him from the family.

MARY: Well, it's hard to find any actual behavior items because I see so little of him. Well, okay, here's one. When he *is* home, he still isn't home. He can be sitting—he can be home, maybe he's home—but he's sitting and sitting and burying his nose in the financial reports and the papers and he doesn't even speak, he doesn't even talk to us at the breakfast table. He might as well be at the office.

THERAPIST: Do you give him a chance?

MARY: Yes, I *try* to talk to him. I try to talk about books that I've read or what's going on at the office or telling him about some of my activities, and he's not even the least bit interested.

BILL: I'm starting to get a head of steam up. I suddenly see what's happening. When I try to get new business, I have to play golf sometimes. And every time I come back from playing golf— it just hit me now—as I enter the door, she'll say, "I just had the most interesting talk with Mommy and Daddy." I think she just calls them to give me a kick in the ass, because she knows it burns me up.

THERAPIST: Neither of you has had much experience arguing, have you? You didn't take debating?

BILL: Experience! That's all she does.

MARY: We never—no, you're right. We don't make sense.

THERAPIST: I used the wrong word. I said "experience" when what I meant was "training." You both are very poor in getting your points across.

BILL: It's no accident that her old man sells phonograph records.

MARY: We never argue in my family. My parents and I get along beautifully; we can discuss things intelligently and have a nice conversation—but not Bill and me!

BILL: What do you want me to do, Mary?

MARY: I certainly don't know. I don't know. Let me say something about the golf. That's a beautiful example. I did try to play golf to be with him.

BILL (*shouts*): Three lessons!

MARY: And he made it so plain that he didn't want me that——

BILL: Goddamn right!

MARY: He was so rude, and he will not let me help him. He treats me like excess baggage.

THERAPIST: I think I'm getting the impression rather clearly of what one of your problems is. You both are trying very hard to save the marriage, and your arguments are not about money, but about who is trying hardest to save the marriage. I think you're staying away from home and trying to make extra money—this way you're staying away from your wife and you can silence her by giving her a few extra bucks. And you, Mary, are trying to save the marriage by turning over your emotional load to your parents, instead of to your husband, and probably looking to your children for emotional support.

MARY: I can't turn it over to him. Every time I even talk to him we fight.

THERAPIST: So really, when both of you are trying so hard to save the marriage by avoiding each other, the question is one of admitting the cause. Is it because neither of you can admit how bad things are? Not how bad the other person is, but how bad the marriage is?

MARY: It is bad. We haven't had a happy day in ten years.

BILL: That's right. As a matter of fact, I get bored at home.

MARY: If you can't talk——

BILL: Wait a minute . . .

THERAPIST: It was all right when you said it was a bad marriage, but when you say you get bored at home, you're putting your finger on your wife. But when you're home, there are two people there.

BILL: I never seem to have any problem knowing what to do with myself until I get around her at home.

THERAPIST: I wonder if that's a myth? How much time at home is there when you're not actually working or eating or sleeping?

BILL: Too damned little.

MARY: That's not the point. I have to keep busy too. Maybe the doctor is saying we don't organize what little free time we do have.

THERAPIST: That's what I mean. You're blaming each other for being too busy instead of cherishing what little time you do have together. Do you think the money arguments are a way of blaming each other for working so hard?

BILL: Could be. That's probably what makes me so mad when she complains about my buying equipment for my office. I am trying to use time-savers.

MARY: You know, we're not quite so broke that I couldn't have a little household help. Maybe I am afraid that it will encourage Bill to outspend me.

THERAPIST: Before we meet again, I want you to sit down separately and work out an ordinary week's apportionment of time. We may find that there is some squandering going on because neither of you is willing to take the first step in rectifying the situation. Don't discuss your time lists until you are here in my office. And if at any time either of you is annoyed with the other, you are to leave the other's presence. Do anything you want—see a movie, walk around the block, read a book alone—but you must avoid pointless quarrels until we can understand things better— okay?

MARY: Yes.

BILL: I'll try—when do we come back?

In this session the professional therapist has tried to find a point of agreement between the husband and wife, and he does in fact accomplish this—by getting them to *agree* that they have a bad marriage. Of course, in saying that the marriage is discordant, each feels that he is accusing the other spouse. But at the same time, each is in agreement with the other *that the marriage is bad*—whereas hitherto neither spouse recognized that they were in agreement on any point.

Because this couple is locked in a status struggle, agreement on something will start a process in which each will try to show that he agrees even more than the other; since they agree that they have a bad marriage, each will be striving to show the other that he takes the bad-marriage idea seriously. Realizing how competitive they are, the therapist knows that when he gives them instructions, each will be comparing the other's performance with his own. In the next session, the instructions will be for them to see as little of each other as possible for a few weeks. This is what they *have* been doing, but now *the therapist takes the situation* under control, ordering them to continue this behavior. He recognizes that both of the Parsons like to be in charge of their own behavior and that the very tactics they are using against each other they will also use against him in order to gain control of the therapeutic relationship. But in opposing him they will unwittingly place themselves in a coalition—together—and they will have to give up some of their habitual tactics in order to get the better of the therapist. Furthermore, they will both find puzzling the fact that the therapist, having established that they appear to have a bad marriage, wants them to stay apart. Couples with a bad marriage expect a counselor to tell them to have fun together, to take a trip together, to recapture the joys of their honeymoon, and so on. But by keeping them apart, the therapist will make them fight to get back together. As they go through a series of struggles with him, it will become increasingly apparent to them that the cost of office equipment and the amount of the telephone bill are not what they are really fighting over, that through the years each has developed so much pride in his hurt position that he would not admit the extent to which he was hurting and attacking the other.

49

THE NECESSITY FOR
MARITAL CHECKUPS

People usually do not attempt to evaluate their marriage until the relationship is in deep trouble and is about to blow up. Unless the behavior of the spouses is obviously destructive and the individuals are extremely miserable, it does not occur to them to examine themselves. They will bring a malfunctioning automobile to a garage for inspection, or at least will lift the hood and take a look at it themselves, but they don't do as much for their marriage. And if they have a quietly negative relationship which is becoming increasingly unhappy, they usually try to keep the worsening condition out of their awareness by denial.

The same defense of self-deceit is also common in relation to physical illnesses. Many a person has symptoms of a serious disease—but (often because of fear) refuses to see a physician. Instead, he rationalizes that he just has a "bad cold," or perhaps a "stomach ache." Only in recent years has an annual physical checkup for adults come to be regarded as almost mandatory. The checkup is performed in the hope that any pathologies present will be discovered while they are still treatable. For example, some forms of high blood pressure respond if treatment is given before irreversible changes have ensued.

It seems to us that marriages deserve the same care and attention given our bodies, or our automobiles. Marital checkups, we believe, can be useful. First, a checkup enables the husband and wife to identify and appraise marital liabilities, and the liabilities may then be reduced by therapy. Also, a marital checkup makes the spouses aware of taken-for-granted assets, and methods of stabilizing or increasing the assets can then be determined.

An individual in good health may be approaching an age where certain aspects of his living, such as diet, exercise, smoking, should be altered to help him maintain this good health. Similarly, marriages have phases, or life stages, that can be met by shifts or changes in the nature of the marital interaction and in some of the spouses' activities. Spouses may not recognize these marital process changes, but an experienced "marriage doctor" will.

There is much evidence that a *competent* third party can exert a therapeutic influence on an ailing marriage. Current statistics indicate that conciliation courts are fairly effective, if the conciliation officers are well trained and competent. For example, the Conciliation Court of Los Angeles has reported that sixty to seventy per cent of the treated spouses, among the first five hundred cases, dropped their requests for divorce actions. In Australia, a conciliation effort is required by law before a divorce can be brought into court. The director of the Government Bureau of Marriage Counselors in the Australian federal government, Lester Harvey, has reported to us that a large percentage of the divorce actions initiated are suspended as a result of the efforts of trained and qualified conciliators, and that the spouses thus helped apparently stay married after learning to understand their marriages. The law making a conciliation effort mandatory was enacted in 1959, so it is still too soon to tell whether these effects of conciliation are lasting, or just transitory. But all indications are that the couples assisted do remain married, and that their marriages function better than they did previously.

The conciliators in these courts help the discordant spouses to understand:

1. What the total assets and the total liabilities of the marriage are. This more objective view of the relationship largely eliminates the feeling, often more emotional than objective in origin, *that the marriage is all wrong.*

2. That the spouses are both part of a joint system. Neither of

them is all "good" or all "bad," and the marital system itself produces great changes in the behavior patterns of the people involved. Every action by Mary results in a reaction by John, and vice versa. The relationship is conjoint, not unilateral.

3. That consciously or unconsciously the primary function of many of the ways in which spouses behave is to take revenge for perceived hurts, or to prove that one spouse is equal to, if not better than, the other. Behavior with these motives can be identified by the competent therapist.

4. That differences in taste and performance levels do not necessarily mean inferiority or superiority.

5. That the communications system between the spouses may have broken down, so that the messages sent are not the messages received.

The conciliators can help the discordant spouses explicitly and consciously to decide whether they wish to stay married and whether they can reasonably expect to make a go of the marriage. If the spouses agree, as they usually do, that it is advantageous for them to remain married, then the conciliators can assist them in several respects. They advise them on how to communicate more effectively with each other. They provide a means for checking the workability level of the marriage. And they help them to establish a *quid pro quo*—the ground rules for a workable marriage—in terms of their particular personalities. (One of the mistakes of popular quickie How-to-Do-It articles is their implication that the roles of husband and wife are fixed and similar in all marriages.)

If the spouses agree, after appraising the advantages and disadvantages, that they should get divorced, the conciliator can advise and assist them in doing so, helping to make the divorce as cooperative, as undamaging, as possible, and enabling each party to assist the other to get a new start with a minimum of difficulty or bitterness.

We believe that yearly marital checkups with a professional would make the majority of marriages more workable, and would result in a vast increase in mental health, physical health, satisfaction, and productivity. However, the chances for such annual checkups becoming widespread in the near future are, indeed, small. For one thing, spouses have a natural reluctance to seek help unless their marriage is in great difficulty. At the same time, psychologists, psychiatrists, and marriage counselors often are hesitant about undertaking marital checkups of this sort. They do not know enough about preventive therapy. Almost all of their training and experience has been in dealing with pathological conditions or states of calamity. There is little literature, few schools, and no backlog of experience to which the professional can go for guidance. Furthermore, it is easier and more profitable to deal with calamities. The chances for apparent success are higher.

The marital checkup by a professional, then, will not be common for many years to come. Therefore, if the idea is sound—and we believe it is—spouses will have to conduct their checkup for themselves. Such a checkup is desirable for many reasons. First, it can be assumed that every marriage has problems. We have never encountered, or even heard of, a problem-free marriage. Correspondingly, it can be assumed that just about every marriage would profit from an evaluation, with the problems viewed in objective perspective.

Second, there is in marriage a process called *tendency:* a movement in the marriage process in one particular direction is apt to increase geometrically in the course of time. Thus, spouses who are drifting apart because of nonreciprocal behavior patterns tend to exaggerate these patterns as they drift apart; and they blame each other for the drifting and for the increase and the acceleration in the rate of drift. As time passes, the marriage becomes increasingly rigid and unbalanced in the particular direction which it happened to take. Usually the spouses caught in such a pathological marital system do not realize that negative tendencies *can* be limited, and often even reversed.

Third, there are natural and unavoidable dangers which occur in almost all marriages. For example, when children are born, when they grow older and eventually leave the household, when economic changes occur within the household, when the spouses acquire more leisure or more responsibility, or a combination of both, when geographical moves occur, new and strong stresses are imposed on the marital relationship. It is difficult (but not impossible) for an individual spouse to sense what these natural changes in the marital conditions will produce—what kind of shift of reciprocal interactions in the marriage will result.

Learning to appraise and diagnose the state of a marriage, it seems to us, is essential for the maintenance of a workable relationship. We wish that our married readers could find well-trained and experienced professionals to help them with such a checkup; and we wish that our readers, if they could find such professionals, had enough money to afford them. But the average married couple in the United States today probably cannot take advantage of professional services; therefore, the next chapter is devoted to methods for checking up on one's own marriage.

50

HOW TO CHECK UP
ON YOUR
OWN MARRIAGE

This chapter concerns methods for checking up on one's own marriage, not ways to improve the marital condition. At this point, the aim is to discover how well the process is operating. Using techniques for self-appraisal, the spouses will determine whether their marriage is functioning satisfactorily. If they decide that the marriage should be continued and they wish to improve it, their next step will be to identify their marital liabilities. Then, the third step, which will be discussed subsequently, is to find ways of reducing or eliminating these liabilities.

There are three recommended methods of appraisal:

Method A. The spouses isolate themselves, and each tries to make the marital appraisal alone. This unilateral do-it-alone method is the least effective of the self-checkup procedures, but under some conditions it is the only one possible. Later we will describe how it can be made most efficacious.

Method B. The two spouses sit down together under conditions to be described later, and perform a joint evaluation of their marital state.

Method C. The two spouses meet in the presence of a third individual, a nonprofessional. The function of the third party is to listen, and to reflect back what he "hears." Often the message sent by one spouse is not the message "heard" by the other, and in this situation a third party frequently can clarify what the message is. Many times, messages are transmitted at least in part by nonverbal behavior of which the sender is not aware. The third party can describe to the spouses their behavior and actions during the discussion. The nonprofessional for this purpose should be someone not related to either spouse—someone who can be trusted not to take sides, and not to gossip about what he hears. Also, he should be someone who is not bitter about marriage even if he has been divorced.

Occasionally, a fourth method is employed. Two couples (that is, a total of four people) meet together in the effort to share the function of judging and appraising each other's marital interactions. It is difficult to find two wives and two husbands who have a functioning four-way communication system, but it can be, and has been, done. We have also observed several larger groups, typically composed of four to six couples meeting under the auspices of a church or social agency to discuss marriage without the benefit of a professional. Some of those with which we were familiar were soon blown apart by arguments, but several continued for as many as ten sessions. We do not know of any such groups which have continued for longer than ten sessions or which have been noticeably profitable without the leadership of a professional—although they may well exist. We do not recommend this method in this book. The presence of any additional couples introduces too many distracting variables.

Method A. Marriage Appraisal by Individual Spouses

Each spouse should locate a place where he can apply himself in quiet and without interruption for a period of approximately two hours, and should try to select the time of highest vitality and least fatigue. Preferably, the test should be taken after the spouses have been apart for several hours, so that if they have been arguing, they have had an opportunity to simmer down. The only equipment needed is a pen or pencil and a pad of lined paper.

The first step is to record, in writing, what are considered to be the marital assets and the marital liabilities. In one column, the individual lists those elements which he likes about the marriage, those which he thinks work well, and in another column he records those which he dislikes, or which appear not to work well.

The next step is to answer the questions listed on the following pages, supplying explanatory information as required. It is essential that the person taking this test *write out the answers*. It is not sufficient just to read the page and answer the questions mentally.

The answers should be numbered to correspond to the questions. All the questions must be answered. Where a question does not apply to the spouse taking the test, he should attempt to answer it as well as possible for the other spouse. For example, in answering questions 15-17, the wife should state whether she believes her husband is getting along better or worse in his job since his marriage, giving the reasons for her conclusion.

1. Do you look forward to rejoining your spouse after being separated during the day? Answer *yes* or *no*.

2. If the answer to question 1 is "No," write out the major single reason why you do not look forward to meeting your spouse at home each evening. Be specific; for example, "My husband starts complaining about the way the house looks and the way I'm mishandling everything from the minute he comes into the house," or "I come home tired from the office and my wife has the house noisy, the television going, or friends in the kitchen, and everything looks like a pigpen."

3. If the answer to question 1 is "No," now write down at least five reasons, in addition to the one given in answering question 2, why the event of meeting at night is considered so unpleasant. Writing these five reasons may be difficult, and to do so will require much objectivity, for often one is ashamed of one's reaction to certain traits in one's spouse. For example, one man wrote, "I simply cannot stand the whining, high-pitched tone of my wife's voice." This husband had known about his wife's voice before he married her, and therefore found it embarrassing to admit that her manner of speech disturbed him. One wife wrote,

"Tom comes home so goddamned jolly and tells of all the interesting people he met during the day. Me, I'm exhausted from cleaning house and looking after three children and I simply resent his noisy cheerfulness. Why can't he come in quietly and just start helping me?" It is essential that at least five reasons be listed. If five important reasons cannot be found, minor ones can be included, to bring the total up to five.

4. In terms of Harry Stack Sullivan's definition of the state of love, do you love your spouse?—is the security and well-being of your wife or husband as significant to you as your own security and well-being? Answer *yes* or *no*.

5. Using this same definition, does your spouse love you? Answer *yes* or *no*.

6. Briefly list five instances of your own loving behavior toward your spouse during the last month.

7. List five instances of your spouse's loving behavior toward you during the last month.

8. List five hateful things you have done—intentionally or unintentionally—to your spouse in the last month.

9. List five hateful things your spouse has done to you during the last month.

10. List five things which you have asked or scolded or nagged your spouse to correct or improve, but which your spouse has not corrected.

11. List five things which your spouse has asked or scolded or nagged you to correct or improve, but which you have not corrected either because you could not or because you did not wish to do so.

12. Of the items listed in your answer to question 11, which could you have corrected if you had really wanted to do so? For example, which would you have been ready and willing to rectify during your courting period?

13. For each of the items listed in your answer to question 12, specify in detail your reasons for not making the changes suggested by your spouse.

14. For each of the items listed in your answer to question 10, put down the reasons why, in your opinion, your spouse did not attempt to please you by making the changes suggested.

15. (*For the husband.*) Have you been getting along better or worse in your job since your marriage? Answer *better* or *worse*.

16. If you are getting along better, describe in what ways your being married has been responsible.

17. If you are getting along worse, describe in what ways your marriage has been responsible.

18. (*For the wife.*) Since marriage, have your days been as fulfilling and as interesting as they were before you were married? Answer *yes* or *no*.

19. If they are at least as fulfilling, describe in what ways your marriage has been responsible.

20. If less fulfilling, describe in what ways your marriage has been responsible.

21. List five ways in which you consider your spouse to be excessively selfish in regard to you.

22. Who do you believe is exerting the greater effort to make the marriage successful, you or your spouse? Give reasons for this answer.

23. Have you considered the possibility of a divorce, even as a fleeting thought? Answer *yes* or *no*.

24. How many times have you considered the possibility of divorce in the last six months?

25. Do you know of a couple with a marriage better than yours? Answer *yes* or *no*.

26. If you know of such a couple, why is their marriage better than yours?

27. Before you got married, you must have thought (unless yours was a shotgun wedding) that your marriage would be a success. List five reasons why you thought it would be a success.

28. Knowing what you do now about your present marriage, would you—if you were again single—still marry the same person? Answer *yes* or *no*.

29. If you could get divorced from your present spouse without any inconvenience, without any major cost or publicity or bitterness, and without inflicting any hardship on your children, would you get divorced? Answer *yes* or *no*.

30. Were you happier during your courting period than you are now? Answer *yes* or *no*.

31. If you were happier, give at least three reasons why.

32. List five negative things (things which you do not like) about your spouse which you learned only after the intimacy of marriage.

33. List ten differences in taste between your spouse and yourself. For example, "He likes jazz; I like opera," or "She dislikes cleaning up the kitchen in the morning, and I object to the mess in the morning."

34. Is your married sex life satisfactory? Answer *yes* or *no*.

35. What behavior or techniques on the part of your spouse would make your sex life more satisfying?

36. If you have children, do they seem to you to help or to hinder your marriage? If you could begin your marriage all over, and be without children, would you prefer to have none?

37. If you do not have children, do you think their presence would improve the marital relationship?

38. Do you like your spouse's relatives? If there are any you dislike, tell why.

39. (*For the wife.*) Would your marriage be better if your husband made more money?

40. Is there any way you can help your husband to get ahead in his business (make more money)?

41. Would your marriage be better if your spouse had some particular skills which you believe he does not now possess?

42. Why does your spouse not have these skills?

43. Can you help him to acquire them?

44. List five reasons why your marriage is advantageous (or satisfying) for you.

45. List ten disadvantages (or unsatisfying aspects) for you in your marriage.

If you have answered all of these questions honestly, a review of your answers will indicate very clearly whether your marriage, in your opinion, is working in a way which is reasonably satisfying to you, whether it needs a major overhaul, or whether the repair work required so outweighs your commitment to the relationship that it should be ended with a divorce to avoid continued destructiveness.

Neither spouse should show his answers to the other. If a

spouse knows his partner will see his written answers, there is an inclination not to do the test with the same objectivity as if it were private.

After both have gone through the test, each should ask the following question of the other: "Do you believe our marriage is much less than we want it to be?" If at least one of the spouses believes that the marriage is very unsatisfactory, then even if the other feels that the marriage is great, they should each answer the following question: "Shall we find out what is wrong with the marriage and try to improve it?"

If the answer for both is "Yes," they should next go to the chapter on "Interpersonal Comparison Tests."

Method B. Joint Evaluation

In this second method for checking up on a marriage, the questions listed for Method A are employed once again. However, instead of writing the answers out, the spouses answer the questions out loud, in each other's presence, taking turns at being the first to answer a question. The answers must be brief (that is, as if they were being written out). *Each spouse must listen to the other's answers without comment.* It is not permissible for one spouse to challenge the other, or to argue, or to attempt to explain actions or episodes referred to by the other, or in any way try to enlarge or negate what the other says—regardless of how much he wishes to do so. Also, no matter how annoyed one or both of the partners may become, the test must be completed at one sitting—and it must be conducted in a quiet place where there can be no interruptions of any kind.

When both spouses have answered all of the questions, they should return to their normal routines without further comment. After a thinking period of about twenty-four hours, each of the spouses should tell the other his answer to the following question: "Is our marriage very unsatisfactory?"

If both parties believe that the marriage is satisfactory and cannot be improved, nothing more need be done. But if one or both of the spouses thinks that the marriage process is not working, *or that it can be improved,* they should ask each other the following question: "Should we try to analyze our marriage to see how it can be improved?" The chapter on "Interpersonal Comparison Tests" may be helpful.

Method C. Appraisal with the Assistance of a Nonprofessional Outsider

As has been mentioned, the third party should be someone who is trusted by both spouses, who can be depended upon to be objective, and who will not gossip.*

This method requires much more time than the others—a minimum of five uninterrupted hours.

Once again, the questions listed for Method A are employed, and as in Method B, they are answered out loud, not in writing. But this time, with a third party present, after one of the spouses has answered a question, the subject is open for discussion. The other spouse may challenge, may argue, may explain, may say anything he wishes, as long as it is relevant. If, as often happens, one of the spouses wanders from the subject, it is the function of the third party to return the discussion to the matter at hand.

In the course of the session, there may be flare-ups of temper or weeping or cursing. When these occur, the third party should calmly remind the spouses that their purpose in coming together was not to argue, but to make an appraisal of the marriage.

Frequently, when one spouse challenges another, asks questions, makes an explanation, open hostility will occur between the spouses. During these times it often happens that the message received by one of the spouses is not the message that the other actually sent. The third party must stay alert for this situation, and try to act as interpreter, making sure that the messages sent by one spouse are accurately received by the other. For example, the third party may have to interrupt a discussion and say, "Mary,

---

* In Chapter 48 (which includes examples of how an incompetent third party operates and how a well-trained professional operates) are many points which the unprofessional third party will find useful. Indeed, it would be desirable for him to read this entire book, so that he and the two spouses concerned are familiar with the same thinking patterns and the same terminology.

I will paraphrase what you have said in the way I understand it."
After completing his paraphrase he asks, "Mary, is that what you
meant?" If Mary says that it is, the third party asks the other
spouse if he understands the statement in the same way also.

At the completion of the session, after all of the questions have
been answered by both spouses, the third party asks both spouses
if they think the marriage can be improved and if they wish to
try to improve it.

If they wish to improve it, they can proceed to the chapter on
"Interpersonal Comparison Tests."

51

HOW TO SELECT
A SPOUSE

The probability of having a workable marriage is highest if one chooses the spouse with whom one can most easily work. Although this thought is obvious, it is seldom put into practice. It is unlikely that the man and woman "in love" will follow their own best judgment in picking a spouse. It is even more unlikely that they will make use of the knowledge accumulated by social scientists. Nature, our culture, and our traditions all distract us, prevent us from being intelligent during the mate-selecting process. Instead, the marriage-bound individual gallops off and gets himself engaged to someone who "attracts" him.

But even now, all need not be lost. Usually there is at least a little time before the marriage when the potential spouses still have the opportunity to make a checklist and estimate if the relationship stands a chance of lasting "till death do us part," although the percentage who have the courage to break a well-announced engagement is small.

But before approaching the marital checklist, a potential spouse must renounce the myth that there's only one person in the world for each of us, and try, for once in his life, to be objective.

The idea that there is only one possible mate for each originated more or less in the church, which long has regarded marriages specifically as created by God. The attitude of the state, as reflected in the civil ceremony, is that marriage is just a legal contract, but the average person, even if he is irreligious, is usually awed by the ritual of a church wedding.

The idea that a marriage was "made in heaven" is certain to be harmful. The thought that each of the spouses selected the other with divine inspiration, from among the three billion people in the world, makes them intolerant of the imperfections of marriage, which are always present. More important, it eliminates the notion of personal *responsibility* both in selecting one's mate and in making the marriage workable.

Probably there are hundreds of other individuals with whom either partner would have done just as well or perhaps even better (as many middle-aged spouses do not have to be told). The recognition of this fact can introduce more realistic assessments and planning into a marriage. Some spouses strive too hard to maintain the illusion of perfect marriage. If one starts out believing that one has chosen the perfect spouse, one becomes too readily disillusioned when the inevitable discovery of imperfection occurs. The result may be resentment and blame, of oneself or one's spouse. Further, the unrealistic idea that there exists somewhere on the globe the "perfect mate" often leads to a lengthy and frustrating search. Many a bachelor or spinster "just never found the perfect mate." And many married people never commit themselves fully to their marriage because they continue to keep one eye open for someone more perfect.

It is worthwhile again to consider why most people happen to get married:

1. There is geographical propinquity; individuals are thrown together simply because they happen to live or to work near each other.

2. They share some valued cultural similarities—for example, both may be white, upper-middle-class, Protestant, college graduates—or each may be reasonably acceptable according to the value system of the other's family or peer group.

3. One or both are pressured by friends, family, or even cultural norms which proclaim that it is time to get married and settled down.

4. They are pressured by sexual urges which they cannot handle outside of a marital relationship.

5. One or both are lonely, and unrealistically believe being married is a cure for loneliness.

6. One or both believe having a child automatically would enhance their life.

7. The individual cannot think of any path of action except marriage to get him out of an unpleasant situation: he may live at home with quarreling parents; a woman may wish to quit an odious job; a man may fear he will succumb to a homosexual relationship with his roommate. Sometimes a person is simply bored by his present circumstances.

8. One or both are seeking the solution to neurotic problems which they feel will be overcome through marriage. (For example, an individual may get a divorce and marry the mistress or lover who, it is hoped, "will solve everything.")

It is not flattering to recognize that one's spouse has not chosen one as a mate solely because of one's personal characteristics. Yet this is inevitably true, and should not be a source of embarrassment. Observe the sudden increase in the marriage rate when the government announces that men married before a certain date will be excused from the draft. Yet the individuals who let such a reason influence their decision to marry deny the nonpersonal stimulus, stating, "Oh, we were in love anyway," or "We planned to get married, so we just moved it up a little." *Believing* this falsehood, they marry in response to a nonpersonal stimulus, and in many instances the result is subsequent difficulty. For they get married before they are ready, ignoring the statistics which make it clear that the younger the marriage age, the shorter the courtship, the more external the reasons for the marriage (for example, the desire for money, or for security, or for immunity from the draft), the higher the divorce rate.

Forty per cent of all marriages occur between people twenty years of age or younger. The earlier the individual drops out of school, the lower his ambitions and his intelligence, the sooner he is likely to get married.

It is evident, then, that nature, society, excessive possessiveness, ambition, or a jittery nervous system often pushes two human beings helter-skelter to the altar. Seldom is the decision to get married made carefully and objectively, on the basis of each individual's intimate knowledge of himself and of the prospective spouse.

The unrecognized forces are so strong that even when persons do attempt to measure the prospective success of their marriage-to-be by means of an objective scoring system, they tend to cheat. They want to believe that the potential mate is indeed the boy or girl of their dreams. But by and large the romantic dreams of what the other person is or will be like are untested by *experience* with that person.

After several years of marriage, people often say, "If I had known as much before I got married as I know now, I'd still be a bachelor." Hogwash. One can learn as much about a possible husband or wife before marriage as ten years after. The unpleasant fact is that the people concerned frequently do not wish to do so.

WHAT SHOULD ONE LOOK FOR IN A SPOUSE?

A "personality" is made up of a repertoire of behavioral tactics. The tactics of a spouse will be either complementary to one's own, nonrelated to one's own, or in conflict with one's own. Environment strongly influences our behavior and values. Just as the person reared in a Southern state develops a Southern accent, so does the person raised in a particular part of the country base his behavior on the values commonly accepted there. The character of the individual's home also affects the nature of his behavioral repertoire. Different biases develop, for example, in such varied environments as a Catholic home, a Protestant home, a rich family, a poor family.

Marriage, it should now be evident, is difficult enough even when the spouses do not have behavioral repertoires which clash or which are mutually incomprehensible. When these avoidable problems are built into the marriage, it is under an extra handicap right from the start. For example, though a girl from an economically and culturally deprived home where listening to music was a rarity can smile and appear to be happy when she accompanies her fiancé to a concert, in most cases she is going along *to be with him,* not to hear the music. In fairy stories (many women's magazines publish them) she learns to love music, and after marriage they both become members of the local string quartet. In real life, this rarely happens. After a few years of marriage, these two spouses may find music an object of mutual resentment. The wife may start skipping a few of the concerts because they bore her, or because the highbrow conversation she hears there excludes her. If she does come to a concert at her husband's urging, she may resent it, and may even fall asleep during the performance. Then *he* resents her not sharing his pleasure spontaneously. But if she and her husband stay home and watch television, as she prefers, he resents being deprived of one of his major interests. *A year's engagement might have exposed the problem.*

Young engaged couples may find pleasure in their political arguments. During courtship, they are mutually considerate, and their dialectic does not include personal invective. After marriage it becomes important that they are canceling out each other's votes. When their children come along, there are battles for the youngsters' political allegiance. The disagreement that once appeared "stimulating" too often becomes a message of rejection after marriage.

Of course, there are exceptions, marriages which seem to thrive despite marked differences between the spouses. There is the famous conductor-composer who married the burlesque queen. Recently they celebrated their silver anniversary with a wonderful party. Hardly anyone knows that he is a homosexual and she is a practicing lesbian. The great conductor spends twelve hours a day at his work and requires a wife mostly as a charming hostess at social gatherings. She enjoys prestige and social acceptance without having to give up her sexual preference. The union is highly functional for this couple.

But marriages of this sort are most unusual. In general, the degree of consonance between the value systems of the spouses is of major importance in determining marital compatibility. Of course, many of us are acquainted with spouses who are opposites in various ways—and still have a successful marriage. But the differences are generally in noncritical areas, and therefore without major significance, just as smoking six cigarettes or less a day is not linked with cancer or circulatory disorders.

Observe, however, the dissimilar environmental backgrounds

and values systems of Mary and John Hawkins. Here is an example of how differing values can lead to trouble.

John was born in a large city on the eastern seaboard. His parents were Irish immigrants. The work ethic was strong in John, and he earned his own way through two years at Boston University before being drafted in World War II. Graduating from officer candidate school, he soon became a second lieutenant.

One evening as he sat alone reading the sports page at a USO dance, a young hostess came up to him and asked if he wanted to dance. This is how John and Mary met. After a few dances it became apparent to Mary that John was reticent; she became a bit aggressive in order to break down his shyness.

During the dates they had in the following month, they learned about each other. Mary was from a wealthy Jewish family which owned a chain of dry-goods stores in Arizona. She was in her junior year at Swarthmore, majoring in music and French.

When Mary was three, her father had walked out and gotten a divorce, and she and her mother had moved into her grandfather's house, which was large and well-staffed with servants. Mary recalled how her grandfather had demanded exquisite manners and had made her recite quotations from books at meals. He had tyrannized her throughout her childhood.

Mary had attended expensive private schools and then Swarthmore. She was unsure of herself with boys, even though she was vivacious and attractive; and she rationalized that getting high grades in school was the important thing. As much as possible she avoided going home during vacations because she did not like to be lectured by her grandfather.

Although John was attracted to Mary, he felt somewhat uneasy with her. At first, he wondered if he reacted this way because she was Jewish. But he rejected this idea because he had never thought of himself as intolerant. As for Mary, going with a Christian created no problems (she thought) since her grandfather made a point of joining clubs and societies where Jewish members were not entirely welcome.

John and Mary did not discuss their religious differences prior to the wedding. (The fact that they avoided the subject indicates that it made them uncomfortable.)

The problem of finances did not come up either. John was

living at the bachelor officers' quarters, and Mary's college expenses had been taken care of. John had to spend money only for weekend-dating with Mary. He noticed her expensive clothes and habits, but since he was in uniform there was no incongruity between his level of attire and hers. John was pleased but uncomfortable about several of Mary's gifts to him, including a gold pocketknife which was expensive and useless.

Soon they were spending weekends in an apartment belonging to one of Mary's friends. Both John and Mary had been virgins, and they were delighted to find that they enjoyed a rewarding sexual compatibility.

In June, John was transferred to military headquarters in London. Mary stayed in Philadelphia, but dropped out of college and went to work for the Red Cross. They corresponded frequently. On John's return, a year later, they married. By eloping, instead of having a formal wedding, they avoided and isolated their two families. At the time, neither John nor Mary thought about this, but years later, Mary (not knowing exactly what was bothering her) complained that she had not had a proper marriage, and blamed this on John. (A psychiatrist would say that actually they had avoided their families for fear that their relatives would recognize that the marriage was not desirable for either of them and would urge them to delay or to abandon the idea altogether.)

They moved to Cambridge, Massachusetts, where John, on the GI bill, completed his college work and obtained a graduate degree in engineering. Those three years were hell for Mary. Their small quarters had no privacy. Living on ninety dollars a month was almost impossible. Mary occasionally dipped into her own private (inherited) income; and John resented this, as if she were blaming him for being a poor provider.

Mary had too much leisure. She could not force herself to get an ordinary job as, say, a clerk or secretary, and she had no qualifications for anything else. She kept insisting that she would start studying music again, but she never did. There was always "something" which stopped her.

Mary did not like the cold New England weather. Hitherto, she had always spent winters in comfortable, well-heated houses, but at Cambridge she had to go into a cold bathroom in the morning. Also, with the cold weather came confinement, and since

John spent most of his time in the laboratory and the library, Mary had little companionship.

She convinced John that they should use some of her money for a winter vacation for both of them in Arizona. They spent a miserable two weeks there. John fought with her grandfather continuously. They disagreed on almost everything—from religion to politics, to financing, to manners. For the first time, Mary found herself agreeing with her grandfather.

Back at Cambridge, John told Mary he had accepted a post as a teaching assistant at Yale. Mary became belligerent. They had never discussed where they would live, and Mary had always assumed it would be in the West or the Southwest. They fought over this for a solid week, and to top it off, during this time Mary learned that she was pregnant. Her annoyance changed into a panic as she realized how her miseries would be increased by the pregnancy.

John did not want to have a child, but he tried hard to hide his reaction. Instead, he attempted to be supportive and thoughtful, but Mary interpreted his quietness as further rejection and criticism.

As the pregnancy progressed, Mary began to fear she might die in childbirth. Neither John nor her physician could relieve her of this apprehension. As a result of this fear and of her general nervousness with the total situation, Mary became physically run-down, and after seven weeks the physician said that her condition was dangerous and suggested that she return to Arizona and have the baby delivered there.

The child was born in Arizona, and several months passed before John could get out there. Mary was resentful over his absence, and when John did come, they fought over what the boy should be named. Mary wanted to name him Isadore after her grandfather. John wanted to call him Patrick. After wrangling, they decided on John junior, a name neither of them particularly liked.

In an effort—however resentful—to give in to Mary's wishes, John gave up his job at Yale and accepted a teaching position in a small California college. He felt this was generous of him, because he liked the eastern milieu and the prestige of Yale.

When Mary joined John in California—in a small, hot college town—it seemed to him that she did not appreciate his sacrifice.

And it seemed to her that he was not understanding of the problems of being a mother—especially on a small income, without help, in a tiny apartment in a hick town.

For the first time, violent quarrels broke out between them. Once, John hit Mary. In his rage, he shouted, "You goddamn kike!"

Both knew the marriage had to end. *They had nothing in common.* Mary returned to Arizona and secured an uncontested divorce.

Some years later (after each had remarried), Mary and John met to discuss some psychological difficulties their young son was having. At this time they were able to view their marriage with considerable objectivity. They discussed their marital mess and concluded that because of the cultural, economic, religious, and geographical differences between them, they hadn't stood a chance. They also concluded there had been enormous squandering of the resources of two young human beings.

If Mary and John had had a means of recognizing the gap between their respective cultural backgrounds and values systems, and a way of estimating its significance, they probably would not have married. Clinical psychologists are able to perform this evaluation by means of interpersonal tests and interviews. But there are not enough psychologists to do this for everyone, and their services are expensive. Therefore, we have devised a series of tests which couples can take by themselves. True, these tests cannot supply the same precise information as would five or six hours with a psychologist who could personally observe the interactions between the two people. But the tests will indicate unmistakable trends to those couples who are intelligently seeking a functional and satisfying marriage.

For those who already are married, the identification of a gap between the spouses' backgrounds and values systems may point to a previously unrecognized source of discord. Once recognized, the destructiveness of the gap can often be reduced.

52

INTERPERSONAL
COMPARISON TESTS

In this section we offer three tests which will aid in determining how close or far apart couples are in their repertoire of values. The amount of difference will indicate the likelihood that the two individuals can form a functional system. Later we will explain how to estimate this.

The tests should be taken by one person at a time in complete privacy. To start the first test, place a piece of white bond paper alongside the first test page. Line up the top of the paper with the top of the page. Now answer the questions by placing an X on the bond paper opposite the horizontal line where it would be put if the answers were being marked in the book. Mark only a single answer for each question, choosing the one which is more true than any of the others. Go through Tests A and B in this manner, using a fresh piece of paper for each page. The instructions for taking Test C are given separately. Be sure to identify each page by writing at the top the number of the corresponding page in the book.

Do not make marks in the book. The second person taking the test would then see your answers, and would be influenced by them.

TEST A

1. I was born
    a. on the Eastern seaboard. _____
    b. in the Southern United States. _____
    c. in the Midwestern United States. _____
    d. in the Southwestern United States. _____
    e. in the Western United States. _____
    f. outside the United States. _____

2. My place of rearing was
    a. a metropolis. _____
    b. suburbia. _____
    c. a medium-sized town. _____
    d. a small town. _____
    e. a rural area. _____

3. My religious background is
    a. Catholic. _____
    b. Jewish. _____
    c. Protestant. _____
    d. Moslem. _____
    e. none. _____
    f. other. _____

4. My parents are
    a. first-generation Americans. _____
    b. second-generation Americans. _____
    c. third-generation Americans (or earlier). _____
    d. not American citizens. _____

5. The highest annual income earned by my father was
    a. over $30,000. _____
    b. over $20,000. _____
    c. over $15,000. _____
    d. over $10,000. _____
    e. over $5,000. _____
    f. $5,000 or less. _____

6. The highest educational level reached by my father was
    a. grade school. _____
    b. high school. _____
    c. college. _____
    d. graduate school. _____
    e. a doctoral degree. _____

7. *The highest educational level reached by my mother was*
   a. grade school.
   b. high school. _____
   c. college. _____
   d. graduate school. _____
   e. a doctoral degree. _____

8. *My position in the family was*
   a. oldest child. _____
   b. middle child. _____
   c. youngest child. _____
   d. only child. _____
   e. one of several in middle. _____

9. *The number of children in my family was*
   a. very large (seven or more). _____
   b. large (five or six). _____
   c. average (three or four). _____
   d. small (two). _____
   e. only one. _____

10. *My parents were*
    a. very close in age. _____
    b. less than five years apart. _____
    c. less than ten years apart. _____
    d. less than fifteen years apart. _____
    e. fifteen or more years apart. _____

11. *My parents' experience with divorce was that*
    a. neither was ever divorced. _____
    b. one had been previously divorced. _____
    c. both had been previously divorced. _____
    d. they were divorced when I was a child (12 or under). _____
    e. they were divorced when I was in my teens or older.

12. *In my parents' families (including grandparents and parents' siblings)*
    a. there have been no divorces. _____
    b. there has been one divorce. _____
    c. there have been two divorces. _____
    d. there have been three or more divorces. _____

13. *In my family rearing the person who seemed most in charge was*
    a. my mother. _____
    b. my father. _____

   c. neither parent. _____
   d. I never thought about who was in charge. _____

14. *In our community my parents were*
   a. considered important people. _____
   b. included among the people of some standing. _____
   c. just average socially. _____
   d. below average socially. _____
   e. considered outsiders. _____

TEST B

I. PAST LIFE EXPERIENCES

1. *My family situation consisted of*
   a. living with both of my biological parents. _____
   b. living with just my mother. _____
   c. living with just my father. _____
   d. living in foster homes or with stepparents. _____
   e. living with my real mother and a stepfather. _____
   f. living with my real father and a stepmother. _____

2. *My own family experience was*
   a. warm and pleasant. _____
   b. pleasant but not intimate. _____
   c. nothing I can particularly remember. _____
   d. unpleasant. _____

3. *As clearly as I can remember my earliest days were*
   a. extremely pleasant. _____
   b. neither pleasant nor unpleasant. _____
   c. pleasant, though I was nervous. _____
   d. unpleasant. _____

4. *The most pleasant aspects of my childhood are associated with experiences*
   a. with both parents. _____
   b. with the parent of the same sex. _____
   c. with the parent of the opposite sex. _____
   d. with my siblings. _____
   e. unconnected with members of my immediate family. _____
   f. I do not recall any particularly pleasant experiences. _____

5. *As a child I was fond of*
   a. reading, solitary hobbies, and daydreaming. _____
   b. sports and outdoor activities. _____

c. being around other people socially as much as possible. _____

d. no particular interests which I can recall. _____

6. *During my growing-up period*
   a. I had many close friends. _____
   b. I had one or two close friends. _____
   c. I had no friends whom I particularly recollect. _____
   d. I was a very solitary person. _____

7. *In my family, my dating*
   a. was something I could easily discuss with my parents. _____
   b. was mentioned rarely, or only in a kidding manner. _____
   c. was something I did not care to discuss. _____
   d. aroused considerable conflict. _____

8. *When I was in high school*
   a. my major interest was in getting good grades as well as maintaining an active social life. _____
   b. my major interest was in maintaining an active social and sports life rather than in getting high grades. _____
   c. I did not want to go to school any longer, and wanted to make money. _____
   d. I felt confused and did not know what I wanted to do. _____

II. PRESENT LIFE EXPERIENCES

1. *Financially and socially I feel the next five years*
   a. will be reasonably successful. _____
   b. will consist of two steps forward and one back. _____
   c. are impossible to predict at present. _____
   d. The future scares me. _____

2. *About my health at the present time, I would say that*
   a. I have always had perfect health, and I am certain I'll stay that way. _____
   b. for the last few years, my general condition has been below par, but I believe I'll regain excellent health in the near future. _____
   c. for some time now I have had a chronic illness (or disability) which is serious, and the probability of improvement is small. _____
   d. I don't know for sure. I guess I'm as healthy as anybody, but I haven't had a physical for years. _____

3. *About my psychological adjustment, I would say that*
   a. I feel fairly secure emotionally. -_____
   b. I am happiest not living alone. _____

    c. I probably do best living alone.   _____
    d. I do not think about my emotions.   _____

4. *Like many people I am*
    a. sometimes uneasy when I am alone.   _____
    b. sometimes uncomfortable when in a crowd.   _____
    c. sometimes concerned about dying.   _____
    d. hardly ever concerned with such matters.   _____

5. *With regard to children*
    a. I have doubts about how good a parent I would be (am).   _____
    b. I very much want (am very glad I have) a child of the same sex as I am.   _____
    c. I am not sure I want children (like having children).   _____
    d. I do not care what sex the child is, but I do want to have one (or perhaps two or three).   _____
    e. I would like to have at least four or five children.   _____
    f. as far as I am concerned, my marriage would be most successful without any children.   _____

6. *With regard to getting married (being married) at this particular time, I feel that*
    a. since most of my friends are already married, I would like to be (am glad I am) too.   _____
    b. marriage would be (is) an important stabilizing influence in my life.   _____
    c. the person I wish (wished) to marry will not wait if we do not get married now (would not have waited if we had not married when we did).   _____
    d. there is (was) no special reason for marrying now (when I did) but I do (did) not wish to disappoint my friends and relatives.   _____
    e. it is (was) as good a time as any to marry.   _____

III. THE PERSON I AM THINKING OF MARRYING (AM MARRIED TO)

1. *My prospective mate (my spouse)*
    a. is extremely attractive physically.   _____
    b. is not unusually attractive physically, but is likeable.   _____
    c. is someone I do not think of in terms of physical beauty or good looks.   _____
    d. embarrasses me because of his (her) looks.   _____

2. *My prospective mate (my spouse)*
    a. comes from a family I greatly admire.   _____

   b. comes from a family I feel very much a part of. _____

   c. has so little family closeness I feel sorry for him (her). _____

   d. has very irritating parents, but I can overlook them. _____

3. *With regard to the family of my intended mate (my spouse)*

   a. I am worried that she may become too much like her mother (or he like his father). _____

   b. I am concerned that she may become too much like her father (or he like his mother). _____

   c. I do not feel his (her) parents will (do) play any significant role in our marriage. _____

   d. I do not think he (she) is like either of his (her) parents. _____

4. *I feel that my intended mate's (my spouse's) parents*

   a. are better educated than my family. _____

   b. have considerably more money than my family. _____

   c. are not as socially acceptable as my family. _____

   d. I do not think about them in this way. _____

5. *In the relationship with my intended mate (my spouse) I feel that*

   a. he (she) is more in charge than I am. _____

   b. we are equally in charge. _____

   c. I am more in charge than he (she) is. _____

   d. neither of us is in charge. _____

6. *With regard to companionship, my intended mate (my spouse) and I*

   a. have many interests in common. _____

   b. have independent interests, but are tolerant and supportive of each other's activities. _____

   c. expect to develop interests in common. _____

   d. seem to have relatively little in common when we are not busy with social activities. _____

7. *With regard to the question of marriage, my intended mate (my spouse) and I*

   a. have discussed our doubts and fears of marriage. _____

   b. have had some doubts, but have not mentioned them. _____

   c. may be afraid of hurting each other by bringing up the question of whether we are making (have made) a mistake. _____

   d. do not have any doubts whatsoever. _____

   e. used to have doubts but overcame them. _____

8. *With regard to our contemplated (present) marriage*
   a. I would like to postpone (leave) it, but am afraid of the consequences. _____
   b. despite my doubts I prefer to go ahead (stay) with it. _____
   c. I feel I can overcome any doubts since my love is great enough for two. _____
   d. I would have doubts no matter whom I was marrying (had married) and should therefore not let these doubts stand in the way now. _____

9. *With regard to religion*
   a. we are of the same faith and there are no conflicts. _____
   b. neither of us has had serious religious training, and we do not intend to become involved with any church. _____
   c. we are of different faiths, but have agreed to rear our children in one of them. _____
   d. we have opposing religious views, but are tolerant of each other's ideas. _____
   e. we would have no problems about religion if other people would stay out of our business. _____

IV. ATTITUDES PRECEDING MARRIAGE (FOR ENGAGED COUPLES)

1. *My plans for marriage include*
   a. a wish to travel as soon as possible. _____
   b. a desire to move from our present area and establish a home elsewhere. _____
   c. a desire to settle down where we are as quickly as possible. _____
   d. I have no plans beyond wishing to get married. _____

2. *With regard to traveling and establishing a home*
   a. my intended mate's plans include nothing that is incompatible with my own wishes. _____
   b. we have not discussed this topic fully. _____
   c. I am leaving the decisions to him (her). _____
   d. he (she) is leaving the decisions to me. _____

3. *With regard to sex*
   a. my intended spouse has had experience, but I have not. _____
   b. I am more experienced than he (she). _____
   c. It is important to me that he (she) has had sexual experience before marriage. _____
   d. we have both had premarital sex experience. _____

    e. we are limiting our sex activity until after marriage. _____

    f. we do not agree on our sex life at present. _____

4. With regard to having children

    a. I would like to have children as soon as possible. _____

    b. I would leave the decision about when to have children to my intended spouse. _____

    c. I would prefer to wait several years before having children. _____

    d. I don't feel this is an important consideration. _____

V. MARRIAGE AND THE FUTURE

1. With regard to my occupational or avocational interests

    a. I feel I have the courage to pursue both my marriage and my interests, even when they conflict. _____

    b. I feel I could sacrifice almost anything in order to have a happy marriage. _____

    c. I see no reason for conflict between marriage and my other interests. _____

    d. my intended mate (my spouse) has no ambitions or professional commitments which will jeopardize or interfere with our marriage. _____

    e. my intended mate's (my spouse's) devotion to his (her) career interest is something I can easily admire and support. _____

    f. my intended mate's (my spouse's) devotion to his (her) career is something I hope I can get more enthusiastic about as I understand him (her) better. _____

2. With regard to the future with my intended mate (my spouse)

    a. I sometimes think he (she) may become ill. _____

    b. I fear that he (she) may become ill. _____

    c. I fear that he (she) will become superior intellectually or more important than I can become. _____

    d. I never have had any doubts. _____

3. With regard to the future of our marriage

    a. I am worried about becoming poor. _____

    b. I am worried about the influence of our in-laws upon us. _____

    c. I am troubled about the question of how many children we should have. _____

d. it sometimes occurs to me that my intended mate
(my spouse) might have an affair.   _____

e. I prefer not to worry about things until they happen.   _____

TEST C

Using a separate sheet of paper, write down in order of preference the three activities listed here which you like most and the
three which you like least.

Motion pictures
Competitive sports (tennis, bowling, and so on)
Spectator sports
Outdoor activities (fishing, walking, bicycling, and so on)
Special gatherings with friends
Reading
Art appreciation (listening to music, visiting art galleries, and so on)
Politics
Hobbies (woodworking, sewing, stamp collecting, and so on)
Membership in organizations (school or college clubs, union activi-
ties, and so on)
Business or professional activities (beyond ordinary office hours)
Creative endeavor (writing, drawing, singing, acting, playing a musi-
cal instrument)
Television
Driving in the automobile
Theater
Night clubs
Dancing
Discussion groups
Civic activities
Being with a few friends of my own sex

When you and your partner compare sheets, first note those
activities which neither of you checked and decide whether you
are both genuinely indifferent to all of these. Perhaps there are
some in this group which you might enjoy trying together.

How to Use the Tests

For Tests A and B lay the two partners' answer sheets for a particular page one on top of the other so that the columns of *X*'s

are side by side. Be sure that the tops of the two sheets are even. (See diagram.)

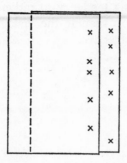

The alternative answers for each question have been arranged in order of increasing differentness (vertically). Therefore, the extent of the vertical distance between the *X*'s for any particular question indicates the degree of difference in cultural and ethnic values between the two people taking the tests.

A scanning of the results of Test C will make the differences in taste between the two people obvious.

In *general*, the greater the gap between the two people in culture and taste, the greater is the likelihood that they will find themselves incompatible and the greater will be their difficulty in forming a highly functional relationship. The reasons for this have been discussed earlier.

This is the rule of thumb, but it is not an absolute law. No generalization about human nature can be absolute, for there is an infinite variety of people, and they relate to each other in an infinite number of different ways. Therefore, the man and woman who have completed the tests should do more than just take note of the differences between them. They should explore them in depth so that they can determine if the "samenesses" can be fully utilized to increase the solidarity of the marriage, and so that they can attempt to turn some of the possibly debilitating differences into advantages, or at least to neutralize them.

One way of achieving these aims is to undertake a *quid pro quo* session, using the information brought out in these tests as the basic material for discussion. Such a session will provide the spouses with a means of beginning, at least, to resolve and adjust differences. But no matter how hard they attempt to be objective, they will have a strong tendency to rationalize. A trusted third party can be helpful in keeping the dialogues on an even keel, and the conclusions objective.

Part V

PROFESSIONAL
HELP

53

HOW TO GET HELP
FROM A PROFESSIONAL

If discordant spouses wish to develop a workable, productive marriage, they must remove or reduce the disruptive forces, behavior patterns, or attitudes of their association. Such a procedure involves several steps:

1. The development of a desire to achieve a more satisfying marriage.
2. The development of communication between spouses, so that the message sent is the message received.
3. The identification of the forces, behavior patterns, and attitudes which are warping the marriage.
4. The development of the recognition that neither spouse is all good or all bad. Marriage is a system, a constant interaction, and therefore neither spouse is to blame for the interactional problems. Both contribute (and probably equally) to the marital discords.
5. The practice of techniques which will assist both spouses in reducing their abrasive interactional characteristics.
6. The practice of techniques which will help spouses fabricate their own *quid pro quo*. In doing so, they acknowledge that no one can be perfect, that no two people can be completely con-

gruous, and that, therefore, the spouses must agree about which faults, which opposing views, which taste differences, each can— voluntarily and with grace—accept from the other.

7. The practice of techniques which will develop collaboration between spouses, techniques which will reduce their deprecatory and disparaging behavior and substitute behavior which supplies positive reinforcement to each.

When spouses see a counselor, or when they sit down together to try to improve their relationship, they are by their actions expressing a desire to develop a workable marriage.

From this point on, the basic essential is that the information and messages which each gives the other be directed toward improving the marriage. *But this seldom happens spontaneously.* No matter how hard the spouses believe they are trying, their well-established relationship system and joint behavioral patterns usually negate their individual efforts. Unless the improve-the-marriage techniques are used skillfully, the spouses may end up defeating the very purpose for which their sessions were intended. Unless the improve-the-marriage techniques are used properly, they may turn out to be a means of escalating the wrangling and the destructive patterns the spouses want to eliminate. Therefore, when spouses have decided they need the help of a third party, they should make every effort to find a counselor who is professionally competent and is suited to dealing with their particular personalities and problems.

Among the various kinds of professionals who undertake marital counseling are psychiatrists, psychologists, social workers, pastoral counselors, and marriage counselors. In Appendix C the requirements for practicing these various specialties in the state of California are listed. The California qualifications have been cited because they are at least as high as those laid down by any state. Indeed, in some states there are no specified requirements for a marriage counselor.

Unfortunately, even when the qualifications of a professional do fulfill certain objective standards, they do not indicate whether he had minimal, uninspired training or the best available. Furthermore, the individuals seeking help have no way of knowing what to expect in the way of attitude biases in the professional to whom they will be entrusting high hopes and a great deal of responsibility, time, and money. And it is probably fair to state that since all forms of psychotherapy, including marital therapy, are more art than science, the personality, the stability, and the skill of the therapist—which cannot be objectively evaluated—are all-important.

Nevertheless, certain basic training requirements are necessary, and the fact that they have been fulfilled gives some assurance that the spouses are not falling into the hands of a quack. It is suggested that the individual or couple desiring professional help for problems call the therapist on the telephone to ask about his training, experience, orientation, and method before setting up an appointment. (The name of a therapist can be obtained from the family physician, a minister, the local Family Service Association, a friend, or the yellow pages of the telephone book.) *It is important that he be prepared to see the couple together (conjointly).* Many therapists have not had experience in this method, which is essential in conducting skilled and expeditious therapy for marital problems. The method of counseling the husband and wife separately, whether by the same or by different counselors involves a number of inherent problems. When a therapist sees only one of a couple, it is natural for him to defend his patient and to accept the patient's picture of his spouse at least to some degree. Further, when the spouses are seen separately, it is not possible to learn what their interactional patterns are—simply because they are not aware of them and cannot describe them. These patterns must be observed by the therapist as the marital pair interact. As we have tried to point out elsewhere in this book, it is not the problems of either spouse that result in a difficult marriage, but their joint problems. The compages of their joined personalities creates their difficulties, and the therapist has to witness their interaction in order to understand it. The disadvantages of separate counseling are discussed more fully in the chapter on unilateral therapy.

Suppose only one spouse has decided that the marriage requires professional help—what to do then? First of all, he should appeal to the other spouse to join in this venture. If the other spouse refuses, the spouse who is seeking help should still consult a professional therapist who works with marital problems, and attempt to enlist his support in bringing the reluctant spouse into the therapy. It is striking to observe how seldom the other spouse refuses when the therapist takes the trouble to call him directly instead of sending the message through the spouse who has initiated therapy. Delivering a message to one spouse through the other is inadvisable, if only because the spouses in a troubled marriage have problems of communication to begin with. The probability is great that the message will be distorted somewhere along the line.

TYPES OF MARITAL THERAPISTS

Since it is important to know something about the several classes of marital therapists, we shall discuss the various different specialists within this group.

The Psychiatrist

Although in the last few years there has been a surge of interest by psychiatrists in the family and in marriage, their training generally does not prepare them to deal with marital problems in conjoint therapy. The ordinary psychiatrist has spent four years in medical school, one year in a general internship, and at least three years in psychiatric residency. A good part of his residency may have been at a large mental institution, such as Bellevue in New York City or a state hospital, and the people with whom he dealt there were primarily individuals hospitalized with severe mental illnesses like schizophrenia or alcoholism. He has spent some of his training period (approximately six months) working with neurological problems (disorders caused by pathological abnormalities of the brain or nerves), and some of his time in an outpatient clinic seeing adults and perhaps also children, usually in individual therapy, once or twice a week. Some institutions do afford the opportunity for a small amount of special training in family and marital work, but this is not yet common.

A number of departments of psychiatry in medical schools have started family-treatment units within the last two or three years. This development is a considerable departure from the viewpoint prevalent between the 1920's and the 1940's that the physician should see each patent separately.

Psychoanalysts (psychiatric M.D.'s who have received psycho-analytic training after their three years of psychiatric residency) are often the best-trained psychiatrists in their area, but the least equipped to handle marital problems. Traditionally, one spouse is seen by one analyst and the other by a second. The two analysts rarely communicate (sometimes *never*), so there is no important sharing of information. Besides, as we have indicated, only by studying the marital interaction can the therapist obtain the important information he requires.

The psychiatrist's methods of practice may be ascertained by asking someone who has seen him in therapy about them. Some-times, as has been suggested, the psychiatrist himself will discuss them briefly in a telephone conversation, in order to give a pro-spective patient his orientation. If the individual knows nothing about the psychiatrist except that he is qualified—that he has his M.D. and has completed the requirements for the American Board of Psychiatry—a shopping expedition is necessary: the individual should arrange to meet the therapist in person and ask him about his methods and point of view. This procedure may seem unnecessarily rude or expensive, but it should be kept in mind that the whole venture is terribly important and its success depends upon the choice of the proper therapist. One may have to visit two or three different psychiatrists before finding an in-dividual with whom one feels confident and compatible. Ob-viously, this kind of shopping around is necessary for locating not only the most suitable psychiatrist, but any other type of marital therapist as well.

If at all possible, spouses who have agreed to seek conjoint marital therapy should interview the prospective therapists *to-gether*. If just one spouse goes on this important shopping expedi-tion, he begins the sessions at an advantage—having already talked to the therapist and having chosen him for personal reasons.

The Clinical Psychologist

A clinical psychologist has completed four years of college and obtained a Ph.D. degree, which usually requires at least an addi-tional four years of study and training. In most states, in order to qualify as a clinical psychologist (that is, someone who may treat patients), he must have had the majority of his training in clinical work rather than in experimental, educational, social, or general psychology. The field of clinical psychology has expanded tremendously in the past few years. It used to be difficult for psychologists to find adequate training centers, and though they might have a good degree of book knowledge, their actual experience with patients was fairly limited. Now most departments of psychiatry, most medical schools, and most Veterans Administration and state hospitals offer training for psychologists, and many departments of psychology manage clinics. Because a psychologist does not have an M.D. degree, he is not allowed to administer drugs or other forms of physical treatment, such as insulin shock or electric shock.

Some universities offer an M.S. in psychology, and give minimal training in counseling and testing in this year of graduate study. *Most of these centers do not teach conjoint marital therapy,* and many put the primary emphasis on diagnostic testing, such as the use of the Rorschach, the Minnesota Multiphasic Personality Inventory, and intelligence tests. Before consulting a psychologist who does not have his doctorate in clinical psychology the prospective patient should be especially careful to check the nature of his training. Recently, conjoint marital work has been increasingly available for psychologists in training, both master's and doctoral candidates. In 1966, fourteen departments of psychology offered *some* training in marital and family work.

The Social Worker

Most social workers today have an M.S.W. (Master of Social Work) degree—earned by the completion of a rigorous two-year program of graduate study in an accredited school of social work. In addition to receiving the required classroom instruction, social-work students work two or three days each week in an agency which offers counseling services, such as a psychiatric clinic, a hospital, a probation department, a welfare department, or a family-counseling agency. This on-the-job training is carefully supervised by an experienced social worker who has an M.S.W. degree. Usually, individuals admitted to a graduate school of social work have received their Bachelor of Arts (or Science) degree in sociology, psychology, or other behavioral sciences.

In only a few agencies, such as departments of county welfare and the American National Red Cross, is the term "social worker" used for individuals who do not have the M.S.W. degree. These workers are normally supervised by experienced social workers who do have the degree. A couple desiring marital therapy would normally seek such a service not from these agencies but from an accredited social worker in private practice or from a family counseling agency, where the M.S.W. degree is required for employment.

The individual pursuing a Master of Social Work degree may find it possible to specialize in psychiatric social work, but increasingly, a generic course is being offered, including instruction in group work, individual casework, and community organization. A few social-work schools now provide opportunities for their students to work in institutions where they receive training in family and marital counseling. A social worker with this experience is as qualified to do conjoint marital therapy as the psychologist or the psychiatrist with training in this area.

As always, both the individual's personality and his experience and training determine his success as a therapist. Most social workers are women, and frequently both spouses object to seeing a woman therapist. It is surprising how many women in marital difficulties downgrade their own sex, having more confidence in a male therapist.

The number of social workers in private practice (as opposed to those working in social-service agencies, hospitals, and the like) is increasing rapidly. Often the social worker joins forces with a psychiatrist, psychologist, or other professional; in any case it is essential that the prospective patient inquire as to the social worker's training and method.

The Pastoral Counselor and the Marriage Counselor

The pastoral counseling group constitutes a rather specialized branch of the ministry; it is increasing in size, but not yet large. Some of its members have a D.D. (Doctor of Divinity) degree, and some have taken additional courses in educational psychology, clinical psychology, or pastoral counseling. However, well-trained pastoral counselors are still rare.

The average nonpastoral marriage counselor has an M.A. degree in the field of psychology, educational psychology, counseling and testing, or religion. Many of these counselors have received neither theoretical instruction nor practical experience related to marital problems. Many older marriage counselors are former ministers who fulfilled joint functions, serving as both pastor and marriage counselor for their church. Some of the older marriage counselors have the benefit of years of experience, but no formal training. Nevertheless, they sometimes do quite an adequate job. One of the problems in selecting such a counselor is that the lack of formal qualifications in most states means that the prospective patient has a difficult time deciding whether a marriage counselor can deal adequately with his particular problem.

Occasionally an M.D. without psychiatric training will eschew the rigors of medicine for the comfort of an easy chair and hang out his shingle as a marriage counselor. Here again—*caveat emptor!*

In some countries marriage counseling is a highly respected field. In Australia, for example, a national act instituted in 1959 requires a couple seeking a divorce to have several sessions with a counselor first. These counselors are trained and licensed by the national government.

The inspiration for men in such a country to enter the marital-counseling field is greater than it is in the United States, and the quality of counselors is apt to be quite high, just as their responsibilities are great. In the United States, the Association of Marital Counselors seeks to keep standards up and to encourage proper training and the dissemination of information for counselors, but considerable policing is still required, since the laws determining who may give marital advice are loose and vary from state to state. Indeed, as has been mentioned, in some states no special education or training is required.

PROSPECTS FOR THE FUTURE
OF MARITAL THERAPY

Taken all together, the psychiatrists, psychologists, social workers, and marital counselors—regardless of their qualifications for the job of treating sick marriages—are not numerous enough to take care of the public's needs, especially in areas outside of the large metropolitan cities. This unfortunate picture is likely to persist for many years; for some time to come the overflow of couples seeking therapy will probably be handled by nonprofessional counselors.

Experiments have already been started, especially at the National Institute of Mental Health under the direction of Dr. Margaret Rioch, in the training of lay persons in basic counseling. Dr. Rioch first selected a group of mature women who were eager for pursuits other than keeping house and who had demonstrated some ability in managing their own lives successfully. She found that the group as a whole developed fairly rapidly skills which allowed them to be useful to other people in counseling, without assuming those responsibilities that a psychiatrist would ordinarily shoulder.

Another trend of particular importance is developing in some primary and secondary schools. A child's performance in school and the state of the parents' marriage are often intimately related. In some schools, when a child appears to be troubled the counselor attempts to see the parents as well as the child. This is an important trend, and one which may gain momentum—partially because it is relatively easy to detect problems in children in the early grades. Spouses who have been delaying their efforts to improve their marriage may be motivated to do so when they learn that their difficulties are interfering with their child's school performance. But here again, there is the problem of finding sufficient individuals to fill the jobs as school counselors, and of providing better training centers for them. In particular, they will require training that concentrates on marital problems and not on long-term individual psychotherapy, still the primary focus of training in most centers.

The possibility that television might become a source of help for unhappy couples has been largely unexplored. The success of the Purex Corporation programs for women suggests that even marital problems might be discussed in some detail and intimacy if the programs were scheduled for the evening and a couple could watch them together after the children were in bed. The development of this type of program would be a most valuable project for educational television, especially if the right teachers could be found and the material could be presented in a compelling fashion.

Another method of helping troubled spouses is the formation, possibly under the auspices of an organization such as the YMCA, of groups in which married couples meet together for joint discussions. When four to six couples get together weekly to discuss marital problems, the presence of the group has the effect of containing the individual couples' quarrels and bitterness. Thus the meeting can be reasonably orderly, and yet a good deal of feeling can still be expressed, *providing the leader is experienced.* The spouses learn that theirs are not the only hates and hurts, and are often able to say things to each other that they cannot mention in private.

There is an increasing tendency for psychiatrists and psychologists interested in marital problems to conduct sessions of this sort, in which four to six couples meet regularly with a therapist. This can be a relatively economical way of obtaining therapy for the couples, but the successful management of this situation is difficult, and requires considerable experience. So-called leaderless groups have been tried, but to our knowledge have not worked out well. Generally, one couple tends to dominate the rest, and the group breaks up as a result of bickering and boredom.

It is interesting that although we have Alcoholics Anonymous to help unfortunate alcoholics, Gamblers Anonymous to aid those who can't help throwing away their money, and Parents Without Partners to enable divorced individuals to share their difficulties, there is no comparable group for those with marital problems. Apparently a marriage is regarded as almost sacrosanct until it has broken up. A Save Our Marriage Society might not be a bad idea; it could offer spouses in difficulty the opportunity to attend group meetings, learn how much their problems resemble or differ from those of other people, find out what others have done to solve such problems in the past, and generally benefit from a clearing of the air. One possible shortcoming in such meetings, we would expect, is that much of the discussion would deal with the battle of the sexes. However—and this would be fortunate—it might occur to someone among the participants that the caricature of men by women or of women by men is highly ridiculous. Such an organization could sponsor educational films for engaged couples, and a marital checkup clinic for spouses not yet in serious trouble. Corporations now spend millions of dollars a year on periodic medical examinations to guard the health of their executives. The malignant marriage is probably the most frequent source of executive ill health, and yet little, if anything, is done about it. Unfortunately, one must start by admitting that the problem exists.

SOME PITFALLS TO BE AVOIDED IN THERAPY

Anyone doing marital therapy, whether a psychiatrist, a psychologist, a social worker, or a marriage counselor, is in a position to make a bad situation worse.

The following observations may be useful both to those who plan to seek marital counseling and to the counselors themselves.

Even the best therapist, with the most adequate training, is bound to have bad days and is certain to do better with some couples than with others. However well intended, his intervention cannot always be correct, and the mark of the honest counselor is that if a mistake is made, he is willing to pick up the pieces and put them together again. To obtain assurance of this kind of professional responsibility is one reason for paying a professional instead of seeking out free advice.

The counselor must be on guard against foisting his own values upon his clients. One cannot help revealing some personal beliefs during therapy, but as long as they are clearly identified as personal biases and dealt with honestly, their presence can be an essential part of therapy. They help identify the therapist as an individual human being rather than a stone god. It is the imposition of personal values which are not so labeled which can be damaging.

The warnings in this section are not offered to provide justifications for couples who wish to avoid seeking marital therapy, or for those who want to quit therapy because the going is a little rough. It is our belief that *good* marital counseling can save a sick marriage. And in most cases, matters must be expected to get worse before they get better. For example, as each spouse learns to air his gripes the other is apt to respond with anger and defensiveness. It takes time for spouses to gain the ability to distinguish differentness from badness and to recognize a justified complaint *without finding it necessary to produce a counter complaint.*

Here we would like to list some of the most obvious therapeutic errors, so that the individual seeking help may be on the lookout for them in his own therapy.

Error 1. The therapist takes sides with one or the other spouse, unintentionally, and not as a temporary therapeutic maneuver. Sometimes this error results when the therapist tries to overcome a natural tendency to identify with the spouse of the same sex by leaning over backward to understand the viewpoint of the spouse of the opposite sex. It usually reflects the therapist's bias and problems with the opposite sex, and is common among inexperienced therapists who have not yet realized that in marriages there are no "good guys" and "bad guys." Culpability is evenly divided.

This error may also occur when the counselor—even the experienced counselor—has a set of values in which he earnestly believes (for example, religious tenets), and the attitudes of one of the spouses therefore strike a responsive chord in him not reached by the other. For example, one young psychologist found it easy to understand the plight of a woman who complained of her husband's handling of their finances. The psychologist was careful with his own income and was eager to save sensibly. After listening to this couple he concluded, from the wife's story, that the husband irresponsibly bought what he wanted when he wanted it. He attempted to get the couple to stay on a budget, overlooking the fact that the husband was proud of his large income and had carefully taken care of the future through sound investments and life insurance. The budget simply functioned as a club wielded by the young wife in her status struggle with her husband. The husband took her messages literally, and his responses added to the problem. This couple finally obtained a divorce.

Only three months after the final decree, the young woman married a merchant seaman whom she had to support during the rare occasions he was at home because he blew his pay the minute he hit port. The psychologist would not have known the outcome of this case except for the fact that the woman wrote him for a letter of reference to a prospective employer. He learned something valuable about himself from the experience.

The overall neutrality of the therapist is essential to successful conjoint marital therapy. Of course, at some point he may take sides with respect to certain particular issues or a specific piece of behavior by one of the spouses. However, in balance he recognizes that the two spouses chose each other in the first place *for some reason*, and that they both are hurting, even though superficially one or the other may appear to have the better deal, or to be more at fault. A young therapist may remark to his colleagues, "I don't see how such a nice guy could marry a bitch like that." His inexperience shows in such a statement.

Error 2. The therapist views his role as a judicial one in which he sifts the evidence presented to him and eventually makes pronouncements.

This approach tends to be extremely damaging because the spouses involved are likely to devote their energy and ingenuity to digging up "evidence" against each other. The result is an escalation of bad feelings and an increasing schism, until the therapy—and the marriage—break down altogether. Even when the judicial therapist attempts to make a pronouncement which does not favor one of the spouses—for example, "From what you both have told me I can see how each of you feels hurt and distressed in the marriage"—it is likely to fall on deaf ears, for warring spouses are in no mood to listen to each other's side of the story, or be told that each is equally in the right.

To force a shift in the spouses' behavior, the therapist has to set specific guidelines, some rules of procedure, some ways of looking at the marriage, *that have not yet occurred to either spouse.* He can only do this by interfering with their customary pattern of behavior, whether it be constant bickering or constant silence.

Error 3. The therapist secretly thinks that the spouses are mismatched and that each would do better with another mate. Instead of referring them to another therapist, he strives to overcome his bias by convincing them that they should try harder to make their marriage work, but since his bias handicaps his being helpful and creative, the spouses are at the same time prodded by the moral cry of "try harder" and blocked by the therapist's inability to function effectively.

The therapist's attitude should be: My job is to help these people stay together more compatibly and productively, or to help them separate as amicably as possible. Since this is not my marriage, it is not my place to tell these people which of these two courses to take.

Error 4. The therapist takes the position that one spouse is sicker than the other and sets up a situation in which he and the "well" spouse are treating the one identified as the patient. The therapist may be aware of his value judgment or, as is usually the case, it may be unconscious. In any case, the result is an imbalance in the marital interaction which may never be overcome. One such situation developed when a therapist saw a married couple shortly after the wife had been released from a week's stay in the mental ward of a private hospital for an impulsive, but not-too-serious, suicide attempt. He was concerned about the possibility of her repeating the attempt, and shared this concern with her husband. He put her on drugs to calm her nerves, and it soon became obvious that though ostensibly he was dealing with the marriage problems by seeing the couple together, actually he and the husband were treating the wife as the patient. Further, the husband derived strength from the wife's weakness. He became more overtly dissatisfied with her "faults," and as she was threatened by his apparent superiority, her level of performance decreased. The husband began taking out a mutual friend, a recently divorced woman, and one day announced to his stricken wife that he was going to Reno to get a quick divorce so that he could marry the other woman.

The wife continued to see the therapist alone, and they agreed that there was no point in fighting the husband's divorce. Feeling guilty about what had happened, the therapist encouraged her to be very demanding in the negotiations for a financial settlement. He helped her find an aggressive lawyer, who soon had the husband in a fury, and the process of making the financial arrangements was long and drawn-out. In the meantime, the wife felt terribly inadequate and depressed. Through mutual friends she learned that her husband had remarried and that he and his new wife were busily turning themselves into alcoholics. The ex-husband made no attempt to keep in touch with his wife, nor did he see their two daughters. About a year later he was killed driving home from a party, when his car went off the road and crashed into a tree.

Until after the divorce, it was apparent not at all to the therapist (and only unconsciously to the wife) that the husband was actually quite insecure, and had relied on his wife's "weakness" to make him look relatively strong. When he married an aggressive and demanding woman, he could not handle her and increasingly tried to reduce his anxiety by drinking.

This story has two morals. First, the identification of who is the strong one and who is the weak one in a marriage is a very tricky proposition. Sometimes a great deal of strength is required to make someone else look stronger, and *being in charge at the overt level is not the same as covertly determining the nature of the marital rules.*

Second, the therapist who identifies one spouse as "healthy and strong" and the other as "sick and weak" may—as he did in this example—help escalate the marital discord until a runaway develops and the marital system flies apart.

Insight into the skills and the precautions required in counseling can best be learned from examples.

In the following example, Mr. and Mrs. McIntosh, who wish to improve their marriage, have just seated themselves in the office of an inexperienced and untrained marriage counselor. The counselor, Miss Valet, approaches therapy from a typical battle-of-the-sexes point of view.

The example includes the dialogue of everyone present. As the session proceeds, the marital interactions become more and more destructive. This occurs because of the counselor's incompetence. The detailed explanation of why this happens is given several times during the dialogue. However, later, when a well-trained and experienced marriage counselor takes the place of the well-meaning but incompetent Miss Valet, the marital discussion begins to straighten out and indicate some progress.

DIALOGUE

COUNSELOR: Very nice seeing you both. Mrs. McIntosh, I gather you're the one who made the phone call. Perhaps you'd like to speak first.

WIFE: Well, I don't know where to start. I thought *you* were the one who would know what to tell us to do.

COUNSELOR: Well, I just am trying to get some idea of what brought you two here to me today.

WIFE: Well, I called you, uh, to talk to my husband, uh, and to me, of course, uh, because it seems to *me*—and my husband doesn't agree with me—uh, that something is very seriously wrong with our marriage. Uh, I, uh, cannot get any cooperation whatsoever from him in anything that we try to do. . . .

HUSBAND: What do you mean, no cooperation? I try to do everything you say. . . .

WIFE: She asked me. Will you let me finish what I'm saying?

COUNSELOR: Yes, you'll have your turn in just a moment.

WIFE: I, uh, my husband will not cooperate with me. He absolutely refuses to participate in the discipline of the children, so that I'm left with the four of them and, uh, with all I have to do, taking care of all the yard work . . .

COUNSELOR: You mean he doesn't do anything at all to help you around the house?

WIFE: That's just it. I, uh, I have an awful lot to do and I try to explain it to him and he just turns me off. I do *all* of the housework, *all* of the laundry, all of everything, and he couldn't care less. I can't keep up with the four children with all I have to do, without getting some help from my husband.

INTERPRETATION

The counselor reinforces the existing pattern by giving the wife the lead, thus determining who is to speak first, rather than waiting to see what pattern emerges spontaneously.

The wife engages in a power struggle with the counselor, attempting to take control of who is to define the relationship, baiting the counselor to act as the authority—*under the wife's direction.*

The counselor shifts responsibility back to the wife and refuses to be trapped by her power maneuver.

The wife accepts the counselor's being in charge. She hints that she thinks her husband is the real problem, but adds as an afterthought that she, too, needs help. She implies conflict between herself and her spouse by quickly mentioning that he doesn't agree with her.

The husband tries to balance the relationship by giving his point of view, but angrily.

The wife undercuts the husband and at the same time reestablishes her control and avoids hearing his viewpoint.

The counselor forms a coalition with the wife, and again reinforces the existing pattern.

The wife gains strength from the coalition. She begins recounting issues probably discussed many times before with the husband. Apparently she is seeking confirmation from the counselor, so that the husband will see the "error of his ways."

The wife counteracts the husband's earlier maneuver by pointing out that her husband doesn't listen to her and doesn't care. She gives a clue to a communication problem not having to do with the specific issue.

DIALOGUE

COUNSELOR: Well, now Mr. McIntosh, you look like a very energetic and charming fellow to me, uh, surely you don't refuse to help your wife at *all*.

HUSBAND: Yes, I do! When we were——

WIFE: That's the first honest thing you've said in months. (*Laughs.*)

HUSBAND: When we were married, at first I tried to help her. But she does everything in such a slow, sloppy way, and she won't go to school, and she'll not learn how! And that house when I come home at night is such a mess . . .

WIFE: Boy, if I haven't heard that before!

COUNSELOR: But, Mr. McIntosh, doesn't that give you all the more feeling of the need to help her?—to pitch in and really get some of these things done? I mean, four children are quite a few, uh . . .

HUSBAND: I didn't want them, she did.

COUNSELOR: Well——

WIFE: That's another story . . .

COUNSELOR: He's joking.

WIFE: The point is that he doesn't see—and I do not keep a sloppy house! I do darn well considering all I have to do. I'm *not* a coffee-klatcher; I *don't* spend time with other women; I *don't* go to bridge parties. I do the best I can.

HUSBAND: No, all you do is attend cocktail parties!

INTERPRETATION

Instead of focusing on the implied communication and relationship problem, the counselor casts the husband in the role of the "bad guy" by suggesting that if he really is energetic and charming, he will surely help his wife.

The husband accepts the role given him.

The wife reinforces her husband's role by ridicule.

The husband starts to hint that he has a reason for not helping, stating that he used to help but does so no longer. Then he ruins the argument by falling into superficial complaints like those the wife makes.

The wife tries to ridicule her husband.

The counselor continues taking sides with the wife, trying to "reach" the husband with "reason" and moralistic pressure, much as the wife has done with little success.

The husband tries to balance the relationship by changing to another provocative topic.

To cover her inadequacy to deal with the husband's ploy, the counselor disregards it.

The wife defines more clearly her role as a martyr, and again implies that her reasoning with the husband changes nothing—a good clue to the counselor that *her* reasoning is an ineffective tactic.

Dialogue

Wife: I *never* attend cocktail parties!

Husband: You went to three last week—the one at the——

Wife: Under *real* protest!

Husband: . . . at the Palo Alto Club. . . .

Counselor: Well, uh, it seems to me that we're getting off the topic here because it doesn't sound as if your wife would really have much *time* for, uh, social activities, uh . . .

Wife: I don't; but when I do, in the evening, my husband keeps telling me that when he comes home in the evenings, he's worn out and tired and doesn't want to do anything. But I've tried to explain to him that after a day's hard work, with all the little kids and not having anyone to talk to, anyone to have fun with, I need activity at night. This is *my* form of relaxation!

Counselor: You'd like to get out some too.

Husband: Miss Valet, I've asked her—would she like to come bowling, would she like to play golf, would she like to see a musical comedy, would she like to see a movie—*no!* she doesn't. She has to see the goddamn opera—uh, long-haired music, uh, big intellectual swamis who I can't understand—and that's all she has an interest in. I——

Wife: All my husband enjoys is TV and beer in the local pub, and this is *not* my idea of relaxation!

Husband: Well, then, you should have married someone else, because you knew it before we got married, but I didn't know about *you*—goddamn it—you held it all in and pretended to love everything I did.

DIALOGUE

COUNSELOR: Uh, I think we're getting off the topic a little here. Uh, what I'm wondering is, now, uh, isn't there the weekend; I mean, uh, isn't it possible that over weekends you could pitch in and help your wife out with some of these kinds of chores?

HUSBAND: Yes, but she and I don't agree on *how*. For example, our lawn—it looks pretty good, but she wants the edges trimmed, every leaf has to be picked up—it takes all morning. . . .

COUNSELOR (*to the wife*): It sounds like you take some pride in the house, don't you?

WIFE: Yes, but it's even more than that—it's that my husband *outlasts* me in everything.

HUSBAND: Ha!

WIFE: I ask him to help me and he'll say, "Okay, get off my back; don't nag me; I'll do it when I get around to it," and so in the *meantime*, I have to watch the lawn die; everything goes to pot, the kids are getting out of hand, everything just goes wild, while my husband is sitting there saying, "Don't nag; get off my back," and it's, uh, not a difference of standards so much—it's just that he knows that if he waits long enough I'll do it—and I *do* —and it makes me angry.

COUNSELOR: Well, uh, it seems to me, Mr. McIntosh, that not being more help and, uh, not participating more would make you feel sort of unmasculine, uh, aren't you really losing something by, uh, by not having more say and, uh—really—uh——

HUSBAND: *No!* If I did what she nagged me on, I'd be nothing but a sponge around the house. . . .

INTERPRETATION

Instead of commenting on the spouses' interaction or trying to focus on underlying messages, the counselor attempts to return to the original topic and suggests a strategy to solve the present issue.

By criticizing the wife for her high standards for the lawn, after criticizing her low standards for the house, the husband gives a good clue that the issues under discussion are but symptoms of a larger problem.

The counselor continues to get caught up in the game between the spouses, failing to challenge the game itself.

The counselor intensifies the battle of the sexes by focusing on the couple's conflict as if it were caused by the genetic differences between male and female; thus she puts the husband in a bind, making it necessary for him to defend (and define?) masculinity in his effort to win the argument.

DIALOGUE

WIFE: That's what you think. He's, he's the type——

COUNSELOR: Well, after all, aren't married people *supposed* to help each other out? I'm, uh, not quite clear—I understand your rather truculent attitude; you seem to feel that you aren't required to do anything more than bring home the paycheck. Is that fair?

HUSBAND: No, it's not, but each has to do *half* of it and she expects me to do half of *her* half. When I come home at night, the goddamn kitchen has dirty dishes in it from lunch—uh, I'm ashamed to have anyone in without giving her twenty-four hours' notice because if he hangs up his coat, everything in the closet might fall out, uh, and——

WIFE: And if you helped me, it wouldn't be that way—uh, he's —uh, he's a typical man. He's scared to death that if he gets in and does the dishes, somehow he's not being, you know, quite masculine. And what I've tried to tell him is that if he took some responsibility—*this* is being a man—that if he took over a little bit and took some responsibility for the relationship and for the home and everything, uh—this is *my* idea of a real man.

COUNSELOR: You know, wouldn't it be rather simple if we could settle on some point, some task, that you feel you *are* willing to do, uh, so that Mrs. McIntosh could know what she can count on . . .?

HUSBAND: You're damned right—if *she* will agree on some items also. . . .

WIFE: Like what?

COUNSELOR: Well, I got the impression that your wife was rather busy already. . . .

HUSBAND: It's only because she's *stupid*—she doesn't know how to do *anything* efficiently. . . .

INTERPRETATION

The counselor escalates the male-female battle, strengthens her coalition with the wife, and gives the wife fuel for continued argument.

The wife picks up the counselor's argument and uses it, with all the greater force because it has the counselor's sanction.

The counselor suggests an approach which cannot be transferred to other areas of conflict, because it concerns a particular issue instead of the basic interactional pattern.

The battle increases, the husband is forced to insist on an equal concession so he will not have lost altogether.

The counselor ignores the real struggle between the spouses and shrugs off the husband's insistence on a *quid pro quo*.

The husband loses ground rapidly by displaying frustrated anger and irrationality, his response to being hopelessly trapped by the wife's coalition with the counselor.

DIALOGUE

COUNSELOR: Oh, come now, I'm sure a smart man like you wouldn't have married a stupid woman.

HUSBAND: But I *did*—I made a mistake!

COUNSELOR: Uh, well now, uh, let me get back on . . .

THERAPIST: Uh, it seems to me that one thing I've noticed, uh, Mr. McIntosh, is that while we've been talking here, *you're* the one who ends up being angry, while your wife just, uh, you know, looks put upon and hurt, but as if she's got something going for her—like she's on the "side of the right." You know—uh, you sort of look like you feel that you get yourself into a corner somehow, like you don't want to be taken advantage of, but, uh . . .

INTERPRETATION

The counselor tries to indicate the husband's irrationality, while soothing him with a compliment. This maneuver can only trap and enrage him further because he doesn't know what he's fighting.

Again the counselor covers her inadequacy to cope with the husband's anger by returning to the immediate issue.

It becomes obvious in the above interchange that the counselor has succeeded primarily in escalating the conflict between the couple, by allowing herself to become caught up in the battle of the sexes. The argument unquestionably promises to continue growing after the session, leading to further estrangement, bitterness, and misunderstanding.

In the following interchange the same couple picks up where they left off with Miss Valet (in their own charming way) but now they are being seen by Mr. Kilpatrick, Miss Valet's supervisor, who has had a little more training and experience. He has been observing the therapy through a one-way mirror, and enters to rescue the session from total disaster.

The therapist shifts away from the superficial issue under discussion and focuses on the basic interaction, giving the husband some recognition of the fact that he is feeling trapped.

DIALOGUE (using experienced therapist)

HUSBAND: I must admit that on this stuff of the opera and cocktail parties—when she asks me and I say no, I don't want to go because I don't like them and I'm exhausted, *she'll* say, "Well, very well, I'll go alone," and she *does*. And she often meets others whom she knows and comes back at midnight or later, after I've been watching the kids, and she's just had one hell of a time. But *I've* had to clean up in the goddamn kitchen, much of which has been left over from lunch and breakfast. . . .

WIFE: I don't do that very often. You make it sound like it's a constant sort of thing, but——

HUSBAND: And I have to fix my own breakfast. . . .

THERAPIST: But why, why is it, that you overstate things? Because it seems to me that you ruin your argument. You, uh, are obviously sore about something and so you must have a good reason—I, uh, just wouldn't doubt it, uh, and I'm sure your wife has a point of view too—but somehow by putting things so strongly as if your wife is a lush and out on the town every night, you put *yourself* in the hole, you know. You strain my credulity, really. What are you being left out of that's really kind of sticking in your craw?

HUSBAND: Well, I, uh, had always looked forward to having a happy home, but I haven't gotten it—it's one *bedlam*. The house, according to my standards, is slovenly. Uh, I always look at it that my home is where I can come and relax, but it never happens.

WIFE: But this is just *my* point and it's what I keep trying to tell him. That if he had a different attitude toward it and saw it as a *team* effort, so that *he* could make some contribution to the home too? Then he *would* have what he wanted. But I get so mad, and the reason that I have to go out——

INTERPRETATION

The husband refocuses on the immediate issue instead of talking about his feelings, but his anger dissipates somewhat and he becomes more rational as he gets the opportunity to "speak his piece" without interruption or disqualification by the therapist.

The therapist forces the husband to leave the immediate issue by refocusing on the behavioral and interactional patterns. He implies that this particular issue is not the basic problem, stating that each spouse has a point of view and a good reason for having it. He tries to get at what is really bothering the husband. Notice that the wife is quiet during most of this discussion, whereas hitherto she was very eager to speak.

The husband returns to his complaint about the housekeeping, but he now relates it to a more basic disillusionment about the marriage and about home life in general.

Dialogue

THERAPIST: May I ask, Mrs. McIntosh, what evidence you have that you could work in a team yourself? Uh, what is there in your own past that tells you that you really *could* work in a team?

WIFE: I don't understand what you mean.

THERAPIST: Uh, well, have you really had any experience—did you come from a home where you *saw* real teamsmanship and cooperation in practice? Are you sure that you're not just talking about a model of operating that you're not up to because you never practiced it?

WIFE: Well, I *am* up to it—uh, I *want* to cooperate and——

HUSBAND: There! You got an example of it! You asked her a question—she comes from a home where she had to be slippery and sly and everybody was always squabbling—and you asked her, "What kind of home are you from?" and she evades the answer. . . .

WIFE: But I didn't *want* to have a home like that. I wanted something better than that. . . . (*Her voice softens and she shows a hint of tears.*)

THERAPIST: No, no, no, I understand your feelings and I know you wouldn't be here if you weren't trying, and trying hard, to change things. What I'm saying is, apart from *wishing*, do you have any experience that tells you that you know you're capable— *right now*—of being a teammate—because that's part of the problem. . . .

INTERPRETATION

The therapist catches the wife up on her theoretical interpretation of what *should* be, by focusing on what is actually possible for her. He tries to get her to apply her point at a more personal level, meanwhile leading her to the possibility that she is accusing the husband of something which is true of herself also. At the same time, he prevents her from *continuing criticisms of the issue under discussion.*

The wife resists the therapist, and by "not understanding," refuses to give him full control.

The wife continues to resist by talking around the central question.

The husband recognizes the wife's ploy and indicates that it is familiar to him. In a prior interchange, the husband himself switched to new issues when he was angry, but this time he is focusing on an interactional aspect of the wife's behavior and identifying it openly.

The wife gives some evidence of feeling trapped, as her husband did previously, but instead of evincing open anger, she begins to cry.

The therapist offers support by recognizing the wife's feelings and efforts, but does not let her avoid the challenge he is presenting.

DIALOGUE

WIFE: I think I *could* be—but not with *Tom*, because *he* doesn't cooperate! I really could! I, uh, we started out like this in our marriage. . . .

THERAPIST: Uh, I'm sorry to keep pressing this, and I'm probably beating a dead horse, but I still don't quite understand where, uh—where did you have the experience of, you know, practicing being a team member?—uh, with whom have you really collaborated in the past? Uh, this is your first marriage?

WIFE: Yes.

THERAPIST: All right.

WIFE: I don't know. I don't think I know what you mean.

THERAPIST: Well, uh, maybe *you* can help me out, Mr. McIntosh. I'm simply trying to say that maybe both of you want something very hard and desperately, but you simply haven't had the practice in how to go about it, so you blame each other for not producing it and the fact is that neither of you——

HUSBAND: Doctor, you've had here a perfect example of what I have to live with. You asked her a question and she says, "I don't know; I don't understand." This is exactly what she pulls on me. We started to fight from the first day we got married——

THERAPIST: We are also having an example of what *she* has to live with—because, you see, you made a very good point and an important observation about your wife, but you put it in such a truculent way again that I'm sure she just kind of shuts her ears and doesn't even really hear you.

(*The wife mumbles something*)

THERAPIST: Louder

INTERPRETATION

The wife continues to resist and to refocus on the husband as the cause of the problem, trying to get back to the original topic, the fact that he doesn't help her.

The wife refuses to give the therapist charge or to cooperate with him, a response which suggests her inability to work as a team-mate.

The therapist draws the husband back into the discussion to prevent his being left out; also the wife refuses cooperation at this time.

The husband points out the communication problem once more, but then overstates his point again by making it a criticism and by overgeneralizing.

The therapist points out the husband's self-defeating maneuver while giving him credit for his observation, and at the same time anticipates verbally the wife's possible reaction. He is still trying to make the interaction pattern explicit to the couple instead of permitting escalation of an issue-oriented argument.

DIALOGUE

WIFE (*almost crying*): He just doesn't understand *anything* I try to get across. . . .

THERAPIST: But you care enough about him to cry about it, so I gather you haven't given up completely.

WIFE: Oh, I vary. (*Tearfully.*) I, uh, sometimes I just think it's not worth it and I'm ready to just walk out and leave the whole mess, just run. And other times, I think that if we keep working at it hard enough, maybe we can make something out of it. But it's just—it's a mess. Neither of us is happy; we can't get along. And it's affecting the kids. . . .

THERAPIST (*to the husband*): You, uh, do you make a reasonable income?

HUSBAND: Twenty-two thousand.

THERAPIST: Uh-huh, and are there any major financial debts that you're concerned about?

HUSBAND: Uh, not major, but I'm still pissed off at the sixteen-hundred-dollar fur coat she charged without consulting me, which I haven't paid for. We owe about four thousand exclusive of the mortgage on the house.

THERAPIST (*to the wife*): And, uh, do you have some feeling that your husband is a good provider?

WIFE: Yes, I think he is. . . .

THERAPIST: It sounds like it.

WIFE: I don't have any complaints about that.

INTERPRETATION

The therapist nips fresh criticism in the bud and focuses on the wife's commitment to working out the problems.

The wife takes this opportunity to state her feelings about the marriage, and begins to grow depressed and defeatist, indicating *nothing* is right or hopeful in the relationship.

The therapist, aware that the husband earns a good income, begins to focus on some of the positive aspects of the marriage, to break the cycle of constant criticism and hopelessness between the spouses.

The husband resists the disruption of his habitual critical pattern and makes the therapist's question an opportunity to complain about the wife again.

The therapist ignores the husband's ploy and invites the wife to comment on a positive aspect of the marriage.

The wife admits that *something* is all right in the relationship.

DIALOGUE

THERAPIST: And, uh, in all of the annoyances you've shown, Mr. McIntosh, you haven't mentioned anything critical about your wife's treatment of the kids, so I gather you feel she is adequate as a mother.

HUSBAND: Yes. . . .

WIFE: Not true.

HUSBAND: Well, you're not strict enough on them, but——

THERAPIST: Now wait a minute! He just said "Yes," so I gather you must believe him *some*.

WIFE: Well, he doesn't like a lot of things that I do with the kids, and *more* important, he doesn't help me do them, uh, so that no matter what I do, right or wrong——

THERAPIST: But he just was saying that he thought you were a good mother and you were saying—

WIFE (*petulantly*): Well, he doesn't tell me that at home.

THERAPIST: Are you sure you could hear it if he did?

WIFE: I think I could hear it if he *ever* said anything complimentary. . . .

THERAPIST: So you've got him labeled as the old bear, the old grouch, the one who always is——

INTERPRETATION

The therapist tries to secure a *quid pro quo* for the wife, since interaction in the past has been symmetrical, with each insisting on getting something for giving something.

The wife refuses the husband's offering, as acceptance would temporarily remove him from the "bad guy" role.

The husband "bites," and slips back into the role of the grouch, upon the wife's insistence.

Instead of getting detoured on a fresh issue (that is, child rearing), the therapist continues focusing on the couple's interaction by commenting on the wife's behavior.

The wife tries to slip off the hook by switching to her old complaint about the husband's lack of cooperation.

The therapist points out the wife's refusal to permit the husband to be a "good guy" occasionally.

Dialogue

WIFE: Oh, he's not a *grouch,* he's just, uh—he really isn't a grouch too much, he's just, uh—it's just that I get the feeling that nothing I do really ever pleases him and, uh, this makes me feel like *I'm* failing somehow, and yet I've been *trying* ever since we got married, I've been knocking myself out trying to do what he wanted me to do.

THERAPIST: Okay, then, I want you to try something. Now, this may sound rather screwy, and I hope you'll realize that I take your problem seriously, so don't think I'm suggesting this simply for no reason at all, but, uh . . . What I want you to do, if you would, is before we meet next week—wait, let's see if we can't set up a time. Is Tuesday all right for you?

HUSBAND: If it's in the late afternoon.

THERAPIST: Yeah, okay. So before next Tuesday in the late afternoon when we meet again—that will be one, two, three, four . . . six days from now—I want you, Mrs. McIntosh, *to try as hard as you can* to do something for your husband. Now I'm sure— you've been married quite a few years—that you know what this could include. It could be something like paying more attention to what the TV room looks like or whatever.

WIFE: But I do this all the time . . . and he doesn't notice it!

THERAPIST: I know, so all I'm asking is that for just these six days, which is not very long, you do it *even more* than you have been. Could you do that if you really tried? I'm not saying that you're in the wrong . . .

WIFE: Well, I will, but he won't even notice, is the point. He doesn't even know——

INTERPRETATION

The therapist has brought into the open the wife's implicit labeling of the husband, thereby revealing the label to be absurd. The
wife reacts by giving it up, reluctantly. Then she focuses on the
more basic problem of her *own* feelings of failure in her efforts to
please her husband, but expresses her difficulty in the form of a
complaint against him. She describes once again how hard she
tries, while her husband doesn't appreciate her efforts.

The therapist employs the strategy of "paradoxical injunction":
he asks the wife to do what she is already doing, only more so.
In this way, he is placing himself in charge of her behavior by
prescribing it. Under direction, her behavior will seem absurd
and will become much more *difficult to continue*. By making it a
chore to maintain the old pattern, the therapist causes the ground
to be broken for developing new, more constructive patterns of
interaction.

The therapist controls the wife's resistance to his authority by
asking her *if* she *can* follow his directions *if she really tries*. The
wife can only comply or admit that she cannot do so. Her past
responses have indicated that she cannot admit that she is incapable of cooperation, so she has no way out of following the
therapist's directions.

Dialogue

THERAPIST: We don't know what he'll do, but if you will break your neck even more than you already do, I realize that you——

WIFE: Yeah, all right.

HUSBAND: Without rubbing my nose in it!

THERAPIST: Now wait a minute, we haven't gotten to you yet—uh, but do try to include some specific things, because he——

WIFE: Okay . . .

THERAPIST: I'm sure you know.

WIFE: Don't ask him what he wants?

THERAPIST: That's the other thing. I would prefer it if you do not discuss this session at all with each other until we meet again. There are plenty of other things you can talk about—the weather, the world series, the kids, but no marital discussions. Okay? (*To wife.*) But you really see what you can do about surprising him. There may have been things that you haven't thought of for some time that he used to appreciate, and they'll come back to you.

WIFE: I'll try.

THERAPIST: Now what I want you to do, Mr. McIntosh, in return, is to be very careful that you *show no unusual appreciation* for her efforts.

HUSBAND: Don't mention it at all?

WIFE: That will be easy for you!

THERAPIST: Just act as you would ordinarily and, uh, in other words, I don't want you to go out of your way at all to show that you appreciate this, because maybe your wife won't carry it out,

INTERPRETATION

The husband tries to take charge of the prescription.

The therapist tries to prevent the couple from making therapy a new issue of argumentation and destroying the therapeutic effects of the session.

The therapist uses the same strategy with the husband as with the wife, putting himself in charge of what the husband has already been doing, and encouraging him to maintain this behavior, so that it will become more difficult to continue.

The therapist recognizes that the wife is more likely than the husband to sabotage the efforts, and again traps her into carrying out the prescription, saying he doesn't know if she'll do it—

but we don't know, we've just got to see. I can't say right now to
you why I'm taking this particular approach because it would
give the game away. You'll have to trust me because we will get to
discuss it.

WIFE: You mean even if he doesn't—well, you told him not to
—okay, so he doesn't say anything to let me know that he even
notices——

THERAPIST: Except he's very free to be critical. . . .

WIFE: . . . and I'm supposed to keep on doing it and still keep
trying?

THERAPIST: This is only for six days, and I would appreciate it
if he is as critical as he usually is.

WIFE: I've been doing it for thirteen years, so I guess I can do
it for six days.

THERAPIST: Except you're going to do it harder, and you (*to
Mr. McIntosh*) are going to try harder to look for small things to
be critical of.

HUSBAND: There'll be lots of them!

THERAPIST: Okay.

WIFE: Doctor, could you tell me——

THERAPIST: Now just don't discuss it, that's all I ask.

WIFE: Could you tell me, uh, you know, if—what are we going
to get out of this? Not this particular thing, but coming here for
couple therapy? Uh, do you think there's anything we can do,
uh . . .

INTERPRETATION

"we've just got to see." Thus he sets up competition between the spouses about how well each does his part: if one of them sabotages the efforts he will have to admit that he failed to cooperate and work as part of a team.

The wife challenges the therapist's authority by questioning the value of therapy.

DIALOGUE

THERAPIST: Well, it's a little early to say yet. The kind of thing I'm trying, which I know may sound a little screwy, will give us a better notion of what some of the underlying problems are. It's not just a matter of housekeeping and opera and so on. I don't think we quite know yet what the basic problems are. Okay, I'll look forward to seeing you next week.

HUSBAND: Doctor, there's one thing I'd like to mention. It's that when she's angry with me, she always has a headache or she's menstrual or something when we get into the sack. . . .

THERAPIST: Yeah, yeah, but hold it for now. During the next six days when she's trying harder, excuses won't be valid. If she does her part—and I'm sure she will—then no matter how she's feeling, she'll be trying harder to please you.

HUSBAND: Well, it sounds like a very interesting six days.

WIFE: Oh, you'll love it, because you won't have to compliment me on it.

THERAPIST: Okay, see you next week then.

INTERPRETATION

The therapist implies the couple's responsibility in making therapy work by the use of the word "we" and by refusing to be cast in the role of the one with all the answers.

The husband makes a last effort to bring the pattern back to normal by throwing in a fresh complaint about a new issue.

The therapist adds final reinforcement to the wife's compliance with the therapeutic prescription, by indicating that he trusts her to do it. He refuses to permit the husband's ploy to begin a new complaint.

Finding the right therapist is often difficult. Sometimes recommendations made by friends are useful; other times they are not: a therapist may be quite helpful to one couple and not helpful at all to another. Public reputation is often a clue, but sometimes the popular therapist is one who pleases his clients instead of helping them.

Unfortunately, the most effective way of locating a good therapist is shopping around. People seeking therapy cannot always determine whether a therapist is suitable for them until they have seen him a few times. This procedure can be expensive. Also, regretably, it provides a good excuse for the couple wishing to avoid the effort and necessary changes inherent in good therapy. When a man and wife have seen a number of therapists and found them all inadequate, the likelihood is great that they are using this activity to give the impression of working at their marriage, while avoiding the real challenge. Those who are genuinely seeking help, and are willing to make the necessary effort to change, can usually find the help they desire. They must, recognize, however, that part of their responsibility in making therapy work for them is to insist on good therapy, and if they decide the therapist they are seeing is really providing no challenge to their pathological system, it is their responsibility to look for another who will. If no one else is available, the spouses may have to face the fact that they are dependent on self-help.

54

WHAT YOU CAN
EXPECT FROM
MARITAL COUNSELING

We have given some idea of the range of training and the variety of techniques employed by those who do marital counseling and have pointed out that there are great differences among counselors in training, experience, and point of view. Obviously, a minister who has been primarily trained in religious doctrine, and who has had only a few months of instruction in how to handle marital problems, will tend in his counseling to rely more on encouraging couples to be kind and to pray than on trying to change their interactional patterns. At the other extreme, a psychoanalyst with many years of medical and psychoanalytic training will look for the hidden and unconscious motives of the husband and wife in an attempt to cure each spouse individually, hoping thereby to cure the marital sickness as well.

We have also stated—and this point cannot be emphasized too strongly—that such elements as the personality, the personal life, the values, the persuasion, of the therapist are of extreme importance in determining his approach, and may even supersede his training or the particular theoretical model to which he adheres intellectually.

Suppose, now, that you and your spouse are in a position to afford marital counseling, and that competent professionals are available in your area. Given these ideal circumstances, what can you reasonably expect from marital counseling?

To understand how a marriage counselor may function, one must recognize, first of all, the nature of the behavior rules or relationship rules which exist among family members. These are highly institutionalized. That is to say, the participants are not conscious of the rules for interaction; these function largely at an unconscious or unnoticed level. In the same way, we are unaware of the regularity of our breathing; when we do become aware of it, breathing becomes more difficult and irregular.

For example, suppose that a family has a rule that no member is to criticize another member. Because of this rule, which is largely unconscious, many unresolved problems and unspoken dissatisfactions exist in this family. Now suppose that someone makes these people aware that this rule is in effect and is causing many of their problems. Member A will then be tempted to say to Member B, "Why haven't I the right to criticize you? You do many things I don't like." And B may then be offended and say to A, "Well, you won't let me criticize you, and there's plenty I dislike about you, too. You're not perfect." And so on. But because these individuals have not yet learned to criticize freely, the exchange may stop right there, and both parties will then be just that much worse off. Each will now know that the other has critical thoughts *but is not expressing them aloud.* Sometimes the conscious, deliberate awareness of such a rule results in a very uncomfortable situation unless both parties understand the function of the rule and the fact that they both support it. Therefore, we believe, one of the prime functions of the marriage counselor is to observe the exchanges of behavior between the spouses, make them aware of those unconscious rules which are causing friction between them, and *help them develop new rules which may be more workable.* Insight alone is insufficient. It is usually not enough simply to tell the spouses that they have been following some particular rule. Such a statement doesn't have much meaning to them, and they still don't know what to do about it.

It is usually necessary to have them consciously engage in behavior that demonstrates the presence or absence of this rule,
and then to help them begin to formulate a new one.

Here is an example. A husband and wife had a covert rule
about their respective roles which resulted in the following
arrangement: he was ostensibly in charge of the children, but in
fact, she was the major force behind their discipline and training.
Thus, when the father arrived home in the evening, the mother
would have the children lined up for various punishments. Yet it
was the mother who determined who was to be punished for
what; the father was simply the executioner. Because he was
expected to punish the children for "crimes" he knew little about,
his discipline was highly inappropriate. He would blow up at the
children, yell, occasionally strike them, while the mother always
appeared serene. The counselor (in order to focus on this particular rule, which he felt was unworkable) asked the mother as a
favor to him to take charge of the children's discipline for the
next few weeks, so that they could study the effects of a new
situation. He did not explain to her what he had in mind. His
basic aim was to *demonstrate* that having a rule which was a
reversal of the real situation had created problems for every
member of the family, and that therefore changing the rule (by
giving the mother both overt and covert charge of discipline)
would eliminate some of the problems.

The therapist next asked the father to cooperate in this new
arrangement, to avoid interfering, and if he had any criticism of
the mother's handling of the children, to speak to her in private,
not in front of the children. In due course, the new explicit rule
had the effect of making the father feel relieved; when he admitted that the mother did a very good job, he not only got rid of
his "bad guy" role, but gave the mother great satisfaction in
fulfilling a role well and receiving credit for it.

The children also responded to this prescription by the therapist—behaving in a more rational fashion. For now they were less
confused about who was doing the punishing and who was really
in charge of their rearing. They could both like their father and
respect their mother more.

Another function which one can reasonably expect from marital counseling is that of enabling the couple to review value

differences which they unwittingly regard as good or bad rather than just different. Most couples have great difficulty doing this on their own. For example, a father may feel that it is better for the children to be polite and well-disciplined, and his wife may feel that it is more important for them to be spontaneous, so that their spirits are not broken. When they attempt to discuss this difference in values, invariably they get into an argument about who is right. The mother says that the father is making repressed neurotics of the children, and the father feels that the mother is turning them into a bunch of ill-mannered hedonists. The therapist may be able to see that in fact the couple is operating as a team: *the father is helping the mother not to be too permissive, and the mother is helping the father not to be too restrictive.* Strange as it seems, such a simple view of their behavior may never have occurred to the couple because they are so concerned about who is correct and who is in the wrong.

Perhaps one of the most important functions that a marriage counselor can fulfill is that of helping the spouses to assess the strengths or assets in their marriage. Again, it may appear at first blush that they should be able to do this themselves without difficulty. After all, if something is good, they should find it easy to congratulate each other about it. But this is rarely true. The spouses are bound to be warring on some points, and therefore each hates to give the other any credit, especially in the realm of personal behavior, for fear that doing so will weaken his own position in regard to the things they do not agree upon. Thus, a woman may be able to congratulate her husband on a business success and the husband may be able to compliment his wife on a tasty dinner, but they may not be able to say to each other, "You know, I like the way you handled that situation in relation to me," or "I like the way you are able to step in and calm me down when I blow up at the kids." A neutral third party, such as the marriage therapist, can help them put labels on the reasons they stay together. It is not uncommon to have a couple come to a marriage counselor with all sorts of complaints even though they have been married for many years and have no intention of divorce. It has never occurred to them that despite these complaints, they have some pretty positive reasons for staying together.

When we speak of "reasons," we are not talking about the kind of claptrap often found in discussions in women's magazines about "counting your blessings." Such reasons are usually of no lasting relevance to the spouses.

WHAT NOT TO EXPECT FROM MARITAL THERAPY

In the first place, if you are dragging your spouse to therapy because you feel that the counselor, being an intelligent individual, will obviously see your side of the marital mess, forget it. If he is experienced, he is not likely to assume such a one-sided position. To do so would only increase your problems.

Also, you should not expect to receive advice that you will accept like homework from a classroom teacher, so that you emerge from the office prepared to carry out instructions on how to live a better life. Of course, the counselor may make certain suggestions, but these will usually be of a nonspecific nature having to do with your relationship—not with how you should lead your life. As we have indicated, marriages vary greatly— different people have different needs and expectations—and it would be impossible for the counselor to know precisely what was best for you and your spouse.

Furthermore, you should not expect that things will get better immediately. As we know, they are very apt to get worse for a while after the visits to a counselor have begun. Change is not easy, and you and your spouse will fight it despite your best intentions. However, some individuals avoid marital counseling because they are afraid that all hell will break loose and believe that it is better to let sleeping dogs lie. Their reasoning resembles that of the person who refrains from visiting a surgeon after discovering a lump on his body that may be cancerous. Such avoidance may endanger the individual's life, and since he cannot really *forget* his fear of cancer, the delay doesn't even give him peace of mind.

Continuing the surgery analogy, we may observe next that the surgeon must cut if he is to diagnose the condition and achieve a cure. The biopsy necessary to determine the extent of the illness is relatively painless. If a malignant cancer is indeed present, the operation which follows will be more painful and time-consuming. It may be too late to cut out the diseased area—but it may not be. If not, the patient can look forward to greater health in compensation for the pain of surgery and convalescence. Correspondingly, in an effort to diagnose and treat the marital illness, the marriage counselor may bring up matters or make remarks that will not please one or both of the spouses. The pained spouse or spouses may withdraw, argue, protest, or even occasionally walk out. Such a response does not mean that the therapy is hopeless or that the errant spouse is hopeless; he has simply displayed an appropriate reaction to stress—and stress is normal when highly-charged learning is occurring. After a breather, or period of reevaluation, the joint effort can be resumed.

Some people seem to expect marital therapy to be a superficial, almost judicial procedure, where they will receive the therapist's wisdom and blessing without being shaken up in the process. They therefore refuse to speak honestly about their thoughts, desires, expectations, and motives, and they steer away from "hot" topics. But if the therapy is to be productive, the basic issues must be exposed. The trained counselor can be trusted to prevent undue and pointless argument; he may even—on the rare occasions when it becomes necessary—employ physical intervention. A variety of measures are available to him for breaking the pattern of constant bickering. For example, he may see one or both members of the couple separately for a number of sessions, or he may invite other important family members or relatives into a session.

There is nothing sadder than hearing the sessions of an inexperienced counselor who allows a husband and wife to engage in bitter quarreling session after session, in the mistaken belief that they are getting something off their chests. The inability of the couple to avoid fighting bitterly during the counseling session does not indicate that they cannot benefit from counseling. *It simply shows that their therapist cannot handle them.* When Freud conceived of psychoanalysis, he discovered (and this observation was supported by his associates) that the method was not suitable for certain kinds of psychiatric problems and certain kinds of people. Over the years this discovery has been interpreted to mean that certain people are unanalyzable, the implication being that there is something "wrong" with these persons, and *not* that there is something wrong with the method. In the same way, when the inadequate marriage counselor finds a couple he cannot deal with, he may tell them, in effect, that they are hopeless. But for him to imply that they are at fault is harmful. Actually, there is no such thing as an impossible couple; there are, however, impossible therapists. The counselor's responsibility and ethical duty is to refer a couple to someone else if he is unable to handle their problem. It is all too easy for a frustrated counselor instead to tell his clients to get a divorce. On the other hand, good counseling does not always result in an improved marriage. It may result in the decision of both spouses to get out of the marriage.

HOW LONG SHOULD THERAPY LAST?

Marital therapists vary in their recommendations concerning the frequency with which a couple should come in for therapy and the length of time the therapy should continue. It is fairly standard procedure for a couple to be seen for one hour once a week, although sometimes one of the spouses may also be seen individually between the conjoint marital sessions. However, there are no magic numbers in this particular game.

If a couple has serious marital problems, they are likely to see their therapists for one or two years. This doesn't mean that they will necessarily see him once a week during the entire period. If they make considerable progress in six months or a year, less frequent sessions may be sufficient thereafter. On the other hand, new and different problems may suddenly occur which require brief periods of more intensive therapy. Even when the process of working out a marital problem involves two steps forward and one step back, the net accomplishment may be considerable.

Some people who believe that they have serious marital problems are able to establish adequate patterns of communication in a relatively short period of time, and can then continue to progress on their own. We have seen couples who have materially benefited from as few as three to ten sessions, although by and large substantially more are required. The number of sessions necessary also depends on certain external circumstances. For example, in one instance a couple came upon difficult times when the husband toyed with the idea of making a job change. They sought help through therapy, and the counselor was honestly able to encourage the husband to make the change despite the wife's fears. The counselor believed that to do so would be sensible, that the husband felt frustrated in his present occupation and that this feeling was feeding back negatively into the marriage. When the husband did transfer successfully to the new job, the marriage benefited materially. Altogether, six sessions were involved, over a total period of approximately one year.

PROBLEMS IN THE TRANSITION FROM INDIVIDUAL TO CONJOINT THERAPY

Very often, just one member of a marital team feels ill, either physically or emotionally, from the strain of a bad marriage and seeks therapy to alleviate his distress. In many instances, the counselor works individually with the spouse who approached him, leaving the other out of the therapy. Then, at some subsequent date (sometimes as long as a year or two later), the therapist or the spouse in treatment may decide that the left-out spouse should now be included. Obviously, this situation presents some difficulties for the spouse who has been hitherto ignored, since he is apt to feel that the spouse who has been seeing the therapist is the "sick" one. Also, he may suspect that the therapist will be biased in favor of the spouse who has been in treatment. Therefore, many people are reluctant to begin conjoint therapy after one spouse has been in individual therapy; if they do begin it, they are often so skeptical and suspicious that they have difficulty continuing the treatment.

There are several possible solutions to this dilemma. In the first place, it usually would have been far better if the therapist had included both spouses early in the game. There seems to be little excuse for treating only one member of a marital pair, regardless of the nature of his psychological complaints. As we have pointed out, the reasons why the two spouses got together in the first place necessarily involve both of them, and these reasons usually pervade the entire marriage; therefore, it is fruitless and sometimes harmful to treat only one spouse. Secondly, the spouse who is invited into therapy relatively late may be helped by the realization that most experienced therapists do not take sides with the original patient, but remain relatively objective. In fact, the therapist may sometimes find himself on the side of the spouse who has hitherto not been in treatment, because he has had time to become aware of many difficult aspects of the behavior of the spouse he has known longer. Also, if the latecomer has doubts and suspicions, he may appropriately ask to see the therapist individually for a few sessions, to get acquainted with him, or suggest that a second therapist take over the marital counseling, so that both spouses start afresh together.

CONCLUSION

We believe that as time goes on, marital problems in this culture will inevitably receive increasing attention from therapists of various sorts, and that facilities for training professionals to handle these problems will improve and expand. At present, it would be misleading to encourage people, particularly outside of large metropolitan areas, to believe that they can easily find a good marriage counselor even if they can afford one.

We do feel that the kind of information supplied in this book may enable a couple to choose and evaluate a marriage counselor (minister, psychologist, psychiatrist, or social worker) with a touch more sophistication than is possessed by the average couple walking naked and yet expectant into the marriage counselor's office.

55

THE POTENTIAL DANGERS IN UNILATERAL THERAPY

Until the 1950's, the generally accepted practice was for a psychotherapist to see only one of the spouses involved in a marital mix-up. If the other partner needed, requested, or could be dragged into therapy, he saw a different therapist. Sometimes a psychiatrist hired several social workers, and farmed out one of the spouses in each of his cases to a social worker, keeping the "sicker" spouse as his own patient. This procedure had certain financial advantages and was rather safe because it supported the couple's own myth that one partner was "sick" and one was "well." We now know that this sick-well dichotomy is an illusion. Loving people do not marry hateful people, and the "well" spouse often keeps his health at the expense of the apparently neurotic or psychotic spouse.

At present, unilateral therapy in which only one spouse is seen, is increasingly being replaced, except in orthodox analytic circles, by the technique of conjoint marital therapy. In the latter method, spouses are seen together by one therapist, so that their habitual patterns of interaction can be directly observed and the therapist can serve both spouses as a model in dealing with the patterns as they occur.

A further extension of this method (not yet in common practice) is for the therapist to treat the couple in their home.* Under these circumstances, the therapist can quickly assess the nature of the home, its accouterments, the position of the bedroom, the relative amount of living space available to each family member, and he is frequently privy to behavior (for example, episodes of irritation) which he would never see in his own office. It appears that many couples are less able to be on "good behavior" in their homes because they are in their natural habitat.

If the conjoint therapy currently gaining favor seems to us to be a more appropriate technique than any which have been employed in the past, it is only fair to explain what we regard as *inappropriate* about unilateral marital therapy.

In the first place, people who are warring wish to have allies, so it is natural that the patient-spouse wants the therapist to be on his side. For this reason, a great deal of what he tells the therapist will be essentially a recitation, a litany, of the other's faults, lies, and deviousness. If the therapist refuses to hear such material or constantly interrupts, the patient often feels hurt or misunderstood. At the same time, since the therapist has no idea of what the other spouse is *really* like, he is in no position to seriously question or challenge any of the statements made. Even when they are so extreme that they seem simply unbelievable, there is always the risk that they may be true. One of the authors well remembers the time a young woman claimed that her husband was trying to break her leg. This seemed like such a peculiar form of destructive behavior that the therapist eliminated it from the discussion. Some nights later he received a call from an orthopedist, informing him that his patient was in the hospital with a broken right tibia. The husband had accomplished the deed using a bed footboard as a fulcrum.

* One of the therapists at the Mental Research Institute, Palo Alto, California, has lived for a week with several families. One or two hour-long home visits are a regular part of many a marital therapist's armamentarium.

The patient-spouse may be expected to use any human trick available to seduce the therapist to his side in the ally-seeking process. In order to convince the therapist of the truth of his own set of biases concerning his spouse, he may lie, or he may unconsciously distort the experiences which he describes.

Suppose, however, that out of this mishmash of marital tales the therapist evolves a belief that the absent marital partner represents the mother or father to the patient, who has therefore assumed the role of a child in this relationship. *Gaining insight* that one is treating one's spouse in terms of the feelings one *supposedly* had toward one's mother or father at the age of five, does not automatically change one's behavior toward the spouse. It is quite unlikely that the spouse is exactly like the patient's mother or father, or that the patient is able to recall precisely how he felt at the age of five. *Current* problems are the sources of marital woes and are the ones which must be dealt with by the therapist. Action, not just understanding, is required.

Another disadvantage in unilateral marital therapy is that the spouse not in treatment is likely to feel left out, even though his resentment at not being included may be assuaged to some extent by his pride in being the "less sick" of the two partners. Furthermore, the fact that he is left out means that he is less involved with the process, and eventually it results in disdain or distaste on his part for the procedure, makes him suspicious of the therapist, and usually separates him further from the spouse in treatment.

Occasionally, though less often, the left-out spouse responds by pumping the patient-spouse for information and interpretation until he vicariously relives every session at home. The result is an untenable situation in which the patient has two therapists who almost invariably disagree, since the left-out spouse tends to agree with the therapist only when he is critical of the patient. However, if the patient reports a comment by the therapist which sounds critical of the left-out spouse, he may justifiably respond angrily that "the son-of-a-bitch doesn't even know me! How could he say such a thing?"

It would be incorrect to suppose that unilateral marital therapy never does any good. However, it is a less desirable form of marital psychotherapeutic practice. It has been our observation from visiting clinics and offices throughout the country that even when two therapists, one seeing each spouse, are housed in the same office and intend to coordinate their efforts, they rarely get together. And when they do, they are faced with the problem that putting together two separate pictures *does not produce the same kind of information which is obtained by watching the marital system at work.*

Unilateral therapy may be beneficial in that a spouse may receive amelioration of hurt feelings, release from pent-up anger, and some insight into how he "asked for it," all of which will take some of the immediate pressure off the marriage and encourage the other spouse to behave in a more loving and tolerant manner. But there is always the danger that if unilateral marital therapy continues for any length of time, the two spouses will grow apart, either because the "well" spouse thinks the other is too sick for him, or because the spouse in treatment begins to understand his marital partner in a new way, is horrified by the picture, and wants out.

There are a few facts and figures available on the results of psychoanalysis and individual, or unilateral, psychotherapy. These suggest that divorce is not uncommon even following prolonged analysis for each of the spouses. Nearly all the psychiatrists and analysts we know—and these are individuals who have personally undergone long and extensive analyses—have been married at least twice. Furthermore, analysts themselves do not claim that their technique is a solution for marital problems; relatively few papers written about marital problems by analysts appear in the analytic journals.

APPENDICES

APPENDICES

APPENDIX A

Suggested Reading List on Marriage and Family Living

BOOKS

* Indicates material more suitable for nonprofessionals.

Bell, Norman W., and Vogel, Ezra F. (editors), *A Modern Introduction to the Family*. Glencoe: The Free Press of Glencoe, 1960. 691 pp.

*Bernard, Jessie, *American Family Behavior*. New York: Harper and Brothers, 1942. 564 pp.

*Blood, Robert O., Jr., *Husbands and Wives*. Glencoe: The Free Press of Glencoe, 1960. 288 pp.

Bossard, James, and Ball, Eleanor S., *Family Situations*. Philadelphia: University of Pennsylvania Press, 1943. 265 pp.

Burgess, Ernest W., and Cottrell, Leonard S., *Predicting Success or Failure in Marriage*. New York: Prentice-Hall, Inc., 1939. 472 pp.

Burgess, Ernest W., and Locke, Harvey J., *The Family*. New York: American Book Company, 1945. 800 pp.

Burgess, Ernest W., and Wallin, Paul, *Courtship, Engagement and Marriage*. Philadelphia: J. B. Lippincott Company, 1952. 819 pp.

Cottrell, Leonard S., and Foote, Nelson N., *Identity and Interpersonal Competence: New Directions of Research on the American Family*. Chicago: University of Chicago Press, 1955. 305 pp.

Davis, Katherine B., *Factors in the Sex Life of Twenty-Two Hundred Women*. New York: Harper and Brothers, 1929. 430 pp.

Emerson, Guy D. (editor), *The Family in a Democratic Society*. New York: Columbia University Press, 1949. 314 pp.

*Glick, Paul, *American Families*. New York: John Wiley & Sons, 1957. 240 pp.

Hamilton, Gilbert V., *A Research in Marriage*. New York: Albert and Charles Boni, Inc., 1929. 570 pp.

Herberg, Will, *Protestant, Catholic and Jew*. Garden City: Doubleday & Company, 1960. 320 pp.

Hess, Robert D., and Handel, Gerald, *Family Worlds—A Psychological Approach to Family Life*. Chicago: University of Chicago Press, 1959. 305 pp.

Hill, Reuben, *Families Under Stress*. New York: Harper and Brothers, 1949. 443 pp.

Laing, R. D., *The Self and Others*. Chicago: Quadrangle Books, 1962. (First published in 1961 by Tavistock Publications, Ltd., London.)

Laing, R. D., Phillipson, H., and Lee, A. R., *Interpersonal Perception: A Theory and a Method of Research*. New York: Springer Publishing Company, 1966.

*Levy, John, and Monroe, Ruth, *The Happy Family*. New York: Alfred A. Knopf, 1939. 319 pp.

Locke, Harvey J., *Predicting Adjustment in Marriage: A Comparison of a Divorced and a Happily Married Group*. New York: Henry Holt and Company, 1951. 407 pp.

Monahan, Thomas P., *The Pattern of Age at Marriage in the United States*. Philadelphia: Stephenson Brothers, 1951. 451 pp.

Mudd, Emily H., Mitchell, H. D., and Taubin, Sara B., *Success in Family Living*. New York: Association Press, 1965.

Selltiz, Claire, Jahoda, Marie, Deutsch, Morton, and Cook, Stuart W., *Research Methods in Social Relations*. New York: Henry Holt and Company, 1959. 622 pp.

Slater, Eliot, and Woodside, Moya, *Patterns of Marriage—A Study of Marriage Relationships in the Urban Working Classes*. London: Cassell and Company, Ltd., 1951. 311 pp.

*Terman, Lewis M., *Psychological Factors in Marital Happiness*. New York: McGraw-Hill Book Company, 1938. 474 pp.

*Terman, Lewis M., and Oden, Melita H., *The Gifted Child Grows Up: Twenty-five Year Follow-up of a Superior Group*. Stanford: Stanford University Press, 1947. 463 pp.

Watzlawick, P., Beavin, Janet H., and Jackson, D. D., *Pragmatics of Human Communication: A Study of Interactional Patterns, Pathologies and Paradoxes*. New York: W. W. Norton & Company, 1967.

*Winch, Robert F., *The Modern Family*. New York: Henry Holt and Company, 1952. 505 pp.

*Zimmerman, Carle C., and Cervantes, Lucius F., *Successful American Families*. New York: Pageant Press, Inc., 1960. 226 pp.

ARTICLES

Baber, Ray E., "Religion and the Family," *Annals of the American Academy of Political and Social Science*, 256:92–101 (March, 1948).

Bernard, Jessie, "An Instrument for Measurement of Success in Marriage," *Publications of the American Sociological Society*, 27:94–106 (July, 1933).

Burchinal, Lee G., Hawkes, Glenn, and Gardner, Bruce, "Marriage Adjustment Personality Characteristics of Parents and Personal Adjustment of Their Children," *Marriage and Family Living*, 19:366–373 (November, 1957).

Burgess, Ernest W., "The Family in a Changing Society," *American Journal of Sociology*, 53:417–431 (November, 1948).

Burgess, Ernest W., "Predictive Methods and Family Stability," *Annals of the American Academy of Political and Social Science*, 272:47–53 (November, 1950).

Burgess, Ernest W., and Wallin, Paul, "Predicting Adjustment in Marriage from Adjustment in Engagement," *American Journal of Sociology*, 49:737–751 (September, 1944).

Christensen, H. T., and Philbrick, R. E., "Family Size As a Factor in the Marital Adjustments of College Students," *American Sociological Review*, 17:306–312 (June, 1952).

Dyer, Dorothy T., "Religious Affiliation and Selected Personality Scores As They Relate to Marital Happiness of Minnesota College Sample," *Marriage and Family Living*, 23:46–48 (May, 1961).

Ellis, Albert, "The Value of Marriage Prediction Tests," *American Sociological Review*, 13:710–718 (May, 1948).

Ferguson, Leonard W., "Correlates of Marital Happiness," *Journal of Psychology*, 6:285–294 (May, 1938).

Goode, William J., "Economic Factors and Marital Stability," *American Sociological Review*, 16:802–811 (December, 1952).

*Hey, Richard N., and Mudd, Emily H., "The American Family," *1948 Encyclopedia Yearbook*. New York: The Grolier Society, Inc., 160.

Hollingshead, August B., "Class Differences in Family Stability," *Annals of the American Academy of Political and Social Science*, 272:39–47 (November, 1950).

Jansen, Luther, "Doing Things Together—Measuring Family Solidarity," *American Sociological Review*, 17:727–734 (December, 1952).

Kelly, Lowell E., "Marital Compatibility As Related to Personality Traits of Husband and Wife As Rated by Self and Spouse," *Journal of Sociol Psychology*, 13:193–198 (May, 1941).

King, Charles E., "The Burgess-Cottrell Method of Measuring Marital

Adjustment Applied to a Non-White Southern Urban Population," *Marriage and Family Living,* 14:280–285 (November, 1952).

Kirkpatrick, Clifford, "Community of Interest and the Measurement of Marital Adjustment," *The Family,* 43:133–137 (May, 1937).

Kirkpatrick, Clifford, "Factors in Marital Adjustment," *American Journal of Sociology,* 43:270–273 (May, 1937).

Landis, Judson T., "A Re-examination of the Role of the Father As an Index of Family Integration," *Marriage and Family Living,* 24:122–129 (May, 1962).

Locke, Harvey J., and Klausner, William J., "Marital Adjustment of Divorced Persons in Subsequent Marriages," *Sociology and Social Research,* 33:97–101 (May, 1948).

Luckey, Eleanor B., "Marital Satisfaction and Parent Concepts," *Journal of Consulting Psychology,* 24:195–204 (May, 1960).

Mitchell, Howard E., Bullard, James W., and Mudd, Emily H., "Areas of Marital Conflict in Successfully and Unsuccessfully Functioning Families," *Journal of Health and Human Behavior,* 3:88–93 (Summer, 1962).

Mowrer, Harriet R., "The Study of Marital Adjustment As a Background for Research in Child Behavior," *Journal of Educational Sociology,* 53:482–492 (July, 1937).

Ogburn, William F., "Education, Income and Family Unity," *American Journal of Sociology,* 53:474–476 (May, 1948).

Ort, R. S., "Happiness in Marriage and Role Conflict," *Journal of Abnormal Sociology and Psychology,* 45:691–699 (May, 1950).

Otto, H., "What Is a Strong Family?" *Marriage and Family Living,* 24:246–249 (February, 1962).

Popenoe, Jaul, "Marital Happiness in Two Generations," *Mental Hygiene,* 21:218–223 (October, 1937).

Remmers, H. H., Drucker, A. J., and Christensen, H. T., "Some Background Factors in Socio-sexual Modernism," *Marriage and Family Living,* 14:334–337 (November, 1952).

Schnepp, Gerald S., and Johnson, Mary M., "Do Religious Background Factors Have Predictive Value?" *Marriage and Family Living,* 14:301–304 (November, 1952).

Strauss, A., "The Influence of Parental Image upon Marriage Choice," *American Sociological Review,* 11:554–559 (June, 1946).

Stroup, A. L., "Marriage Adjustment of the Mother and the Personality of the Child," *Marriage and Family Living,* 18:109–114 (May, 1956).

Stroup, A. L., "Predicting Marital Success or Failure in an Urban Population," *American Sociological Review,* 18:558–563 (October, 1953).

Terman, Lewis M., "Prediction Data: Predicting Marriage Failure from Test Scores," *Marriage and Family Living,* 12:51–54 (July, 1950).

Terman, Lewis M., and Bettenweiser, P., "Personality Factors in Marital Incompatibility," *Journal of Social Psychology,* 6:143–171 (May, 1935).

Terman, Lewis M., and Wallin, Paul, "The Validity of Marriage Prediction and Marital Adjustment Tests," *American Sociological Review,* 14:497–505 (May, 1949).

Tharp, Roland C., "Psychological Patterning in Marriage," *Psychological Bulletin,* 55:97–118 (March, 1963).

Thomas, John L., "The Factor of Religion on the Selection of Marriage Mates," *American Sociological Review,* 16:482–492 (August, 1951).

Weisman, Irving, "Exploring the Effect of the Marital Relationship on Child Functioning and Parental Functioning," *Social Casework,* 44:330–335 (June, 1963).

Williamson, Robert E., "Economic Factors in Marital Adjustment," *Marriage and Family Living,* 14:298–301 (November, 1952).

Woodhouse, Chase G., "A Study of Two-hundred and Fifty Successful Families," *Social Forces,* 8:511–532 (May, 1930).

Yi-chuang Lu, "Predicting Roles in Marriage," *American Journal of Sociology,* 58:51–55 (December, 1952).

APPENDIX B

California Requirements for Professionals Who Work with Marriage Problems

I. The Marriage Counselor

To engage in the business of marriage, family, or child counseling in California an individual must have

1. at *least* a master's degree in marriage counseling, social work, or one of the behavioral sciences, such as sociology or psychology, from an accredited college or university.
2. at least two years' counseling experience, of a nature approved by the director of the Department of Professional Vocational Standards, under the direction of a person who is qualified to do supervision (as defined by the director), *or*
3. at least two years' experience of a type which in the judgment of the director is equivalent to that obtained under the direction of such a person.

Exempted from these requirements are priests, rabbis, ministers of the gospel of any religious denomination, any person licensed to practice medicine or admitted to practice law in the state of California, and the personnel of any organization which is both nonprofit and charitable.

II. The Social Worker

Social workers who are in private practice and do counseling generally have the M.S.W. (Master of Social Work) degree in psychiatric social work. This degree requires four years of college and two years of graduate social work, including one year of supervised work experience in counseling. Some social workers become licensed marriage counselors in the state of California, but they are not required to do so at present. A registered social worker in this state must take an examination in social work, but this does not include clinical questions related to marriage counseling. Membership in the American Council of Social Work (denoted A.C.S.W. after the name) requires two years of supervised social-work practice in addition to the master's degree.

Most psychiatric social workers in the state of California in private practice are well-trained counselors. However, since it is possible for a qualified social worker to see private patients without having had any clinical training specifically in marriage or family counseling, the prospective client should inquire about the social worker's training.

III. The Clinical Psychologist

To obtain a license to practice as a clinical psychologist an individual must

1. possess a doctorate degree (Ph.D.) in social, behavioral, or biological science from a training institution approved by the American Psychological Association, in which at least forty semester hours of successful work at the graduate level have been completed in courses clearly identified by title and content as psychological in nature.

2. have submitted an original research thesis, on a psychological topic, as determined by the psychology examining committee.

3. have had supervised clinical experience (internship) fulfilling the following conditions:

   a. It must be preceded by the completion of two full academic years of graduate training in psychology, and at least forty-eight semester hours.

   b. It must be in the same fields of psychology as the applicant's education and training, or in closely related fields.

   c. It must consist of no less than 1,500 clock hours, completed within twenty-four successive calendar months.

   d. It must include a minimum of one hour each week of face-to-face supervision or similar personal consultation between the supervisor and the applicant.

   e. The supervisor of the applicant must have acquired prior to the period of supervision a doctorate degree in psychology or educational psychology or its equivalent, and must have had three years of professional experience of a type deemed qualifying by the committee. The teaching of psychology may count for half of one year of this experience, provided that it has been in the same field of psychology as the experience, or in a closely related field.

4. pass a written examination (approximately six hours) and a brief oral examination (approximately one-half hour).

IV. The Psychiatrist

To qualify as a psychiatrist an individual must

1. hold an M.D. degree from a recognized medical school.
2. have completed one year of rotating internship.
3. have completed three years of residency training in an approved hospital or institution devoted to the practice of psychiatry.
4. have passed the medical-board examinations of the state of California.

To fulfill the requirements of the American Board of Psychiatry, the individual must, in addition to the preceding qualifications, complete two years of practice and pass a one-day oral examination in neurology and psychiatry. However, a psychiatrist need not pass this examination in order to practice psychiatry in any state in the United States. Doing so is simply another evidence of his competence.

V. The Minister, Priest, or Rabbi

As has been noted, in the state of California, a minister, priest, or rabbi may consult with one or both marital partners without being licensed. Some church orders require courses in pastoral counseling, particularly for individuals who have been out of school for some years and may have had no training at all. Some religious sects encourage some of their students to acquire training in pastoral counseling so that members of the sect who require marital or individual therapy may receive it from them.

Index

Raniero Cantalamessa

232

CAV

JESUS CHRIST
THE HOLY ONE OF GOD

Translated by Alan Neame

A Liturgical Press Book

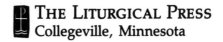

THE LITURGICAL PRESS
Collegeville, Minnesota

Cover design by Ann Blattner.

Cover: Mosaic of Christ Pantocrator in Hagia Sophia, Istanbul (late 12th or 13th century).

Original title: *Gesù Cristo il Santo di Dio,* copyright © 1990 Edizioni Paoline s.r.l., Cinisello Balsamo, Italy. English translation copyright © 1991 St. Paul Publications, Slough, United Kingdom. All rights reserved.

This edition for the United States of America and Canada published by The Liturgical Press, Collegeville, Minnesota. Printed in the United States of America.

2	3	4	5	6	7	8	9

Library of Congress Cataloging-in-Publication Data

Cantalamessa, Raniero.
    [Gesù Cristo, il Santo di Dio. English]
    Jesus Christ, the Holy one of God / Raniero Cantalamessa ; translated by Alan Neame.
        p.   cm.
    Translation of: Gesù Cristo, il Santo di Dio.
    Includes bibliographical references and indexes.
    ISBN 0-8146-2073-6
    1. Jesus Christ—Person and offices—Meditations. I. Title.
BT202.C33513   1991
232—dc20   NA-1939   91-27215
                                                     CIP

Contents

Introduction

The hero and the poet

'My heart overflows with a goodly theme;
I address my verses to the king' (Ps 45).

There are various ways, or methods, of approaching the person of Jesus. One may, for example, set off straight from the Bible and, even in this case, there are various ways that can be taken: the *typological* way, followed in the most ancient catechesis of the Church, which explains Jesus by the light of figures and prophecies in the Old Testament; the *historical* way, which reconstructs the development of faith in Christ on the basis of the various traditions, authors and Christological titles, or of the differing cultural environments of the New Testament. Or one may start from the demands and problems of human beings today; or directly from one's own personal experience of Christ, and from this work one's way back to the Bible. These are all ways widely in use.

Very early, the Tradition of the Church worked out its own way of access to the mystery of Christ, its own way of selecting and organizing the relevant biblical data; this way is known as Christological dogma, the *dogmatic* way. By Christological dogma, I mean the fundamental truths concerning Christ as defined in the early ecumenical councils, most notably the Council of Chalcedon, and in substance summed up in the following three statements: Jesus Christ is true man, he is true God, he is one sole person. To approach Christ by the way of Tradition and dogma is to approach him by the way that, through his Spirit, he himself has traced in order to reach us. As in the quest for the distant sources of great rivers, so here: no surer method exists than to trace the course of the river back to its source.

In these meditations I have tried to approach the person of Jesus Christ precisely by following this classic way of the Church. They consist of six reflections: two are devoted to the humanity of Christ, two to his divinity and two to his unity of

1

person. These are followed by a concluding chapter of somewhat different character, a kind of *excursus* in which I attempt a critical evaluation of the theses recently advanced in certain so-called 'new Christologies', more particularly on the problem of the divinity of Christ.

Christological dogma is not intended to be a synthesis of all the biblical data, a distillation, as it were, containing within itself all the immense wealth of statements about Christ to be found in the New Testament and reducing all this to the meatless and arid formula: '*two natures, one person*'. If this were the case, dogma would be tremendously reductionist and dangerous too. But it is not so. Of Christ, the Church believes and preaches everything the New Testament affirms about him, omitting nothing. By means of dogma, the Church has merely sought to establish a frame of reference, to set out a sort of 'fundamental law' that every statement about Christ should respect. Everything said about Christ should now and henceforth respect this certain and incontrovertible datum; that is to say, that he is God and man at the same time and, what is more, in the same person.

Dogmas are 'open structures', ready to accept whatever new and genuine discovery in the word of God each age makes, which has bearing on those truths they are intended to define, though not to close. They are open to development from within, though always 'in the same sense and in the same direction'. That is to say, in such a way, that the interpretation given in one age does not contradict that of a previous age.

It is certainly true, however, that in the course of centuries dogma's role was sometimes forgotten and its relationship with Scripture was reversed, so that Scripture ceased to be the base and dogma the exponent, while dogma became the base and Scripture the exponent. That is to say, dogma was no longer used to explain Scripture, but Scripture was made use of to explain dogma by being often reduced to so many little detached phrases adduced in proof of dogmatic theses already constituted, as one more set of 'proofs', along with those drawn from reason , from tradition, from the liturgy and so forth.

Once restored to its original function, dogma, today as always, constitutes the surest way to take if we are to discover the true Jesus. Not only is it the surest, but also the loveliest, the freshest, the richest in promise, like all those things that have not been improvized from one day to the next in accordance with the latest fashionable theory but that have slowly matured as it were in the sun and rain of history, each generation having added its own contribution. 'The dogmatic terminology of the primitive Church,' writes Kierkegaard, 'is like an enchanted castle where, locked in slumber, lie the handsomest of princes and the loveliest of princesses. They only need to be aroused, for them to leap to their feet in all their glory.'[1]

So, approaching Christ by way of dogma does not mean we have to resign ourselves wearily to repeating the same things about him over and over again, merely changing the words. It means reading Scripture in the Tradition, with the eyes of the Church; that is to say, reading it in a way ever old and ever new. Revealed truth, St Irenaeus says, is 'like a precious liquor contained in a costly vessel; by the activity of the Holy Spirit, it is forever renewed and likewise renews the vessel that contains it.'[2] The Church is in the position to read Scripture ever anew, since the Church is ever renewed by Scripture. This great yet very simple secret discovered by St Irenaeus explains why the Tradition is perennially fresh and hence too the dogmas that are its highest expression.

Furthermore, in these words St Irenaeus tells us what the condition, or rather the principal agent, of this perennial youth and freshness is: it is the Holy Spirit. The Holy Spirit guides the Church to accept the ever-new stimuli constantly arising from history and human thought (the so-called 'signs of the times') and, under this impulse, to read the word of God in manner ever new and more profound. One of the Fathers of the Church calls the Holy Spirit 'the light of dogmas'. It is a wonderful definition and inspires us with a bold hope. At the present time, when we are praying for and to some degree experiencing a renewal of the Holy Spirit's activity in so many aspects of the Church — in prayer, in religious life, in institutions — we instantly discern another field into which the Holy Spirit can and wills to infuse a new vitality: that of dogma.

Renewing dogma in the Holy Spirit does not mean talking more frequently than we normally would about the Holy Spirit in connection with this or that theological question. The Holy Spirit is like light. Light illuminates and makes things visible, not when we have it shining straight into our eyes or when its source is plain to see, but when we have it behind us and it lights up everything in front of us, keeping itself, as it were, apart. It is the Spirit who projects the light on Jesus Christ and makes him known. St Paul calls Jesus Christ 'the mistery revealed to his holy apostles and prophets by means of the Spirit' (cf Eph 3:5). Just as we cannot proclaim that 'Jesus is the Lord', except 'in the Holy Spirit' (cf 1 Cor 12:3), so we cannot proclaim that he is 'true God and true man', except 'in the Holy Spirit'. The same difference as exists, from the strictly religious point of view of sacred art, between an Orthodox icon of the Mother of God and a Madonna by Leonardo, by Botticelli or by Raphael, also exists between a discourse on Christ made 'in the Holy Spirit' and a discourse, be it ever so wise or technically perfect, but not made in the Holy Spirit. The one helps us to believe and pray; the other does not.

In this respect and due distinctions made, dogma shares the prerogative of Scripture. Scripture, being inspired by the Holy Spirit, cannot be understood in its deepest intention unless it is read 'spiritually', that is to say, in the Holy Spirit; and so too dogma, defined by the Church under the influence of the Holy Spirit, cannot be understood in its deeper nature and dynamic except by the light of that same Holy Spirit.

In these meditations I propose for myself the following aim: to show how the Holy Spirit, who quickens everything in the Church, can also and especially quicken Catholic dogma, make it shine with new light, make believers fall in love with it, having brought it close to their own experience. To show how dogma is not only the bearer of *certitudes* but also of *energies* for the Church. To attempt, in a word, a sketch of 'spiritual' Christology.

In a period such as our own, in which we witness a widespread rejection of everything, in the faith, that is objective, handed down and doctrinally binding, in favour of new forms of extemporary and esoteric religiosity where all is left to the spiritual taste of the individual and to personal 'experience', it seems an urgent and vital task to rediscover the true nature and the true 'face' of the dogmas of the Christian faith. 'One thing only', says Tertullian, addressing the pagans of his day, 'Christian truth demands: not to be condemned before it has been heard: *ne ignorata damnetur*'.[3]

No doubt what I shall succeed in saying will actually be very little, but I shall be content if I have shown that the possibility exists, if I have launched the idea, in the hope that it will be taken up and achieved by others more competent than myself. In this attempt I have found the works of Kierkegaard very helpful, since they — due reservations sustained — have the great merit of immersing the dogmatic truths of the ancient Church in the living element of modern thought, without however dissolving the dogmas in it, thus demonstrating that the two things — dogmas of faith and modern thought — are not in fact, as is sometimes assumed, incompatible one with the other.

Lastly, a word on the practical aim and on the recipients of these reflections. They were first given as meditations to the Pontifical Household during Advent time. I am allowing them to be published in the hope that they may serve as an integrating factor, however modest, and to some degree also as a corrective to hold on to, when studying Christology.

But much more than to *studying*, I want to make my own small contribution to *proclaiming* Christ today. In view of the 'new wave' of evangelization in preparation for the dawning of the third millennium since the birth of Christ, there is a need not only for Christological specialists but also for people in love with Christ and able to talk about him and prepare the way for him as humbly and as ardently as John the Baptist did the first time. 'The God who created man and woman,' Kierkegaard writes elsewhere, 'also fashioned the hero and the poet or orator. The latter cannot do what the former does; he can only admire, love, rejoice with the hero. All the same, he too is happy, no less than the other. Indeed the hero is his better essence, he with whom he is in love, happy in not being him himself. And this is how his love can manifest itself: in admiration. He is the recording genius who can do nothing save record what has been done, do nothing but admire what has been done, does nothing of himself but is jealous of what has been entrusted to him. He follows his heart's choice but, once having found what he seeks, he then goes from door to door with his songs and his speeches, proclaiming that all should admire the hero as he does, should be as proud of the hero

5

as he is. This is his trade, his humble activity, this is his loyal service in the house of the hero.'[4]

I should count myself happy if just one young person, having read these reflections, felt the inner stirring of a vocation to be one of these poets and admirers who go from door to door, from city to city, proclaiming the name and love of Christ, the unique, true 'hero' of the world, of history. Unique since also God.

NOTES

1 S. Kierkegaard, *The Journals*, II A, 110 (OUP 1938, entry 127 adapted).
2 St Irenaeus, *Adv. Haer.*, III, 24, 1.
3 Tertullian, *Apologeticum*, 1, 2 (CC 1, p. 85).
4 S. Kierkegaard, *Fear and Trembling* (Panegyric of Abraham).

Chapter I

'In all things like us, except in sin'

The holiness of Christ's humanity

In the Fourth Gospel there is an episode which has every appearance of being the Johannine equivalent of Peter's confession at Caesarea Philippi. When, after the discourse in the synagogue at Capernaum on the bread of life and the negative reaction of some of the disciples to it, Jesus asks the apostles whether they too wish to leave him, Peter replies: 'Lord, to whom shall we go? You have the words of eternal life; and we have believed, and have come to know that you are the Holy One of God' (Jn 6:68–69).

The 'Holy One of God': this title takes the place here of the title 'Christ' (Mk 8:29), or 'Christ of God' (Lk 9:20), or 'Christ, the Son of the living God' (Mt 16:16) which occurs in Peter's confession at Caesarea. In this case too, Peter's declaration is presented as a revelation from on high and not as the fruit of human reasoning or deduction.

In the gospels we also find this same title 'Holy One of God' in a diametrically opposite context, even though also connected with the synagogue at Capernaum. A man possessed of an unclean spirit began shouting when Jesus appeared: 'What have you to do with us, Jesus of Nazareth? Have you come to destroy us? I know who you are, the Holy One of God' (Lk 4:34). This same awareness of Christ's holiness occurs here by way of contrast. Between the unclean spirit and the Holy Spirit which is in Jesus there is a mortal opposition and the demons are the first to feel its effects. They cannot 'endure' Christ's holiness.

The title 'Holy One of God' recurs at various other times in the New Testament, being mentioned in connection with the Holy Spirit which Jesus received at the moment of his conception (cf Lk 1:35), or at his baptism in the Jordan. The Apocalypse called Jesus simply 'the Holy One': 'Thus says the Holy One . . .' (Rev 3:7). We have here a title surviving 'from among the most ancient and rich in significance', one that can therefore help us to discover a little explored aspect of Christ's person and rekindle within us the desire and yearning for holiness.

1. *An absolute holiness*

It may seem odd to devote this first reflection on the dogma of Christ's humanity to a consideration of his holiness, but the reason for this will become clear later when we move on to consider the problem of Christ's humanity in the world of today. For the time being, suffice it for us to note one thing: that the theme of Christ's holiness, or of the absence of all sin in him, is closely connected in the New Testament with that of his humanity in all respects like our own: '. . . who in every respect has been tempted as we are, yet without sinning' (Heb 4:15).

For the holiness of Jesus is mainly presented in the New Testament in its negative aspect of absence of all sin: 'Which of you can convict me of sin?' Jesus asks his opponents (Jn 8:46). On this point we have a unanimous chorus of apostolic testimony: 'He knew no sin' (2 Cor 5:21); 'He committed no sin; no guilt was found on his lips' (1 Pet 2:22); 'He was in every respect tempted as we are, yet without sinning' (Heb 4:15); 'It was fitting that we should have such a high priest, holy, blameless, unstained, separated from sinners' (Heb 7:26). John in his First Letter never wearies of proclaiming: 'He is pure . . . in him there is no sin . . . he is righteous' (1 Jn 3:3–7).

At this unanimous affirmation of the absolute absence of any sin in the man Jesus of Nazareth, two questions arise: first, what was the source of the *knowledge* the apostles had of the absence of all sin in Jesus, seeing that all the relevant affirmations on this subject can be traced back to them; and secondly, what was the cause of the *fact* of the absence of all sin in Jesus, that is to say, how could Jesus, who was indeed a human being like others, be exempt from all sin?

Traditional theology, both ancient and mediaeval, completely ignored the first of these problems, which is a

8

typically modern, historical and hermeneutic one, and forthwith examined the second question which is of the ontological order. It forthwith sought, as was natural to the culture of the age, the *basis* or principle of the thing, without being too concerned about its *development*. The Fathers always derived the sinlessness of Christ from the hypostatic union, or — as in the case of a few belonging to the Antiochene school — from the moral union which existed, in Jesus, between God and the human race. Since the sinner is not the nature but the person, which in Jesus is represented by the divine person of the Word, to say that he could have sinned is like saying that God himself could sin, which is the absurdity of absurdities.

This is how Origen for instance explains the impeccability of Jesus: 'To all the saints some warmth from the Word of God must be supposed to have passed; and in this soul [Christ's soul] the divine fire itself must be believed to have rested, from which some warmth may have passed to others. Lastly, the expression, "God, your God, has anointed you with the oil of gladness above your fellows" (Ps 45:7) shows that that soul is anointed in one way with the oil of gladness, i.e., with the Word of God and wisdom; and his fellows, i.e., the holy prophets and apostles in another. For they are said to have "run in the odour of his ointments"; and that soul was the vessel which contained that very ointment of whose fragrance all the worthy prophets and apostles were made partakers. As then, the substance of an ointment is one thing and its odour another, so also Christ is one thing and his fellows another. And as the vessel itself, which contains the substance of the ointment, can by no means admit any foul smell; whereas it is possible that those who enjoy its odour may, if they remove a little way from its fragrance, receive any foul odour which comes upon them. So, in the same way, was it impossible that Christ, being as it were the vessel itself in which was the substance of the ointment, should receive an odour of an opposite kind, while they who are his "fellows" will be partakers and receivers of his odour in proportion to their nearness to the vessel.'[1]

Jesus is thus impeccable from this point of view, since his soul is substantially (later the term will be *hypostatically*) united to the very fountain of holiness, which is the Word.

Recent theology known as *kerygmatic* has in a certain sense taken an opposite path. Disregarding the ontological problem — that is to say, the derivation of absence of sin in Christ — it has raised the critical question, that is to say, of where the apostles derived their *knowledge* or certainty of this absence of sin. The answer given is: the resurrection! The certainty of the absence of all sin in Christ is not derived from direct observation of his life. The life or behaviour of Jesus, as others saw it, was ambiguous, that is to say, subject to differing evaluations. He could be taken for the greatest blasphemer and sinner or contrariwise for the greatest saint and quintessentially righteous human being. It was only with the resurrection, as St Paul said while addressing the Areopagus, that God had given 'a sure proof' about Jesus (cf Acts 17:31). Jesus 'was justified in the Spirit' by means of the resurrection, that is to say, he was proclaimed as righteous (cf 1 Tim 3:16). The resurrection was the moment in which the Holy Spirit convinced the world 'of the righteousness' of Christ (cf Jn 16:10). Without this judgement on God's part, all possibility for the apostles or for us to have known would have been precluded. The impeccability of Christ therefore does not derive from an *a priori* but from an *a posteriori*, not from that which is at the beginning of his existence — the hypostatic union — but from that which is at the end: the resurrection.

All this undoubtedly constitutes an advance. Even so, the recent, kerygmatic perspective does not contradict, nor does it render useless or out-of-date, the traditional perspective of the Fathers and general councils (as people sometimes tend to give the impression), but merely completes it and is completed by it. The two thus exist in tandem. In the resurrection Jesus was manifested and recognized as sinless; as, also in the resurrection, he was manifested as 'Son of God with power' (cf Rom 1:4). But perhaps the fact that in the resurrection Jesus was manifested as 'Son of God with power' excludes the fact that he was Son of God even before that moment? The resurrection brought the reality to light, it did not create it out of nothing; to say the contrary would be to relapse into the adoptionist heresy. The same goes for his impeccability. This existed in Jesus' life, even if, just suppose for a moment, no one had perceived it. So the

Fathers are not begging the question when they investigate the basis of this impeccability and find it in the union, operated in him, of the human and divine natures.

So what we should do is not repudiate the traditional, ontological explanation for the modern, kerygmatic one nor, vice-versa, repudiate the fruitful modern explanation to cling exclusively to the ancient one. Rather, what we should do is to make a synthesis between the two. This safeguards the principle of Tradition, which is that of progressive enrichment, whereas the opposite destroys it by replacing the principle of Tradition with that of substitution. We have two sources of light from opposite directions for discovering the holiness of Jesus: the resurrection and the incarnation. The resurrection permits us to affirm that in Christ *was no sin*; the hypostatic union permits us to affirm that in Christ *could be no sin*. The one is the basis for Christ's sinlessness; the other, for his impeccability, which is something more. We should make use of both these sources of light. Taken in isolation, each of the two perspectives has the grave disadvantage of reducing the real holiness of the Jesus of the gospels to virtual irrelevance, whereas this is the most important thing for us to imitate.

To base Christ's holiness one-sidedly on his resurrection can also involve a danger: that of conceiving, tacitly, of Christ's resurrection — in the light of the Lutheran concept of justification — as an imputation of righteousness from outside; as a declaration of righteousness by God's sovereign judgement, regardless of whether or not righteousness and holiness exist in the person concerned. The innocence or absence of sin in Christ would in this case consist in the judgement that God gives on the matter by raising Christ from the dead. 'Thus the righteousness of Jesus,' we read in one of these authors, 'was sited outside himself, in the Father's hands, in the judgement of God.'[2] Certainly it is admitted that 'Jesus was indeed in himself without sin', but this does not seem to count for much; whereas for the New Testament writers this was so important that they constantly revert to it.

2. A holiness lived

So we should not be afraid, even in the theological context of today, of turning again to the gospels to contemplate Christ's holiness in them, even if it was an insight acquired by the apostles only after the Lord's Passover.

An examination of the gospels immediately shows us that Jesus' holiness is no mere abstract principle or metaphysical deduction but a real holiness, lived minute by minute in the most concrete situations of life. The Beatitudes, to take a single example, are not just a beautiful code of life outlined for other people by Jesus; it is his own life and his own experience that he is revealing to the disciples, summoning them to enter into his own sphere of holiness. He teaches what he does; hence he can say: 'Learn from me, for I am gentle and lowly in heart' (Mt 11:29). He tells us to forgive our enemies, nor does he himself hesitate to forgive those who are crucifying him, with the words: 'Father, forgive them, for they know not what they do' (Lk 23:34).

It is not however this or that episode lending itself to illustrate Jesus' holiness, but every action, every word that issues from his mouth. 'Never,' writes Kierkegaard, 'was deceit found on his lips (cf 1 Pet 2:22) but everything in him was truth. There was not the distance of a moment of a feeling, of an intention, between his love and the law's demand for its fulfilment. He did not say "No" as the one brother did; neither did he say "Yes" as the other brother, for his good was to do his Father's will. Thus he was one with the Father, one with every single demand of the law, so that fulfilling it was a need, his only life-necessity. Love in him was pure action. There was not a moment, not a single one in his life, when love in him was merely the inactivity of feeling, which hunts for words while it lets time slip by, or a mood which is self-satisfying, dwelling on itself with no task to perform. No, his love was pure action. Even when he wept, this was not passing time, for Jerusalem did not know what was needed for preserving peace. If those sorrowing at Lazarus' grave did not know what was going to happen, he knew what he would do. His love was completely present in the least things as in the greatest; it

12

did not gather its strength in single great moments as if the hours of everyday life were outside the requirements of the law. It was equally present at every moment, no greater when he breathed his last on the cross at Calvary than when he suffered himself to be born in the Bethlehem cattle-shed.'[3]

This passage illuminates Jesus' perfection, considered from the stand-point of love. The history of Christian spirituality contains examples of every sort of holiness and perfection, all of which are to be attributed in the highest degree to Christ, since they derive from him. One of them is the ideal of sobriety and purity of heart, privately practised in Orthodox monasticism. It consists in ridding the mind, little by little, by means of a fearsome and very delicate inner struggle, of every kind of useless or extraneous thought, so as to leave it with yearning for God and prayer as its sole activity. This sublime state was lived by Jesus throughout his life. He indeed could say that his breath and bread were to do the Father's will.

Christ's holiness represents the infinite in the ethical order and this is no less great and important than the infinite in the metaphysical order. So too, in considering this moral infinite or infinite perfection, mind fails us and we founder. Not one sin, never an instant of separation from the Father's will, never a pause in willing and doing good! 'I *always* do what is pleasing to him' (Jn 8:29).

Christ's holiness results, as is plain, from two elements: one negative, which is the absolute lack of all sin, and one positive, which is the constant and absolute adhesion to the Father's will. In Jesus there was perfect coincidence between *being, ought to be* and *can be*. Thus, he not only did during his life what he *ought to do* but also everything he *could do*, which in his case is infinitely more. His yardstick was not a law, but love.

Today we are in a position to recognise a new aspect of Christ's holiness from which the Fathers were precluded, thanks to certain conditioning due to the culture of their day, as also to their preoccupation with not encouraging the Arian heresy. Basing the holiness of Christ on the hypostatic union, or on the incarnation, they were obliged to attribute to Jesus an essential, and immutable holiness existing in him from the beginning of his life which the passing of the years could at most manifest but not increase. The Holy Spirit received by Jesus at his baptism in the Jordan was not, according to them, destined to sanctify Christ's humanity but ours. 'The descent of the Holy Spirit on Jesus in the Jordan,' says St Athanasius, 'concerns us, for he bore our body; it does not occur for the perfecting of the Word but for sanctifying us.'[4] To admit that the Christ could be perfectible was dangerous at that moment, since the Arians would have instantly concluded that the Word too was perfectible and, if he was perfectible, then he was not truly God.

We are no longer conditioned like this today. Hence we are in a position to recognize a twofold holiness in Jesus' life: an *objective holiness*, whether of personal character, deriving from the hypostatic union, or of ministerial character (that is to say, bound to his messianic office), deriving from the unction of his baptism, and a *subjective holiness*, willed and achieved by him with the passing of time, by his perfect agreement to the Father's will. Jesus is he 'whom the Father has sanctified and sent into the world' (Jn 10:36) but is also he who sanctifies himself (cf Jn 17:19), that is to say, spontaneously offers himself to the Father's will.

Jesus grew in holiness as he grew 'in wisdom and stature' (Lk 2:52). Not that his response to the demands of God's will at such and such a moment was imperfect, but that it was perfect for that moment, in accordance with what the Father asked of him and he was able to give, at that state of development of his human personality and vocation which he had then reached. To think that Christ's holiness was the same before and after the great and awesome '*fiat*' of Gethsemane would be to empty his life and even his paschal mystery of significance. Jesus first lived what we call the 'reaching towards holiness'. Of this tension we have many revelatory signs, as when one day he exclaimed: 'I have a baptism to be baptized with, and how I am constrained until it is accomplished!' (Lk 12:50).

In the gospels we also discover another important thing about Jesus' holiness and that is his own *knowledge* or awareness of being without sin, of always doing the Father's will. Jesus' conscience is a transparent crystal. Never even the slightest admission of guilt, or apology or request for forgiveness, either in his dealings with God or with other people. Always the calm *certainty* of being in the truth and in the right, of having acted well; which is something altogether different from a human assumption of always being right. This absence of guilt and of admission of guilt is not bound up with this or that gospel passage or saying, the historicity of which might be held in doubt, but exudes from the entire gospel. It is a life-style reflected in everything. We may rummage through the obscurest recesses of the gospel but the result is always the same. This is a sign of the all-divine, a sign that this man is no mere man, however exalted. The notion of an exceptionally holy and exemplary human being is not sufficient to explain all this. In fact it would rather belie it. Such assurance, such exclusion of sin as we see in Jesus of Nazareth would indicate an exceptional human being, yes, but exceptional in its pride, not in its holiness. An awareness so constituted is either in itself the greatest sin ever committed, greater even than Lucifer's, or is contrariwise the simple truth. Christ's resurrection shows that it was the simple truth.

Jesus' awareness of being without sin is easier to explain than his awareness of being the Son of God. Guilt indeed, when it exists, manifests itself in the form of a sense of guilt and remorse. There is a phenomenology of sin which comes within our observation. As a human being, Jesus could not have the awareness of being the only-begotten Son of the Father or, if he did, we cannot explain how this came about, since it involves a leap from one nature to the other. But as a human being, he could very well be aware of being without guilt, since this belongs within the sphere of that same human nature. It was this awareness of being without guilt that John wished to affirm by putting into Jesus' mouth those incredible words that we have already quoted: 'Which of you can convict me of sin?' (Jn 8:46).

3. *'Tu solus Sanctus'*

The Church invites us to contemplate Christ's holiness when, turning to him in prayer in the *Gloria*, she exclaims:

15

'*Tu solus Sanctus!*' You alone are Holy. 'Alone' means, not in the bosom of the Trinity, but in the bosom of humanity. You alone are the totally and completely holy human being, the true 'Holy of Holies' (cf Dan 9:24). It is precisely because of his holiness that Jesus constitutes the absolute apex of all reality and history.

Pascal formulated the famous principle of the three orders, or planes of reality: the order of bodies or matter; the order of the mind or the intellect; and the order of holiness. An infinite distance, qualitatively speaking, separates the order of the intellect from that of matter; but an 'infinitely more infinite' distance separates the order of holiness from that of the intellect, since the former is supernatural. The geniuses who belong to the order of the intellect have no need of carnal and material grandeurs; for these can add nothing to them. Likewise the saints, who belong to the order of charity, 'need no worldly or intellectual eminence, for these neither increase nor diminish their stature. They are seen by God and the angels, and not by bodies or inquisitive minds; God is sufficient for them.' Likewise the Holy of holies, Jesus Christ. 'Jesus Christ, without riches and without any external display of knowledge, occupies his own rank of holiness. He never invented anything. He was never a ruler; but he was humble, patient, holy, holy to God, terrible to the demons, without a trace of sin . . . It would have been useless for our Lord Jesus Christ to come as a king, in order to shine in the kingdom of his holiness; but he came with the kind of glory that befitted his rank.'[5]

Jesus is not only the culmination of the order of holiness, he is also its source, since from him, as we shall see later, historically derives all the holiness of the saints and of the Church. Christ's holiness is the reflection of God's own holiness, his visible manifestation, his image. To Christ, the Fathers attribute the title 'image of God's goodness' (Wis 7:26), given to wisdom.[6] That which the Letter to the Hebrews says of Christ with reference to the glory and substance of the Father will also be said with reference to his holiness: 'This Son reflects the glory of God and bears the very stamp of his nature' (Heb 1:3). That same exclamation '*Tu solus Sanctus*' which the Church addresses to Christ

16

is that which in the Apocalypse is addressed to God: 'Who shall not fear and glorify thy name, O Lord? For thou alone art holy' (Rev 15:4).

'Holy', *Qadosh*, is the most numinous title attributed to God in the Bible. Nothing succeeds in giving us so strong a sense of God as the nearness and perception of his holiness. The strongest impression the prophet Isaiah retained of his vision of God was of his holiness, proclaimed by the Seraphim in the words: 'Holy, holy, holy is the Lord of hosts' (Is 6:3). In Jesus' experiences too something similar occurred.

The biblical word *qadosh* suggests the idea of separation, of being different. God is holy because he is the 'Totally Other' as far as everything human beings can think or do is concerned. He is the Absolute, in the original sense of *ab-solutus*, that is to say, loosed from all the rest and apart. He is the Transcendent One, in the sense that he is beyond all our categories. But all this is to be understood in not so much a metaphysical as a moral sense, concerning, that is to say, not only the being but still more the actions of God. In the Bible, God's judgements, his works and his ways above all are called holy or right (cf Deut 32:4; Dan 3:27; Rev 16:17). Holy however is not a primarily negative concept indicating separateness or absence of evil and alloy in God; it is positive in the highest degree. It indicates a 'pure fulness'. In us, 'fulness' never totally accords with 'purity'. The one contradicts the other. Our purity is always obtained 'by means of taking away', that is to say, by purifying ourselves, by ridding our activities of evil. In God and in the man Jesus of Nazareth, not so. Fulness and purity co-exist there and constitute the complete 'simplicity' and holiness of God. The Bible expresses this concept to perfection, by saying that to God 'nothing can be added and nothing taken away' (Sir 42:22). In that he is total purity, nothing *needs* to be taken away from him; in that he is complete fulness, nothing *can* be added to him.

In this sense, the holiness of Christ, as pure fulness, coincides with the *beauty* of Christ. To contemplate the holiness of Jesus is at the same time to contemplate his ineffable beauty. Certain Orthodox icons of Christ as Lord and *Pantocrator*, as for example the one by Rublev, seem

17

to give plastic expression to the concept of the God who is 'majestic in holiness' (cf Ex 15:11).

In the gospels we often find awareness of the goodness and holiness of Jesus expressed by means of the concept of beauty. 'He has done all things beautifully (*kalòs*)', the crowds say of him (cf Mk 7:37). Jesus even describes himself as 'the beautiful (*kalòs*) Shepherd' and says that he has shown his contemporaries many beautiful works (*kalà*) (cf Jn 10:11, 32). Peter exclaims on Mount Tabor, 'Lord, it is beautiful (*kalòn*) that we are here' (Mt 17:4). In the Bible, everything pertaining to God is beautiful, just as it is holy. St Gregory of Nyssa writes: 'Outside you, nothing seems beautiful to me, for you are the only truly beautiful. And not only beautiful but the very eternal and personal essence of beauty.'[7] Dostoevsky, who in one of his characters had tried to portray the ideal of a beauty made of goodness without however entirely succeeding, wrote in a letter more or less excusing himself: 'In the world there only exists one absolutely beautiful being, the Christ, but the appearing of this infinitely beautiful being is assuredly an infinite miracle.'[8] The Church too gives voice to this sensation of beauty experienced in the presence of Christ, by applying to him the Psalmist's exclamation: 'You are the fairest of the sons of men' (Ps 45:37).

4. *'Sanctified in Christ Jesus'*

Let us now move on to see what Christ's holiness means for us and requires of us. Let us move, in other words, from the kerygma to the paraenesis, from the *fact* to the *act*. But first, a piece of good news. There is indeed good news and glad tidings in connection with the holiness of Christ; and this good news, which we shall now try to take in, is not so much that Jesus is the Holy One of God, or the fact that we too ought to be holy and spotless, but that Jesus communicates, gives, presents his holiness to us; that his own holiness is also ours; that he himself is our holiness. For is it not written that he has become our *wisdom, sanctification and redemption* (1 Cor 1:30)?

Every human father can pass on what he has to his

children, but not what he is. He may be an artist, a scientist or even a saint, but there is no saying that his children will themselves be born artists, scientists or saints. He can do his best to make them love these things, can teach them about them, but he cannot pass them on, as it were, by way of inheritance. Jesus, contrariwise, in baptism not only passes on to us what he has, but also what he is. He is holy and makes us holy; he is the Son of God and makes us children of God.

Having contemplated the holiness and impeccability of Christ, it now remains for us to appropriate or make ours this marvellous holiness of his; to put it on and likewise clothe ourselves 'in the robe of righteousness' (cf Is 6:10). It has been written that 'what is of Christ is more ours than what is of us.'[9] Since in fact we belong to Christ more than to ourselves (cf 1 Cor 6:19–20), so, reciprocally, Christ belongs to us more, and more intimately, than we to ourselves. We understand therefore why St Paul wanted to be found, not with his own personal righteousness or holiness derived from observance of the law, but with the holiness or righteousness derived from faith in Christ, that is to say, with the holiness that is derived from God (cf Phil 3:9). He considered his holiness not his own, but Christ's!

In other words, we have reached the doctrine of the grace of Christ, which distinguishes the Christian faith from any other faith and religion known. According to it, Christ is not merely a sublime model of holiness for us, or just a 'Teacher of righteousness', but is something infinitely more. He is the cause and form of our holiness. To grasp the originality of this vision, a comparison with other religions can be helpful, for instance with what happens in Buddhism. Buddhist liberation is individual and incommunicable. The disciple has no model available to be the object of mystical or salvific imitation. The disciple has no grace but must find salvation from within. Buddha provides a doctrine but in no way assists the adept to put it into effect. In contrast, Jesus says: 'If the Son makes you free, you will be free indeed' (Jn 8:36). There is no self-liberation for Christians. If they are *free*, it is because they are *set free* by Christ.

To say that we share in Christ's holiness is as much as to say we share in the Holy Spirit who comes from him.

19

To be or to live 'in Christ Jesus' is the equivalent, for St Paul, of being or living 'in the Holy Spirit'. 'By this,' St John writes in his turn, 'we know that we abide in him and he in us, because he has given us of his own Spirit' (1 Jn 4:13). Christ abides in us and we abide in Christ, thanks to the Holy Spirit. And the Holy Spirit it is therefore who sanctifies us. Not the Holy Spirit as such, but the Holy Spirit who was in Jesus of Nazareth and sanctified his human nature, who was enclosed in Jesus as in an alabaster vessel that at Pentecost he poured out on the Church. Hence the holiness that is in us is not a second and different holiness, though operated by the same Spirit, but is the same holiness as Christ's. We are truly 'sanctified in Christ Jesus' (1 Cor 1:2). As, in baptism, the human body is immersed and washed in the water, so the soul is, so to speak, baptized in the holiness of Christ: 'You were washed, you were sanctified, you were justified in the name of the Lord Jesus Christ and in the Spirit of our God', says the Apostle, referring to baptism (1 Cor 6:11).

Two means in particular are available for us to appropriate Christ's holiness to ourselves: faith and the sacraments. *Faith* is the only possibility we have of entering into contact with Christ. 'Who believes in Christ,' says St Augustine, 'touches Christ.'[10] If we wonder how the experience of God, undergone by a man who lived two thousand years ago at a certain point in time and space, can overcome time and space and so communicate itself to other individuals as to become their own experience and their own holiness, the answer is: by faith. On the part of Christ, who communicates this holiness, this is made possible by the fact that he, being God and man at once, is the mediator; that the salvation operated by him came about within the human sphere; that it had been thought about and willed for all people and therefore that is was *destined* for them and hence, in a sense, theirs by right. But from the point of view of the recipient to whom such holiness is communicated, human beings that is to say, it is made possible only by faith. By faith, St Paul says, Christ dwells in our hearts (cf Eph 3:17). So too, without faith, the sacraments are valid but inefficacious; effected but ineffective.

The second means by which we can appropriate Christ's holiness lies in the *sacraments*, particularly the Eucharist. In the Eucharist we not only enter into contact — as in listening to the Word — with this or that virtue or teaching of Christ, but with the very 'Holy One of God'. In the Eucharist, 'Christ pours into us and fuses with us, changing us and transforming us into himself, like a drop of water in an infinite ocean of scented ointment. These are the effects this ointment can produce in those who encounter it: not merely does it make them sweet-smelling, not only does it make them exhale that scent, but it transforms their very substance into the scent of that ointment and we ourselves become the sweet odour of Christ.'[11]

5. *'Called to be saints'*

So far we have done two things in considering the holiness of Christ: we have first contemplated it and next appropriated it. There yet remains a third thing to do, without which there is the risk of everything being left as it were suspended fruitless in the void; and that is to imitate it. By doing this, we avoid going over from exegesis to ascesis, from theology to pious consideration. This is the mistake that has brought theology to a falsely neutral, falsely scientific approach, as a result of which theological studies of a certain type often dry up rather than increase the faith and piety of the young. As far as the New Testament is concerned, any consideration about Christ not ending in an *appeal*, with a 'therefore', is inconceivable. 'I appeal to you *therefore*, brethren, to present your lives as a living sacrifice, holy and acceptable to God': this is how St Paul concludes his exposition of the mystery of Christ in the Letter to the Romans (Rom 12:1). It has been rightly said that 'from the Christian point of view everything, absolutely everything, should serve for edification. The sort of learning which is not in the last resort edifying is precisely for that reason unchristian.'[12] That is not to say that the edifying dimension should always be present in the same mode and in the same degree of explicitness, but it is certainly necessary that it should be visible as though in transparency and that, on occasion, it should be manifest.

After the *contemplation* of Christ's holiness and its *appropriation* by means of faith, we turn to its *imitation*. But what can we still be lacking if we have already been 'sanctified in Christ Jesus'? We shall find the answer by reading what St Paul says next: 'To those sanctified in Christ Jesus, called to be saints together with all those who in every place call on the name of our Lord Jesus Christ' (1 Cor 1:2). The believers are 'sanctified in Christ Jesus' and at the same time are 'called to be saints'. Sanctified and sanctifying. Directly after the good news that we are holy, that Christ's holiness is ours, there follows forthwith the summons to become saints: 'As he who called you is holy, be holy yourselves in all your conduct, since it is written, "You shall be holy, for I am holy" ' (1 Pet 1:15–16).

We have seen, in his life too, Jesus was sanctified ('he whom the Father sanctified and sent into the world') and sanctified himself ('for their sake I sanctify myself'). In Jesus too there was a given holiness and an acquired holiness. And thus the grand horizon of the imitation of Christ opens up before us. For, it has been said, 'the Middle Ages went further and further astray in stressing the aspect that Christ was the model. Then came Luther and stressed the other aspect, that Christ is a gift which must be received through faith.'[13] But the author who noted this down then added, he too being a Protestant, that 'in our times it is obvious that the aspect of Christ which must be stressed is that he is the model', since the doctrine on faith is little more than a fig-leaf concealing more unchristian omissions.[14]

We have a splendid treatment of this by the Second Vatican Council, where it speaks of the universal summons to holiness addressed to the baptized. The Council too based the call to holiness of all Christians on the holiness of Jesus, who is 'the Holy One of God'. Having run over the biblical texts that treat of the holiness of Christ and of the Church made holy by him, the conciliar text goes on to say: 'Therefore in the Church, everyone belonging to the hierarchy, or being cared for by it, is called to holiness, according to the saying of the Apostle: "For this is the will of God, your sanctification" ' (1 Thess 4:3).[15] This is not a question of a new holiness to be added to that received from

Christ, by means of faith and the sacraments, but of maintaining, developing and manifesting in our lives that same holiness received from Christ: 'Then,' the Council text goes on, 'by God's gifts they must hold on to and complete in their lives this holiness which they have received.'[16] Christ's holiness is refracted in as many thousand different colours as there are saints in the Church, no Christian saint being the same as another; yet all is the product of one single light. 'For no one has holiness of himself; it is not the consequence of human virtue, but comes to all from [Christ] and through him; it is as if we were to place mirrors beneath the sun: each would shine and send forth rays of light, so that one would think there were many suns; yet in truth there is but one sun, which shines in all.'[17]

This summons to holiness is the Council's most needed and most urgent achievement. Without it, all other achievements are either impossible or useless; yet it is the one most in danger of being disregarded since there is only God and conscience to require it and demand it, and not (as in other matters) particular pressure groups and competing interests within the Church at human level. Sometimes one gets the feeling that in certain environments and in certain religious families since the Council, more effort has been put into 'making saints' than into 'making themselves saints', that is to say, into raising their founders or fellow-religious to the altars rather than into imitating their virtuous examples.

6. Setting out again towards holiness

Our reaching out towards holiness is very much like the progress of the Chosen People through the desert, on their way to the Promised Land. It too is a journey made up of endless stops and fresh starts. Every so often the people halted in the desert and pitched their tents, whether because they were tired, or because they had found water and food, or because they felt like doing so. But then, without warning, comes the Lord's command to fold their tents and hit the road once more: 'Up, leave here, you and the people, for the land I have promised', God tells Moses, and the whole community, we read, would strike camp and resume the march (cf Ex 15:22; 17:1).

In the life of the Church, these periodic departures and stages on the road are represented by the beginning of a new liturgical year or of a significant season of the year, such as Advent or Lent. For each of us, taken individually, the time to dismantle our tent and take the road once more is when we become aware, deep within us, of the mysterious summons that comes to us from grace. This is not some desire that may arise 'from flesh and blood', but only from the Father who is in heaven. We are talking of a blissful moment, of an ineffable encounter between God and creature, between grace and free-will, which is to have positive and negative reverberations for all eternity. First, there is a moment when you pause. You stop, in your normal whirl of activity or in the daily round of duties; you step aside for a while. You stand back, as we say, to take stock of your life as though from outside or from above, to see how things are going. This is the moment of truth, of those fundamental questions: 'Why am I? Where have I come from? Where am I going? What do I want?'

It is related that St Bernard too, every once in a while, would stop and, as though beginning a conversation with himself, would ask: '*Bernarde, ad quid venisti?*' Bernard, why have you entered religion and monastic life?[18] And we should do the same. Address ourselves by name (since that is a help) and ask ourselves: '*Ad quid venisti?*' Why are you where you are and doing the work you are doing? Is it in order to do God's will and make yourself holy, or not? And if it is to make yourself holy, are you succeeding? It has been very truly said: there is only one really irreparable misfortune in life and that is not to be holy.

In the New Testament, a type of conversion is described which might be classified as a conversion-awakening, or conversion from tepidity. It occurs in the Apocalypse. There we read seven letters written to the angels (some people would interpret these as 'bishops') of the seven Churches of Asia Minor. The letters are all constructed to a common plan. The speaker is the Risen Christ, the Holy One. In the letter to the angel of Ephesus, he opens by acknowledging the good that the recipient has done: 'I know your works,

24

your toil and your patient endurance. . . You are enduring patiently and bearing up for my name's sake, and you have not grown weary.' Then he passes on to state what by way of contrast he find displeasing in him: 'You have abandoned the love you had at first!' And at this point, there rings out, like a trumpet blast at dead of night when all are sleeping, the shout of the Risen One: *Metanòeson*, that is to say, repent! Rouse up! Awake! (Rev 2:1f).

So much for the first of the seven letters. We know how much severer the last of the seven sounds, the one addressed to the angel of the Church of Laodicea: 'I know your works; you are neither cold nor hot. Would that you were cold or hot!' Repent and be zealous and fervent once more: *Zeleue oun kai metanòeson!* (Rev 3:15f). This letter too, like all the others, ends with the mysterious warning: 'He who has an ear, let him hear what the Spirit says to the Churches' (Rev 3:22). The context leaves us in no doubt over what the Spirit is saying to the Churches. He is saying: Repent, wake up!

So what is to be done? St Augustine offers us one suggestion: to begin by arousing the desire: 'The whole life of a good Christian is an holy desire (or, a desire for holiness): *Tota vita christiani boni, sanctum desiderium est.* By longing, thou art made capable, so that when that is come which thou mayest see, thou shalt be filled. God, by deferring our hope, stretches our desire; by the desiring stretches the mind; by stretching it makes it more capacious. Let us desire, therefore, my brethren, for we shall be filled.'[19] We shall not make ourselves holy unless we have a great desire to become so. Nothing great is achieved without desire. Desire is the wind that swells the sails and drives the ship along; it is the motor of the spiritual life.

But who can have the desire for holiness unless the Holy Spirit imparts it? This is why St Bonaventure concludes his *Itinerary of the mind to God* with these inspired words: 'This mysterious wisdom is hidden, no one knows it who has not received it, no one receives it who has not desired it, and no one desires it unless already inflamed within by the Holy Spirit sent by Christ.'[20]

25

NOTES

1 Origen, *De principiis*, II, 6, 6 (PG 11, 214).
2 W. Pannenberg, *Grundzuege der Christologie*, Guetersloh 1964, pp. 377f.
3 S. Kierkegaard, *Works of Love*, Collins, London 1962, pp. 106–107.
4 St Athanasius, *Contra Arianos*, 1, 47 (PG 26, 108).
5 B. Pascal, *Pensées*, Dent, London 1960: entry 585.
6 Cf Origen, *In Ioh. Evang.*, XIII, 36 (PG 14, 461).
7 St Gregory of Nyssa, *In Cant. hom.*, IV (PG 44, 836).
8 F. Dostoevsky, *Letter to a niece, Sonja Ivanova*.
9 N. Cabasilas, *Vita in Christo*, IV, 6 (PG 150, 613).
10 St Augustine, *Sermo* 243, 2 (PL 38, 1133).
11 N. Cabasilas, *Vita in Christo*, IV, 3 (PG 150, 593).
12 S. Kierkegaard, *The Sickness unto Death*, OUP 1941, p. 3.
13 S. Kierkegaard, *The Journals*, X, 1 A, 154 (OUP 1938, entry 889).
14 *Ibidem*.
15 *Lumen Gentium*, n. 39.
16 *Lumen Gentium*, n. 40.
17 N. Cabasilas, *A Commentary on the Divine Liturgy*, 36, SPCK, London 1960, p. 89 (PG 150, 449).
18 Guillaume de Saint-Thierry, *Vita prima*, I, 4 (PL 185, 238).
19 St Augustine, *In Epist. Ioh.*, 4, 6 (PL 35, 2008).
20 St Bonaventure, *Itinerarium mentis in Deum*, VII, 4.

Chapter II

Jesus Christ, the new human being

Faith in the humanity of Christ today

1. *Christ, 'the perfect human being'*

During the earthly life of Jesus and even after the first Easter, no one ever thought of doubting the reality of Christ's humanity, that is to say, the fact that he was truly human like everyone else. After all, his mother, his brothers, his country, his age, his profession: all this was a matter of common knowledge. What was disputed was not his humanity but his divinity. The Jews' accusation was: 'You, being a man, make yourself God' (Jn 10:33). This is why, when speaking of the humanity of Jesus, the New Testament shows more interest in the holiness than in the truth or reality of it.

Less than a hundred years after Jesus' death, the situation has radically altered. Already in St John's letters we learn that there are people who deny that Christ has come 'in the flesh' (cf 1 Jn 4:2–3; 2 Jn 7). One of the major preoccupations of St Ignatius of Antioch, in his letters, was to demonstrate the *truth* of Jesus' humanity and of the actions he performed in the flesh: that he was really born, that he really suffered, that he really died and 'not merely in appearance as some godless and faithless people say.'[1]

In a word, we have reached the heresy of *docetism*, which denies the reality of the incarnation and the truth of Christ's human body. Tertullian sums up the various forms that this heresy took in his time: 'Marcion, to be able to deny Christ's flesh, also denied his birth. Apelles allowed the flesh but denied the birth. Lastly Valentinus allowed the one and the other, both the flesh and birth, only then to explain them in his own idiosyncratic way. For he regards as belonging to the order of appearance (*to dokein*) and not of reality, not only his flesh but also his very conception, gestation, birth from the Virgin and so on.'[2] 'We ought therefore,' he concluded, 'to concentrate on the Lord's humanity, since his divinity is not in question. It is his human nature that is doubted: the reality and quality of that.' For this author, this is of such vital importance to the faith that it makes him exclaim when he is addressing the heretics: 'Spare what is the whole world's only hope (*parce unicae spei totius orbis*)! Why should you try to destroy the necessary scandal of the faith? What is "unworthy" of God is salvation for me.'[3]

In the New Testament, attention was entirely focused on the *newness* of Christ's humanity (on Christ 'the new man' and 'new Adam'); now it is entirely focused on the *truth* or ontological consistency of this. The commonest affirmation in this new context is that Jesus was 'perfect man' (*teleios anthropos*), meaning 'perfect' not in the moral sense of 'holy', of 'without sin' (as in Eph 4:13), but in the metaphysical sense of 'complete' and of really existing.

What has caused such a total change of perspective in so brief a time? Simply the fact that, by this time, the Christian faith is confronting a new cultural horizon and has been obliged to face the challenges and problems pertaining to this new culture, Hellenistic culture that is to say. For many factors contributed to making the tidings of God in the flesh unacceptable in this new culture. First, a *teleological factor*: how can God, who is immutable and impassive, undergo birth, growth and — more astonishingly — the torment of the cross? A *cosmological factor*: matter is the kingdom of an inferior god (the Demiurge) and is incapable of attaining salvation; how then can one attribute a material body to God? An *anthropological factor*: the soul is what constitutes the true human being and it is by nature heavenly and divine; the body (*soma*) is rather the tomb (*sema*) than the companion of the soul; why should the Saviour, coming to free the soul from its prison of matter, himself have had to be entombed in a body? Lastly, a *Christological factor*: how can Christ be the man 'without sin' if he has been in contact with matter, which is of its nature wicked? How could he belong to the world of God, if he belongs to the physical world which is incompatible with it?[4]

The Church was forced, as it were, to conquer her faith in the full humanity of Christ inch by inch. A conquest that was not to end until the seventh century. First, in the struggle against docetism, she established certainty in the reality of Christ's human body and in his human birth from Mary; then, in the struggle against the heresy of Apollinaris of Laodicea, she established certainty also in the existence of a human soul in Christ; finally, in the seventh century in the struggle against the monothelite heresy, she established certainty in the existence in Christ both of a human will and of human freedom. Christ, then, had a body, this body was endowed with a soul, and this soul was free! He was thus truly 'in all things like us'.

These successive gains, except the last which occurred later, were to find a place in the dogmatic definition of Chalcedon. There we read of Christ that he is 'perfect in divinity and perfect in humanity, true God and true man, having a rational soul and a body, consubstantial with the Father as to his divinity and consubstantial with us as to his humanity, *made in all respects like us, except in sin.*'[5]

Thus the dogma of Christ 'true man' came to be formed, remaining in force and unchanged to our own day.

2. *The dogma of Christ 'true man' in the cultural context of today*

So, as a result of the encounter with the culture of the day and because of certain heresies arising from it, all interest in the human Christ shifted from the problem of the *newness* or holiness of his humanity to that of its *truth* or ontological completeness. Everything was focused on the idea of the assumption of a human nature by the Word. The fundamental fact is that Christ assumes or becomes what we are; rather than objecting to our human nature, he takes it as it is. Only thus could there be any possibility of total salvation for human beings. 'Man could not be saved in his totality, had Christ not put on man in his totality.'[6] Christ had to have a body so that our body could be redeemed; he had to have a soul so that our soul could be redeemed and he had

29

to have free-will so that our freedom could be redeemed. In those days the Church was able, from revelation, to draw the antidote needed for the malady of the moment. The sad fact is that today the cultural situation and type of threat to the faith have changed completely, whereas the response has not changed enough. Indeed, if we look carefully, we shall see that all today's problems about the humanity of Christ (at least when it is a matter of defining the actual person of Christ, that is to say, in Christological discussions) continue to revolve round an ancient problem that no longer exists. No one today denies that Christ was a man, as the docetists used to do. Yet we observe a strange and disturbing phenomenon: the 'true' humanity of Christ is affirmed in tacit alternative to his divinity, as a sort of counterweight. There is a kind of general race to see who can go farthest in affirming the 'full' humanity of Jesus of Nazareth. The fact of being fully and integrally human — we read in a contemporary author — entailed not only suffering, anxiety, temptation and doubt for Jesus, but also 'the possibility of error'.[7] An affirmation, this last, absolutely new to Christian tradition.

And so the dogma of Jesus 'true man' has become either a discounted truth not disturbing or worrying to anyone or, worse still, a dangerous truth serving to legitimize rather than oppose secular thinking. Affirming the full humanity of Christ today is like breaking down an open door.

Signs of this tendency are to be seen in the highest levels of theology as well as in those more attuned to the mentality of the general public and mass media. For some writers, all that the adjective 'true' can denote in the expression 'true man' is that more-than-human element in Christ, the excellence or exemplariness of his humanity, which believers call his 'divinity'. Setting out from a secular concept of human nature and stressing his 'true' humanity, they thus arrive at the point where Christ's divinity becomes superfluous or is denied. The modern, secular concept of human nature indeed requires a total and absolute autonomy, in terms of which God and human nature are incompatible and mutually destructive; 'where God is born, man dies.'

Ideas of this sort are to be found in authors trying to

delineate a 'Jesus for atheists'.[8] But even certain attempts at a modern Christology betray an analagous tendency, in another form. Thus, one writer, in affirming the humanity of Christ, goes even further than the Council of Chalcedon itself, attributing to Christ not only a human body, soul and will, but also a human *personality*, with the consequently inevitable necessity of either affirming that he is not God, or of affirming that he is 'two persons', not 'one person'. There is talk in this connection about Christ's 'human transcendence', by which Christ was to transcend history, not as God, but as human being. There is talk too of 'integral Christological humanism'.[9] Insistence on Christ's humanity, as we see, is more than generous.

The same tendency is encountered at the level of the popular mind. The film *The Last Temptation of Christ*, based on the novel by Nikos Kazantzakis (an Orthodox excommunicated by his Church for this), depicts a Jesus who throughout his life is desperately seeking to evade the requirements of the Father's will and who finally, on the cross, is as though hypnotized by images of sin. We are talking of an extreme and clumsy example of this sort of mentality, but indicative enough. In defence of the film it has been said, even by certain theologians: 'If Jesus was truly human, what is there to be shocked about in all this? That's what real people are like.' Someone made the positive comment that, portrayed like that, this Jesus with his doubts, his uncertainties, his moments of rebellion, felt closer to him and his own experience of life. In a sense this is a repeat of what went on in pagan times; not being disposed to reform their vices such as adultery and theft, what did the pagans do? St Augustine asked long ago. In their myths, they attributed these vices to their gods and goddesses, so as to feel themselves excused in committing them.[10] How can human beings be blamed for things that even the gods cannot manage to avoid?

The reason for all this is that today the affirmation of Christ's full humanity falls on a cultural soil which is the exact opposite of that antique one, where the dogma of Christ 'true man' took form. The Fathers lived in a culture characterized by spiritual values and contempt (at least on the theoretical level) for matter; we for our part live

31

in a culture characterized by materialism and the exaltation of matter and the body. What is the challenge, what are the grounds for disagreement, that modern culture offers to the faith, with regard to human nature? It is certainly not the anti-cosmic and manichean prejudice of man as 'stranger to the world', but the principle of the radical worldliness of man. The argument no longer turns so much on the *nature* of man, or on man as entity, as rather on man as *project*. Two notorious declarations penned in this new context crudely illuminate this concept of the 'earthly' man and the human race 'its own master': 'If God exists, man is nothing. God does not exist . . . No more heaven. No more hell. Just the earth, that's all.'[11] 'There is nothing left in heaven, no right, no wrong, nor anyone to give me orders . . . For I am a man and every man must find out his own way.'[12]

What we have today is a sort of docetism in reverse. No longer is matter the 'projection', shadow or illusory image of the divine and spiritual world, as it was in the Platonic view of things, but contrariwise now the divine world has become the projection and image of the historical human race. Now God is seen as the image of man, not man as the image of God. This is the ideology of radical secularism, which is luckily not the only ideology in existence and being followed in today's world, though certainly widespread and dangerous enough. If Tertullian could say: 'Let us be concerned with the Saviour's humanity, for his divinity is undisputed', we today in the new cultural context should be saying: 'We must quickly safeguard Christ's divinity, for his humanity is all too safe already. We must rediscover what Christ has that is different from what we have, for what he has in common with us is all too bland and safe. Alongside Christ the "true" man, we must rediscover Christ the "new" man!'

What is to be done in this new situation affecting Christological dogma? The history of Christian thought, and of biblical revelation too, is full of examples of affirmation, made in response to particular problems of the moment, which were later taken up again and adapted to respond to new and different demands or to counter new and different heresies. It is easy to demonstrate the process with regard, say, to the dogma of the unity of Christ. The formula that speaks of the 'one and identical' Christ (*unus et idem*), worked out by Irenaeus against the Gnostics,[13] was later taken up by Cyril of Alexandria and the Council of Chalcedon in a very different sense, in which the unique and identical subject is the pre-existent person of the Word made flesh. Dogma is an 'open structure' which hence can be applied in ever new contexts while maintaining its own fundamental identity and thus remaining perennially alive and effective. All that is needed is to let it work, by inserting it into the new situation. Of course, dogma will not apply automatically and in the same fashion to all situations successively down the centuries. For this to happen, it has to be brought back, each time, into contact with its basis, which is Scripture.

Dogma has an exemplary value: it invites us today to do what the Fathers did in their day. Of the biblical datum, they took that part which was needed for meeting the need of the moment and for defending that part of the faith which was then under attack, while leaving aside what as yet was not in dispute. Having to defend the fact that Jesus was human, they found it sufficient to take account, as it were, merely of the incarnation, that being the moment when the Word took human form. If at a certain point it was less necessary to affirm that Jesus was human than to explain what his being human involved, it would obviously no longer be sufficient to confine themselves merely to the incarnation, but would be necessary to take the paschal mystery into account as well, not only Christ's birth therefore, but also his life and death.

In this spirit let us once again examine the New Testament on the subject of the Saviour's human nature. We shall see that this does not involve any diminishing of the importance of the dogma of the 'perfect' humanity of Christ defined at Chalcedon, but the discovery of new riches and implications in it.

3. *Jesus, the 'new' human being*

The New Testament, as I have said, is not so much concerned with affirming that Jesus is a 'true' man as that he is the 'new' man. He is described by St Paul as 'the last Adam' (*eschatos*), that is to say 'the definitive human being', of whom the first Adam was a kind of sketch and imperfect realization (cf 1 Cor 15:45f; Rom 5:14). Christ has revealed the new human being, the one 'created after the likeness of God in true righteousness and holiness' (Eph 4:26; cf Col 3:10).

The 'newness' of the new human being does not consist, we see, in some new component which he has extra, in contrast to the previous human being, but consists in holiness. Christ is the new human being because he is the Holy One, the righteous one, a human being in the image of God. Evidently we are talking of a newness not accidental but essential, not merely affecting the human being's behaviour but also his very being. What in point of fact is a human being? For profane thought and Greek thought in particular, it is essentially a *nature*, a being determined basically by what it has by *birth*: 'a rational animal' or however else one may choose to define this nature. But for the Bible, the human being is not only *nature*, but also, in equal measure, *vocation*; the human being is also that which is called-to-become, by the exercise of free-will in obedience to God. The Fathers expressed this by distinguishing, in Genesis 1:26, between the concepts of 'image' and 'likeness'. Human beings are by nature or birth 'in the image' of God, but become 'in his likeness' only during their lives by an effort to be like God, by obedience. By the fact that we exist, we are in God's image, but by the fact that we obey we are also in his likeness, since we desire the things that he desires. 'In obedience,' says one of the ancient Desert Fathers, 'likeness to God is brought about, and not the mere being in his image.'[14]

Incidentally, we might make the point that this way of defining human beings in function of *vocation* rather than of *nature* is shared by contemporary thought, even if in the latter the dimension of *obedience* (essential for the Bible) is no more and that of *freedom* alone remains intact, and although instead of vocation the term now favoured is *project*. ('Project' is the central category under which human existence is treated in M. Heidegger's *Being and Time* and in J. P. Sartre's *L'Etre et le Néant*.) So, this being the case, the most effective answer to the postulates of modern thought does not come so much from insisting on the dogma of Christ 'true man', understood in the ancient sense of 'naturally complete' as from insisting on that of Christ the 'new man', revealer of the definitive project for the human race.

The Word of God does not therefore confine himself to becoming human, as though there existed a model or mould of human nature, already excellent and complete, into which he, so to speak, descends. He also reveals what human nature is; with him, the model itself appears, since he is himself the true and perfect 'image of God' (Col 1:15). We are the ones who are called to become 'conformed to the image which is the Son' (cf Rom 8:29), much more than Jesus is called to become conformed to any image of ours. The Second Vatican Council rightly says: 'The truth is that only in the mystery of the incarnate Word does the mystery of man take on light. For Adam, the first man, was a figure of him who was to come, namely, Christ the Lord. Christ, the final Adam, by the revelation of the mystery of the Father and his love, fully reveals man to man himself.'[15] 'God became man,' the Fathers of the Church loved to repeat, 'so that man might become God.' That axiom, in our own day, we should supplement with this other: God became man, so that man might become human! Fully, genuinely human.

Jesus thus is not only a human being like all other human beings, he is also the human being whom all other human beings should resemble. This 'definitive human being' is also, in a certain sense, the primal human being, if it is true, as the Fathers used to say, that it was in the image of this future human being — in the image of the Image — that Adam was created. 'He made human beings,' writes Irenaeus, 'in the image of God (Gen 1:2). The image of God is the Son of God (Col 1:15), in whose image the human race was created.'[16]

All this constitutes a consistent application of the Pauline affirmation according to which Christ is 'the first-born of all creation' (Col 1:15) and of the Johannine statement about the Word 'through whom all things were made' (cf Jn 1:3). In Christ, human nature has its model, but also its own 'substantial form'. As, in the carving of a statue, the form or project which in thought precedes the execution exerts its control over both material and moulding, so Christ the archetypal human being moulds us and configures us to himself by defining our true nature for us. 'If by some artifice,' Cabasilas writes, 'it were possible with the naked eye to see the mind of the artist, you would see the house, the statue or whatever other work in immaterial form.'[17] Not by some 'artifice' but by divine revelation did John, Paul and the inspired authors 'see' the mind of the Artist, God, and perceive the ideal human being contained immaterially in Christ. It is pleasing to rediscover this patristic vision of the relationship between human beings and Christ, virtually unchanged, in a modern theologian such as Karl Barth, for this demonstrates that it is by no means incompatible with modern modes of thought but merely incompatible with modern unbelief. 'Man,' says Barth, 'is a *human* being in as much as he is one single being with Jesus, has his basis in the divine election and, furthermore, in as much as he is one sole being with Jesus, he is constituted from attentiveness to the Word of God.'[18]

Considered in the light of this, the expression 'except in sin' (*absque peccato*) used of Jesus (cf Heb 4:15) does not convey some exception to the full and definitive human nature of Christ, as though he were in all respects truly human like ourselves, less one thing: sin — as though sin were an essential and natural characteristic of human nature. Far from derogating from the full humanity of Christ, 'except in sin' constitutes the distinguishing feature of his true humanity, since sin is the only true 'superstructure', the only spurious addition to the divine project of human nature. It is surprising how we have reached the point of regarding as most 'human' the very thing that is least human. 'To this point has human perversity arrived,' says St Augustine, 'that he whom lust overcomes is regarded as a man, whereas he who has overcome lust cannot be a man. Those who overcome evil cannot be men, whereas those whom evil overcomes are men indeed!'[19] 'Human' has come to mean rather what we have in common with the beasts than what distinguishes us from them, such as intelligence, will power, conscience, holiness.

So Jesus is 'true man', not *in spite of* being without sin but precisely *because* he is without sin. In the famous dogmatic letter of St Leo the Great which inspired the Chalcedonian definition and constitutes the best commentary on certain passages in it, we read: 'He, true God, was born in an integral and perfect nature as true man, complete with all prerogatives, as well divine as human. In saying 'human' however, we refer to those things which the Creator originally placed in us and which he then came to restore; whereas in the Saviour there was no trace of those things that the Deceiver added and that man deceived accepted. It is not to be thought that he, because he willed to share our weakness, also participated in our guilt. He assumed the condition of a slave, but without the contamination of sin; he thus enriched mankind but did not diminish God.'[20]

From this text we see how, by revitalizing dogma by starting from Scripture and following Tradition in harmony with the mind of the Church, it ceases to be an antique truth incapable of withstanding the assault of modern thought 'like a leaning wall or a tottering fence', but instead becomes a new, energetic truth with 'the power to demolish fortresses by destroying arguments and every proud obstacle to the knowledge of God and taking every thought captive to obey Christ' (cf 2 Cor 10:4–6). Kierkegaard was right in saying that 'the dogmatic terminology of the primitive Church is like an enchanted castle where, locked in slumber, lie the handsomest of princes and the loveliest of princesses. They only need to be aroused, for them to leap to their feet in all their glory.'[21]

The dogma of Christ 'true man' and 'new man' can cause a complete reversal to the way we think. It constrains us to pass from a Christ who is 'measured' by the yardstick of our humanity to a Christ who 'measures' us, from the Christ judged by philosophers and history to the Christ who judges philosophers and history. 'It is not he,' writes the philosopher just quoted, 'that, after letting himself be born, and making his appearance in Judaea, has presented himself for an examination in history; it is he that is the Examiner, his life is the examination, and that not alone for that race and generation, but for the whole race.'[22]

4. *Obedience and newness*

It now remains for us briefly to illuminate one last point: how is the 'new man' revealed in Christ to be recognized and what is the essential characteristic distinguishing him from the 'old man'? For we ought to know this 'new man', since we are summoned to 'put him on'. Once again we have reached the moment when kerygma must yield to paraenesis, when we pass from *contemplating* Christ the 'new' human being to *imitating* his newness.

The difference between the two types of human nature is summed up by St Paul in the antithesis: disobedience — obedience. 'As by one man's disobedience many were made sinners, so by one man's obedience many will be made righteous' (Rom 5:19). This is why I said earlier that to discover that 'Jesus is man' you only have to look at the incarnation, but to discover what sort of man Jesus is you also have to consider the paschal mystery. For in this the new Adam reveals himself as obedient.

The 'new man' is one who does nothing 'on his own authority' or 'for himself' and for his own glory. He is the one whose food is to do the Father's will. He is the one who carries his obedience to the point of death, death on the cross. The 'new man' is the one who lives in total, absolute dependence on God and in this dependence finds his strength, his joy, his freedom. In it, he finds, not his limitations, but the way to overcome them. In a word, in this dependence he finds his 'being'. 'When you have lifted up the Son of man,' Jesus says, 'then you will know that I Am and that I do nothing on my own authority but speak as the Father taught me' (Jn 8:28). 'I Am' because 'I do nothing on my own authority.' The being of Christ is rooted in his submission to the Father. He 'is' because 'he obeys'.

Our being is measured by our degree of dependence on God our creator, until it coincides, at our ultimate apex (which is Jesus Christ) with the absolute Being who is God himself, when even we as human beings can say: 'I Am'. This is what constitutes the true 'affirmation' of human nature, this is the true 'humanism'. Representatives of other kinds of humanism may not accept this affirmation and may therefore rebel against it, but we for our part know it to be the truth. If we are not only nature but vocation too, this is where our vocation is fulfilled — which is to be 'in the image and likeness of God'.

Believers should do two things with regard to this 'new man': proclaim him and put him on, that is to say, live him. In proclaiming him, we have the great Fathers of the Church of the third and fourth centuries for our exemplars: Basil, Gregory Nazianzen, Gregory of Nyssa, Augustine... They were men imbued with the culture of their times; they could say, when speaking of their pagan counterparts: 'Are they Greeks? I'm one too!' But they became converts, they made themselves foolish in the eyes of the learned by embracing the humility of Christ and so became the 'place' in which a new way of thinking could take shape, a new vision of human destiny, the 'crucible' in which Hellenism became christianized and Christianity became, in the best sense, hellenized, that is to say, became 'Greek with the Greeks'. They took up the notion of human nature current in their own culture, saving what was valid in it, as for instance the affirmation that 'we are the offspring of God' (Acts 17:28) and correcting what was erroneous, as for instance the affirmation that 'the flesh cannot be saved'. And that is what we ought to do today, in our own culture which finds no difficulty in admitting the salvation and goodness of matter, though it does find it hard to admit that we are 'God's offspring' created by him. The Fathers indeed actually saved their own culture by forcing it from within to open up to new horizons. They were wise enough to acknowledge the great achievements of the culture of their times, not merely to point out its defects; and this too is how we should behave.

The sensitive nexus in their day was 'wisdom'; today the hot spot is 'freedom'. St Paul said: 'The Greeks seek *wisdom*, but we preach Christ crucified, a folly to the Gentiles, but to those who are called, the power of God and the wisdom of God' (cf 1 Cor 1:22–24). We for our part might say: 'The people of today seek freedom and independence, but we preach Christ obedient unto death, the power of God and the freedom of God!'

All the aberrations current today over Christ's human nature and his presumed struggles and acts of rebellion, as for instance the idea that Christ is not complete unless he has a 'human personality', derive from the fact that people have tacitly accepted the postulates of atheistic humanism, according to which there exists an underground rivalry and incompatibility between God and human autonomy: 'where God is born, man dies.' Rather than destroying arguments advanced against the faith and taking every thought captive to the faith, the faith itself in this way is being taken captive by modern thought.

5. 'If the Son makes you free. . .'

The purpose of proclaiming Christ the man 'without sin' is certainly not to confound the world and our contemporaries; on the contrary, our aim is to infuse trust and hope. Few gospel themes have the liberating force of this one. I well recall how the 'discovery' of Christ's holiness first came to me. In observing my actions and thoughts, I saw clearly that not one of them could be said to be entirely pure and untainted to some degree by my sinful 'ego'. This situation prompted me to try and think of some way of escape, as when St Paul exclaimed: 'Who will deliver me from this body of death?' (Rom 7:24). Then it was that I discovered the Jesus 'without sin' and for the first time understood the immeasurable importance of that incidental 'absque peccato'. The insight poured great peace and truth into my soul; like a shipwrecked mariner, I had something to grip hold of. Sin, I would repeat to myself, is not omnipresent after all and, since not omnipresent, not omnipotent! There has been — and there still is — a point in the universe where sin has begun to retreat, retreat that will ineluctably end with complete elimination. I then felt an impulse to open the Bible in hopes of finding something that would speak to me somehow or other about this sinless Jesus. My eyes came to rest on the passage in St John where Jesus says: 'Truly, truly, I say to you, everyone who commits sin is a slave to sin . . . So, if the Son makes you free from sin, you will be free indeed' (Jn 8:34–36). I grasped that Jesus was not speaking here of ordinary freedom or freedom in the abstract, but of freedom from sin: if the Son sets you free *from sin* you will indeed be free. One day we too shall be free from sin, that is to say free 'indeed', with a freedom that now we cannot even imagine. Commenting on the text of 2 Corinthians 3:17 ('Where the Spirit of the Lord is, there is freedom'), St Augustine reveals the secret of true freedom: 'Where the Spirit of the Lord is,' he says, 'the pleasure of sinning no longer exerts its attraction, and this is freedom; where the Spirit is absent, the pleasure of sinning exerts its attraction, and this is slavery.'[23] The 'Spirit of the Lord' is the Spirit of the Lord Jesus.

Proclaiming Christ the 'new man' includes all this. But even more than to proclaim the 'new man' to the world, we are called, as I have said, 'to put him on' and to live him: 'Put off your old nature which belongs to your former manner of life and is corrupt through deceitful lusts, and be renewed in the spirit of your minds and put on the new nature created after the likeness of God in true righteousness and holiness' (cf Eph 4:22–24).

We for our part cannot imitate Christ in his being God, in working miracles and rising from the dead. On the other hand, we ought not to imitate him as 'true' man, since as man it is rather he who has imitated us. ('People always talk, says God, about the *imitation of Jesus Christ.* I mean, the imitation, the faithful imitation of my son on the part of human beings . . . But in the end it must not be forgotten that my son began with that remarkable imitation of human nature. A remarkably faithful one. And that this was carried to the point of perfect identity. When he so faithfully, so perfectly, put on the mortal lot. When he so faithfully, so perfectly imitated being born. And suffering. And living. And dying.')[24] We *cannot* therefore imitate Jesus as God and we *ought not* to imitate him as 'true man'. But we can and we should imitate Jesus as 'new man', the human being without sin.

Not everyone can proclaim Christ the 'new man' to the world by speech or pen. The Second Vatican Council made a good job of it; John Paul II proclaims him often in his addresses and especially in the encyclical *Redemptor Hominis.* But all of us can live him and bear witness to him in our own lives. St Francis of Assisi had little to say about the 'new man', but all his biographers expressed the same conviction after his death: that with him the 'new man' had come into the world. 'People of every age and either sex ran to see and hear that new man given by heaven to the world.'[25]

Even those of us who are called to proclaim, by our words, Christ the 'new man' to the world of today, know that in the ultimate analysis our words will only be made credible by the way we live our lives and more especially by the way we die. We believers often feel saddened by the blindness and hardheartedness of our contemporaries, exalting as some of them do the absolute independence and autonomy of human nature even above morality, even above God. We stand rightly dismayed when confronted with the enormity and *hubris* of certain declarations, such as those already mentioned. We accept that we cannot do anything, that words do not suffice, that the most authoritative appeals, such as those of Vatican II, fall on deaf ears. And yet, yes, there is something that we can do and that is not to do as they do, not to copy them! Not for us to turn our freedom and independence into a jealously guarded treasure that no one is allowed to touch. An idol. Indeed I see within myself, without needing to look any further, how easy it would be for me to recognize the enormity of those declarations of absolute autonomy, written in the books of the philosophers and put into effect by my contemporaries, and yet conversely not to be aware how often they are present in my own life and how much they influence my decisions. 'Old nature' has an army deployed in defence of its freedom. It is ready to sacrifice almost everything, even health, but not its freedom. 'Anything,' says our old nature, 'but not my freedom!' And yet it is just this that we should 'render' to God, if we wish to imitate Jesus Christ. This is where our return journey to God should begin; this was where we went astray.

We ought therefore to take the invitation to put off our old nature and its lusts very seriously. Putting off our old nature means putting off our own will, and putting on our new nature means embracing God's will. Every time we decide, even in the most trivial matters, to break our 'will of flesh' and deny ourselves, we approach one step nearer to Christ the 'new man'. Of him it is written that he

42

'did not please himself: *Christus non sibi placuit*' (Rom 15:3). This is a sort of general rule for the discerning of spirits. Not to seek and not immediately to do that which, humanly speaking, would please us to do or say. We cannot know in every circumstance what it is God's will that we should do, what God wants or does not want from us; but we do know, conversely, what it is our will *not* to do. This is recognizable by certain infallible signs, known to anyone at all accustomed to self-examination. Let us too learn to repeat, as a kind of ejaculatory prayer whenever we are faced with difficulty or doubt, what Jesus said: 'I seek not my own will but the will of him who sent me' (Jn 5:30); 'I have come down from heaven, not to do my own will, but the will of him who sent me' (Jn 6:38). I am not here in this post, in this situation, to do my own will but God's will! The 'newness' of the new human being is measured, as we have seen, by obedience and conformity to God's will.

NOTES

1 St Ignatius of Antioch, *Ad Trall.*, 9–10.
2 Tertullian, *De carne Christi*, 1, 2f. (CC 2, 873).
3 *Ibidem*, 5, 3 (CC 2, 881).
4 Cf J. Davies, 'The Origins of Docetism' in *Studia Patristica*, VI (TuU, 81), Berlin 1962, pp. 13–15.
5 Denzinger-Schoenmetzer, *Enchiridion Symbolorum*, Herder 1967, n. 391.
6 Origen, *Dialogue with Heraclides*, 7 (SCh 67, p. 71).
7 H. Küng, *On Being a Christian*, Collins, London 1977, p. 449.
8 Cf M. Machovec, *Gesù per gli atei*, Assisi 1973.
9 Cf P. Schoonenberg, *The Christ*, Sheed and Ward, London 1972, pp. 91f.
10 Cf St Augustine, *Confessions* I, 16, 25.
11 J-P. Sartre, *Le Diable et le Bon Dieu*, Gallimard, Paris 1951.
12 J-P. Sartre, *Les Mouches*, Paris 1943, Act III.
13 St Irenaeus, *Adv. Haer.*, III, 16, 8–9.
14 Diadochus of Photice, *Ascetic Discourses*, 4 (SCh 5 bis, pp. 108f).
15 *Gaudium et Spes*, n. 22.
16 St Irenaeus, *Demonstration of the Apostolic Teaching*, 22.
17 Cabasilas, *Vita in Christo*, V, 2 (PG 150, 629).
18 K. Barth, *Church Dogmatics*, III, 2, 170 (Clark, Edinburgh 1960).
19 St Augustine, *Sermo* 9, 12 (CC 41, 131f).
20 St Leo the Great, *Tomus ad Flavianum*, I, 3 (PL 54, 757f).
21 S. Kierkegaard, *The Journals*, II A, 110.

22 S. Kierkegaard, *Training in Christianity*, OUP 1946, p. 37.
23 St Augustine, *De Spiritu et Littera*, 16, 28 (CSEL 60, 181).
24 Ch. Péguy, *Le mystère des Saints Innocents*, in *Oeuvres poétiques*, Paris, p. 692.
25 St Bonaventure, *Legenda Maior*, IV, 5 (*St Francis of Assisi, Writings and Early Biographies*, Chicago 1983, p. 656).

Chapter III

'Do you believe?'

The divinity of Christ in the gospel of John

1. *'Unless you believe that I Am . . .'*

One day I was saying mass in an enclosed monastery. The gospel passage for the day was that page in John where Jesus keeps repeating his 'I Am': 'You will die in your sins unless you believe that I Am . . . When you have lifted up the Son of man, then you will know that I Am . . . Before Abraham was, I Am' (Jn 8:24, 28, 58). The fact that, contrary to all grammatical rule, I Am was written in the lectionary with two capital letters and evidently implied something more mysterious, struck a spark. The words 'exploded' inside me. Yes, I knew that in John's gospel there were a number of examples of *ego eimi*, 'I Am', pronounced by Jesus and that this was an important feature of John's Christology. But this was an inert, unproductive piece of knowledge. I had never found it in the least disturbing. That day however it was quite different. It happened at Easter time and it seemed to me as though the Risen One himself were proclaiming his divine name in the sight of heaven and earth. His 'I Am!' lit up and filled the universe. I felt myself to be infinitely small, like someone from the side-lines accidentally witnessing an unforeseen and extraordinary event or some great spectacle of nature. It was nothing more than an emotion of faith, but one of those experiences which, once over, leave a deep yearning in the heart.

Anxious to know more about Christ's 'I Am', I consulted the modern commentaries on the Fourth Gospel and found them virtually unanimous in seeing an allusion in these words of Jesus to the divine name, as it appears for instance in Isaiah 43:10: 'That you may know and believe me and understand that I Am.' Centuries before this, St Augustine had associated these words of Jesus with the revelation of the divine name in Exodus 3:14 and concluded, 'It seems to me that, by saying, "Unless you believe that I Am", the Lord Jesus Christ had not meant to tell us anything other than this: "Yes, unless you believe that I am God, you will die in your sins." Thanks be to God that he said "unless you believe", and that he did not instead say "unless you understand". If you cannot understand, faith will come to your rescue.'[1]

I have made bold to begin this treatment of the divinity of Christ with this personal memory, since in the compass of the Fourth Gospel truths of this sort find their most throbbing expression in the 'I Am' of Christ.

It may be objected that these are words of John's, later developments of the faith, and that Jesus has nothing to do with them. But this is the very point. They are indeed words of Jesus; certainly of the Risen Jesus, alive and speaking henceforth 'in the Spirit'; but always of Jesus, the same identical Jesus of Nazareth. Today it is the custom to distinguish between the sayings of Jesus in the gospels as 'authentic' or 'unauthentic'. That is to say, between words actually uttered by him during his lifetime and words attributed to him by the apostles after his death. But this is a very ambiguous distinction and not helpful in the case of Christ as it might be in that of an ordinary human author. There is of course no question here of casting doubt on the fully human and historical character of the New Testament writings with their diversity of literary types and 'forms', much less of returning to the old idea of the literal and quasi-mechanical inspiration of Scripture; but rather of knowing whether biblical inspiration still has any meaning for Christians or not: whether, when we say that the Bible is 'the word of God', that 'of God' means something qualitatively different from all other things for us or if it is merely one form of words among others.

Jesus said that the Spirit would bear witness to him (cf Jn 15:26), that he would 'take what is mine' and declare it to the disciples (Jn 16:14); and where should he bear this witness more clearly than in the Scriptures, which are inspired by him?

But there is more to it. Jesus affirmed that he himself

would continue to speak through his Spirit. 'The hour is coming,' he said, 'when I shall no longer speak to you in figures, but tell you plainly of the Father' (Jn 16:25). I, not someone else, shall tell you about the Father! To what future time is Jesus referring in these words? Not to the time of his earthly life, since he is on the eve of dying; not in eternity, where there will be no more need for him to speak any further about the Father. He is referring to the time following his Passover and Pentecost when, through his Spirit, he would guide the disciples into the full truth about his relationship with the Father (cf Jn 16:13), which is when, historically speaking, we know it came about. Certainly, one might say that even the words 'I shall tell you about the Father' have their source in the evangelist himself; but is it not strange that John should already be affirming this: that he believes, that is to say, that after the Passover of the Lord, Jesus was still actively revealing himself and revealing the Father?

2. 'You are bearing witness to yourself'

So it is Jesus himself, in the Fourth Gospel, who in the 'I Am' and in countless other ways proclaims himself to be God. He thus makes explicit a claim which during his earthly life had already been broached, if only implicitly; for the disciples could not have borne the additional weight of a revelation of this order.

But this was a secondary reason. The reason why Jesus reserves the full comprehension of himself until after his Passover — and hence to the testimony of the apostles — is a far more significant one: since his very death and resurrection were the key to understanding who he was. In this sense, the apostolic testimony — that is to say, in practice, the New Testament writings — are an integral part of Christ's self-revelation. In them, Jesus told, by means of his Spirit, what he could not tell in person without first having died and risen again. Before knowing that 'Jesus was God', it was important to know what sort of God Jesus was, and this is only revealed in the cross and resurrection.

So it is not merely the evangelist who proclaims Jesus to

be 'God', but Jesus who proclaims himself as such. But here we come to the great argument which broke out actually during Christ's lifetime: 'You are bearing witness to yourself; your testimony is not true' (Jn 8:13). Jesus replied: 'Even if I do bear witness to myself, my testimony is true, for I know whence I have come and whither I am going' (Jn 8:14). This reply is only apparently absurd and contrary to our own every notion of evidence. 'If a person had perfect knowledge of himself, a knowledge necessarily shared by no one else, then his own testimony would in fact be the only testimony available.'[2] Now this is just the case with Jesus, and only with him. Only he knows where he has come from and where he is going; only he is from heaven, all the other people are from the earth (cf Jn 8:14, 23). Jesus bears witness to himself for the same reason that God, as the Bible says, 'swore by himself, since he had no one greater by whom to swear' (Heb 6:13).

Jesus illustrates this fact by having recourse to the imagery of light: 'I', he says, 'am the light of the world' (Jn 8:12); he was, the evangelist says, 'the true light' (Jn 1:9). Can the light *of* the world receive light *from* the world? Can the sun receive light from a candle? The characteristic of light is to be light in itself, to light everything up without being able to be lit up by anything else. It can only shine, in the hope that there may be eyes open to receive it. 'The real meaning of Jesus's reply is that his claim is self-evidencing. Indeed, a claim to be "the light" could not possibly be substantiated by anything except the shining of the light. It is the purport of the whole Gospel that the work of Christ is self-evidencing. His *erga* are luminous.'[3] John the Baptist? Yes, he bears witness to the light (cf Jn 1:8), though like a little lantern kept burning in expectation of the dawn but disappearing once the sun has risen. And indeed he does disappear, saying: 'He must increase but I must decrease' (Jn 3:30). Only one person can bear witness to Jesus and he does indeed do so: the Father. Continually and in many ways the Father bears witness to Jesus: with the Scriptures that speak of him (cf Jn 5:39), with the words that he gives him to utter and the works that he gives him to perform. But all this presupposes one condition to be efficacious: of having, within, the 'word', or 'the love of the

Father', or of being 'from God', of loving the light and of wanting to do God's will (cf Jn 5:38, 41; 7:17; 8:47). All these different ways of saying the same thing.

All testimony coming from without fades into the void unless it finds something in the heart that is capable of hearing and accepting it. The light may shine for all it is worth but if the eye that ought to receive it shuts against it, it is as though the light never shone at all. In this case, the fact that someone does not see it, is not a sign that the light is not there, but that the party is blind. Jesus can show his divinity, his origin from above; but if the organ that ought to receive this revelation is lacking or not working, no recognition occurs and no faith is generated. Much as when you address a foreigner who does not know the language you are speaking: the words reach his ears but make no sense, remaining mere sounds. Exactly so, in the context where Jesus pronounces that 'I Am' of his, he says, as though struggling against the state of incommunicability which exists between himself and his listeners: 'Why do you not understand what I say? It is because you cannot bear to hear my word' (Jn 8:43).

The answer that emerges is always the same:. some people do not have the word of God within them, and the sign that they do not have this word is precisely the fact that they do not believe (cf Jn 5:38). If they were from God, they would recognize that he was uttering words of God. It is as though a man, coming from a distant land, were to run into people claiming that they come from the same country. But when he addresses them in his native tongue, they cannot understand him. It is a clear sign that they have been lying and that they are not from his own country, since he knows 'where he comes from'.

After the Passover of the Lord, the apostles were to make the same discovery. In response to the incredulity of the Sanhedrin, Peter was to declare: 'We are witnesses to these things, and so is the Holy Spirit whom God has given to these who obey him' (Acts 5:32). Here the apostles call 'Holy Spirit' what Jesus called 'the Word' or 'the love of the Father', but they are clearly talking of the same reality, that is to say, of the inner correspondence that alone makes it possible to accept external testimony, in the days of Jesus and now in those of the apostles. The field of visibility is restricted to the human heart; this is where it is decided who will be a believer and who not.

3. *'How can you believe?'*

But why is there not something within that 'word' or Spirit that will allow everyone to recognize that what Jesus says about himself is true: that he is truly the Son of God? Does God perhaps discriminate and make blind, does he predestine some people to faith and some to unbelief? We know that some thinkers, notably Calvin, have indeed resolved the problem thus. But, if this is so, how can those who do not believe be held responsible, how be condemned by the word of Jesus and the works that he performs? It is true that John himself writes of certain people: 'They could not believe; for Isaiah again said: "He has blinded their eyes and hardened their heart, lest they should see with their eyes and perceive with their heart, and turn for me to heal them" ' (Jn 12:39–40; Is 6:9f). But we know how scriptural texts of this sort are to be interpreted: not in the sense that God himself blinds and hardens, but that he allows the spirit to be blinded and the heart hardened as a result of people's free choices and previous acts of resistance. 'They did not honour him as God,' St Paul says, 'but they became futile in their thinking . . . And since they did not see fit to acknowledge God, God gave them up to a base mind' (cf Rom 1:21, 28). Who it is who really blinds people, St Paul himself tells us where he writes: 'If our gospel is veiled, it is veiled only to those who are perishing. In their case the god of this world has blinded the minds of the unbelievers, to keep them from seeing the light of the gospel of the glory of Christ, who is the likeness of God' (2 Cor 4:3–4). So too St Augustine writes that God 'will not desert if he is not deserted.'[4] True, even so, there is still an element of mystery in the fact that some believe and some do not, and this should strike us with salutary dread. But we should keep our minds on what is our business, not on what is God's business. Of God, we know that he is ever just and right in what he does, and let that be enough for us!

50

With regard to what *is* our business, Jesus himself pointed out the root from which unbelief springs in human beings, that is to say, why the unbeliever 'cannot' believe: 'How can you believe,' he said, 'who receive glory from one another and do not seek the glory that comes from the only God?' (Jn 5:44). On another occasion, just after recalling those words of Isaiah, the evangelist writes: 'Many indeed of the authorities believed in him but for fear of the Pharisees they did not confess it, lest they should be put out of the synagogue; for they loved the praise of men more than the praise of God' (Jn 12:42–43).

Who then is the enemy of faith in the divinity of Christ? Reason? No: sin is and, to be accurate, the sin of pride, the quest for personal glory. Impossible for anyone to believe who is ruled by the desire for personal glory, because in faith there is no human glory, there is no 'originality'. Quite the reverse: to believe, one is obliged to give way, to 'submit to God', as St Peter said (cf Acts 5:32). It is true that they who believe 'will see the glory of God' (Jn 11:40), but the glory of God, not their own. To believe is constantly to stand against the yardstick of the absolute, constantly aware of one's own nothingness.

By the same token, faith's great ally, its true *preambulum*, is humility. God has hidden his divinity in the humility of 'the flesh and the cross. No one therefore can discover it who does not consent to being humble, who does not become like a little child. It is as though you were looking for something by going in the opposite direction from where it is: you never will find it. You look in vain for Christ's divinity if you do not seek it humbly in humility. The Father, Jesus says, has kept these things hidden — and that is to say, especially the mystery of his person — from the wise and clever and revealed them to little children (cf Mt 11:25).

It has to be said that pride has a powerful ally in inflicting blindness, and that is impurity, the slavery of matter and, generally speaking, a disordered and dishonourable life. The evangelist John affirms this, once again having recourse to the imagery of light: 'The light has come into the world and men loved darkness rather than light, because their deeds were evil. For everyone who does evil hates the light and does not come to the light, lest his deeds should be exposed'

51

(Jn 3:19–20). He is not speaking here exclusively of carnal impurity (light is also love, and darkness hatred), but he is certainly speaking *also* about this, and experience confirms it. Moral disorder quenches the Spirit, which alone allows us to recognize the outward testimony of Jesus and the apostles as true. 'For the desires of the flesh are against the Spirit, and the desires of the Spirit are against the flesh' (Gal 5:17). A society sinking ever deeper into matter and moral disorder will be a society believing progressively less and less in the divinity of Christ. For this becomes a standing rebuke, like an indiscreet light. The unbeliever says, writes Pascal: ' "I would soon have renounced pleasure, if I had faith." And I tell you: "You would soon have had faith, if you had renounced pleasure." ' [5] Conversely, purity is a great sustainer of faith in the divinity of Christ. 'Blessed are the pure in heart, for they shall see God' (Mt 5:8). They will also see God in Jesus, they will recognize his divinity.

There are certainly all sorts of other reasons, some guilty, others not guilty, for not believing in Christ's divinity, but the ones to which I have drawn attention, in particular that of seeking one's own glory, are among the commonest where people who have known Jesus and even at some time believed in him too are concerned — especially among the learned.

4. *'God's work is to believe in him whom he has sent'*

The divinity of Christ — and hence the universality of his mission and of his salvation — is, according to the New Testament, the specific and primary object of belief. 'To believe' without further qualification henceforth means believing in Christ. It can also mean believing in God, but in so far as it was the God who sent the Son into the world. Jesus addresses himself to people who already believe in the true God; all his insistence on faith is concerned henceforward with this new factor: his having come into the world, his speaking in God's name. In a word, in his being God's only-begotten Son.

John furthermore has made Christ's divinity and divine

sonship the primary purport of his gospel, the all-unifying theme. He concludes his gospel by saying: 'These [signs] are written that you may believe that Jesus is the Christ, the Son of God, and that believing you may have life in his name' (Jn 20:31), and he ends his First Letter with almost the same words; 'I write this to you who believe in the name of the Son of God, that you may know that you have eternal life' (1 Jn 5:13).

A rapid perusal of the Fourth Gospel with an eye to faith in Christ's divinity shows how this constitutes both warp and woof. Believing in him whom the Father has sent is seen as 'God's work', that which is pleasing to God, without qualification (cf Jn 6:29). Not believing this is consequently seen as 'sin' *par excellence*: 'The Counsellor,' it is said, 'will convince the world of sin' and the sin is: 'they do not believe in me' (Jn 16:8–9).

A clear line is drawn, dividing the human race into two parts: those who believe and those who do not believe that Jesus is the Son of God. Whoever believes in him will not be condemned; but whoever does not believe is condemned already; whoever believes has life, whoever does not believe will not see life (cf Jn 3:18, 36). Concretely too, as the revelation of Jesus gradually proceeds, we see two bodies of people taking shape. Of the one it is said that 'they believed in him'; of the other, that 'they did not believe in him'. At Cana, his own disciples believed in him (Jn 2:11); many more among the Samaritans 'believed in him because of his word' (Jn 4:41). By contrast, people are mentioned, especially the leaders, who 'did not believe in him' and it is noted that 'even his brothers did not believe in him' (Jn 7:5). Similarly, after his disappearance, faith in him was to remain the great watershed in the heart of the human race: on the one hand there would be those who, despite not having seen him, would believe (cf Jn 20:29); on the other would be the world that refuses to believe. Before this distinction, all other previously known ones sink into second place. The episode of Thomas stands there as a tacit invitation addressed by John to the reader. Having reached the end, he is invited to close the book, bow the knee and in his turn exclaim: 'My Lord and my God!' (Jn 20:29). In this clear and solemn profession of faith in Christ's divinity the purpose for which John wrote his gospel is fulfilled. It only remains for us to marvel at the undertaking that the Spirit of Jesus has allowed John to bring to a conclusion. He has embraced the themes, symbols, expectations, everything indeed that was alive, religiously speaking, whether in the Jewish or in the Hellenistic worlds, making all this serve one single idea or, more correctly, one single person: Jesus Christ the Son of God, the Saviour of the world. John's gospel is not centred on an event but on a person. In this it is different from Paul, whose thought, although this too is dominated by Christ, has at its centre Christ's saving *work*, his paschal mystery, rather than his *person*.

To judge by the books of the 'History of Religion School' (*Religionsgeschichtliche Schule*), the Christian mystery differs only in minor detail from the Gnostic and Mandaean religious myth or from Hellenistic and Hermetic religious philosophy. Boundaries melt away, parallels multiply. The Christian faith, especially that of St John, becomes one more variant of this shifting mythology and this generalized religiosity. But what does this mean? It merely means that the essential thing has been ignored: the life and historic force that lies behind the systems and their performance. Living people differ from one another but their skeletons all look alike. Once reduced to a skeleton, cut off from the life it has produced, that is to say, from the Church, there is a danger of confounding the Christian message with others of the same period.

John has not transmitted a corpus of ancient religious doctrines to us, but a potent kerygma. He has mastered the language of his own contemporaries, in it to shout with all his energy that unique saving truth, the Word *par excellence*, 'the Word of God'. He has indeed 'taken every thought captive to obey Christ'. John's Christ is 'the heir of all things'; he is the 'total Logos' as St Justin calls him, in that within himself he reunites all the molecules of truth, scattered here and there like seeds among the peoples.[6] He is the Christ 'heir of all human effort', the king who 'has received tribute from peoples who did not know they were sending it to him'[7].

An undertaking of this sort is not accomplished by

donkey-work and the use of half a dozen reference books. The Johannine synthesis of faith in Christ has come about 'by fire', that is to say, in prayer, by living in Christ, by talking of him. Who knows? — also by talking to Christ's Mother who shared his home, or merely by being with her and looking after her. One thing however is sure, regardless of any question over the Fourth Gospel's authorship: Mary was present in the circle where the traditions of the Fourth Gospel took shape, for 'the disciple whom Jesus loved' had taken her into his own home. Precisely because of this special origin, the scope of John's synthesis is not to be grasped by donkey-work and half a dozen works of reference, even today.

Only revealed certitude, having behind it the authority and strength of God himself, could be unfolded in any book with such insistence and consistency, arriving from a thousand different points always at the same conclusion: that is to say, at the total identity between the Father and the Son based, for the Father's part, on love for the Son and, for the Son's part, on obedience to the Father. There have however been scholars of great repute in our century who have passed judgement on John's gospel in much the same frame of mind as they would assess their students' doctoral theses: almost entirely concerned over borrowings from other works, with the bibliography, always ready to find fault in one respect or another and unable to perceive the unique and fundamental thing that John was trying so hard to say: that Jesus Christ is the Son of God, that in Jesus the human race makes contact, without any barrier whatever, with eternal life and with God himself.

'Has not God made foolish the wisdom of the world?' (1 Cor: 1:20). Yes, he has indeed shown it to be foolish and the worst of it is that the wisdom of the world is very far from suspecting this or realizing it to be true. Many scholars comment at great length on this saying of Paul's, without realizing that he is talking about them. Since you say: 'We see', your guilt remains, says Jesus. If you were really blind, if you were really foolish, ignorant and aware of your ignorance . . . but since you say or think that you are wise, your guilt remains (cf Jn 9:40–41).

I said that John learned the language of his contemporaries in order to proclaim the saving truth in it: that Jesus Christ is the Son of God, that the Word was God. In Christian tradition, this has earned him the title of 'theologian'. For this word entered the Christian vocabulary with a very precise meaning and a different one from what it had had previously, from Plato onwards. Theologians (*theologountes*), we read in a second century text where the noun makes its first appearance in Christian sources, are those 'who announce Christ as God'.[8] So doing, John shows us what every Christian theologian should be doing, every day, to deserve the title.

5. *'Blessed is he who takes no offence at me'*

The divinity of Christ is the highest peak, the Everest, of faith. Much more difficult than just believing in God. So if, from an objective view point, that is to say, from the *datum* of faith, this — as we have seen so far — is what the New Testament holds to be the most important thing to believe and God's work *par excellence*, from a subjective view point, that is to say, from that of our *act* of faith, this is the most arduous thing to believe.

The difficulty is linked to the possibility of and so to the inevitability of 'scandal': 'Blessed is he,' says Jesus, 'who takes no offence at me' (Mt 11:6). The scandal arises from the fact that the man proclaiming himself to be 'God' is someone about whom everything is known: 'We know where this man comes from', say the Pharisees (Jn 7:27). 'Son of God!' sneered Celsus. 'A man living only a few years ago?' Someone 'of yesterday or the day before?' A man 'who came from a village in Judaea and whose mother was a poor country woman who earned a living by spinning?'[9]

The scandal of this is only overcome by faith. It is a delusion to think that it can be eliminated by piling up historical proofs of the divinity of Christ and Christianity. With regard to the true faith, we are in the same situation as the people whom Jesus encountered during his life, or rather perhaps the same situation as they found themselves in after the first Easter, when they heard John and the other apostles proclaiming that Jesus of Nazareth, that man 'who came from a village in Judaea', rejected by everyone, crucified, was the Son of God, and himself God.

One cannot truly believe, it has been written, except in a situation of contemporaneousness, by making oneself, that is to say, a contemporary of Christ and the apostles. But history, the past: does this not help us to believe? Is it not eighteen hundred years, wrote Kierkegaard, since Christ lived? Is his name not proclaimed and believed in throughout the world? Has his teaching not changed the face of the earth, has it not penetrated victoriously into every environment? And has history not established sufficiently and more than sufficiently who he was: that he was God? No, history has not established it; in all eternity, history could not do it! How can one sum up the results of a human life, such as that of Jesus, by saying: *Ergo*, this man was God? A footprint on the road is the consequence of the fact that someone has passed along that road. I may deceive myself by believing, for example, that it was in fact a bird. By looking more carefully, I may decide that it was not a bird but some other kind of animal. But I cannot, however carefully I look, reach the conclusion that it was neither a bird nor another animal, but a spirit, since a spirit, by its very nature, cannot leave footmarks on the road. This is somewhat the case with Christ. We cannot draw the conclusion that he is God simply by examining what we know about him and about his life, that is to say, by direct observation. Anyone who wishes to believe in Christ is obliged to become his contemporary in abasement. The problem is: do you or do you not want to believe that he was God, as he said he was? In relation to the absolute, there is only one time: the present; for people who are not contemporaneous with it, the absolute does not exist at all. And since Christ is the absolute, it is easy to see that, with regard to him, only one situation is possible: that of contemporaneousness. One hundred, three hundred, one thousand eight hundred years take nothing away from and add nothing to him; they do not change him, nor do they reveal who he was, for who he was can be manifested only by faith.[10]

So, according to this view, we cannot become believers unless we go to Christ in his state of abasement, as giver of scandal and object of faith. He has not yet come again in glory, and is therefore ever he who is abased. To this vision, it is true, something is lacking. And what lacks is due attention to Christ's resurrection. Today we encounter him who *humbled* himself and him who has been *exalted*: not only him who has only been *abased*. What lacks is also due attention to the witness of the apostles. The Holy Spirit, Jesus said, 'will bear witness to me, and you also are witnesses' (Jn 15:26–27). 'To these things,' said St Peter, speaking of Christ's resurrection, 'we are witnesses, and so is the Holy Spirit, whom God has given to those who obey him' (Acts 5:32). It is not therefore entirely accurate to say that 'there is only one proof of the truth of Christianity: the inner proof, *argumentum Spiritus Sancti*.'[11] There is an invisible proof consisting of the Spirit's witness, and a different, exterior proof which is also important, consisting of the apostolic witness. Beyond the personal dimension, in the faith there is also a community dimension: 'That which we have seen and heard we proclaim also to you, so that you may have fellowship with us' (1 Jn 1:3). Kierkegaard's statement that the only true relationship with Christ does not come about owing to the 'eighteen hundred years' of Christian history but owing to contemporaneousness, can therefore be stated more precisely. Eighteen centuries of history and contemporaneousness are not to be placed in antithesis, but maintained together. Contemporaneousness, as the New Testament understands it, is none other than the *Holy Spirit*, who is indeed Jesus' presence and permanence in the world, the one to be with us forever (cf Jn 14:16); the eighteen centuries — now indeed become twenty — are not other, in theological terms, than the Church. In the Catholic view therefore, the Holy Spirit and the Church are the essential conditions making it possible for us to have a relationship with Christ, a relationship only becoming effective, it must be said, through faith and imitation of the model that Christ presents.

Notwithstanding these reservations however, in that description of faith in Christ's divinity there is a profound element of truth, of which we especially as Catholics ought to take account. Put in simpler words, what did all those affirmations of Kierkegaard's really mean: about believing as contemporaries? They meant that believing in Christ's divinity is the task for each individual. Believing in the contemporaneous situation also means believing in solitude. Christ's divinity, as I have already said, is the Everest of faith. But on the climb up this Everest, there are no porters, no *sherpas*, to carry you and your gear up to a certain height, then letting you walk the last few hundred yards on your own. Each of us has to climb the whole way. Indeed it is a matter of making an infinite leap, where a century or a millennium more or less adds nothing, takes nothing away. Where the fact of being one out of two, or two thousand million, believers alike does not essentially modify the difficulty of the thing. True, we can be helped to believe by the fact that others round us are doing so, but this is still not believing in the true sense that has God himself as only reason.

We cannot therefore reason as though the believers who existed before today had done the major part and our job today was merely to carry on and put the finishing touches to their hard work. If it was like this, it ought to get progressively ever easier to believe in Christ as we gradually advance through history, which we see is not at all the case. It is not easier but harder to believe today than it was in the days of St John, of St Athanasius or of Luther. Everything depends on 'the demonstrative force which by its very nature the word of God has when acting in the words and deeds of Jesus' and on whether it finds or does not find a disposition ready to accept it.

There are certainly the 'signs', the 'works'. Jesus often refers to them. He says that we should believe at least on account of the works that he is doing; that if he had not performed so many signs, our blame would have been less (cf Jn 5:36; 10:25–37). But what actually went on when Jesus was there, demonstrates that the signs were not sufficient to make people believe. Even when he was present in person, a hundred reasons could still be found for remaining in unbelief. 'Though he had done so many signs before them, they did not believe in him', says the evangelist (Jn 12:37). The story of the man born blind serves to illustrate this very fact: that even when faced with the most clamorous of signs, there is always the possibility of opening to, or shutting out, the light. On another occasion, Jesus has no sooner performed the great sign of the multiplication of the loaves than people start asking him, 'What sign do you do, that we may believe in you?' (Jn 6:30), as if the previous sign went for nothing. Jesus for his part warns us against a faith based merely on seeing signs: he mistrusts those people who, unless they see signs, will not believe (cf Jn 4:48) and when others 'seeing the signs' did believe in him, it is written that 'Jesus did not trust himself to them' (Jn 2:23).

We should not however disdain the signs. If there is a certain inner predisposition to recognize the truth, Christ's works as such can offer proof that the power of God is acting in them and hence that Jesus was the mediator of eternal life. But what weight could such works and signs have, other than at the moment when they were performed? Were they sufficient to make people conclude that they actually had God to deal with, in person? Could not the Hellenistic world too boast many a thaumaturge, that is to say, miracle-worker? So we must conclude that, for John, Christ's works consisted not so much of a few sporadic cures as his complete work of having brought eternal life to earth. Those who listened to the message were invited to consider whether in effect they might not find a new kind of life in the Church.[12] But such an experience could only be had by coming to Christ, that is to say, by believing. And this proves yet again that only in faith is witness sufficient about Jesus, that faith is witness in itself.

6. *'Corde creditur: we believe with the heart'*

All this spurs us on to effect a purgation of our faith. St Paul says that 'man believes with his heart and so is justified, and he confesses with his lips and so is saved' (Rom 10:10). In the Catholic view, confession of the correct faith, that is to say, the second moment of this process, has often assumed such high relief as to leave the first moment in the shade, although it is the more important and takes place in the hidden depths of the heart. 'Faith springs from the roots of the heart.'[13] *Corde creditur*, we believe with the heart; or again, we cannot truly believe unless with the heart.

This first act of faith, for the very reason that it does take place within the heart, is a 'singular' act, that can only be made singly, in absolute solitude with God. In John's gospel we hear Jesus constantly repeating the question: 'Do you believe?' He puts this question to the man born blind the moment he is healed: 'Do you believe in the Son of man?' (Jn 9:35); he puts it to Martha: 'Do you believe this?' (Jn 11:26); and every time the question raises the answering cry of faith from the heart: 'Yes, Lord, I believe!' Even the Church's Creed begins like this, in the singular: '*Credo* . . . I believe.'

When '*credo*' is pronounced like this as a real confession of faith, it marks the moment when time opens into eternity ('whoever believes in him has eternal life'), even though this moment may very well occur within a permanent state or habit of faith, and not spring unbidden from or finish in the void. This is the most sublime and poetic moment of 'unveiling the being': the hidden being in the man Jesus or in the very word 'God' is unveiled, is illuminated and then — says St John — it comes about that the glory of God is seen. It is not only believed, but known, seen, contemplated: 'We have believed and come to know' (Jn 6:69); 'We have seen his glory' (Jn 1:14); 'We have contemplated the Word of Life' (cf 1 Jn 1:1).

In baptism, the Church has anticipated my faith and promised it to God, standing guarantee for me a child that one day when I have grown up I shall believe. Now I have to show that the Church has not been deceived on my account. I myself have to believe. I cannot go on believing through intermediaries, be they persons or institutions. No more can it be the Church that does the believing for me. 'Do you believe?' That leaves you no way out. There is no taking refuge in the multitude and no, as I said, digging-in behind the Church. We too have to consent to passing through this moment, to submitting to this examination. We must not imagine ourselves to be excused. If we answer Jesus' question immediately and without even pausing to think: 'Of course I believe' and find it funny that this sort of question should be addressed to a believer, to a priest or to a bishop, it probably means that we have not yet discovered what believing that Jesus is God really means, that we have not as yet descended into the depths of faith. We have never experienced that great vertigo of the reason which precedes the act of faith. Ours is a faith that has not yet been subjected to scandal. There was a moment when the disciples thought they had reached the acme of faith: 'Now', they said to Jesus, 'we know that you know all things . . . By this we believe that you have come from God.' Jesus replied, 'So, you believe now?' and predicted that soon afterwards they would take offence at him and run away in all directions, leaving him all alone (cf Jn 16:29–32). How often, in this situation, our faith resembles that of the disciples! We are ingenuously certain of believing firmly and finally from now on, while Jesus, who knows us, knows very well that the moment the test arrives, the reality will be very different, showing that we have not believed seriously in him. That 'Now we believe!' often strikes me as a photograph of our own faith.

True faith is that which comes, having overcome the perilous ford of scandal and ordeal, not that which has never considered the awesomeness of the fact. If we find it more or less natural, from having heard it said so often, that Jesus — this human being — should be God, that God should be a human being, it is a deplorable sign of superficiality, possibly offending God as much as, if not more than, the unbelief of someone who considers such a thing too great, too unworthy of God, impossible. So great is the notion that the latter has of the infinite qualitative difference between God and the human creature. We must not diminish what God has done in taking flesh, by regarding it as something commonplace and easy to understand.

The first thing we must do, we believers and we churchmen, is to break down within ourselves the false conviction that we believe already. We must provoke doubt, not of course in Jesus but in ourselves, so as to put ourselves in quest of a more genuine faith. Who knows but that it may be a benefit, for a little while, not to be trying to prove anything to anyone but to interiorize our faith and rediscover its roots in our heart! Jesus asked Peter three times: 'Do you love me?'. He knew that, the first and second time, the answer came out too glibly to be true. Finally, at the third time, Peter got the idea. So the question about faith ought to be put to us like that: three times, insistently, until we get the point and enter into the truth: 'Do you believe? Do you believe? Do you truly believe?' Then perhaps, at last we shall blurt out: 'No, Lord, to tell the truth, deep down, I don't. Help thou my unbelief!'

7. *Believing 'in' Christ*

In the gospel of John, the personal nature of the act of faith is stressed by the very use of the verb 'to believe'. In the gospel we encounter the expression 'to believe', which means to lend credence or hold to be true. For instance, to believe Scripture (cf Jn 2:22), or Moses, or Christ (cf Jn 5:46). We also encounter the expression 'to believe that' (in Greek: *oti*) meaning to be convinced that, or just to believe. For instance, to believe that Jesus is the Holy One of God, that he is the Christ, that the Father has sent him, and so forth (cf Jn 6:69; 11:27, 42; 14:11).

But alongside these well known usages, there is one unknown to profane language yet most dear to the evangelist, and that is the expression 'to believe in' (in Greek: *eis*), as in the sentence: 'Let not your hearts be troubled. Believe in God, believe also in (*eis*) me' (Jn 14:1). Believe here means have faith in, entrust yourself to the person you believe in, build your own life on that person. It indicates a total and unconditional trust that is to replace all human insecurity. A trust in consequence of which the heart can never again be troubled by anything. Jesus asks the same kind of trust for himself, that God asked of his people in the Old Testament.

Long ago, St Augustine stressed the importance of the expression '*credere in*'. Commenting on John 6:29 ('This is the work of God: that you believe in him whom he has sent'), he writes: 'He says that ye believe *in* him, not that ye believe him. True, if ye believe in him, ye believe him, but it does not follow that whosoever believeth him, believeth in him. Thus the devils too believed him, and yet believed not in him. Again of his Apostles also, we may say we believe Paul, but not, we believe in Paul; we believe Peter, but not, we believe in Peter. For to him that believeth in him that justifieth the ungodly, his faith is counted unto him for righteousness (Rom 4:5). Then what is it to believe in him? By believing to love him, by believing to prize him, by believing to go into him and to be incorporated into his members. Consequently it is none other than faith that God exacteth of us; but this is not to be found in us unless he himself bestows it.'[14]

'*Credere in*', in other words, applies only to God. The Church adheres scrupulously, at least in the Latin text, to this usage: so, in the Creed we say: 'Credo *in* Deum Patrem . . . *in* Jesum Christum . . . *in* Spiritum Sanctum'. And though we say, 'I believe in the Church, in the forgiveness of sins', it would be more proper to say: 'I believe the Church, the forgiveness of sins,' i.e., that sins *are* forgiven, and so forth.

Believing 'in' the Son of God is something different and more than believing 'that' Jesus is the Son of God. This last is an indivisible belief, admitting within itself of no gradations; either he is, or he is not; either you believe it, or you do not. As regards the former however, there are all sorts of degrees and you would never finish progressing through them. In other words, you can always trust more in Christ, by surrendering yourself to him more and more and losing yourself in him, until faith in the Son of God becomes the whole reason for your life. Like Paul, who could say: 'The life I now live in the flesh, I live by faith in the Son of God who loved me and gave himself for me' (Gal 2:20).

8. *The fruits of faith in Christ the Son of God*

The fruits of faith in Christ's divinity possess divine qualities themselves. The first of the fruits is *eternal life*. Whoever believes in him has eternal life (cf Jn 3:5; 5:24, 6:40, 47). The gospel itself was written so that people would believe that Jesus is the Son of God and, believing, would have eternal life (cf Jn 20:31). For John, eternal life is not just the life that begins after death, but the new life of children of God which already opens up now for the believer. Whoever believes in him has already 'passed from death to life' (Jn 5:24). Faith allows the divine world to irrupt into this our world right now. Believing, therefore, means something very different from believing in a 'hereafter', in life after death; it is to experience the life and glory of God here and now. Whoever believes already sees the glory of God, right now (cf Jn 11:40).

This fruit of faith — I mean, life — is also distinguished by other imagery. Whoever believes in the name of Christ 'is born of God' and receives the power to become a child of God (cf Jn 1:12–13), passes from darkness into light (cf Jn 12:46), will do the works that Jesus himself has done (cf Jn 14:12). But above all, whoever believes receives the Holy Spirit, that is, he who concretely bears eternal life within us. 'Whoever believes in me, as the Scripture has said, out of his heart shall flow rivers of living water. Now this he said about the Spirit which those who believed in him were to receive' (Jn 7:38–39). Those who believe in him! Faith establishes contact between Christ and the believer, opens a line of communication, through which the Holy Spirit passes. The Holy Spirit is given to whoever believes in Christ. Faith — and I use a bold image — is now the soldier's lance, with which Christ's side is pierced, so that from it may gush the rivers of living water of the Spirit.

There is a fruit of faith in Christ the Son of God which John discovered towards the end of his life, perhaps having experienced it personally, and which he describes in his First Letter; faith in the divinity of Christ, in it alone, allows us to overcome the world: 'Who is it that overcomes the world but he who believes that Jesus is the Son of God?' (1 Jn 5:15). Overcoming the world means overcoming the world's hostility, unbelief, hatred and persecution. But not only this. It also has a non-polemical, existential meaning: overcoming the world means overcoming time, corruption, worldliness. Who believes, escapes the law of decay and death; rises above time; in a word, shares in Christ's victory, for he said: 'Be of good cheer, I have overcome the world' (Jn 16:33). But this only a faith of special mettle can obtain: that which has passed or is passing through the cross. For it was on the cross that the Lamb won his victory (cf Rev 5:5).

Today as never before, the Church is searching for something that can overcome the world; that can overcome it, not in order to dominate it but to save it, to convert it. Something mightier than its immense power to resist the faith and to seduce our race. The word of God assures us that this something exists and that it is faith in Jesus Christ the Son of God: 'This is the victory that overcomes the world: our faith' (1 Jn 5:4).

This being so, Christ willed to found his Church on nothing else than faith in him as Son of God. Peter becomes Cephas, Rock, the moment when, by revelation from the Father, he believes in the divine origin of Jesus. 'On this rock,' St Augustine comments, 'I shall build the faith which you have professed. On the fact that you have said: "You are the Christ, the Son of the Living God", I shall build my Church.'[15] The Church was founded on the first act of faith, in the temporal order, in Christ's divinity. This remains her basis, this allows her to overcome the world and the gates of hell. How different the works of God are from those of human beings! The whole immense edifice of the Church set on something invisible, very fragile yet invincible: on faith in Christ the Son of God and on the promise made in response to this faith. The Church is, in herself, the tangible proof of the truth of those words: Whoever believes that Jesus is the Son of God overcomes the world.

9. *Invitation to have faith*

In the Bible there is a psalm called 'invitatory' which the Liturgy requires us to recite at the beginning of each new day. It says:

> O come, let us worship and bow down,
> let us kneel before the Lord, our Maker;
> He is our God.   (Ps 95:6–7)

We Christians can and should also apply these words to Christ: 'O come, let us worship and bow down; let us approach him with faith; he is our God.' The best way of concluding a meditation on Christ's divinity is for us to exhort one another to believe. What St John says in his gospel is also helpful for these reflections of ours: 'These things are written that *you may believe* that Jesus is the Son of God.' For no other reason than this.

All the gospels are an exhortation to believe. Jesus' great

66

question throughout the gospels is: Do you all believe? Do you individually believe? The 'I believe' with which the Church responds to this question is an epochal reality. It is the only adequate response. The Church steps forward and declares to the whole world: 'I believe!' And would God not love the Church after that? What new, incalculable effects are seen even today when someone, putting all delay aside, quits the neutral sphere of the world, quits the sphere of simply telling, explaining, discussing or stating, even though with admiration, and says: 'I believe!' Jesus exulted in the Spirit whenever someone believed. Jesus was and is a seeker of faith as, and infinitely more than, some people are seekers of gold.

He it is, the Only-Begotten of the Father, who stands before the human race today and says: 'Be still, and know that I am God' (Ps 46:10). He does not plead for it, he does not beg for faith and recognition, as so many pseudo-prophets and founders of empty religions do. He does not say: 'Believe me, please, be kind enough to listen'; but he says: 'Know that I am God!' Whether you believe it or not, I am God!

Of the Magi it is written that 'they fell down and worshipped him. Then, opening their treasure chests, they offered him gifts of gold, incense and myrrh' (cf Mt 2:11). Let us too open the treasure chest of our heart and offer Jesus the gift of our faith. '*Corde creditur*': believing is done with the heart; the heart is made for believing. If it seems to us to be empty, let us ask the Father to fill it with faith: 'No one can come to me,' Jesus says, 'unless the Father draws him' (Jn 6:44). 'Art thou not drawn? Pray that thou mayest be drawn.'[16] Let us not fall into the error of believing that faith in Christ's divinity can come from within ourselves. That we can climb Everest on our own. It was the Father of Heaven who, that day, 'revealed' to Peter who Jesus was: not flesh and blood. The Father it was who gave him the faith to believe and Jesus pronounced him blessed precisely because of this. Faith is better obtained from prayer than from study.

1 St Augustine, *In Ioh.*, 38, 10 (PL 35, 1680).
2 C. H. Dodd, *The Interpretation of the Fourth Gospel*, CUP 1953, p. 205.
3 *Ibidem.*
4 St Augustine, *De Natura et Gratia*, 26, 29 (CSEL 5, 255): 'Non deserit, si non deseratur.'
5 B. Pascal, *Pensées*, Dent, entry 350.
6 Cf St Justin Martyr, *II Apologia*, 10, 13.
7 Ch. Péguy, *Eve*, in *Oeuvres poétiques*, pp. 1086, 1581.
8 Eusebius of Caesarea, *Ecclesiastical History*, V, 28, 5 (PG 20, 513).
9 Cf Origen, *Contra Celsum*, I, 26, 28; VI, 10 (SCh 132, 146f; SCh 147:202f).
10 Cf S. Kierkegaard, *Training in Christianity*, I–II.
11 S. Kierkegaard, *The Diary*, Peter Owen, London 1961, entry 201 (X 1 A, 481).
12 Cf C. H. Dodd, *op. cit.*, part III.
13 St Augustine, *In Ioh.*, 26, 2 (PL 35, 1607).
14 St Augustine, *In Ioh.*, 29, 6 (PL 35, 1631).
15 St Augustine, *Sermo* 295, 1 (PL 38, 1349).
16 St Augustine, *In Ioh.*, 26, 2 (PL 35, 1607).

Chapter IV

'He is the true God and eternal life'

Divinity of Christ and tidings of eternity

Writing to a cardinal of her day, St Catherine of Siena said that such a 'bellow', that is to say, so loud a roar, should be uttered over the body of Holy Church as would awaken the sons lying dead within her.[1] (The saint shared the popular notion of her times that lion-cubs were born dead and the father-lion brought them to life with his powerful roar.) I do not know what the word was that St Catherine in her day thought ought to be shouted over the body of Holy Church. But I do know the word that ought to be shouted today to wake up those of her children who have fallen asleep. The word is 'Eternity!' This is the shout of Christian awakening; the word that, like the ploughshare, can open the furrow for a new sowing of the Word. To proclaim the Gospel to people who had for instance lost the very notion of eternity, would be like sowing on the rock.

In this chapter I propose to show how the dogma of Christ 'true God and true man' can help us in this task by restoring our courage and the freedom of faith that we need for setting about shouting 'Eternity, eternity!' to the people of today. And we shall see how only faith in the divinity of Christ can make the word 'eternity' a concrete possibility offered to human beings, the very task of life, and not, as it would otherwise be, a mere category of thought or a vague 'yearning for the Totally Other'.[2]

At the same time, this will allow us to grasp the whole enormous existential charge and applicability of Christological dogma today. The kerygmatic theology of our own century has transferred the whole weight of Christology from *'per se'*, that is to say, what Christ is in himself, to *'per me'*, that is to say, what he means for me and for my salvation. But it has often left this 'per me' vague, reducing it to an abstract and formal principle, void of real content. If Christ was born for me, if he became the new human being for my sake, if 'he sanctified himself' for my sake (cf Jn 17:19), if he died for my sins, it follows that these events involve me directly, that they have a meaning that I ought to accept and imitate in my own life. In so doing, we recover one of the most fertile aspects of existential thinking, which was extremely lively in the work of its initiator but which was often lost in that of his continuators: the conviction that the element of 'seriousness' in Christianity resides in living, in doing, much more than in understanding, explaining or relating Christian truth to this or that philosophic system. In other words, the conviction that Christianity needs saints and not professors; or, if it does need professors, this is only in the strong sense of the word: people who 'profess' Christianity, who humbly shoulder its demands while knowing that they can never perfectly discharge them. What really counts, as Kierkegaard reminds us with the title of one of his works, is 'training in Christianity', that is to say, the living of it, the practising of it, the being inside it. Nothing else. 'If you know these things,' said Jesus, 'blessed are you if you put them into practice' (cf Jn 13:17). Blessedness is not promised to *knowing*, but to *putting into practice*.

Wanting to concentrate on our plan to effect a synthesis, this time between Christology's *'per se'* and *'per me'*, I shall divide the reflection into two parts. In the first, we shall reflect on the dogma of the two natures of Christ and how this can be translated and made contemporary for the people of today; in the second, we shall see how the charge of announcing the glad tidings is released by this dogma's renewed presentation and how, in particular, it gives a basis for the cry: 'Eternity, eternity!'

1. *From the two 'times' to the two 'natures' of Christ*

How was the dogma formed of the two natures of Christ, that is to say, of Christ 'true man and true God'? At the outset, immediately after the first Easter, the scheme by which people tried to express the mystery of the person of

Jesus was not that of the two *natures* or substances, of his divinity and humanity, but that of the two *times* or phases, of his story: the phase anterior to the resurrection, lived in the normal conditions of any human being — growth, susceptibility to pain, death — and the phase inaugurated by his resurrection from the dead, marked by entirely different characteristics. We may call the first phase 'life according to the flesh', and the second 'life according to the Spirit'. Romans 1:3–4 expresses itself in precisely these terms. Christ who, by virtue of his human birth from the seed of David existed for a while according to the flesh, since his resurrection lives according to the Spirit and manifests himself in all his power as Son of God. It was an historical schema: the succession *flesh-spirit* corresponding neatly to that of *time-eternity*. More interesting than Christ's *nature*, in this perspective, is Christ's *condition*, his mode of existence: first, in time, and then, outside time. More than in the essence, we should say today, interest lies in the existence.

Starting from this initial comprehension of the mystery of Christ, a process of deepening begins, in which the Church's faith strives to leap ever higher or, which is the same thing, to delve ever deeper, to discover Christ's true identity.

A first but enormous step in this direction consists in standing the schema on its head. No more first the flesh and then the Spirit, no more first time and then eternity, but the other way round: first the Spirit, then the flesh; first eternity, then time. This begins as far back as St Paul. In Philippians 2:6–8, he speaks of Jesus as of him who, being originally 'in the divine state', at a certain moment of history assumes 'the servile state', that is to say, the human condition. But it becomes very clear indeed with John, who speaks of the Word who 'was in the beginning with God' and who, at a certain moment, 'became flesh' (Jn 1:1–14).

Certain passages in the apostolic Fathers allow us to see this transition from one point of view to another actually taking place. On one occasion, St Ignatius of Antioch, following Romans 1:3–4, says that Jesus is 'fleshly and spiritual, of Mary and of God', that he was 'born of the seed of David and of the Holy Spirit';[3] but on another occasion he is already following the new schema and says

71

of Jesus that, being first 'intemporal, invisible and unsusceptible to pain,' he subsequently becomes 'visible and susceptible.'[4] In the first case, the moment of change is still Christ's resurrection; in the second, it is now the incarnation. In the first case the order is: flesh-Spirit; in the second, Spirit-flesh. This new order is also clearly to be seen in another so-called apostolic composition, where we read that Christ, 'being first Spirit, became flesh.'[5]

A second step in this evolution no longer concerns the *order* but the *meaning* of the terms *Spirit-flesh* or what corresponds to them in Johannine language: *Word-flesh*. These no longer serve to indicate merely two different states or modes of existence of Christ, but two realities, two substances or natures. Attention has shifted, we should say today, from existence to essence. The following passage from Tertullian is enough to let us gauge the astonishing distance travelled by the faith in little more than a century and a half. Commenting on the text of Romans 1:3–4, he writes: 'Here the Apostle teaches the two substances of Christ. With the words "descended from David according to the flesh", he indicates the man and the Son of man; with the words, "designated Son of God according to the Spirit", he indicates God, the Word, the Son of God. Thus in him we see a twofold substance.'[6] Another author only a little later clinches the matter: 'We confess that Christ is truly God according to the Spirit and truly man according to the flesh.'[7] The doctrine of the Christ 'according to the flesh and according to the Spirit', that is to say, of the two times, has crystallized as the doctrine of the Christ true God and true man, that is to say, of the two natures.

The Council of Chalcedon does no more than confirm this new understanding of the faith, by speaking of Christ 'perfect in divinity and perfect in humanity, true God and true man . . . begotten of the Father before all ages as regards his divinity and of Mary in these latter days as regards his humanity; one only and identical Christ, Son of God, to be recognized in the two natures, without confusion and without division.'[8]

The reason for this evolution is the same as we have seen earlier when speaking of Christ's humanity. We are witnessing an early and exemplary case of inculturation of the faith. For the same reason as the change from Christ the 'new' man (which refers to time and history) to Christ the 'true' man (which refers to his being), so now there is the change from the two phases or modes of existence of Christ, to his two natures. The reason is that the Gospel has had to be absorbed into a culture where far greater emphasis was laid on the being or immutable essence of things, than in their development and history. For the same reason, Christ's spiritual and eternal dimension is placed earlier than his temporal and historical one. For it is impossible — it was rightly thought — that eternity should spring from time, like any other of its creations; whereas time it is that springs from eternity, that 'follows' eternity, if one can talk of a preceding or a following with respect to what has neither a before nor after. It was certainty over the pre-existence of the Word that induced the inversion of the order between the Christ according to the flesh and the Christ according to the Spirit.

So have we then deserted the Bible to run after the Greeks? Have Christianity and even Jesus Christ himself been hellenized? No, since we have seen that what is being affirmed here was already present in the word of God, in Paul and in John. The pastoral requirement to proclaim the Gospel has merely contributed to throwing full light on a fundamental aspect of the revealed datum, which otherwise might have remained forever in shadow.

But with this, a principle was instantly established affecting even us, though in a different way. The progress of the faith was not cut off by the Chalcedonian definition. Just as the Fathers had a sure sense in seizing on that aspect of the message best suited to establishing a bridge with the culture of the day, so we have to work out what aspect of the message is best fitted to speak to the people of today, if necessary by subjecting this same contemporary culture to the judgement of the word of God and by helping it to overcome its limitations and gaps, as the Fathers did with Greek culture in their day.

2. *Christ, the synthesis of eternity and time*

No sooner do we gird up our loins for the task of setting out afresh from the Bible with an up-to-date proclamation of Jesus Christ in view than we make surprising discoveries. For we see the enormous possibilities, like so many seeds ready to blossom and bear fruit, that this still offers for modern, existential discourse about Christ and hence about human nature.

Natural scientists and botanists fall back in amazement at all the things contained within one tiny seed that science is ever increasingly bringing to light. If all the information contained in one seed had to be put down in writing, you would end up with something like an encyclopaedia. Everything in it is programmed in the minutest particular. A natural computer comes to mind, containing an incalculable mass of data in its memory-bank: when and how to flower, what fruit to produce of what colour and flavour, of what dimensions, how to react to this or that external agent, how to adapt to a change of climate. Sometimes all these pieces of information remain active for centuries, if it is true (as is said) that grains of wheat still alive and able to germinate have been found in the ancient pyramids of Egypt. Under the stimulus of the present ecological crisis, it has been discovered that a better understanding of the seed, of its resources and of its natural allies, can help reduce the need for violent intervention from outside with anti-parasitic chemicals, poisoning the soil and in the long run damaging the plant itself.

The revealed message is also a seed. Jesus himself compares it to 'the smallest of all seeds' (Mt 13:32) and compares himself to a grain of wheat sown in the ground (cf Jn 12:24). Like the seed, the message hides unsuspected resources within itself, which after two thousand years we are far from having finished exploring. This is especially true as regards Christology. In the New Testament kerygma about Jesus Christ there are in-built pieces of information which allow it to burst into flower at any stage of history, to acclimatize itself in every culture, without ever belying itself or changing nature. It possesses its own defence mechanisms within it and it is not kept alive by external human intervention either of polemical or apologetic type.

It is enough for it to be put in the position where it can make use of its own resources, not confined in books and dogmatic formulations as in a greenhouse, but placed in contact with the living and ever new terrain of history and allowed to react to that.

So let us consider how this living terrain of history looks today and what is new about it in relation to the distant age when Christological dogma first assumed fixed form. I do not pretend to be in a position to define the true character of modern culture in a few words. One thing however I believe I can say. Today's people are people who have discovered a 'sense of history', who are interested more in the existence of themselves and things than they are in the essence, more in freedom than in nature. It is not the Gospel preacher's job to establish whether this is a good thing or an evil, whether an advance or a regression. His job is to become modern with the moderns, as Paul, John and the Fathers became 'Greeks with the Greeks' (cf Rom 1:14).

Deep down, in the substance of things, the people of antiquity and those of today do not differ so very radically from one another. Both the one and the other are alike interested in their destiny and react to a message, if this touches them in that deep nucleus of their being which harbours those most worrying of questions: 'Who are we? Where have we come from? Where are we going?' These questions asked by people today were also being asked by people in the second century AD.[9] The problem of salvation, that is to say, soteriology, is the gate of entry to Christology. What has changed is only the way this need for salvation is presented. If in the olden days salvation was thought of as salvation 'from' the world and 'from' the body, today it is thought of more as salvation 'of' the world and 'of' the body, rather than of the soul alone.

Let us therefore see what Christological dogma has to say to the people of our own day, marked, as the title of a famous philosophical work of our century will have it — by the problem of 'being and time'.

In his First Letter, John says of Christ: 'We are in him who is true, in his son Jesus Christ: this is *the true God and eternal life*' (1 Jn 5:20). These two concepts — 'true God' and 'eternal life' — applied to Christ are accorded an

75

equal importance and frequency in the Johannine writings. Of them, in the dogmatic field, ancient thought made use only of one: 'true God', from which it eventually drew the time-honoured formula of the Nicene Creed: 'true God from true God'. It remains in great part to explore what it means, for Christology, to say that Jesus is 'eternal life', that in him not only divinity but eternity too appeared on earth. We are faced here with one of those seeds waiting to germinate or, as I said earlier on, a shout waiting to be uttered over the body of Mother Church.

In the same letter, John, who is regarded as the most metaphysical of the New Testament authors, speaks of Christ as 'the eternal life which was with the Father and was made visible' (cf 1 Jn 1:2). The formula 'the eternal life was made visible' is clearly of the same stamp as that other: 'the Word was made flesh' (Jn 1:14). It expresses by the key-words *eternity* and *time* what is expressed in the Prologue by the key-words *Word* and *flesh*, that is to say, ontological realities. Here too ancient Christology seized on and developed the formula 'Word-flesh', building directly on it, whereas the other expression, which is evidently fraught with great significance for the human race, remains yet to be evaluated. For it proclaims that in Christ eternity has become visible, that is to say, has entered time and has, as it were, come to meet us.

Not only is this aspect of the mystery of Christ still there, intact, in the Bible, where we can draw on it, but in retracing the history of the development of dogma we shall not be slow to observe that it was by no means absent from patristic thought, where it has always been heard, even if mutedly, as a kind of sub-dominant. St Ignatius of Antioch, for instance, speaks of Christ as of him who 'was above time and intemporal (*achronos*) and that he was made visible.'[10] St Leo the Great speaks of the incarnation as the event thanks to which 'he who existed before time began to exist in time.'[11]

In Christ, there is not only therefore the union 'without confusion and without division' between God and the human race, but also between eternity and time. Christ, writes St Maximus the Confessor, explaining the Chalcedonian definition, conjoined in himself the mode of existence according

76

to nature with the mode of existence above nature; he conjoined the extremes, that is to say, immanence and transcendence.'[12]

All this however remained, as I said, a secondary, barely audible note. The man who suddenly made it ring out as a dominant one was Kierkegaard. The mystery of Christ, which in St Maximus and the Fathers in general was expressed for preference as a mystery of transcendence and immanence, that is to say, in terms of *space*, in Kierkegaard is expressed as the paradox of eternity and temporality, that is to say, in relation to *time*. 'The paradox', he writes, 'consists principally in the fact that God, the Eternal One, has come in time as an individual man.'[13] The incarnation is the point at which eternity and time intersect. It is absolute, unrepeatable newness.

This means that Jesus, who is the 'mediator between God and man' (1 Tim 2:5), is also the mediator between eternity and time. He is the bridge thrown across the abyss, which allows transit from one bank to the other. 'The new comes with a leap'[14] and the whole newness of Christ comes precisely from the 'leap' from eternity to time, which occurs in him. Yet a leap entirely special, as of someone who, standing with one foot on the bank where he is, should lean forward to reach the opposite bank with his other foot. For Christ, as St Leo the Great said, 'remaining outside time, begins to exist in time.'

Christ thus represents the unique reality able to save our race from despair. He changes the destiny of our race, and from a 'being-towards-death'[15] makes of us a 'being-towards-eternity'. Christological dogma is unique in being able to give an objective reason for overcoming existential *Angst*.

There is no need here to say what time is and what eternity. We know that eternity and time are no less incommensurable and irreducible, one with the other, than are divinity and humanity, or Spirit and flesh.[16] They are therefore an adequate transposition on the existential and historical plane, of the dogma of Christ God and man. A transposition which does not attenuate the dogma but preserves its absolute and mysterious character intact. The infinite qualitative difference between time and eternity, in him becomes infinite nearness too. He is the one and the other thing at once, in the same person, 'without confusion and without separation'.

3. *From dogma to living*

How apposite and precious this 'bud' of biblical Christology is as it bursts into bloom, under our very eyes, on the trunk of traditional dogma! At a stroke, the dogma is brought very close to everybody's life. Not all perhaps are still able and willing to feel the importance of becoming 'partakers of the divine nature' (2 Pet 1:4). Who, these days, still exults, as happened in the times of St Gregory Nazianzen, at the thought of becoming 'as it were God'?[17] But all feel, as soon as they reflect on it, the dramatic aspect of time passing and the precariousness of human life. They are aware how true, for all without distinction, the words are with which a poet described the situation and state of mind of the soldiers in the trenches at the front during the First World War:

> We are like
> the leaves
> on the trees
> in autumn.
> (G. Ungaretti)

So, if all are not moved today at the prospect of becoming 'partakers in the divine nature', all are certainly moved at the prospect of becoming (as St Maximus the Confessor paraphrased the expression in 2 Peter 1:4) 'partakers in the divine eternity'.[18]

To a friend who reproached him with his yearning for eternity as though it were a form of pride and presumption, Miguel de Unamuno once replied: 'I don't say we deserve a hereafter, nor that logic can demonstrate that there is one; I say we need one, whether we deserve it or not, and that's all. I say that what is transitory does not satisfy me, that I am athirst for eternity, that I am indifferent to everything but this. I need it, I need it! Without it there is no more joy in living, and the joy of life has nothing more to say to me. It is too easy to insist: "You must live, you must be satisfied with life." What about those who are not satisfied with it?'[19] The people who despise the world and life here-below are not the ones who desire eternity; the reverse is true: they are the ones who do not desire it. 'I love life so much', the same author writes, 'that the loss of it strikes me as the worst of evils. They do not truly love life, who enjoy it as it comes, without worrying whether or when they will lose the lot.'[20] 'What is the point', St Augustine asked long ago, 'of living the good life, if it be not granted one to live forever?' (*Quid prodest bene vivere, si non datur semper vivere?*)

But how are we now to pass from dogma to living, from the '*per se*' to the '*per me*' of Christ? How can we make the shout and promise: 'Eternity, eternity!' ring out from what we have considered about Christ? We can do it by applying to the concept of eternity what the Fathers with their doctrine of 'exchange' affirmed about Christ's divinity. They loved to keep repeating: 'God became man, so that man could become God.'[21] We for our part can say: eternity entered time, so that time could obtain eternity. Jesus came to give us eternity, not merely to show it to us in him, just as he came to give us divine life, not merely to show us what it is. Christ's leap from eternity to time makes our leap from time to eternity possible. The hope of an eternity for us is hence an integral part of Christological dogma, springing from it both as purpose and as fruit. The hope of eternity crowns our faith in the incarnation.

Illuminism posed the celebrated problem: how can eternity be obtained while we are in time and how can an eternal consciousness have its starting-point in history?[22] Put another way, how can one justify the Christian religion's pretension to promise eternal life and to threaten equally eternal punishment for acts performed in time? The only viable solution to this problem, known as 'the Gordian knot of the Christian religion' is the one based on faith in God's incarnation. In Christ, the eternal appeared in time; he merited eternal salvation for human beings. Before him therefore – but before him alone – can that act be made which, though performed in time, decides our eternity.[23]

In practice, such an act consists in believing in Christ's divinity: 'I write this to you who *believe* in the name of the

Son of God, so that you may know that you have *eternal life*,' says John the evangelist (1 Jn 5:13); and again: 'Whoever lives and *believes* in me shall *never* die' (Jn 11:26). Faith in Christ's divinity opens the gate to eternal life, allows us to achieve the infinite leap. Before Jesus Christ, precisely because he is at once human being and God, we can take a decision having eternal repercussions.

4. *Eternity, eternity*!

So at last we have reached the moment when we pluck the fruit of the entire journey we have made: eternity. We shall stop here. We shall huddle together round this word in an effort to revive it. We shall warm it, so to speak, with our breath until it returns to life. For eternity is a dead word; we have allowed it to die, as an abandoned baby, whom no one can any longer be bothered to feed, is left to die. As on the caravel bound for the New World, when all hope had been lost of arriving anywhere, there rang out suddenly one morning the look-out's shout: 'Land, land ahoy!' so in the Church must needs ring out the cry: 'Eternity, eternity!'

What has happened to this word, which used once to be the secret motor, or the sail, propelling the pilgrim Church through time, the pole of attraction for the thoughts of believers, the 'mass' attracting hearts upwards as the full moon raises the waters at high tide? The lamp has been quietly put back under the bushel, the flag folded away as of any army in retreat. 'The hereafter has become a joke, an exigency so uncertain that not only does no one any longer respect it but no one even envisages it, so that people are actually amused at the thought that there used to be a time when this idea transformed everyone's existence.'[24]

This phenomenon has a very precise name. Defined in relation to time, it is called *secularism* or temporalism; defined in relation to space, it is called *immanentism*. And this is the point, in our day, at which the faith, having accepted a particular culture, has to show itself capable of contesting some of its assumptions from within by stimulating it into overcoming its arbitrary omissions and inconsistencies.

Secularism means forgetting, or putting in parentheses, the eternal destiny of the human race, by concentrating exclusively on the '*saeculum*', that is to say, on time present and on this world. It is to be seen as the most widespread and most insidious heresy of the modern age and, what is more, we are all in some way or another at risk from it. Even those of us who in theory are struggling against secularism are often its accomplices or victims. We have been 'worldlified', we have lost the sense of, a taste for, familiarity with, eternity. Initially the word 'eternity' (or 'the beyond', which is its equivalent in spatial terms) fell under Marxist suspicion on the grounds that it distracts from the historical task of transforming the world and improving present living conditions and is hence a sort of alibi or evasion. Gradually, owing to the suspicion, forgetfulness and silence have fallen on it too. In affluent societies, materialism and consumerism have done the rest, by making it seem odd and rather bad form still to mention eternity to cultivated, up-to-date people. Who dares talk any more about the 'the four last things' — death, judgement, hell, heaven — which are the beginning and forms of eternity respectively? When did we last hear a sermon on eternal life? And yet you might say that Jesus, in the gospel, never talked about anything else.

What is the practical consequence of the eclipse of the notion of eternity? St Paul quotes the motto of those who do not believe in the resurrection of the dead: 'Let us eat and drink, for tomorrow we die' (1 Cor 15:32). The natural desire to live 'forever', when distorted, becomes a desire or frenzy 'to live it up', that is to say, to have a good time. Quality dissolves into quantity. One of the most efficacious motivations of the moral life is gone.

Perhaps this weakening of the notion of eternity does not affect believers in the same way; it does not lead to as coarse a conclusion as the one mentioned by the Apostle, but it affects them too, more especially by diminishing their capacity for dealing bravely with suffering. Imagine yourself with a balance in your hand: one of those balances which you work with one hand, having a scale pan on the one side, in which you put the things you want to weigh, and on the other a calibrated bar along which you move the weight.

If the weight falls off or is put in the wrong place, whatever happens to be in the scale-pan will make the bar fly up and bring the scale-pan down. Anything can do it, even a handful of feathers: no problem.[25]

Very well, this is what we are like, this is what we are reduced to. We have lost the measure which is eternity, and so earthly things and suffering easily depress our spirit. Everything strikes us as being too heavy, excessive. Jesus said: 'If your hand or your foot causes you to stumble, cut it off; if your eye causes you to stumble, pluck it out; it is better to enter life with one eye, than with two eyes to be thrown into the eternal fire' (cf Mt 18:8–9). Here we see how the measure of eternity acts when it is present and working and to what it is capable of inspiring us. But we, having lost sight of eternity, already find it too much to be asked to avert our eyes from a dubious show.

On the contrary, while you are on earth and about to be overwhelmed by tribulation, summon up your faith and from the other part of the balance throw in that prodigious weight, the thought of eternity, and you will find the weight of tribulation grow lighter, become bearable. Let us say to ourselves: 'What is this when set against eternity?' 'A thousand years are as one day' (2 Pet 3:8), are 'but as yesterday when it is past, or as a watch in the night' (Ps 90:4). But what do I mean: 'one day'? They are an instant, less than one breath.

And while we are talking of weights and measures, let us recall something said by St Paul, who had certainly had an unusually abundant measure of suffering: 'This slight momentary affliction is preparing for us an eternal weight of glory beyond all comparison, because we look not to the things that are seen but to the things that are unseen. The things that are seen are transient, but the things that are unseen are eternal' (2 Cor 4:17–18). The weight of tribulation is 'slight' precisely because it is 'momentary', that of glory is 'beyond all comparison' precisely because it is 'eternal'. This is why St Paul can also say: 'I consider that the sufferings of this present time are not worth comparing with the glory that is to be revealed to us' (Rom 8:18).

St Francis of Assisi, at the famous Chapter of the Rushmats, gave his brethren a memorable address on this subject.

'My sons,' he said, 'we have promised great things to God but much greater are the things that God has promised to us. Let us observe what we have promised to him and confidently expect what he has promised to us. Brief are the delights of this world; the pain which follows after them is perpetual. Little are the pains of this life; but the glory of the other life is infinite.'[26] In more refined language, our friend the philosopher Kierkegaard expresses this same concept of St Francis. 'We suffer only once,' says he, 'but we triumph eternally. So far as that goes, we triumph also only once. Quite true. But the difference is infinite: that the once of suffering is the instant, that of triumph, eternity; the "once" of suffering, therefore, when it is past, is no time, the "once" of triumph is, in another sense, no time, for it is never past; the once of suffering is a transition or a thing we pass through, that of triumph, an eternally enduring triumph.'[27]

A picture comes into my mind. A crowd of people of all sorts and all doing different kinds of things: some working, some laughing, some crying, some going, some coming and some standing disconsolately by themselves. From far away an elderly man arrives, out of breath and whispers something to the first person he meets and then runs on and tells someone else. Each of his hearers runs off to tell another person, and this one in turn tells yet another. And now we witness an unexpected change: the people who were lying gloomily on the ground get up and run off to tell their families at home; those who were running in the first place, stop dead and turn about in their tracks; some who were quarrelling and holding their clenched fists under one another's chin, now throw their arms round one another's neck and burst into tears. What is the word that has produced this remarkable change? The word 'eternity!'

That crowd is the entire human race. And the word that should be running through its midst like a blazing torch, like the beacon-light that watchmen used to send from tower to tower in olden days, is no other than the word: 'Eternity!' The Church should be that elderly messenger. She should make the word ring out in people's ears and proclaim it from the rooftops of the city. Woe if she too were to lose 'the measure'; that would be as though salt had lost its savour.

Who then will preserve life from corruption and vanity? Who will have the guts to repeat, even to the people of to-day, that saying instinct with Christian wisdom; 'Everything in the world, except the eternal, is vain'? Everything but the eternal and whatever in some way leads to it.

Philosophers, poets, everyone indeed, can talk about eternity and the infinite, but only the Church — as guardian of the mystery of the Man-God — can make these words stand for anything more than a vague feeling of 'yearning for the totally other'. There is indeed also this danger: that 'some people bend eternity back into time to please the imagination. Conceived of in this way, it produces an enchanting effect; one does not know whether it is dream or reality; eternity peeps sadly, dreamily, roguishly into the instant.'[28] The Gospel prevents us from *emptying* eternity like this by immediately turning the talk to what has got to be done: 'What shall I do to inherit eternal life?' (Lk 18:18) Eternity becomes life's great task, that to which we must devote ourselves day and night.

5. *Yearning for eternity*

I have already said that, for believers, eternity is not merely a 'yearning for the totally other'. Yet it is this too. Not that I believe in the pre-existence of souls and hence that we have fallen into time, having first lived in eternity and tasted it, as Plato and Origen supposed. I speak of yearning in the sense that we have been created for eternity, we carry the natural desire for it in our hearts, and this is why our hearts are uneasy and dissatisfied until they rest in it. What St Augustine said about happiness, we can also say about eternity: 'Where have I known eternity, for me to remember and desire it?'[29]

What are human beings reduced to, if you take eternity out of their hearts and minds? You de-naturize them, in the strongest sense of the word, if it is true, as the same philosophy says, that human beings are 'finite beings capable of the infinite'. If we deny them the eternal, then they must instantly exclaim with Macbeth once he has killed the king:

'There's nothing serious in mortality.
All is but toys. Renown and grace is dead.
The wine of life is drawn. . .'[30]

But I think we can talk about yearning for eternity in a simpler, more concrete sense too. What man, what woman, is there who looking back over his or her younger days cannot recall a moment, a circumstance, in which they had, as it were, a certain intimation of eternity, as though poised on its threshold, had glimpsed it even if they have never been able to put the experience into words? I recall a moment of that sort in my own life. I was a boy. It was summer and, feeling hot, I stretched out on the grass with my face upwards. My attention was drawn to the blue sky where a few light, very white, clouds were drifting here and there. I thought: "What is beyond that blue vault? and beyond that? and further beyond that?' And so, in successive waves, my mind rose towards the infinite and became lost, as one who staring at the sun grows dazzled and no longer sees at all. Infinite space drew my thoughts on to infinite time. 'What can eternity mean?' I wondered. 'Always, forever, always, forever! A thousand years and that isn't the start of it; millions and thousands of millions of years and it still hasn't begun.' Again, my mind was lost, but it was a wonderful feeling that made me grow. I grasped what the poet Leopardi meant when he wrote in L'infinito: 'To be shipwrecked in this sea is sweet to me.' I intuitively understood what the poet was trying to convey when he spoke of 'endless spaces and superhuman silences' presenting themselves to the mind. So much so that I can hear myself saying to the young people of today: 'Stop, lie down if need be on your back on the grass and look quietly up at the sky for once. Don't seek the shimmering infinite elsewhere, in drugs where there is nothing but delusion and death. Another very different way exists for going beyond our "limitations" and experiencing the genuine feeling of eternity. Seek the infinite on high, not below; above you, not beneath you.'

I know what it is that prevents us — most times — from speaking out like this; it is doubt, that deprives believers of their 'freedom'. The weight of eternity, we think to ourselves, will be so colossal and much greater than the weight of our tribulation. But we carry our crosses in time, not in eternity; we walk by faith, not by sight, as the Apostle says (2 Cor 5:7). In fact we have nothing to oppose to the attraction of things visible but the hope of things invisible; we have nothing to oppose to the immediate enjoyment of the things here-below except the promise of eternal bliss. 'We should like to be happy in this body. This life is so delightful!' people were saying as long ago as the days of St Augustine.

But this is just the mistake that we believers should treat with scorn. It is not entirely true that eternity is only a hope and a promise here-below. It is also a presence and an experience! This is the moment at which to recall what we have learnt from Christological dogma. In Christ, 'the eternal life which was with the Father was made visible.' We, says John, have heard it, seen it with our own eyes, contemplated it, touched it (cf 1 Jn 1:1–3). With Christ the incarnate Word, eternity irrupted into time and we experience this each time we believe, for whoever believes 'already possesses eternal life' (cf 1 Jn 5:13). Each time we receive the body of Christ in the Eucharist, each time we hear 'the words of eternal life' from Jesus (cf Jn 6:68). It is a provisional, imperfect experience but nonetheless a true and sufficient one to give us the certitude that eternity really exists, that time is not all.

The presence, by way of first fruits, of eternity in the Church and in every one of us has a special name: it is called the Holy Spirit. He is defined as 'the guarantee of our inheritance' (Eph 1:14; 2 Cor 5:15), and he is given to us so that, having received the first-fruits, we may long for fulness. 'Christ', says St Augustine, 'has given us the guarantee of the Holy Spirit, with which he, who could in no manner whatever deceive us, has willed to certify us of the fulfilment of his promise, even though without the guarantee he would have certainly kept it. What has he promised? He has promised us eternal life, of which the Holy Spirit that he has given us is the guarantee. Eternal life is possessed by those who have reached their resting-place; his guarantee is the consolation of those who are still on the way. It is more accurate to say guarantee than pledge; the two words seem alike but between them there is a difference in meaning which should not be overlooked. With either a pledge or a guarantee, one may ensure that what is promised will be discharged, but whereas the pledge, once the promise has been performed, gets returned to the person on whose behalf it was received, the guarantee on the other hand does not get given back but the remainder of the debt is added to it.'[31] It is for the Holy Spirit that we groan inwardly, waiting to obtain the glorious liberty of the children of God (cf Rom 8:20–23). He, who is 'an eternal Spirit' (Heb 9:14), is able to kindle in us the true yearning for eternity and make it a living, palpitating word once more arousing joy, not fear.

The Spirit draws us upward. He is the *Ruah Yahweh*, the Breath of God. A method has recently been devised for recovering ships and other objects that have sunk to the bottom of the sea. By means of special air-chambers fitted to the wreckage, air is introduced to lift it off the bottom and gently raise it to the surface by rendering it lighter than water. We people of today are like those bodies that have sunk to the bottom of the sea. We have sunk into temporality and worldliness. We have become 'secularized'. The Holy Spirit has been infused into the Church for a purpose similar to the one I have just described: to raise us from the depths, up, ever higher, so that we can once again contemplate the infinite heavens and, full of joyful hope, exclaim: 'Eternity, eternity!'

NOTES

1   St Catherine of Siena, *Letter 177 to Cardinal Pietro Corsini.*
2   Cf M. Horkheimer, *Die Sehnsucht nach dem ganz Anderen (Yearning for the Totally Other)*, Hamburg 1970.
3   St Ignatius of Antioch, *Letter to the Ephesians*, 7, 2; 20, 2.
4   St Ignatius of Antioch, *Letter to Polycarp*, 3, 2.
5   *Second Letter of Clement*, 9, 5 (ed. Bihlmeyer-Schneemelcher, Tübingen 1956, p. 75).
6   Tertullian, *Adversus Praxean*, 27, 11 (CC 2, p. 1199).
7   Adamantius, *De recta fide*, 5, 11 (GCS, Berlin 1901, p. 194).
8   Denzinger-Schoenmetzer, nn. 301–302.
9   Cf *Excerpta ex Theodoto*, 78 (GCS 17, 2, Berlin 1970, p. 131).
10 St Ignatius of Antioch, *Letter to Polycarp*, 3, 2.
11 Denzinger-Schoenmetzer, n. 294.
12 St Maximus the Confessor, *Ambigua*, 5 (PG 91, 1053 B); cf also St Athanasius, *De incarnatione*, 17 (PG 25, 125). The union between God and man in Christ as the union between eternity

and time is stressed by St Augustine, *Sermones*, 187, 4; 188, 2 (PL 38, 1002, 1004).

13 S. Kierkegaard, *Concluding Postscript*, 5.

14 S. Kierkegaard, *Concept of Dread*, 3 (OUP 1946).

15 Heidegger, *Being and Time*, 2, 1, 51, SCM Press, London 1962.

16 On the relationship between time and eternity, see St Augustine, *Confessions*, XI, 11, 14.

17 Cf St Gregory Nazianzen, *Oratio*, 1, 5 (PG 35, 398 C); 7, 23 (PG 35, 485 B); St Basil, *De Spir.*, 9, 23 (PG 32, 109 C).

18 St Maximus the Confessor, *Capita*, 1, 42 (PG 90, 1193).

19 M. de Unamuno, 'Cartas a J. Ilundain' in *Rev. Univ. Buenos Aires*, 9, p. 135).

20 *Ibidem*, p. 150.

21 Cf St Irenaeus, *Adv. Haer.*, III, 19, 1; V, praef.; St Athanasius, *De incarnatione*, 54 (PG 25, 192); St Maximus the Confessor, *Cap. theol.*, 2, 25 (PG 90, 1136 B).

22 G. E. Lessing, *Über den Beweis des Geistes und der Kraft*, ed. Lachmann, X, p. 36.

23 Cf C. Fabro, Introduction to *Opere di S. Kierkegaard*, Florence 1972, p. XLVI.

24 S. Kierkegaard, *Concluding Postscript*, 4.

25 Cf S. Kierkegaard, *Gospel of Sufferings*, 6 (Clarke, Cambridge 1955).

26 *Little Flowers*, XVII, Burnes Oates & Washbourne, London, no date.

27 S. Kierkegaard, *Christian Discourses*, OUP, New York 1961, p. 103.

28 S. Kierkegaard, *Concept of Dread*, OUP 1946, p. 135.

29 Cf St Augustine, *Confessions*, X, 21.

30 W. Shakespeare, *Macbeth*, II, 3.

31 St Augustine, *Sermo* 378, 1 (PL 39, 1673).

Chapter V

'The sublime knowledge of Christ'

Jesus Christ, a 'person'

The aim of these reflections on the person of Jesus Christ is, as I said at the beginning, to prepare the ground for a new wave of evangelization, to mark the completion of the second millennium since the coming of Christ on earth. But what is the primary aim of all evangelization and of all catechesis? Possibly that of teaching people a certain number of eternal truths, or of passing on Christian values to the rising generation? No, it is to bring people to a personal encounter with Jesus Christ the only Saviour by making them his 'disciples'. Christ's great command to the apostles rings out: 'Go, make disciples of all nations' (Mt 28:19).

1. *The personal encounter with Christ*

At the beginning of his gospel, John tells us how people became Christ's disciples; and he does this by relating his own experience, that is to say, how he personally one day became one of Jesus' disciples. It is worth re-reading the passage, which is one of the first and most moving examples of what today we call bearing personal testimony: 'The next day again John was standing with two of his disciples; and he looked at Jesus as he walked, and said, "Behold, the Lamb of God!" The two disciples heard him say this, and they followed Jesus. Jesus turned, and saw them following, and said to them, "What do you seek?" And they said to him, "Rabbi" (which means Teacher), "where are you staying?" He said to them, "Come and see." They came and saw where he was staying; and they stayed with him that day, for it was about the tenth hour' (Jn 1:35–39).

Nothing abstract or scholastic about this way of becoming

Jesus' disciple. It is a meeting of persons; it is the establishing of a knowledge, friendship and familiarity destined to last for a lifetime and for eternity. Jesus turns round and, realizing that he is being followed, stops and asks: 'What are you looking for?' They reply: 'Rabbi, Master, where are you living?' And so, almost without realizing it, they have proclaimed their master and decided to be his disciples. Jesus does not give them any books to study or precepts to learn by heart, but just says: 'Come along, you'll see.' He invites them to keep him company. They go and stay with him.

And look how three personal encounters are immediately born of the one personal encounter and how someone who has got to know Jesus will make him known to others. See in a word how the good news gets passed on. One of the new disciples was the future writer of the gospel, John, and the other one was Andrew. Andrew went and told his brother Simon: ' "We have found the Messiah." He brought him to Jesus. Jesus looked at him and said: 'So you are Simon the son of John; you shall be called Cephas" ' (Jn 1:41–42). This was how the chief of the apostles himself came to the faith: through the testimony of someone else. Next day, same scene. Jesus says to Philip, 'Follow me!' Philip meets Nathanael and tells him: 'I have found Jesus, him of whom Moses wrote,' and to Nathanael's objections he answers by repeating Jesus' words: 'Come and see' (cf Jn 1:45–46).

If Christianity, as so often and so rightly has been said, is not primarily a doctrine but a person, Jesus Christ, it follows that the proclamation of this person and of one's relationship with him is the most important thing, the beginning of all true evangelization and the very condition for making such a thing possible. To reverse this order and put the doctrines and obligations of the gospel before the discovery of Jesus would be like putting the carriages in front of the railway engine that is supposed to pull them. The person of Jesus opens the highway of the heart for the acceptance of everything else. Anyone who has once known the living Jesus has no further need to be goaded along; we ourselves burn with desire to know his thought, his will, his word. It is not on the authority of the Church that we accept Jesus, but on the authority of Jesus that we accept and love the Church.

So the first thing the Church has to do is not present herself to the world, but present Jesus.

In connection with this, a serious pastoral problem now exists. The defection of many members of the Catholic Church in various countries to other Christian confessions of Protestant type is giving rise to serious concern. If we take the trouble to observe the phenomenon from close up, we see that generally the defectors are attracted by a simpler, more immediate style of preaching, where all the emphasis falls on accepting Jesus as Lord and Saviour of one's life. I am not talking so much about the mainstream Protestant denominations as of small revivalist Churches and other groups and sects that lay stress on a 'second conversion'. The fascination this type of preaching exerts on people is remarkable and cannot be said to be always superficial and ephemeral, since it often changes people's lives.

The Churches belonging to the strong dogmatic and theological tradition and having a big legislative apparatus, sometimes find themselves at a disadvantage, owing to their very wealth and complexity of doctrine, when dealing with a society that has in large degree lost its Christian faith and that consequently needs to start again at the beginning, that is to say, by rediscovering Jesus Christ. It seems we are still lacking a suitable instrument for coping with this new situation, now obtaining in various Christian countries. Owing to our past, we are better prepared to be 'shepherds' than 'fishers' of men; that is to say, better prepared to feed the people who have stayed faithful to the Church than to bring new people in or to 'fish back' those who have wandered away. This shows how urgently we need a new evangelization that, while being truly Catholic, that is to say, open to all the fullness of the truth and the Christian life, will yet be simple and basic; and this is achieved by making Jesus Christ the initial and focal point of everything, the one from whom we always set out and the one to whom we always return.

Insistence on the importance of a personal encounter with Jesus Christ is not a sign of subjectivism or emotionalism but is the translation, on to the spiritual and pastoral plane, of a dogma central to our faith: that Jesus Christ is 'a person'. In this meditation I shall try to show how the dogma proclaiming Christ to be 'a person' is no mere metaphysical statement no longer of interest to anyone or at best only to a few theologians, but, on the contrary, is the very basis of the Christian message and the secret of its strength. The only way of getting to know a living person is of course by entering into a living relationship with that person.

The General Councils of the Church encapsulated the essential aspects of faith in Jesus Christ in three affirmations: Jesus Christ is true man; Jesus Christ is true God; Jesus Christ is one sole person. We have here a sort of dogmatic triangle, of which the humanity and divinity represent the two sides and the unity of person the apex. That is also true historically. First, the humanity of Christ was firmly established during the struggle against the Gnostic heresy. Next, his divinity was firmly established during the struggle against Arianism in the fourth century. And finally, his unity of person during the Christological controversies of the fifth century.

Having reflected in the foregoing chapters on Jesus 'true man' and on Jesus 'true God', we must now reflect on Jesus as 'person'. 'We teach', says the Council of Chalcedon, 'that Christ must be acknowledged as a person, or hypostasis, not separated and divided into two persons, but unique and identical only-begotten Son, Word and our Lord Jesus Christ.'[1]

We are aware of the central importance of this truth; it speaks of an hypostatic or personal union between the human race and God in Christ. It is the 'node' holding Trinity and Christology together. Christ is a person and this person is none other than the person of the Word, the second person of the Trinity who, by taking flesh of Mary, began also to exist as a human being in time. Rather than as two natures, in this light divinity and humanity appear as two phases or two modes of existing for the same person: first, outside time, then within time; first, without flesh, then in the flesh. This insight has our salvation depend in the strictest possible sense on God's free initiative: which best reflects the profundity of the Christian religion at its very root, i.e., of being the religion of grace, of giving, rather than of conquest and works; of the descent of God rather than ascent to God. 'No one', says Jesus in St John's gospel, 'has ascended into heaven except the Son of man who descended from heaven' (Jn 3:13), and this means that we cannot ascend to God unless God himself first descends halfway to us; that no Christology departing radically 'from the base' (from Jesus 'human person') can ever succeed in 'ascending into heaven', that is to say, in rising high enough to attain faith in the divinity and pre-existence of Christ. And this is what recent experience has demonstrated once again.

2. 'That I may know him . . .'

But this is not what I really want to talk about. This dogma too, of the unique person of Christ, is an 'open structure', that is to say, capable of speaking to us today, of answering to new needs of the faith, which are different from those of the fifth century. Today no one denies that Christ is 'one person'. There are, as we have seen, people who deny that he is a 'divine' person, preferring to say that he is a 'human' person. But the unity of Christ's person is not contested by anyone. It is not however on this traditional stamping-ground that the modern applicability of our dogma is to be found.

On the plane of practical life, the most important thing today in the dogma of Christ 'one person' is not so much the adjective 'one' as the noun 'person'. To discover and proclaim that Jesus Christ is not an idea, an historical problem, a mere personage, but a person and a living one at that! For this is what is lacking today and what we desperately need, so as not to allow Christianity to be reduced to ideology or mere theology.

This truth too forms part of that enchanted castle which is the dogmatic terminology of the ancient Church; where, locked in slumber lie the handsomest of princes and the loveliest of princesses who only need to be aroused for them to leap to their feet in all their glory. Following the programme that we have sketched out for ourselves — of revitalizing dogma by starting out once more from its biblical basis — we now turn again to the word of God. And since the matter in hand here is to make a personal encounter with the Risen Christ possible for our contemporaries, I set out from the page in the New Testament that tells us about the most famous 'personal encounter' with the Risen One that ever occurred on earth: that of the Apostle Paul. 'Saul, Saul'. . . 'Who are you, Lord?' . . . 'I am Jesus!' Such was the encounter from which such blessings flowed for the nascent Church (cf Acts 9:4–5).

But let us hear how he himself describes the encounter that was the watershed of his life: 'But whatever gain I had [being circumcised, of the seed of Israel, a Pharisee, blameless], I counted as loss for the sake of Christ. Indeed I count everything as loss because of the surpassing worth of knowing Christ Jesus my Lord. For his sake I have suffered the loss of all things, and count them as refuse, in order that I may gain Christ and be found in him, not having a righteousness of my own, based on law, but that which is through faith in Christ, the righteousness from God that depends on faith; that I may know him' (Phil 3:7–10).

I still recall the moment when this passage became an 'active reality' for me, for the word of God is not truly known in the depths of its nature, except by its fruits, that is to say, by what it has at some time produced either in your own life or the lives of others. While studying Christology, I did a great deal of research into the origins of the concept of 'person' in theology, its definitions and various interpretations. I was familiar with the endless discussions on the unique person and hypostasis of Christ in the Byzantine period, the modern developments over the psychological dimension of the person, with the consequent problem over the 'I' of Christ . . . In one sense I knew everything there was to know about the person of Christ. But, at a given moment, I made a disconcerting discovery: yes, I knew all about the person of Jesus, but I did not know Jesus in person! I knew the notion of person better than the person himself.

It was actually those words of Paul that helped me to grasp the difference. More especially, it was the phrase: 'that I may know him . . .' and, in particular, that pronoun 'him', which struck me. It seemed to me to contain more about Jesus than any number of Christological treatises. 'Him' means Jesus Christ, my Lord 'in flesh and bone'. I realized that I knew books about Jesus, doctrines, heresies about

Jesus, concepts about Jesus, but I did not know him as a concrete, living person. I had not got to know him in the least while approaching him through historical and theological studies. I had hitherto acquired an *impersonal* knowledge of the *person* of Christ. A contradiction and a paradox, alas, all too common!

Why impersonal? Because this knowledge leaves us neutral as regards the person of Christ, while the knowledge that Paul had made him consider everything else as loss, as rubbish, and filled his heart with an irresistible yearning to be with Christ, to divest himself of everything, even of the body, to be with him. The person is a unique reality. Unlike every other created thing, the person can only be known 'personally', that is to say, by establishing a direct personal relationship with it, so that the person ceases to be an 'it' and becomes a 'he' or 'she', or better still a 'you'.

From this point of view, knowledge of the person of Christ differs even from knowledge of his humanity and divinity, that is to say, of his natures. These last, being objects and parts of the whole, may be objectified and studied. But not the person. The person is a living subject and is the whole. For this reason, it cannot be fully appreciated unless by preserving it as such, that is to say, whole, and by entering into relationship with this. Reflecting on the concept of person in God, St Augustine, with all Latin theology behind him, came to the conclusion that person means 'relationship'. Modern thought, though profane, has confirmed the saint's insight. 'True personality consists in rediscovering oneself by immersing oneself in the other' (Hegel). The person is person in so far as opening to a 'you', and by means of comparison acquires self-knowledge. Being a person is a 'being-in-relation-to'. This is eminently true of the divine persons of the Trinity, who are 'pure relationships' even though subsistent ones; but in a different way it is also true of every person, whether it be ours or Christ's. The person then is not known in its reality, except by entering into 'relationship' with it. And this is why one cannot know Christ as person, except by entering into a personal me-you relationship with him. In other words, by recognizing him as one's Lord.

Entering into a personal relationship with Jesus is not

like entering into a relationship with anyone you may run into. To be a 'true' relationship, it has to lead to recognition and acceptance of Jesus for what he is, that is to say, Lord. In the text quoted above, the Apostle speaks of a 'superior', 'eminent' or even 'sublime' (*hyperechon*) knowledge of Christ and different from all other kinds; certainly different from knowing Jesus 'according to the flesh', today we should say as an historical figure, in an external, 'scientific' way. And he also says what this superior knowledge consists in: in acknowledging Christ as one's personal Lord . . . 'Because of the surpassing worth of knowing Christ Jesus my Lord.' The sublime knowledge of Christ, the personal knowledge of him, thus consists in this: that I acknowledge Jesus as my Lord, which is like saying: as my centre, my meaning, my reason for living, my supreme good, my purpose in life, my joy, my glory, my law, my leader, my Saviour, the One to whom I belong.

From this you can see that it is possible to read, and even write, books and books about Jesus Christ and yet not really know Jesus Christ at all. Really knowing Jesus Christ is altogether special. Like knowing one's own mother. Who know their mothers best? The people who have read all the best books on motherhood, or studied the concept of mother in various cultures and religions? Of course not! They who know their mother best are the children who, having outgrown childhood, realize one day that they were formed in their mother's womb and brought into the world through her birth-pangs. They become aware of a bond that is unique in the world, existing between them and her. Often this comes as a 'revelation', as a kind of 'initiation' into the mystery of life.

So it is with Jesus. We know Jesus for what he really is, that is to say, intrinsically, not extrinsically, when one day, by revelation, not now of the flesh and blood, as in the case of our mother, but of the heavenly Father, we discover that we have been born of him, from his death, and that we exist, spiritually, for him. We know it when, reading the famous *Song of the Suffering Servant* in Isaiah, we suddenly perceive all the mysterious strength of that 'we-him' relationship on which the whole song is constructed:

> *He* was wounded for *our* transgressions,
> on *him* was the chastisement that made *us* whole
> and with *his* stripes *we* are healed . . .
> The Lord has laid on *him*
> the iniquity of *us* all.
> (Isaiah 53:5–6)

3. '*The object of faith is a thing*'

To revitalize the dogma that speaks of Jesus 'one person' means passing from consideration of the *essence* of the person to consideration of his *existence*; to perceive, that is to say, that the Risen Jesus is an existing person who stands before me and calls me by name, as he called Saul. In the field of faith too, we have to carry out the programme dear to the philosopher Husserl and to all phenomenology, of 'going to the things'; of going beyond concepts, words, declarations of faith, to attain the realities of faith as they are. In this case, that reality of faith which is Christ Jesus risen and living. 'The object of faith is not a proposition but a thing', St Thomas says.[2] We for ourselves cannot be satisfied with believing in the formula 'one person'; we have to reach the person himself and, in a certain sense, touch him.

There is a knowledge which is experience, that is to say, a tasting and a touching. St Paul is speaking of this when he says: 'That I may know him . . .' Here, 'to know' is very clearly what in biblical language means 'to possess'. Not knowing by concept but by the direct, immediate way. Speaking of the Risen One, St Augustine says: 'But what mortal can touch him when he is seated in heaven, if he does not touch him here on earth? That touch (cf Jn 20:17) moreover signifies faith. Who believes in Christ, touches Christ.'[3] In the knowledge of faith it sometimes happens, of a sudden, that our spirit is 'dazzled by the radiance of the truth as by a lamp' and then 'a sort of spiritual contact' ('*quidam spiritalis contactus*') is established with the reality believed in.[4]

This is not a matter of something far away from you; it is neither in heaven, nor beyond the seas, but in your own heart, and perhaps you only need to know this to recognize it. Has there been a moment in your life when Christ appeared to your inner eye in all his majesty, sweetness and beauty, when you felt, like the Apostle, that Christ had made you his own (cf Phil 3:12)? A moment, however brief, when the mystery of Christ and his mystical body so fascinated you that you even wished 'to depart and be with Christ' and know him as he really is? A moment, possibly when you were young, when for one instant the 'truth' of Christ was so clearly manifested to you that for its sake you could have taken on the whole world? The truth of the prophecies, the truth of the gospels, the truth of everything to do with Christ? If so, that was the sublime knowledge of Christ, worked in you by the Holy Spirit.

The object of faith is truly thus a 'thing'. East and West are in accord in attesting this type of knowledge, attaining to the ultimate reality. 'Our knowledge of things', says Cabasilas, 'is twofold: what can be acquired by listening, and what can be learnt by direct experience. In the first manner, we do not handle the thing but we see it in words as in a picture and by no means an accurate picture of its form. For among all things that exist, it is not possible to find one in all respects like another and that, if used as a model, would suffice for knowledge of the first. To know by experience, however, means to attain the thing itself: for here the form imprints itself in the soul and arouses desire directly proportionate to its beauty. But when we are deprived of a true idea of the object and only receive a weak and obscure picture of it, drawn from its relationships with other objects, our desire corresponds to this image and hence we do not love it as much as it deserves to be loved and through it we do not experience the feeling that could be aroused, because we have not enjoyed its form. For, as the diverse forms of diverse essences, by imprinting themselves in the soul, shape it in diverse ways, so it is with love. So, when love of the Saviour does not allow us to perceive anything extraordinary or supernatural within us, this is a manifest sign that we have only encountered voices talking about him; but how is it possible by such means to come to a good knowledge of the One to whom nothing is similar, who has nothing in common with others, to whom nothing can be compared and who cannot be compared to anything? How are we to learn about his beauty and love him in the manner that his beauty deserves? Those to whom such ardour was given as for them to be drawn out of their own nature and induced to desire and be able to perform greater works than human beings can conceive, were wounded directly by the Bridegroom; he it was who infused a ray of his beauty into their eyes; the size of the wound betrays the arrow; the ardour, he who caused the wound.'[5]

When love of the Saviour does not allow us to perceive anything extraordinary within ourselves, it is a sign that we have only encountered *voices* talking about him. Not *him*! If our proclamation of Christ does not startle anyone, if it is weak and repetitive, it is a sign that hitherto we have only known *voices* talking about him. Not *him*!

But how are we to restore to our vapid faith the realism that was the source of its strength in the Fathers and the saints? Formulas, concepts, words have taken on so much importance as often to turn themselves into a giant 'insulator' cloaking the realities and preventing them from giving us a shock. As, in the Eucharist, the visible signs, the bread and wine, are emptied of themselves, are laid aside, as it were, and reduced to pure signs in order to give place to the reality of the body and blood of Christ which they are to transmit, so, in talking about God, words ought to be humble signs, concerned to convey the living realities and truths that they contain and then to be laid aside. Only thus can Christ's words be revealed for what they are, and that is 'Spirit and life' (cf Jn 6:63).

We should, as I said, pass on from attention to the *essence* of the person, to attention to the *existence* of the person of Christ. This is the way a recent philosopher describes how the sudden discovery of the existence of things can come about: 'I was sitting', he wrote, 'in the public gardens. The root of the chestnut tree plunged into the ground, right under my bench. I no longer remembered it was a root. Words had disappeared and with them the meaning of things, the ways they are used, the tenuous signs of recognition that human beings have traced on their surfaces. I was sitting, rather huddled up, with head bowed, alone, facing that black, knotty, totally ugly mass that made me feel afraid. And then I had this flash of illumination. It took my breath away. Before these recent days, of course, I had anticipated

99

what "to exist" means. I was like other people, like the ones walking along by the sea in their spring clothes. Like them, I said: "The sea is green; that white spot on it is a seagull", but I did not feel that it existed, that the seagull was a "seagull-existing"; normally existence is in hiding. It is there, around us, we cannot say two words without talking about it, and yet we cannot touch it. When I thought I was thinking about it, I was evidently thinking about nothing, my head was empty or with only a word in it, the word "being". And then, look, at a stroke, there it was, as clear as day: existence was suddenly unveiled.'[6]

To know Christ in person, him, 'in flesh and bone', we need to go through this sort of experience. We need to perceive that he *exists*. For this is not only possible as regards the root of a chestnut tree, that is to say, something that can be seen and touched, but, by faith, even things that cannot be seen including God himself. It was like this one night when the believer Blaise Pascal discovered the living God of Abraham and preserved a record of this in short, burning, exclamatory phrases: 'God of Abraham, God of Isaac, God of Jacob. Not of the philosophers and learned. He is kept only by the means taught in the Gospel. Certitude, certitude, love, joy, peace. Forgetfulness of the world and of everything outside God.'[7] For him, that night, God had become an 'active reality'. A person 'who breathes' as Paul Claudel calls him.

4. *The name and heart of Jesus*

How is it possible to have an experience of this sort? Having long sought by every method to attain the being of things and so to speak snatch their mystery out of them, one current of existential philosophy has had to give up and admit (thus approaching, without knowing it, the Christian concept of grace) that the unique manner in which this can happen is for being to reveal itself and come on its own initiative to encounter the human being. And the place where this can happen is language, which is a kind of 'house of being'. Now, that is certainly true, if by 'being' we mean the Being (God, or Risen Christ) and by 'language' we mean the Word or the kerygma. The Risen Christ in person reveals himself to us and we can encounter him personally in his word. That is indeed his 'house', and the Holy Spirit opens its door to anyone who knocks.

In the Apocalypse he meets the Church and says: 'I am the First and the Last and the Living One; I died and behold I am alive' (Rev 1:18). Still it rings out now, after he has died and risen again: Christ's 'I Am'. When God introduced himself to Moses with these words, their meaning seems to have been: 'I am there', that is to say, I exist for you; I am not one of the many gods and idols of the peoples, that have mouths but do not speak, that have eyes but do not see. I really exist! I am not a theoretical God, a God existing mostly in the mind. And now Jesus Christ says the same thing.

Would that we might one day perceive this, undergo this experience, as St Paul did: 'Who are you, Lord?' . . . 'I am Jesus.' Then our faith would change, it would become contagious. We should kick the sandals off our feet as Moses did that day, and say like Job: 'I had heard of thee by the hearing of the ear, but now my eye sees thee' (Job 42:5). We too should have our breath taken away!

All this is possible. This is not mystical exaltation but is based on an objective datum, that is to say, Christ's promise: 'Yet a little while', Jesus said to the disciples at the Last Supper, 'and the world will see me no more, but you will see me; because I live, you will live also' (Jn 14:19). After his resurrection and ascension into heaven — for this was the time to which Jesus was referring — the disciples were to see Jesus with a new, spiritual, inward sight, by faith, but a sight so real that Jesus could simply say: 'You will see me.' And the explanation for all this is that he 'lives'.

There is one extremely simple method that can help in this effort to enter into contact with Jesus, and this is to invoke his name: 'Jesus!' For the Bible, as we know, the name is the most direct representative of the person and in a sense actually is the person. It is a sort of door, allowing entry into the mystery of the person. It does not belong to the category of other titles, concepts and declarations — as does the title 'person' itself — but is something more and different. They are common to many, whereas the name is unique. In the New Testament, to believe in the *name* of Jesus, to pray and suffer for his *name*, means to believe in the *person* of Jesus, to pray and suffer in union with him; to be baptized 'in the name of Jesus' is to be baptized into him, incorporated into him.

Of the Jesus who ascended into heaven, no relics or traces have remained on earth; his name however has remained and numberless are the souls in the East as in the West who by experience throughout the centuries have known the power enclosed in this name. Israel too admitted no pictures or images of God, but in their stead knew the name as a holy path for entering into contact with him. Israel knew 'the majesty of the name of the Lord his God' (Mic 5:4). Now the same majesty is also shared by the glorified Son.

Following St Bernard, the Church sings the sweetness, suavity and strength of the name of Jesus ('*Iesu dulcis memoria* . . .'). St Bernardino of Siena renewed the devotion to it and promoted the feast-day, so re-awakening the torpid faith of entire cities and peoples. Orthodox spirituality has made the name of Jesus the privileged vehicle for bringing God into the heart and for attaining purity of heart. All those who in simplicity learn to utter the name of Jesus, sooner or later experience something that surpasses all explanation. They then begin to hold this name dear, as a treasure, to prefer it to all Christ's other titles designating his nature or function. Nor do they need to say 'Jesus of Nazareth', as historians and scholars commonly call him, since for them to say 'Jesus' is enough. To say 'Jesus' means 'to call him', to establish personal contact with him, as happens when, in a crowd, you call a person by name and the latter turns round to see who is calling.

How many things we succeed in expressing just with the name of Jesus! According to the need or particular grace of the moment and the tone in which we utter it, with it we proclaim that Jesus is the Lord, that is to say, we 'affirm' Jesus against every power of evil and every anxiety; with it, we rejoice, we weep, we implore, we knock, we thank the Father, we adore, we intercede . . .

Another way of cultivating this 'personal' knowledge of Jesus alongside devotion to his name, is devotion to his heart. In the Old Testament, especially in the Psalms, at the time when inspiration grows strongest and most consuming in the praying poet, the desire for union with God always has recourse to a symbol: the face. 'Thou hast said, "Seek ye my face." My heart says to thee, "Thy face, Lord, do I seek. . ." Hide not thy face from me' (Ps 27:8–9). 'My soul thirsts for God, for the living God. When shall I come and behold the face of God?' (Ps 42:2). The 'face' indicates here the living presence of Yahweh; not only his 'aspect' but also, in the active sense, his 'gaze' which meets that of the creature, reassuring, illuminating, raising up. It indicates the very person of God, and indeed the word 'person' is actually derived from this biblical meaning of face, countenance (*prosopon*).

In our relations with Jesus Christ, we have something very much more real to which 'to cling' in order to enter into contact with his living person: we have his heart! The face was only a metaphorical symbol, since everyone knew perfectly well that God has not got a human face; but for us, now, since the incarnation, the heart is a real symbol, that is to say, it is both symbol and reality: that within the Trinity there beats a human heart. For, if Christ has risen from the dead, his heart too has risen from the dead; it is alive, like all the rest of his body, in a different dimension from before, spiritual now, not carnal, but alive. If the Lamb is alive in heaven, 'standing as though it had been slain' (Rev 5:6), his heart too shares the same state; it is a heart transfixed yet living; eternally transfixed, since eternally living.

Perhaps this is the certitude that was lacking (or that was insufficiently expressed) in the traditional cult of the Sacred Heart, and that can contribute to renewing and requickening that devotion. The Sacred Heart is not only the heart that used to beat in Jesus' breast when he was on earth and that was pierced on the cross: of which only faith and devotion or, at most, the Eucharist can perpetuate the presence among us. It does not live only in devotion but also in reality; it is not located only in the past but also in the present. Devotion to the Sacred Heart is not exclusively bound up with a spirituality that gives primacy to the earthly Jesus and the Crucified, as for many hundreds of years the Latin devotion has been, but is equally open to the mystery of the resurrection and of the lordship of Christ. Each time we think of this heart, each time we feel it, so to speak, beating above us, at the centre of the mystical body, we enter into contact with the living person of Jesus.

So devotion to the Sacred Heart has not exhausted its task with the disappearance of Jansenism but still to the present day remains the best antidote to abstraction, intellectualism and that formalism that can make theology and faith so arid. A beating heart is what most clearly distinguishes a living reality from the concept of it, since the concept may contain everything about a person, save his beating heart.

NOTES

1 Denzinger-Schoenmetzer, 302.
2 St Thomas Aquinas, *S. Th.*, II, IIae, Q.1, A.2, ad 2.
3 St Augustine, *Sermo* 243, 1–2, (PL 38, 1144).
4 St Augustine, *Sermo* 52, 6, 16 (PL 38, 360).
5 Cabasilas, *Vita in Christo*, II, 8 (PG 150, 552f).
6 J-P. Sartre, *La Nausée*, in *Oeuvres romanesques*, Gallimard, Paris p. 105f.
7 B. Pascal, *Memorial*, entry 737 in *Pensées*, Dent, London 1960.

Chapter VI

'Do you love me?'

Loving Jesus

St Thomas divides love into two great categories: love-of-desire and love-of-friendship, which correspond roughly to the other more common distinction between *eros* and *agape*, between acquisitive and self-giving love. Love-of-desire, he says, is when someone loves something (*aliquis amat aliquid*), that is to say, when a *person* loves a *thing*, by 'thing' meaning not only a material or spiritual good but also a person, if this last is not loved as a person but is instrumentalized and reduced to a thing. Love-of-friendship is when someone loves someone (*aliquis amat aliquem*), that is to say, a *person* loves another *person*.[1]

The fundamental relationship binding us to Jesus is therefore love. The question put to us concerning Christ's divinity was 'Do you believe?' The question we now have to put to ourselves concerning Christ's person is: 'Do you love me?' There is an exam in Christology that all believers, not merely theologians, have to sit. It consists of two questions obligatory for all candidates. And the examiner this time is Christ himself. On the result of this exam depends not our advancement to the priesthood or to the preaching ministry, not even our advancement to a doctorate in theology, but our advancement to eternal life. And the two questions are just these 'Do you believe?' and 'Do you love me?' Do you believe in Christ's divinity? Do you love Christ's person?

St Paul pronounced these terrible words: 'If anyone has no love for the Lord, let him be anathema' (1 Cor 16:22), and the Lord who is being spoken of here is the Lord Jesus Christ. In the course of the centuries a great many anathemas have been pronounced in connection with Christ: against those denying his humanity, against those denying his divinity, against those dividing his two natures, against those not distinguishing between them . . . but perhaps not enough attention has been paid to the fact that the first Christological anathema, pronounced by an apostle in person, was against those who do not love Jesus Christ.

In this sixth stage of our approach to Jesus Christ by the dogmatic way of the Church, we shall, the Spirit aiding, try to deal with some questions concerned with loving Christ: Why should we love Jesus Christ? What does loving Jesus Christ mean? Is it possible to love Jesus Christ? Do *we* love Jesus Christ?

1. *Why should we love Jesus Christ?*

The first reason why we should love Jesus Christ and the simplest one is that he himself has asked us to do so. In the Risen One's last appearance recorded in St John's gospel, the moment comes when Jesus turns to Simon Peter and asks him three times over: 'Simon, son of John, do you love me?' (Jn 21:15). Twice in the words of Jesus the verb *agapao* occurs, which is normally used to denote the highest form of love, that of *agape* or charity; and once the verb *phileo,* which means love-of-friendship, loving or being fond of someone. 'At the end of life', it has been said, 'we shall be examined about love',[2] from which we see that this was what happened to the apostles too: at the end of their life with Jesus, at the end of the gospel, they were examined about love. Not about anything else.

Like all Christ's great sayings in the gospel, so too this 'Do you love me?' is not addressed only to the person hearing it on the first occasion, in this case Peter, but to all who read the gospel afterwards. If this were not so, the gospel would not be the book it is, the one containing words that do 'not pass away' (Mt 24:35). Besides, how can anyone who knows who Jesus Christ is, hear that question from his own lips and not feel personally summoned, not perceived that the 'you' of 'Do you love me?' is addressed individually to *us*?

This question immediately puts each of us in a unique position, it isolates us from everyone else, it individualizes us, it makes us persons. To the question: 'Do you love me?' we cannot respond through intermediary persons or intermediary institutions. To love Jesus, it is not enough to belong to a body, the Church. We can see this for ourselves in the actual gospel narrative without any need to force the text. Up to that moment, the scene as presented is very crowded and busy: along with Simon Peter, there were Thomas, Nathanael, the two sons of Zebedee and two other disciples. Together they had fished, had eaten, had recognized the Lord. But now, suddenly, at that question from Jesus, everything and everyone fade away as though into nothing, disappearing from the gospel scene. An intimate space is created in which, alone, face to face, stand Jesus and Peter. The apostle is individualized and isolated from everyone by this unexpected question: 'Do you love me?' A question which no one else can answer for him and which he cannot answer — as he had so many other times — on behalf of all the others, but has to answer for himself alone. For we see that Peter is constrained, by the way the questions follow so insistently, to look into himself, passing from the first two replies, immediate but superficial ones, to the last one in which all knowledge of his past and also great humility are seen to flower within him: 'Lord, you know everything; you know that I love you' (Jn 21:17).

So we have to love Jesus because he himself asks us to. But also for another reason: because he loved us first. That more than anything else was what inflamed the apostle Paul. 'He loved me', he said, 'and gave himself for me' (Gal 2:20). 'The love of Christ', he says again elsewhere, 'overwhelms us when we consider that one has died for all' (cf 2 Cor 5:14). The fact that Jesus loved us first and to the point of giving his life for us 'overwhelms us' or — as one may also translate — 'constrains us on all sides', 'urges us on'. It is the business of that well-known law by which love '*a nullo amato amar perdona*',[3] that is to say, does not permit that anyone loved should not love in return. 'Who would not love thee, loving us so dearly?' runs the famous carol.[4] Love can only be repaid by love. No other return will do.

Next, we ought to love Jesus especially because he deserves to be loved and is loveable in himself. In himself, he unites all beauty, all perfection and holiness. Our hearts need 'something majestic' to love; so nothing can satisfy them completely other than he. If the heavenly Father is well pleased with him, as it is written, if the Son is the object of all his love (Mt 3:17; 17:5), how can he not be of ours? If he completely fulfils and satisfies all God the Father's infinite capacity for loving, will he not fulfil ours?

We ought also to love Jesus because everyone who loves him is loved by the Father. 'Whoever loves me', he said, 'will be loved by my Father' and: 'The Father himself loves you because you have loved me' (Jn 14:21–23; 16:27).

We ought to love Jesus because only those who love him can know him: 'To whoever loves me', he said, 'I shall reveal myself' (cf Jn 14:21). If the maxim is true that 'what is not known cannot be loved' (*nihil volitum quin praecognitum*), the opposite is nonetheless true, particularly where divine matters are concerned, by which I mean that unless there is love there cannot be knowledge. St Augustine is saying the same thing, where he remarks: 'There is no entering into truth unless with charity.'[5] This insight has been taken up and affirmed by some currents of modern thought too, such as phenomenology and existentialism.[6] But, as concerning Christ and God, it is above all confirmed by the constant experience of the saints and all believers. Without a true love inspired by the Holy Spirit, the Jesus who can be known as a result of the most brilliant and acute Christological analyses, is not the true Jesus but something different. The true Jesus is not revealed by 'flesh and blood', that is to say, by human brain-power and research, but by 'the Father who is in heaven' (cf Mt 16:17), and the Father does not reveal him to the inquisitive, but to those who love him; not to the wise and clever, but to babes (cf Mt 11:15).

Lastly, we ought to love Jesus because only by loving him is it possible to keep his words and put his commandments into practice. 'If you love me', he said, 'you will keep my commandments', and: 'Whoever does not love me does not keep my words' (Jn 14:15, 24). This means it is not possible to be serious Christians, that is to say, effectively to follow the radical dictates and requirements of the gospel, without having a true love for Jesus Christ. And even if, let us suppose, someone did manage to do this, it would be quite futile: without love, nothing would be gained (cf 1 Cor 13:3).

In contrast, who loves has wings; to such a one, nothing seems impossible or too hard.

2. *What does loving Jesus Christ mean?*

The question 'What does loving Jesus Christ mean?' can have a very practical sense: knowing what is involved in loving Jesus Christ, knowing in what love for him consists. In this case, the answer is very simple, and Jesus Christ himself gives it in the gospel. It does not consist in saying: 'Lord, Lord!' but in doing the Father's will and in keeping his words (cf Mt 7:21). When 'loving' concerns a creature — husband, wife, child, parent, friend — it means seeking the good of the person loved, it means desiring and procuring that person's well being. . . But what 'good' can we desire for the Risen Jesus that he does not already have? Loving, as regards Christ, therefore means something else. The 'good' of Jesus, that is to say, his 'food', is the Father's will. So, loving or desiring Jesus' good essentially means, with him, doing the Father's will. Doing it ever more fully, ever more joyfully. 'Whoever does the will of God', Jesus says, 'is my brother, and sister, and mother' (Mk 3:35). For him, all the loveliest qualities of loving are subsumed into that act: the doing of the Father's will.

Loving Jesus does not, we may say, so much consist in words or pious emotions as in deeds: doing as he has done who has loved us not in word alone but in deed. And what deeds! He humbled himself to nothing for our sake and from being rich became poor. 'My love for you was not make-believe', Blessed Angela of Foligno heard Christ say to her one day and at this word she nearly died of grief, realizing how, in contrast, her love for him till then had been precisely that: make-believe.[7]

But I should like to consider the question 'What does loving Jesus Christ mean?' in a less retributive and work-a-day sense. There are two great commandments concerning love. The first: 'You shall love the Lord your God with all your heart, and with all your soul, and with all your mind'; the second is: 'You shall love your neighbour as yourself' (Mt 22:37–39). In what we have just mentioned, where do we site love for the person of Christ? To which of the two commandments does it belong: to the first or the second? And again: Is Christ the supreme and ultimate object of human love, or only the penultimate? Is he only the way to the love of God, or is he the end of it?

These are questions of the greatest importance for the Christian faith as indeed for the prayer-life of the individual, yet it has to be admitted that uncertainty and ambiguity pervade them, at the practical level, at least. There are treatises on loving God (*De diligendo Deo*), in which loving God is dealt with at large, without however any precise treatment of how loving Christ should be integrated into it; whether it should be regarded as the same thing, or whether instead love for God, without other addition, represents a superior stage, a higher objective for love. Everyone is of course convinced that the problem of how a human being should love God does not take the same form since Christ's coming as it did before he came, or for that matter that it takes outside Christianity. With regard to loving God, what the incarnation of the Word brought into the world was not just an extra reason for loving God, or just one further example — the highest — of this love; it brought something very much newer: it revealed a new face of God and hence a new way to love him, a new 'form' of love for God. But not all conclusions have been drawn from this, nor have those drawn all been made explicit.

True, by the time of the Rule of St Benedict, the maxim was current: 'The love of Christ must come before all else.'[8] the *Imitation of Christ* has a wonderful chapter entitled: 'To love Jesus Christ above all things'[9] and St Alphonsus Maria de Liguori wrote a very popular book called *The Practice of the Love of Jesus Christ*. But in all these cases the comparison is, so to speak, from Christ downwards, that is to say, between him and all creatures, the argument being that one must not put anything in the human sphere before the love of Christ, not even oneself. The question of whether we ought not perhaps to put anything in the divine sphere before the love of Christ is however left open.

We are dealing with a real problem here, arising from events in the past. For Origen, influenced by the Platonic view of the world — permeated through and through by the tendency to despise whatever pertains to this visible world — established a principle which has had great weight in the development of Christian spirituality. He envisages a level beyond that of love for Christ as the incarnate Word; he postulates a more perfect stage of love, in which the Word is contemplated and loved exclusively in his divine form, as he was before he became flesh, hence by-passing his human form. In other words, to be accurate, we love the Word of God, not Jesus Christ. The incarnation was necessary, according to Origen, to attract souls, just as it is necessary for the scent of a perfume to be released from the vessel before it can be enjoyed. But, once attracted by the divine fragrance, souls hasten no longer to attain a mere divine fragrance but its very substance.[10]

This notion that something stands above love for Christ crops up from time to time in the course of the centuries under the form of a 'mysticism of the divine essence'. In this is posited as absolute apex of divine love, contemplation of and union with the absolute, unqualified essence of God, without form and without name, taking place in the depths of the soul, totally devoid of all sensible imagery, even though it is of Christ and his passion. Meister Eckhart speaks of an immersing of the soul 'in the limitless abyss of the Godhead', giving the impression that he thinks of 'the depths of the soul', rather than the person of Christ, as the place and means for encountering God without intermediaries. 'The power of the soul', he writes, 'attains God in his essential being, stripped of everything.'[11]

St Teresa of Avila felt a need to react against this tendency which was also to be found in her day in certain circles of spirituality, and did so with those famous pages in which she very vigorously affirms that there is no stage in the spiritual life, be it however elevated, at which one can or, worse indeed, one should prescind from Christ's humanity to concentrate directly on the divine essence.[12] The saint explains how a little instruction and contemplation had for a while turned her away from the Saviour's humanity, but how conversely progress in instruction and contemplation had led her back to it once and for all.

It is a significant fact, in the history of Christian

spirituality, that the tendency championing a direct union with the divine essence has always been regarded with suspicion (as in the case of the speculative mysticism of the Rhineland in the fifteenth century and later of the so called 'Alumbrados'), and more especially the fact that it has not produced a single saint to be recognized by the Church despite having left behind works of the highest speculative and religious quality.

The problem that I have touched on so far has become one concerning us today, in a different context, owing to the spread among Christians of techniques of prayer and forms of spirituality which have their origins in India and the Far East. As regards the Christian faith, these practices are not in themselves bad; they play a part in that vast 'evangelistic preparation' in the same way as, according to some of the Fathers, certain religious insights of the Greeks also had a part to play. St Justin Martyr used to say that everything true and good said or invented by anyone belongs to Christians, since they adore the total Word of whom these various 'seeds of truth' were no more than partial and provisional manifestations.[13] Indeed, the primitive Church followed this principle, for example in its attitude towards the mystery religions and cults of its day, they too for the most part being of Asiatic origin. While rejecting all the mythological and idolatrous elements in such cults, the Church did not hesitate to appropriate the language and indeed certain ceremonies and symbols from the mystery cults in order to present the Christian mysteries. So, though we ought not to exaggerate the influence of the mystery cults on the Christian liturgy, we must not on the other hand deny it altogether.

Rightly therefore a recent document issued by the Magisterium devoted to the problem of these forms of oriental spirituality affirms that 'these indications are not to be prejudicially disparaged as un-Christian.'[14] Yet that same document of the Magisterium is right in alerting the faithful to the danger of introducing, along with the techniques of prayer and meditation, other elements alien to the Christian faith. The most delicate point is precisely that concerning the position of Jesus Christ, the man-God. In the internal logic of Hinduism and Buddhism, by which these techniques of meditation are generally inspired, the need is to overcome everything that is particular, sensible and historical, so as to immerse oneself in the Divine All or Nothing. There can hence be a tacit tendency to lay meditation on Jesus aside, whereas for us Christians Jesus is the unique possibility offered to the human race for attaining eternity and the Absolute. Not only hence is it not necessary to put Christ aside in order to reach God, but you cannot in fact get to God except 'by means of him' (cf Jn 14:6). He is 'the Way and the Truth', that is to say, not only the means for arriving but also the point of arrival.

These forms of spirituality are therefore positive as regards the way that leads to Christ, but they change entirely and become negative as soon as they, instead of putting Christ first, can be classified as 'after Christ' or 'beyond Christ'. In this latter case, they rejoin the attempt to 'go beyond the faith', for which St John the Evangelist rebuked the Gnostics of old (cf 2 Jn 9). They are a relapse from faith to trusting in works. They are a new making-do with the 'elemental spirits of the universe', having failed to recognize that 'the fulness of the deity' dwells in Christ. This is to repeat the error with which the Apostle reproached the Colossians (cf Col 2:8–9).

Yet perhaps in all this reversal of things with Christians having recourse to forms of oriental spirituality, it is not enough merely to voice a criticism; self-criticism too will not come amiss. We ought, in other words, to be considering why this happens, why so many people in quest of a personal and lived experience of God feel impelled to seek it outside our own structures and communities. If we are witnessing a quest for the Spirit without Christ, perhaps this is because we are offering a Spirit-less Christ and Christianity.

But let us see how the dogma of the unique person of Christ is able to give an adequate reply to all these problems, posed in the past by the mysticism of the divine essence, and today by the spread of forms of oriental spirituality. Let us see, in other words, how a theological justification can be found for the affirmation that absolutely nothing must be allowed to come before love for Christ, either in the human sphere or in the divine. For in whom does the love terminate? Who is the object of it? We have already seen that the love-of-desire, or *eros*, can only terminate at things, whereas the love-of-friendship, or *agape*, with which we are now concerned, can only seek a person as person. But *who* is the person of Christ? Certainly, if we follow that Christology which speaks of Christ as a 'human person', everything is different. Not only is it possible but actually a positive duty, eventually to transcend even Christ, if we are not to remain in the sphere of created things. If however, professing the faith of the Church, we hold that Christ is a 'divine person', the person of the Son of God, then loving Christ is loving God himself. With no qualitative distinction. He is thus the form that loving God has taken for human beings, thanks to his incarnation. He who said: 'Who hates me hates my Father also' (Jn 15:23), can by the same token also say: 'Who loves me loves my Father too.' In Christ we attain God directly, without intermediary. I have already said that loving Jesus, wanting his good, essentially means doing the Father's will; we see however that, far from creating difference and inferiority with respect to the Father, this creates equality. The Son is the equal of the Father, precisely because of his absolute dependence on the Father.

If the perennial meaning of the Nicene definition is that in every age and culture Christ must be proclaimed as 'God', not in some derived or secondary acceptance but in the strongest sense that the word 'God' bears in any given culture, then it is also true that Christ is not to be loved with a secondary or derived love, but by right as God. That in no culture, in other words, is a higher ideal than that of loving Jesus Christ to be conceived.

It is certainly true, all the same, that Jesus is also a human being and as such he is our 'neighbour', one of our 'brothers' as he himself says (cf Mt 28:10), as also 'the first-born among many brothers' (Rom 8:29). So he has to be loved with the other love too. He is the apex, not only of the first commandment, but also of the second. He is the synthesis of the two great commandments, which in a sense become one single commandment in him. He is, as St Leo the Great said, 'Everything from God's part and everything from our part.' He himself, for the rest, identified himself as our neighbour by saying that whatever we do to the least of his brothers, we do it to him (cf Mt 25:37f).

A number of great thinkers and theologians, while not posing the problem in the same terms as we have, have nonetheless perfectly grasped and expressed this central requirement of the Christian faith. One of these is St Bonaventure. As regards the great commandment to love, he posits no difference between Christ and God. Sometimes he writes of 'God', at other times of 'our Lord Jesus Christ'. 'With all our heart and with all our soul', he writes, commenting on this commandment, 'we must love the Lord God Jesus Christ.'[15] For St Bonaventure, loving Christ is the definitive and proper form that loving God has assumed for us: 'This is why I became a visible human being,' he represents the Word of God as saying, 'so that, being seen by you, I could be loved by you — I who was not loved by you while I remained unseen and invisible in my divinity. Give therefore the recompense due to my incarnation and passion, you for whose sake I took flesh and suffered death. I gave myself to you, give yourself to me.'[16]

Even more explicit and courageous is the position taken by Cabasilas, representing a rich vein of Orthodox thought. If I quote this little-known author of the Byzantine Middle Ages so often, I do it because I consider his work *Life in Christ* to be one of the absolute masterpieces of Christian theologico-spiritual literature. It is entirely constructed on this basically simple yet impressive insight: human beings, created in Christ and through Christ, only find their fulfilment and repose in loving Christ. 'The eye', he writes, 'was created for light, the ear for sounds, and everything for what it was ordained. But the soul's desire goes uniquely to Christ. Here is the place of its repose, since he alone is the good, the truth and all that inspires love. Human beings, of their very nature, reach out to Christ, with their will, with their thoughts, not only for the divinity of Christ, which is the end of all things, but also for his humanity. In Christ, human love finds its repose; Christ is the delight of human thought.'[17] Those celebrated words of St Augustine's addressed to God: 'Thou hast made us for thyself and our hearts are restless until they rest in thee',[18] are clearly and perhaps even deliberately applied by Cabasilas to Christ.

He is 'the place of our rest', that to which the most intimate aspirations of the human heart are directed. Not as to a different object, in respect to that indicated by the term 'God', but as to the same object in the form that he was pleased to assume for our sake and which he had planned from all eternity.

That said, we certainly do not mean to refuse to recognize or to conceal the great variety of ways that souls may use for drawing nearer to God, either depending on the diversity of gifts bestowed on each, or on people's differing psychology and mental structure. Some direct their love and prayer-life more towards the Father, others direct it more towards the Son, others towards the Holy Spirit and others towards the whole Trinity, by which love, praise and prayer is constantly offered 'to the Father through the Son in the Holy Spirit'. There are also those who direct their love and prayers simply to 'God', by the word 'God' comprehending the Tri-une God of the Bible: like Angela of Foligno when she cried out: 'I want God!' These are all good ways widely tried by the saints and often alternating in the lifetime and experience of the same individual. Owing to the mutual com-penetration of the divine persons, by loving one, we love all, since each is in all and all in each by virtue of the single nature and will. What I have been trying to say is just this: that whoever loves Jesus Christ does not for this reason move to a lower level, at an imperfect stage, but to the same level as whoever loves the Father.

3. *How are we to cultivate love for Jesus?*

I have done my best to answer the question: 'What does loving Jesus Christ mean?' but I am very conscious that what I have said falls far short of what might have been said and that only the saints could say. A liturgical hymn, often recited on feastdays of Jesus, runs:

> No tongue of mortal can express,
> no letters write its blessedness:
> alone who hath thee in his heart
> knows, love of Jesus! what thou art.[19]

Ours can be no more than a collection of crumbs fallen from the table of the masters (cf Mt 1:27), that is to say, an anthology of the experience of the great lovers of Jesus. To them it is, who have made the experiment, that we should have recourse if we want to learn the art of loving Jesus Christ. To St Paul, for instance, who wished to be released from the body in order 'to be with Christ' (cf Phil 1:23), or to St Ignatius of Antioch who wrote on the eve of martyrdom: 'It is a beautiful thing to set in the world for the Lord's sake and to rise again with him. . . All I desire is to find Jesus Christ. . . I seek him who died for me, I desire him who rose again for me!'[20]

But is it possible to love Jesus, now that the Word of God can no longer be seen, touched and contemplated with our fleshly eyes? St Leo the Great said that 'all visible properties of our Lord Jesus Christ, on his ascension, passed into the sacraments of the Church.'[21] It is therefore through the sacraments and especially through the Eucharist that our love for Christ is nourished, since the ineffable union with him takes place in these. It is possible to love Jesus Christ, for the reason that we have illustrated in the previous chapter: because he is a living and 'existent' person. He is not, that is to say, merely an historical figure or a philosophical concept, but a 'you', a 'friend', who can hence be loved with the love-of-friendship.

There is an infinite number of methods for cultivating this friendship with Jesus and we each have our own preferred means, our own gift, our own way. It may be in his word that we experience him living and conversing with us; it may be in prayer. Yet in every case the Spirit's unction is needful, for only the Holy Spirit knows who Jesus is and can inspire us with love for Jesus.

I should like to draw attention to one method which has always been dear to Tradition, especially to that of the Orthodox Church: *the memory of Jesus*. He entrusted himself, as it were, to the disciples' *memory* when he said: 'Do this in memory of me' (Lk 22:19). Memory is the door of the heart. 'Since a sorrow full of grace', writes Cabasilas again, 'is born from love for Christ, and love from the thoughts that have Christ and his love for the human race as their object, it is very useful to keep such thoughts in the memory,

117

revolving them in the soul and never taking respite from this activity. . . Thinking about Christ is the proper activity for baptized souls.'[22] St Paul had already made the connection between loving Christ and remembering him: 'Love for Christ overwhelms us at the thought that one has died for all' (2 Cor 5:14). When we for our part reflect and in our minds weigh up (*krinantes*) this deed, i.e., that he died for our sake, for all of us, we are as it were constrained to love Jesus in return. The thought or remembrance of him 'kindles' love.

In this sense, we may say that to love Jesus Christ we need to rediscover and cultivate a taste for the inner life and contemplation. The Apostle establishes this correspondence: in so far as 'we are strengthened in the inner man', Christ dwells in our hearts by faith; then, rooted and grounded in love, we come to comprehend the breadth and length and height and depth and to know 'the love of Christ which surpasses knowledge' (cf Eph 3:14–19). So we must begin by strengthening the inner self, which for a believer means believing more, hoping more, praying more, letting ourselves be guided more by the Spirit. 'Christ in us, the hope of glory' (cf Col 1:27): this is the perfect definition of Christian inner life.

The greatest good fortune, or grace, that can befall young people — especially if called to the priesthood or in whatever manner to proclaim Christ to their fellows — is to make him their life's grand ideal, the 'hero' with whom they are in love and whom they want to make known to everyone. To be in love with Christ makes other members of God's people fall in love with him too. There is no finer vocation than this. To set Jesus as a seal upon one's heart. In the Song of Songs, it is in fact the bride, according to the traditional interpretation, the soul, who says to the bridegroom: 'Set me as a seal upon your heart, as a seal upon your arm' (Son 8:6). But the bridegroom, Christ, has already granted this request of his own accord; he has indeed set us as a seal upon his heart and upon his hands. A seal bloody and indelible. But the invitation is reciprocal. The bride too must set Christ as a seal on her heart. And that is why Christ now says to Church and individual soul: 'Set me as a seal upon your heart!' A seal, not there to prevent us from loving other people and other things — wife, husband, children, friends, souls and all good things — but to prevent us from loving them without him, outside him or instead of him.

If the Church in her deepest being is Christ's 'bride' (cf Eph 5:25f; Rev 19:7), what in particular is expected of a bride if not that she should love her husband? Does anything avail, if this is lacking? For loving Christ is 'the proper activity for baptized souls', the proper vocation of the Church.

If a young person feeling a radical call to follow Christ were to ask my advice along these lines: What ought I to do to persevere in my vocation and so one day be an enthusiastic and convinced proclaimer of Christ? I think I should instantly reply: Fall in love with Jesus, with him try to establish a relationship of intimate, humble friendship, then go serenely forward to meet the future. The world will try to beguile you by all sorts of means but it will not succeed, since 'he who is in you is greater than he who is in the world' (1 Jn 4:4).

After Peter had replied: 'Lord, you know that I love you', Jesus said to him: 'Feed my sheep.' For we cannot feed Christ's sheep and we cannot proclaim Jesus Christ to them, unless we love Jesus Christ. We need, as I said at the beginning, in certain respects to become poets in order to hymn the 'Hero', and only love can really make us like that. Would to heaven that when our lives and our 'humble service in the house of the Hero' come to an end, we too may repeat, as our testament, the poet's words:

> This little pipe of cane
> I have carried up-hill and down-dale,
> and through it I have breathed
> melodies eternally new.[23]

The melody eternally new that we ought to carry up-hill and down-dale to the ends of the earth is that sweetest of all names for us: Jesus.

NOTES

1   St Thomas Aquinas, *S. Th.*, I, IIae, Q. 28, A. 1.
2   St John of the Cross, *Sentences*, n. 57.
3   Dante, *Inferno*, V, 103.

4   *Adeste fideles:* 'Sic nos amantem quis non redamaret?'
5   St Augustine, *C. Faust.*, 32, 18 (PL 42, 507).
6   Cf M. Heidegger, *Being and Time*, I, 5, 29.
7   *Il libro della B. Angela da Foligno* (*The book of Bl. Angela of Foligno*), Quaracchi, Grottaferrata 1985, p. 612.
8   *Rule of St Benedict*, IV, 21; but cf earlier St Cyprian, *De orat. domin.*, 15.
9   *Imitation of Christ*, II, 7.
10 Origen, *Commentary on the Song of Songs*, 1, 3–4 (PG 13, 93); *In Ioh.*, 1, 28 (PG 14, 73f); *C. Celsum*, IV, 16 (SCh 136, p. 220) and particularly *Comm. in Rom.*, VII, 7 (PG 14, 1122) where Origen says that those who are beginners in the spiritual life should become conform 'to the form of the servant', that is to say, to Christ the man, whereas the perfect should try to be conformed 'to the form of God', that is to say, to the 'pure Logos'.
11 Eckhart, *Deutsche Predigten und Traktate*, ed. J. Quint, Munich, 1955, pp. 221, 261.
12 St Teresa of Avila, *Vita*, 22, 1f.
13 Cf St Justin Martyr, *II Apologia*, 10, 13.
14 Congregation for the Doctrine of the Faith, *Letter to the Bishops of the Catholic Church on certain aspects of Christian meditation*, V, 16; in *Osservatore Romano* of 15 December 1989.
15 St Bonaventure, *De perf. vitae ad soror.*, 7.
16 St Bonaventure, *Vitis mystica*, 24.
17 Cabasilas, *Vita in Christo*, II, 9; VI, 10 (PG 150, 561, 681).
18 St Augustine, *Confessions*, 1, 1; LX, 9.
19 Hymn *Iesu dulcis memoria*, trans. J. M. Neale.
20 St Ignatius of Antioch, *To the Romans*, 2, 1; 5, 1; 6, 1.
21 St Leo the Great, *Second Discourse on the Ascension*, 2 (PL 54, 398).
22 Cabasilas, *op. cit.*, VI, 4 (PG 150, 653, 660).
23 Tagore, *Gitanjali*, 1.

Chapter VII

'Do not believe every spirit'

Faith in the divinity of Christ today

St John the Evangelist in his First Letter clearly states the problem of the discernment of spirits and opinions concerning Christ. He writes: 'Beloved, do not believe every spirit, but test the spirits to see whether they are of God; for many false prophets have gone out into the world. By this you know the Spirit of God: every spirit which confesses that Jesus Christ has come in the flesh is of God, and every spirit which does not confess Jesus is not of God. This is the spirit of antichrist, of which you heard that it was coming, and now it is in the world already. Little children, you are of God, and have overcome them; for he who is in you is greater than he who is in the world. They are of the world, therefore what they say is of the world, and the world listens to them. We are of God. Whoever knows God listens to us, and he who is not of God does not listen to us. By this we know the spirit of truth and the spirit of error' (1 Jn 4:1–6).

The Evangelist, having already guided us on the way towards the personal *act* of faith in Jesus the Son of God, now introduces us, with the words that I have just quoted, to that other aspect of faith in Christ, which concerns its authenticity and orthodoxy; in other words, the *content* of faith. We must therefore use this inspired passage and, armed with the criteria set out in it by John, practise, we too, discernment of the spirits, that is to say, of the voices and doctrines circulating today in the Church and world with regard to Jesus Christ. We are rapidly approaching the year 2000 and initiatives are now hotting up for devoting the last decade of the century to world-wide ecumenical evangelization. Evangelization carried out by the various Christian Churches in a new spirit: no longer in competition among themselves but in brotherly collaboration, to proclaim to the world what they already have in common, which is immense: faith in Jesus Christ the only Lord and Saviour. But precisely because of this, it is urgent to be clear what the faith is. 'If the bugle gives an indistinct sound,' St Paul writes, 'who will get ready for battle?' (1 Cor 14:8). If the very nucleus of the proclamation wobbles in uncertainty, it is as though the Christians' shout — the kerygma — were to break up at the crucial moment, losing all possibility of transfixing hearts. On this discernment depends whether the year 2000 can be considered the anniversary of a unique and absolute event in history or of an event only relatively so: whether it is the anniversary of the coming of God on earth, or the anniversary of the birth of a human prophet, though he be the greatest of all.

John sets out from the fact that contrasting opinions about Jesus exist; he does not seek to reconcile them at all cost; nor does he list them one after the other in an attempt to display the good sides and the gaps in them, as often is done today in analyses of the various Christologies in circulation. Instead he proceeds frankly, taking position at a level so radical as to let him say: this opinion is of God; this other one is not of God; one is not of the world; the other one is of the world; one is truth; the other is the work of false prophets, even, he says, of anti-Christs.

I should like to follow his example and apply this same criterion, by singling out, from among those doctrines current about Christ, the ones that one may and should say are not of God, but of the world. To the cause of the faith, I should like to make a small contribution of discernment based on history. In the preceding chapters I tried to show how the ancient Christological dogmas are 'open structures', capable of admitting new developments and of responding to new demands, like tree-trunks ever ready to sprout anew. In the present chapter I want to show how the ancient Christological dogmas also constitute a criterion and a fixed, irremovable yardstick by which every new proposition ought to be judged and with which every new one ought to tally. Dogmas are like anti-bodies in the Church's bloodstream. Once a healthy organism has contracted and overcome an infectious disease, such as plague, it remains immunized forever against that particular disease, since henceforth it possesses within itself the efficacious anti-body, ready to spring into action whenever the same disease returns to haunt the neighbourhood. An analagous function is discharged, in the sphere of faith, by a dogmatic definition. It comes into action of its own accord, the moment the same heresy that originally provoked it — Arianism, for instance — returns to worm its way into the Church, though in a different guise. There is no need for the Church to issue a new condemnation. It is judged by the dogma. The dogmas of the Church are not 'hypotheses', they are theses.

1. *An alternative system of faith*

So that everything may be clearer, I anticipate at once the conclusion that I have reached. In the ecclesial sphere and notably in that of the Catholic Church, side by side with various excellent treatises on Christology which are at once up-to-date yet respectful of the traditional datum of faith, today there exist a number of so-called 'new Christologies' which depart, sometimes deliberately, from the datum fixed by the Councils of Nicaea and Chalcedon, with the aim of translating into modern terms that same truth expressed by the Fathers in categories appropriate to their own culture. My own conviction, which I shall seek to prove by reference to history, is that here we do indeed have a translation into modern categories of something ancient, not however of the *truth* of Nicaea but of the *error* condemned at Nicaea, not of the truth of Chalcedon but of the errors condemned at Chalcedon. In other words, there has been a renewal, yes, but of heresy, not of orthodoxy.

The second point is this: these new propositions depend on the assumption that the way of thinking or the cultural climate has altered so radically from ancient times that today it is no longer possible to proclaim the faith in those terms; that modernity, in a word, requires this new solution. My conviction — and again in this case I think it can be proved historically — is that this is all quite inaccurate. The system they advance is not new; it was put forward, discussed and refuted by the Church in ancient times;

irrefutable truth, this, that it is not exclusively a product of the modern age. The antithesis applied in this way between antiquity and modern times is a false one. The true antithesis, existing then as it does today, is rather, in some cases, between faith and unbelief, and in others, between orthodoxy and heresy.

Among recent Christologies by Catholic authors, there are some, as I have said, that — deep divergences between them notwithstanding — have nonetheless a basic *schema* in common, sometimes clear, sometimes implied. The schema is very simple, since reductionist. It is obtained by a systematic elimination of the complexities of the revealed datum and by a rationalizing process aimed at dissolving all tension between the various truths of faith.

The central nucleus of revelation — what used to be defined in the catechism as 'the two great mysteries of our faith' — are the Trinity and the Incarnation. God is *one* and *three*; Jesus Christ is *God* and *man*. In the new system, this nucleus is reduced as follows: God is *one*, and Jesus Christ is man. Christ's divinity has gone, and with it the Trinity. For the 'Catholic' logic of *et-et*: both one thing and the other, has been substituted the dialectical argument of *aut-aut*: either one thing or the other.

I summarize briefly, and in manner accessible to all, the positions of the authors in question, first on the divinity of Christ, then on the Trinity, referring my readers to the notes for a more exact documentation on the thought of the various authors, as also for the notable differences between them. Rather than concentrate on authors and individual books, I am anxious to draw attention to a certain reductionist system of the faith which is now passing out of theological works into the culture-media of people at large, where there is a danger of its becoming received opinion without any proper evaluation of the consequences. For the result of this will be that we shall end up, silently and hypocritically, accepting the existence of two different faiths, two different Christianities, which no longer have anything in common except the name: the Christianity of the Church's Creed, of the common ecumenical declarations, in which faith in the Trinity and in the full divinity of Christ continues to be professed, and the 'real' Christianity of wide strata of society and culture where, in the wake of a few 'noted' theologians, these same truths are interpreted in a totally different way.

To criticize the basic project emerging from these 'new Christologies' does not mean refusing to recognize the merits that they may have had, especially as a stimulus to a return to a more concrete Christology and one nearer to the biblical datum, and to an up-dating of the technical language of theology, which had grown too remote from the Church's life and message. Towards the end of this chapter I shall try to point out some of these positive stimuli, to be drawn, indirectly, from a reading of the works in question.

It may happen that one or another of the authors examined by me will perhaps read what I have written and maintain that it is not what he intended, that I have been mistaken about him. I should be happy to think so. For I take the Church's most traditional schema as my model, in dealing with this problem of discernment of doctrines: '*Si quis dixerit ... anathema sit*': if anyone says such and such, he is to be condemned. That is not what you are saying? All the better for all of us, the Church replies. But then permit me to defend our weak brother, unversed in theological subtleties, who may understand the very opposite of what you are trying to say, and so be scandalized in his faith. 'Who is weak, and I am not weak?' St Paul exclaimed. 'Who is made to fall, and I am not indignant?' (2 Cor 11:29).

At this point, I believe it a matter of duty to denounce the unjustified pretension of a Catholic theologian, who insists that the Church and people of God ought to master his language, laboriously seeking the key with which to penetrate his new and personal system of hermeneutics; who sometimes also makes this impenetrability his alibi and a refuge in which to take cover, so as to neutralize and frustrate any critical judgement on the Church's part, by choosing a point positioned outside the system, outside Tradition and hence incommensurable with it. In Christianity, a theologian should be measured against Tradition, the Magisterium and the actual body of believers, and not the other way round. Novelists, poets, dramatists, sociologists or philosophers can and do create very private and personal languages and symbolic systems of their own, leaving people who wish to enter their world to assume the burden of temporarily abandoning their own language and symbolic system and taking on theirs. Not, however, the theologian. The device of angrily rejecting and ruling out any criticism of one's own theological system from the outset on the grounds that the recondite philosophical, exegetical and hermeneutical presuppositions have not been grasped, has now become so common as to seem little more than a handy cop-out.

2. *'The stone which the builders rejected'*

The basic statement of the Christologies to which I now refer, expressed negatively first and then positively, is this: Jesus Christ *is not* God, but God *is* (or *acts*) in Jesus Christ. This idea originates with R. Bultmann who wrote: 'The formula "Christ is God" is false in every sense, when "God" is considered as objective being, whether this be meant according to Arius or according to Nicaea, in the orthodox sense or the liberal one. It is correct if "God" is meant as the event of divine actuation.'[1] Jesus, Bultmann further says, is 'God's decisive action.' (The action, not the person!)

Drawing inspiration from this concept, the authors of the 'new Christologies' affirm that Christ is God in the sense that God acts in him.[2] He is not the *true God*, but the *revelation* of the true God, which is something very different. Jesus is 'the eschatological prophet', he in whom 'God's cause' is expressed. This, they affirm, is the safest thing we can say, if we stick to the most ancient of the New Testament traditions. To say more and insist on the divinity of Christ, besides being useless in an age when the very word 'God' has lost its meaning, may conceal an attempt to neutralize the critical force of the prophet Jesus of Nazareth.[3] Jesus is 'one person', not two, and this person is a 'human' person. To say that he is also a 'divine person' is not possible except at the price of grave and insurmountable difficulties.[4] (Insurmountable certainly for reason, but not for faith!) For the traditional doctrine, common to Western and Eastern Churches alike, of the *union* of the two natures, human and divine, in the unique person of Christ, is substituted the doctrine of the *presence* of the Godhead in the human person of Christ. For *being* is substituted '*being in*'. As I said above, Christ *is not* God, but God *is in* Christ.

Everything becomes clearer still as soon as we pass on to consider what is thought, in this new system, about the *pre-existence of Christ*. The pre-existence — that is to say, the Christian doctrine according to which the Son of God, before taking flesh of Mary, already existed as a distinct person or distinct entity, with the Father — is to be regarded as a mythological concept derived from Hellenism. It would merely mean that 'the relationship between God and Jesus did not emerge only at a later stage and, as it were, by chance, but existed from the beginning and has its foundation in God himself.'[5] (That which exists *from the beginning*, please note, is the relationship, not Jesus!) In other words, Jesus pre-existed in the intentional sense, but not actually; in the sense, that is to say, that the Father had always foreseen, willed and loved the Jesus that would one day be born of Mary. (He pre-existed therefore not otherwise than any one of us, since everyone has been 'chosen and destined' by God to be his child, before the creation of the world! — cf Eph 1:4–5).

So, what about the *trinitarian climate* of the Christian faith? In some cases it disappears almost entirely or is dangerously attenuated; in others it is reduced to an attempt to salvage the formulae of Tradition and the Creeds, while in practice abandoning every reality intended by the said Tradition and Creeds.[6] God in himself is not threefold; at most he becomes threefold in history, as a result of the coming of Jesus Christ into the world. For the biblical and traditional thesis of the Son of God who becomes flesh is tacitly substituted the thesis of the flesh that becomes the Son of God, in the sense that in the man Jesus of Nazareth we have 'a divine-becoming person of the Word.'[7]

Next comes the inseparable nexus existing between the two principal mysteries of the faith. They are like two doors opening and closing together. The divinity of Christ is the cornerstone holding up the two mysteries of the Trinity and the Incarnation. Take this stone away and the whole structure of Christian faith collapses. This was condemned long ago and unambiguously by St Athanasius when writing against the Arians: 'If the Word does not exist together with the Father from all eternity, then no eternal Trinity exists, but first there was Unity and then, with the passing of time, by increment, there began to be the Trinity . . . There was a time when the Trinity was not, but only the Unity.'[8] In this context, Athanasius makes an observation still relevant in our dealings with those who speak today of a 'divine becoming' on the part of God. How can we know, he asks, when God's growth and becoming is finished? If he has become, he will go on becoming. But long before Athanasius, St John had established this link between the two mysteries: 'No one who denies the Son has the Father; he who confesses the Son has the Father also' (1 Jn 2:23). The two things stand or fall together.

This results in the Christian faith's becoming banal. We have already seen what an immense task Christological dogma can discharge even today, in that it allows a positive answer to be given to the problem: is it possible for an act situated in time to be effective throughout eternity? Yet this is only possible so long as the dogma conserves all the apparently contradictory force it has in the Chalcedonian definition, where God and man, and hence eternity and time, are spoken of as being present in Christ, unconfused and undivided. This task cannot be discharged where — as occurred in the extreme forms of 'death of God' theology — the talk is of a God who 'dies', ceases to exist and disappears to make way for humanity; where time or secularity succeeds to eternity, and where — standing the classic maxim on its head — it is said of the Word that 'ceasing to be what he was, he becomes that which he was not.' Nor can dogma entirely resolve the problem, even in those 'new Christologies' where the idea of an eternal pre-existence of the Word is left in shadow or dropped, and where, for the infinite *leap* between eternity and time is substituted the Hegelian idea of a continual *process* and of 'a divine becoming' on the part of the Son of God.

So we have a systematic abolition of Christianity's newness. No longer is it the religion of the incarnation with all that this signifies in our view of the cosmos and the human race. St Paul's great affirmation about Jesus who, though he was in the form of God, did not count equality with God a thing to be grasped, but emptied himself, taking the form of a servant (cf Phil 2:6f), is, it too, immediately voided of meaning and relegated to the status of mythological imagery. God, furthermore, is no longer 'Father' except in the pre-Christian and metaphorical sense in which, in the Greek world, he was called 'Father of the cosmos', and, in Israel, 'Father of his people'. God is not even love, despite what St John says (1 Jn 4:8). For God is love only when he loves someone who is not in all respects identical to himself, since otherwise it would not be love but egoism or narcissism. Then whom does God love, to be perfect love? The man Jesus of Nazareth? But then God has been love for less than two thousand years, and what was he before that, if he was not love? Does he love the human race? The universe? If so, he has been love for so many million, or so many thousand million, years respectively. And before that, what was he if he was not love? He might perhaps be love, only in the sense that from all eternity he foresaw and predestined his Son Jesus, that is to say, in the sense that he has always loved something that does not yet exist but that one day will? But then God is hope, not charity! Or perhaps God would feel an infinite love for one of his own modes of existence, given that the Son is considered as a mode and not as a real person or hypostasis? But this would be neither hope nor charity, but vanity!

Can we honestly say we are still talking about the same fundamental Christian faith? Further, how are we to distinguish, if so, between Christianity and Islam, leaving aside their ethical content perhaps? The Islamic synthesis is: 'Allah is the only God and Muhammed is his prophet.' The synthesis in this type of Christianity is: 'Yahweh is the only God and Jesus Christ is his prophet', or — which comes to the same thing — his definitive revelation. To prophet, true, we add the adjective 'eschatological', which however makes no difference since Muhammed too is regarded by his followers as the final prophet once and for all.

Though in the case of Islam merely reflecting this history of this religion and its own explanation of itself, this synthesis in the case of Christianity instantly transforms its entire history into a sustained idolatry. Anyone who believes, St Athanasius observes, that the Son is a thing made or created forces Christianity back into idolatry, into worship of the creature in place of the Creator. Having subdued idolatry, Christianity itself becomes idolatry. For the worship and full adoration of Christ has always been a datum of the Church.[9]

The great difference between the Old and New Testaments consists, according to the Letter to the Hebrews, in the fact that in the former God spoke 'through the medium of prophets', whereas in the latter he spoke to us 'by a Son' (cf Heb 1:1–2). In the Old Testament, God spoke through 'intermediaries'; in the New he spoke 'in person'. But this fundamental distinction, this qualitative leap, on which the whole 'newness' of the New Testament depends, is lost if Christ is accorded the title of 'prophet' in preference to that of 'Son'.

One thing emphasized by all the great Fathers involved in the Arian controversy is the absolute homogeneity of the divine Trinity, which cannot be composed of something increate and something created put together.[10] Conversely here, I believe there is a relapse into the serious error of conceiving of the Trinity as a hybrid entity, when it is envisaged — as occurs in one of the cases examined — as a Trinity formed of 'Father, Jesus Christ and the Holy Spirit',[11] where Jesus Christ indicates what is seen herebelow, that is to say, a human, historical person, even though foreseen and loved by the Father from all eternity, that is to say, as the so-called eschatological prophet.[12]

I must admit that in the course of these reflections the phrase has more than once occurred to me, with which St Jerome described the state of Christianity when, after the semi-Arian Synod of Rimini, people woke up from the sleep into which they had fallen: 'The entire world groaned aloud, astonished to find itself Arian.'[13]

3. A 'modern' interpretation of the revealed datum?

But now I come to a matter to which I am more anxious to draw attention. These attempts to reformulate the datum on Jesus Christ from the beginning are based, more or less declaredly, on a presupposition also derived from Bultmann and treated as a certainty, which is as follows: the way of presenting the faith, in the New Testament and ancient Councils, was conditioned by the mythological mentality of the age; it was an obligatory way and the Church had no choice over accepting it. Vice-versa, this new way of presenting the faith — that which has just been described — is required by modern thinking, which rejects every mythological category. So this second is also an obligatory choice which the Church cannot avoid, if the Church's faith is to be made comprehensible today. 'We can no longer accept the mythical ideas of that age about a being descended from God, existing . . . in a heavenly state; a "story of Gods" in which two (or even three) divine beings are involved, is not for us.'[14]

I believe we can show how this assumption, so expressed, is historically false in both cases, that is to say, as touching antiquity and also as touching modern times.

But first, an observation of general character. Is it thinkable that the Church which — as we have seen above — exerted every effort in her opposition to Hellenism and Platonism, in her doctrine of the humanity of Christ, to constrain them to accept the idea of a real incarnation of God and the idea of the salvation *of* the flesh (something very different from their doctrine of salvation *from* the flesh!), should then have uncritically adapted herself to that same Hellenism, in the doctrine of Christ's divinity and pre-existence? Is it not more accurate to state that, in dealing with the positions of the heretics — of the Gnostics on the one hand and of Arius on the other — characterized by a giving of ground to Hellenism and the spirit of the times, orthodoxy invariably reacted by stressing the requirement of the revealed datum?

But I pass on to considering something more directly pertinent to my intent. In antiquity and in parallel to the formation of Christological dogma, there can be traced a doctrinal system containing all the elements and propositions since advanced by the so-called 'new Christologies', and often enough in the same terms. So the Church had various possibilities before her. For orthodoxy is not the fruit of necessity or the by-product of a certain culture, but the fruit of daily pondered and suffered discernment. Conversely, modern thinkers and theologians have existed and still exist, some of them actually regarded as the founders of modern existential thought (such as Soeren Kierkegaard and Karl Barth), who have not found believing, in full and moving sort, be it in Christ's divinity or in the Trinity, to be incompatible with the modern view that they hold of the world and human nature and with their analyses of existence. On this account, it seems to me that the presupposition on which some of these new Christologies rest falls to the ground.

I shall now attempt to prove the first of the two things mentioned previously: that in antiquity it was possible *not to believe* in Christ's divinity. (The second thing, that it is possible today *to believe* in Christ's divinity — as I have just pointed out — is obvious and does not need to be demonstrated.) Just as we know of the existence of a heresy of Hellenistic and Gnostic origin, which denied the real humanity of Christ, i.e., Docetism, so we also know of an opposite heresy of Jewish inspiration, called Ebionism, which held that Jesus was a 'naked man' and did not accept that in Christ there was 'the union of God and man', even though considering Jesus to be the awaited Messiah, destined to return to earth.[15] This line of thought persists through the second and third centuries, first in the heresy of Artemon, who did not acknowledge the divinity of Christ, and in the adoptionism of Theodotus of Byzantium, and then in Paul of Samosata who first presented it in systematic form. For the latter, the Divine Word was not personal, that is to say, endowed with divine hypostasis, but only a *dynamis* or operative faculty of God. The Word is not the Son of God, but only the man Jesus in whom the Word took up its dwelling. Jesus was 'a man like us, though better in all respects by effect of the Holy Spirit.'[16] He was the greatest of the prophets, though constitutionally remaining just a man.

This classic combination of modalism and adoptionism, in contrast to the Greek tendency of the apologists and then of Arius, reached its clearest expression in the fourth century with Marcellus of Ancyra and his disciple Photinus.

Also, according to these two authors, the Word became Son of God and subsistent reality only with the appearance of the man Jesus of Nazareth. Before that, it was only a virtuality within God. 'The disciples of Marcellus and Photinus', we read in the canon of a council held in 345 AD, 'reject the eternal subsistence of Christ, his divinity and his eternal kingdom on the pretext of safeguarding the unity of God, *being in this respect like the Jews.*'[17] 'We declare all those to be anathema', our source-documents continue, 'who say that Christ as Son of God, mediator and image of God, did not exist *ab aeterno* but became such, that is to say, Christ and Son of God, only on assuming our flesh of the Virgin, that is to say, four hundred years ago.'[18] Against their concept of a merely intentional pre-existence of the Word, the orthodox sources say: 'If anyone says that the Son, before being born of Mary, existed only by way of prevision and was not begotten of the Father before all worlds to be God and, by his means, to bring all things into existence, let him be anathema.'[19] So Photinus was already familiar with the idea of a pre-existence of Jesus 'by way of prevision' or 'by way of anticipation'. The union between God and the man in Christ is conceived of in an unstable and exterior manner as by the Adoptionists. The basic structure of Christ is that of a man in whom the divine Word has taken up residence, like the spirit of prophecy in the prophets.[20]

Paul of Samosata and Photinus, speaking in ontological terms, conceive of him as the *greatest* prophet; today, speaking in historical terms, he is conceived of as the *eschatological* prophet, that is to say, the definitive one. But is eschatological something different from supreme? Can the great difference of viewpoint between ancient ontological thought and modern functional thinking lie here? Can one be the greatest prophet, the culmination of the prophets, without also being the definitive prophet, and can the definitive prophet not also be the greatest of the prophets?

The Fathers had seen right: those men, Marcellus and Photinus, are reasoning by the Jewish schema, according to which the Messiah would have existed first as the predestined, and later as the manifested one. (A schema of which there is an echo at the level of language, if not of content, in 1 Peter 1:20.) They expressed the Jewish soul of Christianity which is above all concerned with safeguarding biblical monotheism.

These few indications are enough to prove that the Church from the very outset found herself faced with two possible basic interpretations of the revealed datum: one more consonant with the Hellenistic mentality and one more consonant with the Jewish, and that she chose neither one nor the other, but traced out her own path, thus subjecting the Greek middle-Platonist system to as deep a crisis as the one of Jewish origin. Nicaea threw the Greek schema of the real into crisis or forced it to develop by eliminating the idea of an intermediary between God and the world: the *Logos* or Son of God conceived of as a 'God of the second rank' (*Deuteros theos*). It drew a line clearly distinguishing the only two possible types of being: the Creator and the creatures; and situating Christ, by virtue of his being one sole person with the divine Word, on the side of the Creator. But it also emphasized the newness of the New Testament in respect of the Old Testament phase of Revelation, by accepting the new concept of a divine unity that is not a numerical, static unity but a dynamic one: a unity that is love and hence generation and communion. It implicitly affirmed that, like all other human concepts, this one of unity too comes about in God in a way which is different in creatures; that God can be even beyond our concepts of unity and multiplicity. The Fathers consistently applied the criterion of an apparently paradoxical, apophatic theology all the way to the apex, without stopping short, as people sometimes would today, even at monotheism. Given the esteem in which they held biblical monotheism — that valiant warhorse in the struggle against paganism and idolatry — we may be sure that nothing in the world would have induced the Fathers to give their adversaries so much as the slightest hint that they had abandoned it with their doctrine of the Trinity, had they not been constrained by the very force of revelation and faith.

The Christologies that I have been examining are not therefore situated so much on the side of the Hellenistic schema of Arius, which admits a form of pre-existence, *real* even if not *eternal*, as in the opposing line of Jewish monotheism and messianism. They evince the tendency that responds to every external difficulty by retreating into the maternal womb. In this case, the maternal womb is the monotheistic faith of the Old Testament, which long ago allowed unfettered dialogue to be held with the highest flights of Greek philosophy and today allows unimpeded dialogue (at least as it is supposed) to take place with Islam. The odd thing was that in antiquity this was a *reactionary* line of thought, appropriate to those who were opposed to the new departures of the theologians. Not for nothing were its promoters — Paul of Samosata, Marcellus of Ancyra, Photinus — all bishops, whereas the promoters of the opposing tendency were mere priests and laymen: the Greek apologists, Origen, Arius.

We should add that this line of thought, more concerned about the unity than the trinity of God, is also the reproach which has always been levelled against Latin theology. But whereas the reproach is certainly not deserved by Augustine, Ambrose or other Latin Fathers, it is justified today in the case of those authors who, even when taking the event Jesus Christ as their point of departure, argue from the philosophic presupposition of the unity of God, rather than from the biblical revelation of God the Father, Son and Holy Spirit. Sabellian modalism here is not a bugbear trotted out by Orthodox churchmen to upset the Latins, but actually a declared datum of fact. If such a line were ever to be affirmed in Western theology — which I don't think is likely to happen — then the rift between the Orthodox and Latin Churches would become insuperable.

So, strictly speaking, we are not so much faced with a form of Arianism, as with its opposite. Yet the Fathers did not find it necessary to issue a new definition nor to summon a new ecumenical council but, against Marcellus and Photinus, always appealed to the definition of Nicaea. For Nicaea not only condemned the error of Arius but those of Paul of Samosata, Marcellus and Photinus too.[21]

When we consider what concentrated debate, what a sieving, these phrases and words sanctioned by dogma underwent, before and during the Council, we not longer wonder at the formidable precision, profundity and scope investing them, and are not tempted to attribute this to our own reading of them. We are certainly not the people to improve on such expressions as, for instance, 'begotten not created'. When we read Athanasius, Arius, Basil or Eunomius, we are more likely to be impressed by our own superficiality, our remoteness from their acuteness, rigour and ability to see far into the consequences of each definition.

In general, we remark a great cavalierness and opportunism in the interpreting of the Nicene definition, which is not based on the texts but on a hermeneutic to suit the book.[22] As I see it, if it is legitimate today to try to interpret the basic intention and the actual meaning of Nicaea, it is this: by calling the Word 'consubstantial', *homoousios*, the Council intended to say that in every culture the Word, and hence Christ, was to be held to be 'God' not in some ill-defined or attenuated or derived sense but in the fullest sense that the word 'God' has in that particular culture. Looked at like this, consubstantial, *homoousios*, is an 'open structure', as B. Lonergan defined it.

A text from Isaiah, which Christian writers were early (as early as in *Ad Diognetum*) applying to Christ, runs thus: 'Not a messenger nor an angel, but he himself, the Lord, saved them because he loved them' (Is 63:9 LXX). Nicaea is the definitive consecration of this certitude of faith that, in Christ, we do not obtain a mere intermediary, or a revealer of God, or a prophet, but God himself without intermediaries, and that God obtains us.

Nicaea is quite other than the hallowing of some mythological statement about God. Much confusion has arisen on account of the indiscriminate and acritical use of the category 'mythological'. By means of it, a great part of biblical and patristic thought has had suspicion cast on it and been laid open to every type of manipulation. All religious language is mythological in one way or another, in the sense that it relies on systems and interpretations of our world which are totally different from God's world. In respect of this radical common datum, the distinction between the *ancient* representation of the world and the *modern* representation of the world (always supposing that history may be divided in such a simplistic way) is pretty relative and minor. Is not what is left after de-mythologizing still mythological? What does it mean to say: 'God acted in

Christ', or: 'Christ is the supreme revelation of God'? Even in these sentences, are we not merely flitting from one 'semantic register' to another one? To be consistent, we should have to conclude that the faith itself, in every expression of it, is mythological. And indeed we know that this was the conclusion reached by some of Bultmann's disciples — H. Braun for instance — who carried the master's theory to its extreme and most logical consequences. For them, Jesus is only a man, and Christology is only anthropology. The sole truly radical alternative to mythological speech about God, if in spite of all we still wish to be believers, is total silence about God. But this silence about God would be more dangerous than talking imperfectly about him: 'What can anyone say when he speaks of thee?' says St Augustine. 'Yet woe to them that speak not of thee at all.'[23] The true remedy against the danger of the mythological is to be aware of the inadequacy of all representation and to repeat after every statement about God: 'God is not this, God is not this.'[24]

So the original plan was that of 'systematically translating the truth taught by the ancient Christological councils, out of the socio-cultural Hellenistic context into the mental climate of our own time.'[25] But the result has been that what has been translated into modern terms is not the truth of the ancient councils but the truth that the ancient councils condemned.

In certain cases, to this motive for translating the message into modern categories, is added another. that of re-emphasizing the *humanity* of Christ and, with this, the importance of the *praxis* of the Kingdom. There is the conviction that Christianity has hitherto all too one-sidedly accepted the divinity of Christ, thus making him the 'great Icon', the 'divine Icon', that is to say, a heavenly cultic mystery obscuring the inconvenient prophet Jesus of Nazareth.[26] But can we honestly say, at least today and at least in the West, that Tradition too one-sidedly emphasizes Christ's divinity? Is not the contrary in fact true and obvious to everyone, as I have done my best to demonstrate in the chapter devoted to faith in Christ's humanity today? We find ourselves faced with the same situation as Pascal described so well as follows: 'The source of all heresies is the

137

exclusion of some of these truths: Jesus Christ is God and man. The Arians, unable to reconcile these facts, which they believe incompatible, say that he is man; in this they are Catholics. But they deny that he is God; in this they are heretics. They claim that we deny his humanity; in this they are ignorant.'[27]

4. '*They are of the world*'

Now we shall try to discover how things could have reached such a pass; why this has overtaken theology and Catholic theology in particular. The explanation is to be found in that saying of St John from which we set out and is summed up in the category 'world' or worldliness, or to put it in modern terms, 'secularism', 'secularization'. 'They are of the world,' St John writes, 'therefore what they say is of the world, and the world listens to them' (1 Jn 4:5).

I do not mean to say that these brothers in faith have actually intended to serve the cause of the world, rather than that of Christ. On the contrary! No one has the right to cast doubt on their intentions or on their attachment to the Church. In their efforts however, it seems to me, they have been taken captive by the logic of the world, which only acknowledges and takes account of that which fits into its own categories, these being by definition 'worldly' categories, that is to say, human and historical. Perhaps the explanation for this secularism lies precisely in their inability to make the connection between Spirit and history, and hence time and eternity. The *historical sense*, which is without doubt one of the most notable conquests of modern Western culture, turns into a fearful impoverishment and indeed a sort of prison, once it is no longer able to accept the *spiritual sense*. The reproach levelled against patristic thought of often sacrificing the historical sense to the spiritual, we now see being stood on its head in present-day thought — but rather more radically.

I think we find ourselves faced with the umpteenth episode in the conflict between *kerygma* and *sophia*, that is to say, between the Christian proclamation and human wisdom; indeed in certain extreme cases we find ourselves confronted by a reduction of the kerygma purely and simply to wisdom, achieved by an undiscriminating use of hermeneutics. It has been said that the fundamental sin of modern Christian thought has been to make use of the Holy Spirit as 'a substitute for cogency, authorization, plausibility, intrinsic credibility, objective discussion',[28] whereas the opposite is certainly the case where, especially in a certain type of European theology, cogency, plausibility and intrinsic, that is to say, rational credibility, have been substituted for the Holy Spirit, thus reversing the method of St Paul, who said: 'My speech and my message (*kerygma*) were not in plausible words of wisdom (*sophia*), but in demonstration of the Spirit and power, that your faith might not rest in the wisdom of men but in the power of God' (1 Cor 2:4–5).

In the reduction of the *kerygma* to *sophia* and of the Spirit to history, hermeneutics, that is to say, the modern science of textual interpretation, have played a decisive part. Hermeneutics should be a kind of lye, into which the web of faith is dipped, to come out cleansed of human and contingent incrustations. But this lye has turned out to be so strong and corrosive that, rather than cleansed, the web of faith comes out dissolved. The first thing to be half-destroyed by the treatment has been Scripture. Biblical inspiration ends by being regarded as a 'late-ancient' doctrine only appearing towards the end of the New Testament canon, it too being suspected of Hellenistic influences, particularly of divination.[29] It is certainly the case that with a number of the authors discussed, this no longer constitutes an absolute criterion. Hermeneutics permit one to take what one wants or what serves the argument and to pass over as 'secondary' or 'late' or as mythological costume, that which does not serve. The authority of the Fourth Gospel evaporates, more or less. It represents an acute moment in the hellenization of Christianity. No line of demarcation exists, setting the canonical writings apart from others. The division is rather of an historical or ideological character and passes elsewhere, as was the case in the days of liberal theology and the comparative history of religions, in W. Bousset for instance.

One effect of this substitution of the critical criterion for that of faith is, in my opinion, the preference granted to the category of eschatological prophet as against that of Christ, Word, Son of man or Son of God. It takes on so much importance since it is the most ancient that can be documented historically, going back to Jesus himself. True, therefore it is not the *whole* thing, which we get at the end of the historical process, but a part. It is the *old* part. According to this criterion, betraying as it does a residual element of romanticism, one would have to say that the most genuine form of biblical monotheism is not that which evolved, but that original form in the earliest traditions of the Pentateuch; that the monotheism, in the radical form in which it is found for instance in Isaiah, is the historical adaptation, due to external circumstances, of a faith which initially did not make such great demands and by no means excluded the existence of other, though subordinate, gods.

This secular hermeneutic manifests itself even more clearly in its method of dealing with the councils and in the choice of what should be the sources of faith, or theological *loci*. Conciliar definitions are regarded as 'hypotheses', not as theses. For an interpretation taking account of experience drawn from faith and Christian living, is substituted the appeal to a *praxis*, the nature of which is never clearly defined, and above all a massive recourse to philosophy in all its forms, even those most alien from a vision of faith. Careful examination of the index of authors quoted in these Christologies tells all.

And thus we witness an incredible fact: twenty centuries of experience of Christ's divinity and of worshipping Christ, twenty centuries of trinitarian theology, liturgy and mysticism, during which the doctrine of the Trinity has nourished and modelled the Church's holiness, setting a trinitarian imprint on it in all its manifestations: all this is overlooked and cancelled, as though with one sweep of a sponge, thanks to the expedient of hermeneutics, explaining it all as simply due to the influence of the *theology* of the Trinity, but not of the *Trinity* itself, on the life of the Church. And all this while at the same time it is affirmed that the fundamental criterion for interpreting the faith ought to start from the praxis and experience of salvation in Christ!

In all this I detect the influence of the modern secular

prejudice, by which only those who are neutral as regards the faith can say anything objective about it. In all matters today we take our stand on experimentation as the criterion for discovering the truth: except the faith. The assumption is that the only people who can say anything objective and worthwhile about the faith are those who are outside it, who look at it from outside, in accordance with the scientific principle that the scholar should be impartial with regard to the object of research. Sometimes they behave towards the believer exactly as they would towards a maniac. The last person able to say anything useful about madness is obviously the maniac. Similarly, it is assumed, the last person to be able to say anything worthwhile about the faith is someone who believes and admits to believing.

John wrote to the early Christians: 'You have been anointed by the Holy One and you all know the anointing you received from him abides in you, and you have no need that anyone should teach you' (1 Jn 2:20, 27). What do these words about inner teaching mean? That the individual Christian knows everything and has nothing to learn from other people? Certainly not! Here too the background is the Christian community and the world. You do not need anyone from outside the anointing to instruct you, that is to say, from outside the environment in which the anointing is at work, which is of course the environment of the Church; you have no need to, nor can you, in what specifically concerns the faith, go to school to people of the world who do not have the anointing and do not believe.

Today one type of hermeneutics has become the ground for reason's return-match against faith. With this, we take away with one hand what faith has rendered to God with the other. Enough for instance to affirm without actually needing to demonstrate it, that 'all statements about divine sonship, pre-existence, creation mediatorship and incarnation — often clothed in the mythological forms of the time — are meant in the last resort to do no more and no less than substantiate the uniqueness, underivability and unsurpassability of the call ... made known in Jesus',[30] for at a stroke we are dispensed from believing in Christ's pre-existence and incarnation. By a skilful move, the difficulty of having to believe is avoided and the real act of faith is postponed *sine die*.

Here is another example of drastic reduction of the faith by hermeneutics or interpretation: 'We cannot', it is said, 'make of Christianity just what we fancy.' This is quite right. So what is the criterion? The criterion is orthopraxis, that is to say, 'an authentic Christianity true to Jesus' message, life and death.' And how can we tell what this right praxis may be? 'Orthopraxis . . . is only feasible through a grasp of the point at issue.'[31] And so we come back to the interpreters, to whom the last word in matters of faith belongs.

Kierkegaard illustrated this abusive application of hermeneutics to the Bible with a parable that seems even truer today than when he actually wrote it: 'Imagine a country. A royal command is issued to all the office-bearers and subjects, in short, to the whole population. A remarkable change comes over them all: they all become interpreters, the office-bearers become authors; every blessed day there comes out an interpretation more learned than the last, more acute, more elegant, more profound, more ingenious, more wonderful, more charming, and more wonderfully charming. Criticism which ought to survey the whole can hardly attain survey of this prodigious literature, indeed criticism itself has become a literature so prolix that it is impossible to attain a survey of the criticism; everything became interpretation — but no one read the royal command with a view to acting in accordance with it. And it was not only that everything became interpretation, but at the same time the point of view for determining what seriousness is was altered, and to be busy about interpretation became real seriousness.'[32]

In Kierkegaard's thought there is a truly biblical prophetic component, of which the philosopher himself became aware towards the end of his life; this cannot however be grasped except in the spirit, that is to say, by seeing things from Kierkegaard's point of view. From the days when Hegel, in his system, placed philosophy above religion and faith as the supreme manifestation of the Spirit, there followed a succession of attempts by reason and by theology to go 'beyond' faith, as though there were anything beyond. Abraham, Kierkegaard was to observe, did not presume to go beyond faith but was content to believe. Believing seemed to him a serious enough matter in the first place. At this point, how can we not recall the words with which John once again takes up the theme, so dear to him, of the discernment of spirits, in his Second Letter? 'Many deceivers have gone out into the world, men who will not acknowledge the coming of Jesus Christ in the flesh. . . Anyone who goes beyond (*proagon*) and does not abide in the doctrine of Christ does not have God' (cf 2 Jn 7–9). Even in those days there were people who went 'beyond'.

If the cause of this straying from the ways of faith is, as John says, the 'world' — one of the world's activities being to pass judgement on the faith, instead of being judged by it — then the way to escape from this situation can only be a conversion from the world: 'If anyone among you thinks that he is wise in this age, let him become a fool that he may become wise, for the wisdom of this world is folly with God' (1 Cor 3:18). This is a sort of law: anything written by someone who has not undergone this conversion is suspect; it is the wisdom of this world and therefore folly in God's eyes. Even the Fathers had to undergo this conversion. St Augustine — and before him the philosopher Victorinus, whose conversion the saint relates in his *Confessions* — had to become fools, had to lose face in the eyes of their colleagues, be 'cast out of the synagogue', leave the circle, before they could attain to the mystery and to Christian wisdom. They too tried to resist, they procrastinated, they suffered, but they too, like 'the man born blind' in the gospel before them, having once been cast out of the synagogue, found it was much easier to believe (cf Jn 9:35). A certain academic environment — where theology lives cheek by jowl with other purely human disciplines and has to defend its claim to be, it too, scientific — can easily become the 'synagogue' for those who fear to be kicked out if they believe in a God made flesh (cf Jn 9:22).

In the Bible there is a conversion for everyone and every situation: for sinful women like Mary Magdalene and the Samaritan woman; for businessmen like Zacchaeus; for Church leaders like Peter and the other apostles who had to be converted from the urge to be the greatest (cf Mt 18:1f). There is also a conversion for the learned and the theologians and it is this: the conversion from false wisdom to true, from the wisdom of the world to that of God. Paul experienced this conversion himself, which is why he can talk about it to others. Jesus says that the Father has revealed the mysteries of the Kingdom, and firstly the mystery of his own person, to babes. A genuine faith in the divinity of Christ can only be born of this sort of conversion. Paraphrasing a famous saying of Jesus, one may say: If human intelligence and reason, having fallen into the ground, do not die, they stay as they are: mere human reason, mere nature. If however they die, they bear much fruit (cf Jn 12:24). What fruit it bore in Paul, what fruit it bore in Augustine and thousands of others! If we have not undergone this experience, we cannot truly attain to the mystery; if we talk about it, while unwittingly remaining on the outside, we shall be dealing with the shell, not with the kernel. Until Jesus, from being the *object* of study which we analyse and master and imprison in a Christological treatise, has become the *subject* by whom we are mastered and subjugated and to whom we have surrendered, everything we write will be 'the letter' and sometimes the letter 'that kills'. No one apart from the person in question can know with any certainty whether a theologian has or has not undergone this experience of 'being crucified' to the world. No one therefore has the right to pass judgement and decide from outside whether you are a new theologian or an old theologian, of the spirit or of the letter. But the person in question can know it, so we can and should pass judgement on ourselves.

5. '*He who is in you is greater than he who is in the world*'

Does the error therefore reside in applying hermeneutics to the faith? No. That was what, in different ways, the Fathers themselves did. The alternative to this would be biblical fundamentalism and a Christianity made of pure and dead repetition. The error lies rather in ignoring the fact that hermeneutics has one impassable limitation and this is constituted by the datum revealed in Scripture and made explicit in councils by means of dogma. It is a bit like the musical interpretation of a symphony or a well-known oratorio: it is certainly different, depending on the sensibility of the moment and the conductor, but this cannot go to the point of altering the original score of the work, without its turning into something else.

The error thus lies in assigning to hermeneutics the task of re-inventing faith in Christ over and over again, in every age, founding Christianity's claim to universality on this and not on something objective existing from the outset, i.e., Jesus himself.[33] A similar explanation for the universality of the Christian faith might perhaps be thinkable if Christian salvation were no more than a response to human yearnings. In this case, by radically changing the yearnings (if that were possible), one should also be able to change the response. But Christian salvation is something other than just a response to human aspirations; it is something forever springing anew in the human heart; it is an unforeseen gift surpassing all expectation; it is grace. From a doctrine of the type where Christ's significance is seen in his praxis, independently of his person, a doctrine of grace can only follow in which 'the grace of Christ' will be reduced, as in Pelagianism, to Christ's example.

We know what this project can lead to: of giving every age the task of defining the essence of Christianity anew without any sense of being bound once and for all by the datum. Albert Schweitzer showed in his *Quest of the Historical Jesus* how it worked out in the last century. Each generation of theologians had set out intent on releasing Christ from the shackles of ecclesiastical dogmatics, so as to bring him nearer to the writer and his pre-occupations. The result was that each age clothed Christ in the ideas and tendencies successively pre-occupying society. It dressed him in the clothes then in fashion. They used Christ as a laboratory for trying out their own theories. It is odd that there is no modern Christology that does not set out from the change illustrated in this book and that does not base itself in part on its findings, to justify the abandoning of liberal tendencies, without perceiving that the same identical change is being repeated in our own century and that, in some cases — those examined here — the wheel has come full circle. All that is needed is someone with the patience and courage of Albert Schweitzer, when our own century comes to an end, who can hand on, with a few additions, that same heritage that we received from the last one. What happened within the liberal theology of the last century is what has happened in ours within kerygmatic theology: a 'pendulum' effect as regards the central nucleus of faith in Christ, notwithstanding undeniable advances whether of method or of content, that have been notched up on particular issues. The faith in Christ which, following this method, every age will elaborate for itself, will never be other than 'a pattern created on the seashore by one wave and washed away by the next.'

Albert Schweitzer brought his book to a close with an evocative image: 'The study of the life of Jesus has had a curious history. It set out in quest of the historical Jesus, believing that when it had found him, it could bring him straight into our time as a teacher and saviour. It loosed the bands by which he had been riveted for centuries to the stony rocks of ecclesiastical doctrine, and rejoiced to see life and movement coming into the figure once more, and the historical Jesus advancing, as it seemed, to meet it. But he does not stay; he passes by our time and returns to his own. . . He returned . . . by the same necessity by which the liberated pendulum returns to its original position.'[34]

Christ, this author writes, always returns to his own *time*; I however say that Christ always returns to his own *place*. He returns to the Church, from which time after time efforts are made to release him, since, as it was in the early days, so too today, he is only significant for the community that lives by faith in him and in what he is: in a real and not merely metaphorical sense, 'the living one'.

6. *Releasing Christ from the shackles of ecclesiastical dogmatism*

But here something important has to be said. The Church — and by Church I mean here the hierarchy as well as theology and the pastoral work of proclaiming the Gospel — cannot behave as though nothing has happened, merely muttering: 'There, I told you so!' Church and Christian orthodoxy have a duty to show that it is possible to baptize and make room for the new insights advanced by these theologians, and yet remain within the channel of the traditional faith. To show that Tradition is capable of accepting progress, even where progress has not been capable of accepting Tradition. In other words, that the traditional dogmatic formulae of ontological sort are capable of accepting the modern, in character more functional and dynamic, reading even if the contrary is not always the case. To say that Jesus Christ is 'true God' does not exclude but actually includes his being the definitive 'self-revelation of God' and his self-communication to the human race, whereas to say that he is the definitive 'self-revelation of God' does not always include and safeguard the affirmation that he is the 'true God'.

More particularly it is up to the Church and specifically to her pastors and those who proclaim the Gospel to show that it is not true that 'to fight for the divinity of Christ' means silencing the disconcerting voice of the prophet Jesus of Nazareth, when he attacks the rigidified forms of religiosity, the hypocrisies, the formalisms and that so ancient tendency to pass off things that *we do not want* to change as things instituted by God himself and hence that *we cannot* change. It is up to us to see that proclaiming Christ's divinity does not diminish the critical force of Jesus human being and prophet, but immeasurably increases it. Human beings, it is written, see the outward appearance, but God sees into the heart (cf 1 Sam 16:7; Prov 15:11). If Jesus is only a man, be he even the eschatological prophet, he cannot see into the hearts of all human beings, let alone of the people of today, separated from him by two thousand years. He can only do this if he is God too. And indeed he does it because he is God too!

Should it not be for the Church herself to perform the operation that no one else has yet been able to effect, that is to say, 'to release', in the constructive sense, Christ from the shackles of ecclesiastical dogmatics? The Christological dogma of Nicaea and Chalcedon was formed by a process of selection and reduction. Out of all the possible titles and ways of speaking about Jesus, the ones that were chosen were the ones which gradually showed themselves to be the most efficacious in dialogue with Hellenistic culture and in resisting heresies. This explains the preference accorded to the title *Logos* or Word of God. In the theological debate, the biblical datum grew more and more constricted until, cone-like, reaching its apex in the Chalcedonian definition, where Christ is defined as true God and true man, that is to say, 'one person in two natures'. Releasing Jesus from the constraints of ecclesiastical dogma certainly cannot mean disregarding Chalcedon or, worse still, going actually against it; it can however mean setting out again in every age from the complete, concrete, biblical datum on Jesus and reappraising those ways of speaking of him (among which, why not that of eschatological prophet) which were neglected in earlier cultural contexts, if and when they reveal themselves to be useful and meaningful today. This means not constructing all Christological discourse, as used to occur in the manuals until recently, on the schema of a big inverted cone, supporting everything on the apex of the preceding cone, that is to say, on the formula 'one person in two natures', but, rather, as a cone which, by taking as its base the entire biblical datum and incorporating within itself the synthesis of the patristic age and modern thought, stretches out towards a new apex and a new synthesis. This can be done, and some of the best of today's treatments of Christology are getting near it. This then would be to take Chalcedon 'not only as end but also as beginning.'[35]

In ecclesiastical dogmatics — especially, I repeat, in the manuals — the ancient formulae are sometimes dealt with in too material or logical a sense, as though they were chemical formulae that say all there is to be said about the thing and which you only need to handle in the right way for everything to come good. To release Christ, in a positive sense, from the shackles of Church dogma could mean the recovery of the apophatic value of the dogmas and that freedom in using the formulae which the best of the Fathers had. St Athanasius, at a certain moment, shows himself disposed to leave even the term *homoousios* aside, provided that what the Nicene Fathers had intended to affirm was not being held in question. And St Augustine openly declared that in theology we use the term *persona* for want of a better one, but that it is inadequate for expressing the divine realities of the Father, the Son and the Holy Spirit.[36]

7. 'Who is it that overcomes the world?'

We must re-create conditions for a recovery of faith in Christ's divinity. Again we must produce an outburst of faith, giving birth to the act of faith: 'I believe in one Lord, Jesus Christ, the only-Son of God, eternally begotten of the Father, God from God, Light from Light, true God from true God, begotten, not made, of one Being with the Father.' Once long ago, the body of the Church made a supreme effort, rising in faith above all human systems and all the objections of reason. The fruit of this effort remains today. The tide rose once to its highest level and the mark of this has been left on the rock. Now we need the high tide repeated; the tide-mark is not enough. It is not enough to repeat the Nicene Creed; we need to renew the outburst of faith which there was then in the divinity of Christ, the like of which has not been seen since. And we need it now. There was a moment in the Church, when the faith of Nicaea held out, you might say, in the heart of one man alone: Athanasius. But this was enough for it to survive and resume its victorious march. This shows that even a few faithful people, willing to stake their lives on this, can do much to reverse the present tendency in theology of introducing basically Arian theses, according to which 'there was a time when the Son was not.'

What we have been discussing has important consequences for Christian *ecumenism*. For there are two ecumenisms in existence: one of faith and one of unbelief; one uniting all who believe that Jesus is the Son of God and that God is Father, Son and Holy Spirit, and another uniting all who confine themselves to 'interpreting' these things. An ecumenism in which, in the ultimate analysis, everyone believes in the same things because no one any longer really believes in anything, using 'believe' in the strongest sense of the word. There is a new, invisible unity taking shape and running through the various Churches. From that text in John, quoted initially, may be deduced that in the sphere of faith the fundamental distinction between spirits is not what distinguishes Catholics from the Orthodox, or the Orthodox from Protestants, but what distinguishes those who believe in Christ the Son of God from those who do not.

This invisible unity, in its turn, has the greatest need of theological discernment and the discernment of the hierarchy if it is not to lapse into a dangerous fundamentalism or into the vain presumption of being able to form a species of transversal Church, outside the existing Churches and the Catholic Church in particular. But even when this risk has been avoided, we are faced with a fact that we can no longer allow ourselves to ignore. What would be the good of my remaining formally within the institutional environment of the Catholic Church if I had lost all faith in the Christ of the Catholic Church?

So what we have been saying is particularly important for a new *evangelization*. There are buildings or metal structures so made that if they are struck at a certain point or if a certain stone is moved, the whole thing collapses. Such is the edifice of Christian faith, and its particular cornerstone is the divinity of Christ. Take that away and everything falls to pieces and before everything else, as we have seen, the Trinity. St Augustine said: 'It is not a great thing to believe that Christ died; this the pagans also, and the Jews, and all the wicked believe. This all believe: that he died. The resurrection of Christ is the faith of Christians; this we hold a great thing, that we believe that he rose from the dead.'[37] As well as about his death and resurrection, the same thing has to be said about Christ's humanity and divinity, of which death and resurrection are the respective manifestations. Everyone believes that Jesus was a man; what makes the difference between believers and non-believers is believing that he is God. Christ's divinity is the Christian's faith. There is one thing alone, John again reminds us, that is stronger than the world and able to overcome its tremendous resistance to the message: believing that Jesus is the Son of God. Believing it and then proclaiming it and proving it to others: 'Who is it that overcomes the world but he who believes that Jesus is the Son of God?' (1 Jn 5:5).

At all levels today we need the whole. From ancient times the Catholic and Orthodox Churches stressed the importance of the believed faith (*fides quae*). From the Arian controversy onwards, all patristic treatises 'on faith' (*de fide*) were exclusively concerned with establishing what the true and orthodox faith was. There was no trace of interest in the structure of the act of faith or the subjective dimension of belief. In contrast, the Churches of the Reform stressed the importance of the believing faith (*fides qua*), of the personal act of faith, defining faith as trust. The one however cannot stand without the other. Objective faith, or orthodoxy, of its own does not convert; it does not affect those far away; subjective or personal faith of itself leads to subjectivism and to endless divisions, and in extreme cases boils down to having an unshakable faith and trust, but in oneself, in one's own opinion or in one's own little group, rather than in God.

Faced with the infinite number of scholastic distinctions about God, someone in the Middle Ages with contemplation in mind launched the cry: 'I need the whole!'[38] Today, with evangelization in mind, an analogous cry should be raised in the Church: 'We need the whole!' We need the whole content of the faith: God one and threefold; Jesus Christ God and man, and we need the Church's whole capacity for believing. We need all our forces — Catholic, Orthodox, Protestant — if we seriously hope to give real thrust to evangelization. No one Christian Church can hope to accomplish this gigantic task on its own.

The rest is in God's hands. We must however not fall into the temptation of millenarianism or of bi-millenarianism. We must not repeat the mistakes the first disciples made when they questioned Jesus, saying: 'Is this the time?' (cf Acts 1:6). Is the two thousandth anniversary the time when the Kingdom of God will be established everywhere on earth? 'It is not for you', Christ still replies today, 'to know the times or seasons . . . but you will receive power when the Holy Spirit has come upon you and you will be my witnesses' (Acts 1:7–8). For this is exactly how the Kingdom of God does come: by receiving strength from the Holy Spirit to bear witness to Jesus.

NOTES

1   R. Bultmann, *Glauben und Verstehen*, II, Tübingen 1938, p. 258 (*Existence and Faith*, Hodder & Stoughton, London 1961).

2   H. Küng, *On Being a Christian*, Collins, London 1977, p. 444: 'How can Jesus's relationship to God be positively expressed? We might

put it in this way: the *true man* Jesus of Nazareth is for faith the real revelation of the one true God.' According to this author, the titles Image of God, Son of God, Word of God, do not denote the divine being of Jesus, but 'the human face' of God: 'The man Jesus shows, manifests, reveals this human visage in his whole being, speech, action and suffering. He might almost be called the visage or face of God or, as in the New Testament itself, the image or likeness of God. The same thing is expressed also in other terms: when Jesus is called the Word of God or even the Son of God' (*loc. cit.*).

3   E. Schillebeeckx, *Jesus, an Experiment in Christology*, Seabury Press, New York 1979, p. 655, writes: 'However intimately this union with God is displayed in a historical human being, we can never speak of two *components*: humanity and divinity, only of two total *aspects*: a real humanity in which "being of God", in this case "being of the Father" is realized.' 'To contend for the divinity of Jesus in a world of which God has long since taken his leave, may well be a battle lost before it has begun. It also fails to grasp the deepest intention of God's plan of salvation, namely, God's resolve to encounter us "in fashion as a man", so that indeed we might eventually be enabled to find him' (*ibid.* p. 671).

4   According to P. Schoonenberg, *The Christ*, Sheed and Ward, London 1972, pp. 87f, in Christ, it is not the human nature that subsists in God, that is to say, in the person of the Word, but God who subsists in the human person: 'Now, not the human,' he writes, 'but the divine nature in Christ is anhypostatic [that is to say, without independent existence]. . . . Our concept could now be called the theory of the enhypostasia of the Word. Or in other words: of the presence of God's Word, or of God through his Word, in Jesus Christ.' So here, for the two natures in a single person is substituted 'God's presence' determining everything in this human person. What we have therefore is a Christology of 'God's presence' in Christ (*ibid.* p. 91). Even if one should say, in the dynamic sense, that Jesus 'is' God, this has to be understood in fact as meaning that 'there is' God in him. So in this Christology, it is hard to see what force can be attached to the 'I Am' (*Egô eimi*) uttered by Jesus in the gospel of John and equivalent, according to the exegetes, to claiming the name and absolute being of God. At the most, Jesus could have said: 'In me there is', not 'I am' God. In this perspective, the basic personality of Jesus does not differ qualitatively from that of Moses, the prophets, Paul or anyone else to whom God has been present and spoken.

5   Cf H. Küng, *op. cit.*, p. 446. To say that Jesus existed as Word and Son of God, before being born of Mary, means that he was 'chosen and destined as God's son from the beginning, from eternity' (*ibid.*, p. 456). Schillebeeckx adopts an independent position, different from the other two; he says that the pre-existence was 'the unique orientation of the Father towards Jesus', whom Christian tradition calls 'the Word' (*op. cit.*). Such a way of putting it does however

leave a doubt that here too we are dealing with an only-intentional pre-existence, in the sense that God the Father foresaw, fore-loved, fore-chose Jesus, of whom hence it cannot be said that 'he was from the beginning' (cf 1 Jn 1:1), but only that 'he was *foreseen* from the beginning'. The New Testament not only speaks of the orientation or of the eternal love of the Father for the Son, but also of an eternal orientation of the Son towards the Father (cf Jn 1:1). Only in this second case can one speak of a real pre-existence and not of one merely foreseen. After such premises one can therefore see how falsely reassuring the subsequent statement is that 'the Word of God is the supportive foundation to the whole figure of Jesus' (*op. cit.*); for we are talking of a 'non-existent' foundation, or one only coming into existence at the moment of Christ's human birth.

P. Schoonenberg in his turn writes: 'It is now only a matter of drawing a conclusion from this association, namely, that what is contained in Scripture, Tradition and the teaching Magisterium on the divine and pre-existent person of the Son can never be in conflict with what is preached about Jesus Christ: . . . that he is one person and that he is a human person. What is said of the pre-existent divine person can never nullify this one and human person' (*op. cit.*, p. 82). Everything one reads in the Bible about the Son of God and the pre-existent Word is therefore to be understood in relation to the historical Jesus. It is in Jesus that the Son of God becomes a person. Before that, he existed at most as a mode or potentiality in God. The Son of God does not pre-exist, but comes into existence with and in Jesus of Nazareth (cf *op. cit.*, p. 86).

6 Cf H. Küng, *op. cit.*, p. 476: 'The monotheistic faith taken over from Israel and held in common with Islam must never be abandoned in any doctrine of the Trinity. There is no god but God!' 'The Christological element is the specific feature [of Christianity] and it is from this that everything about the Trinity appears to be deduced' (*ibid.*, p. 474). 'Nowhere in the New Testament,' Küng writes, 'is a mythological two-gods doctrine (bitheism) developed' (p. 444). 'We can no longer accept the mythical ideas of that age about a being descended from God, existing before time and beyond this world in a heavenly state; "a story of Gods" in which two (or even three) divine beings are involved, is not for us' (p. 446). The recent laudable effort of this author to foster a dialogue between world religious is unfortunately still based on this practical "bracketing" of the divinity of Christ and of the Trinity. What he proposes as a theological standpoint for Christians in the dialogue is: "a priori acknowledge their own conviction of faith (Jesus is normatively and definitively the Christ) and at the same time take seriously the function, say, of Muhammad as an authentic (post-Christian) prophet—*especially his 'warning' against a deviation from belief in one God in Christology"* (H. Küng, *Global Responsibility. In Search of a New World Ethic.* SCM Press, London 1991, 102: italics mine). The highest claim Christians should make for Jesus, to be faithful to the Scripture, is that he is the normative and definitive "Christ of God" (*ibid.* p. 99), (not "Christ God"!).

7 'Can we say', writes Schoonenberg, 'that God is "already" threefold in his pre-existence? [It would seem not.] There are many who conclude to a pre-existent Trinity from the divinity of Christ and of the Spirit sent to us, but they do so . . . via a concept of God's immutability that is open to criticism. Thus we do not consider it justified . . . to say that God is "already" threefold in his pre-existence' (*op. cit.*, pp. 82–3). 'The Christological titles of the New Testament can be interpreted in the sense that only from the incarnation does the Logos obtain his being-person towards the Father (his being-Son). But this in no way derogates from his divinity defined at Nicaea, for we can speak of a divine becoming person of the Logos' (P. Schoonenberg, 'Monophysitisches und dyophysitisches Sprechen ueber Christus' in *Wort und Wahrheit*, 27, 1972, p. 261). E. Schillebeeckx, *op. cit.*, p. 668, dissociates himself from this conclusion of Schoonenberg's, writing that 'God does not become "Trinitarian" only when Jesus Christ becomes a man. . . I find the very idea inconceivable'. But, frankly, even in him it is impossible to see what the alternative can be to this radical conclusion of Schoonenberg's. If such an alternative does exist, it must be, as he himself defines it, 'theology to the power of three', that is to say, virtually incomprehensible. Besides, what he excludes is that God becomes Trinitarian 'only when Jesus Christ becomes a man', not that God 'becomes Trinitarian'. In these authors, it seems to me, we have the dynamic and unitary Christological *schema* of the Alexandrians (the Word that becomes flesh), filled moreover with a typically Antiochene content, being that of the absolute integrity, both physical and personal, of the human nature of Christ. For the thesis of the Son of God who becomes flesh, is substituted the thesis, in a word, of the flesh that becomes the Son of God.

8 St Athanasius, *Contra Arianos*, I, 17–18 (PG 26, 48).

9 St Athanasius, *Contra Arianos*, I, 8 (PG 26, 28).

10 St Athanasius, *Ad Serapionem*, I, 28 (PG 26, 294).

11 E. Schillebeeckx, *op. cit.*, p. 631.

12 E. Schillebeeckx, *op. cit.*, p. 27. Schillebeeckx set out with the intention of removing Jesus from the undue monopoly of the Churches and of listening to what outsiders might have to say about him, 'the resultant knowledge yielding a view of Jesus that can also be a touchstone for the pictures that believers have formed of Jesus down the centuries' (*ibid.*, p. 27). The intention was a good one, but the result, I believe, has been a tacit reversal of the positions to be found in Matthew 16, in the dialogue between Jesus and the apostles at Caesarea Philippi. 'Who do men say', Jesus asks, 'that the Son of man is?' And the reply was: 'A prophet!' But Jesus, not apparently satisfied with this, pursues the matter: 'But who do you say that I am?' To which, Peter by divine revelation replies: 'You are the Christ, the Son of the living God!' In the theory according to which Jesus is 'the eschatological prophet', the positions appear to be reversed, as though the evangelist had made a mistake over the order in which he set down the questions and answers. The truest

and most satisfying answer is no longer that of 'Son of the living God', but that of 'prophet', not the answer of the apostles but that of the outsiders.

13 St Jerome, *Dialogus contra Luciferianos*, 19 (PL 23, 181): 'Ingemuit totus orbis et arianum se esse miratus est.'

14 H. Küng, *op. cit.*, p. 505. According to Küng, the doctrine of pre-existence 'was in the air', in the culture of late-antiquity. 'In this mental climate similar ideas of a pre-existence of Jesus, God's Son and God's Word . . . must have seemed extremely plausible.' 'It was natural to think in Hellenistic physical-metaphysical categories. Mythical elements played a large part, but never became absolutely dominant' (*op. cit.*, pp. 445–6). In saying that 'the mythical ideas of the age . . . a "story of Gods" in which two divine beings are involved, can no longer be ours,' Küng is not only saying that the concepts of Nicaea can no longer be ours, but more important still that those of the Fourth Gospel can no longer be ours either. For in it what he describes as a 'story of Gods' in which several divine persons are involved is even more accentuated than in the terse definition of Nicaea. There it speaks of a Father who teaches the Son, who sends him into the world, who waits for him, and of a Son who sees what the Father does, who is with him in the creation . . . I do not think that all this can be explained away by saying that 'in those days they did not have any other conceptual instruments at their disposal' (*op. cit.*, p. 448).

15 St Irenaeus, *Adv. Haer.*, V, 1, 3.

16 Paul of Samosata, Syriac fragment 26 (ed. H. de Riedmatten, *Les actes du procés de Paul de Samosate*, Fribourg 1952).

17 *Creed* of the Third Synod of Antioch (ed. A. Hahn, *Bibliothek der Symbole und Glaubensregeln in der alten Kirche*, Hildesheim 1962, p. 194).

18 *Ibidem.* The above-mentioned thesis (*vide supra* n. 7) according to which 'the son of man became Son of God, but the Son of God did not become son of man' is also to be found formulated in Photinus, cf St Augustine, *Sermo* 186, 2 (PL 39, 999).

19 *Formula* of the Synod of Sirmiun of 351 AD (ed. A. Hahn, *op. cit.*, p. 197). Besides the expression 'by way of prevision' (*katà prognôsin, prokatangeltikôs*), in the source documents we also find the expression 'by way of anticipation' (*prochrestikôs*).

20 Cf St Hilary of Poitiers, *De Trinitate*, X, 21, 50 (PL 10, 358, 385); against those who say that in Christ the divine nature operated 'by grace, as in a prophet', cf St Gregory Nazianzen, *Letter I to Cledonius*, 22 (PG 37, 180).

21 The expression 'begotten, not made' (*genitus, non factus*) of the Nicene Creed has a multipurpose significance and offers a yardstick for every Christology. Of the Son of God, it says what he is and what he is not. All attempts to explain the divinity of Christ as coming about at some given moment and more particularly: (*a*) at the creation of the world (Arius), (*b*) when born of Mary (Hippolytus, Marcellus of Ancyra), (*c*) at his baptism in the Jordan or at the resur-

rection (adoptionists): all these attempts are as it were ruled out by that *non factus*, not made, that is to say, not become. All those Christologies in which it is possible to say that 'There was a time when the Son was not' are thus debarred forever. Conversely, all efforts to deny or attenuate the divinity of Christ by reducing him to a prophet or to a human being in whom the Spirit and the Word of God act, are ruled out by that *genitus*, begotten, understood in the strong and absolute sense that the Council of Nicaea understood it. Here the Nicene definition does no more than faithfully interpret the Fourth Gospel. For John takes position only one step away from the '*genitus, non factus*' of Nicaea and in point of fact contains it by anticipation. The Jesus of John affirms: 'Before Abraham was (*genesthai*), I Am (*Egô eimi*)' (Jn 8:58). 'The point of this, in the first place, lies in the contrast of the verbs *genesthai*, to come into being, in the aorist, and *einai*, to be, in the continuous present,' writes an eminent modern exegete. 'The implication is that Jesus does not stand within the temporal series of great men, beginning with Abraham and continuing through the succession of the prophets, so as to be compared with them. His claim is not that he is the greatest of the prophets, or even greater than Abraham himself. He belongs to a different order of being. The verb *genesthai* is not applicable to the Son of God at all. He stands outside the range of temporal relations. He can say *Egô eimi*. This is the' *anî hû* of the Old Testament, the declaration of the unique and eternal self-existence of God' (C. H. Dodd, *The Interpretation of the Fourth Gospel*, CUP 1953, pp. 261–2). It is not only Tradition and the Councils thus that get rejected on the score of having interpreted the faith according to contingent schemes and demands, but Holy Scripture too. R. Bultmann's criticism of the formula 'Christ is God', mentioned above, is not merely levelled against the Council of Nicaea but against something very much more authoritative. His question, whether it would not be better to avoid such formulae altogether, is not addressed merely to the Nicene Fathers but to the very authors of the New Testament, and in particular, as we have seen, to John.

22 According to H. Küng, what Nicaea intended to condemn in Arius was only a form of polytheism, not the denial of the full divinity and eternity of the Word, as though Arius seriously intended 'a disguised introduction of polytheism into Christianity' (*op. cit.*, p. 448). According to Schillebeeckx, Nicaea was no more than an attempt to interpret the faith on the basis of liturgical praxis and salvation-experience, the implication here being that today too an interpretation of the divinity of Christ can only be arrived at from a reading of our own praxis and salvation-experience, which are different from those of antiquity (*op. cit.*, p. 576). As against this, it must be noted that the soteriological argument was developed principally by Athanasius who wrote after, and not before, the Council of Nicaea. The conciliar discussion was not based chiefly on that argument but on scriptural texts. If it is true that the soteriological argument influenced the development of Christological dogma, it is also

true to say that the dogmatic definition helped to develop and make people aware of the Christological implications of salvation.

23   St Augustine, *Confessions*, I, 4.
24   St Augustine, *Enarr. in Ps*. 85, 12 (PL 36, 1090). On the contrary, in the Nicene definition, and above all in John, I see the most de-mythologizing statements that can possibly be made about God. John's Jesus says: 'You are from below, I am from above; you are of this world, I am not of this world' (Jn 8:23). This looks like the quintessence of mythological language (below — above), yet is no other than what is meant in modern dialectic theology when we speak of the infinite qualitative difference between time and eternity, between God and the world.
25   H. Küng, *op. cit.*, p. 449.
26   E. Schillebeeckx, *op. cit.*, p. 671.
27   B. Pascal, *Pensées* (Dent), entry 462.
28   H. Küng, *op. cit.*, p. 468.
29   *Ibidem*, pp. 463f.
30   *Ibidem*, pp. 448f.
31   E. Schillebeeckx, *op. cit.*, pp. 611f.
32   S. Kierkegaard, *For Self-Examination*, OUP 1946, p. 58.
33   E. Schillebeeckx, *op. cit.*, p. 611: 'It follows that Christianity only stays alive and real if each successive period, from out of its rela-tionship to Jesus Christ, declares anew for Jesus of Nazareth. Then it is impossible to determine "first" the essence of the Christian faith in order subsequently — "in the second instance", as it were — to interpret it as accommodated to our own time. Anyone who, with the Christian Churches, affirms the universal significance of belief in Jesus must have the humility loyally to shoulder, along with that, the difficulties accruing to it — or else must surrender the claim to universality. Only these two possibilities are genuine and consistent. To accept the universality while at the same time denying the hermeneutical problem — thereby positing one exclusive definition, *ne varietur*, of essential Christianity — is neither an accessible road nor an authentic possibility; it is to disregard and evacuate of all substance the true universality of the Christian faith.'
34   A. Schweitzer, *The Quest of the Historical Jesus*, A. & S. Black, London (3rd edn.) 1954, p. 397 (chapter XX).
35   Cf K. Rahner, 'Calkedon — Ende oder Anfang?' in *Das Konzil von Calkedon*, III, Wuerzburg 1954.
36   St Augustine, *De Trinitate*, VII, 6, 11 (PL 42, 943f).
37   St Augustine, *Enarr. in Ps*. 120, 6 (PL 36, 1609).
38   Cf Anon., *The Cloud of Unknowing*, 7.

Index of authors

Thematic Index

controversy 13, 14, 123, 128, 131, 138, 150; Jesus' knowledge 14; "Tu solus Sanctus" 15ff; beauty of Christ 17f; *Pantocrator* 17f; Teacher of righteousness 19; Holy One of God 21; Christ the model 22, 35, 36; Lutheran: Christ is a gift through faith 22, 59; the Risen Christ 24f; Christ the perfect human being 27f; Christ new Adam, new human being 28, 33ff, 130; personality of Christ 31, 54, 148; John's Christology 45, 54, 54; natures of Christ 2, 28, 34, 71; divinity of Christ 69ff; Christology *per se* and *per me* 69, 70; new scheme, *schema* 71f,124; the synthesis of eternity and time 74ff; Jesus Christ, a person 89ff; Trinity and Christology 92f, 154; God is one and three 124, 153; Byzantine period 94; Byzantine Middle Ages 115; impersonal knowledge of the person of Christ 95; voices about Christ 99; essence and existence of Christ 97, 99; the name and heart of Jesus 100ff, 119; the Sacred Heart 103f; loving Jesus 106ff, 116ff; exam in Christology 105; Christological analyses 108; Christian mystery 112, 143; and cultic mysteries 137; Spirit-less Christ 113; Nicene definition 114, 123, 135, 148, 155; memory of Jesus 117f; faith in the divinity of Christ 121ff, 150; Bultmann's Christology, 126f, 131, 137, 151, 156; pre-existence of Christ 127; see *Dogma, Heresy, Chalcedon*

Church 30, 61, 149-150; Second Vatican Council 22, 23, 41; the Chosen People 23; local Churches 24f; foundation on Peter 66, 67, 154; pilgrim Church 80; Magisterium 112, 125, 153; Christ's bride 119; ancient councils 131; Christological councils 137; Orthodox and Latin Churches 135, 149, 150; Protestants 149; Churches of the Reform 151; see *Orthodox*

Congregation for the Doctrine of the Faith 120

Contemplation 22; contemplating Christ 38, 111

Corde creditur 60, 67; see *Faith*

Credo 61, 124, 149, 150; *credere in* 63, 64; Nicene Creed 76, 114, 135, 136, 148, 149, 155, 156; Creed of the Third Synod of Antioch 155; Traditions and Creeds 127; see *Faith*

Deceiver 37

Demiurge 28

Discernment 150

Disobedience 38; see *Obedience*

Docetism 27f, 29, 32, 132; *The Origins of Docetism* 43; see *Heresy*

Dogma: dogmatic way 1; "two natures, one person", Christological dogma 2, 70, 126f, 128, 131, 147, 148, 156; Christ as a unique person 91f, 93, 101f, 156; dogmatic terminology 3, 37, 93; technical language of theology 125; dogma bearer of certitudes and energies 4; of Christ true man and true God 29f, 35, 37, 69, 70, 75, 77, 79, 86; unity of Christ 32f; an open structure 33, 122, 136; revitalizing dogma from Scripture and Tradition 37; development of dogma 76; from dogma to living 78ff; theses not hypotheses 123, 140; ecclesiastical dogmatics 146ff; see *Christology, Theology*

Dokein 27

Dynamis faculty of God, 132

Easter, first Easter 27, 45, 70; paschal mystery 54; see *Passover*

Ebionism 132; see *Heresy*

164